# SCIENCE FICTION

This is a volume in the
Arno Press collection

# SCIENCE FICTION

# A

# CHECKLIST OF

# SCIENCE-FICTION

# ANTHOLOGIES

*Edited by*

Walter R. Cole

**ARNO PRESS**

A New York Times Company

New York — 1975

Reprint Edition 1974 by Arno Press Inc.

Copyright © 1964 by W. R. Cole

Reprinted by permission of Walter R. Cole

Reprinted from a copy in The Library
of the University of California, Riverside

SCIENCE FICTION
ISBN for complete set: 0-405-06270-2
See last pages of this volume for titles.

Manufactured in the United States of America

———◆———

Library of Congress Cataloging in Publication Data

Cole, Walter R
    A checklist of science-fiction anthologies.

    (Science fiction)
    1. Science fiction--Bibliography.   I.   Title.
II.   Series.
Z5918.S36C6  1974        016.823'0876        74-15956
ISBN 0-405-06323-7

A Checklist of
Science – Fiction
Anthologies

Compiled by
W. R. COLE

# CONTENTS ...

ANTHOLOGIES LISTED IN THIS VOLUME....................................page 1

The INDEX BY EDITORS....................................................page 11

The INDEX BY STORY TITLES............................................page 91

The INDEX BY AUTHORS..................................................page 188

    SUPPLEMENT: 1962-1963 ANTHOLOGIES.............................page 9

    The INDEX BY EDITORS  (1962-1963)...........................page 298

    The INDEX BY STORY TITLES  (1962-1963)....................page 316

    The INDEX BY AUTHORS  (1962-1963)..........................page 342

       Preface....................................................page V

       HOW TO HATCH A HASSEL by Theodore Sturgeon........page VII

       How to use The Checklist..........................page XI

       Abbreviations used in The Checklist..............page XIII

# PREFACE...

If scholars of science fiction would delve deeply enough into the dusty shelves of libraries and collectors they would find that although Science Fiction is thousands of years old, it has been less than half a century since the publication of what we consider to be the first Science Fiction anthology. During that period over two hundred anthologies have been published. As a matter of fact, it was only within the last decade that over 80% of the collections listed in this checklist were published.

Science Fiction has had its ups and downs during the previously alluded to ten year period with the anthology still going strong. In the 227 anthologies we have listed there were almost 2700 stories published. Of this figure, 243, or slightly over 9%, were anthologized twice; 72 three times; 18 four times and only 3, thank goodness, were re-printed five times. With a total of 331 we arrive at a figure of 12.5% that have been anthologized more than once. Isn't that going a bit too far? Surely there are thousands of stories in the magazines that have not been touched. The cynics say, and we do not participate in this line of thinking, that anthologies are just another medium for an author to obtain an extra buck for his story. To the best of our knowledge, however, no one begrudges a writer the opportunity to make a living, but it seems to us that anthologists habitually double and triple-print a story.

Amongst the authors, Dr. Isaac Asimov leads the field with 56 stories anthologized and Theodore Sturgeon second with 52 stories published. With reference to the magazines, we found that the "Big-3", Analog (Astounding) Science Fact Science Fiction, Fantasy & Science Fiction and Galaxy took the honors with the greatest number of stories published. Since both Galaxy and F&SF were first published at different times, we found it necessary to formulate the following chronological breakdown:

| | | |
|---|---|---|
| Galaxy | From October 1950 to April 1963 | 164 stories |
| ASF | From October 1949 to September 1950 | 17 stories |
| | From October 1950 to April 1962 | 136 stories |
| F&SF | From Summer 1949 to Summer 1950 | 6 stories |
| | From Fall 1950 to October 1962 | 187 stories |

Statistics alone will not prove too much. It was not, and is not, our intention, with these figures, to indorse any one magazine nor any one writer. As Joe Friday of Dragnet fame put it, "Just presenting the facts, ma'm."

The idea for this checklist was originally conceived when we started a series of articles for Gnome Press' SCIENCE FICTION WORLD. At that time, both Martin Greenberg of Gnome Press and this compiler discovered that there was a definite need for a checklist of anthologies. The foundational question was what to list. The inclusion of every type of fantasy and science fiction anthology would make this an encyclopedia. Rather than have that happen, we decided to elicit the advise of other collectors in the attempt to establish a practical criterion by which we could select our material.

We entreated and cajoled, begged and borrowed, enlisted and drafted, until we had emassed a considerable cross section of opinion. This was subjected to much ruminating and culling until we finally pieced the puzzle together in this fashion: Weird and Ghost anthologies were excluded along with other types of supernatural anthologies. Anthologies of the Weird and Horror type have been published for over a century and to locate them all would take to much time. In the same vein, to trace a good percentage of the stories published in the Weird anthologies would be a tremendous undertaking in itself. One must have a cut-off place somewhere but the decision as to its location should rest, certainly, in the laps of the Gods. We ignored the saw about angels and fools and after months of research, and numerous inquiries, we found what we considered the happy medium that comprises our checklist. This was predicated upon the feature which distinguishes science fiction from the rest of the fiction milieu; that feature is an intangible, a relationship, if you will. Science Fiction, in common with all literature, is a symbolic abstraction, but with the difference being that its content must reasonably adhere to the multifaced bounds of reality; it may postulate any sort of phenomena which are not mutually exclusive or contradictory, and it may do this without the acknowledgement of a single BEM or paralysis ray. We regretted leaving out such outstanding collections like August Derleth's NIGHT'S YAWNING PEAL but we decided to keep to the happy medium described above.

Once we decided upon a definite course of action, the task began of formulating the index. We found that the most utilitarian arrangement would be to divide the checklist into four sections. Full details on this arrangement will be located on Pages XI and XII.

There is always the possibility of error where the human element is involved. If there are any existing errors in this checklist, our sincere apologies. Every story and anthology was traced to the best of this editor's ability but during our research something might have been overlooked. We would appreciate hearing from any literary detectives who feel we have been guilty of some negligence; at the same time we would like to receive additional data for use in future supplements.

All works of this type have involved the help of many individuals. Without the assistance of the following this listing would have been an unsurmountable task; on many occasions they have been our only source of information concerning a particular story, and consequently the leads they furnished have been invaluable. We would, therefore, like to extend our thanks and appreciation to Forrest J Ackerman, Nelson Bond, August Derleth, Judith Merril and Donald A. Wollheim. Special thanks go to Anthony Boucher, Will F. (Murray Leinster) Jenkins, and James Sieger, for their valuable help and criticisms; Theodore Sturgeon for his introduction; and last, but certainly not least, to James V. Taurasi, Sr., Sam Moskowitz and Frank Dietz for their council and encouragement during the preparation of this manuscript. Special thanks go to Marty Greenberg for his efforts during the early stages of this checklist and Al Schuster, Jr. for his outstanding job in printing this index. Of course it has been impossible, regretfully, to mention everyone who have been of inestimable help. Their absence from this acknowledgement is a matter of physical limitations and should not be misconstrued. To all those, be they fan, editor or writer alike, we can merely express the hope and wish that the publication of this index will provide some measure of gratification as a recompense for their unflagging interest. Tim Dumont also deserves a vote of thanks for his fine jacket design.

W. R. Cole

Brooklyn, New York
June 1964

# HOW TO HATCH A HASSEL
## by THEODORE STURGEON

Some years ago the redoubtable Fletcher Pratt drew a bead on (as it were) a thorn in our side. He had, I think, heard too many comments and criticisms of speculative fiction running like this:

"It's good, but it isn't science fiction."

"That isn't science fiction; it's fantasy."

"He's running a strictly sci-fantasy magazine."

"There hasn't been any *real* science fiction since Clayton's *Astounding*."

"What, in other words, *is* Science Fiction?"

So he researched the matter, and an engaging research it was. To a series of klatsches he invited people in and around science fiction — writers, editors, even an agent or so. From time to time he invited people who were specifically not science fiction: people who didn't give a damn one way or the other, people who ardently and cordially did. They had in common one thing: opinions; and you just wouldn't believe how many were bruited about, and how hot some of those bruitings became.

At first blush it's easy to say what science fiction is. It's the stuff published in science fiction magazines. Or it's stories about the future. Or it's fiction based on known and recognized science.

Likewise one can blurt out what science fiction isn't. It doesn't have ghosts in it, or witchcraft. It doesn't deal with any un-extrapolated (i. e., real) problems of the here and now. It is always about ideas and devices, never about people.

Anyone who has read more than four science fiction stories can attest that all these attempts at delineation are spacious, or partial, or nonsense, or all three. The interesting thing is that everyone who has read forty, or four thousand stories will go at the argument as heatedly and heavily as the rest.

But back to Fletcher Pratt's research. One evening the discussion had got itself to the stage of trying to find the demarcation between science fiction and fantasy. And suddenly Fletcher Pratt leapt to his feet, thrust a sharp forefinger at the top north bookshelf, and said, "*All* fiction is fantasy!"

Now, I shall not go into the conclusions reached by these discussions and their interlocutor; they have been adequately expounded by Mr. Pratt elsewhere. And I surely don't have to explain that I know his remark was jocose. Yet in a lifetime of playing this game of definitions — and what else is a writer's life but that? — I cannot recall having been quite so electrified.

*All* fiction is fantasy.

HOW TO HATCH A HASSEL [Continued]

It is worth bringing up in terms of this book, because Mr. Cole is about to receive on the top of his capable head such a cargo of shards and ashtrays, bricks and bullets, that he will wonder (if the labor of the lists hasn't already made him wonder) why he bothered. He is going to be cuffed and castigated six ways from Sunday for stopping where he did; for going as far as he did; for including, and for excluding, what he has.

All the man wanted to do initially was to compile an index of anthologies. That sounds as simple as completing this sentence: Science Fiction is ——. — But look what he's gone and done — never even mentioned the book in which Ezekial saw the flying saucer. And what about Dorothy Sayer's Lord Peter Wimsey stories? Wasn't one of them about a girl whose evil husband made her a monster by denying her the old extract: Isn't that science in fiction? Over here's a collection of six out-and-out fantasies and four science fiction stories; should he include it? Over there's a collection of Western stories plus one science fiction: how about that? What about the juveniles, foreign language, or British-only volumes?

And anyway, in a world which reviews Philip Wylie's THE DISAPPEARANCE and Vercors' YOU SHALL KNOW THEM as mainstream fiction and Pangborn's A MIRROR FOR OBSERVERS under *Spaceman's Realm* in the New York Times...what is science fiction?

The only conceivable safe way out would be to reason thus: if all fiction is fantasy, and if science fiction is a branch of fantasy, then let's get up an index of all fiction. Then we'll have an index of science fiction and the critics can stop their particular carping and go back to fishing in generalities.

Failing that, the only thing to do is draw the line somewhere. What, to begin with, *is* a science fiction anthology? Is it a book consisting solely of "pure" science fiction (and let the pure among you cast the first definition)? If a book contains one fantasy, should the whole book be excluded? A Third? Half? Should the presence of one unavailable science fiction opus qualify any collection of stories? And again (because it must always come back to that) what of the stories that some people just don't think *are* science fiction?

There then are the limits Mr. Cole drew. Yours might be laid down differently, but if they were, they would still be arbitrary. Then so are his. The careful reader will, however, allow that Walter Cole's limits are wide and his compromise, in this perplexing task, a rational one.

The earliest book in the Checklist is THE MOON TERROR published in 1927. The latest is Groff Conklin's 12 GREAT CLASSICS OF SCIENCE FICTION (Dec. 1963).

The checklist *does* include British, juvenile, and foreign-language but *does not* include one author collections.

No anthologies of pure (i. e., fairy-tale, or Gothic, or hobgoblin type) fantasies are included; but where a book contains stories of a real science-fiction coloration, it and its contents are listed. Hence the presence, in a science fiction checklist, of such titles as THE SATURDAY EVENING POST FANTASY STORIES and THE MOONLIGHT TRAVELER. August Derleth is present with THE OTHER SIDE OF THE MOON but not with THE NIGHT SIDE. Groff Conklin is also present with SCIENCE FICTION TERROR TALES but IN THE GRIP OF TERROR is not listed.

viii

Mr. Cole has made some interesting discoveries and has also developed some towering peeves. Among the former is a pinpointing of the percentage of stories anthologized more than once in the period covered by the Checklist. These stories have been a sore point to certain reviewers and editors, and a good many readers who, the bookdealers tell me, glance through their stock, see just one story in a collection which they've read before, and refuse to buy. Well, it's 12%. Whether that's 12% or I-told-you-so 12% depends on how you feel about it. Then there's the matter of which magazine had had the greatest number of antholozations. Adjusting the figures for the varying lifetimes of the Big Three (not counting what might be called "house" publications [ASF anthologies, The Best from F&SF Series, The Galaxy Readers] Fantasy & Science Fiction seems to have the highest percentage. But see Mr. Cole's preface for the figures. Go pick up your bar bets. And one more: What was, quantitively at least, science fiction's biggest year? 1963.

The peeve department is something the well-mannered Mr. Cole wouldn't write about, so allow me. Splittingest of all his headaches were the anthologists who veiled the sources of stories, giving only by-line or magazine credit. Tracking down over 2600 stories from close to two hundred thirty anthologies made Mr. Cole's task much harder than it had to be, this way. Then there's the editor who changes the title of a story for his book and doesn't say so in his credits. And the author who does what I did to Don Day several years ago, to my lasting shame — ignores quiries as to which stories appeared under which pseudonym.

The other side of the peeves, of course, is the kudos. These are covered by Mr. Cole in his acknowledgements. A number of people have certainly gone far out of their way for Mr. Cole and his labor of love. Let me add my thanks to his. If you haven't gathered it by now, let me say here that I'm pretty impressed by the size of a task so well done by a man who is, after all, not a publisher or editor or writer in the field but just someone who cares about it more than most professionals.

Woodstock, New York

# *How To Use The Checklist*

In a work of this sort, it is important to make the information as accessible as possible to the reader — any reference material is only as useful as its catalogue raisonne. The following explanatory notes, therefore, are designed to provide a profile of method and what, we like to think, is the exacting order which has been incorporated into this volume.

As we pointed out in our preface, this index was divided into four sections. The first section is an alphabetical listing, by title, of the various anthologies, their editors and the pages upon which they can be found. Section two, our main listing, is also an alphabetical listing, by editor, of the anthologies, the stories found in these collections, and all important data available. The third section is a register of story titles, again in alphabetical order; while the fourth section is comprised of a list of authors, inescapably alphabetically arranged, with the individual stories of each accompanying his name. The 1962-1963 supplement follows the same format as the main sections. The only basic difference lies in the listing of stories that were re-printed in collections covered by the supplement. Example:

> \*BEYOND BEDLAM by Wyman Guin............................Glxy Aug 1951

The asterik shows that this story is also listed in the main section.

By further explanation of our alphabetical arrangement described above, we are giving examples of each section in order. We find firstly that all anthologies are arranged in alphabetical order together with their editors, the year of publication and the pages on which they can be found. Example:

> ADVENTURES IN THE FAR FUTURE......................................85
> (Edited by Donald A. Wollheim — 1954)

In the section devoted to the list of editors, we have presented all the pertinent data available such as number of stories, publisher, data of publication (when known), etc. Example:

> CONKLIN, GROFF
> SCIENCE FICTION TERROR TALES (Gnome Press; New York, N. Y.)
> 15 stories 262 pages $3.50 February 20, 1955
>
> PUNISHMENT WITHOUT CRIME by Ray Bradbury...............OW Mar 1950

This example indicates that SCIENCE FICTION TERROR TALES was published by Gnome Press on February 20, 1955, it contained 15 stories, 262 pages and had a list price of $3.50. We have transferred the story titles from the anthologies into this index section in the sequence in which they appeared.

Our section of story titles is simply that. In it are listed all the stories anthologized together with the author, magazine or book, date or year of the original publication and the anthology in which it was re-printed. There are some stories that have made several appearances in anthologies and those are listed in the order of publication. Example:

> "Hobbyist" by Eric Frank Russell........................ASF Sep 1947
> THE ASTOUNDING SCIENCE FICTION ANTHOLOGY [ J. W. Campbell — 1952]
> BEST SF FOUR SCIENCE FICTION STORIES [Crispin — 1961]

# HOW TO USE THE CHECKLIST [Continued]

When a story was expressly written for inclusion in an anthology, i. e.; INVASION FROM INNER SPACE by Howard Koch; it is simply listed as an original story for the anthology in which it appeared; as in this case Howard Koch's story was written for STAR SCIENCE FICTION STORIES #6.

The author section is arranged according to the principles that was used by Don Day in his INDEX TO THE SCIENCE FICTION MAGAZINES. By this criterion, the author's name is followed by a list of his anthologized stories. Example:

VAN VOGT, A. E. (28)
Asylum....................................................ASF Mar 1945
ADVENTURES IN TIME AND SPACE [Healy & McComas - 1946]

This shows that Van Vogt has had 28 stories anthologized. The example of ASYLUM is typical of the listings throughout the author section. In cases where the bylines of the various stories are not uniform the original by-lines are given parenthetically. Example:

CLARKE, ARTHUR C.
Fires Within, The...................................Fty Aug 1947
(Originally appeared under pseudonym E. G. O'Brien)

Where the title in the anthology is different from the magazine version the earliest title is listed also. Example:

BOND, NELSON
Cunning of the Beast...............................BB Nov 1942
(Originally appeared under title ANOTHER WORLD BEGINS)

The preceeding guide is not meant to be all-inclusive. The scope of this work is such that we would require many more pages for a thorough description of what the reader may expect to glean herein. The best guide can do no more than indicate the way; the reader's interest should furnish the impetus to direct his quest for information. The checklist is in a logical form and once the reader familiarizes himself with one portion of the list the entire book will become his to command.

We have used abbreviations throughout this book and on the following pages the reader will find a register of abbreviations which will serve to interpret them. As a final word, we would like to express the hope that this checklist will fill a void in the Science Fiction world and that it will be useful to our readers.

# # #

# ABBREVIATIONS USED IN THE CHECKLIST

| | |
|---|---|
| AASW | Argosy & All-Story Weekly |
| Adt | Audit |
| ALM | American Legion Magazine |
| AlS | All-Story Magazine |
| AmB | American Boy |
| Amz | Amazing Stories |
| AP | Associated Press |
| Aprd/Aprd | Appeared |
| Apr | April |
| Arg | Argosy |
| Ark | The Arkham Sampler |
| Art | article |
| ASF | Astounding Science Fiction/Analog Science Fact — Science Fiction |
| Ash | Astonishing Stories |
| ASQ | Amazing Stories Quarterly |
| Ast | Astounding Stories |
| Atl | Atlantic Monthly |
| ATYA | All The Year Around |
| Aug | August |
| Aut | Autumn |
| Auth | Authentic Science Fiction |
| AvR | Avon Science Fiction & Fantasy Reader |
| AWR | American Whig Review |
| B&W | Black & White |
| BGM | Burton's Gentlemen's Magazine |
| BJG | Boston University Graduate Journal |
| Bkm | The Bookman |
| BLM | Boy's Life Magazine |
| BV | Bratsky Vistnik |
| Bynd | Beyond/Beyond Fantasy Fiction |
| Cas | Cassell's Magazine |
| Cav | Caviler |
| CF | Captain Future |
| Chm | Charm |
| Cmt | Comment |
| Cnt | Coronet |
| Cny | Century |
| Col | Collier's |
| Com | Comet Stories |
| Copyr | Copyright |
| Cpln | Cosmopolitan |
| Csm | Cosmic Stories |
| CYE | Collins Young Elizabethan |
| DLM | Dublin Literary Magazine |
| DM | Dime Mystery |
| DP | Daily Post |
| DR | Democratic Review |
| DSF | Dynamic Science Fiction |
| DSS | Dynamic Science Stories |
| Dude | The Dude |
| EM | Elks Magazine |
| Epch | Epoch |
| EQMM | Ellery Queen's Mystery Magazine |

ABBREVIATIONS USED IN THE CHECKLIST [Continued]

| | |
|---|---|
| Escp | Escapade |
| Esq | Esquire |
| FA | Fantastic Adventures |
| Fal | Fall |
| F&SF | The Magazine of Fantasy & Science Fiction |
| FB | Fantasy Book |
| Fctn | Fiction |
| Fnt | Fantastic |
| For | Forum |
| fr | From |
| FSF | Future Science Fiction |
| FSFS | Future Science Fiction Stories |
| FSM | Fantasy Story Magazine |
| FSQ | Fantastic Story Quarterly |
| FTM | Ford Times Magazine |
| Ftn | Fortune |
| Fty | Fantasy |
| FU | Fantastic Universe Science Fiction |
| Fw/SF | Future combined w/ Science Fiction |
| Fw/SFS | Future combined w/ Science Fiction Stories |
| Fym | Fantasy Magazine |
| Gft | Gift |
| GLB | Godey's Lady's Book |
| GLGM | Graham's Lady's and Gentleman's Magazine |
| Glxy | Galaxy Science Fiction/Galaxy Magazine |
| Grp | The Graphic |
| Gst | Ghost Stories |
| h ps | House pseudonym |
| H pseud | House pseudonym |
| HBZ | Harper's Bazaar |
| HN | Histoires Naturalles |
| Hpr | Harper's Magazine |
| HS | Hall Syndicate |
| If | If: Worlds of Science Fiction |
| ill feat | Illustrated feature |
| ILN | Illustrated London News |
| Im | Imagination |
| ImT | Imaginative Tales |
| Inf | Infinity Science Fiction |
| Jan | January |
| Jul | July |
| Jun | June |
| LHJ | Ladies Home Journal |
| LM | London Magazine |
| LnM | London Mercury |
| Lpt | Lilliput |
| Mar | March |
| Mcl | McCall's |
| McM | MacLean's Magazine (Canadian) |
| Mdm | Madamoiselle |
| Mncl | Monacle |
| MnW | Man's World |
| MoF | The Magazine of Fantasy |
| Mpln | Metropolitan Magazine |

ABBREVIATIONS USED IN THE CHECKLIST [Continued]

| | |
|---|---|
| MS | Marvel Stories |
| MSF | Marvel Science Fiction |
| MSS | Marvel Science Stories |
| n/d | No date/Not dated |
| n/d/a | No data (date) available |
| NEA | NEA Service, Inc. |
| Neb | Nebula Science Fiction |
| NEM | New England Magazine |
| No. | Number |
| Nov. | November |
| NS | The New Statesman |
| NW | New Worlds Science Fiction |
| NwR | New Review |
| NwS | New Story Magazine |
| NYEJ | New York Evening Journal |
| NYHT | New York Herald Tribune |
| NYTM | New York Times Magazine |
| OAW | Once A Week |
| Obs | London Observer |
| Oct | October |
| Org | Original (ly) |
| Org Sty | Original Story |
| OS | Oriental Stories |
| OSF | Orbit Science Fiction |
| OSFS | Original Science Fiction Stories |
| OTWA | Out of this World Adventures |
| OW | Other Worlds Science Fiction |
| Pch | Punch |
| Phi | Philadelphia Inquirer |
| Plby | Playboy |
| Pln | Pelican Magazine |
| PMB | Pall Mall Budget |
| Prn | Pearson's Magazine |
| PS | Planet Stories |
| ps | pseudonym (of) |
| pseud | pseudonym (of) |
| Rp | Reprint |
| Rpnt | Reprint |
| Rptr | Reporter |
| RvP | Revue Parisenne |
| SA | Scientific American |
| S&I | Science and Invention |
| Sch | Scholastic |
| SEP | Saturday Evening Post |
| Sep | September |
| SF | Science Fiction |
| SF # | Science-Fantasy (Numbered) |
| SFA | Science Fiction Adventures |
| SFAd | Science Fiction |
| SF+ | Science Fiction Plus |
| SFQ | Science Fiction Quarterly |
| SFS | Science Fiction Stories |
| Slp | The Salopian |
| SM | Scribner's Magazine |

ABBREVIATIONS USED IN THE CHECKLIST [Continued]

| | |
|---|---|
| Snd | Strand |
| Snt | Slant |
| Spc | Space Science Fiction |
| Spr | Spring |
| SRL | Saturday Review of Literature |
| SS | Science Stories |
| SSS | Super Science Stories |
| ST | Strange Tales |
| Stg | Startling Stories |
| Sti | Stirring Science Stories |
| Stp | Story Parade |
| StrSF | Star Science Fiction |
| Sty | Story |
| Sum | Summer |
| Sup | Super Science Stories (New Series) |
| Sus | Suspense |
| SWS | Science Wonder Stories |
| TB | Thrill Book |
| TEN | Tech Engineering News |
| IOSF | Ten Story Fantasy |
| tld | Titled |
| Tmw | Tomorrow Magazine |
| TOW | Tales Of Wonder |
| Tr fr | Translated from |
| TW | This Week |
| 2CB | Two Complete Science Adventure Books |
| TWS | Thrilling Wonder Stories |
| UCLR | University of Chicago Law Review |
| UCM | University of Chicago Magazine |
| USF | Universe Science Fiction |
| UW | Unknown Worlds |
| Var | Variety |
| Vge | Vogue |
| Vlg | The Village Voice |
| Vol | Volume |
| VSF | Venture Science Fiction |
| Vtx | Vortex |
| w/ | with |
| WB | Worlds Beyond |
| Wdg | What's Doing |
| WM | Westminster Magazine |
| WR | World Review |
| WS | Wonder Stories |
| WSQ | Wonder Stories Quarterly |
| WT | Weird Tales |
| YR | Yale Review |

# ANTHOLOGY LISTING BY TITLE

Page

A. D. 2500.................................................................84
    (Edited by Angus Wilson)
ADVENTURES IN DIMENSION...............(See SCIENCE FICTION ADVENTURES IN DIMENSION)
ADVENTURES IN THE FAR FUTURE.............................................85
    (Edited by Donald A. Wollheim - 1954)
ADVENTURES IN TIME AND SPACE.............................................58
    (Edited by Raymond J. Healy and J. Francis McComas - 1946)
ADVENTURES IN TOMORROW...................................................39
    (Edited by Kendall Foster Crossen - 1951)
ADVENTURES ON OTHER PLANETS..............................................85
    (Edited by Donald A. Wollheim - 1954)
ADVENTURES TO COME.......................................................47
    (Edited by J. Berg Esenwein - 1937)
ALL ABOUT THE FUTURE.....................................................55
    (Edited by Martin Greenberg - 1955)
ASPECTS OF SCIENCE FICTION...............................................47
    (Edited by G. D. Doherty - 1959)
ASSIGNMENT IN TOMORROW...................................................74
    (Edited by Frederik Pohl - 1954)
ASTOUNDING SCIENCE FICTION ANTHOLOGY, THE................................24
    (Edited by John W. Campbell, Jr. - 1952)
ASTOUNDING TALES OF SPACE AND TIME.......................................
      (See THE ASTOUNDING SCIENCE FICTION ANTHOLOGY)
BEACHHEADS IN SPACE......................................................41
    (Edited by August Derleth - 1954)
BEST FROM FANTASY & SCIENCE FICTION, THE.................................17
    (Edited by Anthony Boucher & J. Francis McComas - 1952)
BEST FROM FANTASY & SCIENCE FICTION: Second Series, THE..................13
    (Edited by Anthony Boucher & J. Francis McComas - 1953)
BEST FROM FANTASY & SCIENCE FICTION: Third Series, THE...................19
    (Edited by Anthony Boucher & J. Francis McComas - 1954)
BEST FROM FANTASY & SCIENCE FICTION: Fourth Series, THE..................19
    (Edited by Anthony Boucher - 1955)
BEST FROM FANTASY & SCIENCE FICTION: Fifth Series, THE...................20
    (Edited by Anthony Boucher - 1956)
BEST FROM FANTASY & SCIENCE FICTION: Sixth Series, THE...................20
    (Edited by Anthony Boucher - 1957)
BEST FROM FANTASY & SCIENCE FICTION: Seventh Series, THE.................21
    (Edited by Anthony Boucher - 1958)
BEST FROM FANTASY & SCIENCE FICTION: Eighth Series, THE..................21
    (Edited by Anthony Boucher - 1959)
BEST FROM FANTASY & SCIENCE FICTION: Ninth Series, THE...................69
    (Edited by Robert P. Mills - 1960)
BEST FROM FANTASY & SCIENCE FICTION: Tenth Series, THE...................70
    (Edited by Robert P. Mills - 1961)
BEST FROM NEW WORLDS, THE................................................26
    (Edited by E. J. Carnell - 1955)
BEST FROM STARTLING STORIES, THE.........................................71
    (Edited by Samuel S. Mines - 1953)

BEST OF SCIENCE FICTION, THE...........................................................27
      (Edited by Groff Conklin - 1946)
BEST SCIENCE FICTION STORIES, THE....(See THE BEST SCIENCE FICTION STORIES: 1950)
BEST SCIENCE FICTION STORIES: 1949, THE.................................................13
      (Edited by Everett F. Bleiler & T. E. Dikty - 1949)
BEST SCIENCE FICTION STORIES: 1950, THE.................................................13
      (Edited by Everett F. Bleiler & T. E. Dikty - 1950)
BEST SCIENCE FICTION STORIES: 1951, THE.................................................14
      (Edited by Everett F. Bleiler & T. E. Dikty - 1951)
BEST SCIENCE FICTION STORIES: 1952, THE.................................................14
      (Edited by Everett F. Bleiler & T. E. Dikty - 1952)
BEST SCIENCE FICTION STORIES: 1953, THE.................................................15
      (Edited by  Everett F. Bleiler & T. E. Dikty - 1953)
BEST SCIENCE FICTION STORIES: 1954, THE.................................................15
      (Edited by Everett F. Bleiler & T. E. Dikty - 1954)
BEST SCIENCE FICTION STORIES: 2nd Series, THE...........................................
                                   (See THE BEST SCIENCE FICTION STORIES: 1951)
BEST SCIENCE FICTION STORIES: 3rd Series, THE...........................................
                                   (See THE BEST SCIENCE FICTION STORIES: 1952)
BEST SCIENCE FICTION STORIES: 4th Series, THE...........................................
                                   (See THE BEST SCIENCE FICTION STORIES: 1953)
BEST SCIENCE FICTION STORIES: 5th Series, THE...........................................
                                   (See THE BEST SCIENCE FICTION STORIES: 1954)
BEST SCIENCE FICTION STORIES & NOVELS: 1955, THE........................................46
      (Edited by T. E. Dikty - 1955)
BEST SCIENCE FICTION STORIES & NOVELS: 1956, THE........................................46
      (Edited by T. E. Dikty - 1956)
BEST SCIENCE FICTION STORIES & NOVELS: 9th SERIES, THE..................................47
      (Edited by T. E. Dikty - 1958)
BEST SF SCIENCE FICTION STORIES........................................................38
      (Edited by Edmund Crispin - 1955)
BEST SF TWO SCIENCE FICTION STORIES....................................................38
      (Edited by Edmund Crispin - 1956)
BEST SF THREE SCIENCE FICTION STORIES..................................................38
      (Edited by Edmund Crispin - 1958)
BEST SF FOUR SCIENCE FICTION STORIES...................................................39
      (Edited by Edmund Crispin - 1961)
BEYOND HUMAN KEN.......................................................................63
      (Edited by Judith Merril - 1954)
BEYOND THE BARRIERS OF SPACE AND TIME..................................................64
      (Edited by Judith Merril - 1954)
BEYOND THE END OF TIME.................................................................74
      (Edited by Frederik Pohl - 1952)
BEYOND THE STARS AND OTHER STORIES.....................................................11
      (Anonymous - 1958)
BEYOND TIME AND SPACE..................................................................41
      (Edited by August Derleth - 1950)
BIG BOOK OF SCIENCE FICTION, THE.......................................................28
      (Edited by Groff Conklin - 1950)
BODYGUARD AND FOUR OTHER SHORT NOVELS FROM GALAXY......................................51
      (Edited by H. L. Gold - 1960)
CATEGORY PHOENIX...............(See THE YEAR'S BEST SCIENCE FICTION NOVELS: 1953)
CHILDREN OF WONDER.....................................................................83
      (Edited by William Tenn - 1953)

COMING ATTRACTIONS.....................................................55
     (Edited by Martin Greenberg)
CROSSROADS IN TIME.....................................................29
     (Edited by Groff Conklin - 1953)
CRUCIBLE OF POWER, THE...................(See FIVE SCIENCE FICTION NOVELS)
DECADE OF FANTASY & SCIENCE FICTION, A.................................70
     (Edited by Robert P. Mills - 1960)
EARTH IN PERIL, THE....................................................85
     (Edited by Donald A. Wollheim - 1957)
EDITOR'S CHOICE IN SCIENCE FICTION.....................................74
     (Edited by Sam Moskowitz - 1954)
END OF THE WORLD, THE..................................................85
     (Edited by Donald A. Wollheim - 1956)
ESCALES DANS L'INFINI [Scales of the Infinite]........................50
     (Edited by Georges H. Gallet - 1954)
EVERY BOY'S BOOK OF OUTER SPACE STORIES...............................47
     (Edited by T. E. Dikty - 1960)
EVERY BOY'S BOOK OF SCIENCE FICTION...................................86
     (Edited by Donald A. Wollheim - 1951)
FAMOUS SCIENCE FICTION STORIES.............(See ADVENTURES IN TIME AND SPACE)
FANTASIA MATHEMATICA..................................................48
     (Edited by Clifton Fadiman - 1958)
FANTASTIC UNIVERSE OMNIBUS, THE.......................................79
     (Edited by Hans Stefan Santesson - 1960)
FAR BOUNDARIES.......................................................42
     (Edited by August Derleth - 1951)
FIFTH ANNUAL OF THE YEAR'S BEST SF....................................68
     (Edited by Judith Merril - 1960)
FIFTH GALAXY READER, THE.............................................54
     (Edited by H. L. Gold - 1961)
FIRST ASTOUNDING SCIENCE FICTION ANTHOLOGY, THE..........................
                    (See THE ASTOUNDING SCIENCE FICTION ANTHOLOGY).....78
FIRST WORLD OF IF, THE...............................................
     (Edited by James L. Quinn & Eve Wulff - 1957)
FIVE GALAXY SHORT NOVELS............................................51
     (Edited by H. L. Gold - 1958)
FIVE SCIENCE FICTION NOVELS.........................................55
     (Edited by Martin Greenberg - 1952)
FIVE TALES FROM TOMORROW.....(See THE BEST SCIENCE FICTION STORIES & NOVELS: 1955)
FLIGHT INTO SPACE...................................................86
     (Edited by Donald A. Wollheim - 1950)
FOUR FOR THE FUTURE.................................................29
     (Edited by Groff Conklin - 1959)
FOURTH GALAXY READER OF SCIENCE FICTION, THE........................54
     (Edited by H. L. Gold - 1959)
FROM OFF THIS WORLD.................................................62
     (Edited by Leo Margulies & Oscar J. Friend - 1949)
FROM UNKNOWN WORLDS.................................................25
     (Edited by John W. Campbell, Jr. - 1948)
FRONTIERS OF SPACE.......(See THE BEST SCIENCE FICTION STORIES: 1951, 1952, 1953)
FUTURE TENSE.......................................................40
     (Edited by Kendall Foster Crossen - 1953)
GALAXY OF GHOULS, A................................................64
     (Edited by Judith Merril - 1955)
GALAXY READER OF SCIENCE FICTION, THE..............................51
     (Edited by H. L. Gold - 1952)
GALAXY SCIENCE FICTION OMNIBUS..(See THE SECOND GALAXY READER OF SCIENCE FICTION)

GARDEN OF FEAR AND OTHER STORIES, THE...........................................37
    (Edited by William C. Crawford - 1945)
GATEWAY TO THE STARS...........................................................26
    (Edited by E. J. Carnell - 1955)
GATEWAY TO TOMORROW............................................................26
    (Edited by E. J. Carnell - 1954)
GET OUT OF MY SKY..............................................................62
    (Edited by Leo Margulies & Oscar J. Friend - 1954)
GIRL WITH THE HUNGRY EYES AND OTHER STORIES, THE...............................86
    (Edited by Donald A. Wollheim - 1949)
GREAT STORIES OF SCIENCE FICTION...............................................60
    (Edited by Murray Leinster - 1951)
GREAT TALES OF FANTASY & IMAGINATION.................(See THE MOONLIGHT TRAVELER)
HIDDEN PLANET, THE.............................................................86
    (Edited by Donald A. Wollheim - 1959)
HUMAN?.........................................................................65
    (Edited by Judith Merril - 1954)
IMAGINATION UNLIMITED..........................................................16
    (Edited by Everett F. Bleiler & T. E. Dikty - 1952)
INVADERS OF EARTH..............................................................29
    (Edited by Groff Conklin - 1952)
INVASION FROM MARS.............................................................83
    (Edited by Orson Welles - 1949)
INVISIBLE MEN..................................................................40
    (Edited by Basil Davenport - 1960)
JOURNEY TO INFINITY............................................................55
    (Edited by Martin Greenberg - 1951)
JOURNEYS IN SCIENCE FICTION....................................................61
    (Edited by Richard L. Loughlin & Lilian M. Popp - 1961)
LOOKING FORWARD................................................................61
    (Edited by Milton Lesser - 1953)
MEN AGAINST THE STARS..........................................................56
    (Edited by Martin Greenberg - 1950)
MEN OF SPACE AND TIME.............................(See IMAGINATION UNLIMITED)
MEN ON THE MOON................................................................87
    (Edited by Donald A. Wollheim - 1958)
MIND PARTNER AND EIGHT OTHER NOVELETS FROM GALAXY..............................54
    (Edited by H. L. Gold - 1961)
MOMENT WITHOUT TIME....................(See THE BEST FROM STARTLING STORIES)
MOON TERROR AND OTHER STORIES, THE.............................................12
    (Anonymous - 1927)
MOONLIGHT TRAVELER, THE........................................................80
    (Edited by Philip Van Doren Stern - 1943)
MORE ADVENTURES IN TIME AND SPACE.............(See ADVENTURES IN TIME AND SPACE)
MY BEST SCIENCE FICTION STORY..................................................53
    (Edited by Leo Margulies & Oscar J. Friend - 1949)
NEW TALES OF SPACE AND TIME....................................................57
    (Edited by Raymond J. Healy - 1951)
NINE TALES OF SPACE AND TIME...................................................58
    (Edited by Raymond J. Healy - 1954)
NO PLACE LIKE EARTH............................................................26
    (Edited by E. J. Carnell - 1952)
OFF THE BEATEN ORBIT...................................(See GALAXY OF GHOULS)
OMNIBUS OF SCIENCE FICTION, THE................................................30
    (Edited by Groff Conklin - 1952)
OPERATION FUTURE...............................................................32
    (Edited by Groff Conklin - 1955)

ANTHOLOGY LISTING BY TITLE [Continued]                                      Page

OTHER SIDE OF THE MOON, THE.............................................43
   (Edited by August Derleth - 1949)
OTHER WORLDS, THE.......................................................82
   (Edited by Phil Stong - 1941)
OUT OF THIS WORLD.......................................................49
   (Edited by Julius Fast - 1944)
OUT OF THIS WORLD 1.....................................................84
   (Edited by Amabel Williams-Ellis & Mably Owen - 1960)
OUT OF THIS WORLD 2.....................................................84
   (Edited by Amabel Williams-Ellis & Mably Owen - 1961)
OUTER REACHES, THE......................................................43
   (Edited by August Derleth - 1951)
OUTSIDERS: CHILDREN OF WONDER.........................(See CHILDREN OF WONDER)
PENGUIN SCIENCE FICTION.................................................11
   (Edited by Brian Aldiss - 1961)
PETRIFIED PLANET, THE...................................................77
   (Edited by Fletcher Pratt - 1952)
PLANET OF DOOM AND OTHER STORIES........................................11
   (Anonymous - 1958)
POCKET BOOK OF SCIENCE FICTION, THE.....................................87
   (Edited by Donald A. Wollheim - 1943)
PORTABLE NOVELS OF SCIENCE..............................................87
   (Edited by Donald A. Wollheim - 1945)
PORTALS OF TOMORROW.....................................................44
   (Edited by August Derleth - 1954)
POSSIBLE WORLDS OF SCIENCE FICTION......................................32
   (Edited by Groff Conklin - 1951)
PRIZE SCIENCE FICTION...................................................87
   (Edited by Donald A. Wollheim - 1953)
PRIZE STORIES OF SPACE AND TIME...................(See PRIZE SCIENCE FICTION)
RACE TO THE STARS...............(See THE GIANT ANTHOLOGY OF SPACE AND TIME)
ROBOT AND THE MAN, THE..................................................56
   (Edited by Martin Greenberg - 1953)
SAINT'S CHOICE, THE.....................................................27
   (Edited by Leslie Charteris - 1945)
SANDS OF MARS AND OTHER STORIES, THE....................................11
   (Anonymous - 1958)
SATURDAY EVENING POST FANTASY STORIES, THE..............................50
   (Edited by Barthold Fles - 1951)
SCIENCE AND SORCERY.....................................................50
   (Edited by Garrett Ford - 1953)
SCIENCE FICTION ADVENTURES IN DIMENSION.................................33
   (Edited by Groff Conklin - 1953)
SCIENCE FICTION ADVENTURES IN MUTATION..................................33
   (Edited by Groff Conklin - 1956)
SCIENCE FICTION & READER'S GUIDE........................................12
   (Edited by Marjorie Barrows - 1954)
SCIENCE FICTION CARNIVAL................................................24
   (Edited by Fredric Brown & Mack Reynolds - 1953)
SCIENCE FICTION GALAXY..................................................34
   (Edited by Groff Conklin - 1950)
SCIENCE FICTION OMNIBUS........(See THE BEST SCIENCE FICTION STORIES: 1949, 1950)
SCIENCE FICTION OMNIBUS....(Groff Conklin)...(See THE OMNIBUS OF SCIENCE FICTION)
SCIENCE FICTION SHOWCASE................................................59
   (Edited by Mary Kornbluth - 1959)
SCIENCE FICTION TERROR TALES............................................35
   (Edited by Groff Conklin - 1955)

SCIENCE FICTION THINKING MACHINES.................................................35
    (Edited by Groff Conklin - 1954)
SCIENCE-FICTIONAL SHERLOCK HOLMES, THE...........................................73
    (Edited by Robert C. Peterson - 1960)
SCIENCE IN FICTION...............................................................13
    (Edited by A. E. M. & J. C. Bayliss - 1957)
SECOND ASTOUNDING SCIENCE FICTION ANTHOLOGY, THE.................................
                            (See THE ASTOUNDING SCIENCE FICTION ANTHOLOGY)
SECOND GALAXY READER OF SCIENCE FICTION, THE.....................................52
    (Edited by H. L. Gold - 1954)
SECOND WORLD OF IF, THE..........................................................78
    (Edited by James L. Quinn & Eve Wulff - 1958)
SELECTIONS FROM BEYOND HUMAN KEN.........................(See BEYOND HUMAN KEN)
SF: THE YEAR'S GREATEST SF AND FANTASY...........................................66
    (Edited by Judith Merril - 1956)
SF: 57 THE YEAR'S GREATEST SF AND FANTASY........................................66
    (Edited by Judith Merril - 1957)
SF: 58 THE YEAR'S GREATEST SF AND FANTASY........................................67
    (Edited by Judith Merril - 1958)
SF: 59 THE YEAR'S GREATEST SF AND FANTASY........................................67
    (Edited by Judith Merril - 1959)
SHADOW OF TOMORROW...............................................................74
    (Edited by Frederik Pohl - 1953)
SHANADU..........................................................................23
    (Edited by Robert E. Briney - 1953)
SHOT IN THE DARK.................................................................65
    (Edited by Judith Merril - 1950)
SIX FROM WORLDS BEYOND....(See THE BEST SCIENCE FICTION STORIES AND NOVELS: 1956)
SIX GREAT SHORT NOVELS OF SCIENCE FICTION........................................36
    (Edited by Groff Conklin - 1954)
6 GREAT SHORT SCIENCE FICTION NOVELS.............................................36
    (Edited by Groff Conklin - 1960)
SIXTH ANNUAL OF THE YEAR'S BEST SF...............................................68
    (Edited by Judith Merril - 1961)
SPACE PIONEERS...................................................................72
    (Edited by Andre Norton - 1954)
SPACE POLICE.....................................................................73
    (Edited by Andre Norton - 1956)
SPACE SERVICE....................................................................73
    (Edited by Andre Norton - 1953)
SPACE, SPACE, SPACE..............................................................79
    (Edited by William Sloane - 1953)
SPACE STATION 42 AND OTHER STORIES...............................................12
    (Anonymous - 1958)
SPECTRUM.........................................................................11
    (Edited by Kingsley Amis & Robert Conquest - 1961)
STAR OF STARS....................................................................77
    (Edited by Frederik Pohl - 1960)
STAR SCIENCE FICTION STORIES.....................................................75
    (Edited by Frederik Pohl - 1953)
STAR SCIENCE FICTION STORIES #2..................................................75
    (Edited by Frederik Pohl - 1953)
STAR SCIENCE FICTION STORIES #3..................................................76
    (Edited by Frederik Pohl - 1954)
STAR SCIENCE FICTION STORIES #4..................................................76
    (Edited by Frederik Pohl - 1958)
STAR SCIENCE FICTION STORIES #5..................................................76
    (Edited by Frederik Pohl - 1959)

ANTHOLOGY LISTING BY TITLE [Continued]                                    Page
STAR SCIENCE FICTION STORIES #6.............................................76
    (Edited by Frederik Pohl - 1959)
STAR SHORT NOVELS...........................................................77
    (Edited by Frederik Pohl - 1954)
STARTLING STORIES........................(See THE BEST FROM STARTLING STORIES)
STORIES FOR TOMORROW........................................................79
    (Edited by William Sloane - 1954)
STORIES OF SCIENTIFIC IMAGINATION...........................................50
    (Edited by Joseph Gallant - 1954)
STRANGE ADVENTURES IN SCIENCE FICTION............(See OMNIBUS OF SCIENCE FICTION)
STRANGE PORTS OF CALL.......................................................44
    (Edited by August Derleth - 1948)
STRANGE TRAVELS IN SCIENCE FICTION..............(See OMNIBUS OF SCIENCE FICTION)
TALES OF OUTER SPACE........................................................88
    (Edited by Donald A. Wollheim - 1954)
TERROR IN THE MODERN VEIN...................................................88
    (Edited by Donald A. Wollheim - 1955)
THIRD GALAXY READER OF SCIENCE FICTION, THE.................................53
    (Edited by H. L. Gold - 1958)
13 GREAT STORIES OF SCIENCE FICTION.........................................36
    (Edited by Groff Conklin - 1960)
THREE FROM OUT THERE........................................................62
    (Edited by Leo Margulies - 1959)
THREE TIMES INFINITY........................................................62
    (Edited by Leo Margulies - 1958)
TIME TO COME................................................................45
    (Edited by August Derleth - 1954)
TIMELESS STORIES FOR TODAY AND TOMORROW.....................................23
    (Edited by Ray Bradbury - 1952)
TOMORROW, THE STARS.........................................................59
    (Edited by Robert A. Heinlein - 1952)
TOMORROW'S UNIVERSE.........................................................24
    (Edited by H. J. Campbell - 1954)
TRAVELERS IN TIME...........................................................81
    (Edited by Philip Van Doren Stern - 1947)
TRAVELERS OF SPACE..........................................................56
    (Edited by Martin Greenberg - 1952)
TREASURY OF GREAT SCIENCE FICTION, A........................................22
    (Edited by Anthony Boucher - 1959)
TREASURY OF SCIENCE FICTION, A..............................................36
    (Edited by Groff Conklin - 1948)
TREASURY OF SCIENCE FICTION CLASSICS, A.....................................59
    (Edited by Harold W. Kuebler - 1955)
UBERWINDUNG VON RAUM UND ZEIT [Conquest of Space and Time].................59
    (Edited by Gotthard Gunther - 1952)
ULTIMATE INVADER AND OTHER SCIENCE FICTION, THE.............................89
    (Edited by Donald A. Wollheim - 1954)
WITCHES THREE...............................................................77
    (Edited by Fletcher Pratt - 1952)
WORLD OF WONDER.............................................................77
    (Edited by Fletcher Pratt - 1952)
WORLD THAT COULDN'T BE AND EIGHT OTHER NOVELETS FROM GALAXY, THE............54
    (Edited by H. L. Gold - 1959)
WORLDS OF TOMORROW..........................................................45
    (Edited by August Derleth - 1953)
YEAR AFTER TOMORROW, THE....................................................40
    (Edited by Lester del Rey, Cecille Matschat and Carl Carmer - 1952)

⑦

YEAR'S BEST SCIENCE FICTION NOVELS.............................................
                          (See YEAR'S BEST SCIENCE FICTION NOVELS: 1952)
YEAR'S BEST SCIENCE FICTION NOVELS: 1952......................................17
    (Edited by Everett F. Bleiler & T. E. Dikty — 1952)
YEAR'S BEST SCIENCE FICTION NOVELS: 1953......................................17
    (Edited by Everett F. Bleiler & T. E. Dikty — 1953)
YEAR'S BEST SCIENCE FICTION NOVELS: 1954......................................17
    (Edited by Everett F. Bleiler & T. E. Dikty — 1954)
YEAR'S BEST SCIENCE FICTION NOVELS: SECOND SERIES.............................
                          (See YEAR'S BEST SCIENCE FICTION NOVELS: 1954)
ZACHERLY'S MIDNIGHT SNACKS....................................................89
    (Edited by Zacherly — 1960)
ZACHERLY'S VULTURE STEW.......................................................89
    (Edited by Zacherly — 1960)

# 1962 - 1963 Supplement

## ANTHOLOGY LISTING BY TITLE

Page

ANALOG 1................................................................301
   (Edited by John W. Campbell - 1963)
ASLEEP IN ARMAGEDDON..................................................315
   (Edited by Michael Sissons - 1962)
BEST FROM FANTASY & SCIENCE FICTION: 12th Series, THE.................304
   (Edited by Avram Davidson - 1963)
BEST SF FIVE SCIENCE FICTION STORIES.................................304
   (Edited by Edmund Crispin - 1963)
BEYOND..............................................................298
   (Anonymous - 1963)
CENTURY OF SCIENCE FICTION, A.......................................310
   (Edited by Damon Knight - 1962)
COMING OF THE ROBOTS, THE...........................................313
   (Edited by Sam Moskowitz - 1963)
CONTACT.............................................................310
   (Edited by Noel Keyes - 1963)
DESTINATION: AMALTHEIA..............................................305
   (Edited by Richard Dixon - 1963)
8th ANNUAL OF THE YEAR'S BEST SF....................................312
   (Edited by Judith Merril - 1963)
ESCAPE TO EARTH.....................................................308
   (Edited by Ivan Howard - 1963)
EXPLORING OTHER WORLDS..............................................313
   (Edited by Sam Moskowitz - 1963)
EXPERT DREAMERS, THE................................................314
   (Edited by Frederik Pohl - 1962)
FIFTY SHORT SCIENCE FICTION TALES...................................300
   (Edited by Isaac Asimov & Groff Conklin - 1963)
FIRST FLIGHT: Maiden Voyages of Space and Time......................311
   (Edited by Damon Knight - 1963)
GREAT SCIENCE FICTION ABOUT DOCTORS.................................303
   (Edited by Groff Conklin & Noah D. Fabricant M. D. - 1963)
GREAT SCIENCE FICTION ADVENTURES....................................314
   (Edited by Larry T. Shaw - 1963)
GREAT SCIENCE FICTION BY SCIENTISTS.................................302
   (Edited by Groff Conklin - 1962)
GREAT STORIES OF SPACE TRAVEL.......................................302
   (Edited by Groff Conklin - 1963)
HEART OF THE SERPENT, THE...........................................299
   (Anonymous - 1961)
HELL HATH FURY......................................................308
   (Edited by George Hay - 1963)
HUGO WINNERS, THE...................................................299
   (Edited by Isaac Asimov - 1962)
HUMAN AND OTHER BEINGS..............................................305
   (Edited by Allen DeGraeff - 1963)

MATHEMATICAL MAGPIE, THE..................................................305
    (Edited by Clifton Fadiman - 1962)
MORE ADVENTURES ON OTHER PLANETS..........................................315
    (Edited by Donald A. Wollheim - 1963)
MORE PENGUIN SCIENCE FICTION..............................................298
    (Edited by Brian W. Aldiss - 1963)
MORE SOVIET SCIENCE FICTION.........................(See The Heart of the Serpent)
NOVELETS OF SCIENCE FICTION...............................................309
    (Edited by Ivan Howard - 1963)
OUT OF THIS WORLD 3.......................................................315
    (Edited by Amabel Williams-Ellis & Mably Owen - 1962)
PROLOGUE TO ANALOG........................................................301
    (Edited by John W. Campbell - 1962)
RARE SCIENCE FICTION......................................................309
    (Edited by Ivan Howard - 1963)
ROD SERLING'S TRIPLE W: WITCHES, WARLOCKS AND WEREWOLVES...................314
    (Edited by Rod Serling - 1963)
6 AND THE SILENT SCREAM...................................................309
    (Edited by Ivan Howard - 1963)
17 X INFINITY.............................................................303
    (Edited by Groff Conklin - 1963)
7th ANNUAL OF THE YEAR'S BEST SF..........................................311
    (Edited by Judith Merril - 1962)
SOVIET SCIENCE FICTION......................(See A Visitor From Outer Space)
SPECTRUM II...............................................................298
    (Edited by Kingsley Amis & Robert Conquest - 1962)
SPECTRUM III..............................................................298
    (Edited by Kingsley Amis & Robert Conquest - 1963)
THREE IN ONE..............................................................311
    (Edited by Leo Margulies - 1963)
TIME WAITS FOR WINTHROP AND FOUR OTHER SHORT NOVELS FROM GALAXY...........314
    (Edited by Frederik Pohl - 1962)
12 GREAT CLASSICS OF SCIENCE FICTION......................................303
    (Edited by Groff Conklin - 1963)
UNKNOWN, THE..............................................................301
    (Edited by D. R. Benson - 1963)
VISITOR FROM OUTER SPACE, A...............................................299
    (Anonymous - undated)
WAY OUT...................................................................309
    (Edited by Ivan Howard - 1963)
WEIRD ONES, THE...........................................................309
    (Edited by Ivan Howard - 1963)
WORLDS OF SCIENCE FICTION, THE............................................313
    (Edited by Robert P. Mills - 1963)
WORLDS OF WHEN............................................................303
    (Edited by Groff Conklin - 1962)

# Alphabetical Listing by Editor

ALDISS, BRIAN                                                           Mag.    Year
    PENGUIN SCIENCE FICTION          Penguin Books Ltd.; London, England
    12 stories  236 pages  3/6 (.50¢) October 26, 1961

| | | |
|---|---|---|
| SOLE SOLUTION by Eric Frank Russell | FU | Apr 1956 |
| LOT by Ward Moore | F&SF | May 1953 |
| THE SHORT-SHORT STORY OF MANKIND by John Steinbeck | Plby | Apr 1958 |
| SKIRMISH by Clifford Simak | Amz | Dec 1950 |

    (Originally appeared under title BATHE YOUR BEARINGS IN BLOOD)

| | | |
|---|---|---|
| POOR LITTLE WARRIOR! by Brian W. Aldiss | F&SF | Apr 1958 |
| GRANDPA by James H. Schmitz | ASF | Feb 1955 |
| THE HALF PAIR by Bertram Chandler | NW #65 | Nov 1957 |
| COMMAND PERFORMANCE by Walter M. Miller | Glxy | Nov 1952 |
| NIGHTFALL by Isaac Asimov | ASF | Sep 1941 |
| THE SNOWBALL EFFECT by Katherine MacLean | Glxy | Sep 1952 |
| THE END OF SUMMER by Algis Budrys | ASF | Nov 1954 |
| TRACK 12 by J. G. Ballard | NW # 70 | Apr 1958 |

AMIS, KINGSLEY & ROBERT CONQUEST
    SPECTRUM                         Victor Gollancz Ltd.; London, England
    10 stories  304 pages  18/ ($2.50) September 1961

| | | |
|---|---|---|
| THE MIDAS PLAGUE by Frederik Pohl | Glxy | Apr 1954 |
| LIMITING FACTOR by Clifford D. Simak | Stg | Nov 1949 |
| THE EXECUTIONER by Algis Budrys | ASF | Jan 1956 |
| NULL-P by William Tenn ps (Philip Klass) | WB | Jan 1951 |
| THE HOMING INSTINCTS OF JOE VARGO by Stephen Barr | F&SF | Dec 1959 |
| SPECIAL FLIGHT by John Berryman | ASF | May 1939 |
| INANIMATE OBJECTION by H. Chandler Elliott | Glxy | Feb 1954 |
| PILGRIMAGE TO EARTH by Robert Sheckley | Plby | Sep 1956 |

    (Originally appeared under title Love, Inc.)

| | | |
|---|---|---|
| UNHUMAN SACRIFICE by Katherine MacLean | ASF | Nov 1958 |
| BY HIS BOOTSTRAPS by Robert A. Heinlein | ASF | Oct 1941 |

    (Originally appeared under pseudonym Anson MacDonald)

ANONYMOUS
    BEYOND THE STARS AND OTHER STORIES     Jubilee Publications Pty., Ltd.
    7 stories  114 pages  2/ (.25¢)  1958  Satellite Series #21 (Sydney, Austr.)

| | | |
|---|---|---|
| BEYOND THE STARS by John Berryman | ASF | Oct 1939 |

    (Originally appeared under title SPACE RATING)

| | | |
|---|---|---|
| THE COLD EQUATIONS by Tom Godwin | ASF | Aug 1954 |
| LIMITING FACTOR by Clifford D. Simak | Stg | Nov 1949 |
| ASLEEP IN ARMAGEDDON by Ray Bradbury | PS | Win 1948 |
| EXPLOITERS END by James Causey | Orb #2 | n/d 1954 |
| POTENTIAL ENEMY by Mack Reynolds | Orb #2 | n/d 1954 |
| CENTURY JUMPER by August Derleth | Orb #2 | n/d 1954 |

    (Originally appeared under title A TRAVELER IN TIME)

    THE MOON TERROR & OTHER STORIES  Popular Fiction Pub. Co.; Indianapolis, Ind
    4 stories  192 pages  $1.25  1927
                ALL STORIES FROM WEIRD TALES

| | |
|---|---|
| THE MOON TERROR by A. G. Birch | May 1923 |
| OOZE by Anthony M. Rud | March 1923 |

PENELOPE by Vincent Starrett                                      May 1923
AN ADVENTURE IN THE FOURTH DIMENSION by Farnsworth Wright        October 1923


   PLANET OF DOOM AND OTHER STORIES   Jubilee Publications Pty. Ltd Sydney, Austr.
   8 stories  114 pages 2/              1958 Satellite Series #211

PLANET OF DOOM by Malcolm Jameson                               ASF   Feb 1945
   (Originally appeared under title LILIES OF LIFE)
LUNAR ESCAPADE by H. B. Fyfe                                  Orb #2   n/d 1954
RETREAT FROM RIGEL by Philip K. Dick                          Orb #2   n/d 1954
   (Originally appeared under title TONY AND THE BEETLES)
THE LAST WAR by Arthur Dekker Savage                          Orb #2   n/d 1954
   (Originally appeared under title THE BUTTERFLY KISS)
THE MATING OF THE MOONS by Kenneth O'Hara ps (Bryce Walton)   Orb #2   n/d 1954
THE IMAGE OF THE GODS by Alan E. Nourse                       Orb #4   Sep 1954
PLACE OF MEETING by Charles Beaumont                          Orb #2   n/d 1954
THE LAST NIGHT OF SUMMER by Alfred Coppell                    Orb #4   Sep 1954


   THE SANDS OF MARS & OTHER STORIES Jubilee Publications Pty. Ltd  Sydney  ustr.
   6 stories  114 pages  2/            1958   Satellite Series #213

THE SANDS OF MARS by A. E. Van Vogt                             OW   Jul 1954
   (Originally appeared under title ENCHANTED VILLAGE)
THE PILLOWS by Margaret St. Clair                             TWS   Jun 1950
OPERATION ZERO by Milton Lesser                              Orb #4   Sep 1954
   (Originally appeared under title INTRUDER ON THE RIM)
ADJUSTMENT TEAM by Philip K. Dick                            Orb #4   Sep 1954
THINKERS, MARK VII by August Derleth                         Orb #4   Sep 1954
   (Originally appeared under title THE THINKER AND THE THOUGHT)
NO MORE THE STARS by Irving E. Cox                           Orb #4   Sep 1954


   SPACE STATION 42 & OTHER STORIES  Jubilee Publications Pty. Ltd  Sydney Austr.
   6 stories  114 pages  2/            1958   Satellite Series # 212

SPACE STATION 42 by Charles E. Fritch                        Orb #5   Nov 1954
   (Originally appeared under title MANY DREAMS OF EARTH)
CONTROLLED EXPERIMENT by Chad Oliver                         Orb #5   Nov 1954
THE LAST OF THE MASTERS by Philip K. Dick                    Orb #5   Nov 1954
THE LAST MAN by Charles Beckman, Jr.                         Orb #5   Nov 1954
   (Originally appeared under title NOAH)
BETWEEN TWO WORLDS by Anthony Riker                          Orb #5   Nov 1954
   (Originally appeared under title AUNT ELSIE'S STAIRWAY)
THE DREAMER by Jack Vance                                    Orb #5   Nov 1954
   (Originally appeared under title THE ENCHANTED VILLAGE)


BARROWS, MARJORIE
   SCIENCE FICTION AND READER'S GUIDE  (VOLUME 16: THE CHILDREN'S HOUR)
   9 stories  376 pages  June 30, 1954  Spencer Press — Chicago, Ill.

   Note: SCIENCE FICTION & READER'S GUIDE was published as Volume 16 of a set  of
         books entitled "THE CHILDREN'S HOUR.  This set  is a collection   of
         stories for children and Volume 16 was not sold as a seperate book.

         This volume has two sections: Section One is comprised of nine science
         fiction stories  and a glossary  of science  fiction terms while Section
         Two is a collection of articles on children's literature.


WHAT TIME IS IT? by Richard M. Elam, Jr.
   (From TEEN AGE SCIENCE FICTION STORIES; 1952)
ADVENTURES ON MARS by Richard M. Elam, Jr.                       Stp Dec 1952
MARS & MISS PICKERELL by Ellen MacGregor    (Fr MISS PICKERELL GOES TO MARS; 1951)

Mag.    Year

THE STAR DUCKS by Bill Brown
LANCELOT BIGGS ON THE SATURN by Nelson Bond    (From LANCELOT BIGGS: SPACEMAN; 1950)
THE TRUTH ABOUT PYECRAFT by H. G. Wells
THE BLACK PITS OF LUNA by Robert A. Heinlein
IS THERE LIFE ON THE MOON? by H. Percy Wilkins                (article)
TRAIL TO THE STARS by Capt. Burr W. Leyson                    (article)

F&SF  Fal 1950
ST    Apr 1903
SEP   1/10/41
CYE   Jan 1953
BLM   Feb 1950

BAYLISS, A. E. & J. C. BAYLISS
    SCIENCE IN FICTION            University of London  (England)
    12 stories  191 pages  4/3  (.60¢)  1957

PRELUDE TO SPACE by Arthur C. Clarke              (excerpts)
    (Originally published by World Editions; 1951)
THE STAR by H. G. Wells
                                                  Grp Xmas 1897
AN ANCIENT GULLIVER by Lucien      (From A TRUE HISTORY; written about 165 A.D.)
THE FLYING ISLAND by Jonathan Swift    (From THE THIRD VOYAGE OF GULLIVER; 1726 )
A RACE WITH A DINOSAUR by A. Conan Doyle          (From THE LOST WORLD; 1912)
AN EARLY TIME-TRAVELLER by Louis Sebastian Mercier
    (From Journal of the Year 2440; 1795)
ADVENTURE IN A SPACE SHIP by C. S. Lewis    (From OUT OF THE SILENT PLANET; 1938)
THE EXPERIMENTAL FARM by H. G. Wells       (From THE FOOD OF THE GODS; 1904)
THE AVENGING RAY by Seamark ps (Austin J. Small)        (excerpts)
    (Originally published in 1930)
CAPTAIN NEMO'S THUNDERBOLT by Jules Verne
    (From 20,000 Leagues Under The Sea; 1873)
THE TRIFFID by John Wyndham ps (John Beynon Harris)
    (From The Day of The Triffids; 1951)
OFF FOR THE MOON by Edwin F. Northrup             (From ZERO TO EIGHTY; 1937 )
    (Originally appeared under pseudonym Akkad Pseudoman)

BLEILER, EVERETT F. & T. E. DIKTY
    THE BEST SCIENCE FICTION STORIES: 1949  Frederick Fell, Inc.; New York, N. Y.
    12 stories  314 pages  $2.94  September 12, 1949

    Note:  THE BEST  SCIENCE FICTION STORIES: 1949  and THE  BEST SCIENCE FICTION
           STORIES: 1950 were published under one title [SCIENCE FICTION OMNIBUS]
           by Garden City Books in January 1952.

MARS IS HEAVEN! by Ray Bradbury
EX MACHINA by Lewis Padgett ps (Henry Kuttner and C. L. Moore)
THE STRANGE CASE OF JOHN KINGMAN by Murray Leinster ps (Will F. Jenkins)

PS    Fal 1948
ASF   Apr 1948

DOUGHNUT JOCKEY by Erik Fennel
THANG by Martin Gardner
PERIOD PIECE by J. J. Coupling ps (John R. Pierce)
KNOCK by Fredric Brown
GENIUS by Poul Anderson
...AND THE MOON BE STILL AS BRIGHT by Ray Bradbury
NO CONNECTION by Isaac Asimov
IN HIDING by Wilmar H. Shiras
HAPPY ENDING by Henry Kuttner

ASF   May 1948
BB    May 1948
Cmt   Fal 1948
ASF   Nov 1948
TWS   Dec 1948
ASF   Dec 1948
TWS   Dec 1948
ASF   Jun 1948
ASF   Nov 1948
TWS   Aug 1948

    THE BEST SCIENCE FICTION STORIES: 1950  Frederick Fell, Inc.; New York, N. Y.
    13 stories  347 pages  $2.95  August 19, 1950

    Note:  THE BEST  SCIENCE FICTION STORIES: 1949  and THE  BEST SCIENCE FICTION
           STORIES: 1950 were published under one title [SCIENCE FICTION OMNIBUS]
           by Garden City Books in January 1952.

    Canadian Edition:  George J. McLeod Ltd.    (No change from American edition)

THE BEST SCIENCE FICTION STORIES: 1950 [Continued]          Mag.    Year

English Edition:  Grayson & Grayson Ltd.  8 stories  256 pages 8/6  ($1.20)
     Titled:  THE BEST SCIENCE FICTION STORIES          June 1951

|   |   |   |
|---|---|---|
| PRIVATE EYE by Henry Kuttner | ASF | Jan 1949 |
| (Originally appeared under pseudonym Lewis Padgett) | | |
| DOOMSDAY DEFERRED by Will F. Jenkins | SEP | 9/24/49 |
| THE HURKLE IS A HAPPY BEAST by Theodore Sturgeon | MoF | Fal 1949 |
| ETERNITY LOST by Clifford D. Simak | ASF | Jul 1949 |
| EASTER EGGS by Robert Spencer Carr | SEP | 9/24/49 |
| OPENING DOORS by Wilmar H. Shiras | ASF | Mar 1949 |
| FIVE YEARS IN THE MARMALADE by Robert W. Krepps | FA | Jul 1949 |
| (Originally appeared under pseudonym Geoff St. Reynard) | | |
| DWELLERS IN SILENCE by Ray Bradbury | PS | Spr 1949 |
| MOUSE by Fredric Brown | TWS | Jun 1949 |
| REFUGE FOR TONIGHT by Robert Moore Williams | BB | Mar 1949 |
| THE LIFE WORK OF PROFESSOR MUNTZ by Murray Leinster ps (Will F. Jenkins) | TWS | Jun 1949 |
| | Stg | Jan 1949 |
| FLAW by John D. MacDonald | TWS | Feb 1949 |
| THE MAN by Ray Bradbury | | |

THE BEST SCIENCE FICTION STORIES: 1951  Frederick Fell, Inc.; New York, N. Y.
18 stories  351 pages  $2.95  August 5, 1951

     Canadian Edition:  George J. McLeod Ltd.   (No change from American Edition)
     Pocket Book Edition:  Bantam Books; New York, N. Y. #1328  .35¢  1955
          Selections from THE BEST SCIENCE FICTION STORIES: 1951, 1952, 1953
               Titled:  FRONTIERS OF SPACE
     English Edition:  Grayson & Grayson Ltd.  14 stories  240 pages  9/6 ($1.35)
          Titled:  THE BEST SCIENCE FICTION STORIES: 2nd Series    July 10, 1952

|   |   |   |
|---|---|---|
| THE SANTA CLAUS PLANET by Frank M. Robinson | ORIGINAL STORY | |
| THE GNURRS COME FROM THE VOODVORK OUT by R. Bretnor | F&SF | Spr 1950 |
| THE MINDWORM by Cyril M. Kornbluth | WB | Dec 1950 |
| THE STAR DUCKS by Bill Brown | F&SF | Fal 1950 |
| NOT TO BE OPENED — by Roger Flint Young | ASF | Jan 1950 |
| PROCESS by A. E. Van Vogt | F&SF | Dec 1950 |
| FORGET-ME-NOT by William F. Temple | OW | Sep 1950 |
| CONTAGION by Katherine MacLean | Glxy | Oct 1950 |
| TRESPASS! by Poul Anderson and Gordon R. Dickson | FSQ | Spr 1950 |
| ODDY AND ID by Alfred Bester | ASF | Aug 1950 |
| (Originally appeared under title THE DEVIL'S INVENTION) | | |
| TO SERVE MAN by Damon Knight | Glxy | Nov 1950 |
| SUMMER WEAR by L. Sprague de Camp | Stg | May 1950 |
| BORN OF MAN AND WOMAN by Richard Matheson | F&SF | Sum 1950 |
| THE FOX IN THE FOREST by Ray Bradbury | Col | 5/13/50 |
| THE LAST MARTIAN by Fredric Brown | Glxy | Oct 1950 |
| THE NEW REALITY by Charles L. Harness | TWS | Dec 1950 |
| TWO FACE by Frank Belknap Long | WT | Mar 1950 |
| COMING ATTRACTION by Fritz Leiber | Glxy | Oct 1950 |

THE BEST SCIENCE FICTION STORIES: 1952  Frederick Fell, Inc.; New York, N. Y.
18 stories  288 pages  $2.95  August 19, 1952
     Canadian Edition:  George J. McLeod, Ltd.   (No Change from American edition)
     Pocket Book Edition:  Bantam Books; New York, N. Y. #1328  .35¢  1955
          Selections from THE BEST SCIENCE FICTION STORIES: 1951, 1952, 1953
               Titled:  FRONTIERS OF SPACE
     English Edition:  Grayson & Grayson Ltd.  16 stories  256 pages  9/6  ($1.35)
          Titled:  THE BEST SCIENCE FICTION STORIES: 3rd SERIES    9/21/53

| | | |
|---|---|---|
| THE OTHER SIDE by Walter Kubilius | Sup | Apr 1951 |
| OF TIME AND THIRD AVENUE by Alfred Bester | F&SF | Oct 1951 |
| THE MARCHING MORONS by Cyril M. Kornbluth | Glxy | Apr 1951 |
| A PECULIAR PEOPLE by Betsy Curtis | F&SF | Aug 1951 |
| EXTENDING THE HOLDINGS by David Grinnell | F&SF | Apr 1951 |
| THE TOURIST TRADE by Arthur Wilson Tucker | WB | Jan 1951 |
| (Originally appeared under Bob Tucker byline) | | |
| THE TWO SHADOWS by William F. Temple | Stg | Mar 1951 |
| BALANCE by John Christopher ps (Christopher S. Youd) | NW #9 | Spr 1951 |
| BRIGHTNESS FALLS FROM THE AIR by Idris Seabright ps (Margaret St. Clair) | | |
| | F&SF | Apr 1951 |
| WITCH WAR by Richard Matheson | F&SF | Jul 1951 |
| AT NO EXTRA COST by Peter Phillips | MSF | Aug 1951 |
| NINE-FINGER JACK by Anthony Boucher | Esq | May 1951 |
| APPOINTMENT IN TOMORROW by Fritz Leiber | Glxy | Jul 1951 |
| THE RATS by Arthur Porges | MnW | Feb 1951 |
| MEN OF THE TEN BOOKS by Jack Vance | Stg | Mar 1951 |
| GENERATION OF NOAH by William Tenn ps (Philip Klass) | Sus | Spr 1951 |
| DARK INTERLUDE by Mack Reynolds and Fredric Brown | Glxy | Jan 1951 |
| THE PEDESTRIAN by Ray Bradbury | Rptr | 9/7/51 |

THE BEST SCIENCE FICTION STORIES: 1953   Frederick Fell Inc.  New York, N. Y.
15 stories  279 pages  $3.50  September 6, 1953

Pocket Book Edition:  Bantam Books; New York #1328  .35¢  1955
    Selections from THE BEST SCIENCE FICTION STORIES: 1951; 1952; 1953
        Titled:  FRONTIERS OF SPACE
English Edition:  Grayson & Grayson Ltd.  13 stories 239 pages 9/6 (1/14/55)
    Titled:  THE BEST SCIENCE FICTION STORIES: FOURTH SERIES

| | | |
|---|---|---|
| THE FLY by Arthur Porges | F&SF | Sep 1952 |
| ARARAT by Zeena Henderson | F&SF | Oct 1952 |
| COUNTER-TRANSFERENCE by William F. Temple | TWS | Apr 1952 |
| THE CONQUEROR by Mark Clifton | ASF | Aug 1952 |
| MACHINE by John W. Jakes | F&SF | Apr 1952 |
| THE MIDDLE OF THE WEEK AFTER NEXT by Murray Leinster ps (Will F. Jenkins) | | |
| | TWS | Aug 1952 |
| THE DREAMER by Alfred Coppel | F&SF | Apr 1952 |
| THE MOON IS GREEN by Fritz Leiber | Glxy | Apr 1952 |
| I AM NOTHING by Eric Frank Russell | ASF | Jul 1952 |
| COMMAND PERFORMANCE by Walter M. Miller Jr | Glxy | Nov 1952 |
| SURVIVAL by John Wyndham ps (John Beynon Harris) | TWS | Feb 1952 |
| GAME FOR BLONDES by John D. MacDonald | Glxy | Oct 1952 |
| THE GIRLS FROM EARTH by Frank M. Robinson | Glxy | Jan 1952 |
| LOVER, WHEN YYOURE NEAR ME by Richard Matheson | Glxy | May 1952 |
| FAST FALLS THE EVENTIDE by Eric Frank Russell | ASF | May 1952 |

THE BEST SCIENCE FICTION STORIES: 1954   Frederick Fell, Inc.  New York, N.Y.
13 stories  316 pages  $3.50  November 16, 1954

English Edition:  Grayson & Grayson Ltd.  9 stories 207 pages 10/6 (2/17/56)
    Titled:  THE BEST SCIENCE FICTION STORIES: FIFTH SERIES

D P ! by Jack Vance                                          F&SF  Jan 1953

THE BEST SCIENCE FICTION STORIES: 1954 [Continued]  Mag.  Year

| | Mag. | Year |
|---|---|---|
| THE BIG HOLIDAY by Fritz Leiber | F&SF | Jan 1953 |
| THE COLLECTORS by G. Gordon Dewey and Max Dancey | Amz | Jul 1953 |
| ONE IN THREE HUNDRED by J. T M'Intosh ps (James J. MacGregor) | F&SF | Feb 1953 |
| WONDER CHILD by Joseph Shallit | Fnt | Feb 1953 |
| CRUCIFIXUS ETIAM by Walter M. Miller Jr. | ASF | Feb 1953 |
| THE MODEL OF A JUDGE by William Morrison ps (Joseph Samachson) | Glxy | Oct 1953 |
| THE LAST DAY by Richard Matheson | Amz | May 1953 |
| TIME IS THE TRAITOR by Alfred Bester | F&SF | Sep 1953 |
| LOT by Ward Moore | F&SF | May 1953 |
| YANKLE EXODUS by Ruth M. Goldsmith | F&SF | Jul 1953 |
| WHAT THIN PARTITIONS by Mark Clifton and Alex Apostolides | ASF | Sep 1953 |
| A BAD DAY FOR SALES by Fritz Leiber | Glxy | Jul 1953 |

INDEX: THE BEST SCIENCE FICTION STORIES: 1949 THROUGH 1954

IMAGINATION UNLIMITED        Farrar, Strauss·and Young  New York, N. Y.
13 stories   430 pages  $3.50  March 21, 1952

Pocket Book Edition:  Berkley Publishing Corp; New York
    # G233  7 stories  172 pages  April 1959
English Editions:  John Lane The Bodley Head Ltd.
     6 stories  175 pages  8/6  1953
               John Lane The Bodley Head Ltd.
     7 stories  221 pages  8/6  1953  (Titled MEN OF SPACE AND TIME)

### MATHEMATICS AND PHILOSOPHY

MATHEMATICS

| WHAT DEAD MEN TELL by Theodore Sturgeon | ASF | Nov 1949 |
|---|---|---|

PHILOSOPHY

REFERENT by Ray Bradbury — TWS Oct 1948
        (Originally appeared under house pseudonym Brett Sterling)

### THE PHYSICAL SCIENCES

GEOLOGY AND GEOGRAPHY

BLIND MAN'S BUFF by Malcolm Jameson — ASF Oct 1944

CHEMISTRY

PRESSURE by Ross Rocklynne — ASF Jun 1939

PHYSICS

THE XI EFFECT by Philip Latham ps (Robert S. Richardson) — ASF Jan 1950

ASTRONOMY

OLD FAITHFUL by Raymond Z. Gallun — Ast Dec 1934

### THE BIOLOGICAL SCIENCES

BIOLOGY

ALAS, ALL THINKING! by Harry Bates — Ast Jun 1935

BIO-CHEMISTRY

DUNE ROLLER by Julian C. May — ASF Dec 1951

PALEONTOLOGY

EMPLOYMENT by L. Sprague deCamp — ASF May 1939
        (Originally appeared under pseudonym Lyman R. Lyon)

### THE SOCIAL SCIENCES

(16)

PSYCHOLOGY | Mag. | Year
DREAMS ARE SACRED by Peter Phillips — ASF Sep 1948
SOCIOLOGY
HOLD BACK TOMORROW by Kris Neville — Im Sep 1951
LINGUISTICS
BEROM by John Berryman — ASF Jun 1951
ANTHROPOLOGY
THE FIRE AND THE SWORD by Frank Robinson — Glxy Aug 1951

YEAR'S BEST SCIENCE FICTION NOVELS: 1952  Frederick Fell Inc.  New York, N. Y.
5 stories  351 pages  $3.50  June 9, 1952

English Edition:  Grayson & Grayson Ltd.  4 stories  263 pages  9/6  (4/7/53)
Titled:  YEAR'S BEST SCIENCE FICTION NOVELS

IZZARD AND THE MEMBRANE by Walter M. Miller Jr. — ASF May 1951
...AND THEN THERE WERE NONE by Eric Frank Russell — ASF Jun 1951
FLIGHT TO FOREVER by Poul Anderson — Sep Nov 1950
THE HUNTING SEASON by Frank M. Robinson — ASF Nov 1951
SEEKER OF THE SPHINX by Arthur C. Clarke — 2CB Spr 1951

YEAR'S BEST SCIENCE FICTION NOVELS: 1953  Frederick Fell Inc.  New York, N. Y.
5 stories  315 pages  $3.50  June 2, 1953

English Edition:  The Bodley Head Ltd.  3 stories  192 pages  9/6
Titled:  CATEGORY PHOENIX                  Copyright: 1955

FIREWATER by William Tenn ps (Philip Klass) — ASF Feb 1952
CATEGORY PHOENIX by Boyd Ellanby ps (William C. and Lyle G. Boyd) — Glxy May 1952
SURFACE TENSION by James Blish — Glxy Aug 1952
THE GADGET HAD A GHOST by Murray Leinster ps (Will F. Jenkins) — TWS Jun 1952
CONDITIONALLY HUMAN by Walter M. Miller Jr. — Glxy Feb 1952

YEAR'S BEST SCIENCE FICTION NOVELS: 1954  Frederick Fell Inc.  New York, N. Y.
5 stories  317 pages  $3.50  June 2, 1954

English Edition:  Grayson & Grayson Ltd.  4 stories 240 pages 10/6  (12/2/55)
Titled:  YEAR'S BEST SCIENCE FICTION NOVELS: SECOND SERIES

THE ENORMOUS ROOM by H. L. Gold and Robert W. Krepps — Amz Nov 1953
ASSIGNMENT TO ALDEBARAN by Kendall Foster Crossen — TWS Feb 1953
THE OCEANS ARE WIDE by Frank M. Robinson — SS Apr 1954
THE SENTAMENTALISTS by Murray Leinster ps (Will F. Jenkins) — Glxy Apr 1953
SECOND VARIETY by Philip K. Dick — Spc May 1953

BOUCHER, ANTHONY & J. FRANCIS McCOMAS
THE BEST FROM FANTASY AND SCIENCE FICTION     Little Brown & Co.; Mass.
19 stories  214 pages  $2.75  March 3, 1952

[Editor's Note:  There are stories listed in The BEST FROM FANTASY & SCIENCE FIC-
TION SERIES that were originally published elsewhere.  In these cases, the original book and/or magazine is given when known.  As all stories listed in the

next four pages  were reprinted  from FANTASY & SCIENCE FICTION only the issue
is given.

HUGE BEAST by Cleve Cartmill                                    Summer 1950
JOHN THE REVELATOR by Oliver La Farge                         February 1951
GAVAGAN'S BAR by L. Sprague de Camp and Fletcher Pratt          Spring 1950
THE FRIENDLY DEMON by Daniel Defoe                            February 1951
        (Originally printed by J. Roberts; London: 1726)
OLD MAN HENDERSON by Kris Neville                                 June 1951
THE THREEPENNY PIECE by James Stephens                           June 1951
        (From HERE ARE LADIES; 1913)
NO-SIDED PROFESSOR by Martin Gardner                          February 1951
        (Originally appeared in Esquire January 1947)
THE LISTENING CHILD by Idris Seabright ps (Margaret St. Clair)  December 1950
DRESS OF WHITE SILK by Richard Matheson                        October 1951
THE MATHEMATICAL VOODOO by H. Nearing Jr.                         April 1951
THE HUB by Philip MacDonald                                     August 1951
        (Originally appeared under title SOLITARY CONFINEMENT)
BUILT UP LOGICALLY by Howard Schoenfeld                           Fall 1950
        (Originally aprd under title THE UNIVERSAL PANACEA in Retort, Winter 1949)
THE RAT THAT COULD SPEAK by Charles Dickens                     August 1951
        (Org aprd in ALL THE YEAR AROUND — Vol. III [Nurse's Stories: Sept 8, 1960])
NARAPOIA by Alan Nelson                                           April 1951
        (Originally aprd under title THE ORIGIN OF NARAPOIA in What's Doing Apr 1948)
POSTPAID TO PARADISE by Robert Arthur                           Spring 1950
        (Originally aprd under title POSTMARKED FOR PARADISE in Argosy: June 15, 1940)
IN THE DAYS OF OUR FATHERS by Winona McClintic                    Fall 1949
BARNEY by Will Stanton                                            April 1951
THE COLLECTOR by H. F. Heard                                    August 1951
FEARSOME FABLE by Bruce Elliott                               February 1951


        THE BEST FROM FANTASY AND SCIENCE FICTION  (2nd Series)
        18 stories  270 pages  $3.00  March 16, 1953  Little Brown & Co.; Mass.


BUDDING EXPLORER by Ralph Robin                             September 1952
THE SHOUT by Robert Graves                                       April 1952
        (Originally published by Elkins Mathews & Marlot Ltd.; 1929)
THE TOOTH by G. Gordon Dewey                                    August 1952
UGLY SISTER by Jan Struther ps (Joyce Maxtone Graham)         February 1952
        (Originally appeared in London Mercury: December 1935)
THE BLACK BALL by L. Sprague de Camp and Fletcher Pratt        October 1952
THE HOLE IN THE MOON by Idris Seabright ps (Margaret St. Clair) February 1952
THE THIRD LEVEL by Jack Finney                                 October 1952
        (Originally appeared in Collier's: October 7, 1950)
THE CHERRY SOUL by Elizabeth Bowen                               April 1952
        (From IVY GRIPPED THE STEPS; 1945)
RANSOM by H. B. Fyfe                                          February 1952
THE EARLIER SERVICE by Margaret Irwin                         December 1951
        (From MADAME FEARS THE DARK: SEVEN STORIES AND A PLAY; 1935)
THE HYPERSPHERICAL BASKETBALL by H. Nearing Jr.               December 1951
THE DESRICK ON YANDRO by Manly Wade Wellman                       June 1952
COME ON WAGON! by Zeena Henderson                             December 1951
JIZZLE by John Wyndham ps (John Beynon Harris)                February 1952
        (Originally appeared in Collier's January 8, 1949 under pseudonyn John Beynon)
                (Revised for publication in Fantasy & Science Fiction

STAIR TRICK by Mildred Clingerman                                    August 1952
THE SOOTHSAYER by Kem Bennett                                        August 1952
HOBSON'S CHOICE by Alfred Bester                                     August 1952
LETTERS TO THE EDITOR by Ron Goulart                                 April 1952
   (Originally appeared in Pelican Magazine; October 1961)

THE BEST FROM FANTASY AND SCIENCE FICTION: 3rd SERIES
16 stories   252 pages   $3.25   February 18, 1954   Doubleday & Co.; New York

Pocket Book Edition: Ace Books; New York   D-422 .35¢          (2/15/60)

ATTITUDES by Philip Jose Farmer                                      October 1953
MAYBE JUST A LITTLE ONE by R. Bretnor                               February 1953
   (Originally appeared in Harper's; August 1947)
THE STAR GYPSIES by William Lindsay Gresham                           July 1953
THE UNTIMELY TOPER by L. Sprague de Camp and Fletcher Pratt          July 1953
VANDY, VANDY by Manly Wade Wellman                                    March 1953
EXPERIMENT by Kay Rogers                                           February 1953
LOT by Ward Moore                                                       May 1953
MANUSCRIPT FOUND IN A VACUUM by P. M. Hubbard                        August 1953
   (Originally appeared in Punch; 12/17/52)
THE MALADJUSTED CLASSROOM by H. Nearing Jr.                           June 1953
CHILD BY CHRONOS by Charles L. Harness                               June 1953
NEW RITUAL by Idris Seabright ps (Margaret St. Clair)              January 1953
DEVLIN by W. B. Ready                                                April 1953
CAPTIVE AUDIENCE by Ann Warren Griffith                             August 1953
SNULBUG by Anthony Boucher                                             May 1953
   (Originally appeared in Unknown Worlds; December 1941)
SHEPARD'S BOY by Richard Middleton                                   March 1953
STAR SLIGHT, STAR BRIGHT by Alfred Bester                            July 1953

BOUCHER, ANTHONY

THE BEST FROM FANTASY AND SCIENCE FICTION: 4th SERIES
15 stories 6 verses 250 pages $3.50   January 6, 1955   Doubleday & Co.; N. Y.

Pocket Book Edition: Ace Books; New York   D-455 .35¢          (8/15/60)

FONDLY FAHRENHEIT by Alfred Bester                                   August 1954
I NEVER AST NO FAVORS by C. M. Kornbluth                             April 1954
SOME FACTS ABOUT ROBOTS by Leonard Wolfe        (verse)              July 1954
HEIRS APPARENT by Robert Abernathy                                   June 1954
$1.98 by Arthur Porges                                                 May 1954
THE IMMORTAL GAME by Poul Anderson                                February 1954
ALL SUMMER IN A DAY by Ray Bradbury                                  March 1954
THE ACCOUNTANT by Robert Sheckley                                    July 1954
EPITAPH NEAR MOONPORT by Sherwood Springer      (verse)             July 1954
BRAVE NEW WORLD by J. Francis McComas                            September 1954
MY BOY FRIEND'S NAME IS JELLO by Avram Davidson                      July 1954
THE TEST by Richard Matheson                                      November 1954
CARELESS LOVE by Albert Compton Friborg                              July 1954
REPORT ON THE SEXUAL BEHAVIOR OF THE EXTRA-SENSORY PERCEPTOR by Herman W. Mudgett
                                               (verse)         August 1954
BULLETIN by Shirley Jackson                                          March 1954

| | |
|---|---|
| SANCTUARY by Daniel F. Galouye | February 1954 |
| MISADVENTURE by Lord Dunsany | October 1954 |
| MORE FACTS ABOUT ROBOTS by Leonard Wolfe      (verse) | January 1954 |
| THE LITTLE BLACK TRAIN by Manly Wade Wellman | August 1954 |
| COWBOY LAMENT by Norman R. Jaffray      (verse) | January 1954 |
| THE FOUNDATION OF SCIENCE FICTION SUCCESS by Isaac Asimov  (verse) | October 1954 |

THE BEST FROM FANTASY AND SCIENCE FICTION: 5th SERIES
20 stories 6 verses 256 pages $3.50  January 5, 1956  Doubleday & Co.; N. Y.

Pocket Book Edition:  Ace Books; New York  F-105  .40¢          (7/15/61)

| | |
|---|---|
| IMAGINE: A PROEM by Fredric Brown | May 1955 |
| YOU'RE ANOTHER by Damon Knight | June 1955 |
| SURVIVAL by Carlyn Coffin      (verse) | June 1955 |
| THIS EARTH OF MAJESTY by Arthur C. Clarke | July 1955 |
| BIRDS CAN'T COUNT by Mildred Clingerman | February 1955 |
| THE GOLEM by Avram Davidson | March 1955 |
| 1980 OVERTURES by Winona McClintic      (verse) | April 1955 |
| POTTAGE by Zeena Henderson | September 1955 |
| THE VANISHING AMERICAN by Charles Beaumont | August 1955 |
| CREATED HE THEM by Alice Eleanor Jones | June 1955 |
| SILENT, UPON TWO PEAKS by Herman W. Mudgett      (verse) | July 1955 |
| FOUR VIGNETTES | |
| TOO FAR by Fredric Brown | September 1955 |
| A MATTER OF ENERGY by James Blish | May 1955 |
| (Excerpt from WITH MALICE TO COME — 3 vignettes) | |
| NELLTHU by Anthoby Boucher | August 1955 |
| DREAMWORLD by Isaac Asimov | November 1955 |
| ONE ORDINARY DAY, WITH PEANUTS by Shirley Jackson | January 1955 |
| THE GLASS OF THE FUTURE by Herman W. Mudgett   (verse) | January 1955 |
| THE SHORT ONES by Raymond E. Banks | March 1955 |
| THE LAST PROPHET by Mildred Clingerman | August 1955 |
| BOTANY BAY by P, M. Hubbard | February 1955 |
| A CANTICLE FOR LEIBOWITZ by Walter M. Miller Jr. | April 1955 |
| LAMENT FOR A MAKER by L. Sprague deCamp      (verse) | January 1955 |
| THE DOCTRINE OF ORIGINAL DESIGN by Winona McClintic  (verse) | March 1955 |
| PATTERN FOR SURVIVAL by Richard Matheson | May 1955 |
| THE SINGING BELL by Isaac Asimov | January 1955 |
| THE LAST WORD by Chad Oliver and Charles Beaumont | April 1955 |

THE BEST FROM FANTASY AND SCIENCE FICTION: 6th Series
15 stories 8 verses 255 pages $3.50  January 10, 1957  Doubleday & Co.; N.Y.

| | |
|---|---|
| THE COSMIC EXPENSE ACCOUNT by C. M. Kornbluth | January 1956 |
| BLAZE OF GLORY by Randall Garrett      (verse) | December 1955 |
| MR. SAKRISON'S HALT by Mildred Clingerman | January 1956 |
| THE WOODS GROW DARKER by Leah Bodine Drake      (verse) | November 1955 |
| THE ASA RULE by Jay Williams | June 1956 |
| KING'S EVIL by Avram Davidson | October 1956 |
| INTERVIEW by Bird Ferguson      (verse) | December 1955 |
| THE CENSUS TAKERS by Frederik Pohl | February 1956 |
| FLYING CHAUCER by Anthony Brode      (verse) | March 1956 |
| THE MAN WHO CAME EARLY by Poul Anderson | June 1956 |

THE BEST FROM FANTASY AND SCIENCE FICTION: 6th SERIES [Continued]    Year

THE ANTI-CLIMAX by Winona McClintic          (verse)          January 1956
FINAL CLEARANCE by Rachel Maddux                              February 1956
THE SILK AND THE SONG by Charles L. Fontenay                     July 1956
THE SHODDY LANDS by C. S. Lewis                              February 1956
I WANT MY NAME IN THE TITLE by Winona McClintic  (verse)        July 1956
THE LAST PRESENT by Will Stanton                              August 1956
NO MAN PURSUETH by Ward Moore                                  April 1956
I DON'T MIND by Ron Smith                                    October 1956
THE BARBARIAN by Poul Anderson                                  May 1956
BRIGHT DESTRUCTION by Winona McClintic       (verse)           June 1956
AND NOW THE NEWS... by Theodore Sturgeon                    December 1956
ICARUS MONTGOLFIER WRIGHT by Ray Bradbury                      May 1956
FREE FLIGHT by P. M. Hubbard                 (verse)          April 1956

        THE BEST FROM FANTASY AND SCIENCE FICTION: 7th SERIES
        17 stories 3 verses 264 pages $3.75  January 16, 1958  Doubleday & Co.; N. Y.

THE WINES OF EARTH by Idris Seabright ps (Margaret St. Clair)    September 1957
IN MEMORIAM: FLETCHER PRATT by James Blish       (verse)         January 1957
ADJUSTMENT by Ward Moore                                          May 1957
THE CAGE by Bertram Chandler                                     June 1957
MR. STILWELL'S STAGE by Avram Davidson                      September 1957
VENTURE TO THE MOON by Arthur C. Clarke      (article)       December 1956
EXPEDITION by Fredric Brown                                  February 1957
LYRIC FOR ATOM-SPLITTERS by Doris Pitkin Buck  (verse)          May 1957
RESCUE by G. C. Edmondson                                        June 1957
HORROR STORY SHORTER BY ONE LETTER THAN THE SHORTEST HORROR STORY EVER WRITTEN
    by Ron Smith                                            Original Story
BETWEEN THE THUNDER AND THE SUN by Chad Oliver                   May 1957
A LOINT OF PAW by Isaac Asimov                                August 1957
THE WILD WOOD by Mildred Clingerman                          January 1957
DODGER FAN by Will Stanton                                       June 1957
GODDESS IN GRANITE by Robert F. Young                       September 1957
YES, BUT... by Anthony Brode                                September 1957
MS. FOUND IN A CHINESE FORTUNE COOKIE by C. M. Kornbluth        July 1957
JOURNEY'S END by Poul Anderson                              February 1957
FULL CIRCLE by Dorothy Cowles Pinkney        (verse)        December 1957
THE BIG TREK by Fritz Leiber                                October 1957

        THE BEST FROM FANTASY AND SCIENCE FICTION: 8th SERIES
        15 stories 7 verses 240 pages $3.75  January 8, 1959  Doubleday & Co.; N. Y.

MINISTERING ANGELS by C. S. Lewis                               January 1958
THROUGH TIME AND SPACE WITH FERDINAND FEGHOTT (VII) by Grendel Briarton
    ps (R. Bretnor)                                             March 1958
BACKWARDNESS by Poul Anderson                                   March 1958
THE WAIT by Kit Reed                                            April 1958
ORIGIN OF THE SPECIES by Karen Anderson      (verse)            June 1958
THE UP-TO-DATE SORCERER by Isaac Asimov                         July 1958
EPITHALAMIUM by Doris Pitkin Buck                            January 1958
A DESKFUL OF GIRLS by Fritz Leiber                             April 1958
THE WATCHERS by Anthony Brode                 (verse)          April 1958
POOR LITTLE WARRIOR! by Brian W. Aldiss                        April 1958
THE BETTER BET by Anthony Brode              (verse)        February 1958

THE BEST FROM FANTASY AND SCIENCE FICTION: 8th SERIES [Continued]     Year

THE OMEN by Shirley Jackson                          (verse)                    March 1958
YE PHANTASIE WRITER AND HIS CATTE by Winona McClintic      (verse)    March 1958
GIL BRALTER by Jules Verne                                                          July 1958
     (From LE CHEMIN DE FRANCE; 1887)     Translated from French by I. O. Evans
IN MEMORIAM: HENRY KUTTNER by Karen Anderson            (verse)        May 1958
THE GRANTHA SIGHTING by Avram Davidson                                      April 1958
THEORY OF ROCKETRY by C. M. Kornbluth                                         July 1958
A NEW LO! by Ron Goulart                            (article)            January 1958
GORILLA SUIT by John Shepley                                                       May 1958
CAPTIVITY by Zeena Henderson                                                       June 1958
THE MEN WHO MURDERED MOHAMMED by Alfred Bester                    October 1958
THROUGH TIME AND SPACE WITH FERDINAND FEGHOOT (VIII) by Grendel Briarton
     ps (R. Bretnor)                                                             August 1958


A TREASURY OF GREAT SCIENCE FICTION  [2 Volumes]           Mag.     Year
     24 stories  527 pages (Volume I)  522 pages (Volume 2)  $5.95
          Doubleday & Co.; New York       November 19, 1959
                              VOLUME I
RE-BIRTH by John Wyndham ps (John Beynon Harris)
     (Originally published by Ballantine Books; 1955)
THE SHAPE OF THINGS TO COME by Richard Deming                    F&SF   Oct 1951
PILLAR OF FIRE by Ray Bradbury                                            PS   Sum 1948
WALDO by Robert A. Heinlein                                              ASF   Aug 1942
     (Originally appeared under pseudonym Anson MacDonald)
THE FATHER-THING by Phillip K. Dick                             F&SF   Dec 1954
THE CHILDREN'S HOUR by Henry Kuttner and C. L. Moore            ASF   Mar 1944
     (Originally appeared under pseudonym Lawrence O'Donnell)
GOMEZ by C. M. Kornbluth                                       NW #32   Jan 1955
THE [WIDGET], THE [WADGETT], AND BOFF by Theodore Sturgeon   F&SF   Nov 1955
SANDRA by George P. Elliott                                     Epch   Fal 1953
BEYOND SPACE AND TIME by Joel Townsley Rogers                   SSS   Sep 1950
THE MARTIAN CROWN JEWELS by Poul Anderson                      EQMM   Feb 1958
THE WEAPON SHOPS OF ISHER by A. E. Van Vogt
     (Originally published by Greenberg Publishers; 1951)
                              VOLUME 2

BRAIN WAVE by Poul Anderson
     (Originally published by Ballantine Books; 1954)
BULLARD REFLECTS by Malcolm Jameson                            ASF   Dec 1941
THE LOST YEARS by Oscar Lewis
     (Originally published by Alfred A. Knopf; 1951)
DEAD CENTER by Judith Merril                                   F&SF   Nov 1954
LOST ART by George O. Smith                                     ASF   Dec 1957
THE OTHER SIDE OF THE SKY by Arthur C. Clarke                   Inf   Sep 1957
THE MAN WHO SOLD THE MOON by Robert A. Heinlein
     (Originally published by Shasta; 1950)
MAGIC CITY by Nelson S. Bond                                   ASF   Feb 1941
THE MORNING OF THE DAY THEY DID IT by E. B. White             Nykr   2/25/50
     (Re: The Second Tree From The Corner; 1950
PIGGY BANK by Henry Kuttner  (Org aprd under pseud Lewis Padgett)  ASF  Dec 1942
LETTERS FROM LAURA by Mildred Clingerman                       F&SF   Oct 1954
THE STARS MY DESTINATION by Alfred Bester                      Glxy   Oct 1954

BRADBURY, RAY
    TIMELESS STORIES FOR TODAY AND TOMORROW    Bantam Books; New York
    25 stories  306 pages  #A-944  .35¢  September 10, 1952

|  | Mag. | Year |
|---|---|---|
| THE HOUR AFTER WESTERLY by Robert M. Coates | Nykr | 11/1/47 |
| HOUSING PROBLEM by Henry Kuttner | Chm | Oct 1944 |
| THE PORTABLE PHONOGRAPH by Walter Van Tilburg Clark |  |  |
| (From THE WATCHFUL GODS AND OTHER STORIES; 1941) |  |  |
| NONE BEFORE ME by Sidney Carroll | Cpln | Jul 1949 |
| PUTZI by Ludwig Bemelmanns |  |  |
| (From SMALL BEER; 1939) |  |  |
| THE DEMON LOVER by Shirley Jackson |  |  |
| (From THE LOTTERY; 1949) |  |  |
| MISS WINTERS AND THE WIND by Christine Noble Govan | Tmw | May 1946 |
| MR. DEATH AND THE REDHEADED WOMAN by Helen Eustis | SEP | 2/11/50 |
| (Originally aprd under title THE RIDER ON THE PALE HORSE) |  |  |
| JEREMY IN THE WIND by Nigel Kneale |  |  |
| (From TOMATO CAIN; 1950) |  |  |
| THE GLASS EYE by John Kier Cross |  |  |
| (From THE OTHER PASSENGER; 1946) |  |  |
| SAINT KATY THE VIRGIN by John Steinbeck |  |  |
| (From THE LONG VALLEY; 1938) |  |  |
| NIGHT FLIGHT by Josephine W. Johnson | Hpr | Feb 1944 |
| THE COCOON by John B. L. Goodwin | Sty | Oct 1946 |
| THE HAND by Wessell Hyatt Smitter | Sty | Feb 1947 |
| THE SOUND MACHINE by Roald Dahl | Nykr | 9/17/49 |
| I AM WAITING by Christopher Isherwood | Nykr | 10/21/39 |
| THE WITNESSES by William Sansom |  |  |
| (From FIREMAN FLOWER AND OTHER FLOWERS; 1944) |  |  |
| THE ENORMOUS RADIO by John Cheever | Nykr | 5/17/47 |
| HEARTBURN by Hortense Calisher |  |  |
| (From IN THE ABSENCE OF ANGELS; 1951) |  |  |
| THE SUPREMACY OF URUGUAY by E. B. White | Nykr | 11/25/33 |
| THE PEDESTRIAN by Ray Bradbury | Rptr | 8/5/51 |
| A NOTE FOR THE MILKMAN by Sidney Carroll | Tdw | Apr 1950 |
| THE EIGHT MISTRESSES by Jean Hrolda | Esq | Aug 1937 |
| IN THE PENAL COLONY by Franz Kafka    Translated by Willa and Edmin Muir |  |  |
| (From THE PENAL COLONY; 1948) |  |  |
| INFLEXIBLE LOGIC by Russell Maloney | Nykr | 2/3/40 |

BRINEY, ROBERT E.
    SHANADU                SSR Publications; North Tonawanda, New York
    3 stories  101 pages  $1.50  November 1953

ALL ORIGINAL STORIES

QUEST OF THE VEIL by Eugene Deweese

THE FIRE BORN by Toby Duane ps (W. Paul Ganley)

THE BLACK TOWER by Brian J. McNaughton and Andrew Duane
    (Andrew Duane is a pseudonym of Robert E. Briney)

```
BROWN, FREDRIC & MACK REYNOLDS                                        Mag.    Year
     SCIENCE FICTION CARNIVAL          Shasta Publishers; Chicago, Ill.
     13 stories  315 pages  $3.25  December 8, 1953


     Pocket Book Edition:  Bantam Books; Chicago, Ill.  # A 1615
          10 stories  .35¢  1957

THE WHEEL OF TIME by Robert Arthur                                    Sup   Mar 1950
SRL AD by Richard Matheson                                            F&SF  Apr 1952
A LOGIC NAMED JOE by Murray Leinster ps (Will F. Jenkins)             ASF   Mar 1946
     (Originally appeared under byline of Will F. Jenkins)
SIMWORTHY'S CIRCUS by Larry Shaw                                      WB    Dec 1950
THE WELL-OILED MACHINE by H. B. Fyfe                                  F&SF  Dec 1950
VENUS AND THE SEVEN SEXES by William Tenn ps (Philip Klass)
     (From THE GIRL WITH THE HUNGRY EYES & OTHER STORIES; 1949)
SWORDSMAN OF VARNIS by Clive Jackson                                  OW    Sep 1950
PARADOX LOST by Fredric Brown                                         ASF   Oct 1943
MUTEN by Eric Frank Russell                                          ASF   Oct 1948
     (Originally appeared under psuedonvm Duncan H. Munro)
THE MARTIANS AND THE COYS by Mack Reynolds                            Im    Jun 1951
THE EGO MACHINE by Henry Kuttner                                      Spc   May 1952
THE COSMIC JACKPOT by George O. Smith                                 TWS   Oct 1948
THE ABDUCTION OF ABNER GREEN by Nelson Bond                           BB    Jun 1941


CAMPBELL, H. J.
     TOMORROW'S UNIVERSE          Hamilton and Co. (Stafford) Ltd; London)
     8 stories  224 pages  8/6  May 1954


     Pocket Book Edition:  Pr#101  2/   (Same as hard cover edition)

HERITAGE by Charles L. Harness                                        F&SF  Fal 1950
IT PAYS TO ADVERTISE by Kris Neville                                  F&SF  Jun 1953
TICKING HIS LIFE AWAY by T. D. Hamm                                   ORIGINAL STORY
M 33 IN ANDROMEDA by A. E. Van Vogt                                   ASF   Aug 1943
THE IMMORTAL by Ross Rocklynne                                        Com   Mar 1941
THE SHORE OF TOMORROW by Chad Oliver                                  Stg   Mar 1953
THE SOARING STATUE by L. Sprague de Camp                              ORIGINAL STORY
EXTERRAN by Milton Lesser                                             ORIGINAL STORY


CAMPBELL, JOHN W. JR.
     THE ASTOUNDING SCIENCE FICTION ANTHOLOGY   Simon & Schuster; New York, N. Y.
     23 stories  585 pages  $3.95  February 20, 1952


     Pocket Book Editions:  Berkeley Publishing Corp.; New York  #G41  .35¢  12/56
          Titled: THE ASTOUNDING SCIENCE FICTION ANTHOLOGY 8 stories 188 pages
          Berkeley Publishing Corp.; New York  #G47  .35¢  February 1957 7 stories
          Titled: ASTOUNDING TALES OF SPACE AND TIME  189 pages

     English Editions:  Grayson & Grayson Ltd.  8 stories  240 pages  9/6
          Titled:  THE FIRST ASTOUNDING SCIENCE FICTION ANTHOLOGY  March 22, 1954
               Grayson & Grayson Ltd.  8 stories  224 pages  9/6
     Titled: THE SECOND ASTOUNDING SCIENCE FICTION ANTHOLOGY November 12, 1954

               ALL STORIES FROM ASTOUNDING SCIENCE FICTION

BLOWUPS HAPPEN by Robert A. Heinlein                            September 1940
```

| | |
|---|---|
| HINDSIGHT by Jack Williamson | May 1940 |
| VAULT OF THE BEAST by A. E. Van Vogt | August 1940 |
| THE EXALTED by L. Sprague de Camp | November 1940 |
| NIGHTFALL by Isaac Asimov | September 1941 |
| WHEN THE BOUGH BREAKS by Lewis Padgett ps (Henry Kuttner & C. L. Moore) | |
| | November 1944 |
| CLASH BY NIGHT by Lawrence O'Donnell ps (C. L. Moore) | March 1943 |
| INVARIANT by John R. Pierce | April 1944 |
| FIRST CONTACT by Murray Leinster ps (Will F. Jenkins) | May 1945 |
| MEIHEM IN CE KLASRUM by Dolton Edwards | September 1946 |
| "HOBBYIST" by Eric Frank Russell | September 1947 |
| E FOR EFFORT by T. L. Sherred | May 1947 |
| CHILD'S PLAY by William Tenn ps (Philip Klass) | March 1947 |
| THUNDER AND ROSES by Theodore Sturgeon | November 1947 |
| LATE NIGHT FINAL by Eric Frank Russell | December 1948 |
| COLD WAR by Kris Neville | October 1949 |
| ETERNITY LOST by Clifford D. Simak | July 1949 |
| THE WITCHES OF KARRES by James L. Schmitz | December 1949 |
| OVER THE TOP by Lester del Rey | November 1949 |
| METEOR by William T. Powers | September 1950 |
| LAST ENEMY by H. Beam Piper | August 1950 |
| HISTORICAL NOTE by Murray Leinster ps (Will F. Jenkins) | February 1951 |
| PROTECTED SPECIES by H. B. Fyfe | March 1951 |

FROM UNKNOWN WORLDS          13 stories   4 verses

   Paperback Edition:  Street & Smith Publications; New York, N. Y.
      130 pages   .25¢  July 1948

   Hard Cover Edition:  Atlas Publishing & Distributing Co., Ltd.  (England)
      124 pages   .75¢  March 1952

                         ALL STORIES FROM UNKNOWN WORLDS

| | |
|---|---|
| THE ENCHANTED WEEKEND by John McCormac | October 1939 |
| NOTHING IN THE RULES by L. Sprague de Camp | July 1939 |
| THE COMPLEAT WEREWOLF by Anthony Boucher | April 1942 |
| THE REFUGEE by Jane Rice | October 1943 |
| THE CLOAK by Robert Bloch | May 1939 |
| YESTERDAY WAS MONDAY by Theodore Sturgeon | June 1941 |
| TROUBLE WITH WATER by H. L. Gold | March 1939 |
| ANYTHING by Philip St. John ps (Lester del Rey) | October 1939 |
| THE DEVIL WE KNOW by Henry Kuttner | August 1941 |
| THE PSYCHOMORPH by E. A. Grosser | February 1940 |
| THE HEXER by H. W. Guernsey ps (Howard Wandrei) | June 1939 |
| THE SUMMONS by Don Evans | June 1939 |
| JESUS SHOES by Allan R. Bosworth | April 1942 |

VERSES

| | |
|---|---|
| FICTION by Allen Grant | February 1941 |
| LURANI by Paul Dennis Lavond  hs pseud (Robert W. Lowndes) | February 1940 |
| BLACK CATS by Christel Hastings | December 1940 |
| THE DAWN OF REASON by James E. Beard | October 1939 |

CARNELL, JOHN

    THE BEST FROM NEW WORLDS     T. V. Boardman & Co.; Ltd.; England   Year
    8 stories  190 pages  #163  2/  February 24, 1955

### ALL STORIES FROM NEW WORLDS

| | | |
|---|---|---|
| THE HARD WAY by Alan Barclay | #21 | June 1953 |
| CROSSFIRE by James White | #21 | June 1953 |
| JETSAM by A. Bertram Chandler | #20 | March 1953 |
| ROCKETS AREN'T HUMAN by E. C. Tubb | #20 | March 1953 |
| SHIP FROM THE STARS by Peter Hawkins | #25 | July 1954 |
| ROBOTS DON'T BLEED by J. W. Groves | #8 | Winter 1950 |
| THE BROKEN RECORD by J. T. M'Intosh ps (James J. MacGregor) | #17 | Sep 1952 |
| UNKNOWN QUANTITY by Peter Phillips | #5 | n/d 1949 |

    GATEWAY TO THE STARS     Museum Press; London, England  Mag.    Year
    9 stories  191 pages  March 16, 1955  9/6

| | | |
|---|---|---|
| STITCH IN TIME by J. T. McIntosh ps (James J. MacGregor) | SF #5 | Aut 1952 |
| ONLY AN ECHO by Alan Barclay | NW #22 | Apr 1954 |
| CONSPIRACY by John Christopher ps (Christopher S. Youd) | Auth #53 | Jan 1955 |
| STRANGER FROM SPACE by Gene Lees | SF #7 | Mar 1954 |
| NEVER ON MARS by John Beynon Harris | FU | Jan 1954 |
| ASSISTED PASSAGE by James White | NW #19 | Jan 1955 |
| CIRCUS by Peter Hawkins | SF #5 | Aut 1952 |
| UNFORTUNATE PASSAGE by E. C. Tubb | SF #7 | Mar 1954 |
| OPERATION EXODUS by Lan Wright | NW #13 | Jan 1952 |

    GATEWAY TO TOMORROW     Museum Press; London, England
    10 stories  192 pages  9/6  February 1954

| | | |
|---|---|---|
| DUMB MARTIAN by John Wyndham ps (John Beynon Harris) | Glxy | Jul 1952 |
| HIDE AND SEEK by Arthur C. Clarke | ASF | Sep 1949 |
| HOME IS THE HERO by E. C. Tubb | NW #15 | May 1952 |
| LOST MEMORY by Peter Phillips | Glxy | May 1952 |
| OF THOSE WHO CAME by George Langdon | NW #18 | Nov 1952 |
| THE BLISS OF SOLITUDE by J. T. M'Intosh ps (James J. MacGregor) | Glxy | Jan 1952 |
|    (Originally appeared under title HALLUCINATION ORBIT) | | |
| A FINISHING TOUCH by A. Bertram Chandler | NW #16 | Jul 1952 |
| THE DROP by John Christopher ps (Christopher S. Youd) | Glxy | Mar 1953 |
| EMERGENCY WORKING by E. R. James | NW #17 | Sep 1952 |
| LIFE CYCLE by Peter Hawkins | NW #9 | Spr 1951 |

    NO PLACE LIKE EARTH     T. V. Boardman & Co., Ltd.; England

    Hard Cover Edition:  10 stories  255 pages  9/6  October 1952
    Paper Bound Edition:  7 stories  192 pages  2/  February 26, 1954

| | | |
|---|---|---|
| NO PLACE LIKE EARTH by John Beynon ps (John Beynon Harris) | | |
|    (Original version appeared in New Worlds #9 Spring 1951) | | |
|    (This version incorporates TIME TO REST from the Arkham Sampler; Winter 49) | | |
| BREAKING STRAIN by Arthur C. Clarke | TWS | Dec 1949 |
|    (Originally appeared under title THIRTY SECONDS — THIRTY DAYS) | | |
| SURVIVAL by John Beynon ps (John Beynon Harris) | TWS | Feb 1952 |
| THE TWO SHADOWS by William F. Temple | Stg | Mar 1951 |
| BALANCE by John Christopher ps (Christopher S. Youd) | NW #9 | Spr 1951 |
| UNKNOWN QUANTITY by Peter Phillips | NW #5 | n/d 1949 |
| ROBOTS DON'T BLEED by J. W. Groves | NW #8 | Win 1950 |
| CASTAWAY by George Whitley ps (A. Bertram Chandler) | WT | Nov 1947 |
| MACHINE MADE by J. T. M'Intosh ps (James J. MacGregor) | NW #10 | Sum 1951 |
| CHEMICAL PLANT by Ian Williamson | NW #8 | Win 1950 |

CHARTERIS, LESLIE                                              Mag.    Year
     THE SAINT'S CHOICE     Bond-Charteris Publications; Hollywood, Calif.
     5 stories   125 pages   .25¢   1945

THE GOLD STANDARD by Leslie Charteris     (From THE SAINT AND MR. TEALE; 1933)
THE IMPOSSIBLE HIGHWAY by Oscar J. Friend                     TWS    Aug 1940
PLANETS MUST SLAY by Frank Belknap Long                       TWS    Apr 1942
                                                              TWS    Fal 1943
DAYMARE by Fredric Brown                                      TWS    Win 1944
TROPHY by Henry Kuttner
     (Originally appeared under psuedonym Scott Morgan)


CONKLIN, GROFF
     THE BEST OF SCIENCE FICTION     Crown Publishers; New York, N. Y.
     40 stories   785 pages   $3.50   February 11, 1946

PART ONE     THE ATOM
     SOLUTION UNSATISFACTORY by Anson MacDonald ps (Robert A. Heinlein)
                                                              ASF    May 1941
     THE GREAT WAR SYNDICATE by Frank R. Stockton             OAW    12/22/88
     THE PIPER'S SON by Lewis Padgett ps (Henry Kuttner and C. L. Moore)
                                                              ASF    Feb 1945
     DEADLINE by Cleve Cartmill                               ASF    Mar 1944
     LOBBY by Clifford D. Simak                               ASF    Apr 1944
     BLOWUPS HAPPEN by Robert A. Heinlein                     ASF    Sep 1940
     ATOMIC POWER by Don A. Stuart ps (John W. Campbell, Jr.) Ast    Dec 1934

PART TWO     THE WONDERS OF EARTH
     KILLDOZER! by Theodore Sturgeon                          ASF    Nov 1944
     DAVY JONES' AMBASSADOR by Raymond Z. Gallun              Ast    Dec 1935
     GIANT IN THE EARTH by Morrison Colladay                  WS     Apr 1933
     GOLDFISH BOWL by Anson MacDonald ps (Robert A. Heinlein) ASF    Mar 1942
     THE IVY WAR by David H. Keller                           Amz    May 1930
     LIQUID LIFE by Ralph Milne Farley ps (Roger Sherman Hoar) TWS   Oct 1936

PART THREE   THE SUPERSCIENCE OF MAN
     A TALE OF THE RAGGED MOUNTAIN by Edgar Allan Poe         GLB    Apr 1944
     THE GREAT KEINPLATZ EXPERIMENT by Arthur Conan Doyle
          (Originally published by Rand McNally and Co.; 1895)
     THE REMARKABLE CASE OF DAVIDSON'S EYES by H. G. Wells    PMB    3/28/95
     THE TISSUE CULTURE KING by Julian Huxley                 Amz    Aug 1927
     THE ULTIMATE CATALYST by John Taine ps (Eric Temple Bell) TWS   Jun 1939
     THE TERRIBLE SENSE by Calvin Peregoy ps (Thomas Calvert McClery) ASF Aug 1938
     A SCIENTIST DIVIDES by Donald Wandrei                    Ast    Sep 1934

PART FOUR    DANGEROUS INVENTIONS
     TRICKY TONNAGE by Malcolm Jameson                        ASF    Dec 1944
     THE LANSON SCREEN by Arthur Leo Zagat                    TWS    Dec 1936
     THE ULTIMATE METAL by Nat Schachner                      Ast    Feb 1935
     THE MACHINE by Don A. Stuart ps (John W. Campbell, Jr.)  Ast    Feb 1935

PART FIVE    ADVENTURES IN DIMENSION
     SHORT-CIRCUITED PROBABILITY by Norman L. Knight          ASF    Sep 1941
     THE SEARCH by A. E. van Vogt                             ASF    Jan 1943
     THE UPPER LEVEL ROAD by Warner Van Lorne ps (F. Orlin Tremaine) Ast Aug 1935
     THE THIRTY SECOND OF MAY by Paul Ernst                   Ast    Apr 1935
     *THE MONSTER FROM NOWHERE by Nelson Bond                 FA     Jul 1939


PART SIX     FROM OUTER SPACE

THE BEST OF SCIENCE FICTION [Continued]

| | Mag. | Year |
|---|---|---|
| FIRST CONTACT by Murray Leinster ps (Will F. Jenkins) | ASF | May 1945 |
| UNIVERSE by Robert A. Heinlein | ASF | May 1941 |
| BLIND ALLEY by Isaac Asimov | ASF | Mar 1945 |
| EN ROUTE TO PLUTO by Wallace West | Ast | Aug 1936 |
| THE RETREAT TO MARS by Cecil B. White | Amz | Aug 1927 |
| THE MAN WHO SAVED THE EARTH by Austin Hall | Amz | Apr 1926 |
| SPAWN OF THE STARS by Charles W. Diffin | Ast | Feb 1930 |
| THE FLAME MIDGET by Frank Belknap Long, Jr. | Ast | Dec 1936 |
| EXPEDITION by Anthony Boucher | TWS | Aug 1943 |
| CONQUEST OF GOLA by Leslie F. Stone ps (Mrs. William Silberberg) | WS | Apr 1931 |
| JACKDAW by Ross Rocklynne | ASF | Aug 1942 |

* [Editor's Note: THE MONSTER FROM NOWHERE was erroneously credited to Donald
     Wandrei in the first edition. The second edition carried an errata  slip
     while the third edition contained the proper byline to the story.]

THE BIG BOOK OF SCIENCE FICTION     Crown Publishers; New York, N. Y.
32 stories  545 pages  $3.00  September 8, 1950

   Pocket Book Edition:     Berkley Publishing Corp.; New York, N. Y.
     10 stories  187 pages  .35¢  #G-53  April 1957

PART ONE:   INVENTIONS, DANGEROUS AND OTHERWISE

| | Mag. | Year |
|---|---|---|
| MR. MURPHY OF NEW YORK by Thomas McMorrow | SA | 3/27/50 |
| THE DIMINISHING DRAFT by Waldemar Kaempffert | AIS | 2/9/18 |
| PEACEBRINGER by Ward Moore | Amz | Mar 1950 |
| (Originally appeared under title SWORD OF PEACE) | | |
| A MATTER OF FORM by H. L. Gold | ASF | Dec 1938 |

PART TWO:   WONDERS OF EARTH AND MAN

| | | |
|---|---|---|
| THE PLANETOID OF DOOM by Morrison Colladay | WS | Dec 1932 |
| ONE LEG TOO MANY by W. Alexander | Amz | Oct 1929 |
| THE MAN WITH THE STRANGE HEAD by Miles J. Breuer, M. D. | Amz | Jan 1927 |
| DEFENSE MECHANISM by Katherine MacLean | ASF | Oct 1949 |
| MARGIN FOR ERROR by Lewis Padgett ps (Henry Kuttner & C.L. Moore) | ASF | Nov 1947 |

PART THREE:   FROM OUTER SPACE

| | | |
|---|---|---|
| ISOLATIONIST by Mack Reynolds | FA | Apr 1950 |
| NOBODY SAW THE SHIP by Murray Leinster ps (Will F. Jenkins) | Fw/SFS | Jun 1950 |
| MEWHU'S JET by Theodore Sturgeon | ASF | Nov 1946 |
| THE OUTER LIMIT by Graham Doar | SEP | 12/24/49 |
| RAT RACE by Dorothy and John DeCourcy | Stg | Sep 1948 |
| DEAR DEVIL by Eric Frank Russell | OW | May 1950 |

PART FOUR:   ADVENTURES IN DIMENSION

| | | |
|---|---|---|
| EMERGENCY LANDING by Ralph Williams | ASF | Jul 1940 |
| THE SHIP THAT TURNED ASIDE by Green Peyton ps (G. Peyton Wertembaker) | | |
| (Originally appeared under byline G. Peyton Wertembaker) | Amz | Mar 1930 |
| MANNA by Peter Phillips | ASF | Feb 1949 |
| THE LONG DAWN by Noel Loomis | Sup | Jan 1950 |
| E FOR EFFORT by T. L. Sherred | ASF | May 1947 |

PART FIVE:   FAR TRAVELING

| | | |
|---|---|---|
| THE ROGER BACON FORMULA by Fletcher Pratt | Amz | Jan 1929 |
| (Originally appeared under joint byline Irvin Lester and Fletcher Pratt) | | |
| (Story revised for inclusion in this anthology.) | | |
| THE WINGS OF NIGHT by Lester del Rey | ASF | Mar 1942 |
| DESERTION by Clifford D. Simak | ASF | Nov 1944 |

| | Mag. | Year |
|---|---|---|
| CONTACT, INC. by Robertson Osborne | PS | Fal 1949 |
| (Originally appeared under title ACTION ON AZURA) | | |
| ARENA by Fredric Brown | ASF | Jun 1944 |
| CULTURE by Jerry Shelton | ASF | Sep 1944 |

### PART SIX:  WORLD OF TOMORROW

| | Mag. | Year |
|---|---|---|
| IN THE YEAR 2889 by Jules Verne | For | Feb 1889 |
| FOREVER AND THE EARTH by Ray Bradbury | PS | Spr 1950 |
| THE MINIATURE by John D. MacDonald | Sup | Spr 1949 |
| (Originally appeared under pseudonym Peter Reed) | | |
| SANITY by Fritz Leiber, Jr. | ASF | Apr 1944 |
| THE ONLY THING WE LEARN by C. M. Kornbluth | Stg | Jul 1949 |
| NOT WITH A BANG by Damon Knight | F&SF | Spr 1950 |

CROSSROADS IN TIME          Doubleday and Co.; New York, N. Y.
18 stories   312 pages   .35¢   Permabook #P254   November 2, 1953

| | Mag. | Year |
|---|---|---|
| ASSUMPTION UNJUSTIFIED by Hal Clement ps (Harry Clement Stubbs) | ASF | Oct 1946 |
| THE EAGLE'S GATHER by Joseph E. Kelleam | ASF | Apr 1942 |
| THE QUEEN'S ASTROLOGER by Murray Leinster ps (Will F. Jenkins) | TWS | Oct 1949 |
| "DERM FOOL" by Theodore Sturgeon | Unk | Mar 1940 |
| COURTESY by Clifford D. Simak | ASF | Aug 1951 |
| SECRET by Lee Cahn | ASF | Jan 1953 |
| THIRSTY GOD by Margaret St. Clair | F&SF | Mar 1953 |
| (Originally appeared under pseudonym Idris Seabright) | | |
| THE MUTANT'S BROTHER by Fritz Leiber, Jr. | ASF | Aug 1943 |
| STUDENT BODY by F. L. Wallace | Glxy | Mar 1953 |
| MADE IN U. S. A. by J. T. M'Intosh ps (James J. MacGregor) | Glxy | Apr 1953 |
| TECHNICAL ADVISOR by Chad Oliver | F&SF | Feb 1953 |
| FEEDBACK by Katherine MacLean | ASF | Jul 1951 |
| THE CAVE by P. Schuyler Miller | ASF | Jan 1943 |
| VOCATION by George O. Smith | ASF | Apr 1945 |
| THE TIME DECELERATOR by A. Macfadyen, Jr. | Ast | Jul 1936 |
| ZEN by Jerome Bixby | Glxy | Oct 1952 |
| LET THERE BE LIGHT by H. B. Fyfe | If | Nov 1952 |
| THE BRAIN by W. Norbert ps (Dr. Norbet Weiner) | TEN | Apr 1952 |
| (Originally appeared under byline Dr. Norbet Weiner) | | |

FOUR FOR THE FUTURE          Pyramid Press; New York, N. Y.
4 stories          pages   .35¢   #G434   August 15, 1959

| | Mag. | Year |
|---|---|---|
| ENOUGH ROPE by Poul Anderson | ASF | Jul 1953 |
| THE CLAUSTROPHILE by Theodore Sturgeon | Glxy | Aug 1956 |
| THE CHILDREN'S HOUR by Henry Kuttner | ASF | Mar 1944 |
| PLUS X by Eric Frank Russell | ASF | Jun 1956 |

INVADERS OF EARTH          Vanguard Press; New York
22 stories   333 pages   $2.95   March 11, 1952

Pocket Book Edition:          Pocket Books, Inc.; New York, N. Y.
15 stories   257 pages   .35¢   #1074   1955

English Editions:                    Weidenfeld Nicholson; England
        14 stories  256 pages  10/6  1953
English paperback edition:           Weidenfeld Nicholson; England
        14 stories  256 pages   5/   1955

PROLOGUE
THE DISTANT PART 1

THIS STAR SHALL BE FREE by Murray Leinster ps (Will F. Jenkins)    Sup  Nov 1949
PART ONE
THE IMMEDIATE PAST

CASTAWAY by Robert Moore Williams                                  ASF  Feb 1941
IMPULSE by Eric Frank Russell                                      ASF  Sep 1938
TOP SECRET by David Grinnell                                       Sir  Jul 1949
AN EEL BY THE TAIL by Allen K. Lang                                 Im  Apr 1951
A DATE TO REMEMBER by William F. Temple                            TWS  Aug 1949
STORM WARNING by Donald A. Wollheim                               FFSF  Oct 1942
    (Originally appeared under pseudonym Millard Verne Gordon)
CHILD OF VOID by Margaret St. Clair                                Sup  Nov 1949
TINY AND THE MONSTER by Theodore Sturgeon                          ASF  May 1947
THE DISCORD MAKERS by Mack Reynolds                               OTWA  Jul 1950
PEN PAL by Milton Lesser                                          Glxy  Jul 1951
NOT ONLY DEAD MEN by A. E. Van Vogt                                ASF  Nov 1942

PART TWO
THE IMMEDIATE FUTURE

ENEMIES OF SPACE by Karl Grunert    (Translated from German by Willy Ley)
    (From ENEMIES OF SPACE; 1907)
INVASION FROM MARS by Howard Koch    (Copyright 1940; Princeton University Press)
    [The radio  script of Orson Welles' broadcast  of H. G. Wells' THE WAR OF THE
    WORLDS over the Columbia Broadcasting System, October 30, 1938.]
MINISTER WITHOUT PORTFOLIO by Mildred Clingerman                   F&SF  Feb 1952
THE WAVERIES by Fredric Brown                                      ASF  Aug 1945
CRISIS by Edward Grendon                                           ASF  Jun 1951
ANGEL'S EGG by Edgar Pangborn                                      ASF  Jun 1951
"WILL YOU WALK A LITTLE FASTER!" by William Tenn ps (Philip Klass)  MSF  Nov 1951
THE MAN IN THE MOON by Henry Norton                                ASF  Feb 1943
PICTURES DON'T LIE by Katherine MacLean                           Glxy  Aug 1951

EPILOGUE
THE DISTANT FUTURE

THE GREATEST TERTIAN by Anthony Boucher                            ORIGINAL STORY

    THE OMNIBUS OF SCIENCE FICTION      Crown Publishers; New York, N. Y.
    43 stories  562 pages  $3.50  November 21, 1952

    Pocket Book Edition: Berkeley Publishing Corp.; New York, N. Y.  #G-31
        Titled: SCIENCE FICTION OMNIBUS  11 stories  187 pages .35¢  August 1956

    English Editions:        Grayson and Grayson, Ltd.; London, England
        Titled:  STRANGE TRAVELS IN SCIENCE FICTION
            13 stories  256 pages  9/6  January 11, 1954
        Titled:  STRANGE ADVENTURES IN SCIENCE FICTION
            9 stories  240 pages  9/6  June 18, 1954

PART I:  WONDERS OF EARTH AND MAN

JOHN THOMAS'S CURE by John Leimert                                    Atl  Aug 1945
HYPERPILOSITY by L. Sprague de Camp                                   ASF  Apr 1938
THE THING IN THE WOODS by Fletcher Pratt and B. F. Ruby              Amz  Feb 1935
     [Editors Note:  Although this story has a joint byline both in this  anthology
     and in its original magazine appearance our research brought forth the  factor
     that the  late Fletcher Pratt  had a hobby  of listing  his friends on the by-
     line of his stories  even if they did not collaborate with him.  This particu-
     lar story was written by Fletcher Pratt alone.]
AND BE MERRY by Katherine MacLean                                    ASF  Feb 1950
THE BEES FROM BORNEO by Will H. Gray                                 Amz  Feb 1931
THE RAG THING by David Grinnell                                     F&SF  Oct 1951
THE CONQUEROR by Mark Clifton                                        ASF  Aug 1952


PART 2:  INVENTIONS, DANGEROUS AND OTHERWISE

NEVER UNDERESTIMATE... by Theodore Sturgeon                            If  Jan 1952
THE DOORBELL by David H. Keller, M. D.                                WS  Jun 1934
A SUBWAY NAMED MOBIUS by A. J. Deutsch                               ASF  Dec 1950
BACKFIRE by Ross Rocklynne                                           ASF  Jan 1943
THE BOX by James Blish                                               TWS  Apr 1949
ZERITSKY'S LAW by Ann Griffith                                      Glxy  Nov 1951
THE FOURTH DYNASTY by R. R. Winterbotham                             Ast  Dec 1936


PART 3:  FROM OUTER SPACE

THE COLOUR OUT OF SPACE by H. P. Lovecraft                           Amz  Sep 1927
THE HEAD HUNTERS by Ralph Williams                                   ASF  Oct 1951
THE STAR DUMMY by Anthony Boucher                                    Fnt  Fal 1952
CATCH THAT MARTIAN by Damon Knight                                  Glxy  Mar 1952
SHIPSHAPE HOME by Richard Matheson                                  Glxy  Jul 1952
HOMO SOL by Isaac Asimov                                             ASF  Sep 1940


PART 4:  FAR TRAVELING

ALEXANDER THE BAIT by William Tenn ps (Philip Klass)                 ASF  May 1946
KALEIDOSCOPE by Ray Bradbury                                         TWS  Oct 1949
"NOTHING HAPPENS ON THE MOON" by Paul Ernst                          ASF  Feb 1939
TRIGGER TIDE by Wyman Guin                                           ASF  Oct 1950
     (Originally appeared under pseudonym Norman Menasco)
PLAGUE by Murray Leinster ps (Will F. Jenkins)                       ASF  Feb 1944
WINNER LOSE ALL by Jack Vance                                       Glxy  Dec 1951
TEST PIECE by Eric Frank Russell                                      OW  Mar 1951
ENVIRONMENT by Chester S. Geier                                      ASF  May 1944


PART 5:  ADVENTURES IN DIMENSION

HIGH THRESHOLD by Alan E. Nourse                                     ASF  Mar 1951
SPECTATOR SPORT by John D. MacDonald                                 TWS  Feb 1950
RECRUITING STATION by A. E. Van Vogt                                 ASF  Mar 1942
A STONE AND A SPEAR by Raymond F. Jones                             Glxy  Dec 1950
WHAT YOU NEED by Lewis Padgett ps (Henry Kuttner and C. L. Moore)    ASF  Oct 1945
THE CHOICE by W. Hilton Young                                        Pch  3/19/52

PART 6:  WORLDS OF TOMORROW

THE WAR AGAINST THE MOON by Andre Maurois
   (From THE NEXT CHAPTER: THE WAR AGAINST THE MOON; 1928)
PLEASANT DREAMS by Ralph Robin                              Glxy    Oct 1951
MANNERS OF THE AGE by H. B. Fyfe                            Glxy    Mar 1952
THE WEAPON by Fredric Brown                                 ASF     Apr 1951
THE SCARLET PLAGUE by Jack London                           ASMN    8/8/13
HERITAGE by Robert Abernathy                                ASF     Jun 1942
HISTORY LESSON by Arthur C. Clarke                          Stg     May 1949
INSTINCT by Lester del Rey                                  ASF     Jan 1952
COUNTER CHARM by Peter Phillips                             Stn     Spr 1951


OPERATION FUTURE            Doubleday and Co.; Garden City, N. Y.
  19 stories  356 pages  .35¢  Permabook M-4022  July 1, 1955

THE EDUCATION OF DRUSILLA STRANGE by Theodore Sturgeon      Glxy    Mar 1954
C/O MR. MAKEPEACE by Peter Phillips                         F&SF    Feb 1954
TECHNICAL SLIP by John Beynon                               Im      Dec 1950
SHORT IN THE CHEST by Idris Seabright ps (Margaret St. Clair)  FU   Jul 1954
CURE FOR A YLITH by Murray Leinster ps (Will F. Jenkins)    Stg     Nov 1949
EXPOSURE by Eric Frank Russell                              ASF     Jul 1950
WORRYWART by Clifford D. Simak                              Glxy    Sep 1953
DAY IS DONE by Lester del Rey                               ASF     May 1939
QUIT ZOOMIN' THOSE HANDS THROUGH THE AIR by Jack Finney     Col     8/4/51
HILDA by H. B. Hickey ps (Herb Livingston)                 F&SF    Sep 1952
BLOOD'S A ROVER by Chad Oliver                              ASF     May 1952
CALL ME ADAM by Winston K. Marks                           F&SF    Feb 1954
SPECIAL DELIVERY by Damon Knight                            Glxy    Apr 1954
THE GARDEN IN THE FOREST by Robert F. Young                 ASF     Sep 1953
THE SORCERER'S APPRENTICE by Malcolm Jameson                ASF     Dec 1941
GAMES by Katherine MacLean                                  Glxy    Mar 1953
THE HOLES AROUND MARS by Jerome Bixby                       Glxy    Jan 1954
PROJECT by Lewis Padgett ps (Henry Kuttner and C. L. Moore)  ASF    Apr 1947
THE FUN THEY HAD by Isaac Asimov                            NEA     12/1/51


POSSIBLE WORLDS OF SCIENCE FICTION        Vanguard Press; New York, N. Y.
22 stories  372 pages  $2.95  April 26, 1951

  Pocket Book Edition:    Berkley Publishing Corp.; New York, N. Y.
    10 stories  189 pages  .35¢  #G-3  July 15, 1955

  English Edition:        Grayson & Grayson, Ltd.; London, England
   13 stories  254 pages  9/6  June 22, 1952

PART ONE:  THE SOLAR SYSTEM

OPERATION PUMICE by Raymond Z. Gallun                       TWS     Apr 1949
THE BLACK PITS OF LUNA by Robert A. Heinlein                SEP     1/10/49
ENCHANTED VILLAGE by A. E. Van Vogt                         OW      Jul 1950
LILIES OF LIFE by Malcolm Jameson                           ASF     Feb 1945
ASLEEP IN ARMAGEDDON by Ray Bradbury                        PS      Win 1948
NOT FINAL! by Isaac Asimov                                  ASF     Oct 1941
CONES by Frank Belknap Long, Jr.                            Ast     Feb 1936
MOON OF DELIRIUM by D. L. James                             ASF     Jan 1940
COMPLETELY AUTOMATIC by Theodore Sturgeon                   ASF     Feb 1941
THE DAY WE CELEBRATE by Nelson Bond                         ASF     Jan 1941
THE PILLOWS by Margaret St. Clair                           TWS     Jun 1950
PROOF by Hal Clement ps (Harry Clement Stubbs)              ASF     Jun 1942

PART TWO:  THE GALAXY

PROPAGANDIST by Murray Leinster ps (Will F. Jenkins)           ASF   Aug 1947
IN VALUE DECEIVED by H. B. Fyfe                                ASF   Nov 1950
HARD LUCK DIGGINGS by Jack Vance                               Stg   Jul 1948
SPACE RATING by John Berryman                                  ASF   Oct 1939
CONTAGION by Katherine MacLean                                 Glxy  Oct 1950
LIMITING FACTOR by Clifford D. Simak                           Stg   Nov 1949
EXIT LINE by Sam Merwin, Jr.                                   Stg   Sep 1950
     (Originally appeared under pseudonym Matt Lee)
SECOND NIGHT OF SUMMER by James H. Schmitz                     Glxy  Dec 1950
A WALK IN THE SUN by Arthur C. Clarke                          TWS   Aug 1950
THE HELPING HAND by Poul Anderson                              ASF   May 1950

     SCIENCE FICTION ADVENTURES IN DIMENSION   Vanguard Press; New York, N. Y.
     23 stories  354 pages  $2.95  March 19, 1953

PART ONE:  TIME TALES
PRESENT TO FUTURE

YESTERDAY WAS MONDAY by Theodore Sturgeon                      Unk   Jun 1941
AMBITION by William L. Bade                                    Glxy  Oct 1951
THE MIDDLE OF THE WEEK AFTER NEXT by Murray Leinster ps (Will F. Jenkins)
                                                               TWS   Aug 1952
...AND IT COMES OUT HERE by Lester del Rey                     Glxy  Feb 1951

PRESENT TO PAST

CASTAWAY by A. Bertram Chandler                                WT    Nov 1947
     (Originally appeared under pseudonym George Whitley)
THE GOOD PROVIDER by Marion Gross                              F&SF  Sep 1952
REVERSE PHYLOGENY by Amelia R. Long                            Ast   Jun 1937
OTHER TRACKS by William Sell                                   ASF   Oct 1938

PAST TO PRESENT

"WHAT SO PROUDLY WE HAIL..." by Day Keene                      Im    Dec 1950
NIGHT MEETING by Ray Bradbury             (From THE MARTIAN CHRONICLES; 1950)

FUTURE TO PRESENT

PERFECT MURDER by H. L. Gold                                   TWS   Mar 1940
THE FLIGHT THAT FAILED by E. Mayne Hull  (Mrs. A. E. Van Vogt) ASF   Dec 1942
ENDOWMENT POLICY by Lewis Padgett ps (Henry Kuttner and C. L. Moore) ASF  Aug 1943
PETE CAN FIX IT by Raymond F. Jones                           ASF   Feb 1947

PART TWO:  PARRALLEL WORLDS

THE MIST by Peter Cartur                                       F&SF  Sep 1952
THE GOSTAK AND THE DOSHES by Miles J. Breuer, M. D.            Amz   Mar 1930
WHAT IF... by Isaac Asimov                                     Fnt   Sum 1952
RING AROUND THE REDHEAD by John D. MacDonald                   Stg   Nov 1948
TIGER BY THE TAIL by Allan E. Nourse                           Glxy  Nov 1951
WAY OF ESCAPE by William F. Temple                             TWS   Jun 1948
SUBURBAN FRONTIERS by Roger Flint Young                        ASF   Feb 1950
BUSINESS OF KILLING by Fritz Leiber, Jr.                       ASF   Sep 1944
TO FOLLOW KNOWLEDGE by Frank Belknap Long, Jr.                 ASF   Dec 1942

     SCIENCE FICTION ADVENTURES IN MUTATION   Vanguard Press; New York, N. Y.
     20 stories  316 pages  $3.75  January 11, 1956

CHAIN OF COMMAND by Stephen Arr ps (Stephen A. Rynas)         Glxy    May 1954
BATTLE OF THE UNBORN by James Blish                           Fw/SFS  Jun 1950
THE HUNGRY GUINEA PIG by Miles J. Breuer, M. D.               Amz     Jan 1950

```
KEEP OUT by Fredric Brown                                          Amz    Mar 1954
THE SMALL WORLD OF M-75 by Ed M. Clinton Jr.                       If     Jul 1954
LIMITING FACTOR by Theodore R. Cogswell                            Gixy   Apr 1954
THE LYSENKO MAZE by David Grinnell                                 F&SF   Jul 1954
THE PATIENT by E. Mayne Hull  (Mrs. A. E. Van Vogt)                UW     Oct 1943
COLD WAR by Henry Kuttner                                          TWS    Oct 1949
SKAG WITH THE QUEER HEAD by Murray Leinster ps (Will F. Jenkins)   MSF    Aug 1951
VEILED ISLAND by Emmet McDowell                                    ASF    Jan 1946
EXPERIMENT STATION by Kris Neville                                 Sup    Sep 1950
    Revised for publication in this anthology.   (Org aprd under title THE FIRST)
FAMILY RESEMBLANCE by Alan E. Nourse                               ASF    Apr 1953
AND THOU BESIDE ME by Mack Reynolds                                F&SF   Apr 1954
THIS ONE'S ON ME by Eric Frank Russell                             NSF    Aug 1953
THE AGE OF PROPHECY by Margaret St. Clair                          Fw/SFS Mar 1951
THE LOVE OF HEAVEN by Theodore Sturgeon                            ASF    Nov 1948
THE IMPOSSIBLE VOYAGE HOME by F. L. Wallace                        Gixy   Aug 1954
THE CONSPIRATORS by James White                                    NW #24 Jun 1954
THE BETTER CHOICE by S. Fowler Wright                              ORIGINAL STORY
```

THE SCIENCE FICTION GALAXY     Garden City Publishing Co.; Garden City, N. Y.
12 stories   242 pages   .35¢   Permabook #67  February 6, 1950

### WORLDS OF TOMORROW

```
THE MACHINE STOPS by E. M. Forster
    (From THE ETERNAL MOMENT AND OTHER STORIES; 1928)
EASY AS A.B.C. by Rudyard Kipling                                  LM     Mar 1912
```

### WONDERS OF TOMORROW

```
THE DERELECT by William Hope Hodgson             (From MEN OF DEEP WATERS; 1914)
THE FIRES WITHIN by Arthur C. Clarke                               Fty    Aug 1947
    (Originally appeared under pseudonym E. G. O'Brien)
```

### DANGEROUS INVENTIONS

```
A CHILD IS CRYING by John D. MacDonald                             TWS    Dec 1948
QUIS CUSTODIET..? by Margaret St. Clair                            Stg    Jul 1948
```

### OTHER DIMENSIONS

```
THE LIFE WORK OF PROFESSOR MUNTZ by Murray Leinster ps (Will F. Jenkins)
                                                                   TWS    Jun 1949
THE APPENDIX AND THE SPECTACLES by Miles J. Breuer, M. D.
```

### FROM OUTER SPACE

```
DEATH FROM THE STARS by A. Rowley Hilliard                         WS     Oct 1931
THE HURKLE IS A HAPPY BEAST by Theodore Sturgeon                   MoF    Fal 1949
```

### FAR TRAVELING

```
KING OF THE GREY SPACES by Ray Bradbury                            FFM    Dec 1943
THE LIVING GALAXY by Laurence Manning                              WS     Sep 1934
```

SCIENCE FICTION TERROR TALES  Gnome Press Inc.; New York, N.Y. Mag.    Year
15 stories  262 pages  $3.50  February 20, 1955

Pocket Book Edition:       Pocket Books. Inc.; New York, N. Y.
15 stories  262 pages  .25¢  #1045  March 1, 1955

| | | | |
|---|---|---|---|
| PUNISHMENT WITHOUT CRIME by Ray Bradbury | OW | Mar | 1950 |
| ARENA by Fredric Brown | ASF | Jun | 1944 |
| THE LEECH by Robert Sheckley | Glxy | Dec | 1952 |
| THROUGH CHANNELS by Richard Matheson | F&SF | Apr | 1951 |
| LOST MEMORY by Peter Phillips | Glxy | May | 1952 |
| MEMORIAL by Theodore Sturgeon | ASF | Apr | 1946 |
| PROTT by Margaret St. Clair | Glxy | Jan | 1953 |
| FLIES by Isaac Asimov | F&SF | Jun | 1953 |
| THE MICROSCOPIC GIANTS by Paul Ernst | TWS | Oct | 1936 |
| THE OTHER INAUGUARATION by Anthony Boucher | F&SF | Mar | 1953 |
| NIGHTMARE BROTHER by Alan E. Nourse | ASF | Feb | 1953 |
| PIPELINE TO PLUTO by Murray Leinster ps (Will F. Jenkins) | ASF | Aug | 1945 |
| IMPOSTER by Philip K. Dick | Glxy | Jun | 1953 |
| THEY by Robert A. Heinlein | Unk | Apr | 1941 |
| LET ME LIVE IN A HOUSE by Chad Oliver | USF | Mar | 1954 |

SCIENCE FICTION THINKING MACHINES      Vanguard Press; New York, N. Y.
20 stories  367 pages  $3.50  May 13, 1954

Pocket Book Edition:       Bantam Books; New York, N. Y.
12 stories  183 pages  .25¢  #1352  August 1955

PART ONE:  ROBOTS

| | | | |
|---|---|---|---|
| AUTOMATA: I by S. Fowler Wright | WT | Sep | 1929 |
| MOXON'S MASTER by Ambrose Bierce | (From CAN SUCH THINGS BE?; 1893) | | |
| ROBBIE by Isaac Asimov | (From I, ROBOT; 1950) | | |
| THE SCARAB by Raymond Z. Gallun | Ast | Aug | 1936 |
| THE MECHANICAL BRIDE by Fritz Leiber | ORIGINAL STORY | | |
| VIRTUOSO by Herbert Goldstone | F&SF | Feb | 1953 |
| AUTOMATA: II by S. Fowler Wright | WT | Sep | 1929 |
| BOOMERANG by Eric Frank Russell | FU | Sep | 1953 |
| THE JESTER by William Tenn ps (Philip Klass) | TWS | Aug | 1951 |
| R. U. R. [Rossum's Universal Robots] by Karel Capek | (A Fantastic Melodrama) | | |
| (Copyright 1923 by Doubleday, Page and Co.) | | | |
| SKIRMISH by Clifford D. Simak | Amz | Dec | 1950 |
| (Originally appeared under title BATHE YOUR BEARINGS IN BLOOD) | | | |
| SOLDIER BOY by Michael Shaara | Glxy | Jul | 1953 |
| AUTOMATA: III by S. Fowler Wright | WT | Sep | 1929 |
| MEN ARE DIFFERENT by Alan Bloch | ORIGINAL STORY | | |

PART TWO:  Androids

| | | | |
|---|---|---|---|
| LETTER TO ELLEN by Chan Davis | ASF | Jun | 1947 |
| SCULPTORS OF LIFE by Wallace West | ASF | Dec | 1939 |
| THE GOLDEN EGG by Theodore Sturgeon | Unk | Aug | 1941 |
| DEAD END by Wallace MacFarlane | Glxy | Jan | 1952 |

PART THREE:  Computors

| | | | |
|---|---|---|---|
| ANSWER by Hal Clement ps (Harry Clement Stubbs) | ASF | Apr | 1947 |
| SAM HALL by Poul Anderson | ASF | Aug | 1953 |
| DUMB WAITER by Walter M. Miller, Jr. | ASF | Apr | 1952 |
| PROBLEM FOR EMMY by Robert Sherman Townes | Stg | Jun | 1952 |

6 GREAT SHORT NOVELS OF SCIENCE FICTION    Dell Publishing Co.; New York, N.Y.
6 stories  384 pages  .35¢  #D9  January 26, 1954

NOTE:  ALL STORIES REVISED FOR INCLUSION IN THIS COLLECTION

THE BLAST by Stuart Cloete    (Original version aprd in Collier s  April 12, 1947)
COVENTRY by Robert A. Heinlein
            (Original version appeared in Astounding Science Fiction July  1940)
THE OTHER WORLD by Murray Leinster ps (Will F. Jenkins)
            (Original version appeared in Startling Stories November 1949)
THE BARRIER by Anthony Boucher
            (Original version appeared in Astounding Science Fiction September  1942)
SURFACE TENSION by James Blish
            (Original version appeared in Galaxy Science Fiction  August 1952)
MATURITY by Theodore Sturgeon
            (Original version appeared in Astounding Science Fiction February 1947)

    SIX GREAT SHORT SCIENCE FICTION NOVELS    Dell Publishing Co.; New York, N. Y.
    6 stories  250 pages  .50¢  #C111            1960

|  | Mag. | Year |
|---|---|---|
| GALLEY SLAVE by Isaac Asimov | Glxy | Dec 1957 |
| PROJECT NURSEMAID by Judith Merril | F&SF | Oct 1955 |
| FINAL GENTLEMAN by Clifford D. Simak | F&SF | Jan 1960 |
| CHAIN REACTION by Algis Budrys | ASF | Apr 1957 |
| (Originally appeared under pseudonym John A. Sentry) | | |
| RULE GOLDEN by Damon Knight | SFAd | May 1954 |
| INCOMMUNICADO by Katherine MacLean | ASF | Jun 1950 |

    13 GREAT STORIES OF SCIENCE FICTION    Fawcett Publications; Greenwich, Conn.
    13 stories  192 pages  .35¢  Gold Medal Book #S997  May 1960

| THE WAR IS OVER by Algis Budrys | ASF | Feb 1957 |
|---|---|---|
| THE LIGHT by Poul Anderson | Glxy | Mar 1957 |
| COMPASSION CIRCUIT by John Wyndham ps (John Beynon Harris) | FU | Dec 1954 |
| VOLPA by Wyman Guin | Glxy | May 1956 |
| SILENCE, PLEASE! by Arthur C. Clarke | SF #2 | Win 1950 |
| ALLEGORY by William T. Powers | ASF | Apr 1953 |
| SOAP OPERA by Alan Nelson | F&SF | Apr 1953 |
| SHIPPING CLERK by William Morrison ps (Joseph Samachson) | Glxy | Jun 1952 |
| TECHNOLOGICAL RETREAT by G. C. Edmondson | F&SF | May 1956 |
| THE AVAILABLE DATA ON THE WORP REACTION by Lion Miller | F&SF | Sep 1953 |
| THE SKILLS OF XANADU by Theodore Sturgeon | Glxy | Jul 1956 |
| THE MACHINE by Richard Gehman | Col | 12/14/46 |
| THE ANALOGUES by Damon Knight | ASF | Jan 1952 |

    A TREASURY OF SCIENCE FICTION    Crown Publishers; New York, N. Y.
    30 stories  517 pages  $3.00  March 12, 1948

    Pocket Book Edition:    Berkeley Publishing Corp.; New York, N. Y.
        8 stories  186 pages  .35¢  #G-63  August 1957

PART ONE:  THE ATOM AND AFTER

| THE NIGHTMARE by Chan Davis | ASF | May 1946 |
|---|---|---|
| TOMORROW'S CHILDREN by Poul Anderson and F. N. Waldrop | ASF | Mar 1947 |
| THE LAST OBJECTIVE by Paul Carter | ASF | Aug 1946 |
| LOOPHOLE by Arthur C. Clarke | ASF | Apr 1946 |
| THE FIGURE by Edward Grendon | ASF | Jul 1947 |

A TREASURY OF SCIENCE FICTION [Continued]                    Mag.    Year

PART TWO:  THE WONDERS OF EARTH

 THE GREAT FOG by H. F. Heard
  (From THE GREAT FOG AND OTHER WEIRD TALES; 1944)
 THE CHRYSALIS by P. Schuyler Miller                     Ast   Apr 1936
 LIVING FOSSIL by L. Sprague de Camp                     ASF   Feb 1939
 N DAY by Philip Latham ps (Robert S. Richardson)        ASF   Jan 1946

PART THREE:  THE SUPERSCIENCE OF MAN

 WITH FOLDED HANDS by Jack Williamson                    ASF   Jul 1947
 NO WOMAN BORN by C. L. Moore  (Mrs. Henry Kuttner)      ASF   Dec 1944
 WITH FLAMING SWORDS by Cleve Cartmill                   ASF   Sep 1942
 CHILDREN OF THE "BETSY-B" by Malcolm Jameson            ASF   Mar 1947

PART FOUR:  DANGEROUS INVENTIONS

 CHILD'S PLAY by William Tenn ps (Philip Klass)          ASF   Mar 1947
 THE PERSON FROM PORLOCK by Raymond F. Jones             ASF   Aug 1947
 JUGGERNAUT by A. E. Van Vogt                            ASF   Aug 1944
 THE ETERNAL MAN by D. D. Sharp                          SWS   Aug 1929

PART FIVE:  ADVENTURES IN DIMENSION

 MIMSY WERE THE BOROGOVES by Lewis Padgett ps (Henry Kuttner & C. L. Moore)
                                                     ASF   Feb 1943
 TIME AND TIME AGAIN by H. Beam Piper                    ASF   Apr 1947
 HOUSING SHORTAGE by Harry Walton                        ASF   Jan 1947
 FLIGHT OF THE DAWN STAR by Robert Moore Williams        ASF   Mar 1938
 VINTAGE SEASON by Lawrence O'Donnell ps (C. L. Moore)   ASF   Sep 1946

PART SIX:  FROM OUTER SPACE

 OF JOVIAN BUILD by Oscar J. Friend                      TWS   Oct 1938
 WINGS ACROSS THE COSMOS by Polton Cross ps (John Russell Fearn) TWS   Jun 1938
 THE EMBASSY by Martin Pearson ps (Donald A. Woolheim)   ASF   Mar 1942
 DARK MISSION by Lester del Rey                          ASF   Jul 1940

PART SEVEN:  FAR TRAVELING

 THE ETHICAL EQUATIONS by Murray Leinster ps (Will F. Jenkins)  ASF   Jun 1945
 IT'S GREAT TO BE BACK by Robert A. Heinlein             SEP   7/26/47
 TOOLS by Clifford D. Simak                              ASF   Jul 1942
 RESCUE PARTY by Arthur C. Clarke                        ASF   May 1946

CRAWFORD, WILLIAM C.

 THE GARDEN OF FEAR AND OTHER STORIES Crawford Publications, Los Angeles Cali.
 5 stories  79 pages  .25¢  Copyright: 1945

 [Editor's Note:  Although no editor's byline was given on this collection  we
 were advised by the publishers that William C. Crawford compiled this book.]

ALL STORIES FROM MARVEL TALES

THE GARDEN OF FEAR by Robert E. Howard                       July 1934
THE MAN WITH THE HOUR GLASS by L. A. Eshbach                 May 1934
CELEPHAIS by H. P. Lovecraft                                 May 1934
MARS COLONIZERS by Miles J. Breuer, M. D.                    Summer 1935
THE GOLDEN BOUGH by David H. Keller, M. D.                   Winter 1934

CRISPIN, EDMUND ps (R. B. Montgomery)                        Mag.    Year
      BEST SF SCIENCE FICTION STORIES      Faber & Faber, Ltd.; London, England
      14 stories  368 pages  15/ February 11, 1955

DORMANT by A. E. Van Vogt                                    Stg  Nov 1948
PICTURES DON'T LIE by Katherine MacLean                      Glxy Aug 1951
DUMB MARTIAN by John Wyndham ps (John Beynon Harris)         Glxy Jul 1952
OR ELSE by Henry Kuttner                            (From AHEAD OF TIME; 1953)
NO WOMAN BORN by C. L. Moore  (Mrs. Henry Kuttner)           ASF  Dec 1944
THE FIRE BALLOONS by Ray Bradbury                            Im   Apr 1951
      (Originally appeared under title "IN THIS SIGN...")
THE NEW WINE by John Christopher ps (Christopher S. Youd)
      (From THE TWENTY-SECOND CENTURY; 1954)
PROTT by Margaret St. Clair                                  Glxy Jan 1953
A PRESENT FROM JOE by Eric Frank Russell                     ASF  Feb 1949
THE CEREBRATIVE PSITTACOID by H. Nearing, Jr.                F&SF Aug 1953
FIRST LADY by J. T. McIntosh ps (James J. MacGregor)         Glxy Jun 1953
THE RUUM by Arthur Porges                                    F&SF Oct 1953
THE XI EFFECT by Philip Latham ps (Robert S. Richardson)     ASF  Jan 1950
A CASE OF CONSCIENCE by James Blish                          If   Sep 1953

      BEST SF TWO  SCIENCE FICTION STORIES    Faber & Faber, Ltd.; London, England
      14 stories  296 pages  15/ September 28, 1956

THE ALTER AT MIDNIGHT by C. M. Kornbluth                     Glxy Mar 1952
HOBSON'S CHOICE by Alfred Bester                             F&SF Aug 1952
OUTSIDE by Brian W. Aldiss                                   NW #31 Jan 1955
ANGEL'S EGG by Edgar Pangborn                                Glxy Jun 1951
PLACET IS A CRAZY PLACE by Fredric Brown                     ASF  May 1946
LITTLE LOST ROBOT by Isaac Asimov                            ASF  Mar 1947
THE COPPER DAHLIA by Gerald Kersh
      (From THE BRIGHTON MONSTER AND OTHER STORIES; 1953)
WHEN YOU'RE SMILING by Theodore Sturgeon                     Glxy Jan 1955
ZERO HOUR by Ray Bradbury                                    PS   Fal 1947
WORRYWART by Clifford D. Simak                               Glxy Sep 1953
UNA by John Wyndham ps (John Beynon Harris)                  F&SF Jun 1953
      (Originally appeared under title THE PERFECT CREATURE)
BLOWUPS HAPPEN by Robert A. Heinlein                         ASF  Sep 1940
IMPOSTER by Philip K. Dick                                   Glxy Jun 1953
THE NINE BILLION NAMES OF GOD by Arthur C. Clarke
      (From STAR SCIENCE FICTION STORIES; 1953 - Edited by Frederik Pohl)

      BEST SF THREE  SCIENCE FICTION STORIES  Faber & Faber, Ltd.; London, England
      11 stories  224 pages  15/ June 20, 1958

GRENVILLE'S PLANET by Michael Shaara                         F&SF Oct 1952
FOOD TO ALL FLESH by Zeena Henderson                         F&SF Dec 1953
THE GIFT OF GAB by Jack Vance                                ASF  Sep 1955
FOUR IN ONE by Damon Knight                                  Glxy Feb 1953
THE GAME OF RAT AND DRAGON by Cordwainer Smith               Glxy Oct 1955
THE WABBLER by Murray Leinster ps (Will F. Jenkins)          ASF  Oct 1942
THE ANSWER by Fredric Brown                      (From ANGELS AND SPACESHIPS; 1954)
COUNTERSPY by Kelly Edwards                                  ASF  Dec 1953
THE AVAILABLE DATA ON THE WARP REACTION by Lion Miller       F&SF Sep 1953
HE WALKED AROUND THE HORSES by H. Beam Piper                 ASF  Apr 1948
THE COLD EQUATIONS by Tom Godwin                             ASF  Aug 1954

BEST SF FOUR  SCIENCE FICTION STORIES          Mag.    Year
10 stories 224 pages 15/ **March 10, 1961**    Faber & Faber Ltd. London

THE SHORT LIFE by Francis Donovan                ASF   Oct 1955
A SUBWAY NAMED MOBIUS by A. J. Deutsch         ASF   Dec 1950
IT'S A GOOD LIFE by Jerome Bixby
     (From STAR SCIENCE FICTION STORIES #2; 1953 — Edited by Frederik Pohl)
FLOWERS FOR ALGERNON by Daniel Keyes          F&SF   Apr 1959
BALAAM by Anthony Boucher
     (From 9 TALES OF SPACE AND TIME; 1954 — Edited by Raymond J. Healy)
THE YELLOW PILL by Rog Phillips               ASF   Oct 1958
THE BLISS OF SOLITUDE by J. T. McIntosh ps (James J. MacGregor)   Glxy   Jan 1952
     (Originally appeared under title HALLUCINATION ORBIT)
PSYCLOPS by Brian W. Aldiss               NW #49   Jul 1956
"HOBBYIST" by Eric Frank Russell             ASF   Sep 1947
   D
   A
BAXBR by Evelyn E. Smith      (From TIME TO COME; 1954 — Edited by August Derleth)
   B
   R


CROSSEN, KENDALL FOSTER
     ADVENTURES IN TOMORROW      Greenberg: Publishers; New York, N. Y.
     15 stories 278 pages $3.50 April 12, 1951

     Canadian Edition: Ambassador   $4.50   (No further data available)
     English Edition: The Bodley Head Ltd. 13 stories 240 pages 10/6   1953
     Hebrew Edition:   Titled HAYO HAYA BEATID [Once Upon the Future]
         9 stories 166 pages (Published in Jerusalem, Isreal; 1952)

ATOMIC AGE:    1960 A. D. — 2100 A. D.
                                         ORIGINAL STORY
     FLYING DUTCHMAN by Ward Moore             Col   5/6/50
     THERE WILL COME SOFT RAINS by Ray Bradbury
     THE MUTE QUESTION by Forrest J Ackerman       OW   Sep 1950
     THE PORTABLE PHONOGRAPH by Walter Van Tilburg Clark
         (From THE WATCHFUL GODS AND OTHER STORIES; 1941)

GALACTIC AGE:   2100 A. D. — 3000 A. D.
     AUTOMATON by A. E. Van Vogt                OW   Sep 1950
     RESTRICTED CLIENTELE by Kendall Foster Crossen    TWS   Feb 1951
     SHAMBLEAU by C. L. Moore (Mrs. Henry Kuttner)      WT   Nov 1933
     CHRISTMAS ON GANYMEDE by Isaac Asimov        Stg   Jan 1942

STELLAR AGE:    3000 A. D. — 10,000 A. D.
     MEMORY by Theodore Sturgeon               TWS   Aug 1948
     EXILED FROM EARTH by Sam Merwin Jr.          TWS   Dec 1940
     RETREAT TO THE STARS by Leigh Brackett (Mrs. Edmond Hamilton)   Ash   Nov 1941
     THE VOICE OF THE LOBSTER by Henry Kuttner      TWS   Feb 1950

DELPHIC AGE:    10,000 A. D. — 1,000,000 A. D.
     EVOLUTION'S END by Robert Arthur            TWS   Apr 1941
     TRANSFER POINT by Anthony Boucher          Glxy   Nov 1950
     THE DEVIL WAS SICK by Bruce Elliott         F&SF   Apr 1951

FUTURE TENSE        Greenberg Publishers; New York, N. Y.        Mag.    Year
14 stories  364 pages  $3.50  January 20, 1953

English Edition:  The Bodley Head Ltd.  7 stories  216 pages  10/6  (1954)

ON THE RECORD

    PLAGARIST by Peter Phillips                           NW #7   Sum 1950
    THE AMBASSADORS by Anthony Boucher                    Stg   Jun 1952
    DREAM'S END by Henry Kuttner                          Stg   Jul 1947
    WE THE PEOPLE by Ward Moore                           SFQ   May 1952
    THROWBACK by Miriam Allen DeFord                      Stg   Oct 1952
    THINGS OF DISTINCTION by Kendall Foster Crossen       Stg   Mar 1952
    SCARLET DREAM by C. L. Moore  (Mrs. Henry Kuttner)    WT    May 1934
                    ALL ORIGINAL STORIES

OFF THE RECORD

    CYCLOPS by H. F. Heard
    THE BATTLE OF THE S...S by Bruce Elliott
    ISLAND OF FINE COLORS by Martin Gardner
    BABY KILLERS by Rose Bedrick Elliott
    BEANSTALK by James Blish
    INCUBATION by John D. MacDonald
    LOVE STORY by Christopher Monig

DAVENPORT, BASIL

    INVISIBLE MEN          Ballantine Books, Inc.; New York, N. Y.
    11 stories  158 pages  .35¢  #401K  June 1960

THE WEISSENBROCH SPECTACLES by L. Sprague DeCamp & Fletcher Pratt   F&SF  Nov 1954
THE SHADOW AND THE FLASH by Jack London                            Bkm   Jun 1903
THE NEW ACCELERATOR by H. G. Wells                                 Snd   Dec 1901
INVISIBLE BOY by Ray Bradbury                                      Mdm   Nov 1945
THE INVISIBLE PRISONER by Maurice LeBlanc                        (No data available)
LOVE IN THE DARK by H. L. Gold                                     Sus   Fal 1951
    (Originally appeared under title LOVE ETHERAL)
WHAT WAS IT? by Fitz-James O'Brien                                 Hpr   Mar 1859
THE INVISIBLE DOVE DANCER OF STRATHPHEEN ISLAND by John Collier
    (From PRESENTING MOONSHINE; 1941)
THE VANISHING AMERICAN by Charles Beaumont                         F&SF  Aug 1955
SHOTTLE BOP by Theodore Sturgeon                                   Unk   Feb 1941
THE INVISIBLE MAN MURDER CASE by Henry Slesar                      Fnt   May 1958

DEL REY, LESTER, Cecile Matschat & Carl Carmer

    THE YEAR AFTER TOMORROW        John C. Winston Co.; Philadelphia, Pa.
    9 stories  339 pages  $3.00  April 19, 1952


THE LUCK OF IGNATZ by Lester del Rey                              ASF   Aug 1939

THE MASTER MINDS OF MARS by Carl H. Claudy                        AmB   Sep 1931
    (This story originally appeared under the joint byline of Carl H. Claudy
        and Dr. John C. Paige)
BY VIRTUE OF CIRCUMFERENCE by Peter van Dresser                   AmB   Nov 1937

THE RED DEATH OF MARS by Robert Moore Williams                    ASF   Jul 1940

THE LAND OF NO SHADOW by Carl H. Claudy                           AmB   Feb 1931

PLUM DUFF by Peter van Dresser                                    AmB   Dec 1935

KINDNESS by Lester del Rey                                        ASF   Oct 1944

TONGUE OF BEAST by Carl H. Claudy                                 AmB   May 1939
ROCKET TO THE SUN by Peter van Dresser                           AmB   Jul 1939

DERLETH, AUGUST

BEACHHEADS IN SPACE      Pellegrini and Cudahy; New York, N. Y.  Mag.    Year
14 stories  320 pages  $3.95  September 19, 1954

English Edition:     Weidenfeld Nicholson  7 stories  224 pages  9/6    1954
Pocket Book Edition:  Berkeley Publishing Corp.; New York, N. Y.
    7 stories  190 pages  #G-77  .35¢  August 1957

PROLOGUE

THE STAR by David H. Keller, M. D.                              ORIGINAL STORY
EXPLORATION

THE MAN FROM OUTSIDE by Jack Williamson                  ASF    Mar 1951
BEACHHEAD by Clifford D. Simak                           FA     Jul 1951
"THE YEAR'S DRAW NIGH" by Lester del Rey                 ASF    Oct 1951
METAMORPHOSITE by Eric Frank Russell                     ASF    Dec 1946
THE ORDEAL OF PROFESSOR KLEIN by L. Sprague DeCamp       SFA    Oct 1952
REPITITION by A. E. Van Vogt                             ASF    Apr 1940

INVASION

"BREEDS THERE A MAN...?" by Isaac Asimov                 ASF    Jun 1951
METEOR by John Beynon Harris                             Amz    Mar 1941
    (Originally appeared under title PHONY METEOR under pseudonym John Beynon)
AND THE WALLS CAME TUMBLING DOWN by John Wyndham ps (John Beynon Harris)
                                                         Stg    May 1951
THE BLINDING SHADOWS by Donald Wandrei                   Ast    May 1934
THE METAMORPHOSIS OF EARTH by Clark Ashton Smith         WT     Sep 1951
THE AMBASSADORS FROM VENUS by Kendall Foster Crossen     PS     Mar 1951

EPILOGUE

TO PEOPLE A NEW WORLD by Nelson Bond                     BB     Nov 1950

BEYOND TIME AND SPACE         Pellegrini and Cudahy; New York, N. Y.
34 stories  643 pages  $4.50  May 12, 1950

Pocket Book Edition:          Berkeley Publishing Corp.; New York, N. Y.
    8 stories  174 pages  #G-104  .35¢  February 1958

ATLANTIS by Plato                              Written about 370 B. C.
A TRUE HISTORY by Lucian                       Written about 165 A.D.
THE SOCIAL SCIENTISTS

    1.  UTOPIA by Thomas More      Written about 1516; Published in English 1551
    2.  PHALANSTERY OF THELME by Francis Rabelais      (From GARGANTUA; 1534)
    3.  THE CITY OF THE SUN by Giovanni Domenico Campenella
            Written 1623; published in Paris, France: 1634
    4.  THE NEW ATLANTIS by Francis Bacon  (Originally published in London; 1624)
    5.  LAPUTA by Jonathan Swift                  (From GULLIVER'S TRAVELS; 1726)
SOMNIUM by Johannes Keppler         (English translation by Everett F. Bleiler)
    (Posthoumously published in Latin [Frankfurt: 1634])
THE MAN IN THE MOONE by Francis Godwin     (Org aprd under pseud Domingo Gonsales)
    (Originally published in London by Ioshua Kirton and Thomas Warren; 1638)
THE TREE MEN OF POTU by Lewis Holberg
    (From A JOURNEY TO THE WORLD UNDER-GROUND; Prussia; 1741)
THE THOUSANDTH & SECOND TALE OF SCHEHERAZADE by Edgar Allen Poe     GLB  Feb 1843
DR. OX'S EXPERIMENT by Jules Verne  (From DOCTOR OX & OTHER STORIES; Paris: 1874)

PAUSODYNE by Grant Allen                    (From STRANGE STORIES; London: 1884)
A TALE OF NEGATIVE GRAVITY by Frank R. Stockton
    (From THE CHOSEN FEW, SHORT STORIES; 1895)
THE BLINDMAN'S WORLD by Edward Bellamy
    (From THE BLINDMAN'S WORLD AND OTHER STORIES; 1898)
THE BATTLE OF THE MONSTERS by Morgan Robertson
    (From WHERE ANGELS FEAR TO TREAD AND OTHER STORIES OF THE SEA; 1899)
THE NEW ACCELERATOR by H. G. Wells                         Snd    Dec 1901
THE NOISE IN THE NIGHT by William Hope Hodgson
    (From THE HOUSE ON THE BORDERLAND; 1908)
                                                          LvA    6/17/11
SPACE by John Buchan
WHEN THE GREEN STAR WANED by Nictzin Dyalhis              WT     Apr 1925
THE REVOLT OF THE PEDESTRIANS by David H. Keller          Amz    Feb 1928
THE FLYING MEN by Olaf Stapledon      (From THE LAST AND FIRST MEN; London: 1930)
A VOYAGE TO SFANMOE by Clark Ashton Smith                 WT     Aug 1931
COLOSSUS by Donald Wandrei                                Ast    Jan 1934
    (Originally appeared under title COLOSSUS ETERNAL)
THE LOTUS EATERS by Stanley G. Weinbaum                   Ast    Apr 1935
FESSENDEN'S WORLDS by Edmond Hamilton                     WT     Apr 1937
THE SEESAW by A. E. Van Vogt                              ASF    Jul 1941
WINGLESS VICTORY by H. F. Heard     (From THE GREAT FOG & OTHER WEIRD TALES; 1944)
WHEN THE BOUGH BREAKS by Lewis Padgett ps (Henry Kuttner & C. L. Moore)
                                                          ASF    Nov 1944
WANTED — AN ENEMY — by Fritz Leiber, Jr.                  ASF    Feb 1945
HUMPTY DUMPTY HAD A GREAT FALL by Frank Belknap Long, Jr. Stg    Nov 1948
MINORITY REPORT by Theodore Sturgeon                      ASF    Jun 1949
THE LONG WATCH by Robert A. Heinlein                      ALM    Dec 1949
THE EXILES by Ray Bradbury                                MMC    9/15/49
    (Originally appeared under title THE MAD WIZARDS OF MARS)


FAR BOUNDARIES                    Pellegrini and Cudahy; New York, N. Y.
20 stories  292 pages  $2.95  April 30, 1951


Canadian Edition:     George J. McLeod, Ltd.   $3.95    (No further data available)


PART ONE:  PRIMITIVES

    FROM A PRIVATE MAD-HOUSE by Humphrey Repton             Var n/d/a 1787
    MISSING ONE'S COACH: AN ANACHROMISM — Anonymous         DLM n/d/a 1838
    TALE OF A CHEMIST — Anonymous
        (From THE STORY-TELLER; or TABLE-BOOK OF POPULAR LITERATURE; 1843)
    THE LAST AMERICAN by J. A. Mitchell
        (Originally published by Frederick A. Stokes Co.; 1889)

PART TWO:  MID-PERIOD PIECES

    INFINITY ZERO by Donald Wandrei                        Ast   Oct 1936
    FRANKENSTEIN-UNLIMITED by H. A. Highstone              Ast   Dec 1936
    OPEN, SESAME by Stephen Grendon ps (August Derleth)    Ark   Win 1949
    TEPONDICON by Carl Jacobi                               PS   Win 1946
    THE FEAR PLANET by Robert Bloch                        Sup   Feb 1943

PART THREE:  THE CONTEMPORARY SCENE

    DE PROFUNDIS by Murray Leinster ps (Will F. Jenkins)   TWS   Win 1945
    INVASION by Frank Belknap Long                         Stg   Jul 1950

DEAR PEN PAL by A. E. Van Vogt                                                 Ark   Win 1949
TIME TO REST by John Beynon Harris                                             Ark   Win 1949
AN OUNCE OF PREVENTION by Philip Carter                                        F&SF  Sum 1950
THE SONG OF THE PEWEE by Stephen Grendon ps (August Derleth)                   Ark   Aut 1949
AND LO! THE BIRD by Nelson Bond                                                BB    Sep 1950
VIGNETTES OF TOMORROW by Ray Bradbury

    THE ONE WHO WAITS                                       Ark   Sum 1949
     HOLIDAY                                           Ark   Aut 1949
THE MAN WHO RODE THE SAUCER by Kenyon Holmes ps (August Derleth)               ORIGINAL STORY
LATER THAN YOU THINK by Fritz Leiber                                           Glxy  Oct 1950


THE OTHER SIDE OF THE MOON                    (Pellegrini and Cudady; New York, N. Y.)
20 stories   461 pages   $3.75   April 1949

English Edition: Grayson & Grayson, Ltd.  11 stories 238 pages  10/6    (4/13/56)
Pocket Book Edition: Berkley Publishing Corp.; New York, N. Y.
   10 stories   172 pages   .35¢  #G-249  June 1959

THE APPEARANCE OF MAN by John D. Beresford           (From SIGNS AND WONDERS; 1921)
THE STAR by H. G. Wells                                            Grp Xmas 1897
THE THING ON OUTER SHOAL by P. Schuyler Miller                     ASF  Sep 1947
THE STRANGE DRUG OF DR. CABER by Lord Dunsany
   (From THE FOURTH BOOK OF JORKENS; 1948)
THE WORLD OF WULKINS by Frank Belknap Long, Jr.                    TWS  Apr 1948
THE CITY OF THE SINGING FLAME by Clark Ashton Smith               WS   Jul 1931
BEYOND THE WALL OF SLEEP by H. P. Lovecraft                       WT   Mar 1938
THE DEVIL OF EAST LUPTON by Murray Leinster ps (Will F. Jenkins)   TWS  Aug 1948
   (Org aprd under title THE DEVIL OF EAST LUPTON, VERMONT under Wm. Fitzgerald)
CONQUEROR'S ISLE by Nelson Bond                                   BB   Jun 1946
SOMETHING FROM ABOVE by Donald Wandrei                            WT   Dec 1930
PILLAR OF FIRE by Ray Bradbury                                    PS   Sum 1948
THE MONSTER by Gerald Kersh                                       SEP  2/21/48
SYMBIOSIS by Will F. Jenkins                                      Col  6/14/47
THE CURE by Lewis Padgett ps (Henry Kuttner and C. L. Moore)      ASF  May 1946
VAULT OF THE BEAST by A. E. Van Vogt                              ASF  Aug 1940
THE EARTH MEN by Ray Bradbury                                     TWS  Aug 1948
ORIGINAL SIN by S. Fowler Wright            (From THE THRONE OF SATURN; 1948)
SPIRO by Eric Frank Russell                                       WT   Mar 1947
   (Originally appeared under title VENTURER OF THE MARTIAN MIMICS)
MEMORIAL by Theodore Sturgeon                                     ASF  Apr 1946
RESURRECTION by A. E. Van Vogt                                    ASF  Aug 1948
   (Originally appeared under title THE MONSTER)


THE OUTER REACHES                     Pellegrini and Cudahy; New York, N. Y.
17 stories  342 pages  $3.95  October 16, 1951

Pocket Book Edition: Berkley Publishing Corp.; New York, N. Y.
   10 stories  174 pages  .35¢  #G-116   April 1958

INTERLOPER by Poul Anderson                                       F&SF Apr 1951
DEATH SENTENCE by Isaac Asimov                                    ASF  Nov 1943
THIS IS THE LAND by Nelson Bond                                   BB   Apr 1951
YLLA by Ray Bradbury                          (From THE MARTIAN CHRONICLES; 1950)
THE GREEN CAT by Cleve Cartmill                                   WB   Jan 1951

| | Mag. | Year |
|---|---|---|
| GIT ALONG! by L. Sprague de Camp | ASF | Aug 1950 |
| SERVICE FIRST by David H. Keller, M. D. | ASQ | Win 1931 |
| SHOCK by Henry Kuttner | ASF | Mar 1943 |
| (Originally appeared under pseudonym Lewis Padgett) | | |
| THE SHIP SAILS AT MIDNIGHT by Fritz Leiber, Jr. | FA | Sep 1950 |
| THE POWER by Murray Leinster ps (Will F. Jenkins) | ASF | Sep 1945 |
| THE CRITTERS by Frank Belknap Long | ASF | Nov 1945 |
| PARDON MY MISTAKE by Fletcher Pratt | TWS | Dec 1946 |
| GOOD NIGHT, MR. JAMES by Clifford D. Simak | Glxy | Mar 1951 |
| THE PLUTONIAN DRUG by Clark Ashton Smith | Amz | Sep 1934 |
| FAREWELL TO EDEN by Theodore Sturgeon | | |
| (From INVASION FROM MARS; 1949 – Edited by Orson Welles) | | |
| CO-OPERATE – OR ELSE! by A. E. Van Vogt | ASF | Apr 1942 |
| FINALITY UNLIMITED by Donald Wandrei | Ast | Sep 1936 |

PORTALS OF TOMORROW                    Rhinehart and Co., Inc.; New York, N. Y.
16 stories  371 pages  $3.75  May 27, 1954

Canadian Edition:  Irwin Clarke  $4.25  (No further data available)  (16 stories)
English Edition:  Cassell and Co., Ltd.  16 stories  214 pages  12/6  1956

| | | |
|---|---|---|
| THE HYPNOGLYPH by John Anthony ps (John Ciardi) | F&SF | Jul 1953 |
| TESTAMENT OF ANDROS by James Blish | FSF | Jan 1953 |
| THE PLAYGROUND by Ray Bradbury | Esq | Oct 1953 |
| GRATITUDE GUARANTEED by R. Bretnor and Kris Neville | F&SF | Aug 1953 |
| RUSTLE OF WINGS by Fredric Brown | F&SF | Aug 1953 |
| THE OTHER TIGER by Arthur C. Clarke | FU | Jul 1953 |
| CIVILIZED by Mark Clifton and Alex Apostolides | Glxy | Aug 1953 |
| (Originally appeared under title WE'RE CIVILIZED) | | |
| STICKENEY AND THE CRITIC by Mildred Clingerman | F&SF | Feb 1953 |
| THE WORD by Mildred Clingerman | F&SF | Nov 1953 |
| HERMIT ON BIKINI by John Langdon | BB | Mar 1953 |
| JEZEBEL by Murray Leinster ps (Will F. Jenkins) | Stg | Oct 1953 |
| D. P. FROM TOMORROW by Mack Reynolds | Orb #1 | n/d 1953 |
| THE ALTRUISTS by Idris Seabright ps (Margaret St. Clair) | F&SF | Nov 1953 |
| POTENTIAL by Robert Sheckley | ASF | Nov 1953 |
| EYE FOR INIQUITY by T. L. Sherred | BFF | Jul 1953 |
| KINDERGARTEN by Clifford D. Simak | Glxy | Jul 1953 |

APPENDIX

OUTSTANDING COLLECTION OF FANTASTIC STORIES PUBLISHED DURING 1953
CHECKLIST OF NEW FANTASTIC STORIES PUBLISHED IN AMERICAN MAGAZINES IN 1953
A CHECKLIST OF THE BEST NEW FANTASTIC STORIES PUBLISHED IN BOOKS IN 1953

STRANGE PORTS OF CALL              Pellegrini and Cudahy; New York, N. Y.
19 stories  393 pages  $4.00  April 12, 1948

Pocket Book Edition: Berkley Publishing Corp.; New York, N. Y.
    10 stories  173 pages  .35¢  #G-131  June 1958

| | | |
|---|---|---|
| THE CUNNING OF THE BEAST by Nelson Bond | BB | Nov 1942 |
| (Originally appeared under title ANOTHER WORLD BEGINS) | | |
| THE WORM by David H. Keller | Amz | Mar 1929 |
| THE CRYSTAL BULLET by Donald Wandrei | WT | Mar 1941 |
| THE THING FROM OUTSIDE by George Allan England | S&I | Apr 1923 |
| AT THE MOUNTAINS OF MADNESS by H. P. Lovecraft | Ast | Feb 1936 |
| MARS ON THE ETHER by Lord Dunsany | Crnt | Sep 1937 |
| THE GOD BOX by Howard Wandrei | Ast | Apr 1934 |
| (Originally appeared under pseudonym Howard Von Drey) | | |
| MR. BAUER AND THE ATOMS by Fritz Leiber, Jr. | WT | Jan 1946 |
| THE CRYSTAL EGG by H. G. Wells | NwR | May 1897 |

JOHN JONES' DOLLAR by Harry Stephen Keeler
CALL HIM DEMON by Henry Kuttner
   (Originally appeared under pseudonym Keith Hammond)
MASTER OF THE ASTEROID by Clark Ashton Smith
A GUEST IN THE HOUSE by Frank Belknap Long
THE LOST STREET by Carl Jacobi and Clifford D. Simak
   (Originally appeared under title THE STREET THAT WASN'T THERE)
FAR CENTAURUS by A. E. Van Vogt
THUNDER AND ROSES by Theodore Sturgeon
THE GREEN HILLS OF EARTH by Robert A. Heinlein
BLUNDER by Philip Wylie
THE MILLION YEAR PICNIC by Ray Bradbury

| | Mag. | Year |
|---|---|---|
| JOHN JONES' DOLLAR | Amz | Apr 1927 |
| CALL HIM DEMON | TWS | Fal 1946 |
| MASTER OF THE ASTEROID | WS | Oct 1932 |
| A GUEST IN THE HOUSE | ASF | May 1946 |
| THE LOST STREET | Com | Jul 1941 |
| FAR CENTAURUS | ASF | Jan 1944 |
| THUNDER AND ROSES | ASF | Nov 1947 |
| THE GREEN HILLS OF EARTH | SEP | 2/8/47 |
| BLUNDER | Col | 1/12/46 |
| THE MILLION YEAR PICNIC | PS | Sum 1946 |

TIME TO COME                    Farrar, Straus and Young, Inc.; New York, N. Y.
12 stories  311 pages  $3.50  April 23, 1954

ALL ORIGINAL STORIES

BUTCH by Poul Anderson
THE PAUSE by Isaac Asimov
KEEPER OF THE DREAM by Charles Beaumont
NO MORNING AFTER by Arthur C. Clarke
THE BLIGHT by Arthur J. Cox
HOLE IN THE SKY by Irving Cox, Jr.
JON'S WORLD by Philip K. Dick
THE WHITE PINNACLE by Carl Jacobi
WINNER TAKE ALL by Ross Rocklynne
PARADISE II by Robert Sheckley
PHOENIX by Clark Ashton Smith
  D
  A
BAXBR by Evelyn E. Smith
  B
  R

WORLDS OF TOMORROW                    Pellegrini and Cudahy; New York, N. Y.
19 stories  351 pages  $3.95  March 16, 1953

English Edition:  Weidenfeld Nicholson  15 stories  224 pages  9/6    1955
Pocket Book Edition:  Berkley Publishing Corp.; New York, N. Y.
   10 stories  172 pages  .35¢  #G-163  October 1958

THE TINKLER by Poul Anderson
THE SMILE by Ray Bradbury
THE FIRES WITHIN by Arthur C. Clarke
   (Originally appeared under pseudonym E. G. O'Brien)
SUPERIORITY by Arthur C. Clarke
McILVAINE'S STAR by August Derleth
BROTHERS BEYOND THE VOID by Paul W. Fairman
BEAUTIFUL, BEAUTIFUL, BEAUTIFUL! by Stuart Friedman
THE DEAD PLANET by Edmond Hamilton
LIKE A BIRD, LIKE A FISH by H. B. Hickey ps (Herb Livingston)
THE GENTLEMAN IS AN EPWA by Carl Jacobi
THE ENCHANTED FOREST by Fritz Leiber
THE GREAT COLD by Frank Belknap Long, Jr.
FROM BEYOND by H. P. Lovecraft

| | Mag. | Year |
|---|---|---|
| THE TINKLER | WB | Feb 1951 |
| THE SMILE | Fnt | Sum 1952 |
| THE FIRES WITHIN | Fty | Aug 1947 |
| SUPERIORITY | F&SF | Aug 1951 |
| McILVAINE'S STAR | If | Jul 1952 |
| BROTHERS BEYOND THE VOID | FA | Mar 1952 |
| BEAUTIFUL, BEAUTIFUL, BEAUTIFUL! | FSFS | Mar 1952 |
| THE DEAD PLANET | Stg | Spr 1946 |
| LIKE A BIRD, LIKE A FISH | WB | Feb 1951 |
| THE GENTLEMAN IS AN EPWA | ORIGINAL STORY | |
| THE ENCHANTED FOREST | ASF | Oct 1950 |
| THE GREAT COLD | Ast | Feb 1935 |
| FROM BEYOND | WT | Feb 1938 |

| | | |
|---|---|---|
| LINE TO TOMORROW by Lewis Padgett ps (Henry Kuttner & C.L. Moore) | ASF | Nov 1945 |
| THE BUSINESS, AS USUAL by Mack Reynolds | F&SF | Jun 1952 |
| THE GARDNER by Margaret St. Clair | TWS | Oct 1949 |
| THE MARTIAN AND THE MORON by Theodore Sturgeon | WT | Mar 1949 |
| NULL-P by William Tenn ps (Philip Klass) | WB | Jan 1951 |
| STRANGE HARVEST by Donald Wandrei | WT | May 1953 |

DIKTY, T. E.

THE BEST SCIENCE FICTION STORIES AND NOVELS: 1955
20 stories  544 pages  $4.50 October 27, 1955  Frederick Fell, Inc.; N.Y.N Y

Pocket Book Edition:   Fawcett Publications, Inc.; Greenwich, Conn.
5 stories 176 pages .35¢ Crest # S-197  December 1957
Titled:  5 TALES FROM TOMORROW

| | | |
|---|---|---|
| THE COLD EQUATIONS by Tom Godwin | ASF | Aug 1954 |
| OF COURSE by Chad Oliver | ASF | May 1954 |
| DOMINIONS BEYOND by Ward Moore | SEP | 8/28/54 |
| GUILTY AS CHARGED by Arthur Porges | ORIGINAL STORY | |
| CARELESS LOVE by Albert Compton Friborg | F&SF | Jul 1954 |
| MOMENTO HOME by Walter M. Miller, Jr. | Amz | Mar 1954 |
| MOUSETRAP by Andre Norton ps (Alice Mary Norton) | F&SF | Jun 1954 |
| CHRISTMAS TROMBONE by Raymond E. Banks | F&SF | Jan 1954 |
| ONE THOUSAND MILES UP by Frank M. Robinson | SS | Apr 1954 |
| HOW-2 by Clifford D. Simak | Glxy | Nov 1954 |
| HEIRS APPARENT by Robert Abernathy | F&SF | Jun 1954 |
| JOHN'S OTHER PRACTICE by Winston Marks | Im | Jul 1954 |
| THE INNER WORLDS by William Morrison ps (Joseph Samachson) | F&SF | Apr 1954 |
| THE WILL by Walter M. Miller, Jr. | Fnt | Feb 1954 |
| FELONY by James Causey | Glxy | Jul 1954 |
| THE LITTLEST PEOPLE by Raymond E. Banks | Glxy | Mar 1954 |
| ONE WAY STREET by Jerome Bixby | Amz | Jan 1954 |
| AXOLOTL by Robert Abernathy | F&SF | Jan 1954 |
| EXILE by Everett B. Cole | ASF | Jan 1954 |
| NIGHTMARE BLUES by Frank Herbert | ASF | Jun 1954 |
| THE SCIENCE-FICTION BOOK INDEX [1954]   Compiled by Earl Kemp | | |

THE BEST SCIENCE-FICTION STORIES AND NOVELS: 1956
13 stories 256 pages $3.95 November 15, 1956 Frederick Fell, Inc.; N. Y., N. Y.

Pocket Book Edition:   Fawcett Publications, Inc.; Greenwich, Conn.
6 stories  160 pages  .35¢  Crest # S-258  December 1958
Titled:  6 FROM WORLDS BEYOND

| | | |
|---|---|---|
| JUNGLE DOCTOR by Robert F. Young | Stg | Fal 1955 |
| JUDGEMENT DAY by L. Sprague DeCamp | ASF | Aug 1955 |
| THE GAME OF RAT AND DRAGON by Cordwainer Smith | Glxy | Oct 1955 |
| THE MAN WHO ALWAYS KNEW by Algis Budrys | ASF | Apr 1956 |
| DREAM STREET by Frank M. Robinson | ImT | Mar 1955 |
| YOU CHEATED US by Tom Godwin | FU | Oct 1955 |
| SWENSON, DISPATCHER by R. DeWitt Miller | Glxy | Apr 1956 |
| THING by Ivan Janvier ps (Algis Budrys) | FU | Mar 1955 |
| I DO NOT LOVE THEE, DOCTOR FELL by Robert Bloch | F&SF | Mar 1955 |
| CLERICAL ERROR by Mark Clifton | ASF | Feb 1956 |
| A CANTICLE FOR LEIBOWITZ by Walter M. Miller, Jr. | F&SF | Apr 1955 |
| THE CYBER AND JUSTICE HOLMES by Frank Riley | If | Mar 1955 |

THE SHORES OF NIGHT by Thomas N. Scortia   (Portion entitled SEA CHANGE appeared
in ASF June 1956; balance of story written for this anthology)
THE SCIENCE-FICTION BOOK INDEX [1955]   Compiled by Earl Kemp

THE BEST SCIENCE-FICTION STORIES AND NOVELS: Ninth Series          Mag.    Year
12 stories  258 pages  $3.50  October 19, 1958  Advent Publishers, Chicago, Ill.

| | | |
|---|---|---|
| 2066: ELECTION DAY by Michael Shaara | ASF | Dec 1956 |
| THE MILE-LONG SPACESHIP by Kate Wilhelm | ASF | Apr 1957 |
| THE LAST VICTORY by Tom Godwin | If | Aug 1957 |
| CALL ME JOE by Poul Anderson | ASF | Apr 1957 |
| DIDN'T HE RAMBLE by Chad Oliver | F&SF | Apr 1957 |
| THE QUEEN'S MESSENGER by John J. McGuire | ASF | May 1957 |
| THE OTHER PEOPLE by Leigh Brackett  (Mrs. Edmond Hamilton) | Ven | Mar 1957 |
| (Originally appeared under title THE QUEER ONES) | | |
| INTO YOUR TENT I'LL CREEP by Eric Frank Russell | ASF | Sep 1957 |
| NOR DUST CORRUPT by James McConnell | If | Feb 1957 |
| NIGHTSOUND by Algis J. Budrys | Stl | Feb 1957 |
| THE TUNESMITH by Lloyd Biggle, Jr. | If | Aug 1957 |
| HUNTING MACHINE by Carol Emshwiller | SFS | May 1957 |
| THE SCIENCE-FICTION BOOK INDEX [1956 and 1957]  Compiled by Earl Kemp | | |

EVERY BOY'S BOOK OF OUTER SPACE STORIES
11 stories  283 pages  $3.95      1960              Frederick Fell, Inc.; N. Y., N.Y.

| | | |
|---|---|---|
| "...AND A STAR TO STEER BY..." by Lee Correy ps (G. Harry Stine) | ASF | Jun 1953 |
| SITTING DUCK by Oliver Saari | ASF | Jan 1952 |
| BLIND MAN'S BUFF by Malcolm Jameson | ASF | Oct 1944 |
| GYPSY by Poul Anderson | ASF | Jan 1950 |
| THE CANAL BUILDERS by Robert Abernathy | ASF | Jan 1945 |
| STAR OF WONDER by Julian May | TWS | Feb 1953 |
| THE RELUCTANT HEROES by Frank M. Robinson | Glxy | Jan 1951 |
| THAT SHARE OF GLORY by C. M. Kornbluth | ASF | Jan 1952 |
| MEN AGAINST THE STARS by Manly Wade Wellman | ASF | Jun 1938 |
| MAN IN THE SKY by Algis Budrys | ASF | Mar 1956 |
| A ROVER I WILL BE by Robert Courtney | ORIGINAL STORY | |

DOHERTY, G. D.

ASPECTS OF SCIENCE FICTION          John Murray; London, England
12 stories  218 pages  8/  November 30, 1959

SPACE

| | | |
|---|---|---|
| PICTURES DON'T LIE by Katherine MacLean | Glxy | Aug 1951 |
| THE COLD EQUATIONS by Tom Godwin | ASF | Aug 1954 |

TIME AND THE FOURTH DIMENSION

| | | |
|---|---|---|
| A SOUND OF THUNDER by Ray Bradbury  (From GOLDEN APPLES OF THE SUN; 1953) | | |
| HE WALKED AROUND THE HORSES by H. Beam Piper | ASF | Apr 1948 |

INVASION

| | | |
|---|---|---|
| ZERO HOUR by Ray Bradbury | PS | Fal 1947 |

OTHER WORLDS

| | | |
|---|---|---|
| THE CRYSTAL EGG by H. G. Wells | NwR | May 1897 |
| DORMANT by A. E. Van Vogt | Stg | Nov 1948 |

REALISM

THE SEA RAIDERS by H. G. Wells    (From THE PLATTNER STORY AND OTHERS;  1897)

WARFARE

| | | |
|---|---|---|
| DUMB SHOW by Brian W. Aldiss | Neb #19 | Dec 1956 |

CATASTROPHE

THE NINE BILLION NAMES OF GOD by Arthur C. Clarke
    (From STAR SCIENCE FICTION STORIES; 1953 — Edited by Frederik Pohl)

THE WORLD OF TOMORROW

| | | |
|---|---|---|
| PANEL GAME by Brian W. Aldiss | NW #42 | Dec 1955 |

HUMOUR

THE MAN IN ASBESTOS: AN ALLEGORY OF THE FUTURE by Stephen Leacock
    (From NONSENSE NOVELS; 1941)

ESENWEIN, J. BERG

ADVENTURES TO COME  9 stories 187 pages .50¢ 9/18/37 McLaughlin Bros; Mass.

ADVENTURES TO COME [Continued]

| | Mag. | Year |
|---|---|---|
| A MAN IN THE MOON COMES DOWN by Berger Copeman | ORIGINAL STORY | |
| A LIFE BY TELEVISION by Jack Arnold | " | " " |
| THE CRUISE OF THE S-900 by Russell Kent | " | " " |
| TWENTY-FIVE MILES ALOFT by Raymond Watson | " | " " |
| SCIENCE STEALS A MATCH by Nelson Richards | " | " " |
| DAWN ATTACK by Berger Copeman | " | " " |
| PIRATE OF THE AIR by James S. Bradford | " | " " |
| SIX HUNDRED FATHOMS by Norman Leslie | " | " " |
| IT'S GOING TO BE TRUE! by Burke Franthway | " | " " |

FADIMAN, CLIFTON
    FANTASIA MATHEMATICA    Simon and Schuster, Inc.; New York, N. Y.
    36 stories 19 verses 298 pages $4.95 February 21, 1958

I.  ODD NUMBERS

YOUNG ARCHIMEDES by Aldous Huxley    (From YOUNG ARCHIMEDES; 1924)
PYTHAGORAS AND THE PSYCHOANALYST by Arthur Koestler
    (From Arrival and Departure; 1943)
MOTHER AND THE DECIMAL POINT by Richard Llewellyn
    (From How Green Was My Valley; 1940)
JURGEN PROVES IT BY MATHEMATICS by James Branch Cabell  (From JURGEN; 1919)
PETER LEARNS ARITHMETIC by H. G. Wells
    (From Joan and Peter [The New Republic]; 1918)
SOCRATES AND THE SLAVE by Plato    [Translated by Benjamin Jowett ]
    (From The Meno of Plato; Oxford University Press; 1892)
THE DEATH OF ARCHIMEDES by Karl Capek  (From APOCRYPHAL STORIES; 1949 )

II.  IMAGINARIES

| | | |
|---|---|---|
| THE DEVIL AND SIMON FLAGG by Arthur Porges | F&SF | Aug 1954 |
| " — AND HE BUILT A CROOKED HOUSE — " by Robert A. Heinlein | ASF | Feb 1941 |
| INFLEXIBLE LOGIC by Russell Maloney | Nykr | 2/3/40 |
| NO-SIDED PROFESSOR by Martin Gardner | Esq | Jan 1947 |
| SUPERIORITY by Arthur C. Clarke | F&SF | Aug 1951 |
| THE MATHEMATICAL VOODOO by H. Nearing, Jr. | F&SF | Apr 1951 |
| EXPEDITION by Fredric Brown | F&SF | Feb 1957 |
| THE CAPTURED CROSS-SECTION by Miles J. Breuer, M. D. | Amz | Dec 1929 |
| A. BOTTS AND THE MOEBIUS STRIP by William Hazlett Upson | SEP | 12/22/45 |
| GOD AND THE MACHINE by Nigel Balchin | | |
|     (From Last Recollections of My Uncle Charlie; 1951) | | |
| THE TACHYPOMP by Edward Page Mitchell | SM | n/d 1873 |
| ISLAND OF FINE COLORS by Martin Gardner | | |
|     (From Future Tense; 1953 — Edited by Kendall Foster Crossen) | | |
| THE LAST MAGICIAN by Bruce Elliot | F&SF | Jan 1953 |
| A SUBWAY NAMED MOBEIUS by A. J. Deutsch | ASF | Dec 1950 |
| THE UNIVERSAL LIBRARY by Kurd Lasswitz | (From Seifenblasen; 1903) | |
|     (Translated from German by Willy Ley) | | |
| POSTSCRIPT TO "THE UNIVERSAL LIBRARY" by Willy Ley | ORIGINAL STORY | |
| JOHN JONES'S DOLLAR by Harry Stephen Keeler | Amz | Sep 1927 |

III.  FRACTIONS

A NEW BALLARD OF SIR PATRICK SPENS by Arthur T. Quiller-Couch  (verse)
    (No data available)
THE UNFORTUNATE TOPOLOGIST by Cyril Kornbluth  (verse)  F&SF  Jul 1957
    (Originally appeared under pseudonym S. D. Gottesman)
THERE ONCE WAS A BREATHY BABOON by Sir Arthur Eddington  (verse)  n/d/a

ADVENTURES TO COME [Continued]

A MAN IN THE MOON COMES DOWN by Berger Copeman
A LIFE BY TELEVISION by Jack Arnold
THE CRUISE OF THE S-900 by Russell Kent
TWENTY-FIVE MILES ALOFT by Raymond Watson
SCIENCE STEALS A MATCH by Nelson Richards
DAWN ATTACK by Berger Copeman
PIRATE OF THE AIR by James S. Bradford
SIX HUNDRED FATHOMS by Norman Leslie
IT'S GOING TO BE TRUE! by Burke Franthway

```
ORIGINAL STORY
   "   "    "
   "   "    "
   "   "    "
   "   "    "
   "   "    "
   "   "    "
   "   "    "
   "   "    "
```

FADIMAN, CLIFTON

Mag.    Year

FANTASIA MATHEMATICA        Simon and Schuster, Inc.; New York, N. Y.
36 stories  19 verses  298 pages  $4.95  February 21, 1958

I.  ODD NUMBERS

YOUNG ARCHIMEDES by Aldous Huxley            (From YOUNG ARCHIMEDES; 1924)
PYTHAGORAS AND THE PSYCHOANALYST by Arthur Koestler
    (From Arrival and Departure; 1943)
MOTHER AND THE DECIMAL POINT by Richard Llewellyn
    (From How Green Was My Valley; 1940)
JURGEN PROVES IT BY MATHEMATICS by James Branch Cabell   (From JURGEN; 1919)
PETER LEARNS ARITHMETIC by H. G. Wells
    (From Joan and Peter [The New Republic]; 1918)
SOCRATES AND THE SLAVE by Plato            [Translated by Benjamin Jowett ]
    (From The Meno of Plato; Oxford University Press; 1892)
THE DEATH OF ARCHIMEDES by Karel Capek    (From APOCRYPHAL STORIES; 1949)

II.  IMAGINARIES

THE DEVIL AND SIMON FLAGG by Arthur Porges               F&SF   Aug 1954
" — AND HE BUILT A CROOKED HOUSE —" by Robt A. Heinlein   ASF   Feb 1941
INFLEXIBLE LOGIC by Russell Maloney                      Nykr    2/3/40
NO-SIDED PROFESSOR by Martin Gardner                      Esq   Jan 1947
SUPERIORITY by Arthur C. Clarke                          F&SF   Aug 1951
THE MATHEMATICAL VOODOO by H. Nearing, Jr.               F&SF   Apr 1951
EXPEDITION by Fredric Brown                              F&SF   Feb 1957
THE CAPTURED CROSS-SECTION by Miles J. Breuer, M. D.      Amz   Dec 1929
A. BOTTS AND THE MOEBIUS STRIP by William Hazlett Upson   SEP  12/22/45
GOD AND THE MACHINE by Nigel Balchin
    (From Last Recollections of My Uncle Charlie; 1951)
THE TACHYPOMP by Edward Page Mitchell                     SM   n/d/a 1873
ISLAND OF FINE COLORS by Martin Gardner
    (From FUTURE TENSE; 1953 — Edited by Kendall Foster Crossen)
THE LAST MAGICIAN by Bruce Elliot                        F&SF   Jan 1953
A SUBWAY NAMED MOEBIUS by A. J. Deutsch                   ASF   Dec 1950
THE UNIVERSAL LIBRARY by Kurd Lasswitz       (From SEIFENBLASEN; 1903)
    (Translated from German by Willy Ley)
POSTSCRIPT TO "THE UNIVERSAL LIBRARY" by Willy Ley       ORIGINAL STORY
JOHN JONES'S DOLLAR by Harry Stephen Keeler               Amz  Sep 1927

III.  FRACTIONS

A NEW BALLARD OF SIR PATRICK SPENS by Arthur T. Quiller-Couch   (verse)
                                              (No data available)
THE UNFORTUNATE TOPOLOGIST by Cyril Kornbluth   (verse)   F&SF   Jul 1957
    (Originally appeared under pseudonym S. D. Gottesman)
THERE ONCE WAS A BREATHY BABOON by Sir Arthur Eddington (verse)    n/d/a
YET WHAT ARE ALL... by Lewis Carroll ps (Charles Lutwidge Dodgson) (verse)
                                              (No data available)

(49)

FANTASIA MATHEMATICA [Continued]

TWINKLE, TWINKLE, LITTLE STAR by Ralph Burton　(verse)
　　(From Science In Rhyme and Without Reason; 1924)
MATHEMATICAL LOVE by Andrew Marvell　(verse)
　　(From The Definition of Love; 1650)　　　　　(No data available)
THE CIRCLE by Christopher Morley
THE CIRCLE AND THE SQUARE by Thomas Dekker　　(verse)
　　(From The Honest Whore, Part ii, Act I, Scene 3; 1650)
EUCLID ALONE HAS LOOKED ON BEAUTY BARE by Edna St. Vincent Millay　(verse)
　　(From Collected Poems; 1920)
EUCLID by Vachel Lindsay　(verse)　　(From THE CONGO AND OTHER POEMS; 1914)
TO THINK THAT TWO AND TWO ARE FOUR by A. E. Housman　　(verse)
　　(From The Collected Poems of A. E. Housman; 1940)
THE USES OF MATHEMATICS by Samuel Butler (verse) (Fr COMPLETE POEMS: 1959)
THREES (To Be Sung by Niels Bohr) by John Atherton　　　　Nykr　3/2/57
PLANE GEOMETRY by Emma Rounds　　(verse)　(From CREAITVE YOUTH; 1925)
HE THOUGHT HE SAW ELECTRONS SWIFT by Herbert Dingle　(verse)　n/d/a
FEARSOME FABLE by Bruce Elliott　　　　　　　　　　　　　F&SF　Feb 1951
BERTRAND RUSSELL'S DREAM by G. H. Hardy
　　(From A Mathematician's Apology; 1948)
FOR ALL PRACTICAL PURPOSES by C. Stanley Ogilivy
　　(From Through The Microscope; 1956)
ETERNITY: A NIGHTMARE by Lewis Carroll ps (Charles Lutwidge Dodgson)
　　(From Sylvie and Bruno Concluded, Chapter XVI; 1893)
AN INFINITY OF GUESTS by George Gamow
　　(From One, Two, Three...Infinity; 1947)　(From NEW PATHWAYS OF SCIENCE; 1935)
∞ by Sir Arthur Eddington　　　　　　(verse)　　(Revised Version)
NO POWER ON EARTH by William Whewell
　　(Original version aprd in An Elementary Treatise on Mechanics; 1819)
　　　　　　　　　　　　　　　　　　　　　　(No data available)
X + I by Edgar Allen Poe
THE RECEPTIVE BOSOMS by Edward Shanks
　　(Fr a (London) Sunday Times review of H. McKay's The World of Numbers)
LEINBACH'S PROOF by Arthur Schnitzer　　(From FLIGHT INTO DARKNESS; 1931)
PROBLEM [untitled special feature] Anonymous　　　　　　Nykr　3/2/57
A LETTER TO TENNYSON — Anonymous　(From THE MATHEMATICAL GAZETTE ; n/d/a)
A FABLE — Anonymous　(Fr THE MATHEMATICAL GAZETTE; Vol 38, 1954, Page 308)
THERE WAS A YOUNG MAN FROM TRINITY — Anonymous　(verse)(No data available)
THERE WAS AN OLD MAN WHO SAID, "DO" — Anonymous (verse)　(No data available)
RELATIVITY — Anonymous　　　　　　　(verse)
THERE WAS A YOUNG FELLOW NAMED FISK — Anonymous (verse) (No dta available)


FAST, JULIUS
OUT OF THIS WORLD　　　　　Penguin Books; New York, N. Y.
14 stories　245 pages　.25¢　June 17, 1944

EVENING PRIMROSE by John Collier　　　　(From THE TOUCH OF NUTMEG; 1943)
LAURA by Saki ps (H. H. Munro)　　　　(From BEAST AND SUPER BEASTS; 1914)
SAM SMALL'S TYKE by Eric Knight　　　(From SAM SMALL FLIES AGAIN; 1942)
SATAN AND SAM SHAY by Robert Arthur　　　　　　　　　　EM　Aug 1942
A DISPUTED AUTHORSHIP by John Kendrick Bangs
　　(From A Houseboat on the Styx; 1895)　　　　　　SM　Nov 1937
MR. MERGENTHWIRKER'S LOBBLIES by Nelson Bond
A VISION OF JUDGEMENT by H. G. Wells
　　(From The Time Machine and Other Stories; 1895)　(From THE TOUCH OF NUTMEG; 1943)
THUS I REFUTE BEELZY by John Collier　　　　　　　　HBZ　Feb 1929
THE KING OF THE CATS by Stephen Vincent Benet　　C&SR　3/2/1887
THE CANTERVILLE GHOST by Oscar Wilde　　　　　ORIGINAL STORY
MY FRIEND MERTON by Julius Fast　(From THIS FREEDOM: 13 NEW RADIO PLAYS; 1942)
AND ADAM BEGOT by Arch Oboler　　　　　　　　　　HBZ　Feb 1929
CLUB SECRETARY by Lord Dunsany　(From JORKENS REMEMBERS AFRICA; 1934)
THE SCARLET PLAGUE by Jack London　　　　　　　ASMM　6/8/13

FLES, BARTHOLD

    THE SATURDAY EVENING POST FANTASY STORIES          Mag.    Year
    9 stories  126 pages  .25¢  (#389)  October 30, 1951
    Avon Publishing Co., Inc.; New York, N. Y.

            ALL STORIES FROM THE SATURDAY EVENING POST

THE ENEMY PLANET by Rear Admiral D. V. Gallery, USN           9/30/50
THE CHILD WHO BELIEVED by Grace Amundson              12/16/50
SCENE FOR SATAN by Noel Langley                  1/25/47
DOOMSDAY DEFERRED by Will F. Jenkinss              9/24/49
THE ETERNAL DUFFER by Willard Temple             1/18/46
NOTE ON DANGER B by Gerald Kersh                  4/4/47
THE TERRIBLE ANSWER by Paul Gallico             1/17/50
THE VOICE IN EARPHONES by Wilbur Schramm      Rpnt—5/29/47
    (From WINDWAGON SMITH AND OTHER YARNS; 1947)
DOCTOR HANRAY'S SECOND CHANCE by Conrad Richter       1/10/50


FORD, GARRETT

    SCIENCE AND SOCERY     Fantasy Publishing Co., Inc.; Los Angeles, Calif.
    15 stories  327 pages  $3.00  December 2, 1953

SCANNERS LIVE IN VAIN by Cordwainer Smith         FB #6  n/d 1950
THE LITTLE MAN ON THE SUBWAY by Isaac Asimov & James MacCreigh ps (Frederik Pohl)
                                     FB #6  n/d 1950
WHAT GOES UP by Alfred Coppel, Jr.              FB #6  n/d 1950
KLEON OF THE GOLDEN SUN by Ed Earl Repp         FB #7  n/d 1950
HOW HIGH ON THE LADDER? by Leo Paige           FB #7  n/d 1950
FOOTPRINTS by Robert Ernest Gilbert            FB #8  n/d 1951
THE NAMING OF NAMES by Ray Bradbury             TWS  Aug 1949
THE EYES by Henry Hasse                    FB #8  n/d 1951
THE SCARLET LUNES by Stanton A. Coblentz        FB #6  n/d 1951
DEMOBILIZATION by George R. Cowie
    (Originally appeared in VORTEX, a fan magazine published in Germany; 1947)
VOICES FROM THE CLIFF by John Martin Leahy        WT  May 1925
THE LOST CHORD by Sam Moskowitz          ORIGINAL STORY
THE WATCHERS by R. H. Deutsch           ORIGINAL STORY
THE PEACEFUL MARTIAN by J. T. Oliver         FB #8  n/d 1951
ESCAPE INTO YESTERDAY by Arthur J. Burks      ORIGINAL STORY


GALLANT, JOSEPH

    STORIES OF SCIENTIFIC IMAGINATION     (Oxford Book Co.; New York, N. Y.)
    9 stories  152 pages  .70¢  April 6, 1954

THE BLACK PITS OF LUNA by Robert A. Heinlein      SEP  1/10/48
PLANET PASSAGE by Donald A. Wollheim          FFSF  Oct 1942
    (Originally appeared under pseudonym Martin Pearson)
IN VALUE DECEIVED by H. B. Fyfe            ASF  Nov 1950
PERIL OF THE BLUE WORLD by Robert Abernathy      PS   Win 1942
PROPOGANDIST by Murray Leinster ps (Will F. Jenkins)   ASF  Aug 1947
SYMBIOSIS by Will F. Jenkins              Col  1/14/47
CONQUERORS' ISLE by Nelson Bond             BB   Jun 1946
THE WHITE ARMY by Dr. Daniel Dressler        Amz  Sep 1929
A CONNECTICUT YANKEE IN KING ARTHUR'S COURT by Mark Twain ps (Samuel L. Clemens)
    (Condensed version)  (Originally published by Harper and Brothers; 1889)


GALLET, GEORGES H.

    ESCALES DANS L'INFINI  [SCALES OF THE INFINITE]
    10 stories 256 pages 225 francs April 15, 1954
        Librairie Hachette  Paris, France

ESCALES DANS L'INFINI [Continued]    Mag.    Year

ODYSSEE MARTIENNE [A Martian Odyssey] by Stanley G. Weinbaum    WT    Jul 1934
TQUSISTES DES TEMPS FUTURS [Pawley's Peepholes]
    by John Wyndham ps (John Beynon Harris)    Sus    Sum 1951
       (Originally appeared under title OPERATION PEEP)
LA GIRAFE BLEUE [The Blue Giraffe] by L. Sprague de Camp    ASF    Aug 1939
SHAMBLEAU by C. L. Moore (Mrs. Henry Kuttner)    WT    Nov 1933
COLIN—MAILLARD [Blind Man's Buff] by J. U. Giesy    AIS    1/24/20
L'HOMME—MACHINE D'ARDATHIA [The Machine Man of Ardathia]
    by Francis Flagg ps (George Henry Weiss)    Amz    Nov 1927
LA BETE DU VIDE [A Beast of the Void] by Raymond Z. Gallun    Ast    Sep 1936
TROIS LIGNES DE VIEUX FRANCAIS [Three Lines of Old French] by A. Merritt
                                                                Arg    8/9/19
STATION INTERPLANETAIRE #1 [Space Station #1] by Manly Wade Wellman
                                                                Arg    10/10/36
LE SOURIRE DU SPHINX [The Smile of the Sphinx] by William F. Temple
                                                                ToW    Aut 1938


GOLD, H. L.
    BODYGUARD AND FOUR OTHER SHORT NOVELS FROM GALAXY    Doubleday & Co.; N.Y.N.Y.
    5 stories   312 pages   $3.95   September 9, 1960

                ALL STORIES FROM GALAXY SCIENCE FICTION

BODYGUARD by Christopher Grimm    February 1956
HOW—2 by Clifford D. Simak    November 1954
DELAY IN TRANSIT by F. L. Wallace    September 1952
THE CITY OF FORCE by Daniel F. Galouye    April 1959
WHATEVER COUNTS by Frederik Pohl    June 1959


    FIVE GALAXY SHORT NOVELS    Doubleday & Co., Inc.; New York, N. Y.
    5 stories   287 pages   $3.95   October 2, 1958

                ALL STORIES FROM GALAXY SCIENCE FICTION

TANGLE HOLD by F. L. Wallace    June 1953
WORLD WITHOUT CHILDREN by Damon Knight    December 1951
WHEREVER YOU MAY BE by James E. Gunn    May 1953
MIND ALONE by J. T. McIntosh ps (James J. MacGregor)    August 1953
GRANNY WON'T KNIT by Theodore Sturgeon    March 1954


    THE GALAXY READER OF SCIENCE FICTION    Crown Publishers; New York, N. Y.
    33 stories   566 pages   $3.50   February 28, 1952

    English Edition:  Grayson & Grayson Ltd.   13 stories 254 pages 9/6    3/6/53

                ALL STORIES FROM GALAXY SCIENCE FICTION

PART I — IT HAPPENED TOMORROW
    HONEYMOON IN HELL by Fredric Brown    November 1950
    COMING ATTRACTION by Fritz Leiber, Jr.    November 1950
    RULE OF THREE by Theodore Sturgeon    January 1951
    THIRD FROM THE SUN by Richard Matheson    October 1950
    THE LAST MARTIAN by Fredric Brown    October 1950

PART II — SOONER THAN YOU THINK

    JAYWALKER by Ross Rocklynne    December 1950

THE GALAXY READER OF SCIENCE FICTION [Continued]              Year

THE RELUCTANT HEROES by Frank M. Robinson                January 1951
A LITTLE JOURNEY by Ray Bradbury                         August 1951
VENUS IS A MAN'S WORLD by William Tenn ps (Philip Klass)    July 1951
PART III — THE WORLDS WE MADE
BEYOND BEDLAM by Wyman Guin                              August 1951
THE STARS ARE THE STYX by Theodore Sturgeon             October 1950
INSIDE EARTH by Poul Anderson                            April 1951
I, THE UNSPEAKABLE by Walt Sheldon                       April 1951
PART IV — AREN'T YOU AN EXTERRESTRIAL
THE PILOT AND THE BUSHMAN by Sylvia Jacobs              August 1951
JUDAS RAM by Sam Merwin, Jr.                           December 1951
HOSTESS by Isaac Asimov                                     May 1951
BETELGEUSE BRIDGE by William Tenn ps (Philip Klass)     April 1951
CABIN BOY by Damon Knight                            September 1951
FIELD STUDY by Peter Phillips                            April 1951
PART V — LET'S BUILD SOMEBODY
GOOD NIGHT, MR. JAMES by Clifford D. Simak               March 1951
SYNDRONE JOHNNY by Charles Dye                            July 1951
MADE TO MEASURE by William Campbell Gault               January 1951
PART VI — NOT AROUND THE CORNER
ASK ME ANYTHING by Damon Knight                            May 1951
IF YOU WAS A MAKLIN by Murray Leinster ps (Will F. Jenkins)  September 1951
MAN OF DESTINY by John Christopher ps (Christopher S. Youd     May 1951
SUSCEPTIBILITY by John D. MacDonald                     January 1951
PART VII — THE END OF HISTORY AND BEYOND
THE WAKER DREAMS by Richard Matheson                   December 1950
COMMON DENOMINATOR by John D. MacDonald                  July 1951
SECOND CHILDHOOD by Clifford D. Simak                  February 1951
PART VIII — ABOUT TIME
DON'T LIVE IN THE PAST by Damon Knight                     June 1951
THE BIOGRAPHY PROJECT by Dudley Dell ps (H. L. Gold)   September 1951
DARK INTERLUDE by Mack Reynolds and Fredric Brown       January 1951
THE OTHER NOW by Murray Leinster ps (Will F. Jenkins)     March 1951

THE [SECOND] GALAXY READER OF SCIENCE FICTION  Crown Publishers, N.Y., N.Y.
31 stories  504 pages  $3.50  April 1, 1954

English Edition: Grayson & Grayson Ltd.  20 stories  350 pages 13/6  1/27/56
      Titled:  GALAXY SCIENCE FICTION OMNIBUS
                ALL STORIES FROM GALAXY SCIENCE FICTION
PART ONE  TOMORROW'S THE DAY

THE YEAR OF THE JACKPOT by Robert A. Heinlein            March 1952
A BAD DAY FOR SALES by Fritz Leiber                       July 1953
THE MISOGYNIST by James E. Gunn                       November 1952
SAUCER OF LONLINESS by Theodore Sturgeon              February 1953
TEETHING RING by James Causey                          January 1953
A GLEEB FOR EARTH by Charles Schafhauser                   May 1953
PART TWO  THE WILD BLUE YONDER
HALLUCINATION ORBIT by J. T. M'Intosh ps (James J. MacGregor)  January 1952

THE [SECOND] GALAXY READER OF SCIENCE FICTION [Continued]    Year

C-CHUTE by Isaac Asimov                                    October 1951
JUNKYARD by Clifford D. Simak                                  May 1953
PROBLEM ON BALAK by Roger Dee ps (Roger D. Aycock)       September 1953

PART THREE  ADAPT OR ELSE
    SURFACE TENSION by James Blish                         August 1952
    SPECIALIST by Robert Sheckley                             May 1953
    FOUR IN ONE by Damon Knight                         February 1953
    CARETAKER by James H. Schmitz                            July 1953
    LOST MEMORY by Peter Phillips                             May 1952

PART FOUR  WORLDS OF OTHERS
    NOT FIT FOR CHILDREN by Evelyn E. Smith                  May 1953
    STUDENT BODY by F. L. Wallace                          March 1953
    LOVER WHEN YOU'RE NEAR ME by Richard Matheson           May 1953

PART FIVE  IT'S ALL IN THE MIND
    COMMAND PERFORMANCE by Walter M. Miller, Jr.       November 1952
    STAR BRIGHT by Mark Clifton                             July 1952
    WARM by Robert Sheckley                                 June 1953
    UNREADY TO WEAR by Kurt Vonnegut, Jr.                  April 1953

PART SIX  BLUEPRINT FOR CHAOS
    TIGER BY THE TAIL by Alan E. Nourse                 November 1951
    SELF PORTRAIT by Bernard Wolfe                      November 195
    THE SNOWBALL EFFECT by Katherine MacLean          September 1952

PART SEVEN  TIME AND TIME AGAIN
    PILLAR TO POST by John Wyndham ps (John Beynon Harris)  December 195
    MINIMUM SENTENCE by Theodore R. Cogswell             August 195
    A GAME FOR BLONDES by John D. MacDonald              October 195

PART EIGHT  THE NTH GENERATION
    UNIVERSITY by Peter Phillips                            April 195
    TEA TRAY IN THE SKY by Evelyn E. Smith            September 195
    A PAIL OF AIR by Fritz Leiber                       December 195

THE [THIRD] GALAXY READER OF SCIENCE FICTION  Doubleday & Co.; New York N.Y
15 stories  262 pages  $3.95  June 19, 1958
                ALL STORIES FROM GALAXY SCIENCE FICTION

LIMITING FACTOR by Theodore R. Cogswell                    April 195
PROTECTION by Robert Sheckley                              April 195
THE VILBAR PARTY by Evelyn E. Smith                      January 195
END AS A WORLD by F. L. Wallace                        September 195
TIME IN THE ROUND by Fritz Leiber                           May 195
HELP! I AM DR. MORRIS GOLDPEPPER by Avram Davidson        July 195
A WIND IS RISING by Finn O'Donnevan                       July 195
IDEAS DIE HARD by Isaac Asimov                          October 195
DEAD RINGER by Lester del Rey                          November 195
THE HAUNTED CORPSE by Frederik Pohl                     January 195
THE MODEL OF A JUDGE by William Morrison ps (Joseph Samachson)  October 195
MAN IN THE JAR by Damon Knight                            April 195
VOLPA by Wyman Guin                                         May 195
HONORABLE OPPONENT by Clifford D. Simak                  August 195

THE GAME OF RAT AND DRAGON by Cordwainer Smith          October 195

(54)

THE [FOURTH] GALAXY READER OF SCIENCE FICTION Doubleday & Co.; New York N.Y.
15 stories   264 pages   $3.95   April 19, 1959

ALL STORIES FROM GALAXY SCIENCE FICTION                     Year

| | |
|---|---|
| I AM A NUCLEUS by Stephen Barr | February 1957 |
| NAME YOUR SYMPTON by Jim Harmon | May 1956 |
| HORROR HOWCE by Margaret St. Clair | July 1956 |
| MAN OF DISTINCTION by Michael Shaara | October 1956 |
| THE BOMB IN THE BATHTUB by Thomas N. Scortia | February 1957 |
| YOU WERE RIGHT, JOE by J. T. McIntosh ps (James J. MacGregor) | November 1957 |
| WHAT'S HE DOING IN THERE? by Fritz Leiber | December 1957 |
| THE GENTLEST UNPEOPLE by Frederik Pohl | June 1958 |
| THE HATRED by Paul Flehr | January 1958 |
| KILL ME WITH KINDNESS by Richard Wilson | January 1958 |
| OR ALL THE SEAS WITH OYSTERS by Avram Davidson | May 1958 |
| THE GUN WITHOUT A BANG by Finn O'Donnevan | June 1958 |
| MAN IN A QUANDRY by L. J. Stecher, Jr. | July 1958 |
| BLANK FORM by Arthur Sellings | July 1958 |
| THE MINIMUM MAN by Robert Sheckley | June 1958 |

THE [FIFTH] GALAXY READER        Doubleday and Co.; New York, N. Y.
15 stories   260 pages   $3.95   February 10, 1961

ALL STORIES FROM GALAXY SCIENCE FICTION

| | |
|---|---|
| INSIDE JOHN BARTH by William W. Stuart | June 1960 |
| THE LAST LETTER by Fritz Leiber | June 1958 |
| PERFECT ANSWER by L. J. Stecher, Jr. | June 1958 |
| DOUBLE DARE by Robert Silverberg | November 1956 |
| PASTORAL AFFAIR by Charles A. Stearns | February 1959 |
| BLACK CHARLIE by Gordon R. Dickson | April 1954 |
| $1,000 A PLATE by Jack McKenty | October 1954 |
| TAKE WOODEN INDIANS by Avram Davidson | June 1959 |
| THE BITTEREST PILL by Frederik Pohl | April 1959 |
| THIS SIDE UP by Raymond E. Banks | July 1954 |
| THE EEL by Miriam Allen DeFord | April 1958 |
| A FEAST OF DEMONS by William Morrison ps (Joseph Samachson) | March 1958 |
| NIGHTMARE WITH ZEPPLINS by Frederik Pohl & C. M. Kornbluth | December 1958 |
| WE NEVER MENTION AUNT NORA by Paul Flehr | July 1958 |
| WHEN THE PEOPLE FELL by Cordwainer Smith | April 1959 |

MIND PARTNER AND 8 OTHER NOVELETS FROM GALAXY   Doubleday & Co.; New York, N.Y.
9 stories   263 pages   $3.95   November 1961

ALL STORIES FROM GALAXY MAGAZINE

| | |
|---|---|
| MIND PARTNER by Christopher Anvil | August 1960 |
| THE LADY WHO SAILED THE SOUL by Cordwainer Smith | April 1960 |
| THE STENTORII LUGGAGE by Neal Barrett, Jr. | October 1960 |
| SNUFFLES by R. A. Lafferty | December 1960 |
| THE SLY BUNGERHOP by William Morrison ps (Joseph Samachson) | September 1957 |
| BLACKSWORD by A. J. Offutt | December 1959 |
| THE CIVILIZATION GAME by Clifford D. Simak | November 1958 |
| THE HARDEST BARGAIN by Evelyn E. Smith | June 1957 |
| WITH REDFERN ON CAPELLA XII by Charles Satterfield | November 1955 |

THE WORLD THAT COULDN'T BE AND 8 OTHER NOVELETS FROM GALAXY
9 stories   288 pages   $3.95   September 3, 1959 Doubleday & Co.; New York, N.Y.

ALL STORIES FROM GALAXY SCIENCE FICTION

| | |
|---|---|
| THE WORLD THAT COULDN'T BE by Clifford D. Simak | January 1958 |
| BRIGHTSIDE CROSSING by Alan E. Nourse | January 1956 |

| | |
|---|---|
| MEZZEROW LOVES COMPANY by F. L. Wallace | June 1956 |
| AN EYE FOR A WHAT? by Damon Knight | March 1957 |
| A WOMAN'S PLACE by Mark Clifton | May 1955 |
| A GUN FOR DINOSAUR by L. Sprague de Camp | March 1956 |
| ONE FOR THE BOOKS by Richard Matheson | September 1955 |
| THE MUSIC MASTER OF BABYLON by Edgar Pangborn | November 1954 |
| ONCE A GREECH by Evelyn E. Smith | April 1957 |

GREENBERG, MARTIN

ALL ABOUT THE FUTURE        Gnome Press; New York, N. Y.        Mag.    Year
12 stories   374 pages   $3.50   February 1955

"ADVENTURES IN SCIENCE FICTION" SERIES

INTRODUCTIONS:

| | | |
|---|---|---|
| WHERE TO? by Robert A. Heinlein | Glxy | Feb 1952 |
| LET'S NOT by Isaac Asimov | BJG | Dec 1954 |
| THE MIDAS PLAGUE by Frederik Pohl | Glxy | Apr 1954 |
| UN-MAN by Poul Anderson | ASF | Jan 1953 |
| GRANNY WON'T KNIT by Theodore Sturgeon | Glxy | May 1954 |
| NATURAL STATE by Damon Knight | Glxy | Jan 1954 |
| HOBO GOD by Malcolm Jameson | ASF | Sep 1944 |
| BLOOD BANK by Walter M. Miller, Jr. | ASF | Jun 1952 |

EXCERPTS FROM ENCYCLOPEDIA OF GALACTIC CULTURE —— Edited by Edward Wellen

| | | |
|---|---|---|
| ORIGINS OF GALACTIC ETIQUETTE | Glxy | Oct 1953 |
| ORIGINS OF GALACTIC LAW | Glxy | Apr 1953 |
| ORIGINS OF GALACTIC SLANG | Glxy | Jul 1952 |
| ORIGINS OF GALACTIC MEDICINE | Glxy | Dec 1953 |

COMING ATTRACTIONS        Gnome Press; New York, N. Y.
11 articles   254 pages   $3.50   February 28, 1957

"ADVENTURES IN SCIENCE FICTION" SERIES

| | | |
|---|---|---|
| A LETTER TO THE MARTIANS by Willy Ley | TWS | Nov 1940 |
| (Originally appeared under title CALLING ALL MARTIANS) | | |
| HOW TO LEARN MARTIAN by Charles F. Hockett | ASF | May 1955 |
| LANGUAGE FOR TIME TRAVELERS by L. Sprague de Camp | ASF | Jul 1938 |
| GEOGRAPHY FOR TIME TRAVELERS by Willy Ley | ASF | Jul 1939 |
| TIME TRAVEL AND THE LAW by C. M. Kornbluth | ORIGINAL STORY | |
| SPACE FIX by R. S. Richardson | ASF | Mar 1943 |
| SPACE WAR by Willy Ley | ASF | Aug 1939 |
| SPACE WAR TACTICS by Malcolm Jameson | ASF | Aug 1939 |
| FUEL FOR THE FUTURE by Jack Hatcher | ASF | Mar 1940 |
| INTERPLANETARY COPYRIGHT by Donald F. Reines | ORIGINAL STORY | |
| HOW TO COUNT ON YOUR FINGERS by Frederik Pohl | SFS | Sep 1956 |

FIVE SCIENCE FICTION NOVELS        Gnome Press; New York, N. Y.
5 stories   382 pages   $3.50   April 1, 1952

| | | |
|---|---|---|
| BUT WITHOUT HORNS by Norvell W. Page | Unk | Jun 1940 |
| DESTINY TIMES THREE by Fritz Leiber, Jr. | ASF | Apr 1945 |
| CRISIS IN UTOPIA by Norman L. Knight | ASF | Jul 1940 |
| THE CHRONICLER by A. E. Van Vogt | ASF | Oct 1946 |
| THE CRUCIBLE OF POWER by Jack Williamson | ASF | Feb 1939 |

JOURNEY TO INFINITY        Gnome Press; New York, N. Y.

12 stories   381 pages   $3.50   January 3, 1951

"ADVENTURES IN SCIENCE FICTION" SERIES

| | | |
|---|---|---|
| FALSE DAWN by A. Bertram Chandler | ASF | Oct 1946 |
| ATLANTIS by E. E. Smith | (Excerpts from TRIPLANETARY; 1950) | |
| LETTER TO A PHOENIX by Fredric Brown | ASF | Aug 1949 |
| UNITE AND CONQUER by Theodore Sturgeon | ASF | Oct 1948 |
| BREAKDOWN by Jack Williamson | ASF | Jan 1942 |

DANCE OF A NEW WORLD by John D. MacDonald                           ASF     Sep 1948
MOTHER EARTH by Isaac Asimov                                        ASF     May 1949
THERE SHALL BE DARKNESS by C. L. Moore  (Mrs. Henry Kuttner)        ASF     Feb 1942
TABOO by Fritz Leiber, Jr.                                          ASF     Feb 1944
OVERTHROW by Cleve Cartmill                                         ASF     Nov. 1942
BARRIER OF DREAD by Judith Merril                                   Fw/SFS  Aug 1950
METAMORPHOSITE by Eric Frank Russell                               ASF     Dec 1946

> MEN AGAINST THE STARS              Gnome Press; New York, N. Y.
> 12 stories  351 pages  $2.95  March 20, 1950
>                "ADVENTURES IN SCIENCE FICTION" SERIES

English Edition:   Grayson & Grayson Ltd.
    8 stories  256 pages  8/6  June 1951
Pocket Book Edition:        Pyramid Books; New York, N. Y.
    9 stories  191 pages  .35¢  #G 234  December 15, 1956

TRENDS by Isaac Asimov                                              ASF     Jul 1939
MEN AGAINST THE STARS by Manly Wade Wellman                         ASF     Jun 1938
THE RED DEATH OF MARS by Robert Moore Williams                      ASF     Jul 1940
LOCKED OUT by H. B. Fyfe                                            ASF     Feb 1940
THE IRON STANDARD by Lewis Padgett ps (Henry Kuttner & C. L. Moore) ASF    Dec 1945
SCHEDULE by Harry Walton                                            ASF     Jun 1945
FAR CENTAURUS by A. E. Van Vogt                                     ASF     Jan 1944
COLD FRONT by Hal Clement ps (Harry Clement Stubbs)                 ASF     Jul 1946
THE PLANTS by Murray Leinster ps (Will F. Jenkins)                 ASF     Jan 1946
COMPETITION by E. Mayne Hull (Mrs. A. E. Van Vogt)                 ASF     Jun 1943
BRIDLE AND SADDLE by Isaac Asimov                                  ASF     Jun 1942
WHEN SHADOWS FALL by L. Ron Hubbard                                Stg     Jul 1948

> THE ROBOT AND THE MAN              Gnome Press; New York, N. Y.
> 10 stories  251 pages  $2.95  March 15, 1953
>                "ADVENTURES IN SCIENCE FICTION" SERIES
English Edition:   Grayson & Grayson Ltd.
    10 stories  224 pages  9/6  May 17, 1954

THE MECHANICAL ANSWER by John D. MacDonald                          ASF     May 1948
SELF PORTRAIT by Bernard Wolfe                                      Glxy    Nov 1951
DEADLOCK by Lewis Padgett ps (Henry Kuttner and C. L. Moore)       ASF     Aug 1942
ROBINIC by H. H. Holmes ps (Anthony Boucher)                       ASF     Sep 1943
BURNING BRIGHT by John S. Browning ps (Robert Moore Williams)       ASF     Jul 1948
FINAL COMMAND by A. E. Van Vogt                                     ASF     Nov 1948
THOUGH DREAMERS DIE by Lester del Rey                               ASF     Oct 1939
RUST by Joseph E. Kelleam                                           ASF     Oct 1939
ROBOTS RETURN by Robert Moore Williams                             ASF     Sep 1938
INTO THY HANDS by Lester del Rey                                    ASF     Aug 1945

> TRAVELERS OF SPACE                Gnome Press; New York, N. Y.
> 14 stories  400 pages  $3.95  January 3, 1952
>                "ADVENTURES IN SCIENCE FICTION" SERIES
Articles
    Preface to Science Fiction Dictionary by Samuel Anthony Peeples

Science Fiction Dictionary

Fiction

THE ROCKETEERS HAVE SHAGGY EARS by Keith Bennett                   PS    Spr 1950
CHRISTMAS TREE by Christopher S. Youd                              ASF   Feb 1949
THE FORGIVENESS OF TENCHU TAEN by F. A. Kummer, Jr.                ASF   Nov 1938
EPISODE ON DHEE MINOR by Harry Walton                             ASF   Oct 1939
THE SHAPE OF THINGS by Ray Bradbury                                TWS   Feb 1948
COLUMBUS WAS A DOPE by Lyle Monroe ps (Robert A. Heinlein)         Stg   May 1947
    (Originally appeared under byline Robert A. Heinlein)
ATTITUDE by Hal Clement ps (Harry Clement Stubbs)                  ASF   Sep 1943
THE IONIAN CYCLE by William Tenn ps (Philip Klass)                 TWS   Aug 1949
TROUBLE ON TANTALUS by P. Schuyler Miller                          ASF   Feb 1941
PLACET IS A CRAZY PLACE by Fredric Brown                           ASF   May 1946
ACTION ON AZURA by Robertson Osborne                               PS    Fal 1949
THE RULL by A. E. Van Vogt                                         ASF   May 1946
THE DOUBLE-DYED VILLAINS by Poul Anderson                          ASF   Sep 1949
BUREAU OF SLICK TRICKS by H. B. Fyfe                               ASF   Dec 1948

Illustrations

LIFE ON OTHER WORLDS by Edd Cartier            (Original illustrated feature)
    With special ·descriptive story: THE INTERSTELLAR ZOO by David Kyle
                                                          ORIGINAL STORY


GUNTHER, GOTTHARD

UBERWINDUNG VON RAUM UND ZEIT [Conquest of Space and Time] Copyright: 1952
7 stories 237 pages American Price: $3.75   Karl Rauch Publishers (W. Germany)


FLUCHT [Desertion] by Clifford D. Simak                            ASF   Nov 1944
EINBRUCH DER NACHT [Nightfall] by Isaac Asimov                     ASF   Sep 1941
WER DA? [Who Goes There?] by John W. Campbell, Jr.                 ASF   Aug 1938
    (Originally appeared under pseudonym Don A. Stuart)
DIE LOTUS ESSER [The Lotus Eaters] by Stanley G. Weinbaum          Ast   Apr 1935
ZEIT AND WEIDER ZEIT [Time and Time Again] by H. Beam Piper        ASF   Apr 1947
WEIDERERWECKUNG [Resurrection] by A. E. Van Vogt                   ASF   Aug 1948
    (Originally appeared under title THE MONSTER)
ERBARMLICH WAR'N DIE BURGERBEINE [Mimsy Were The Borogoves]
    by Lewis Padgett ps (Henry Kuttner and C. L. Moore)           ASF   Feb 1943


HEALY, RAYMOND J.

NEW TALES OF SPACE AND TIME            Henry Holt and Co.; New York, N. Y.
10 stories  294 pages  $3.50 November 5, 1951

English Edition: Weidenfeld Nicolson 10 stories 279 pages  10/6  (1952)
Pocket Book Editions: Pocket Books, Inc.; New York, N. Y.
    10 stories  273 pages  .25¢  #908  December 1, 1952
    10 stories  273 pages  .35¢  (Cardinal Edition C319)               1958

ALL ORIGINAL STORIES

HERE THERE BE TYGERS by Ray Bradbury
"IN A GOOD CAUSE ——" by Isaac Asimov
TOLLIVER'S TRAVELS by Frank Fenton and Joseph Petracca
BETTYANN by Kris Neville
LITTLE ANTON by R. Bretnor
STATUS QUONDAM by P. Schuyler Miller
B + M — PLANET 4 by Gerald Heard
YOU CAN'T SAY THAT by Cleve Cartmill
FULFILLMENT by A. E. Van Vogt
QUEST FOR SAINT AQUIN by Anthony Boucher

9 TALES OF SPACE AND TIME        Henry Holt and Co.; New York, N. Y.
9 stories  307 pages  $3.50  May 24, 1954

English Edition: Weidenfeld Nicolson  9 stories  272 pages  9/6  (1955)

ALL ORIGINAL STORIES

THE IDEALISTS by John W. Campbell, Jr.
SHOCK TREATMENT by J. Francis McComas
GENIUS OF THE SPECIES by R. Bretnor
OVERTURE by Kris Neville
COMPOUND B by David Harold Fink, M. D.
THE CHICKEN OR THE EGGHEAD by Frank Fenton
THE GREAT DEVON MYSTERY by Raymond J. Healy
BALAAM by Anthony Boucher
MAN OF PARTS by H. L. Gold

HEALY, RAYMOND J.  w/ J. Francis McComas                          Mag.    Year
    ADVENTURES IN TIME AND SPACE      Random House; New York, N. Y.
    35 stories  997 pages  $2.95  August 26, 1946

    Other American Edition:  Modern Library  997 pages #G-31  $2.95
        Titled:  FAMOUS SCIENCE FICTION STORIES        33 stories  (1957)
    Canadian Edition:  Random House  $3.45  33 stories (No further data available)
        Titled:  FAMOUS SCIENCE FICTION STORIES
    English Edition: Grayson & Grayson Ltd.  11 stories 326 pages 9/6  (12/1/52)
    Pocket Book Editions: Pennant Books; New York, N. Y.
        8 stories  200 pages  .25¢  P 44  April 1954
        Bantam Books; New York, N. Y.  7 stories 142 pages .25¢ #1310 March 1955
            Bantam Edition Titled:  MORE ADVENTURES IN TIME AND SPACE

REQUIEM by Robert A. Heinlein                                     ASF   Jan 1940
FORGETFULNESS by Don A. Stuart ps (John W. Campbell, Jr.)         Ast   Jun 1937
NERVES by Lester del Rey                                          ASF   Sep 1942
THE SANDS OF TIME by P. Schuyler Miller                          Ast   Apr 1937
THE PROUD ROBOT by Lewis Padgett ps (Henry Kuttner and C. L. Moore)  ASF   Oct 1943
BLACK DESTROYER by A. E. Van Vogt                                ASF   Jul 1939
SYMBIOTICA by Eric Frank Russell                                 ASF   Oct 1943
SEEDS OF THE DUSK by Raymond Z. Gallun                           ASF   Jun 1938
HEAVY PLANET by Lee Gregor ps (Milton A. Rothman)                ASF   Aug 1939
TIME LOCKER by Lewis Padgett ps (Henry Kuttner and C. L. Moore)  ASF   Jan 1943
THE LINK by Cleve Cartmill                                       ASF   Aug 1942
MECHANICAL MICE by Maurice G. Hugi ps (Eric Frank Russell)       ASF   Jan 1941
V-2; ROCKET CARGO SHIP by Willy Ley        (article)             ASF   May 1945
ADAM AND NO EVE by Alfred Bester                                 ASF   Sep 1941
NIGHTFALL by Isaac Asimov                                        ASF   Sep 1941
A MATTER OF SIZE by Harry Bates                                  Ast   Apr 1934
AS NEVER WAS by P. Schuyler Miller                               ASF   Jan 1944
Q.U.R. by Anthony Boucher                                        ASF   Mar 1943
    (Originally appeared under pseudonym H. H. Holmes)
WHO GOES THERE? by Don A. Stuart ps (John W. Campbell, Jr.)       ASF   Aug 1938
THE ROADS MUST ROLL by Robert A. Heinlein                        ASF   Jun 1940
ASYLUM by A. E. Van Vogt                                         ASF   May 1942
QUIETUS by Ross Rocklynne                                        ASF   Sep 1940
THE TWONKY by Lewis Padgett ps (Henry Kuttner & C. L. Moore)     ASF   Sep 1942
TIME-TRAVEL HAPPENS! by A. M. Phillips        (article)          Unk   Dec 1939
ROBOTS RETURN by Robert Moore Williams                           ASF   Sep 1938

(59)

THE BLUE GIRAFFE by L. Sprague de Camp                              ASF    Aug 1939
FLIGHT INTO DARKNESS by Webb Marlowe ps (J. Francis McComas)        Amz    Feb 1943
THE WEAPON SHOP by A. E. Van Vogt                                   ASF    Dec 1942
FAREWELL TO THE MASTER by Harry Bates                               ASF    Dec 1940
WITHIN THE PYRAMID by R. DeWitt Miller                              Ast    Mar 1937
HE WHO SHRANK by Henry Hasse                                        Amz    Aug 1936
BY HIS BOOTSTRAPS by Anson MacDonald ps (Robert A. Heinlein)        ASF    Oct 1941
THE STAR MOUSE by Fredric Brown                                      PS    Spr 1942
CORRESPONDENCE COURSE by Raymond F. Jones                           ASF    Apr 1945
BRAIN by S. Fowler Wright                        (From THE NEW GODS LEAD; 1932)


HEINLEIN, ROBERT A.
    TOMORROW, THE STARS              Doubleday and Co.; New York, N. Y.
    14 stories  249 pages  $2.95  February 7, 1952

    Pocket Book Edition: 207 pages  14 stories  .25¢  Signet #1044  (8/26/53)
        New American Library of World Literature, Inc.; New York, N. Y.

I'M SCARED by Jack Finney                                           Col    9/15/51
THE SILLY SEASON by C. M. Kornbluth                                F&SF    Fal 1950
THE REPORT ON THE BARNHOUSE EFFECT by Kurt Vonnegut, Jr.            Col    9/11/50
THE TOURIST TRADE by Bob Tucker                                      WB    Jan 1951
RAINMAKER by John Reese                                            SEP    2/19/49
ABSALOM by Henry Kuttner                                           Stg    Fal 1946
THE MONSTER by Lester del Rey                                      Arg    Jun 1951
JAY SCORE by Eric Frank Russell                                    ASF    May 1941
BETELGEUSE BRIDGE by William Tenn ps (Philip Klass)               Glxy    Apr 1951
SURVIVAL SHIP by Judith Merril                                      WB    Jan 1951
KEYHOLE by Murray Leinster ps (Will F. Jenkins)                   TWS    Dec 1951
MISBEGOTEN MISSIONARY by Isaac Asimov                             Glxy    Nov 1950
THE SACK by William Morrison ps (Joseph Samachson)                 ASF    Sep 1950
POOR SUPERMAN by Fritz Leiber                                     Glxy    Jul 1951
    (Originally appeared under title APPOINTMENT IN TOMORROW)


KORNBLUTH, MARY
    SCIENCE FICTION SHOWCASE         Doubleday and Co.; New York, N. Y.
    12 stories  264 pages  $3.95  September 17, 1959

TICKET TO ANYWHERE by Damon Knight                                Glxy    Apr 1952
THAT LOW by Theodore Sturgeon                                     FFM    Oct 1948
OR THE GRASSES GROW by Avram Davidson                            F&SF    Nov 1958
THE MAN WHO ATE THE WORLD by Frederik Pohl                        Glxy    Nov 1956
THE LONG REMEMBERING by Poul Anderson                            F&SF    Nov 1957
THE END OF THE BEGINNING by Ray Bradbury                          McM        1956
    (Originally appeared under title NEXT STOP: THE STARS)
A WORK OF ART by James Blish                                      SFS    Jul 1956
THE COLD GREEN-EYE by Jack Williamson                            Fnt    Mar 1953
MED SERVICE by Murray Leinster ps (Will F. Jenkins)               ASF    Aug 1957
EXPENDABLE by Philip K. Dick                                     F&SF    Jul 1953
MANTAGE by Richard Matheson                              ORIGINAL STORY
NIGHTMARE NUMBER FOUR by Robert Bloch         (This verse first appeared in a
    fanzine.  This is its first professional appearance.)


KUEBLER, HAROLD W.
    THE TREASURY OF SCIENCE FICTION CLASSICS   Doubleday & Co.; New York, N. Y.
    17 stories  694 pages  $2.95  January 3, 1955
WORLDS IN COLLISION
    THE CONVERSATION BETWEEN EIROS AND CHARMION by Edgar Allen Poe   BGM  Dec 1839

THE STAR by H. G. Wells                                        Grp Xmas 1897
WHEN WORLDS COLLIDE by Edwin Balmer and Philip Wylie     (excerpts)
    (Published by Frederick A. Stokes Co.; 1932)
THE GREAT ADVENTURE
    THE MARACOT DEEP by Arthur Conan Doyle
        (From THE MARACOT DEEP AND OTHER STORIES; 1929)
    ROUND THE MOON by Jules Verne    (Originally published by Hetzel [Paris]; 1870)
    THE LAST TERRESTRIALS by Olaf Stapledon     (From THE LAST AND FIRST MEN; 1930)
THE WORLD OF THE FUTURE
    THE MACHINE STOPS by E. M. Forster
        (From THE ETERNAL MOMENT AND OTHER STORIES; 1928)
    R. U. R. [Rossum's Universal Robots] by Karel Capek
        Copyright 1923 by Doubleday, Page and Co.
    BRAVE NEW WORLD by Aldous Huxley    (Excerpts)
        (Published by Harper and Bros.; 1932)
WORLDS IN CONFLICT
    INVASION FROM MARS by Howard Koch        The radio script of the Orson Welles
        broadcast of H. G. Wells' THE WAR OF THE WORLDS over  the  Columbia Broad-
        casting System, October 30, 1938.
                    (Copyright 1940 by Princeton University Press)
    EDISON'S CONQUEST OF MARS by Garrett P. Serviss  (Abridged)
        Editor's Note:  This novel  originally appeared  serially in the NEW  YORK
        EVENING JOURNAL from January 12 to February 10, 1898.  It was reprinted in
        book form by Carcosa House [Los Angeles, Calif.] in 1947.
    THE MARTIANS by Olaf Stapledon              (From THE LAST AND FIRST MEN; 1930)
ADVENTURES IN TIME
    THE TIME MACHINE by H. G. Wells                            NwR   Jan 1895
    THE CURIOUS CASE OF BENJAMIN BUTTON by F. Scott Fitzgerald
        (From TALKERS OF THE JAZZ AGE; 1920)
    THE RAT by S. Fowler Wright                                WT    Mar 1929
BEYOND TIME AND SPACE
    THE DAMNED THING by Ambrose Bierce           (From CAN SUCH THINGS BE?; 1893)
    MR. STRENBERRY'S TALE by J. B. Priestly          (From FOUR-IN-HAND; 1934)

LEINSTER, MURRAY ps (Will F. Jenkins)
    GREAT STORIES OF SCIENCE FICTION        Random House; New York, N. Y.
    12 stories   321 pages   $2.95  May 12, 1951

    English Edition:  Cassell and Co. Ltd. 12 stories  318 pages  15/      1955

THE FASCINATING STRANGER by Michael Fessier                   SEP     5/22/48
LIQUID LIFE by Ralph Milne Farley ps (Roger Sherman Hoar)     TWS     Oct 1936
SYMBIOSIS by Will F. Jenkins                                  Col     1/14/47
NUMBER NINE by Cleve Cartmill                                 ASF     Feb 1950
BLIND ALLEY by Malcolm Jameson                               UW      Jun 1943
IN HIDING by Wilmar H. Shiras                                 ASF     Nov 1948
NO WOMAN BORN by C. L. Moore  (Mrs. Henry Kuttner)            ASF     Dec 1944
THE STRANGE CASE OF JOHN KINGMAN by Murray Leinster ps (Will F. Jenkins)
                                                             ASF     May 1948
THE IMPOSSIBLE HIGHWAY by Oscar J. Friend                     TWS     Aug 1940
OPEN SECRET by Lewis Padgett ps (Henry Kuttner and C. L. Moore)  ASF Apr 1943
THE CHRONOKINESIS OF JONATHAN HULL by Anthony Boucher         ASF     Jun 1946
THE CHROMIUM HELMET by Theodore Sturgeon                      ASF     Jun 1946

LESSER, MILTON

    LOOKING FORWARD           Beechhurst Press; New York, N. Y.
    20 stories  400 pages  $4.95  November 20, 1953

    English Edition: Cassell and Co. Ltd.  20 stories  400 pages  15/    1955

### TODAY — AND TOMORROW

| | Mag. | Year |
|---|---|---|
| THE MAN FROM OUTSIDE by Jack Williamson | ASF | Mar 1951 |
| WE KILL PEOPLE by Lewis Padgett ps (Henry Kuttner and C. L. Moore) | ASF | Mar 1946 |
| WIN THE WORLD by Chad Oliver | Stg | Feb 1952 |
| THE LITTLE CREEPS by Walter M. Miller, Jr. | Amz | Dec 1951 |
| HIGHWAY by Robert W. Lowndes | SFQ | Fal 1942 |
| (Originally appeared under pseudonym Wilfred Owen Morley) | | |
| EXILE by Edmond Hamilton | Sup | May 1943 |
| THE POWER by Murray Leinster ps (Will F. Jenkins) | ASF | Sep 1945 |

### THE DAY AFTER TOMORROW

| | Mag. | Year |
|---|---|---|
| THE MAN IN THE MOON by Mack Reynolds | Amz | Jul 1950 |
| PRODUCTION TEST by Raymond F. Jones | ASF | Oct 1949 |
| LION'S MOUTH by Stephen Marlowe ps (Milton Lesser) | FA | Jun 1952 |
| IN THIS SIGN by Ray Bradbury | Im | Apr 1951 |
| VICTORY UNINTENTIONAL by Isaac Asimov | Sup | Aug 1942 |
| THE VOYAGE THAT LASTED SIX HUNDRED YEARS by Don Wilcox | Amz | Oct 1940 |

### IMAGINATION UNLIMITED

| | Mag. | Year |
|---|---|---|
| THE LAST MONSTER by Poul Anderson | Sup | Aug 1951 |
| THE KING OF THIEVES by Jack Vance | Stg | Jul 1949 |
| MAN OF DESTINY by John Christopher ps (Christopher S. Youd) | Glxy | May 1951 |
| LULUGOMEENA by Gordon R. Dickson | Glxy | Jan 1954 |
| ULTIMA THULE by Eric Frank Russell | ASF | Oct 1951 |
| INTO THY HANDS by Lester del Rey | ASF | Aug 1945 |
| TRANSIENCE by Arthur C. Clarke | Stg | Jul 1949 |

LOUGHLIN, RICHARD L. & Lilian M. Popp
    JOURNEYS IN SCIENCE FICTION      Globe Book Co.; New York, N. Y.
    17 stories  656 pages  $3.50        1961

DAEDALUS by Thomas Bulfinch              (From THE AGE OF FABLE; 1855)
THE BIRTHMARK by Nathaniel Hawthorne      (From Mosses From An Old Manse; 1846)
A DESCENT INTO THE MAELSTROM by Edgar Allan Poe      GLGM May 1841
A JOURNEY TO THE CENTER OF THE EARTH by Jules Verne
    (From A VOYAGE TO THE CENTER OF THE EARTH; Hetzel [Paris], 1864)
MOXON'S MASTER by Ambrose Bierce        (From CAN SUCH THINGS BE?; 1893)
A TALE OF NEGATIVE GRAVITY by Frank R. Stockton    (From A BORROWED MONTH; 1887)
THE DISINTEGRATION MACHINE by Arthur Conan Doyle
    (From THE MARACOT DEEP AND OTHER STORIES; 1929)
AEPYORNIS ISLAND by H. G. Wells                PMB Xmas 1894
"WIRELESS" by Rudyard Kipling                  SM Aug 1902
TOBERMORY by Saki  (H. H. Munro)          (No data available)
THE ROADS MUST ROLL by Robert A. Heinlein        ASF  Jun 1940
VISIT TO A SMALL PLANET by Gore Vidal  (A Play)  (Copyright 1955 by Gore Vidal)
QUIT ZOOMIN' THOSE HANDS THROUGH THE AIR by Jack Finney    Col  8/4/51
THE FUN THEY HAD by Isaac Asimov               NEA  12/1/51
TRIGGERMAN by J. F. Bone                  ASF  Dec 1958
THE REPORT ON THE BARNHOUSE EFFECT by Kurt Vonnegut, Jr.    Col  2/11/50
    D
    A
BAXBR by Evelyn E. Smith    (From TIME TO COME; 1954 — Edited by August Derleth)
    B
    R

MARGULIES, LEO                                              Mag.     Year
    GET OUT OF MY SKY          Fawcett Publications, Inc.  Greenwich, Conn.
    3 stories  176 pages  .35¢  Crest Book S362  March 1960

GET OUT OF MY SKY by James Blish                           ASF   Jan 1957
SISTER PLANET by Poul Anderson                             SSF   May 1959
ALIEN NIGHT by Thomas N. Scortia                           SFad  Aug 1957

    THREE FROM OUT THERE       Fawcett Publications, Inc.; Greenwich, Conn.
    3 stories  192 pages  .35¢  Crest S282  March 1959

MOTHER EARTH by Isaac Asimov                               ASF   May 1949
DOUBLE MEANING by Damon Knight                             Stg   Jan 1953
SON OF TWO WORLDS by Edmond Hamilton                       TWS   Aug 1941

    THREE TIMES INFINITY   (3 × ∞) Fawcett Publications, Inc.; Greenwich, Conn.
    3 stories  176 pages  .35¢  Gold Medal Giant S726  January 1958

LORELI OF THE RED MIST by Ray Bradbury and Leigh Brackett  TWS   Fal 1953
THE GOLDEN HELIX by Theodore Sturgeon                      TWS   Sum 1954
DESTINATION MOON by Robert A. Heinlein                     SS    Sep 1950

MARGULIES, LEO & OSCAR J. FRIEND
    FROM OFF THIS WORLD         Merlin Press, Inc.; New York, N. Y.
    18 stories  448 pages  $2.95  October 15, 1949
                       HALL OF FAME CLASSICS
BOOK 1
    THE LAST WOMAN by Thomas S. Gardner                    WS    Apr 1932
    THE MAN WHO EVOLVED by Edmond Hamilton                 WS    Apr 1931
    THE WORLD WITHOUT by Benson Herbert                    WS    Feb 1931
    THE GREEN TORTURE by A. Rowley Hilliard                WS    Mar 1931
    THE LITERARY CORKSCREW by David H. Keller, M. D.       WS    Mar 1934
    THE MAN FROM MARS by P. Schuyler Miller                WSQ   Sum 1931
    THE ANCIENT BRAIN by A. G. Stangland                   SWS   Oct 1929
    THE CITY OF THE SINGING FLAME by Clark Ashton Smith    WS    Jul 1931
    BEYOND THE SINGING FLAME by Clark Ashton Smith         WS    Nov 1931
BOOK 2
    THE ETERNAL MAN by D. D. Sharp                         SWS   Aug 1929
    HORNETS OF SPACE by R. F. Starzl                       WS    Nov 1930
    THE CUBIC CITY by Louis Tucker                         SWS   Sep 1929
    A MARTIAN ODYSSEY by Stanley G. Weinbaum               WS    Jul 1934
    VALLEY OF DREAMS by Stanley G. Weinbaum                WS    Nov 1934
    THROUGH THE PURPLE CLOUD by Jack Williamson            WS    May 1931
    THE MICROSCOPIC GIANTS by Paul Ernst                   TWS   Oct 1936
    WHEN THE EARTH LIVED by Henry Kuttner                  TWS   Oct 1937
    CONQUEST OF LIFE by Eando Binder ps (Otto Binder)      TWS   Aug 1937

    THE GIANT ANTHOLOGY OF SCIENCE FICTION     Merlin Press, Inc.; New York, N. Y.
    10 stories  $3.95  580 pages  May 25, 1954
    Pocket Book Edition: Fawcett Publications, Inc.; Greenwich, Conn.
        4 stories  224 pages  .35¢ Crest S245  October 1958
             Titled:  RACE TO THE STARS
ENCHANTRESS OF VENUS by Leigh Brackett  (Mrs. Edmond Hamilton)  PS  Fal 1949

| | Mag. | Year |
|---|---|---|
| GATEWAY TO DARKNESS by Fredric Brown | Sup | Nov 1949 |
| THE GIRL IN THE GOLDEN ATOM by Ray Cummings | AIS | 3/15/19 |
| FORGOTTEN WORLD by Edmond Hamilton | TWS | Win 1946 |
| BY HIS BOOTSTRAPS by Robert A. Heinlein | ASF | Oct 1941 |
| (Originally appeared under pseudonym Anson MacDonald) | | |
| SWORD OF TOMORROW by Henry Kuttner | TWS | Fal 1945 |
| THINGS PASS BY by Murray Leinster ps (Will F. Jenkins) | TWS | Sum 1945 |
| ROGUE SHIP by A. E. Van Vogt | Sup | Mar 1950 |
| ISLAND IN THE SKY by Manly Wade Wellman | TWS | Oct 1941 |
| THE SUN MAKERS by Jack Williamson | TWS | Jun 1940 |

MY BEST SCIENCE FICTION STORY          Merlin Press, Inc.; New York, N. Y.
25 stories   556 pages   $3.95   December 1, 1949

Pocket Book Edition:   Pocket Books, Inc.; New York, N. Y.
12 stories   263 pages   .25¢   #1007   July 1, 1954

| | | |
|---|---|---|
| ROBOT AL 76 GOES ASTRAY by Isaac Asimov | Amz | Feb 1942 |
| GRIEF OF BAGDAD by Arthur K. Barnes | TWS | Jun 1943 |
| (Originally appeared under pseudonym Kelvin Kent) | | |
| THE TEACHER FROM MARS by Eando Binder ps (Otto Binder) | TWS | Feb 1941 |
| ALMOST HUMAN by Robert Bloch | FA | Jun 1943 |
| (Originally appeared under pseudonym Tarleton Fiske) | | |
| ZERO HOUR by Ray Bradbury | PS | Fal 1947 |
| NOTHING SIRIUS by Fredric Brown | CF | Spr 1944 |
| BLINDNESS by John W. Campbell, Jr. | Ast | Mar 1935 |
| (Originally appeared under pseudonym Don A. Stuart) | | |
| VISITING YOKEL by Cleve Cartmill | TWS | Aug 1943 |
| THE HIBITED MAN by L. Sprague de Camp | TWS | Oct 1949 |
| THE THING IN THE POND by Paul Ernst | Ast | Jun 1934 |
| WANDERER OF TIME by John Russell Fearn | Stg | Sum 1934 |
| (Originally appeared under pseudonym Polton Cross) | | |
| THE INN OUTSIDE OF THE WORLD by Edmond Hamilton | WT | Jul 1945 |
| THE GREEN HILLS OF EARTH by Robert A. Heinlein | SEP | 2/8/47 |
| THE PROFESSOR WAS A THIEF by L. Ron Hubbard | ASF | Feb 1940 |
| DON'T LOOK NOW by L. Ron Hubbard | Stg | Mar 1948 |
| THE LOST RACE by Murray Leinster ps (Will F. Jenkins) | TWS | Apr 1949 |
| THE HOUSE OF RISING WINDS by Frank Belknap Long, Jr. | Stg | Mar 1948 |
| THE CARRIERS by Sam Merwin, Jr. | TWS | Feb 1949 |
| DOCTOR GRIMSHAW'S SANITARIUM by Fletcher Pratt | Amz | May 1934 |
| THE UNCHARTERED ISLE by Clark Ashton Smith | WT | Nov 1950 |
| THUNDER AND ROSES by Theodore Sturgeon | ASF | Nov 1947 |
| THE ULTIMATE CATALYST by John Taine ps (Eric Temple Bell) | TWS | Jun 1929 |
| PROJECT SPACESHIP by A. E. Van Vogt | TWS | Aug 1949 |
| SPACE STATION NO. 1 by Manly Wade Wellman | Arg | 10/10/36 |
| STAR BRIGHT by Jack Williamson | Arg | 11/29/39 |

MERRIL, JUDITH
    BEYOND HUMAN KEN                    Random House; New York, N. Y.
    21 stories   334 pages   $2.95   October 10, 1952

    English Edition:  Grayson & Grayson  15 stories 240 pages  9/6  July 10, 1953

    Pocket Book Edition:  Pennant Books; New York, N. Y.  #P 56  June 1954
        Titled: SELECTIONS FROM BEYOND HUMAN KEN  12 stories  248 pages  .25¢

| | | |
|---|---|---|
| THE FITTEST by Katherine MacLean | WB | Jan 1951 |
| THE HOUSE DUTIFUL by William Tenn ps (Philip Klass) | ASF | Apr 1948 |
| PRIDE by Malcolm Jameson | ASF | Sep 1942 |
| UNWELCOME TENANT by Roger Dee ps (Roger D. Aycock) | PS | Sum 1950 |

THE GLASS EYE by Eric Frank Russell                                     ASF    Mar 1949
UNDERGROUND MOVEMENT by Kris Neville                                    F&SF   Jun 1952
A GNOME THERE WAS by Lewis Padgett ps (Henry Kuttner & C. L. Moore)     UW     Oct 1941
    (Originally appeared under Henry Kuttner byline)
SOLAR PLEXUS by James Blish                                             Ash    Sep 1941
OUR FAIR CITY by Robert A. Heinlein                                     WT     Jan 1949
THE FLY by Arthur Porges                                                F&SF   Sep 1952
AFTERTHOUGHT by H. B. Fyfe                                              Fw/SFS Jan 1951
THE COMPLEAT WEREWOLF by Anthony Boucher                                UW     Apr 1942
THE MAN WHO SOLD ROPE TO THE GNOLES by Idris Seabright ps (Margaret St. Clair)
                                                                        F&SF   Oct 1951
THE WABBLER by Murray Leinster ps (Will F. Jenkins)                     ASF    Oct 1942
WHAT HAVE I DONE? by Mark Clifton                                       ASF    May 1942
THE ANGEL WAS A YANKEE by Stephen Vincent Benet                         Mcl    Oct 1940
HELEN O'LOY by Lester del Rey                                           ASF    Dec 1938
SOCRATES by John Christopher ps (Christopher S. Youd)                   Glxy   Mar 1951
GOOD-BYE, ILHA! by Laurence Manning                                     ORIGINAL STORY
THE FOXHOLES OF MARS by Fritz Leiber                                    TWS    Jun 1952
THE PERFECT HOST by Theodore Sturgeon                                   WT     Nov 1948

    BEYOND THE BARRIERS OF SPACE AND TIME      Random House; New York, N. Y.
    19 stories  295 pages  $2.95  October 28, 1954


    English Edition:  Sidgwick & Jackson Ltd. 19 stories 292 pages 10/6  10/27/55

WOLF PACK by Walter M. Miller, Jr.                                      Fnt    Oct 1953
NO ONE BELIEVED ME by Will Thompson                                     SEP    4/24/48
PERFORCE TO DREAM by John Wyndham ps (John Beynon Harris)               BFF    Jan 1954
THE LAOCOÖN COMPLEX by J. C. Furnas                                     Esq    Apr 1937
CRAZY JOEY by Mark Clifton and Alex Apostolides                        ASF    Aug 1953
THE GOLDEN MAN by Philip K. Dick                                        If     Apr 1954
MALICE AFORETHOUGHT by David Grinnell                                   F&SF   Nov 1952
THE LAST SEANCE by Agatha Christie                                      Gst    n/d/a 1926
MEDICINE DANCER by Bill Brown                                           BFF    Nov 1952
BEHOLD IT WAS A DREAM by Rhoda Broughton        (From TALES FOR CHRISTMAS EVE; 1873)
THE BELIEF by Isaac Asimov                                              ASF    Oct 1953
THE VELDT by Ray Bradbury                                               SEP    9/23/50
    (Originally appeared under title THE WORLD THE CHILDREN MADE)
MR. KINCAID'S PESTS by J. J. Coupling ps (John R. Pierce)               F&SF   Aug 1953
THE WARNING by Peter Phillips                                           F&SF   Sep 1953
THE GHOST OF ME by Anthony Boucher                                      UW     Jun 1942
THE WALL AROUND THE WORLD by Theodore R. Cogswell                       BFF    Sep 1953
OPERATING INSTRUCTIONS by Robert Sheckley                               ASF    May 1953
INTERPRETATION OF A DREAM by John Collier                               Nykr   5/5/51
DEFENSE MECHANISM by Katherine MacLean                                  ASF    Oct 1949

    GALAXY OF GHOULS              Lion Books, Inc.; New York, N. Y.
    16 stories  192 pages  .35¢  May 1955

        Second Edition:  Pyramid Books; New York, N. Y. G-397          1959
            Titled:  OFF THE BEATEN ORBIT  16 stories  192 pages  .35¢

WOLVES DON'T CRY by Bruce Elliott                                       F&SF   Apr 1954
THE AMBASSADORS by Anthony Boucher                                      Stg    Jun 1952
SHARE ALIKE by Jerome Bixby and Joe E. Dean                            BFF    Jul 1953

GALAXY OF GHOULS [Continued]                              Mag.    Year

BLOOD by Fredric Brown                                       F&SF    Feb 1955
A WAY OF THINKING by Theodore Sturgeon                       Amz     Nov 1953
CHILD'S PLAY by William Tenn ps (Philip Klass)               ASF     Mar 1947
O UGLY BIRD! by Manly Wade Wellman                           F&SF    Dec 1951
THE WHEELBARROW BOY by Richard Parker                        Lpt     Oct 1950
FISH STORY by Leslie Charteris                               BB      Nov 1953
DESERTION by Clifford D. Simak                               ASF     Nov 1944
TRIFLIN' MAN by Walter M. Miller, Jr.                        FU      Jan 1955
THE NIGHT HE CRIED by Fritz Leiber
    (From STAR SCIENCE FICTION STORIES; 1953 — Edited by Frederik Pohl)
THE DEMON KING by J. B. Priestly                (From FOUR-IN-HAND; 1934)
PROOF OF THE PUDDING by Robert Sheckley                      Glxy    Aug 1952
HOMECOMING by Ray Bradbury                                   Mdm     Oct 1946
MOP-UP by Arthur Porges                                      F&SF    Jul 1953

    HUMAN?                        Lion Books, Inc.; New York, N. Y.
    15 stories  190 pages  .25¢  #205  May 7, 1954              *

I.  AS OTHERS SEE US

    THE BIG CONTEST by John D. MacDonald                     WB      Dec 1950
    THE BOY NEXT DOOR by Chad Oliver                         F&SF    Jun 1951
    TAKE A SEAT by Eric Frank Russell                        Stg     May 1952
    AN EGG A MONTH FROM ALL OVER by Idris Seabright ps (Margaret St. Clair)
                                                             F&SF    Oct 1952
    RIYA'S FOUNDLING by Algis Budrys                         SFS #1  n/d 1953

II. EARTHLINGS ALL

    ghosts by don marquis    (FROM the lives and times of archy and mehitabel; 1927)
    SMOKE GHOST by Fritz Leiber, Jr.                         Unk     Oct 1941
    "WHO SHALL I SAY IS CALLING?" by August Derleth          F&SF    Aug 1952
    THE GNARLY MAN by L. Sprague de Camp                     Unk     Jun 1939
    THE TEMPTATION OF HARRINGAY by H. G. Wells
        (From THE STOLEN BACILLUS AND OTHER INCIDENTS; 1920)
    THE ULTIMATE EGOIST by Theodore Sturgeon                 Unk     Feb 1941
        (Originally appeared under pseudonym E. Hunter Waldo)
    ROPE ENOUGH by John Collier                              Nykr    11/18/39

III. TOMORROW WILL BE BETTER?

    LIAR! by Isaac Asimov                                    ASF     May 1941
    WHO KNOWS HIS BROTHER by Graham Doar                     Stg     Feb 1952
    CRUCIFIXUS ETIAM by Walter M. Miller, Jr.                ASF     Feb 1953

    SHOT IN THE DARK             Bantam Books; New York, N. Y.
    23 stories  310 pages  .25¢  #751  January 11, 1950

THE SKY WAS FULL OF SHIPS by Theodore Sturgeon               TWS     Jun 1947
THE HALFLING by Leigh Brackett  (Mrs. Edmond Hamilton)       Ash     Feb 1943
KNOCK by Fredric Brown                                       TWS     Dec 1948
VOICES IN THE DUST by Gerald Kersh                           SEP     9/13/47
A HITCH IN TIME by James MacCreigh ps (Frederik Pohl)        TWS     Jun 1947
GENTLEMEN, BE SEATED by Robert A. Heinlein                   Arg     May 1948
NIGHTMARE NUMBER THREE by Stephen Vincent Benet      (verse)
    (From BURNING CITY; 1936)
THE STAR by H. G. Wells                                      Grp     Xmas 1897
THE DARK ANGEL by Lewis Padgett ps (Henry Kuttner and C. L. Moore)  Stg  Mar 1946
    (Originally appeared under Henry Kuttner byline)
MR. LEPESCU by Anthony Boucher                               WT      Sep 1945
THE DAY OF THE DEEPIES by Murray Leinster ps (Will F. Jenkins)  FFM  Oct 1947
THE SHADOW AND THE FLASH by Jack London                      Bkm     Jun 1903
SPOKEMAN FOR TERRA by Hugh Raymond ps (John Michael)         Stl     Jun 1941
SHE WAS ASKING FOR YOU by Margarey Allingham (From WANTED: SOMEONE INNOCENT; 1946)

(66)

SHOT IN THE DARK [Continued]                                    Mag.    Year

STRANGE PLAYFELLOW by Isaac Asimov                              Sup   Sep 1940
BROOKLYN PROJECT by William Tenn ps (Philip Klass)              PS    Fal 1948
INTERVIEW WITH A LEMMING by James Thurber
  (From My Worlds and Welcome To It; 1943)
MARS IS HEAVEN! by Ray Bradbury                                 APS   Fal 1948
WHO IS CHARLES AVISON? by Edison Tesla Marshall                 Arg   Apr 1916
THE FACTS IN THE CASE OF M. VALDEMAR by Edgar Allan Poe         AWR   Dec 1845
THE BRONZE PARROT by Austin Freeman      (From THE GREAT PORTRAIT MYSTERY; 1924)
LIFE ON THE MOON by Alexander Samalman                          TWS   Dec 1946
BLUNDER by Philip Wylie                                         Col   1/12/46

        SF:  THE YEAR'S GREATEST SCIENCE-FICTION AND FANTASY      July 1956
        18 stories   352 pages   $3.95   Gnome Press; New York, N. Y.

        Pocket Book Edition:  Dell Publishing Co., Inc.; New York, N. Y. # B-103
             18 stories   342 pages   .35¢   May 22, 1956

THE STUTTERER by R. R. Merliss                                  ASF   Apr 1955
THE GOLEM by Avram Davidson                                     F&SF  Mar 1955
JUNIOR by Robert Abernathy                                      Glxy  Jan 1956
THE CAVE OF NIGHT by James E. Gunn                              Glxy  Feb 1955
THE HOOFER by Walter M. Miller, Jr.                             FU    Sep 1955
BULKHEAD by Theodore Sturgeon                                   Glxy  Mar 1955
  (Originally appeared under title WHO?)
SENSE FROM THOUGHT DIVIDE by Mark Clifton                       ASF   Mar 1955
POTTAGE by Zeena Henderson                                      F&SF  Sep 1955
NOBODY BOTHERS GUS by Algis Budrys                              ASF   Nov 1955
  (Originally appeared under pseudonym Paul Janvier)
THE LAST DAY OF SUMMER by E. C. Tubb                            SF #12 Feb 1955
ONE ORDINARY DAY, WITH PEANUTS by Shirley Jackson               F&SF  Jan 1955
THE ETHICATORS by Willard Marsh                                 If    Aug 1955
BIRDS CAN'T COUNT by Mildred Clingerman                         F&SF  Feb 1955
OF MISSING PERSONS by Jack Finney                               GH    Mar 1955
DREAMING IS A PRIVATE THING by Isaac Asimov                     F&SF  Dec 1955
THE COUNTRY OF THE KIND by Damon Knight                         F&SF  Feb 1956
THE PUBLIC HATING by Steve Allen                                BB    Jan 1955
HOME THERE'S NO RETURNING by Henry Kuttner & C.L. Moore  (Fr NO BOUNDARIES; 1955)
S-F: 1955 by Judith Merril           (Summation and Honorable Mentions)

        SF: 57  THE YEAR'S GREATEST SCIENCE FICTION AND FANTASY
        18 stories   320 pages   $3.95   July 1957  Gnome Press; New York, N. Y.

        Pocket Book Edition:  Dell Publishing Co., Inc.; New York, N. Y. # B-110
             18 stories   320 pages   .35¢   July 9, 1957

THE MAN WHO LIKED LIONS by John Bernard Daley                   Inf   Oct 1956
THE COSMIC EXPENSE ACCOUNT by C. M. Kornbluth                   F&SF  Jan 1956
THE FAR LOOK by Theodore L. Thomas                              ASF   Aug 1956
WHEN GRANDFATHER FLEW TO THE MOON by E. L. Malpass              Obs   1/2/55
  (Originally appeared under title RETURN TO THE MOON)
THE DOORSTEP by R. Bretnor                                      ASF   Nov 1956
SILENT BROTHER by Algis Budrys                                  ASF   Feb 1956
STRANGER STATION by Damon Knight                                F&SF  Dec 1956
EACH AN EXPLORER by Isaac Asimov                                Fut #30 n/d 1956
ALL ABOUT "THE THING" by Randall Garrett       (Parody)         SFS   May 1956
        (Originally appeared as a feature under general title PARODIES TOSSED.  This
        parody appeared under title JOHN W. CAMPBELL JR.'S WHO GOES THERE?)

SF: 57 THE YEAR'S GREATEST SCIENCE-FICTION & FANTASY [Continued] Mag.    Year

PUT THEM ALL TOGETHER, THEY SPELL MONTSER by Ray Russell        Plby   Oct 1956
DIGGING THE WEANS by Robert Nathan                             Hpr   Nov 1956
TAKE A DEEP BREATH by Roger Thorne                            Tgr  n/d/a 1956
GRANDMA'S LIE SOAP by Robert Abernathy                         FU   Feb 1956
COMPOUNDED INTEREST by Mack Reynolds                          F&SF   Aug 1956
PRIMA BELLADONNA by J. G. Ballard                            SF #20  Dec 1956
THE OTHER MAN by Theodore Sturgeon                           Glxy   Sep 1956
THE DAMNEDEST THING by Garson Kanin                           Esq   Feb 1956
ANYTHING BOX by Zeena Henderson                              F&SF   Oct 1956
THE YEAR'S S-F by Judith Merril        (Summation and Honorable Mentions)

    SF: 58 THE YEAR'S GREATEST SCIENCE-FICTION AND FANTASY  (Third Annual Volume)
    17 stories  255 pages  $3.50  December 1958      Gnome Press; New York, N. Y.

    Pocket Book Edition:  Dell Publishing Co., Inc.; New York, N. Y.  #B 119
       17 stories  255 pages  .35¢  July 15, 1958

LET'S BE FRANK by Brian W. Aldiss                            SF #23  Jun 1957
THE FLY by George Langelaan                                   Plby   Jun 1957
LET'S GET TOGETHER by Isaac Asimov                            Inf   Feb 1957
THE WONDER HORSE by George Byram                              Atl   Aug 1957
YOU KNOW WILLIE by Theodore R. Cogswell                      F&SF   May 1957
NEAR MISS by Henry Kuttner
    (Copyright 1958 by Dell Publishing Co. and Western Printing and Litho. Co.)
GAME PRESERVE by Rog Phillips ps (Roger Phillips Graham)       If   Oct 1957
NOW LET US SLEEP by Avram Davidson                           Ven   Sep 1957
WILDERNESS by Zeena Henderson                               F&SF   Jan 1957
FLYING HIGH by Eugene Ionesco                                Mdm   Oct 1957
THE EDGE OF THE SEA by Algis Budrys                         Ven   Mar 1958

From Science Fiction to Science Fact:
       Sputnik and Beyond              (Articles)

HOW NEAR IS THE MOON? by Judith Merril                           ORIGINAL STORY
TRANSITION — FROM FANTASY TO SCIENCE by Arthur C. Clarke
    (From THE MAKING OF A M ON; 1957)
SPUTNIK: ONE REASON WHY WE LOST by G. Harry Stine             F&SF   Jan 1958
GOING UP! by Dennis Driscoll                                 BLM   May 1957
    (Condensed from article "SPACE TRAVEL")
WHERE DO WE GO FROM HERE? by Willy Ley                           ORIGINAL STORY
SCIENCE FICTION STILL LEADS SCIENCE FACT by Anthony Boucher   NYTM   12/1/57
THE YEAR'S S-F by Judith Merril        (Summary and Honorable Mentions)

    SF: 59  THE YEAR'S GREATEST SCIENCE-FICTION AND FANTASY
    18 stories  256 pages  $3.50  June 1959      Gnome Press; New York, N. Y.

    Pocket Book Edition:  Dell Publishing Co., Inc.; New York, N. Y.
       18 stories  256 pages  .35¢  June 30, 1959

PELT by Carol Emshwiller                                      F&SF   Nov 1958
TRIGGERMAN by J. F. Bone                                      ASF   Dec 1958
THE PRIZE OF PERIL by Robert Sheckley                        F&SF   May 1958
HICKORY, DICKORY, KEROUAC by Richard Gehman                   Plby   Mar 1958
    (Originally appeared under pseudonym Martin Scott)
THE YELLOW PILL by Rog Phillips ps (Roger Phillips Graham)     ASF   Oct 1958
RIVER OF RICHES by Gerald Kersh                               SEP   3/8/58
SATELLITE PASSAGE by Theodore L. Thomas                        If   Dec 1958

CASEY AGONISTES by R. M. McKenna                                    F&SF   Sep 1958
SPACE TIME-FOR SPRINGERS by Fritz Leiber
    (From STAR SCIENCE FICTION STORIES #4; 1958 — Edited by Frederik Pohl)
OR ALL THE SEAS WITH OYSTERS by Avram Davidson          Glxy   May 1958
TEN-STORY JIGSAW by Brian W. Aldiss                    Neb #26  Jan 1958
FRESH GUY by E. C. Tubb                                 SF #29  Jun 1958
THE BEAUTIFUL THINGS by Arthur Zirul                    FU     May 1958
THE COMEDIAN'S CHILDREN by Theodore Sturgeon            VSF    May 1958
THE SHORT-SHORT STORY OF MANKIND by John Steinbeck      Plby   Apr 1958

    FROM SCIENCE FICTION TO SCIENCE FACT:  The Universe and Us   (Articles)

MAN IN SPACE by Daniel Lang                            Nykr   11/15/58
ROCKETS TO WHERE? by Judith Merril                     ORIGINAL STORY
THE THUNDER-THIEVES by Isaac Asimov                    ORIGINAL STORY
    Note:  This article contains a verse that originally appeared in Future Science
        Fiction #39 (October 1958) under the title IT'S ALL HOW YOU LOOK AT IT.
THE YEAR'S S-F by Judith Merril           (Summary and Honorable Mentions)

    THE FIFTH ANNUAL OF THE YEAR'S BEST S-F    Simon & Schuster; New York, N. Y.
    22 stories  320 pages  $3.95  September 1960

THE HANDLER by Damon Knight                            Rog   Aug 1960
THE OTHER WIFE by Jack Finney                          SEP   1/30/60
NO FIRE BURNS by Avram Davidson                        Plby  Jul 1959
NO, NO, NOT ROGOV! by Cordwainer Smith                 If    Feb 1959
SHORELINE AT SUNSET by Ray Bradbury          (From MEDICINE FOR MELANCHOLY; 1959)
THE DREAMSMEN by Gordon R. Dickson
    (From STAR SCIENCE FICTION STORIES #6; 1959 — Edited by Frederik Pohl)
MULTUM IN PARVO by Jack Sharkey                        Gent  Dec 1959
FLOWERS FOR ALGERNON by Daniel Keyes                   F&SF  Apr 1959
"WHAT DO YOU MEAN...HUMAN?" by John W. Campbell, Jr.   ASF   Sep 1959
SIERRA SAM by Ralph Dighton                            AP    1/10/60
A DEATH IN THE HOUSE by Clifford D. Simak              Glxy  Oct 1959
MARIANNA by Fritz Leiber                               Fnt   Feb 1960
AN INQUIRY CONCERNING THE CURVATURE OF THE EARTH'S SURFACE AND DIVERS
    INVESTIGATIONS OF A METAPHYSICAL NATURE by Roger Price    Mncl  Win 1959
DAY AT THE BEACH by Carol Emshwiller                   F&SF  Aug 1959
HOT ARGUMENT by Randall Garrett           (verse)      F&SF  Feb 1960
WHAT THE LEFT HAND WAS DOING by Darrel T. Langart      ASF   Feb 1960
THE SOUND SLEEP by J. G. Ballard                       SF #39 Feb 1960
PLENITUDE by Will Worthington                          F&SF  Nov 1959
THE MAN WHO LOST THE SEA by Theodore Sturgeon          F&SF  Oct 1959
MAKE A PRISON by Lawrence Block                        OrSFS Jan 1959
WHAT NOW, LITTLE MAN? by Mack Clifton                  F&SF  Dec 1959
ME by Hilbert Schenck, Jr.                             F&SF  Aug 1959

    SIXTH ANNUAL OF THE YEAR'S BEST S-F    Simon & Schuster; New York, N. Y.
    36 stories  384 pages  $3.95  October 2, 1961

DOUBLE, DOUBLE, TOIL AND TROUBLE by Holley Cantine     F&SF  Jan 1960
THE NEVER ENDING PENNY by Bernard Wolfe                Plby  Sep 1960
THE FELLOW WHO MARRIED THE MAXILL GIRL by Ward Moore   F&SF  Feb 1960
SOMETHING INVENTED ME by R. C. Phelan                  Rptr  10/13/60
A SIGH FOR CYBERNETICS by Felica Lamport  (verse)      Hpr   Jan 1961

OBVIOUS! by Michael Ffolkes                    (carton)               Pch     10/3/56
I REMEMBER BABYLON by Arthur C. Clarke                                Plby    May 1960
THE LAGGING PROFESSION by Leonard Lockhard ps (Theodore L. Thomas)    ASF     Jan 1961
THE DISTORTION by Shel Silverstein             (carton)               Plby    May 1960
REPORT ON THE NATURE OF THE LUNAR SURFACE by John Brunner             ASF     Aug 1960
J. G. by Roger Price                    (From J. G., THE UPRIGHT APE; 1960)
CHIEF by Henry Slesar                                                 Plby    Jun 1960
        (Originally appeared under general heading Four Fables)
PSALM by Lester del Rey                                               FU      Mar 1960
THE LARGE ANT by Howard Fast                                          FU      Feb 1960
A ROSE BY OTHER NAME by Christopher Anvil                             ASF     Jan 1960
ENCHANTMENT by Elizabeth Emmett                                       SEP     10/1/60
THIOTIMOLINE AND THE SPACE AGE by Isaac Asimov                        ASF     Oct 1960
BEACH SCENE by Marshall King                                          Glxy    Oct 1960
CREATURE OF THE SNOWS by William Sambrot                              SEP     10/29/60
ABOMINABLE by Fredric Brown                                           Dude    Mar 1960
THE MAN ON TOP by R. Bretnor                                          Sch     10/24/51
                                                             Rpnt-F&SF  Sep 1960
DAVID'S DADDY by Rosel George Brown                                   Fnt     Jun 1960
THE THINKERS by Walt Kelly                     (carton)      Hall Syndicate  1/29/61
SOMETHING BRIGHT by Zeena Henderson                                   Glxy    Feb 1960
IN THE HOUSE, ANOTHER by Joseph Whitehill                             F&SF    Apr 1960
A SERIOUS SEARCH FOR WEIRD WORLDS by Ray Bradbury                     Life    10/24/60
ED LEAR WASN'T SO CRAZY by Herbert Schenck, Jr.                       F&SF    Jun 1960
INSTRUCTOR by Thelwell                         (carton)               Pch     1/18/61
THE BROTHERHOOD OF KEEPERS by Dean McLaughlin                         ASF     Jul 1960
HEMINGWAY IN SPACE by Kingsley Amis                                   Pch     12/21/60
MINE OWN WAYS by Richard McKenna                                      F&SF    Feb 1960
OLD HUNDREDTH by Brian W. Aldiss                                      NW #100 Dec 1960
BLUES AND BALLARD
    RADIATION BLUES by Theodore R. Cogswell        (Song)        ORIGINAL STORY
    BLOWUP BLUES by Theodore R. Cogswell           (Song)        ORIGINAL STORY
    BALLARD OF THE SHOSHONU by Gordon R. Dickson   (Song)        ORIGINAL STORY
    HOW TO THINK A SCIENCE FICTION STORY by G. Harry Stine
        (Excerpt from SCIENCE FICTION IS TOO CONSERVATIVE)           ASF     May 1961


MILLS, ROBERT P.

    THE BEST FROM FANTASY & SCIENCE FICTION: 9th Series
    30 stories  264 pages  $3.95  February 4, 1960  Doubleday & Co.; New York N.Y.

            ALL STORIES FROM FANTASY & SCIENCE FICTION

FLOWERS FOR ALGERNON by Daniel Keyes                              April     1959
ME by Herbert Schenck, Jr.                     (verse)            August    1959
A DIFFERENT PURPOSE by Kem Bennett                               November  1958
A VAMPIRE'S SAGA by Norman Belkin              (verse)            May       1959
RALPH WOLLSTONECRAFT HEDGE: A MEMOIR by Ron Goulart              May       1959
SPORTSMAN'S DIFFICULTY by Doris Pitkin Buck    (verse)            March     1959
"ALL YOU ZOMBIES —" by Robert A. Heinlein                        March     1959
AN EXPOSTULATION by C. S. Lewis                (verse)            June      1959
CASEY AGONISTES by R. M. McKenna                                September 1958
THROUGH TIME AND SPACE WITH FERDINAND FEGHOTT: XI by Grendel Briarton
    ps (R. Bretnor)                                               February  1959
EASTWARD HO! by William Tenn ps (Philip Klass)                    October   1958
THROUGH TIME AND SPACE WITH FERDINAND FEGHOTT: XIV by Grendel Briarton
    ps (R. Bretnor)                                               May       1959

SOUL MATE by Lee Sutton                                              June 1959
CALL ME MISTER by Anthony Brode              (verse)            February 1959
WHAT ROUGH BEAST? by Damon Knight                              February 1959
CLASSICAL QUERY COMPOSED WHILE SHAMPOOING by Doris Pitkin Buck     (verse)
                                                                   July 1959
FAR FROM HOME by Walter S. Tevis                               December 1959
SPACE BURIAL by Brian W. Aldiss              (verse)               July 1959
INVASION OF THE PLANET OF LOVE by George P. Elliott             January 1959
THROUGH TIME AND SPACE WITH FERDINAND FEGHOTT: X by Grendel Briarton
     ps (R. Bretnor)                                           January 1959
DAGON by Avram Davidson                                         October 1959
PACT by Winston P. Sanders                                       August 1959
TO GIVE THEM BEAUTY FOR ASHES by Winona McClintic     (verse)  September 1959
NO MATTER WHERE YOU GO by Joel Townsley Rogers                 February 1959
THROUGH TIME AND SPACE WITH FERDINAND FEGHOTT: XII by Grendel Briarton
     ps (R. Bretnor)                                              March 1959
THE WILLOW TREE by Jane Rice                                   February 1959
THROUGH TIME AND SPACE WITH FERDINAND FEGHOTT: XIII by Grendel Briarton
     ps (R. Bretnor)                                              April 1959
THE PI MAN by Alfred Bester                                     October 1959
THE MAN WHO LOST THE SEA by Theodore Sturgeon                  ·October 1959
THROUGH TIME AND SPACE WITH FERDINAND FEGHOTT: XV by Grendel Briarton
     ps (R. Bretnor)                                               June 1959

       THE BEST FROM FANTASY & SCIENCE FICTION: 10th SERIES
       17 stories  262 pages  $3.95  May 12, 1961  Doubleday & Co., Inc.; N.Y., N. Y.

               ALL STORIES FROM FANTASY & SCIENCE FICTION

NIKITA EISENHOWER JONES by Robert F. Young                       August 1960
WHO DREAMS OF IVY by Will Worthington                          November 1960
MINE OWN WAYS by Richard McKenna                               February 1960
THE RAINBOW GOLD by Jane Rice                                  December 1959
CRAZY MARO by Daniel Keyes                                        April 1960
SOMETHING by Allen Drury                                        October 1960
IT'S A GREAT BIG WONDERFUL UNIVERSE by Vance Aandahl           November 1960
MAN OVERBOARD by John Collier                                     March 1960
THE BLIND PILOT by Charles Henneberg                           January 1960
     (Translated by Damon Knight)
A DIVVIL WITH THE WOMEN by Niall Wilde                         January 1960
THE MARTYR by Poul Anderson                                       March 1960
DOUBLE, DOUBLE, TOIL AND TROUBLE by Holley Cantine            January 1960
APRES NOUS by Avram Davidson                                      March 1960
INTERBALANCE by Katherine MacLean                              October 1960
INFINITY by Rosser Reeves                    (verse)          December 1960
THE REPLACEMENT by Robert Murray                              February 1960
THE FELLOW WHO MARRIED THE MAXILL GIRL by Ward Moore          February 1960

       A DECADE OF FANTASY & SCIENCE FICTION   Doubleday & Co., Inc.; New York, N. Y.
       25 stories  406 pages  $4.50  December 2, 1960

               ALL STORIES FROM FANTASY & SCIENCE FICTION

THE MARTIAN SHOP by Howard Fast                                November 1959
WALK LIKE A MOUNTAIN by Manly Wade Wellman                         June 1955
MEN OF IRON by Guy Endore            (Copyright 1940; Black & White Press )
                                                              Rpnt-Fall 1949
RABBITS TO THE MOON by Raymond E. Banks                            July 1959
THE CERTIFICATE by Avram Davidson                                 March 1959
THE SEALMAN by John Masefield                                 Rpnt-July 1955
     (From MAINSAIL HAUL; 1913)
THE SKY PEOPLE by Poul Anderson                                   March 1959
THE CAUSES by Idris Seabright ps (Margaret St. Clair)              June 1952
THE HYPNOGLYPH by John Anthony                                     July 1953
A TALE OF THE THIRTEENTH FLOOR by Ogden Nash                       July 1955
SPUD AND COCHISE by Oliver La Farge                        Forum  Jan 1936
                                                          Rpnt-December 1957
UNTO THE FOURTH GENERATION by Isaac Asimov                        April 1959
JORDAN by Zeena Henderson                                         March 1959
WILL YOU WAIT? by Alfred Bester                                   March 1959
PROOF POSITIVE by Graham Greene                              Hpr  Oct 1947
                                                            Rpnt-August 1952
SHOCK TREATMENT by J. Francis McComas                             April 1956
GANDOLPHUS by Anthony Boucher                                  December 1956
THE LAST SHALL BE FIRST by Robert P. Mills                       August 1958
A TRICK OR TWO by John Novotny                                     July 1957
LOT'S DAUGHTER by Ward Moore                                    October 1954
SATURNIAN CELIA by Horace Walpole                            Rpnt-April 1957
     (From THE LETTERS OF HORACE WALPOLE by Mrs. Paget Toynbee; 1903)
FEAR IS A BUSINESS by Theodore Sturgeon                         August 1956
MEETING OF RELATIONS by John Collier                         YR  Dec 1941
                                                           Rpnt-January 1959
FIRST LESSON by Mildred Clingerman                             December 1956
TO FELL A TREE by Robert F. Young                                  July 1959

MINES, SAMUEL S.
     THE BEST FROM STARTLING STORIES      Henry Holt & Co.; New York, N. Y.
     11 stories  301 pages  $3.50 October 4, 1953

     English Edition: Cassell and Co. Ltd.  11 stories  301 pages  12/6
          Titled:  STARTLING STORIES              (1954)

             ALL STORIES FROM STARTLING & THRILLING WONDER STORIES
THE WAGES OF SYNERGY by Theodore Sturgeon                    Stg  Aug 1953
THE PERFECT GENTLEMAN by R. J. MacGregor                     Stg  Sep 1952
MOMENT WITHOUT TIME by Joel Townsley Rogers                  TWS  Apr 1952
NAMING OF NAMES by Ray Bradbury                              TWS  Aug 1952
NO LAND OF NED by Sherwood Springer                          TWS  Dec 1952
WHO'S CRIBBING? by Jack Lewis                                Stg  Jan 1953
THIRTY SECONDS — THIRTY DAYS by Arthur C. Clarke             TWS  Dec 1949
NOISE by Jack Vance                                          Stg  Aug 1952
WHAT'S IT LIKE OUT THERE? by Edmond Hamilton                 TWS  Dec 1952
DORMANT by A. E. Van Vogt                                    Stg  Nov 1948

DARK NUPTIAL by Robert Donald Locke                          TWS  Feb 1953

MOSKOWITZ, SAM                                          Mag.    Year

EDITOR'S CHOICE IN SCIENCE FICTION    The McBride Co., Inc.; New York, N. Y.
12 stories  286 pages  $3.50  March 10, 1954


Canadian Edition:  McClelland and Stewart Ltd.; Toronto  $4.00
    (No further data available)


THE WALL OF FIRE by Jack Kirkland                                BB   Jul 1932
    (Story selected by Donald Kennicott)
WHAT THIN PARTITIONS by Mack Clifton and Alex Apostolides        ASF  Sep 1953
    (Story selected by John W. Campbell, Jr.)
I, ROBOT by Eando Binder ps (Otto Binder)                       Amz   Jan 1939
    (Story selected by Howard Browne)
AND SOMEDAY TO MARS by Frank Belknap Long                       TWS   Feb 1952
    (Story selected by Samuel Mines)
WALL OF DARKNESS by Arthur C. Clarke                            Sup   Jul 1949
    (Story selected by Ejler Jakobsson)
ALL ROADS by Mona Farnsworth                                    Unk   Aug 1940
    (Story selected by John W. Campbell, Jr.)
EXIT by Wilson Tucker                                           Ash   Apr 1943
    (Story selected by Alden H. Norton)  (Originally aprd under byline Bob Tucker)
THE SUBLIME VIRGIL by Chester D. Cuthbert                        WS   Feb 1934
    (Story selected by Hugo Gernsback)
FAR BELOW by Robert Barbour Johnson                              WT   Jul 1939
    (Story selected by Dorothy McIlwraith)
DEATH OF A SENSITIVE by Harry Bates                            SF+   May 1953
    (Story selected by Sam Moskowitz)
THE DEMOISELLS D'YS by Robert W. Chambers              Rpnt—FFM  Nov 1942
    (Story selected by Mary Gnaedinger)      (From THE KING IN YELLOW; 1895)
STOLEN CENTURIES by Otis Adelbert Kline               Rpnt—FSQ  Sep 1953
    (Story selected by Oscar J. Friend)   (Originally appeared in TWS; June 1939)


NORTON, ANDRE ps (Alice Mary Norton)

SPACE PIONEERS               World Publishing Co.; Cleveland, Ohio
9 stories  294 pages  $2.75  February 22, 1954

THE EXPLORERS
    EARTH
        THE ILLUSIONARIES by Eric Frank Russell                 PS   Nov 1951
    MOON
        MOONWALK by H. B. Fyfe                                 Spc   Nov 1952
    MARS
        TRAIL BLAZER by Raymond Z. Gallun                      FSM   Fal 1951
    OTHER SYSTEMS
        THOU GOOD AND FAITHFUL by K. Houston Brunner           ASF   Mar 1953
            (Originally appeared under pseudonym John Loxsmith
        THE END OF THE LINE by James H. Schmitz                ASF   Jul 1951
THE SETTLERS
    EARTH
        A PAIL OF AIR by Fritz Leiber                         Glxy   Dec 1951
    MARS
        THE FARTHEST HORIZON by Raymond F. Jones               ASF   Apr 1952
    ASTEROID BELT

ASTEROID OF FEAR by Raymond Z. Gallun                        PS   Mar 1951

OTHER SYSTEMS
PAGE AND PLAYER by Jerome Bixby                              Stg  Aug 1952


SPACE POLICE              World Publishing Co.; Cleveland, Ohio
9 stories  255 pages  $2.75              1956

WE POLICE OURSELVES: FUTURE TENSE
BAIT by Roy L. Clough, Jr.                                   ASF  Jun 1951
THE CLOSED DOOR by Kendall Foster Crossen                    Amz  Sep 1953
BEEP by James Blish                                          Glxy Feb 1954

WE ARE POLICED
OF THOSE WHO CAME by George Longdon                          NW #18 Nov 1952
POLICE OPERATION by H. Beam Piper                            ASF  Jun 1948
PAX GALACTICA by Ralph Williams                             ASF  Nov 1952

GALACTIC AGENTS
TOUGH OLD MAN by L. Ron Hubbard                              Stg  Nov 1950
AGENT OF VEGA by James H. Schmitz                            ASF  Jun 1949
THE SUB-STANDARD SARDINES by Jack Vance                      Stg  Jan 1949


SPACE SERVICE             World Publishing Co.; Cleveland, Ohio
10 stories  277 pages  $2.50  January 19, 1953

COMMAND by Bernard I. Kahn                                   ASF  Jan 1947
STAR-LINED by H. B. Fyfe                                     ASF  Feb 1952
CHORE FOR A SPACEMAN by Walt Sheldon                         TWS  Dec 1950
THE SPECTOR GENERAL by Theodore R. Cogswell                  ASF  Jun 1952
IMPLODE AND PEDDLE by H. B. Fyfe                             ASF  Nov 1951
STEEL BROTHER by Gordon R. Dickson                          ASF  Feb 1952
FOR THE PUBLIC by Bernard I. Kahn                            ASF  Dec 1946
EXPEDITION POLYCHROME by J. A. Winter, M. D.                 ASF  Jan 1949
RETURN OF A LEGEND by Raymond Z. Gallun                      PS   Mar 1952
THAT SHARE OF GLORY by C. M. Kornbluth                       ASF  Jan 1952


PETERSON, ROBERT C.
THE SCIENCE-FICTIONAL SHERLOCK HOLMES   The Council of Four; Denver, Colo.
8 stories  137 pages  $2.50  1960

THE MARTIAN CROWN JEWELS by Poul Anderson                    EQMM Feb 1958
HALF A HOKA — POUL ANDERSON by Gordon R. Dickson
    (From the Program Booklet of the 17th World Science Fiction Convention 1960)
THE ADVENTURE OF THE MISPLACED HOUND by Poul Anderson and Gordon R. Dickson
                                                            USF  Dec 1953
THE ANOMALY OF THE EMPTY MAN by Anthony Boucher              F&SF Apr 1952
THE GREATEST TERTIAN by Anthony Boucher
    (From INVADERS OF EARTH; 1952 — Edited by Groff Conklin)
THE ADVENTURE OF THE SNITCH IN TIME by Mack Reynolds and August Derleth
                                                            F&SF Jul 1953
THE ADVENTURE OF THE BALL OF NOSTRADAMUS by Mack Reynolds and August Derleth
                                                            F&SF Jul 1955
THE RETURN by H. Beam Piper and John J. McGuire  (Original Version) ASF Jan 1954
    (Revised for publication in this anthology)

POHL, FREDERIK                                               Mag.     Year
    ASSIGNMENT IN TOMORROW          Hanover House; Garden City, N. Y.
    15 stories  317 pages  $2.95  September 7, 1954

MR. COSTELLO, HERO by Theodore Sturgeon                    Glxy   Dec 1953
ANGELS IN THE JETS by Jerome Bixby                           FA   Fal 1952
THE ADVENTURER by C. M. Kornbluth                           Spc   May 1953
SUBTERFUGE by Ray Bradbury                                  Ash   Apr 1943
HELEN O'LOY by Lster del Rey                                ASF   Dec 1938
5,271,009 by Alfred Bester                                 F&SF   Mar 1954
THE BIG TRIP UP YONDER by Kurt Vonnegut, Jr.               Glxy   Jan 1954
THE PEDDLER'S NOSE by Jack Williamson                       ASF   Apr 1951
THE FRIGHTENED TREE by Algis Budrys                        Glxy   Feb 1953
    (Originally appeared under title PROTECTIVE MIMICRY)
A MATTER OF FORM by H. L. Gold                              ASF   Dec 1938
BACK TO JULIE by Richard Wilson                            Glxy   May 1954
SHE WHO LAUGHS by Peter Phillips                           Glxy   Apr 1952
OFFICIAL RECORD by Fletcher Pratt                           Spc   Sep 1952
HALL OF MIRRORS by Fredric Brown                           Glxy   Dec 1953
MOTHER by Philip Jose Farmer                                TWS   Apr 1953


    BEYOND THE END OF TIME          Doubleday and Co.; New York, N. Y.
    19 stories  407 pages  .35¢  Permabook P 145  January 7, 1952

THE EMBASSY by Martin Pearson ps (Donald A. Wollheim)      ASF   Mar 1942
THE HUNTED by John D. MacDonald                            Sup   Jul 1949
HEREDITY by Isaac Asimov                                   Ash   Apr 1941
THE LITTLE BLACK BAG by C. M. Kornbluth                    ASF   Jul 1950
THE LONELY PLANET by Murray Leinster ps (Will F. Jenkins)  TWS   Dec 1949
OPERATION PEEP by John Wyndham ps (John Beynon Harris)     Sus   Sum 1951
    (Originally appeared under title PAWLEY'S PEEPHOLES)
LET THE ANTS TRY by James MacCreigh ps (Frederik Pohl)      PS   Win 1949
THERE WILL COME SOFT RAINS by Ray Bradbury                 Col    5/6/50
SCANNERS LIVE IN VAIN by Cordwainer Smith                FB #6   n/d 1950
SUCH INTERESTING NEIGHBORS by Jack Finney                  Col    1/6/51
BRIDGE CROSSING by Dave Dryfoos                            Glxy   May 1951
LETTER FROM THE STARS by A. E. Van Vogt                   OTWA   Jul 1950
LOVE IN THE DARK by H. L. Gold                             Sus   Fal 1951
    (Originally appeared under title LOVE ETHERAL)
OBVIOUSLY SUICIDE by S. Fowler Wright                      Sus   Spr 1951
BEYOND DOUBT by Robert A. Heinlein and Elma Wentz          Ash   Apr 1951
    (Originally appeared under byline Lyle Monroe (pseudonym) and Elma Wentz)
DEATH IS THE PENALTY by Judith Merril                      ASF   Jan 1949
ROCK DRIVER by Harry Harrison                               WB   Feb 1951
STEPSON OF SPACE by Raymond Z. Gallun                      Ash   Apr 1940
RESCUE PARTY by Arthur C. Clarke                           ASF   May 1946


    SHADOW OF TOMORROW             Doubleday and Co.; New York, N. Y.
    17 stories  379 pages  .35¢  August 3, 1953
THE YEAR OF THE JACKPOT by Robert A. Heinlein             Glxy   Mar 1952
A BAD DAY FOR SALES by Fritz Leiber                       Glxy   Jul 1953
C-CHUTE by Isaac Asimov                                   Glxy   Oct 1951
PERFECT CREATURE by John Wyndham ps (John Beynon Harris)  F&SF   Jan 1953
THE MARCHING MORONS by C. M. Kornbluth                    Glxy   Apr 1951
TRANSFER POINT by Anthony Boucher                         Glxy   Nov 1950

WATCHBIRD by Robert Sheckley                                      Glxy   Feb 1953
TO A RIPE OLD AGE by Wilson Tucker                               F&SF   Dec 1952
ORPHANS OF THE VOID by Michael Shaara                            Glxy   Jun 1952
THE OLD ORDER by Lester del Rey                                   MSF   Feb 1951
    (Originally appeared under title THE NEW GODS LEAD)
GENESIS by H. Beam Piper                                        Fw/SFS  Nov 1951
HALO by Hal Clement ps (Harry Clement Stubbs)                    Glxy   Oct 1952
COMMON TIME by James Blish                                        SFQ   Aug 1953
LOVE by Richard Wilson                                           F&SF   Jun 1952
THE MISOGYNIST by James E. Gunn                                  Glxy   Nov 1952
LUCKIEST MAN IN DENV by Simon Eisner                            Glxy   Jun 1952
NOT A CREATURE WAS STIRRING by Dean Evans                       Glxy   Dec 1951

      STAR SCIENCE FICTION STORIES      Ballantine Books; New York, N. Y.  #16
      15 stories   202 pages   February 18, 1953
          Hard Cover Edition:  $1.50   Pocket Book Edition:  .35¢

                          ALL ORIGINAL STORIES

COUNTRY DOCTOR by William Morrison ps (Joseph Samachson)
DOMINOES by C. M. Kornbluth
IDEALIST by Lester del Rey
THE NIGHT HE CRIED by Fritz Leiber
CONTRAPTION by Clifford D. Simak
THE CHRONOCLASM by John Wyndham ps (John Beynon Harris)
THE DESERTER by William Tenn ps (Phillip Klass)
THE MAN WITH ENGLISH by H. L. Gold
SO PROUDLY WE HAIL by Judith Merril
A SCENT OF SARSAPARILLA by Ray Bradbury
"NOBODY HERE BUT — " by Isaac Asimov
THE LAST WEAPON by Robert Sheckley
A WILD SURMISE by Henry Kuttner and C. L. Moore
THE JOURNEY by Murray Leinster ps (Will F. Jenkins)
THE NINE BILLION NAMES OF GOD by Arthur C. Clarke

      STAR SCIENCE FICTION STORIES #2  Ballantine Books; New York, N. Y.  #55
      14 stories   195 pages   December 31, 1953
          Hard Cover Edition:  $2.00   Pocket Book Edition:  .35¢
                          ALL ORIGINAL STORIES

DISAPPEARING ACT by Alfred Bester
THE CLINIC by Theodore Sturgeon
THE CONGRUENT PEOPLE by A. J. Budrys
CRITICAL FACTOR by Hal Clement ps (Harry Clement Stubbs)
IT'S A GOOD LIFE by Jerome Bixby
A POUND OF CURE by Lester del Rey
THE PURPLE FIELDS by Robert Crane
F   Y   I by James Blish
CONQUEST by Anthony Boucher
HORMONES by Fletcher Pratt
THE ODOR OF THOUGHT by Robert Sheckley
THE HAPPIEST CREATURE by Jack Williamson
THE REMORSEFUL by C. M. Kornbluth
FRIEND OF THE FAMILY by Richard Wilson

STAR SCIENCE FICTION STORIES #3    Ballantine Books; New York, N. Y. #96
10 stories  186 pages  December 20, 1954
    Hard Cover Edition:  $2.00  Pocket Book Edition:  .35¢

ALL ORIGINAL STORIES

IT'S SUCH A BEAUTIFUL DAY by Isaac Asimov
THE STRAWBERRY WINDOW by Ray Bradbury
THE DEEP RANGE by Arthur C. Clarke
ALIEN by Lester del Rey
FOSTER, YOU'RE DEAD by Philip K. Dick
WHATEVER HAPPENED TO CORPORAL CUCKOO? by Gerald Kersh
    (From THE BRIGHTEN MONSTER; 1953)
DANCE OF THE DEAD by Richard Matheson
ANY MORE AT HOME LIKE YOU? by Chad Oliver
THE DEVIL ON SALVATION BLUFF by Jack Vance
GUINEVERE FOR EVERYBODY by Jack Williamson


STAR SCIENCE FICTION STORIES #4   Ballantine Books; New York, N. Y.
9 stories  157 pages  .35¢  #272 K  November 28, 1958

ALL ORIGINAL STORIES

A CROSS OF CENTURIES by Henry Kuttner
THE ADVENT ON CHANNEL TWELVE by C. M. Kornbluth
SPACE-TIME FOR SPRINGERS by Fritz Leiber
MAN WORKING by Richard Wilson
HELPING HAND by Lester del Rey
THE LONG ECHO by Miriam Allen DeFord
TOMORROW'S GIFT by Edmund Cooper
IDIOT STICK by Damon Knight
THE IMMORTALS by James E. Gunn


STAR SCIENCE FICTION STORIES #5   Ballantine Books; New York, N. Y.
9 stories  159 pages  .35¢  #308 K  May 27, 1959

ALL ORIGINAL STORIES

TROUBLE WITH TREATIES by Katherine MacLean and Tom Condit
A TOUCH OF GRAPEFRUIT by Richard Matheson
COMPANY STORE by Robert Silverberg
ADRIFT ON THE POLICY LEVEL by Chan Davis
SPARKIE'S FALL by Gavin Hyde
STAR DESCENDING by Algis Budrys
DIPLOMATIC COOP by Daniel F. Galouye
THE SCENE SHIFTER by Arthur Sellings
HAIR-RAISING ADVENTURE by Rosel George Brown


STAR SCIENCE FICTION STORIES #6   Ballantine Books; New York, N. Y.
8 stories  156 pages  .35¢  #353 K  December 28, 1959
ALL ORIGINAL STORIES

DANGER! CHILD AT LARGE by C. L. Cottrell
TWIN'S WAIL by Elizabeth Mann Borgese
THE HOLY GRAIL by Tom Purdom
ANGERHELM by Cordwainer Smith
THE DREAMSMAN by Gordon R. Dickson
TO CATCH AN ALIEN by John J. McGuire
PRESS CONFERENCE by Miriam Allen deFord
INVASION FROM INNER SPACE by Howard Koch

STAR OF STARS          Doubleday and Co., Inc.; New York, N. Y.
14 stories  240 pages  $3.50  October 14, 1960          Mag.      Year

## SELECTIONS FROM THE STAR SCIENCE FICTION SERIES

WHATEVER HAPPENED TO CORPORAL CUCKOO? by Gerald Kersh
    (From The Brighton Monster; 1953)
THE ADVENT ON CHANNEL TWELVE by C. M. Kornbluth
DISAPPEARING ACT by Alfred Bester
TWIN'S WAIL by Elizabeth Mann Borgese
COUNTRY DOCTOR by William Morrison ps (Joseph Samachson)          StrSF   Jan 1958
DAYBROKE by Robert Bloch
THE DEEP RANGE by Arthur C. Clarke
A CROSS OF CENTURIES by Henry Kuttner
THE MAN WITH ENGLISH by H. L. Gold
SPARKIE'S FALL by Gavin Hyde
SPACE-TIME FOR SPRINGERS by Fritz Leiber
DANCE OF THE DEAD by Richard Matheson
THE HAPPIEST CREATURE by Jack Williamson
IT'S A GOOD LIFE by Jerome Bixby

STAR SHORT NOVELS          Ballantine Books; New York, N. Y.
3 stories  163 pages  #H-89  September 23, 1954
    Hard Cover Edition: $2.00  Pocket Book Edition:  .35¢

## ALL ORIGINAL STORIES

LITTLE MEN by Jessamyn West
FOR I AM A JEALOUS PEOPLE! by Lester del Rey
TO HERE AND THE EASEL by Theodore Sturgeon

    Editor's Note:  Although there was no Editor's byline given in "THE PETRIFIED
    PLANET" and "WITCHES THREE" the publishers stated that Fletcher Pratt can
    be considered the editor of both collections.

PRATT, FLETCHER
    THE PETRIFIED PLANET     Twayne Publishers; New York, N. Y.
    3 stories  263 pages  $2.95  December 5, 1952

## ALL ORIGINAL STORIES

THE LONG VIEW by Fletcher Pratt
ULLR UPRISING by H. Beam Piper
DAUGHTERS OF EARTH by Judith Merril

WITCHES THREE          Twayne Publishers; New York, N. Y.
3 stories  423 pages  $3.95  August 12, 1952

                                                              ORIGINAL STORY
THE BLUE STAR by Fletcher Pratt                               UW   Apr 1943
CONJURE WIFE by Fritz Leiber, Jr.                             TWS  Apr 1950
THREE SHALL BE NO DARKNESS by James Blish

WORLD OF WONDER          Twayne Publishers; New York, N. Y.
19 stories  445 pages  $3.95  August 6, 1951
                                                              ASF   Apr 1948
HE WALKED AROUND THE HORSES by H. Beam Piper
ROADS OF DESTINY by O. Henry ps (Wm. Sydney Porter) (From ROADS OF DESTINY; 1909)
THE RED QUEEN'S RACE by Isaac Asimov                          ASF   Jan 1949
CHILD'S PLAY by William Tenn ps (Philip Klass)                ASF   Mar 1947

THE FINEST STORY IN THE WORLD by Rudyard Kipling      (From MANY INVENTIONS; 1893)
ETAOIN SHRDLU by Fredric Brown                                       UW   Feb 1942
MISTAKE INSIDE by James Blish                                       Stg   Mar 1948
PRIVATE — KEEP OUT! by Philip MacDonald                             MoF   Fal 1949
THEY by Robert A. Heinlein                                          Unk   Apr 1941
METAMORPHOSIS by Franz Kafka                        (From THE METAMORPHOSIS; 1937)
BACK THERE IN THE GRASS by Gouvernour Morris         (From IT & OTHER STORIES; 1922)
THE MARK OF THE BEAST by Rudyard Kipling                (From LIFE'S HANDICAP; 1891)
MUSEUM PIECE by Esther Carlson              (From MOON OVER THE BACK FENCE; 1947)
THE BLUE GIRAFFE by L. Sprague de Camp                              ASF   Aug 1939
THAT ONLY A MOTHER by Judith Merril                                 ASF   Jun 1948
OPERATION RSVP by H. Beam Piper                                     Amz   Jan 1951
CONQUERORS' ISLE by Nelson Bond                                      BB   Jun 1946
GIANT KILLER by A. Bertram Chandler                                 ASF   Oct 1945
THE MILLION YEAR PICNIC by Ray Bradbury                             PS    Sum 1946


QUINN, JAMES L. and EVE WULFF
        THE FIRST WORLD OF IF       (Quinn Publishing Co., Inc.; Kingston, N. Y.
        20 stories  160 pages  .50¢  January 10, 1957
                        ALL STORIES FROM IF

LET THERE BE LIGHT by H. B. Fyfe                                 November 1952
THE ROTIFERS by Robert Abernathy                                   March 1953
THE BATTLE by Robert Sheckley                                  September 1954
A PATTERN FOR PENELOPE by Robert F. Young                       November 1954
DISQUALIFIED by Charles L. Fontenay                            September 1954
A COLD NIGHT FOR DYING by Milton Lesser                         December 1954
FIRST STAGE: MOON by Dick Hetschel                             December 1954
THE SMALL WORLD OF M-75 by Ed M. Clinton, Jr.                       July 1954
JOURNEY WORK by Dave Dryfoos                                      January 1955
THE LAST CRUSADE by George H. Smith                             February 1955
THE CYBER AND JUSTICE HOLMES by Frank Riley                        March 1955
CAPTIVE MARKET by Philip K. Dick                                   April 1955
WATERSHED by James Blish                                             May 1955
THE TWILIGHT YEARS by Kirk and Garen Drussai                       June 1955
FRANCHISE by Isaac Asimov                                           July 1955
LAST RITES by Charles Beaumont                                   October 1955
LABORATORY by Jerome Bixby                                       December 1955
THE MARGENES by Miriam Allen deFord                             February 1956
THE DRIVERS by Edward W. Ludwig                                    March 1956
SHOCK TROOP by Richard Bolton                                    October 1956


        THE SECOND WORLD OF IF       Quinn Publishing Co., Inc.; Kingston, N. Y.
        9 stories  160 pages  .50¢  January 10, 1958
                        ALL STORIES FROM IF

THE COLONISTS by Raymond F. Jones                                   June 1954
THE THING IN THE ATTIC by James Blish                              July 1954
A MONSTER NAMED SMITH by James E. Gunn                             July 1954
THE JUNGLE by Charles Beaumont                                  December 1954
THE ODD ONES by Gordon Dickson                                  February 1955
THE MOLD OF YANCY by Philip K. Dick                                July 1955
CHROME PASTURES by Robert F. Young                                 April 1956
Z by Charles L. Fontenay                                            June 1956
THE HAPPY HERD by Bryce Walton                                   October 1956

SANTESSON, HANS STEFAN                                           Mag.    Year

    THE FANTASTIC UNIVERSE OMNIBUS    Prentice-Hall, Inc.; Englewood Cliffs, N. J.
    19 stories    270 pages    $3.95    April 1960

ALL STORIES FROM FANTASTIC UNIVERSE

| | |
|---|---|
| FIRST LAW by Isaac Asimov | October 1956 |
| SHE ONLY GOES OUT AT NIGHT by William Tenn ps (Philip Klass) | October 1956 |
| THE PACIFIST by Arthur C. Clarke | October 1956 |
| THE BOUNTY HUNTER by Avram Davidson | March 1958 |
| THE MUTED HORN by Dorothy Salisbury Davis | May 1957 |
| A WAY OF LIFE by Robert Bloch | October 1956 |
| IN LONELY HANDS by Harlan Ellison | January 1959 |
| FALL OF KNIGHT by A. Bertram Chandler | June 1958 |
| SIT BY THE FIRE by Myrle Benedict | May 1958 |
| A THING OF CUSTOM by L. Sprague de Camp | January 1957 |
| EXILE FROM SPACE by Judith Merril | November 1956 |
| MEX by Larry M. Harris | January 1957 |
| THE AMAZING MRS. MIMMS by David C. Knight | August 1958 |
| MY FATHER, THE CAT by Henry Slesar | December 1957 |
| TITLE FIGHT by William Campbell Gault | December 1956 |
| THE GOLDEN PYRAMID by Sam Moskowitz | November 1956 |
| THE ROBOT WHO WANTED TO KNOW by Felix Boyd | March 1958 |
| ROAD TO NIGHTFALL by Robert Silverberg | July 1958 |
| THE VELVET GLOVE by Harry Harrison | November 1956 |


SLOANE, WILLIAM

    SPACE, SPACE, SPACE                   Franklin Watts, Inc.; New York, N. Y.
    10 stories    288 pages    $2.50    October 20, 1953

| | | |
|---|---|---|
| NO MOON FOR ME by Walter M. Miller, Jr. | ASF | Sep 1952 |
| TRIP ONE by Edward Grendon | ASF | Jul 1949 |
| TOOLS OF THE TRADE by Raymond F. Jones | ASF | Nov 1950 |
| HIDE AND SEEK by Arthur C. Clarke | ASF | Sep 1949 |
| MASTER RACE by Richard Ashby | Im | Sep 1951 |
| DEAR DEVIL by Eric Frank Russell | OW | May 1950 |
| COURTESY by Clifford D. Simak | ASF | Aug 1951 |
| NIGHTMARE BROTHER by Alan E. Nourse | ASF | Feb 1953 |
| SECOND CHANCE by Walter Kubilius and Fletcher Pratt | FSM | Sep 1952 |
| LIKE GODS THEY CAME by Irving Cox, Jr. | AvR | Jan 1953 |

    STORIES FOR TOMORROW           Funk and Wagnalls Co.; New York, N. Y.
    29 stories    628 pages    $3.95    June 21, 1954

    English Edition:  Eyre & Spottiswoode  22 stories 476 pages  18/  (1955)

    THE HUMAN HEART

| | | |
|---|---|---|
| THE WILDERNESS by Ray Bradbury | Phl | 4/6/52 |
| STARBRIDE by Anthony Boucher | TWS | Dec 195 |
| SECOND CHILDHOOD by Clifford D. Simak | Glxy | Feb 195 |
| HOMELAND by Mari Wolf | If | Jan 195 |

        (Originally appeared under title THE STATUE)
LET NOTHING YOU DISMAY by William Sloane                    ORIGINAL STOR'
A SCENT OF SARSAPARILLA by Ray Bradbury
        (From STAR SCIENCE FICTION STORIES; 1953 - Edited by Frederik Pohl)

II   THERE ARE NO EASY ANSWERS

    THE EXILE by Alfred Coppell                              ASF   Oct 195

STORIES FOR TOMORROW [Continued]                          Mag.    Year

    THE FARTHEST HORIZON by Raymond F. Jones
    NOISE LEVEL by Raymond F. Jones                        ASF   Apr 1952
    FIRST CONTACT by Murray Leinster ps (Will F. Jenkins)  ASF   Dec 1952
III  SWEAT OF THE BROW                                     ASF   May 1945

    FRANCHISE by Kris Neville
    IN VALUE DECEIVED by H. B. Fyfe                         ASF   Feb 1951
    OKIE by James Blish                                     ASF   Nov 1950
    BLACK EYES AND THE DAILY GRIND by Milton Lesser         ASF   Apr 1950
IV  DIFFERENCE WITH DISTINCTION                             If    Mar 1952

    SOCRATES by John Christopher ps (Christopher S. Youd)
    IN HIDING by Wilmar H. Shiras                           Glxy  Mar 1951
    BETTY ANN by Kris Neville                               ASF   Nov 1948
        (From NEW TALES OF SPACE AND TIME; 1951 — Edited by Raymond J. Healy)
V   THE TROUBLE WITH PEOPLE IS PEOPLE

    THE ANT AND THE EYE by Chad Oliver
    BEEP by James Blish                                     ASF   Apr 1953
    AND THEN THERE WERE NONE by Eric Frank Russell          Glxy  Feb 1954
    THE GIRLS FROM EARTH by Frank M. Robinson               ASF   Jun 1951
VI  VISITORS                                               Glxy  Jan 1952

    MINISTERS WITHOUT PORTFOLIO by Mildred Clingerman
    THE HEAD-HUNTERS by Ralph Williams                      F&SF  Feb 1952
    DUNE ROLLER by Julian C. May                            ASF   Oct 1951
    DISGUISE by Donald A. Wollheim                          ASF   Dec 1951
    THE SHED by E. Everett Evans                            OW    Feb 1953
VII  THREE EPILOGS                                          AvR   Jan 1953

    THE NINE BILLION NAMES OF GOD by Arthur C. Clarke
        (From STAR SCIENCE FICTION STORIES; 1953 — Edited by Frederik Pohl)
    FORGOTTEN ENEMY by Arthur C. Clarke                     NW #5  n/d 1949
    THE ANSWERS by Clifford D. Simak                        FSF   MAR 1953
        (Originally appeared under title AND THE TRUTH SHALL MAKE YOU FREE)

STERN, PHILIP VAN DOREN

    THE MOONLIGHT TRAVELER          Doubleday and Co.; New York, N. Y.
    21 stories  488 pages  $2.50  May 7, 1943

    Canadian Edition:  McClelland & Stewart Ltd.; Toronto  $3.25
        No further data available
    English Edition:   The Bodley Head Ltd. 21 stories  487 pages  12/6  (1949)
            "      "      "     "      "                            7/6  (1952)
    Pocket Book Edition:  Pocket Books, Inc.; New York, N. Y.  .35¢  C-156
        Titled GREAT TALES OF FANTASY AND IMAGINATION  November 1, 1954

THE CELESTIAL OMNIBUS by E. M. Forster
    (From THE CELESTIAL OMNIBUS AND OTHER STORIES; 1923)
DESIRE by James Stephens                    (From ETCHED IN MOONLIGHT; 1928)
ENOCH SOAMES by Max Beerbohm                      (From SEVEN MEN; 1919)
THE MAN WHO COULD WORK MIRACLES by H. G. Wells
THE BOTTLE IMP by Robert Louis Stevenson              ILN   Jul 1898
ADAM AND EVE AND PINCH ME by A. E. Coppard            B&W   Mar 1891
    (From ADAM AND EVE AND PINCH ME; 1921)

(81)

THE MOONLIGHT TRAVELER [Continued]

LORD MOUNTDRAGO by W. Somerset Maugham    (From THE MIXTURE AS BEFORE; 1939)
ALL HALLOWS by Walter de la Mare    (From THE CONNOISSEUR; 1926)
OUR DISTANT COUSINS by Lord Dunsany
   (From THE TRAVEL TALES OF MR. JOSEPH JORKENS; 1931)
COBBLER, COBBLER, MEND MY SHOE by Jan Struther ps (Mrs. Joyce Maxtone Graham)
                                                      WR    11/9/29

THE MAN WHO MISSED THE BUS by Stella Benson ps (Mrs. Jo Anderson)
   (From COLLECTED SHORT STORIES OF STELLA BENSON; 1936)
SAM SMALL'S BETTER HALF by Eric Knight    (From SAM SMALL FLIES AGAIN; 1942)
MR. ARCULURIS by Conrad Aiken    (From AMONG THE LAST PEOPLE; 1934)
THE DIAMOND AS BIG AS THE RITZ by F. Scott Fitzgerald
   (From TALES OF THE JAZZ AGE; 1922)
WILLIAM WILSON by Edgar Allan Poe    Gft  n/d 1840
THE CURFEW TOLLS by Stephen Vincent Benet    SEP    10/5/35
MOST MADDENING STORY IN THE WORLD by Ralph Straus
   (From A SECOND CENTURY OF CREEPY STORIES; 1937 — Edited by Hugh Walpole )
PHANTAS by Oliver Onions    (From WIDDERSHINS; 1911)
ROADS OF DESTINY by O. Henry ps (Willam Sydney Porter)
   (From ROADS OF DESTINY; 1909)
                                                      SM  Aug 1902
"WIRELESS" by Rudyard Kipling
THE MUSIC ON THE HILL by Saki ps (H. H. Munro)
   (From THE CHRONICLES OF CLOVIS; 1912)

   TRAVELERS IN TIME    Doubleday and Co.; New York, N. Y.
   24 stories  48 pages  $3.50  July 24, 1947
                     THROUGH THE CLOCK
                                                 NwR  Jan 1895
THE TIME MACHINE by H. G. Wells
ELSEWHERE AND OTHERWISE by Algernon Blackwood    (From SHOCKS; 1936
ENOCH SOAMES by Max Beerbohm    (From SEVEN MEN; 1919)
BETWEEN THE MINUTE AND THE HOUR by A. M. Burrage    (From SOME GHOST STORIES; 1927)
                THE SHAPE OF THINGS TO COME
                                           (From THE LOVELY LADY; 1933)
THE ROCKING-HORSE WINNER by D. H. Lawrence
ON THE STAIRCASE by Katherine Fullerton Gerould    (From VAIN OBLIGATIONS; 1914)
AUGUST by W. F. Harvey    (From THE BEAST WITH FIVE FINGERS AND OTHER TALES; 1928)
THE ANTICIPATOR by Morley Roberts
   (From THE KEEPER OF THE WATERS AND OTHER STORIES; 1898)
THE OLD MAN by Holloway Horn
   (From THE SECOND OMNIBUS OF CRIME; 1932 — Edited by Dorothy Sayers)
THE TAIPAN by W. Somerset Maugham    (From ON A CHINESE SCREEN; 1922)
THE HOUSING OF MR. BRADEGAR by H. F. Heard
   (From THE GREAT FOG AND OTHER WEIRD TALES; 1944)
                  THE PAST REVISITED
"THE FINEST STORY IN THE WORLD" by Rudyard Kipling    (From MANY INVENTIONS; 1893
ETCHED IN MOONLIGHT by James Stephens    (From ETCHED IN MOONLIGHT; 1928
A VIEW FROM A HILL by M. R. James
   (From A WARNING TO THE CURIOUS AND OTHER GHOST STORIES; 1926)
A FRIEND TO ALEXANDER by James Thurber    (From MY WORLDS AND WELCOME TO IT; 1943
THE SILVER MIRROR by A. Conan Doyle    (From TALES OF LONG AGO; 1925
                 WHEN TIME STOOD STILL
                                                 Cas Apr 193
NO SHIPS PASS by Lady Eleanor Smith
THE CLOCK by A. E. W. Mason    (From THE FOUR CORNERS OF THE WORLD; 1917
OPENING THE DOOR by Arthur Machen    (From THE COZY ROOM; 1936

TIME OUT OF JOINT

THE CURIOUS CASE OF BENJAMIN BUTTON by F. Scott Fitzgerald
    (From TALES OF THE JAZZ AGE; 1920)
THE ALTERNATIVE by Maurice Baring
    (From HALF A MINUTE'S SILENCE AND OTHER STORIES; 1925)

VISITORS FROM OUT OF TIME

MR. STRENBERRY'S TALE by J. B. Priestly         (From FOUR-IN-HAND; 1934)
PHANTAS by Oliver Onions                  (From WIDDERSHINS; 1911)
THE HOMELESS ONE by A. E. Coppard      (From FEARFUL PLEASURES; 1946)

STONG, PHIL

    THE OTHER WORLDS            Wilfred Funk; New York, N. Y.
    25 stories  466 pages  $2.50  May 6, 1941

    2nd American Edition:  Garden City Books; Garden City, N. Y.  $1.00 25 stories
        Titled:  25 MODERN STORIES OF MYSTERY AND IMAGINATION  466 pages  (1942)

    Canadian Editions:  Longmans-Green; Toronto  25 stories  $3.00
        (No further data available)
                   Blue Ribbon Books $1.79 25 stories
                    (No further data available)

PART I — STRANGE IDEAS

| | | |
|---|---|---|
| THE CONSIDERATE HOSTS by Thorp McClusky | WT | Dec 1939 |
| THE MAN IN THE BLACK HAT by Michael Fessier | Esq | Feb 1934 |
| NAKED LADY by Mindret Lord | WT | Sep 1934 |
| THE HOUSE OF ECSTASY by Ralph Milne Farley ps (Roger Sherman Hoar) | WT | Apr 1938 |
| ESCAPE by Paul Ernst | WT | Jul 1938 |
| THE ADAPTIVE ULTIMATE by John Jessell ps (Stanley G. Weinbaum | Ast | Nov 1935 |
| THE WOMAN IN GREY by Walter G. Everett | WT | Jun 1935 |
| THE PIPES OF PAN by Lester del Rey | Unk | May 1940 |
| AUNT CASSIE by Virginia Swain | ORIGINAL STORY | |

PART II — FRESH VARIANTS

| | | |
|---|---|---|
| A GOD IN A GARDEN by Theodore Sturgeon | Unk | Oct 1939 |
| THE MAN WHO KNEW ALL THE ANSWERS by Donald Bern | Amz | Aug 1940 |
| ADAM LINK'S VENGEANCE by Eando Binder ps (Otto Binder) | Amz | Feb 1940 |
| TRUTH IS A PLAGUE by David Wright O'Brien | Amz | Feb 1940 |
| THE FOURTH DIMENSIONAL DEMONSTRATOR by Murray Leinster ps (Will F. Jenkins) | Ast | Dec 1935 |
| ALAS, ALL THINKING! by Harry Bates | Ast | Jun 1935 |
| THE COMEDY OF ERAS by Kelvin Kent ps (Henry Kuttner) | TWS | Sep 1940 |
| A PROBLEM FOR BIOGRAPHERS by Mindret Lord | ORIGINAL STORY | |

PART III — "HORRORS"

| | | |
|---|---|---|
| IN THE VAULT by H. P. Lovecraft | WT | Apr 1932 |
| SCHOOL FOR THE UNSPEAKABLE by Manly Wade Wellman | WT | Mar 1940 |
| THE HOUSE WHERE TIME STOOD STILL by Seabury Quinn | WT | Mar 1939 |
| THE MYSTERY OF THE LAST GUEST by John Flanders ps (Jean Ray) | WT | Oct 1935 |
| THE SONG OF THE SLAVES by Manly Wade Wellman | WT | Mar 1940 |
| THE PANNELLED ROOM by August Derleth | WM | Sep 1933 |
| THE GRAVEYARD RATS by Henry Kuttner | WT | Mar 1936 |
| THE RETURN OF ANDREW BENTLEY by August Derleth and Mack Schorer | WT | Sep 1933 |

TENN, WILLIAM ps (Philip Klass)                                    Mag.    Year
    CHILDREN OF WONDER          Simon and Schuster, Inc.; New York, N. Y.
    21 stories  336 pages  $2.95  March 19, 1953

    Pocket Book Edition:  Doubleday and Co.; New York, N. Y.  Permabook P291
       21 stories  355 pages  .35¢  June 7, 1954
          Titled: OUTSIDERS: CHILDREN OF WONDER
                        PART I.  WILD TALENTS
THE ROCKING HORSE WINNER by D. H. Lawrence          (From THE LOVELY LADY; 1933)
THE WORDS OF GURU by C. M. Kornbluth                             Stl  Jun 1941
    (Originally appeared under pseudonym Kenneth Falconer)
BABY IS THREE by Theodore Sturgeon                              Glxy  Oct 1952
                        PART 2.  THE CHILD POSSESSED
SMALL ASSASIN by Ray Bradbury                                    DM  Nov 1946
STORY OF A PANIC by E. M. Forster    (From COLLECTED TALES OF E. M. FORSTER; 1947)
THE PIPER'S SON by Lewis Padgett ps (Henry Kuttner and C. L. Moore)  ASF  Feb 1945
                        PART 3.  THE STUFF OF DREAMS
MIRIAM by Truman Capote            (From TREE OF NIGHT AND OTHER STORIES; 1945)
ADAM AND EVE AND PINCH ME by A. E. Coppard  (From ADAM AND EVE AND PINCH ME; 1921)
CHILD'S PLAY by Mary Alice Schnirring                           WT  Mar 1942
THE OPEN WINDOW by Saki ps (H. H. Munro)    (From BEAST AND SUPER BEASTS; 1914)
                        PART 4.  TERROR IN THE NURSERY
THE END OF THE PARTY by Graham Greene          (From NINETEEN STORIES; 1947)
THE IDOL OF THE FLIES by Jane Rice                              UW  Jun 1942
THAT ONLY A MOTHER by Judith Merril                            ASF  Jun 1948
                        PART 5.  ALIEN BROTHERS
BORN OF MAN AND WOMAN by Richard Matheson                      F&SF  Sum 1950
KEYHOLE by Murray Leinster ps (Will F. Jenkins)                TWS  Dec 1951
TERMINAL QUEST by Poul Anderson                                Sup  Aug 1951
                        PART 6.  LITTLE SUPERMAN, WHAT NOW?
THE ORIGIN OF THE SPECIES by Katherine MacLean               ORIGINAL STORY
IN HIDING by Wilmar H. Shiras                                  ASF  Nov 1948
                        PART 7.  IN TIMES TO COME
"THE HATCHERY" by Aldous Huxley               (From BRAVE NEW WORLD; 1932)
ERRAND BOY by William Tenn ps (Philip Klass)                   ASF  Jun 1947
NIGHTMARE FOR FUTURE REFERENCE: A narrative poem by Stephen Vincent Benet
                                                               Sch  9/17/38

WELLES, ORSON

    INVASION FROM MARS          Dell Publishing Co.; New York, N. Y.
    10 stories  191 pages  .25¢  #305  May 24, 1949

INVASION FROM MARS by Howard Koch          The radio script of the Orson Welles
    broadcast of H. G. Wells' THE WAR OF THE WORLDS over the Columbia Broadcasting
    System, October 30, 1938.      (Copyright 1940 by Princeton University Press)
THE GREEN HILLS OF EARTH by Robert A. Heinlein              SEP    2/8/47
ZERO HOUR by Ray Bradbury                                   PS  Fal 1947
EXPEDITION by Anthony Boucher                              TWS  Aug 1943
INCIDENT ON CALYPSO by Murray Leinster ps (Will F. Jenkins)  Stg  Fal 1945
THE STAR-MOUSE by Fredric Brown                             PS  Spr 1942
THE CASTAWAY by Nelson Bond (Org aprd under pseud George Danzell)  PS  Win 1940

                              (84)

INVASION FROM MARS [Continued]

VICTORY UNINTENTIONAL by Isaac Asimov
FAREWELL TO EDEN by Theodore Sturgeon
THE MILLION YEAR PICNIC by Ray Bradbury

Sup  Aug 1942
ORIGINAL STORY
PS   Sum 1946

WILLIAMS-ELLIS, AMABEL & MABLY OWEN

OUT OF THIS WORLD 1        Blackie & Son Ltd.; London, England
8 stories  197 pages  12/6  September 18, 1960

BREAKING STRAIN by Arthur C. Clarke                         TWS   Dec 1949
    (Originally appeared under title THIRTY SECONDS-THIRTY DAYS)
NO PLACE LIKE EARTH by John Wyndham ps (John Beynon Harris)  NW #9   Spr 1951
THE RUUM by Arthur Porges                                   F&SF   Oct 1953
FRIDAY by John Kippax                                       NW #80  Feb 1959
THE MIDDLE OF THE WEEK AFTER NEXT by Murray Leinster ps (Will F. Jenkins)
                                                            TWS   Aug 1952
PLACET IS A CRAZY PLACE by Fredric Brown                    ASF   May 1946
CHEMICAL PLANT by Ian Williamson                            NW #8   Win 1950
MEN OF THE TEN BOOKS by Jack Vance                          Stg   Mar 1951

OUT OF THIS WORLD 2        Blackie & Son Ltd.; London, England
8 stories  188 pages  12/6  April 13, 1961

THE TROUBLE WITH EMILY by James M. White                    NW #77  Nov 1958
THE DUSTY DEATH by John Kippax                              NW #77  Nov 1958
ANOTHER WORD FOR MAN by Robert Presslie                     NW #78  Dec 1958
THE RAILWAYS UP ON CANNIS by Colin Kapp                     NW #87  Oct 1959
MACHINE MADE by J. T. McIntosh ps (James J. MacGregor)      NW #10  Sum 1951
BUT WHO CAN REPLACE A MAN? by Brian Aldiss                  Inf   Jun 1958
THE GIFT OF GAB by Jack Vance                               ASF   Sep 1955
THE STILL WATERS by Lester del Rey                          NW #78  Dec 1958

WILSON, ANGUS

A. D. 2500 [THE OBSERVER PRIZE STORIES 1954]  Wm. Heinemann Ltd.; London
21 stories  241 pages  15/  October 31, 1955

Editors Note:  The stories in this anthology were all submitted in the contest
    The LONDON OBSERVER conducted in 1954. Of the entries received, the judges
    narrowed the stories down to three which were then published in The Obser-
    ver for the readers to decide which was the best story.  THE RETURN OF THE
    MOON MAN by E. L. Malpass was the winner.  The balance of the stories were
    not previously published.

THE RETURN OF THE MOON MAN by E. L. Malpass              January 2, 1955
NOT FOR AN AGE by Brian W. Aldiss                        January 9, 1955
THE RIGHT THING by William Andrew
JACKSON WONG'S STORY by John Bolsover
VOICE FROM THE GALLERY by Catherine Brownlow
WALKABOUT by Stephen Earl
THE SHADOW — LAY by E. D. Fitzpatrick
VENUS AND THE RABBIT by E. M. Fitzpatrick
THE PLACE OF THE TIGRESS by Isobel Mayne
ANOTHER ANTIGONE by D. A. C. Morrison
SPUD FAILURE DEFINITE by Noel Peart
THE THREE BROTHERS by William Moy Russell              December 26, 1954

THE ATAVISTS by G. A. Rymer
THE MISSION by Arthur Sellings
ALPHA IN OMEGA by Jonathan Stones
THE BLOND KID by Herb Sutherland
THE CASE OF OMEGA SMITH by Buthram Walsh
THE MACHINE THAT WAS LONELY by Robert Wells
HITCH-HIKE TO PARADISE by Geoffrey Whybrow
THE KNITTING by Margaret Wood
MAN MANIFOLD by Peter Young


WOLLHEIM, DONALD A.
    ADVENTURES IN THE FAR FUTURE        Ace Books, Inc.; New York, N. Y.
    5 stories   177 pages   .35¢   D-73   September 7, 1954

        (Double binding of two anthologies — See listing TALES OF OUTER SPACE

| | | |
|---|---|---|
| THE MIND BETWEEN THE WORLDS by Lester del Rey | Glxy | Mar 195 |
| STARDUST by Chad Oliver | ASF | Jul 195 |
| OVERDRIVE by Murray Leinster ps (Will F. Jenkins) | Stg | Jan 195 |
| THE MILLIONTH YEAR by Martin Pearson ps (Donald A. Wollheim) | SFS | Apr 194 |
| THE CHAPTER ENDS by Poul Anderson | DSF | Jan 195 |


    ADVENTURES ON OTHER PLANETS        Ace Books, Inc.; New York, N. Y.
    5 stories   160 pages   .25¢   S-133   December 15, 1955

ON VENUS
    THE OBLIGATION by Roger Dee ps (Roger D. Aycock)            Stg   Sep 195

ON MARS
    THE SOUND OF BUGLES by Robert Moore Williams                Stg   Mar 194

ON A PLANET OF SIGMA DRACONIS
    OGRE by Clifford D. Simak                                   ASF   Jan 194

ON A WORLD IN THE "BORNIK" STAR CLUSTER
    ASSIGNMENT ON PASIK by Murray Leinster ps (Will F. Jenkins)  TWS   Feb 194
        (Originally appeared under pseudonym William Fitzgerald)

ON LAERTES III
                                                                ASF   May 194
    THE RULL by A. E. Van Vogt


    THE EARTH IN PERIL            Ace Books, Inc.; New York, N. Y.
    6 stories   158 pages   .35¢   D-205   February 1957

| | | |
|---|---|---|
| THINGS PASS BY by Murray Leinster ps (Will F. Jenkins) | TWS | Sum 194 |
| LETTER FROM THE STARS by A. E. Van Vogt | OTWA | Jul 19 |
| THE SILLY SEASON by C. M. Kornbluth | F&SF | Fal 19 |
| THE PLANT REVOLT by Edmond Hamilton | WT | Apr 19 |
| MARY ANONYMOUS by Bryce Walton | PS | Sum 19 |
| THE STAR by H. G. Wells | Grp | Xmas 18 |


    THE END OF THE WORLD            Ace Books, Inc.; New York, N. Y.
    6 stories   159 pages   .35¢   S-183   October 1956

| | | |
|---|---|---|
| THE YEAR OF THE JACKPOT by Robert A. Heinlein | Glxy | Mar 19 |
| LAST NIGHT OF SUMMER by Alfred Coppell | Orb #4 | Sep 19 |
| IMPOSTER by Philip K. Dick | Glxy | Jun 19 |
| RESCUE PARTY by Arthur C. Clarke | ASF | May 19 |
| OMEGA by Amelia Reynolds Long | Amz | Jul 19 |
| IN THE WORLD'S DUSK by Edmond Hamilton | WT | Mar 19 |

EVERY BOY'S BOOK OF SCIENCE FICTION  Frederick Fell, Inc., New York, N. Y.
10 stories   254 pages   $2.75   March 26, 1951                    Mag.     Year

   Canadian Edition:  Geo. J. McLeod Ltd.; Toronto  10 stories $3.75
      (No further data available)

THE GRAVITY PROFESSOR by Ray Cummings                            AASW    5/7/21
THE FOUR-DIMENSIONAL-ROLLER-PRESS by Bob Olsen ps (Alfred John Olsen, Jr.)
                                                                Amz   Jun 1927
INFRA-MEDIANS by Sewell Peaslee Wright                          Ast   Dec 1931
THE WHITE ARMY by Daniel Dressler, M. D.                        Amz   Sep 1929
DR. LU-MIE by Clifton B. Kruse                                  Ast   Jul 1934
THE LIVING MACHINE by David H. Keller, M. D.                    WS    May 1935
THE CONQUEST OF TWO WORLDS by Edmond Hamilton                   WS    Feb 1932
THE ASTEROID OF GOLD by Clifford D. Simak                       WS    Nov 1932
IN THE SCARLET STAR by Jack Williamson                         Amz   Mar 1933
KING OF THE GREY SPACES by Ray Bradbury                        FFM   Dec 1943

   FLIGHT INTO SPACE                        Frederick Fell, Inc.; New York, N. Y.
   12 stories  251 pages   $2.75   June 12, 1950

   English Edition:  Kemsley; London  11 stories 190 pages 1/6 CT403 1951
      INTERPLANETARY TRAVEL SCIENCE FICTION STORIES

SUNWARD by Stanton A. Coblentz                                  TWS   Apr 1940
THE MERCURIAN by Frank Belknap Long, Jr.                        PS    Win 1941
PARASITE PLANET by Stanley G. Weinbaum                          Ast   Feb 1935
PERIL OF THE BLUE WORLD by Robert Abernathy                     PS    Win 1942
THE DEATH OF THE MOON by Alexander M. Phillips                  Amz   Feb 1929
THE SEEKERS by Robert Moore Williams                            Stg   May 1948
AJAX OF AJAX by Martin Pearson ps (Donald A. Wollheim)        Fw/SF  Aug 1942
RED STORM ON JUPITER by Frank Belknap Long, Jr.                Ast   May 1936
HERMIT OF SATURN'S RING by Neil R. Jones                        PS    Fal 1940
PLANET PASSAGE by Donald A. Wollheim                           FFSF  Oct 1942
   (Originally appeared under pseudonym Martin Pearson)
A BABY ON NEPTUNE by Clare Winger Harris & Miles J. Breuer, M.D.   Amz  Dec 1929
THE RAPE OF THE SOLAR SYSTEM by Leslie F. Stone ps (Mrs. William Silberberg)
                                                                Amz   Dec 1934

   THE GIRL WITH THE HUNGRY EYES AND OTHER STORIES
   6 stories  127 pages  .25¢  #184  1949   Avon Publishing Co.; New York, N. Y.
                          ALL ORIGINAL STORIES
THE GIRL WITH THE HUNGRY EYES by Fritz Leiber, Jr.
VENUS AND THE SEVEN SEXES by William Tenn ps (Philip Klass)
MRS. MANIFOLD by Stephen Grendon ps (August Derleth)
DAYDREAM by P. Schuyler Miller
MATURITY NIGHT by Frank Belknap Long, Jr.
COME INTO MY PARLOR by Manly Wade Wellman

   THE HIDDEN PLANET  [Science Fiction Adventures On Venus]
   5 stories  190 pages  .35¢  D-354  April 1959 Ace Books, Inc.; N. Y., N. Y.

FIELD EXPERIMENT by Chad Oliver                                ASF   Jan 1955
VENUS MISSION by J. T. McIntosh ps (James J. MacGregor)        PS    Jul 1951
THE LUCK OF IGNATZ by Lester del Rey                          ASF   Aug 1939
THE LOTUS EATERS by Stanley G. Weinbaum                       ASF   Apr 1935
TERROR OUT OF SPACE by Leigh Brackett   (Mrs. Edmond Hamilton)   PS   Sum 1944

MEN ON THE MOON                    Ace Books, Inc.; New York, N. Y.
5 stories  137 pages  .35¢  D-277  March 1958          Mag.      Year

OPERATION PUMICE by Raymond Z. Gallun                  TWS   Apr 1949
JETSAM by A. Bertram Chandler                          NW #20 Mar 1953
THE RELUCTANT HEROES by Frank M. Robinson              Glxy  Jan 1951
MOONWALK by H. B. Fyfe                                 Spc   Nov 1952
KEYHOLE by Murray Leinster ps (Will F. Jenkins)        TWS   Dec 1951


   THE POCKET BOOK OF SCIENCE FICTION     Pocket Books, Inc.; New York, N. Y.
   10 stories  310 pages  .25¢  #214  May 1, 1943

BY THE WATERS OF BABYLON by Stephen Vincent Benet            SEP    7/31/37
   (Originally appeared under title THE PLACE OF THE GODS)
MOXON'S MASTER by Ambrose Bierce             (From CAN SUCH THINGS BE?; 1893)
GREEN THOUGHTS by John Collier              (From PRESENTING MOONSHINE; 1941)
IN THE ABYSS by H. G. Wells                                  Prn   Aug 1896
THE GREEN SPLOTCHES by T. S. Stribling                       Adv    1/3/20
THE LAST MAN by Wallace G. West                              Amz   Feb 1929
A MARTIAN ODYSSEY by Stanley G. Weinbaum                     WS    Jul 1934
TWILIGHT by Don A. Stuart ps (John W. Campbell, Jr.)         Ast   Nov 1934
MICROCOSMIC GOD by Theodore Sturgeon                         ASF   Apr 1941
" — AND HE BUILT A CROOKED HOUSE — " by Robert A. Heinlein   ASF   Feb 1941


   THE PORTABLE NOVELS OF SCIENCE      Viking Press; New York, N. Y.
   4 stories  737 pages  $2.50  December 24, 1945

THE FIRST MEN IN THE MOON by H. G. Wells                     Cpln  Nov 1900
BEFORE THE DAWN by John Taine ps (Eric Temple Bell)
   (Originally published by Williams & Wilkins Co.; 1934)
THE SHADOW OUT OF TIME by H. P. Lovecraft                    Ast   Jun 1936
ODD JOHN by Olaf Stapledon
   (Originally published by Methuen and Co. [London]; 1935)

   PRIZE SCIENCE FICTION        The McBride Co., Inc.; New York, N. Y.
   12 stories  230 pages  $3.00  May 15, 1953

   Canadian Edition:  McClelland and Stewart Ltd.; Toronto  12 stories  $4.00
        No further data available
   English Edition:   Weidenfeld Nicolson; London  248 pages  10/6  12 stories
        Titled:  PRIZE STORIES OF SPACE AND TIME                  (1953)

ALL THE TIME IN THE WORLD by Arthur C. Clarke               Stg   Jul 1952
McILVAINE'S STAR by August Derleth                          If    Jul 1952
DEMOTION by Robert Donald Locke                             ASF   Sep 1952
THE MASK OF DEMETER by Martin Pearson ps (Donald A. Wollheim) and Cecil Corwin
   ps (C. M. Kornbluth)                                     F&SF  Jan 1953
THE BEAUTIFUL WOMAN by Charles Beaumont                     If    Sep 1952
   (Originally appeared under title THE BEAUTIFUL PEOPLE)
THE ALTAR AT MIDNIGHT by C. M. Kornbluth                    Glxy  Nov 1952
THE LAST DAYS OF SHANDAKER by Leigh Brackett  (Mrs. Edmond Hamilton) Stg  Apr 1952
THE PEACEMAKER by Alfred Coppel                             If    Jan 1953
LISTEN by Gordon R. Dickson                                 F&SF  Aug 1952
STAR, BRIGHT by Mark Clifton                                Glxy  Jul 1952
THE TIMELESS ONES by Eric Frank Russell                     SFQ   Nov 1952
THE BIG HUNGER by Walter M. Miller, Jr.                     ASF   Oct 1952

TALES OF OUTER SPACE          Ace Books, Inc.; New York, N. Y.      Mag.    Year
5 stories   140 pages   .35¢   D-73   September 7, 1954

To the Moon
    DOORWAY IN THE SKY by Ralph Williams                           ASF    Jan 1954
        (Originally appeared under title BERTHA)
To Mars
    HERE LIE WE by Fox B. Holden                                   Stg    Jun 1953
To the Sun's Edge
    OPERATION MERCURY by Clifford D. Simak                         ASF    Mar 1941
        (Originally appeared under title MASQUERADE)
To the Stars
    LORD OF A THOUSAND SUNS by Poul Anderson                        PS    Sep 1951
Beyond the Stars
    BEHIND THE BLACK NEBULA by L. Ron Hubbard                      ASF    Jan 1942
        (Originally appeared under title THE INVADERS)
    (Double binding of two anthologies — See listing ADVENTURES IN THE FAR FUTURE)


    TERROR IN THE MODERN VEIN          Hanover House; Garden City, N. Y.
    17 stories   315 pages   $3.95   April 4, 1955


THE CROQUET PLAYER by H. G. Wells              (From THE CROQUET PLAYER; 1936)
THEY by Robert A. Heinlein                                        Unk    Apr 1941
FRITZCHEN by Charles Beaumont                                  OSF #1    n/d 1953
THE GIRL WITH THE HUNGRY EYES by Fritz Leiber, Jr.
        (From THE GIRL WITH THE HUNGRY EYES & OTHER STORIES; 1949)
            Edited by Donald A. Wollheim
THE FISHING SEASON by Robert Sheckley                            TWS    Aug 1952
THE CROWD by Ray Bradbury                                         WT    May 1943
HE by H. P. Lovecraft                                             WT    Sep 1926
THE STRANGE CASE OF LEMUEL JENKINS by Philip M. Fisher, Jr.      AIs    7/26/19
THE RAG THING by David Grinnel                                   F&SF   Oct 1951
THE BURROW by Franz Kafka
        (From THE GREAT WALL OF CHINA; 1946)
GONE AWAY by A. E. Coppard
        (From FEARFUL PLEASURES; 1946)
THE SILENCE by Bernard McLaughlin                                StI    Jun 1941
MIMIC by Donald A. Wollheim                                      Ash    Dec 1942
        (Originally appeared under pseudonym Martin Pearson)
SHIPSHAPE HOME by Richard Matheson                               GIxy   Jul 1952
THE DREAM MAKERS by Robert Bloch                                 BFF    Sep 1953
THE REPUBLIC OF THE SOUTHERN CROSS by Valery Brussof

        (From THE SOUTHERN CROSS AND OTHER STORIES; 1919)
THE INHERITORS by Robert W. Lowndes and John Michael             FFSF   Oct 1942

THE ULTIMATE INVADER AND OTHER SCIENCE FICTION          Mag.    Year
4 stories  139 pages  .35¢  D-44  March 7, 1954    Ace Books, Inc.; N. Y. N.Y.

STORIES FROM THE FOUR CORNERS OF TIME

The Farthest Future
    THE ULTIMATE INVADER by Eric Frank Russell          PS    Jan 1953

The Near Future
    ALIEN ENVOY by Malcolm Jameson                      ASF   Nov 1944

The Near Past
    MALIGNANT MARAUDER by Murray Leinster ps (Will F. Jenkins)   TWS   Sum 1946
      (Originally appeared under title DEAD CITY)

The Farthest Past
    THE TEMPORAL TRANSGRESSOR by Frank Belknap Long, Jr.    ASF   Aug 1944
      (Originally appeared under title BRIDGEHEAD)

ZACHERLY
    ZACHERLY'S MIDNIGHT SNACKS          Ballantine Books, Inc.; New York, N. Y.
    9 stories  157 pages  .35¢  #370K  February 1960

SORRY, RIGHT NUMBER by Richard Matheson                Bynd  Nov 1953
SHARE ALIKE by Jerome Bixby and Joe E. Dean            Bynd  Jul 1953
TALENT by Theodore Sturgeon                            Bynd  Sep 1953
LISTEN, CHILDREN, LISTEN by Wallace West               FU    Nov 1953
THE WHISPERING GALLERY by William F. Temple            FU    Nov 1953
THE PIPING DEATH by Robert Moore Williams              Unk   May 1939
THE GHOST by A. E. Van Vogt                            Unk   Aug 1942
CARILLON OF SKULLS by Philip James                     Unk   Feb 1941
PILE OF TROUBLE by Henry Kuttner                       TWS   Apr 1948

    ZACHERLY'S VULTURE STEW          Ballantine Books, Inc.; New York, N. Y.
    9 stories  160 pages  .35¢  #417K  August 1960

HE DIDN'T LIKE CATS by L. Ron Hubbard                  Unk   Feb 1942
DR. JACOBUS MELIFLORE'S LAST PATIENT by Mindret Lord   F&SF  Nov 1953
THE DEVIL IS NOT MOCKED by Manly Wade Wellman          Unk   Jun 1943
BONES by Donald A. Wollheim                            Sti   Feb 1941
OUT OF THE JAR by Charles Tanner                       Sti   Feb 1941
THE WITCH by A. E. Van Vogt                            Unk   Feb 1943
THEY BITE by Anthony Boucher                           Unk   Aug 1943
THE SHED by E. Everett Evans                           AvR   Jan 1953
THERE SHALL BE NO DARKNESS by James Blish              TWS   Apr 1950

Mag.    Year

A. Botts and the Moebius Strip by William Hazlett Upson..............SEP  12/22/45
    FANTASIA MATHEMATICA [Fadiman-1958]
Abominable by Fredric Brown.......................................Dude  Mar 1960
    SIXTH ANNUAL OF THE YEAR'S BEST SF [Merril-1961]
Abduction of Abner Green, The by Nelson Bond......................BB  Jun 1941
    SCIENCE FICTION CARNIVAL [Brown & Reynolds - 1953]
Absalom by Henry Kuttner..........................................Stg  Fal 1946
    TOMORROW, THE STARS [Heinlein-1952]
Accountant, The by Robert Sheckley................................F&SF  Jul 1954
    THE BEST FROM FANTASY & SCIENCE FICTION: 4th SERIES [Boucher - 1955]
Action On Azura by Robertson Osborne....................(See Listing Contact Inc.)
Adam and Eve and Pinch Me by A. E. Coppard...................................
    (From Adam and Eve and Pinch Me; 1921)
        THE MOONLIGHT TRAVELER [Stern - 1943]
        CHILDREN OF WONDER [Tenn - 1953]
Adam and No Eve by Alfred Bester..................................ASF  Sep 1941
    ADVENTURES IN TIME AND SPACE [Healy & McComas - 1946]
Adam Link's Vengeance by Eando Binder ps (Otto Binder)............Amz  Feb 1940
    THE OTHER WORLDS [Stong - 1941]
Adaptive Ultimate, The by John Jessell ps (Stanley G. Weinbaum)......Amz  Nov 1953
    THE OTHER WORLDS [Stong - 1941]
Adjustment by Ward Moore..........................................F&SF  May 1957
    THE BEST FROM FANTASY & SCIENCE FICTION: 7th SERIES [Boucher - 1958]
Adjustment Team by Philip K. Dick.................................Orb #4  Sep 1954
    THE SANDS OF MARS AND OTHER STORIES [Anonymous - 1958]
Adrift On The Policy Level by Chan Davis.........................ORIGINAL STORY
    STAR SCIENCE FICTION STORIES #5 [Pohl - 1959]
Advent On Channel Twelve, The by C. M. Kornbluth.................ORIGINAL STORY
    STAR SCIENCE FICTION STORIES #4 [Pohl - 1958]
    STAR OF STARS [Pohl - 1960]
Adventure in a Space Ship by C. S. Lewis.....(From Out of the Silent Planet; 1938)
    SCIENCE IN FICTION [A. E. M. & J. C. Bayliss - 1957]
Adventure in The Fourth Dimension, An by Farnsworth Wright...........WT  Oct 1923
    THE MOON TERROR AND OTHER STORIES [Anonymous - 1927]
Adventure Of The Ball Of Nostradamus, The by Mack Reynolds & August Derleth.......
                                         F&SF  Jul 1955

    THE SCIENCE FICTIONAL SHERLOCK HOLMES [Peterson - 1960]
Adventure Of The Misplaced Hound, The by Poul Anderson & Gordon R. Dickson........
                                         USF  Dec 1953

    THE SCIENCE FICTIONAL SHERLOCK HOLMES [Peterson - 1960]
Adventure Of The Snitch In Time, The by Mack Reynolds & August Derleth............
    THE SCIENCE FICTIONAL SHERLOCK HOLMES [Peterson - 1960]     F&SF  Jul 1953

                                                              Mag.    Year

Adventure On Mars by Richard M. Elam, Jr. .......................SP  Dec 1952
    SCIENCE FICTION AND READER'S GUIDE [Barrows - 1954]
Adventurer, The by C. M. Kornbluth................................Spc  May 1953
    ASSIGNMENT IN TOMORROW [Pohl - 1954]
Aepyornis Island by H. G. Wells................................PMB  Xmas 1894
    JOURNEYS IN SCIENCE FICTION [Loughlin & Popp - 1961]
Afterthought by H. B. Fyfe....................................Fw/SFS  Jan 1951
    BEYOND HUMAN KEN [Merril - 1952]
Age of Prophecy, The by Margaret St. Clair...................Fw/SFS  Mar 1951
    SCIENCE FICTION ADVENTURES IN MUTATION [Conklin - 1956]
Agent of Vega by James H. Schmitz................................ASF  Jun 1949
    SPACE POLICE [Norton - 1956]
Alas, All Thinking! by Harry Bates..............................Ast  Jun 1935
    THE OTHER WORLDS [Stong - 1941]
    IMAGINATION UNLIMITED [Bleiler & Dikty - 1952]
Alexander The Bait by William Tenn ps (Philip Klass).............ASF  May 1946
    THE OMNIBUS OF SCIENCE FICTION [Conklin - 1952]
Alien by Lester del Rey....................................ORIGINAL STORY
    STAR SCIENCE FICTION STORIES #3 [Pohl - 1954]
Alien Envoy by Malcolm Jameson.................................ASF  Nov 1944
    THE ULTIMATE INVADER AND OTHER SCIENCE FICTION [Woolheim - 1954]
Alien Night by Thomas N. Scortia.............................SFAd  Aug 1957
    GET OUT OF MY SKY [Margulies - 1960]
All About the Thing by Randall Garrett.............(Parody).........SFS  May 1956
    (Originally appeared as a feature under general title PARODIES TOSSED.  This
    parody appeared under title JOHN W. CAMPBELL JR.'S WHO GOES THERE?)
    SF: 57 THE YEAR'S GREATEST SCIENCE FICTION AND FANTASY [Merril - 1957]
All Hallows by Walter de la Mare.....................(From The Connosseur; 1926)
    THE MOONLIGHT TRAVELER [Stern - 1943]
All Roads by Mona Farnsworth..................................Unk  Aug 1940
    EDITOR'S CHOICE IN SCIENCE FICTION [Moskowitz - 1954]
    (Story selected by John W. Campbell, Jr.)
All Summer In a Day by Ray Bradbury...........................F&SF  Mar 1954
    THE BEST FROM FANTASY & SCIENCE FICTION: 4th SERIES [Boucher - 1955]
All The Time In the World by Arthur C. Clarke...................Stg  Jul 1952
    PRIZE SCIENCE FICTION [Wollheim - 1953]
"All You Zombies ——" by Robert A. Heinlein....................F&SF  Mar 1959
    THE BEST FROM FANTASY & SCIENCE FICTION: 9th SERIES [Mills - 1960]
Allegory by William T. Powers..................................ASF  Apr 1953
    13 GREAT STORIES OF SCIENCE FICTION [Conklin - 1960]
Almost Human by Robert Bloch....................................FA  Jun 1943
    (Originally appeared under pseudonym Tarleton Fiske)
    MY BEST SCIENCE FICTION STORY [Margulies & Friend - 1949]
Alpha In Omega by Jonathan Stones...................(London Observer Prize Story)
    A. D. 2500 [Wilson - 1955]
Altar at Midnight, The by C. M. Kornbluth.....................Glxy  Mar 1952
    BEST SF TWO SCIENCE FICTION STORIES [Crispin - 1956]
Alternative, The by Maurice Baring.............................
    (From Half A Minute's Silence and Other Stories; 1925)
    TRAVELERS IN TIME [Stern - 1947]
Altruists, The by Idris Seabright ps (Margaret St. Clair)..........F&SF  Nov 1953
    PORTALS OF TOMORROW [Derleth - 1954]
Amazing Mrs. Mimms, The by David C. Knight.......................FU  Aug 1958
    THE FANTASTIC UNIVERSE OMNIBUS [Santesson - 1960]
Ambassadors, The by Anthony Boucher.............................Stg  Jun 1952
    FUTURE TENSE [Crossen - 1953]
    GALAXY OF GHOULS [Merril - 1955]
Ambassadors from Venus, The by Kendall Foster Crossen..............PS  Mar 1951
    BEACHHEADS IN SPACE [Derleth - 1954]

                                                                    Mag.    **Year**
Ambition by William L. Bade.............................................Glxy   Oct 1951
    SCIENCE FICTION ADVENTURES IN DIMENSION [Conklin - 1953]
Analogues, The by Damon Knight......................................ASF    Jan 1952
    13 GREAT STORIES OF SCIENCE FICTION [Conklin - 1960]
Ancient Brain, The by A. G. Stangland...............................SWS    Oct 1929
    FROM OFF THIS WORLD [Margulies & Friend - 1949]
Ancient Gulliver, An by Lucien......(From A True History; Written about 165 A.D.)
    SCIENCE IN FICTION [A. E. M. and J. C. Bayliss - 1957]
"...And a Star To Steer By..." by Lee Correy ps (G. Harry Stine)....ASF  Jun 1953
    EVERY BOY'S BOOK OF OUTER SPACE STORIES [Dikty - 1960]
And Adam Begot by Arch Oboler..(From This Freedom: Thirteen New Radio Plays;1942)
    OUT OF THIS WORLD [Fast - 1944]
And Be Merry by Katherine MacLean...................................ASF    Feb 1950
    THE OMNIBUS OF SCIENCE FICTION [Conklin - 1952]
" — And He Built a Crooked House — " by Robert A. Heinlein........ASF   Feb 1941
    THE POCKET BOOK OF SCIENCE FICTION [Wollheim - 1943]
    FANTASIA MATHEMATICA [Fadiman - 1958]
...And It Comes Out Here by Lester del Rey..........................Glxy   Feb 1951
    SCIENCE FICTION ADVENTURES IN DIMENSION [Conklin - 1953]
And Lo! The Bird by Nelson Bond.....................................BB     Sep 1950
    FAR BOUNDARIES [Derleth - 1951]
And Now the News... by Theodore Sturgeon............................F&SF   Dec 1956
    THE BEST FROM FANTASY & SCIENCE FICTION: 6th SERIES [Boucher - 1957]
And Someday To Mars by Frank Belknap Long...........................TWS    Feb 1952
    EDITOR'S CHOICE IN SCIENCE FICTION [Moskowitz - 1954]
    (Story selected by Samuel Mines)
...And the Moon Be Still as Bright by Ray Bradbury..................TWS    Jun 1948
    THE BEST SCIENCE FICTION STORIES: 1949 [Bleiler & Dikty - 1949]
And The Truth Shall Make You Free by Clifford D. Simak..(See listing The Answers)
And The Walls Came Tumbling Down by John Wyndham ps (John Beynon Harris).........
                                                                   Stg   May 1951
    BEACHHEADS IN SPACE [Derleth - 1954]
And Then There Were None by Eric Frank Russell......................ASF    Jun 1951
    YEAR'S BEST SCIENCE FICTION NOVELS: 1952 [Bleiler & Dikty - 1952]
    STORIES FOR TOMORROW [Sloane - 1953]
And Thou Beside Me by Mack Reynolds.................................F&SF   Apr 1954
    SCIENCE FICTION ADVENTURES IN MUTATION [Conklin - 1956]
Angel Was A Yankee, The by Stephen Vincent Benet...................Mcl    Oct 1940
    BEYOND HUMAN KEN [Merril - 1952]
Angel's Egg by Edgar Pangborn......................................Glxy   Jun 1951
    INVADERS OF EARTH [Conklin - 1952]
    BEST SF TWO SCIENCE FICTION STORIES [Crispin - 1956]
Angels In The Jets by Jerome Bixby.................................FA     Fal 1952
    ASSIGNMENT IN TOMORROW [Pohl - 1954]
Angerhelm by Cordwainer Smith....................................ORIGINAL STORY
    STAR SCIENCE FICTION STORIES #6 [Pohl - 1959]
Anomaly of the Empty Man, The by Anthony Boucher...................F&SF   Apr 1952
    THE SCIENCE FICTIONAL SHERLOCK HOLMES [Peterson - 1960]
Another Antigone by D. A. C. Morrison..............London Observer Prize Story
    A. D. 2500 [Wilson - 1955]
Another Word for Man by Robert Presslie.............................NW #78 Dec 1958
    OUT OF THIS WORLD 2 [Williams-Ellis & Owen - 1961]
Answer by Hal Clement ps (Harry Clement Stubbs).....................ASF    Apr 1947
    SCIENCE FICTION THINKING MACHINES [Conklin - 1954]
Answer, The by Fredric Brown...................(From Angels and Spaceships; 1954)
    BEST SF THREE SCIENCE FICTION STORIES [Crispin - 1958]
Answers, The by Clifford D. Simak..................................Fut    Mar 1953
    STORIES FOR TOMORROW [Sloane-1953] (Org aprd as "AND THE TRUTH SHALL MAKE YOU FREE
Ant and the Eye, The by Chad Oliver................................ASF    Apr 1953
    STORIES FOR TOMORROW [Sloane - 1953]

                                                              Mag.    Year
Anti-Climax, The by Winona McClintic..........(verse)..............F&SF  Jul 1956
    THE BEST FROM FANTASY & SCIENCE FICTION: 6th SERIES [Boucher - 1957]
Anticipator, The by Morley Roberts.........................................
    (From The Keepers Of The Waters and Other Stories; 1898)
    TRAVELERS IN TIME [Stern - 1947]
Any More At Home Like You? by Chad Oliver.........................ORIGINAL STORY
    STAR SCIENCE FICTION STORIES #3 [Pohl - 1954]
Anything by Philip St. John ps (Lester del Rey)..................Unk  Oct 1939
    FROM UNKNOWN WORLDS [Campbell - 1948]
Anything Box by Zeena Henderson.................................F&SF  Oct 1956
    SF: 57 THE YEAR'S GREATEST SCIENCE FICTION AND FANTASY [Merril - 1957]
Appearance of Man, The by John D. Beresford.........(From Signs and Wonders; 1921)
    THE OTHER SIDE OF THE MOON [Derleth - 1949]
Appendix and the Spectacles, The by Miles J. Breuer.................Amz  Dec 1928
    THE SCIENCE FICTION GALAXY [Conklin - 1950]
Appointment In Tommorow by Fritz Leiber, Jr.......................Glxy  Jul 1951
    THE BEST SCIENCE FICTION STORIES: 1952 [Bleiler & Dikty - 1952]
    TOMORROW, THE STARS [Heinlein - 1952] (Appeared under title POOR SUPERMAN)
Apres Nous by Avram Davidson.....................................F&SF  Mar 1960
    THE BEST FROM FANTASY & SCIENCE FICTION: 10th SERIES [Mills - 1961]
Ararat by Zeena Henderson........................................F&SF  Oct 1952
    THE BEST SCIENCE FICTION STORIES: 1953 [Bleiler & Dikty - 1953]
Arena by Fredric Brown...........................................ASF  Jun 1944
    THE BIG BOOK OF SCIENCE FICTION [Conklin - 1950]
    SCIENCE FICTION TERROR TALES [Conklin - 1955]
Arithmetic by Carl Sandburg..........(verse)...........(From COMPLETE POEMS; 1950)
    FANTASIA MATHEMATICA [Fadiman - 1958]
As Never Was by P. Schuyler Miller. .............................ASF  Jan 1944
    ADVENTURES IN TIME AND SPACE [Healy & McComas - 1946]
Asa Rule, The by Jay Williams....................................F&SF  Jun 1956
    THE BEST FROM FANTASY & SCIENCE FICTION: 6th SERIES [Boucher - 1957]
Ask Me Anything by Damon Knight..................................Glxy  May 1951
    THE GALAXY READER OF SCIENCE FICTION [Gold - 1952]
Asleep In Armageddon by Ray Bradbury.............................PS  Win 1948
    POSSIBLE WORLDS OF SCIENCE FICTION [Conklin - 1951]
    BEYOND THE STARS AND OTHER STORIES [Anonymous - 1958]
Assignment On Pasik by Murray Leinster ps (Will F. Jenkins)..........TWS  Feb 1949
    ADVENTURES ON OTHER PLANETS [Wollheim - 1955]
Assignment To Aldebaran by Kendall Foster Crossen.................TWS  Feb 1953
    YEAR'S BEST SCIENCE FICTION NOVELS: 1954 [Bleiler & Dikty - 1954]
Assisted Passage by James White..................................NW #19  Jan 1953
    GATEWAY TO THE STARS [Carnell - 1955]
Assumption Unjustified by Hal Clement ps (Harry Clement Stubbs)......ASF  Oct 1946
    CROSSROADS IN TIME [Conklin - 1953]
Asteroid Of Fear by Raymond Z. Gallun............................PS  Mar 1951
    SPACE PIONEERS [Norton - 1954]
Asteroid Of Gold, The by Clifford D. Simak.......................WS  Nov 1932
    EVERY BOY'S BOOK OF SCIENCE FICTION [Wollheim - 1951]
Asylum by A. E. Van Vogt.........................................ASF  May 1942
    ADVENTURES IN TIME AND SPACE [Healy & McComas - 1946]
At No Extra Cost by Peter Phillips...............................Mvl  Aug 1951
    THE BEST SCIENCE FICTION STORIES: 1952 [Bleiler & Dikty - 1952]
At The Mountains Of Madness by H. P. Lovecraft...................Ast  Feb 1936
    STRANGE PORTS OF CALL [Derleth - 1948]
Atavists, The by G. A. Rymer.....................(London Observer Prize Story)
    A. D. 2500 [Wilson - 1955]
Atlantis by Plato................................(Written about 370 B. C.)
    BEYOND TIME AND SPACE [Derleth - 1950]

(94)

Mag.     Year

Atlantis by E. E. Smith...........(Excerpts).............(From Triplanetary; 1950)
    JOURNEY TO INFINITY [Greenberg - 1951]
Atomic Power by Don A. Stuart ps (John W. Campbell, Jr.).............Ast  Dec 1934
    THE BEST OF SCIENCE FICTION [Conklin - 1946]
Attic Voice, The by Algis J. Budrys................(See listing under Nightsound)
Attitude by Hal Clement ps (Harry Clement Stubbs)...................ASF  Sep 1943
    TRAVELERS OF SPACE [Greenberg - 1952]
Attitudes by Philip Jose Farmer......................................F&SF  Oct 1953
    THE BEST FROM FANTASY & SCIENCE FICTION: 3rd SERIES [Boucher & McComas-1954]
August Heat by W. F. Harvey...(Fr The Beast With Five Fingers & Other Tales; 1928)
    TRAVELERS IN TIME [Stern - 1947]
Aunt Cassie by Virginia Swain...............................ORIGINAL STORY
    THE OTHER WORLDS [Stong - 1941]
Aunt Elsie's Stairway by Anthony Riker............(See listing Between Two Worlds)
Automata by S. Fowler Wright..........................................WT  Sep 1929
    SCIENCE FICTION THINKING MACHINES [Conklin - 1954]
Automaton by A. E. Van Vogt...........................................OW  Sep 1950
    ADVENTURES IN TOMORROW [Crossen - 1951]
Available Data On The Warp Reaction, The by Lion Miller.............F&SF  Sep 1953
    BEST SF THREE SCIENCE FICTION STORIES [Crispin - 1958]
    13 GREAT STORIES OF SCIENCE FICTION [Conklin - 1960]
Avenging Ray, The by Seamark ps (Austin J. Hall)...................................
    (Originally published in 1930)     (excerpts)
    SCIENCE IN FICTION [A.E.M. & J.C. Bayliss - 1957]
Axolotl by Robert Abernathy.........................................F&SF  Jan 1954
    THE BEST SCIENCE FICTION STORIES AND NOVELS: 1955 [Dikty - 1955]

# B

B + M —— 4 by Gerald Heard.................................ORIGINAL STORY
    NEW TALES OF SPACE AND TIME [Healy - 1951]
Baby Is Three by Theodore Sturgeon................................Glxy  Oct 1952
    CHILDREN OF WONDER [Tenn - 1953]
Baby Killers by Rose Bedrick Elliot.......................ORIGINAL STORY
    FUTURE TENSE [Crossen - 1953]
Baby On Neptune, A by Clare Winger Harris & Miles J. Breuer, M.D. ...Amz  Dec 1929
    FLIGHT INTO SPACE [Wollheim - 1950]
Back There In The Grass by Gouverneur Morris.....(From It and Other Stories; 1922)
    WORLD OF WONDER [Pratt - 1951]
Back To Julie by Richard Wilson.................................Glxy  May 1954
    ASSIGNMENT IN TOMORROW [Pohl - 1954]
Backfire by Ross Rocklynne......................................ASF  Jan 1943
    THE OMNIBUS OF SCIENCE FICTION [Conklin - 1952]
Backwardness by Poul Anderson...................................F&SF  Mar 1958
    THE BEST FROM FANTASY & SCIENCE FICTION: 8th SERIES [Boucher - 1959]
Bad Day For Sales, A by Fritz Leiber.............................Glxy  Jul 1953
    SHADOW OF TOMORROW [Pohl - 1953]
    THE SECOND GALAXY READER OF SCIENCE FICTION [Gold - 1954]
    THE BEST SCIENCE FICTION STORIES: 1954 [Bleiler & Dikty - 1954]
Bait by Roy L. Clough Jr. ......................................ASF  Jun 1951
    SPACE POLICE [Norton - 1956]

Balance by John Christopher ps (Christopher S. Youd)                NW #9  Spr 1951
    THE BEST SCIENCE FICTION STORIES: 1952 [Bleiler & Dikty - 1952]
    NO PLACE LIKE EARTH [Carnell - 1952]
Balaam by Anthony Boucher.......................................ORIGINAL STORY
    9 TALES OF SPACE AND TIME [Healy - 1954]
    BEST SF FOUR SCIENCE FICTION STORIES [Crispin - 1961]
Ballard Of The Shoshonu by Gordon R. Dickson.........(Song).........ORIGINAL STORY
    SIXTH ANNUAL OF THE YEAR'S BEST SF [Merril - 1961]
Barbarian, The by Poul Anderson...................................F&SF  May 1956
    THE BEST FROM FANTASY & SCIENCE FICTION: 6th SERIES [Boucher - 1957]
Barney by Will Stanton............................................F&SF  Feb 1951
    THE BEST FROM FANTASY & SCIENCE FICTION [Boucher & McComas - 1952]
Barrier, The by Anthony Boucher....................................ASF  Sep 1942
    6 GREAT SHORT NOVELS OF SCIENCE FICTION [Conklin - 1954]
Barrier Of Dread by Judith Merril.............................Fw/SFS  Aug 1950
    JOURNEY TO INFINITY [Greenberg - 1951]
Bathe Your Bearings In Blood by Clifford D. Simak.....(See listing under SKIRMISH)
Battle, The by Robert Sheckley......................................If  Sep 1954
    THE FIRST WORLD OF IF [Quinn & Wulff - 1957]
Battle Of The Monsters, The by Morgan Robertson.................................
    (From Where The Angels Fear To Tread and Other Tales Of The Sea; 1899)
    BEYOND TIME AND SPACE [Derleth - 1950]
Battle of The S...s, The by Bruce Elliott.....................ORIGINAL STORY
    FUTURE TENSE [Crossen - 1953]
Battle Of The Unborn by James Blish..........................Fw/SFS  Jun 1950
    SCIENCE FICTION ADVENTURES IN MUTATION [Conklin - 1956]
    D
    a
Baxbr by Evelyn E. Smith.......................................ORIGINAL STORY
    b    TIME TO COME [Derleth - 1954]
    r    BEST SF FOUR SCIENCE FICTION STORIES [Crispin - 1961]
         JOURNEYS IN SCIENCE FICTION [Loughlin & Popp - 1961]
Beach Scene by Marshall King......................................Glxy  Oct 1960
    SIXTH ANNUAL OF THE YEAR'S BEST SF [Merril - 1961]
Beanstalk by James Blish.......................................ORIGINAL STORY
    FUTURE TENSE [Crossen - 1953]
Beast Of The Void, A [La Bete Du Vide] by Raymond Z. Gallun.........Ast  Sep 1936
    ESCALES DANS L'INFINI [Gallet - 1954]
Beautiful, Beautiful, Beautiful! by Stuart Friedman.................Fut  Mar 1952
    WORLDS OF TOMORROW [Derleth - 1953]
Beautiful People, The by Charles Beaumont..(See listing under THE BEAUTIFUL WOMAN)
Beautiful Things, The by Arthur Zirul.............................FU  May 1958
    SF 59 THE YEAR'S GREATEST SCIENCE FICTION AND FANTASY [Merril - 1959]
Beautiful Woman, The by Charles Beaumont..........................If  Jan 1953
    (Originally appeared under title The Beautiful People)
    PRIZE SCIENCE FICTION [Wollheim - 1953]
Beep by James Blish................................................Glxy  Feb 1954
    STORIES FOR TOMORROW [Sloane - 1954]
    SPACE POLICE [Norton - 1956]
Bees From The Borneo, The by Will H. Gray.........................Amz  Feb 1931
    THE OMNIBUS OF SCIENCE FICTION [Conklin - 1952]
Before The Dawn by John Taine ps (Eric Temple Bell)...........................
    (Originally published in 1934 by the Williams & Wilkins Co.)
    THE PORTABLE NOVELS OF SCIENCE [Wollheim - 1945]
Behind The Black Nebula by L. Ron Hubbard.........................ASF  Jan 1942
    (Originally appeared under title The Invaders)
    TALES OF OUTER SPACE [Wollheim - 1954]

Mag.    Year

Behold It Was A Dream by Rhoda Broughton......(From Tales For Christmas Eve; 1873)
    BEYOND THE BARRIERS OF SPACE AND TIME [Merril - 1954]
Belief by Isaac Asimov...............................................ASF  Oct 1953
    BEYOND THE BARRIERS OF SPACE AND TIME [Merril - 1954]
Berom by John Berryman...............................................ASF  Jan 1951
    IMAGINATION UNLIMITED [Bleiler & Dikty - 1952]
Bertha by Ralph Williams............................(See listing Doorway In The Sky)
Bertrand Russell's Dream by G. H. Hardy.....(From A Mathematician's Apology; 1948)
    FANTASIA MATHEMATICA [Fadiman - 1958]
Betelgeuse Bridge by William Tenn ps (Philip Klass).................Glxy  Apr 1951
    TOMORROW, THE STARS [Heinlein - 1952]
    THE GALAXY READER OF SCIENCE FICTION [Gold - 1952]
Better Bet, The by Anthony Brode.............(verse).................F&SF  Feb 1958
    THE BEST FROM FANTASY & SCIENCE FICTION: 8th SERIES [Boucher - 1959]
Better Choice, The by S. Fowler Wright...........................ORIGINAL STORY
    SCIENCE FICTION ADVENTURES IN MUTATION [Conklin - 1956]
Betty Ann by Kris Neville........................................ORIGINAL STORY
    NEW TALES OF SPACE AND TIME [Healy - 1951]
Between The Minute And The Hour by A.M. Burrage....(From Some Ghost Stories; 1927)
    TRAVELERS IN TIME [Stern - 1947]
Between The Thunder And The Sun by Chad Oliver.....................F&SF  May 1957
    THE BEST FROM FANTASY & SCIENCE FICTION: 7th SERIES [Boucher - 1958]
Between Two Worlds by Anthony Riker...............................Orb #5  Nov 1954
    (Originally appeared under title Aunt Elsie's Stairway)
    SPACE STATION 42 AND OTHER STORIES [Anonymous - 1958]
Beyond Bedlam by Wyman Guin.......................................Glxy  Aug 1951
    THE GALAXY READER OF SCIENCE FICTION [Gold - 1952]
Beyond Doubt by Robert A. Heinlein and Elma Wentz..................Ash  Apr 1941
    (Originally appeared under byline Lyle Monroe (pseudonym) and Elma Wentz)
    BEYOND THE END OF TIME [Pohl - 1952]
Beyond Space And Time by Joel Townsley Rogers.....................SSS  Sep 1950
    A TREASURY OF GREAT SCIENCE FICTION [Boucher - 1959]
Beyond The Singing Flame by Clark Ashton Smith....................WS  Nov 1931
    FROM OFF THIS WORLD [Margulies & Friend - 1949]
Beyond The Stars by John Berryman......................(See listing Space Rating)
Beyond The Wall Of Sleep by H. P. Lovecraft.......................WT  Mar 1938
    THE OTHER SIDE OF THE MOON [Derleth - 1949]
Big Contest, The by John D. MacDonald.............................WB  Dec 1950
    HUMAN? [Merril - 1954]
Big Holiday, The by Fritz Leiber..................................F&SF  Jan 1953
    THE BEST SCIENCE FICTION STORIES: 1954 [Bleiler & Dikty - 1954]
Big Hunger, The by Walter M. Miller, Jr...........................ASF  Oct 1952
    PRIZE SCIENCE FICTION [Wollheim - 1953]
Big Trek, The by Fritz Leiber.....................................F&SF  Oct 1957
    THE BEST FROM FANTASY & SCIENCE FICTION: 7th SERIES [Boucher - 1958]
Big Trip Up Yonder, The by Kurt Vonnegut, Jr......................Glxy  Jan 1954
    ASSIGNMENT IN TOMORROW [Pohl - 1954]
Biography Project, The by Dudley Dell ps (H. L. Gold).............Glxy  Sep 1951
    THE GALAXY READER OF SCIENCE FICTION [Gold - 1952]
Birds Can't Count by Mildred Clingerman...........................F&SF  Feb 1955
    THE BEST FROM FANTASY & SCIENCE FICTION: 5th SERIES [Boucher - 1956]
    SF: THE YEAR'S GREATEST SCIENCE FICTION AND FANTASY [Merril - 1956]
Birthmark, The by Nathaniel Hawthorne........(From Mosses From An Old Manse; 1846)
    JOURNEYS IN SCIENCE FICTION [Loughlin & Popp - 1961]
Bite, They by Anthony Boucher.....................................Unk  Aug 1943
    ZACHERLY'S VULTURE STEW [Zacherly - 1960]
Bitterest Pill, The by Frederik Pohl..............................Glxy  Apr 1959
    THE FIFTH GALAXY READER [Gold - 1961]
Black Ball, The by Fletcher Pratt and L. Sprague de Camp..........F&SF  Oct 1952
    THE BEST FROM FANTASY & SCIENCE FICTION: 2nd SERIES [Boucher & McComas-1953]

|  | Mag. | Year |
|---|---|---|

Black Cats by Christel Hastings.............(verse)...............Unk  Dec 1940
    FROM UNKNOWN WORLDS [Campbell - 1948]
Black Charlie by Gordon R. Dickson...................................Glxy  Apr 1954
    THE FIFTH GALAXY READER [Gold - 1961]
Black Destroyer by A. E. Van Vogt...................................ASF  Jul 1939
    ADVENTURES IN TIME AND SPACE [Healy & McComas - 1946]
Black Eyes and the Daily Grind by Milton Lesser.....................If  Mar 1952
    STORIES FOR TOMORROW [Sloane - 1954]
Black Pits of Luna, The by Robert A. Heinlein.......................SEP  1/10/48
    POSSIBLE WORLDS OF SCIENCE FICTION [Conklin - 1951]
    STORIES OF SCIENTIFIC IMAGINATION [Gallant - 1954]
    SCIENCE FICTION AND READER'S GUIDE [Barrows - 1954]
Black Tower, The by Brian J. McNaughton & Andrew Duane ps (Robert W. Briney).....
    SHANADU [Briney - 1953]  ·ORIGINAL STORY
Blacksword by A. J. Offutt.........................................Glxy  Dec 1959
    MIND PARTNER AND 8 OTHER NOVELETS FROM GALAXY [Gold - 1961]
Blank Form by Arthur Sellings.....................................Glxy  Jul 1958
    FOURTH GALAXY READER OF SCIENCE FICTION [Gold - 1959]
Blast, The by Stuart Cloete.......................................Col  4/12/47
    SIX GREAT SHORT NOVELS OF SCIENCE FICTION [Conklin - 1954]
Blaze of Glory by Randall Garrett............(verse)..............F&SF  Dec 1955
    THE BEST FROM FANTASY & SCIENCE FICTION: 6th SERIES [Boucher - 1957]
Blight, The by Arthur J. Cox......................................ORIGINAL STORY
    TIME TO COME [Derleth - 1954]
Blind Alley by Isaac Asimov.......................................ASF  Mar 1945
    THE BEST OF SCIENCE FICTION [Conklin - 1946]
Blind Alley by Malcolm Jameson....................................Unk  Jun 1943
    GREAT STORIES OF SCIENCE FICTION [Leinster - 1951]
Blind Man's Buff [Colin-Maillard] by J. U. Giesy..................AIS  1/24/20
    ESCALES DANS L'INFINI [Gallet - 1954]
Blind Man's Buff by Malcolm Jameson...............................ASF  Oct 1944
    IMAGINATION UNLIMITED [Bleiler and Dikty - 1952]
    EVERY BOY'S BOOK OF OUTER SPACE STORIES [Dikty - 1960]
Blind Pilot, The by Charles Henneberg............................F&SF  Jan 1960
    (Translated from French by Damon Knight)
    THE BEST FROM FANTASY & SCIENCE FICTION: 10th SERIES [Mills - 1961]
Blinding Shadows, The by Donald Wandrei...........................Ast  May 1934
    BEACHHEADS IN SPACE [Derleth - 1954]
Blindman's World, The by Edward Bellamy...........................
    (From The Blindman's World and Other Stories; 1898)
    BEYOND TIME AND SPACE [Derleth - 1950]
Blindness by John W. Campbell, Jr.................................Ast  Mar 1935
    (Originally appeared under psuedonym Don A. Stuart)
    MY BEST SCIENCE FICTION STORY [Margulies and Friend - 1949]
Bliss of Solitude, The by J.T. M'Intosh...(See listing under Hallucination Orbit)
Blond Kid, The by Herb Sutherland...................London Observer Prize Story
    A. D. 2500 [Wilson - 1955]
Blood by Fredric Brown.............................................. F&SF  Feb 1955
    GALAXY OF GHOULS [Merril - 1955]
Blood Bank by Walter M. Miller, Jr. ..............................ASF  Jun 1952
    ALL ABOUT THE FUTURE [Greenberg - 1955]
Blood's A Rover by Chad Oliver....................................ASF  May 1952
    OPERATION FUTURE [Conklin - 1955]
Blowup Blues by Theodore R. Cogswell...........(song)............ORIGINAL STORY
    SIXTH ANNUAL OF THE YEAR'S BEST SF [Merril - 1961]

```
                                                              Mag.    Year
Blowups Happen by Robert A. Heinlein...............................ASF   Sep 1940
     THE BEST OF SCIENCE FICTION [Conklin - 1946]
     THE ASTOUNDING SCIENCE FICTION ANTHOLOGY [J. W. Campbell Jr - 1952]
     BEST SF TWO SCIENCE FICTION STORIES [Crispin - 1956]
Blue Giraffe, The [La Girafe Bleue] by L. Sprague de Camp..........ASF   Aug 1939
     ADVENTURES IN TIME AND SPACE [Healy & McComas - 1946]
     WORLD OF WONDER [Pratt - 1951]
     ESCALES DANS L'INFINI [Gallet - 1954]
Blue Star, The by Fletcher Pratt.................................ORIGINAL STORY
     WITCHES THREE [Pratt - 1952]
Blunder by Philip Wylie............................................Col    1/12/46
     STRANGE PORTS OF CALL [Derleth - 1948]
     SHOT IN THE DARK [Merril - 1950]
Bodyguard by Christopher Grimm.....................................Glxy   Feb 1956
     BODYGUARD AND FOUR OTHER SHORT NOVELS FROM GALAXY [Gold - 1960]
Bomb In The Bathtub, The by Thomas N. Scortia......................Glxy   Feb 1957
     THE FOURTH GALAXY READER OF SCIENCE FICTION [Gold - 1959]
Bones by Donald A. Wollheim........................................Sti    Feb 1941
     ZACHERLY'S VULTURE STEW [Zacherly - 1960]
Boomerang by Eric Frank Russell.....................................FU    Sep 1953
     SCIENCE FICTION THINKING MACHINES [Conklin - 1954]
Born Of Man And Woman by Richard Matheson..........................F&SF   Sum 1950
     THE BEST SCIENCE FICTION STORIES: 1951 [Bleiler & Dikty - 1951]
     CHILDREN OF WONDER [Tenn - 1953]
Botany Bay by P. M. Hubbard........................................F&SF   Feb 1955
     THE BEST FROM FANTASY & SCIENCE FICTION: 5th SERIES [Boucher - 1956]
Bottle Imp, The by Robert Louis Stevenson..........................B&W    Mar 1891
     THE MOONLIGHT TRAVELER [Stern - 1943]
Bounty Hunter, The by Avram Davidson................................FU    Mar 1958
     THE FANTASTIC UNIVERSE OMNIBUS [Santesson - 1960]
Boy Next Door, The by Chad Oliver..................................F&SF   Jun 1951
     HUMAN? [Merril - 1954]
Box, The by James Blish............................................TWS    Apr 1949
     THE OMNIBUS OF SCIENCE FICTION [Conklin - 1952]
Brain by S. Fowler Wright...........................(From The New Gods Lead; 1932 )
     ADVENTURES IN TIME AND SPACE [Healy & McComas - 1946]
Brain, The by W. Norbet ps (Dr. Norbett Weiner)....................TEN    Apr 1952
     CROSSROADS IN TIME [Conklin - 1953]
Brain Wave by Poul Anderson.......(Originally published by Ballantine Books; 1954)
     A TREASURY OF GREAT SCIENCE FICTION [Boucher - 1959]
Brave New World by Aldous Huxley.....................(excerpts)..............
     (Originally published by Garden City Publishing Co.; 1933)
     THE TREASURY OF SCIENCE FICTION CLASSICS [Kuebler - 1955]
Brave New World by J. Francis McComas..............................F&SF   Sep 1954
     THE BEST FROM FANTASY & SCIENCE FICTION: 4th SERIES [Boucher - 1955]
Breakdown by Jack Williamson.......................................Ast    Sep 1948
     JOURNEY TO INFINITY [Greenberg - 1951]
Breaking Strain by Arthur C. Clarke.....(See l'sting Thirty Seconds — Thirty Days)
"Breeds There A Man...?" by Isaac Asimov...........................ASF    Jun 1951
     BEACHHEADS IN SPACE [Derleth - 1954]
Bridge Crossing by Dave Dryfoos....................................Glxy   May 1951
     BEYOND THE END OF TIME [Pohl - 1952]
Bridgehead by Frank Belknap Long.....(See listing under The Temporal Transgressor)
Bridle And Saddle by Isaac Asimov..................................ASF    Jun 1942
     MEN AGAINST THE STARS [Greenberg - 1950]
```

                                                                  Mag.     Year
Bright Destruction by Winona McClintic.........(verse).............F&SF  Jun 1956
    THE BEST FROM FANTASY & SCIENCE FICTION: 6th SERIES [Boucher - 1957]
Brightness Fall From The Air by Idris Seabright ps (Margaret St. Clair)
                                                                  F&SF  Apr 1951
    THE BEST SCIENCE FICTION STORIES: 1952 [Bleiler & Dikty - 1952]
Brightside Crossing by Alan E. Nourse..........................Glxy  Jan 1956
    THE WORLD THAT COULDN'T BE AND 8 OTHER NOVELETTES FROM GALAXY [Gold - 1959]
Broken Record, The by J. T. McIntosh ps (James J. MacGregor)......NW #17  Sep 1952
    THE BEST FROM NEW WORLDS [Carnell - 1955]
Bronze Parrot, The by R. Austin Freeman....(From The Great Portrait Mystery; 1924)
    SHOT IN THE DARK [Merril - 1950]
Brooklyn Project by William Tenn ps (Philip Klass)...................PS  Fal 1948
    SHOT IN THE DARK [Merril - 1950]
Brotherhood of Keepers, The by Dean McLaughlin...................ASF  Jul 1960
    SIXTH ANNUAL OF THE YEAR'S BEST SF [Merril - 1961]
Brothers Beyond The Void by Paul W. Fairman....................FA  Mar 1952
    WORLDS OF TOMORROW [Derleth - 1953]
Budding Explorer by Ralph Robin.................................F&SF  Sep 1952
    THE BEST FROM FANTASY & SCIENCE FICTION: 2nd SERIES [Boucher & McComas-1953]
Built Up Logically by Howard Schoenfeld..........................Retort  Win 1949
    (Originally appeared under title The Universal Tancea)   Rpnt - F&SF  Fal 1950
    THE BEST FROM FANTASY & SCIENCE FICTION [Boucher & McComas - 1952]
Bulkhead by Theodore Sturgeon..................................Glxy  Mar 1955
    (Originally appeared under title WHO?)
    SF: THE YEAR'S GREATEST SCIENCE FICTION AND FANTASY [Merril - 1956]
Bullard Reflects by Malcolm Jameson..............................ASF  Dec 1941
    A TREASURY OF GREAT SCIENCE FICTION [Boucher - 1959]
Bulletin by Shirley Jackson....................................F&SF  Mar 1954
    THE BEST FROM FANTASY & SCIENCE FICTION: 4th SERIES [Boucher - 1955]
Bureau of Slick Tricks by H. B. Fyfe............................ASF  Dec 1948
    TRAVELERS OF SPACE [Greenberg - 1952]
Burning Bright by John S. Browning ps (Robert Moore Williams)........ASF  Jul 1948
    THE ROBOT AND THE MAN [Greenberg - 1953]
Burrow, The by Franz Kafka...............(From The Great Wall of China; 1946)
    TERROR IN THE MODERN VEIN [Wollheim - 1955]
Business, As Usual, The by Mack Reynolds.......................F&SF  Jun 1952
    WORLDS OF TOMORROW [Derleth - 1953]
Business of Killing by Fritz Leiber, Jr. .......................ASF  Sep 1944
    SCIENCE FICTION ADVENTURES IN DIMENSION [Conklin - 1953]
But Who Can Replace A Man? by Brian Aldiss.....................Inf  Jun 1958
    OUT OF THIS WORLD 2 [Williams-Ellis & Owen - 1961]
But Without Horns by Norvell W. Page...........................Unk  Jun 1940
    FIVE SCIENCE FICTION NOVELS [Greenberg - 1952]
Butch by Poul Anderson..................................ORIGINAL STORY
    TIME TO COME [Derleth - 1954]
Butterfly Kiss, The by Arthur Dekker Savage.............(See listing The Last Man)
By His Bootstraps by Anson MacDonald ps (Robert A. Heinlein).........ASF  Oct 1941
    ADVENTURES IN TIME AND SPACE [Healy & McComas - 1946]
    THE GIANT ANTHOLOGY OF SCIENCE FICTION [Margulies & Friend - 1954]
        (Appeared under Robert A. Heinlein byline)
    SPECTRUM [Amis & Conquest - 1961]
By The Waters of Babylon by Stephen Vincent Benet...................SEP  7/31/37
    (Originally appeared under title The Place Of The Gods)
    THE POCKET BOOK OF SCIENCE FICTION [Wollheim - 1943]
By Virtue Of Circumference by Peter van Dresser...................AmB  Nov 1937
    THE YEAR AFTER TOMORROW [Del Rey, Matschat & Carmer - 1952]

# C

|  | Mag. | Year |
|---|---|---|

C-Chute by Isaac Asimov............................................Glxy  Oct 1951
    SHADOW OF TOMORROW [Pohl - 1953]
    THE SECOND GALAXY READER OF SCIENCE FICTION [Gold - 1954]
Cabin Boy by Damon Knight........................................Glxy  Sep 1951
    THE GALAXY READER OF SCIENCE FICTION [Gold - 1952]
Cage, The by Bertram Chandler....................................F&SF  Jun 1957
    THE BEST FROM FANTASY & SCIENCE FICTION: 7th SERIES [Boucher - 1958]
Call Him Demon by Henry Kuttner..................................TWS   Fal 1946
    (Originally appeared under pseudonym Keith Hammond)
    STRANGE PORTS OF CALL [Derleth - 1948]
Call Me Adam by Winston K. Marks.................................F&SF  Feb 1954
    OPERATION FUTURE [Conklin - 1955]
Call Me Joe by Poul Anderson.....................................ASF   Apr 1957
    THE BEST SCIENCE FICTION STORIES AND NOVELS: 9th SERIES [Dikty - 1958]
Call Me Mister by Anthony Brode...........(verse)...............F&SF  Feb 1959
    THE BEST FROM FANTASY & SCIENCE FICTION: 9th SERIES [Mills - 1960]
Calling All Martians by Willy Ley.......(See listing A Letter to the Martians)
Canal Builders, The by Robert Abernathy.........................ASF   Jan 1945
    EVERY BOY'S BOOK OF OUTER SPACE STORIES [Dikty - 1960]
Canterville Ghost, The by Oscar Wilde..........................C&SR  3/2/1887
    OUT OF THIS WORLD [Fast - 1944]
Canticle For Leibowitz, A by Walter M. Miller, Jr. ............F&SF  Apr 1955
    THE BEST FROM FANTASY & SCIENCE FICTION: 5th SERIES [Boucher - 1956]
    THE BEST SCIENCE FICTION STORIES AND NOVELS: 1956 [Dikty - 1956]
Captain Nemo's Thunderbolt by Jules Verne.......................................
    (From 20,000 Leagues Under The Sea; 1873)
    SCIENCE IN FICTION [A. E. M. & J. C. Bayliss - 1957]
Captive Audience by Ann Warren Griffith.........................F&SF  Aug 1953
    THE BEST FROM FANTASY & SCIENCE FICTION: 3rd SERIES [Boucher & McComas-1954]
Captive Market by Philip K. Dick.................................If    Apr 1955
    THE FIRST WORLD OF IF [Quinn & Wulff - 1957]
Captivity by Zeena Henderson....................................F&SF  Jun 1958
    THE BEST FROM FANTASY & SCIENCE FICTION: 8th SERIES [Boucher - 1959]
Captured Cross-Section, The by Miles J. Breuer...................Amz   Feb 1929
    FANTASIA MATHEMATICA [Fadiman - 1958]
Careless Love by Albert Compton Friborg.........................F&SF  Jul 1954
    THE BEST FROM FANTASY & SCIENCE FICTION: 4th SERIES [Boucher - 1955]
    THE BEST SCIENCE FICTION STORIES AND NOVELS: 1955 [Dikty - 1955]
Caretaker by James H. Schmitz...................................Glxy  Jul 1953
    THE SECOND GALAXY READER OF SCIENCE FICTION [Gold - 1954]
Carillon of Skulls by Philip James..............................Unk   Feb 1941
    ZACHERLY'S MIDNIGHT SNACKS [Zacherly - 1960]
Carriers, The by Sam Merwin, Jr. ...............................TWS   Feb 1949
    MY BEST SCIENCE FICTION STORY [Margulies & Friend - 1949]
Case of Conscience, A by James Blish............................If    Sep 1953
    BEST SF SCIENCE FICTION STORIES [Crispin - 1955]

                                                          Mag.    Year
Case Of Omega Smith, The by Buthram Walsh............(London Observer Prize Story)
   A. D. 2500 [Wilson - 1955]
Casey Agonistes by R. M. McKenna.....................................F&SF  Sep 1958
   THE BEST FROM FANTASY & SCIENCE FICTION: 9th SERIES [Mills - 1960]
Castaway by George Whitley ps (A. Bertram Chandler)...................WT  Nov 1947
   NO PLACE LIKE EARTH [Carnell - 1952]
   SCIENCE FICTION ADVENTURES IN DIMENSION [Conklin - 1953]
      (Appeared under A. Bertram Chandler byline)
Castaway by Robert Moore Williams....................................ASF  Feb 1941
   INVADERS OF EARTH [Conklin - 1952]
Castaway, The by Nelson Bond.........................................PS   Win 1940
   (Originally appeared under pseudonym George Danzell)
   INVASION FROM MARS [Welles - 1949]
Catch That Martian by Damon Knight..................................Glxy  Mar 1952
   THE OMNIBUS OF SCIENCE FICTION [Conklin - 1952]
Category Phoenix by Boyd Ellanby ps (William C. & Lyle G. Boyd).....Glxy  May 1952
   YEAR'S BEST SCIENCE FICTION NOVELS: 1953 [Bleiler & Dikty - 1953]
Causes, The by Idris Seabright ps (Margaret St. Clair)..............F&SF  Jun 1952
   A DECADE OF FANTASY & SCIENCE FICTION [Mills - 1960]
Cave, The by P. Schuyler Miller.....................................ASF  Jan 1943
   CROSSROADS IN TIME [Conklin - 1953]
Cave Of Night, The by James E. Gunn................................Glxy  Feb 1955
   SF: THE YEAR'S GREATEST SCIENCE FICTION & FANTASY [Merril - 1956]
Celephais by H. P. Lovecraft.........................................MT   May 1934
   THE GARDEN OF FEAR AND OTHER STORIES [Crawford - 1945]
Celestial Omnibus, The by E. M. Forster..............................
   (From The Celestial Omnibus and Other Stories; 1923)
   THE MOONLIGHT TRAVELER [Stern - 1943]
Census Takers, The by Frederik Pohl.................................F&SF  Feb 1956
   THE BEST FROM FANTASY & SCIENCE FICTION: 6th SERIES [Boucher - 1957]
Century Jumper by August Derleth...................................Orb #2  n/d 1954
   (Originally appeared under title A Traveler In Time)
   BEYOND THE STARS AND OTHER STORIES [Anonymous - 1958]
Cerebrative Psittacoid, The by H. Nearing, Jr......................F&SF  Aug 1953
   BEST SF SCIENCE FICTION STORIES [Crispin - 1955]
Certificate, The by Avram Davidson.................................F&SF  Mar 1959
   A DECADE OF FANTASY & SCIENCE FICTION [Mills - 1960]
Chain Of Command by Stephen Arr ps (Stephen A. Rynas)..............Glxy  May 1954
   SCIENCE FICTION ADVENTURES IN MUTATION [Conklin - 1956]
Chain Reaction by Algis Budrys.....................................ASF  Apr 1957
   (Originally appeared under pseudonym John A. Sentry)
   SIX GREAT SHORT NOVELS OF SCIENCE FICTION [Conklin - 1960]
Chapter Ends, The by Poul Anderson.................................DSF  Jan 1954
   ADVENTURES IN THE FAR FUTURE [Wollheim - 1954]
Cheery Soul, The by Elizabeth Bowen.............(From Ivy Gripped The Steps; 1941)
   THE BEST FROM FANTASY & SCIENCE FICTION: 2nd SERIES [Boucher & McComas-1953]
Chemical Plant by Ian Williams.....................................NW #8  Win 1950
   NO PLACE LIKE EARTH [Carnell - 1952]
   OUT OF THIS WORLD 1 [Williams-Ellis & Owen - 1960]
Chicken Or The Egghead, The by Frank Fenton.....................ORIGINAL STORY
   9 TALES OF SPACE AND TIME [Healy - 1954]
Chief by Henry Slesar...............................................Plby  Jun 1960
   (Originally appeared under general heading Four Fables)
   SIXTH ANNUAL OF THE YEAR'S BEST SF [Merril - 1961]
Child By Chronos by Charles L. Harness.............................F&SF  Jun 1953
   THE BEST FROM FANTASY & SCIENCE FICTION: 3rd SERIES [Boucher & McComas-1954]

| | Mag. | Year |
|---|---|---|
| Child Is Crying, A by John D. MacDonald............................... | TWS | Dec 1948 |
|     THE SCIENCE FICTION GALAXY [Conklin - 1950] | | |
| Child Of Void by Margaret St. Clair.................................. | SSS | Nov 1949 |
|     INVADERS OF EARTH [Conklin - 1952] | | |
| Child Who Believed, The by Grace Amundson........................... | SEP | 12/16/50 |
|     THE SATURDAY EVENING POST FANTASY STORIES [Fles - 1951] | | |
| Children Of The "Betsy-B." by Malcolm Jameson....................... | ASF | Mar 1939 |
|     A TREASURY OF SCIENCE FICTION [Conklin - 1948] | | |
| Children's Hour, The by Henry Kuttner................................ | ASF | Mar 1944 |
|     (Originally appeared under pseudonym Lawrence O'Donnell) | | |
|     FOUR FOR THE FUTURE [Conklin - 1959] | | |
|     A TREASURY OF GREAT SCIENCE FICTION [Boucher - 1959] | | |
| Child's Play by Mary-Alice Schnirring............................... | WT | Mar 1942 |
|     CHILDREN OF WONDER [Tenn - 1953] | | |
| Child's Play by William Tenn ps (Philip Klass)...................... | ASF | Mar 1947 |
|     A TREASURY OF SCIENCE FICTION [Conklin - 1948] | | |
|     WORLD OF WONDER [Pratt - 1951] | | |
|     THE ASTOUNDING SCIENCE FICTION ANTHOLOGY [Campbell - 1952] | | |
|     GALAXY OF GHOULS [Merril - 1955] | | |
| Choice, The by W. Hilton Young...................................... | Pch | 3/19/52 |
|     THE OMNIBUS OF SCIENCE FICTION [Conklin - 1952] | | |
| Chore For A Spaceman by Walt Sheldon................................ | TWS | Dec 1950 |
|     SPACE SERVICE [Norton - 1953] | | |
| Christmas On Ganymede by Isaac Asimov............................... | Stg | Jan 1942 |
|     ADVENTURES IN TOMORROW [Crossen - 1951] | | |
| Christmas Tree by Christopher S. Youd............................... | ASF | Feb 1949 |
|     TRAVELERS OF SPACE [Greenberg - 1952] | | |
| Christmas Trombone by Raymond E. Banks.............................. | F&SF | Jan 1954 |
|     THE BEST SCIENCE FICTION STORIES AND NOVELS: 1955 [Dikty - 1955] | | |
| Chrome Pastures by Robert F. Young.................................. | If | Apr 1956 |
|     THE SECOND WORLD OF IF [Quinn & Wulff - 1958] | | |
| Chromium Helmet, The by Theodore Sturgeon........................... | ASF | Jun 1946 |
|     GREAT STORIES OF SCIENCE FICTION [Leinster - 1951] | | |
| Chronicler, The by A. E. Van Vogt................................... | ASF | Nov 1946 |
|     FIVE SCIENCE FICTION NOVELS [Greenberg - 1952] | | |
| Chronoclasm, The by John Wyndham ps (John Beynon Harris)............ | ORIGINAL STORY |
|     STAR SCIENCE FICTION STORIES [Pohl - 1953] | | |
| Chronokinesis Of Jonathan Hull, The by Anthony Boucher.............. | ASF | Jun 1946 |
|     GREAT STORIES OF SCIENCE FICTION [Leinster - 1951] | | |
| Chrysalis, The by P. Schuyler Miller............................... | Ast | Apr 1936 |
|     A TREASURY OF SCIENCE FICTION [Conklin - 1948] | | |
| Circle, The by Christopher Morley.................................. | (No data available) |
|     FANTASIA MATHEMATICA [Fadiman - 1958] | | |
| Circle And The Square, The by Thomas Dekker........................ | |
|     (verse)    (From The Honest Whore, Part II, Act I, Scene 3; 1650) | | |
|     FANTASIA MATHEMATICA [Fadiman - 1958] | | |
| Circus by Peter Hawkins............................................. | SF #5 | Aug 1952 |
|     GATEWAY TO THE STARS [Carnell - 1955] | | |
| City Of Force, The by Daniel F. Galouye............................. | Glxy | Apr 1959 |
|     BODYGUARD AND FOUR OTHER SHORT NOVELS FROM GALAXY [Gold - 1960] | | |
| City Of The Singing Flame, The by Clark Ashton Smith................ | WS | Jul 1931 |
|     THE OTHER SIDE OF THE MOON [Derleth - 1949] | | |
|     FROM OFF THIS WORLD [Margulies & Friend - 1949] | | |
| City Of The Sun, The by Giovanni Domenico Campenella............... | |
|     (Written 1623; published in Paris, France: 1634) | | |
|     BEYOND TIME AND SPACE [Derleth - 1950] | | |

```
                                                            Mag.    Year
Civilization Game, The by Clifford D. Simak........................Glxy  Nov 1958
    MIND PARTNER AND 8 OTHER NOVELETS FROM GALAXY [Gold - 1961]
Civilized by Mark Clifton and Alex Apostolides.....................Glxy  Aug 1953
    (Originally appeared under title We're Civilized)
    PORTALS OF TOMORROW [Derleth - 1954]
Clash by Night by Lawrence O'Donnell ps (Henry Kuttner & C. L. Moore)...........
                                                            ASF    Mar 1943
    THE ASTOUNDING SCIENCE FICTION ANTHOLOGY [J. W. Campbell - 1952]
Classical Query Composed While Shampooing by Doris Pitkin Buck.........(verse)....
                                                            F&SF   Jul 1959
    THE BEST FROM FANTASY & SCIENCE FICTION: 9th SERIES [Mills - 1960]
Claustrophile, The by Theodore Sturgeon............................Glxy  Aug 1956
    FOUR FOR THE FUTURE [Conklin - 1959]
Clerical Error by Mark Clifton.......................................ASF Feb 1956
    THE BEST SCIENCE FICTION STORIES & NOVELS: 1956 [Dikty - 1956]
Clinic, The by Theodore Sturgeon................................ORIGINAL STORY
    STAR SCIENCE FICTION STORIES #2 [Pohl - 1953]
Cloak, The by Robert Bloch........................................Unk  May 1939
    FROM UNKNOWN WORLDS [J. W. Campbell - 1948]
Clock, The by A. E. W. Mason...........(From The Four Corners Of The World; 1917)
    TRAVELERS IN TIME [Stern - 1947]
Closed Door, The by Kendall Foster Crossen........................Amz  Sep 1953
    SPACE POLICE [Norton - 1956]
Club Secretary by Lord Dunsany..........(From Mr. Jorkens Remembers Africa; 1934)
    OUT OF THIS WORLD [Fast - 1944]
C/o Mr. Makepeace by Peter Phillips...............................F&SF Feb 1954
    OPERATION FUTURE [Conklin - 1955]
Co-operate - or Else! by A. E. Van Vogt............................ASF Apr 1942
    THE OUTER REACHES [Derleth - 1951]
Cobbler, Cobbler, Mend My Shoe by Jan Struther ps (Joyce Maxtone Graham)..........
                                                            WR     11/9/29
    THE MOONLIGHT TRAVELER [Stern - 1947]
Cocoon, The by John B. L. Goodwin.................................Stry Sep 1946
    TIMELESS STORIES FOR TODAY AND TOMORROW [Bradbury - 1952]
Cold Equations, The by Tom Godwin.................................ASF  Aug 1954
    THE BEST SCIENCE FICTION STORIES & NOVELS: 1955 [Dikty - 1955]
    BEST SF THREE SCIENCE FICTION STORIES [Crispin - 1958]
    BEYOND THE STARS AND OTHER STORIES [Anonymous - 1958]
    ASPECTS OF SCIENCE FICTION [Doherty - 1959]
Cold Front by Hal Clement ps (Harry Clement Stubbs).................ASF Jul 1946
    MEN AGAINST THE STARS [Greenberg - 1950]
Cold Green-eye, The by Jack Williamson.............................Fnt  Mar 1953
    SCIENCE FICTION SHOWCASE [M. Kornbluth - 1959]
Cold Night For Dying, A by Milton Lesser...........................If   Dec 1954
    THE FIRST WORLD OF IF [Quinn & Wulff - 1957]
Cold War by Henry Kuttner..........................................TWS  Oct 1949
    SCIENCE FICTION ADVENTURES IN MUTATION [Conklin - 1956]
Cold War by Kris Neville...........................................ASF  Oct 1949
    THE ASTOUNDING SCIENCE FICTION ANTHOLOGY [Campbell - 1952]
Collector, The by H. F. Heard.....................................F&SF Aug 1951
    THE BEST FROM FANTASY & SCIENCE FICTION [Boucher & McComas - 1952]
Collectors, The by G. Gordon Dewey and Max Dancey.................Amz  Jun 1953
    THE BEST SCIENCE FICTION STORIES: 1954 [Bleiler & Dikty - 1954]
Colonists, The by Raymond F. Jones.................................If   Jun 1954
    THE SECOND WORLD OF IF [Quinn & Wulff - 1958]
```

                                                                    Mag.     Year
Colossus by Howard Wandrei................................................Ast    Jan 1934
    (Originally appeared under title Colossus Eternal)
    BEYOND TIME AND SPACE [Derleth - 1950]
Colour Out Of Space, The by H. P. Lovecraft............................Amz    Sep 1927
    THE OMNIBUS OF SCIENCE FICTION [Conklin - 1952]
Columbus Was A Dope by Lyle Monroe ps (Robert A. Heinlein)...........Stg    May 1947
    (Originally appeared under byline Robert A. Heinlein)
    TRAVELERS OF SPACE [Greenberg - 1952]
Come Into My Parlor by Manly Wade Wellman......................ORIGINAL STORY
    THE GIRL WITH THE HUNGRY EYES AND OTHER STORIES [Wollheim - 1949]
Come On Wagon! by Zeena Henderson......................................F&SF   Dec 1951
    THE BEST FROM FANTASY & SCIENCE FICTION: 2nd SERIES [Boucher & McComas-1953]
Comedian's Children, The by Theodore Sturgeon.........................VSF    May 1958
    SF: 59 THE YEAR'S GREATEST SCIENCE FICTION & FANTASY [Merril - 1959]
Comedy Of Eras, The by Kelvin Kent ps (Henry Kuttner)................TWS    Sep 1940
    THE OTHER WORLDS [Stong - 1941]
Coming Attractions by Fritz Leiber, Jr...............................Glxy   Nov 1950
    THE BEST SCIENCE FICTION STORIES: 1951 [Bleiler & Dikty - 1951]
    THE GALAXY READER OF SCIENCE FICTION [Gold - 1952]
Command by Bernard I. Kahn...........................................ASF    Jan 1947
    SPACE SERVICE [Norton - 1953]
Command Performance by Walter M. Miller, Jr..........................Glxy   Nov 1952
    THE BEST SCIENCE FICTION STORIES: 1953 [Bleiler & Dikty - 1953]
    THE GALAXY READER OF SCIENCE FICTION [Gold - 1954]
    PENGUIN SCIENCE FICTION [Aldiss - 1961]
Common Denominator by John D. MacDonald..............................Glxy   Jul 1951
    THE GALAXY READER OF SCIENCE FICTION [Gold - 1952]
Common Time by James Blish...........................................SFQ    Aug 1953
    SHADOW OF TOMORROW [Pohl - 1953]
Compassion Circuit by John Wyndham ps (John Beynon Harris)...........FU     Dec 1954
    13 GREAT STORIES OF SCIENCE FICTION [Conklin - 1960]
Company Store by Robert Silverberg...........................ORIGINAL STORY
    STAR SCIENCE FICTION STORIES #5 [Pohl - 1959]
Competition by E. Mayne Hull (Mrs. A. E. Van Vogt)...................ASF    Jun 1943
    MEN AGAINST THE STARS [Greenberg - 1950]
Compleat Werewolf, The by Anthony Boucher............................Unk    Apr 1942
    FROM UNKNOWN WORLDS [J. W. Campbell - 1948]
    BEYOND HUMAN KEN [Merril - 1952]
Completely Automatic by Theodore Sturgeon............................ASF    Feb 1941
    POSSIBLE WORLDS OF SCIENCE FICTION [Conklin - 1951]
Compound B by David Harold Fink, M. D. ......................ORIGINAL STORY
    9 TALES OF SPACE AND TIME [Healy - 1954]
Compounded Interest by Mack Reynolds.................................F&SF   Aug 1956
    SF: 57 THE YEAR'S GREATEST SCIENCE FICTION AND FANTASY [Merril - 1957]
Conditionally Human by Walter M. Miller, Jr..........................Glxy   Feb 1952
    YEAR'S BEST SCIENCE FICTION NOVELS: 1953 [Bleiler & Dikty - 1953]
Cones by Frank Belknap Long, Jr......................................Ast    Feb 1936
    POSSIBLE WORLDS OF SCIENCE FICTION [Conklin - 1951]
Congruent People, The by A. J. Budrys.......................ORIGINAL STORY
    STAR SCIENCE FICTION STORIES #2 [Pohl - 1953]
Conjure Wife by Fritz Leiber, Jr.....................................Unk    Apr 1943
    WITCHES THREE [Pratt - 1952]
Connecticut Yankee In King Arthur's Court by Mark Twain ps (Samuel L. Clements)...
    (Condensed Version)  (Originally published by Harper and Brothers; 1889)
    STORIES OF SCIENTIFIC IMAGINATION [Gallant - 1954]

                                                              Mag.    Year
Conqueror, The by Mark Clifton........................................ASF  Aug 1952
    THE OMNIBUS OF SCIENCE FICTION [Conklin - 1952]
    THE BEST SCIENCE FICTION STORIES: 1953 [Bleiler & Dikty - 1953]
Conquerors' Isle by Nelson S. Bond....................................BB  Jun 1946
    THE OTHER SIDE OF THE MOON [Derleth - 1949]
    WORLD OF WONDER [Pratt - 1951]
    STORIES OF SCIENTIFIC IMAGINATION [Gallant - 1954]
Conquest by Anthony Boucher......................................ORIGINAL STORY
    STAR SCIENCE FICTION STORIES #2 [Pohl - 1953]
Conquest Of Gola, The by Leslie F. Stone ps (Mrs. Wm. Silberberg).....WS  Apr 1931
    THE BEST OF SCIENCE FICTION [Conklin - 1946]
Conquest Of Life by Eando Binder ps (Otto Binder)....................TWS  Aug 1937
    FROM OFF THIS WORLD [Margulies & Friend - 1949]
Conquest Of Two Worlds, A by Edmond Hamilton.........................WS  Feb 1932
    EVERY BOY'S BOOK OF SCIENCE FICTION [Wollheim - 1951]
Considerate Hosts, The by Thorp McClusky.............................WT  Dec 1939
    THE OTHER WORLDS [Stong - 1941]
Conspiracy by John Christopher ps (Christopher S. Youd).........Auth #53  Jan 1955
    GATEWAY TO THE STARS [Carnell - 1955]
Conspirators, The by James White................................NW #24  Jun 1954
    SCIENCE FICTION ADVENTURES IN MUTATION [Conklin - 1956]
Contagion by Katherine MacLean......................................Glxy  Oct 1950
    POSSIBLE WORLDS OF SCIENCE FICTION [Conklin - 1951]
    THE BEST SCIENCE FICTION STORIES: 1951 [Bleiler & Dikty - 1951]
Contact, Inc. by Robertson Osborne...................................PS  Fal 1949
    (Originally appeared under title Action On Azura)
    THE BIG BOOK OF SCIENCE FICTION [Conklin - 1950]
    TRAVELERS OF SPACE [Greenberg - 1952]    (Aprd under title Action On Azura)
Contraption by Clifford D. Simak................................ORIGINAL STORY
    STAR SCIENCE FICTION STORIES [Pohl - 1953]
Controlled Experiment by Chad Oliver.............................Orb #5  Nov 1954
    SPACE STATION 42 AND OTHER STORIES [Anonymous - 1958]
Conversation Of Eiros And Charmion, The by Edgar Allen Poe...........BGM  Dec 1839
    THE TREASURY OF SCIENCE FICTION CLASSICS [Kuebler - 1955]
Copper Dahlia, The by Gerald Kersh...................................
    (From The Brighton Monster and Other Stories; 1953)
    BEST SF TWO SCIENCE FICTION STORIES [Crispin - 1956]
Correspondence Course by Raymond F. Jones............................ASF  Apr 1945
    ADVENTURES IN TIME AND SPACE [Healy & McComas - 1946]
Cosmic Expense Account, The by C. M. Kornbluth.....................F&SF  Jan 1956
    THE BEST FROM FANTASY & SCIENCE FICTION: 6th SERIES [Boucher - 1957]
    SF: 57 THE YEAR'S GREATEST SCIENCE FICTION AND FANTASY [Merril - 1957]
Cosmic Jackpot, The by George O. Smith.............................TWS  Oct 1958
    SCIENCE FICTION CARNIVAL [Brown & Reynolds - 1953]
Counter Charm by Peter Phillips....................................SInt  Spr 1951
    THE OMNIBUS OF SCIENCE FICTION [Conklin - 1952]
Counter-transference by William F. Temple..........................TWS  Apr 1952
    THE BEST SCIENCE FICTION STORIES: 1953 [Bleiler & Dikty - 1953]
Counterspy by Kelly Edwards.........................................ASF  Dec 1953
    BEST SF THREE SCIENCE FICTION STORIES [Crispin - 1958]
Country Doctor by William Morrison ps (Joseph Samachson)........ORIGINAL STORY
    STAR SCIENCE FICTION STORIES [Pohl - 1953]
    STAR OF STARS [Pohl - 1960]
Country Of The Kind, The by Damon Knight..........................F&SF  Feb 1956
    SF: THE YEAR'S GREATEST SCIENCE FICTION AND FANTASY [Merril - 1956]

                                                              Mag.    Year
Courtesy by Clifford D. Simak.........................................ASF   Aug 1951
     SPACE, SPACE, SPACE [Sloane - 1953]
     CROSSROADS IN TIME [Conklin - 1953]
Coventry by Robert A. Heinlein.......................................ASF   Jul 1940
     6 GREAT SHORT NOVELS OF SCIENCE FICTION [Conklin - 1954]
Cowboy Lament by Norman R. Jaffrey...........(verse)...............F&SF   Jan 1954
     THE BEST FROM FANTASY & SCIENCE FICTION: 4th SERIES [Boucher - 1955]
Crazy Joey by Mark Clifton and Alex Apostolides....................ASF   Aug 1953
     BEYOND THE BARRIERS OF SPACE AND TIME [Merril - 1954]
Crazy Maro by Daniel Keyes..........................................F&SF   Apr 1960
     THE BEST FROM FANTASY & SCIENCE FICTION: 10th SERIES [Mills - 1961]
Created He Them by Alice Eleanor Jones..............................F&SF   Jun 1955
     THE BEST FROM FANTASY & SCIENCE FICTION: 5th SERIES [Boucher - 1956]
Creature of the Snows by William Sambrot...........................SEP   10/29/60
     SIXTH ANNUAL OF THE YEAR'S BEST SF [Merril - 1961]
Crisis by Edward Grendon.............................................ASF   Jun 1951
     INVADERS OF EARTH [Conklin - 1952]
Crisis In Utopia by Norman L. Knight................................ASF   Jul 1940
     FIVE SCIENCE FICTION NOVELS [Greenberg - 1952]
Critical Factor by Hal Clement ps (Harry Clement Stubbs)...........ORIGINAL STORY
     STAR SCIENCE FICTION STORIES #2 [Pohl - 1953]
Critters, The by Frank Belknap Long, Jr. .........................ASF   Nov 1945
     THE OUTER REACHES [Derleth - 1951]
Croquet Player, The by H. G. Wells................(From The Croquet Player; 1936)
     TERROR IN THE MODERN VEIN [Wollheim - 1955]
Cross of Centuries, A by Henry Kuttner............................ORIGINAL STORY
     STAR SCIENCE FICTION STORIES #4 [Pohl - 1958]
     STAR OF STARS [Pohl - 1960]
Crowd, The by Ray Bradbury...........................................WT   May 1943
     TERROR IN THE MODERN VEIN [Wollheim - 1955]
Crucible of Power, The by Jack Williamson..........................ASF   Feb 1939
     FIVE SCIENCE FICTION NOVELS [Greenberg - 1952]
Crucifixus Etiam by Walter M. Miller, Jr. .........................ASF   Feb 1953
     HUMAN? [Merril - 1954]
     THE BEST SCIENCE FICTION STORIES: 1954 [Bleiler & Dikty - 1954]
Cruise of The S-900, The by Russell Kent..........................ORIGINAL STORY
     ADVENTURES TO COME [Esenwein - 1937]
Crystal Bullet, The by Donald Wandrei...............................WT   Mar 1941
     STRANGE PORTS OF CALL [Derleth - 1948]
Crystal Egg, The by H. G. Wells.....................................NR   May 1897
     STRANGE PORTS OF CALL [Derleth - 1948]
     ASPECTS OF SCIENCE FICTION [Doherty - 1959]
Cubic City, The by Rev. Louis Parker, D. D. ......................SWS   Sep 1929
     FROM OFF THIS WORLD [Margulies & Friend - 1949]
Culture by Jerry Shelton............................................ASF   Sep 1944
     THE BIG BOOK OF SCIENCE FICTION [Conklin - 1950]
Cunning of the Beast, The by Nelson Bond..........................BB   Nov 1942
     (Originally appeared under title Another World Begins)
     STRANGE PORTS OF CALL [Derleth - 1948]
Cure, The by Lewis Padgett ps (Henry Kuttner and C. L. Moore).......ASF   May 1946
     THE OTHER SIDE OF THE MOON [Derleth - 1949]
Cure For A Ylith by Murray Leinster ps (Will F. Jenkins............Stg   Nov 1949
     OPERATION FUTURE [Conklin - 1955]
Curfew Tolls, The by Stephen Vincent Benet........................SEP   10/5/35
     THE MOONLIGHT TRAVELER [Stern - 1943]
Curious Case of Benjamin Button, The by F. Scott Fitzgerald......................
     (From Tales of the Jazz Age; 1920)
     TRAVELERS IN TIME [Stern - 1947]
     THE TREASURY OF SCIENCE FICTION CLASSICS [Kuebler - 1955]

                                                        Mag.    Year
Cyber and Justice Holmes, The by Frank Riley.........................If  Mar 1955
    THE BEST SCIENCE FICTION STORIES AND NOVELS: 1956 [Dikty - 1956]
    THE FIRST WORLD OF IF [Quinn & Wulff - 1957]
Cyclops by H. F. Heard.............................................ORIGINAL STORY
    FUTURE TENSE [Crossen - 1953]


# D


Dagon by Avram Davidson..........................................F&SF  Oct 1959
    THE BEST FROM FANTASY & SCIENCE FICTION: 9th SERIES [Mills - 1960]
Damned Thing, The by Ambrose Bierce..............(From Can Such Things Be?; 1893)
    THE TREASURY OF SCIENCE FICTION CLASSICS [Kuebler - 1955]
Damnedest Thing, The by Garson Kanin..............................Esq  Feb 1956
    SF: 57 THE YEAR'S GREATEST SCIENCE FICTION AND FANTASY [Merril - 1957]
Dance Of A New World by John D. MacDonald.........................ASF  Sep 1948
    JOURNEY TO INFINITY [Greenberg - 1951]
Dance Of The Dead by Richard Matheson............................ORIGINAL STORY
    STAR SCIENCE FICTION STORIES #3 [Pohl - 1954]
    STAR OF STARS [Pohl - 1960]
Danger! Child At Large by C. L. Cottrell.........................ORIGINAL STORY
    STAR SCIENCE FICTION STORIES #6 [Pohl - 1959]
Dark Angel, The by Lewis Padgett ps (Henry Kuttner & C. L. Moore)...Stg  Mar 1946
    (Originally appeared under byline Henry Kuttner)
    SHOT IN THE DARK [Merril - 1950]
Dark Interlude by Mack Reynolds and Fredric Brown.................Glxy  Jan 1951
    THE GALAXY READER OF SCIENCE FICTION [Gold - 1952]
    THE BEST SCIENCE FICTION STORIES: 1952 [Bleiler & Dikty - 1952]
Dark Mission by Lester del Rey....................................ASF  Jul 1940
    A TREASURY OF SCIENCE FICTION [Conklin - 1948]
Dark Nuptial by Robert Donald Locke..............................TWS  Feb 1953
    THE BEST FROM STARTLING STORIES [Mines - 1953]
Date To Remember, A by William F. Temple.........................TWS  Aug 1949
    INVADERS OF EARTH [Conklin - 1952]
Daughters Of Earth by Judith Merril..............................ORIGINAL STORY
    THE PETRIFIED PLANET [Pratt - 1952]
David's Daddy by Rosel George Brown..............................Fnt  Jun 1960
    SIXTH ANNUAL OF THE YEAR'S BEST SF [Merril - 1961]
Davy Jones' Ambassador by Raymond Z. Gallun......................Ast  Dec 1935
    THE BEST OF SCIENCE FICTION [Conklin - 1946]
Dawn Attack by Berger Copeman....................................ORIGINAL STORY
    ADVENTURES TO COME [Eisenwein - 1937]
Dawn Of Reason, The by James H. Beard..............(verse).........Unk  Oct 1939
    FROM UNKNOWN WORLDS [J. W. Campbell - 1948]
Day At The Beach by Carol Emshwiller.............................F&SF  Aug 1959
    THE FIFTH ANNUAL OF THE YEAR'S BEST SF [Merril - 1960]
Day Is Done by Lester del Rey....................................ASF  May 1939
    OPERATION FUTURE [Conklin - 1955]
Day Of The Deepies, The by Murray Leinster ps (Will F. Jenkins).....FFM  Oct 1947
    SHOT IN THE DARK [Merril - 1950]
Day We Celebrate, The by Nelson S. Bond..........................ASF  Jan 1941
    POSSIBLE WORLDS OF SCIENCE FICTION [Conklin - 1951]
Daybroke by Robert Bloch.........................................Star  Jan 1958
    STAR OF STARS [Pohl - 1960]

                                                                    Mag.     Year
Daydream by P. Schuyler Miller........................................ORIGINAL STORY
      THE GIRL WITH THE HUNGRY EYES AND OTHER STORIES [Wollheim - 1949]
Daymare by Fredric Brown.....................................................TWS   Fal 1943
      THE SAINT'S CHOICE [Charteris - 1945]
De Profundis by Murray Leinster ps (Will F. Jenkins).................TWS   Win 1945
      FAR BOUNDARIES [Derleth - 1951]
Dead Center by Judith Merril.................................................F&SF  Nov 1954
      A TREASURY OF GREAT SCIENCE FICTION [Boucher - 1959]
Dead End by Wallace MacFarlane..............................................Glxy  Jan 1952
      SCIENCE FICTION THINKING MACHINES [Conklin - 1954]
Dead Planet, The by Edmond Hamilton.........................................Stg   Spr 1946
      WORLDS OF TOMORROW [Derleth - 1953]
Dead Ringer by Lester del Rey...............................................Glxy  Nov 1956
      THE THIRD GALAXY READER OF SCIENCE FICTION [Gold - 1958]
Deadalus by Thomas Bulfinch........................(From The Age of Fable; 1855)
      JOURNEYS IN SCIENCE FICTION [Loughlin & Popp - 1961]
Deadline by Cleve Cartmill...................................................ASF   Mar 1944
      THE BEST OF SCIENCE FICTION [Conklin - 1948]
Deadlock by Lewis Padgett ps (Henry Kuttner & C. L. Moore)..........ASF   Aug 1942
      THE ROBOT AND THE MAN [Greenberg - 1953]
Dear Devil by Eric Frank Russell............................................OW    May 1950
      THE BIG BOOK OF SCIENCE FICTION [Conklin - 1950]
      SPACE, SPACE, SPACE [Sloane - 1953]
Dear Pen Pal by A. E. Van Vogt..............................................Ark   Aut 1949
      FAR BOUNDARIES [Derleth - 1951]
Death From The Stars by A. Rowley Hilliard..................................WS    Oct 1931
      THE SCIENCE FICTION GALAXY [Conklin - 1950]
Death In The House, A by Clifford D. Simak..................................Glxy  Oct 1959
      THE FIFTH ANNUAL OF THE YEAR'S BEST SF [Merril - 1960]
Death Is The Penalty by Judith Merril.......................................ASF   Jan 1949
      BEYOND THE END OF TIME [Pohl - 1952]
Death Of Archimedes, The by Karel Capek............(From Apocryphal Stories; 1949)
      FANTASIA MATHEMATICA [Fadiman - 1958]
Death Of A Sensitive by Harry Bates.........................................SF+   May 1953
      EDITOR'S CHOICE IN SCIENCE FICTION [Moskowitz - 1954]
      (Story selected by Sam Moskowitz)
Death Of The Moon, The by Alexander M. Phillips.............................Amz   Feb 1929
      FLIGHT INTO SPACE [Wollheim - 1950]
Death Sentence by Isaac Asimov..............................................ASF   Nov 1943
      THE OUTER REACHES [Derleth - 1951]
Deep Range, The by Arthur C. Clarke.........................................ORIGINAL STORY
      STAR SCIENCE FICTION STORIES #3 [Pohl - 1954]
      STAR OF STARS [Pohl - 1960]
Defense Mechanism by Katherine MacLean......................................ASF   Oct 1949
      THE BIG BOOK OF SCIENCE FICTION [Conklin - 1950]
      BEYOND THE BARRIERS OF SPACE AND TIME [Merril - 1954]
Delay In Transit by F. L. Wallace...........................................Glxy  Sep 1952
      BODYGUARD AND FOUR OTHER SHORT NOVELS FROM GALAXY [Gold - 1960]
Demobilization by George R. Cowie...........................................Vtx   n/d 1947
      SCIENCE AND SORCERY [Ford - 1953]
Demoisells D'Ys, The by Robert W. Chambers.........(From The King In Yellow; 1895)
      (Story selected by Mary Gnaedinger)                    Rpnt — FFM  Nov 1942
      EDITOR'S CHOICE IN SCIENCE FICTION [Moskowitz - 1954]
Demon King, The by J. B. Priestly...................(From My Best Thriller; 1934)
      GALAXY OF GHOULS [Merril - 1955]
Demon Lover, The by Shirley Jackson......................(From The Lottery; 1949)
      TIMELESS STORIES FOR TODAY AND TOMORROW [Bradbury - 1952]

Demotion by Robert Donald Locke........................................ASF  Sep 1952
    PRIZE SCIENCE FICTION [Wollheim - 1953]
Derelict by William Hope Hodgson..............(From Men Of The Deep Waters; 1914)
    THE SCIENCE FICTION GALAXY [Conklin - 1950]
Derm Fool by Theodore Sturgeon.........................................Unk  Mar 1940
    CROSSROADS IN TIME [Conklin - 1953]
Descent Into The Maelstrom, A by Edgar Allan Poe.................GLGM  May 1841
    JOURNEYS IN SCIENCE FICTION [Loughlin & Popp - 1961]
Deserter, The by William Tenn ps (Philip Klass)..................ORIGINAL STORY
    STAR SCIENCE FICTION STORIES [Pohl - 1953]
Desertion by Clifford D. Simak.........................................ASF  Nov 1944
    THE BIG BOOK OF SCIENCE FICTION [Conklin - 1950]
    UBERWINDUNG VON RAUM UND ZEIT [Gunther - 1952]
        (Appeared under German translation Flucht)
    GALAXY OF GHOULS [Merril - 1955]
Design For Great Day by Eric Frank Russell......(See listing The Ultimate Invader)
Desire by James Stephens.........................(From Etched In Moonlight; 1928)
    THE MOONLIGHT TRAVELER [Stern - 1943]
Deskful Of Girls, A by Fritz Leiber....................................F&SF  Apr 1958
    THE BEST FROM FANTASY & SCIENCE FICTION: 8th SERIES [Boucher - 1959]
Desrick On Yandro, The by Manly Wade Wellman...........................F&SF  Jun 1952
    THE BEST FROM FANTASY & SCIENCE FICTION: 2nd SERIES [Boucher & McComas-1953]
Destination Moon by Robert A. Heinlein.................................SS  Sep 1950
    THREE TIMES INFINITY [Margulies - 1958]
Destiny Times Three by Fritz Leiber Jr. ...............................ASF  Mar 1945
    FIVE SCIENCE FICTION NOVELS [Greenberg - 1952]
Devil And Simon Flagg, The by Arthur Porges............................F&SF  Aug 1954
    FANTASIA MATHEMATICA [Fadiman - 1958]
Devil Is Not Mocked, The by Manly Wade Wellman.........................Unk  Jun 1943
    ZACHERLY'S VULTURE STEW [Zacherly - 1960]
Devil Of East Lupton, The by Murray Leinster ps (Will F. Jenkins)....TWS  Aug 1948
    (Originally appeared under title The Devil Of East Lupton, Vermont under
        byline William Fitzgerald)
    THE OTHER SIDE OF THE MOON [Derleth - 1949]
Devil On Salvation Bluff, The by Jack Vance............................ORIGINAL STORY
    STAR SCIENCE FICTION STORIES #3 [Pohl - 1954]
Devil Was Sick, The by Bruce Elliot....................................F&SF  Apr 1951
    ADVENTURES IN TOMORROW [Crossen - 1951]
Devil We Know, The by Henry Kuttner....................................Unk  Aug 1941
    FROM UNKNOWN WORLDS [Campbell, J. W. - 1948]
Devil's Invention, The by Alfred Bester................(See listing Oddy And Id)
Devlin by W. B. Ready..................................................F&SF  Apr 1953
    THE BEST FROM FANTASY & SCIENCE FICTION: 3rd SERIES [Boucher & McComas-1954]
Diamond As Big As The Ritz, The by F. Scott Fitzgerald.................
    (From Tales Of The Jazz Age; 1922)
    THE MOONLIGHT TRAVELER [Stern - 1943]
Didn't He Ramble by Chad Oliver.......................................F&SF  Apr 1957
    THE BEST SCIENCE FICTION STORIES & NOVELS: 9th SERIES [Dikty - 1958]
Different Purpose, A by Kem Bennett....................................F&SF  Nov 1958
    THE BEST FROM FANTASY & SCIENCE FICTION: 9th SERIES [Mills - 1960]
Digging The Weans by Robert Nathan....................................Hpr  Nov 1956
    SF: 57 THE YEAR'S GREATEST SF AND FANTASY [Merril - 1957]
Diminishing Draft, The by Waldemar Kaempffert.........................ASM  2/9/18
    THE BIG BOOK OF SCIENCE FICTION [Conklin - 1950]

                                                                    Mag.   Year
Diplomatic Coop by Daniel F. Galouye.........................................ORIGINAL STORY
    STAR SCIENCE FICTION STORIES #5 [Pohl - 1959]
Disappearing Act by Alfred Bester............................................ORIGINAL STORY
    STAR SCIENCE FICTION STORIES #2 [Pohl - 1953]
    STAR OF STARS [Pohl - 1960]
Discord Makers, The by Mack Reynolds....................................OTWA   Jul 1950
    INVADERS OF EARTH [Conklin - 1952]
Disguise by Donald A. Wollheim.........................................OW   Feb 1953
    STORIES FOR TOMORROW [Sloane - 1954]
Disintergration Machine, The by Arthur Conan Doyle...........................
    (From The Maracot Deep and Other Stories; 1929)
    JOURNEYS IN SCIENCE FICTION [Loughlin & Popp - 1961]
Disputed Authorship, A by John Kendrick Bangs...(Fr A Houseboat On The Styx; 1895)
    OUT OF THIS WORLD [Fast - 1944]
Disqualified by Charles L. Fontenay..................................If   Sep 1954
    THE FIRST WORLD OF IF [Quinn & Wulff - 1957]
Distortion, The by Shel Silverstein.............(carton)...........Plby   May 1960
    SIXTH ANNUAL OF THE YEAR'S BEST SF [Merril - 1961]
Divvil With The Women, A by Niall Wilde..............................F&SF   Jan 1960
    THE BEST FROM FANTASY & SCIENCE FICTION] 10th SERIES [Mills - 1961]
Doctor Grimshaw's Sanitarium by Fletcher Pratt......................Amz   May 1934
    MY BEST SCIENCE FICTION STORY [Margulies & Friend - 1949]
Doctor Hanray's Second Chance by Conrad Richter....................SEP   1/10/50
    THE SATURDAY EVENING POST FANTASY STORIES [Fles - 1951]
Doctrine Of Original Design, The by Winona McClintic....(verse).....F&SF   Mar 1955
    THE BEST FROM FANTASY & SCIENCE FICTION: 5th SERIES [Boucher - 1956]
Dodger Fan by Will Stanton...........................................F&SF   Jun 1957
    THE BEST FROM FANTASY & SCIENCE FICTION: 7th SERIES [Boucher - 1958]
Dominoes by C. M. Kornbluth..................................ORIGINAL STORY
    STAR SCIENCE FICTION STORIES [Pohl - 1953]
Dominions Beyond by Ward Moore.....................................SEP   8/28/54
    THE BEST SCIENCE FICTION STORIES AND NOVELS: 1955 [Dikty - 1955]
Don't Live In The Past by Damon Knight.............................Glxy   Jun 1951
    THE GALAXY READER OF SCIENCE FICTION [Gold - 1952]
Don't Look Now by Henry Kuttner....................................Stg   Mar 1948
    MY BEST SCIENCE FICTION STORY [Margulies & Friend - 1949]
Doomsday Deferred by Will F. Jenkins...............................SEP   9/24/49
    THE BEST SCIENCE FICTION STORIES: 1950 [Bleiler & Dikty - 1950]
    THE SATURDAY EVENING POST FANTASY STORIES [Fles - 1951]
Doorbell, The by David H. Keller, M. D. ..............................WS   Jun 1934
    THE OMNIBUS OF SCIENCE FICTION [Conklin - 1952]
Doorstep, The by R. Bretnor.........................................ASF   Nov 1956
    SF: 57  THE YEAR'S GREATEST SCIENCE FICTION & FANTASY [Merril - 1957]
Doorway In The Sky by Ralph Williams................................ASF   Jan 1954
    (Originally appeared under title Bertha)
    TALES OF OUTER SPACE [Wollheim - 1954]
Dormant by A. E. Van Vogt...........................................Stg   Nov 1948
    THE BEST FROM STARTLING STORIES [Mines - 1953]
    BEST SF SCIENCE FICTION STORIES [Crispin - 1955]
    ASPECTS OF SCIENCE FICTION [Doherty - 1959]
Double Dare by Robert Silverberg...................................Glxy   Nov 1956
    THE FIFTH GALAXY READER [Gold - 1961]
Double, Double, Toil And Trouble by Holley Cantine.................F&SF   Jan 1960
    THE BEST FROM FANTASY & SCIENCE FICTION: 10th SERIES [Mills - 1961]
    SIXTH ANNUAL OF THE YEAR'S BEST SF [Merril - 1961]

|  | Mag. | Year |
|---|---|---|

Double-Dyed Villians, The by Poul Anderson..............................ASF  Sep 1949
    TRAVELERS OF SPACE [Greenberg - 1952]
Double Meaning by Damon Knight.........................................Stg  Jan 1953
    THREE FROM OUT THERE [Margulies - 1959]
Doughnut Jockey by Erik Fennel........................................BB  May 1948
    THE BEST SCIENCE FICTION STORIES: 1949 [Bleiler & Dikty - 1949]
D.P.! by Jack Vance...................................................ASF&F  Apr 1953
    THE BEST SCIENCE FICTION STORIES: 1954 [Bleiler & Dikty - 1954]
D.P. From Tomorrow by Mack Reynolds....................................Orb #1  n/d 1953
    PORTALS OF 'TOMORROW [Derleth - 1954]
Dr. Jacobus Mellflore's Last Patient by Mindret Lord.................F&SF  Nov 1953
    ZACHERLY'S VULTURE STEW [Zacherly - 1960]
Dr. Lu-Mie by Clifton B. Kruse.........................................Ast  Jul 1934
    EVERY BOY'S BOOK OF SCIENCE FICTION [Wollheim - 1951]
Dr. Ox's Experiment by Jules Verne..(Fr Dr. Ox's Experiment & Other Stories; 1874)
    BEYOND TIME AND SPACE [Wollheim - 1950]
Dream Makers, The by Robert Bloch.....................................BFF  Sep 1953
    TERROR IN THE MODERN VEIN
Dream Street by Frank M. Robinson.......................................ImT  Mar 1955
    THE BEST SCIENCE FICTION STORIES AND NOVELS: 1956 [Dikty - 1956]
Dreamer, The by Alfred Coppel.........................................F&SF  Apr 1952
    THE BEST SCIENCE FICTION STORIES: 1953 [Bleiler & Dikty - 1953]
Dreamer, The by Jack Vance...........................................Orb #5  Nov 1954
    (Originally appeared under title The Enchanted Village)
    SPACE STATION 42 AND OTHER STORIES [Anonymous - 1958]
Dreaming Is A Private Thing by Isaac Asimov...........................F&SF  Dec 1955
    SF: THE YEAR'S GREATEST SF AND FANTASY [Merril - 1956]
Dreams Are Sacred by Peter Phillips...................................ASF  Sep 1948
    IMAGINATION UNLIMITED [Bleiler & Dikty - 1952]
Dream's End by Henry Kuttner...........................................Stg  Jul 194
    FUTURE TENSE [Crossen - 1953]
Dreamsman, The by Gordon R. Dickson...................................ORIGINAL STOR
    STAR SCIENCE FICTION STORIES #6 [Pohl - 1959]
    THE FIFTH ANNUAL OF THE YEAR'S BEST SF [Merril - 1960]
Dreamworld by Isaac Asimov...........................................F&SF  Nov 1955
    THE BEST FROM FANTASY & SCIENCE FICTION: 5th SERIES [Boucher - 1956]
Dress Of White Silk by Richard Matheson...............................F&SF  Oct 195
    THE BEST FROM FANTASY & SCIENCE FICTION [Boucher & McComas - 1952]
Drivers, The by Edward W. Ludwig.......................................If  Mar 195
    THE FIRST WORLD OF IF [Quinn & Wulff - 1957]
Drop, The by John Christopher ps (Christopher S. Youd)...............Glxy  Mar 195
    GATEWAY TO TOMORROW [Carnell - 1954]
Dumb Martian by John Wyndham ps (John Beynon Harris)................Glxy  Jul 195
    GATEWAY TO TOMORROW [Carnell - 1954]
    BEST SF SCIENCE FICTION STORIES [Crispin - 1955]
Dumb Show by Brian W. Aldiss.........................................Neb #19  Dec 1956
    ASPECTS OF SCIENCE FICTION [Doherty - 1959]
Dumb Waiter by Walter M. Miller, Jr. .................................ASF  Apr 195
    SCIENCE FICTION THINKING MACHINES [Conklin - 1954]
Dune Roller by Julian C. May.........................................ASF  Dec 195
    IMAGINATION UNLIMITED [Bleiler & Dikty - 1952]
    STORIES FOR TOMORROW [Sloane - 1954]
Dusty Death, The by John Kippax.......................................NW #77  Nov 1956
    OUT OF THIS WORLD 2 [Williams-Ellis & Owen - 1961]
Dwellers In Silence by Ray Bradbury...................................PS  Spr 194
    THE BEST SCIENCE FICTION STORIES: 1950 [Bleiler & Dikty - 1950]

# E

E For Effort by T. L. Sherred.................................................ASF   May 1947
    THE BIG BOOK OF SCIENCE FICTION [Conklin - 1950]
    THE ASTOUNDING SCIENCE FICTION ANTHOLOGY [J. W. Campbell - 1952]
Each An Explorer by Isaac Asimov..................................Fut #30  n/d 1956
    SF: 57 THE YEAR'S GREATEST SF AND FANTASY [Merril - 1957]
Eagles Gather, The by Joseph E. Kelleam.....................................ASF   Apr 1942
    CROSSROADS IN TIME [Conklin - 1953]
Earlier Service, The by Margaret Irwin.........................Rpnt-F&SF  Dec 1951
    (From Madame Fears The Dark: Seven Stories and a Play; 1935)
    THE BEST FROM FANTASY & SCIENCE FICTION: 2nd SERIES [Boucher & McComas-1953]
Early Time-Traveler, An by Louis Sebastian Mercier.................................
    (From Journal Of The Year 2440; 1795)
    SCIENCE IN FICTION [A. E. M. & J. C. Bayliss - 1957]
Earth Men, The by Ray Bradbury.............................................TWS   Aug 1948
    THE OTHER SIDE OF THE MOON [Derleth - 1949]
Easter Eggs by Robert Spencer Carr.........................................SEP   9/24/49
    THE BEST SCIENCE FICTION STORIES: 1950 [Bleiler & Dikty - 1950]
Eastward Ho! by William Tenn ps (Philip Klass)......................F&SF   Oct 1958
    THE BEST FROM FANTASY & SCIENCE FICTION: 9th SERIES [Mills - 1960]
Easy As A.B.C. by Rudyard Kipling............................................LM   Mar 1912
    THE SCIENCE FICTION GALAXY [Conklin - 1950]
Ed Lear Wasn't So Crazy by Herbert Schenck, Jr. .....................F&SF   Jun 1960
    SIXTH ANNUAL OF THE YEAR'S BEST SF [Merril - 1961]
Edge Of The Sea, The by Algis Budrys.......................................Ven   Mar 1958
    SF: 58 THE YEAR'S GREATEST SCIENCE FICTION AND FANTASY [Merril - 1958]
Edison's Conquest Of Mars by Garrett P. Service...........(Abridged).............
    Editor's Note: This novel  originally appeared serially in the NEW YORK EVEN-
    ING JOURNAL from January 12 to February 10, 1898. It was reprinted in   book
    form by Carcosa House [Los Angeles, Calif.] in 1947.
    THE TREASURY OF SCIENCE FICTION CLASSICS [Kuebler - 1955]
Education of Drusilla Strange, The by Theodore Sturgeon.............Glxy   Mar 1954
    OPERATION FUTURE [Conklin - 1955]
Eeel By The Tail, An by Allan K. Lang......................................Im   Apr 1951
    INVADERS OF EARTH [Conklin - 1952]
Eel, The by Miriam Allen DeFord............................................Glxy   Apr 1958
    THE FIFTH GALAXY READER [Gold - 1961]
Egg a Month From All Over, An by Idris Seabright ps (Margaret St. Clair)..........
                                                              F&SF   Oct 1952
    HUMAN? [Merril - 1954]
Ego Machine, The by Henry Kuttner...................................Spc   May 1952
    SCIENCE FICTION CARNIVAL [Brown & Reynolds - 1953]
Eight Mistresses, The by Jean Hrolda.......................................Esq   Aug 1937
    TIMELESS STORIES FOR TODAY AND TOMORROW [Bradbury - 1952]
Elsewhere And Otherwise by Algernon Blackwood...................(From Shocks; 1936)
    TRAVELERS IN TIME [Stern - 1947]

|  | Mag. | Year |
|---|---|---|

Embassy, The by Martin Pearson ps (Donald A. Wollheim)...............ASF   Mar 1942
    A TREASURY OF SCIENCE FICTION [Conklin - 1948]
    BEYOND THE END OF TIME [Pohl - 1952]............................ASF   Jul 1940
Emergency Landing by Ralph Williams................................
    THE BIG BOOK OF SCIENCE FICTION [Conklin - 1950]
Emergency Working by E. R. James...................................NW #17  Sep 1952
    GATEWAY TO TOMORROW [Carnell - 1954]
Employment by L. Sprague de Camp..................................ASF   May 1939
    (Originally appeared under pseudonym Lyman E. Lyon)
    IMAGINATION UNLIMITED [Bleiler & Dikty - 1952]..............Ast   Aug 1936
En Route To Pluto by Wallace West.................................
    THE BEST OF SCIENCE FICTION [Conklin - 1946]
Enchanted Forest, The by Fritz Leiber.............................ASF   Oct 1950
    WORLDS OF TOMORROW [Derleth - 1953]
Enchanted Village by A. E. Van Vogt...............................OW   Jul 1950
    POSSIBLE WORLDS OF SCIENCE FICTION [Conklin - 1951]
    THE SANDS OF MARS AND OTHER STORIES [Anonymous - 1958]
    (Appeared under title The Sands Of Mars)
Enchanted Village, The by Jack Vance....................(See listing The Dreamer)
Enchanted Weekend, The by John MacCormac..........................Unk   Oct 1939
    FROM UNKNOWN WORLDS [J. W. Campbell - 1948]
Enchantment by Elizabeth Emmett...................................SEP   10/1/60
    SIXTH ANNUAL OF THE YEAR'S BEST SF [Merril - 1961]
Enchantress Of Venus by Leigh Brackett  (Mrs. Edmond Hamilton)........PS   Fal 1949
    THE GIANT ANTHOLOGY OF SCIENCE FICTION [Margulies & Friend - 1954]
End As a World by F. L. Wallace..................................Glxy   Sep 1955
    THE THIRD GALAXY READER OF SCIENCE FICTION [Gold - 1958]
End Of Summer, The by Algis Budrys...............................ASF   Nov 1954
    PENGUIN SCIENCE FICTION [Aldiss - 1961]
End Of The Beginning, The by Ray Bradbury........................MMC   1958
    (Originally appeared under title Next Stop: The Stars)
    SCIENCE FICTION SHOWCASE [M. Kornbluth - 1959]
End Of The Line, The by James H. Schmitz.........................ASF   Jul 1951
    SPACE PIONEERS [Norton - 1954]
End Of The Party, The by Graham Greene.............(From Nineteen Stories; 1947)
    CHILDREN OF WONDER [Tenn - 1953]
Endowment Policy by Lewis Padgett ps (Henry Kuttner & C. L. Moore)...ASF   Aug 1943
    SCIENCE FICTION ADVENTURES IN DIMENSION [Conklin - 1953]
Enemies Of Space by Karl Grunert...................(First published in 1907)
    (Translated from German by Willy Ley)
    INVADERS OF EARTH [Conklin - 1952]
Enemy Planet, The by Rear Admiral D. V. Gallary, USN .................SEP   9/30/50
    THE SATURDAY EVENING POST FANTASY STORIES [Fles - 19951]
Enoch Soames by Max Beerbohm...........................(From Seven Men; 1919)
    THE MOONLIGHT TRAVELER [Stern - 1943]
    TRAVELERS IN TIME [Stern - 1947].............................Nykr   5/17/47
Enormous Radio, The by John Cheever...............................
    TIMELESS STORIES FOR TODAY AND TOMORROW [Bradbury - 1952]
Enormous Room, The by H. L. Gold & Robert W. Krepps..............Amz   Nov 1952
    YEAR'S BEST SCIENCE FICTION NOVELS: 1954 [Bleiler & Dikty - 1954]
Enough Rope by Poul Anderson.....................................ASF   Jul 1953
    FOUR FOR THE FUTURE [Conklin - 1959]
Environment by Chester S. Geier..................................ASF   May 1944
    THE OMNIBUS OF SCIENCE FICTION [Conklin - 1952]
Episode On Dhee Minor by Harry Walton............................ASF   Oct 1939
    TRAVELERS OF SPACE [Greenberg - 1952]

                                                                    Mag.     Year
Epitaph Near Moonport by Sherwood Springer........(verse)...........F&SF  Jul 1954
    THE BEST FROM FANTASY & SCIENCE FICTION: 4th SERIES [Boucher - 1955]
Epithalamium by Doris Pitkin Buck................(verse)...........F&SF  Jan 1958
    THE BEST FROM FANTASY & SCIENCE FICTION: 8th SERIES [Boucher - 1959]
Errand Boy by William Tenn ps (Philip Klass)........................ASF  Jun 1947
    CHILDREN OF WONDER [Tenn - 1953]
Escape by Paul Ernst................................................WT   Jul 1938
    THE OTHER WORLDS [Stong - 1941]
Escape Into Yesterday by Arthur J. Burks..............■..........ORIGINAL STORY
    SCIENCE AND SORCERY [Ford - 1953]
Etaoin Shrdlu by Fredric Brown....................................Unk  Feb 1942
    WORLD OF WONDER [Pratt - 1951]
Etched In Moonlight by James Stephens............(From Etched In Moonlight; 1928)
    TRAVELERS IN TIME [Stern - 1947]
Eternal Duffer, The by Willard Temple...........................SEP    5/18/46
    THE SATURDAY EVENING POST FANTASY STORIES [Fles - 1951]
Eternal Man, The by D. D. Sharp..................................SWS  Aug 1929
    A TREASURY OF SCIENCE FICTION [Conklin - 1948]
    FROM OFF THIS WORLD [Margulies & Friend - 1949]
Eternity: A Nightmare by Lewis Carroll...........................................
    (From Sylvie And Bruno Concluded; Chapter XVI; 1893)
    FANTASIA MATHEMATICA [Fadiman - 1958]
Eternity Lost by Clifford D. Simak................................ASF  Jul 1949
    THE BEST SCIENCE FICTION STORIES: 1950 [Bleiler & Dikty - 1950]
    THE ASTOUNDING SCIENCE FICTION ANTHOLOGY [J. W. Campbell - 1952]
Ethical Equations, The by Murray Leinster ps (Will F. Jenkins).......ASF  Jun 1945
    A TREASURY OF SCIENCE FICTION [Conklin - 1948]
Ethicators, The by Willard Marsh.................................If  Aug 1955
    SF: THE YEAR'S GREATEST SCIENCE FICTION & FANTASY [Merril - 1956]
Euclid by Cachel Lindsay......(verse).......(From The Congo and Other Poems; 1914)
    FANTASIA MATHEMATICA [Fadiman - 1958]
Euclid Alone Has Looked On Beauty Bare by Edna St. Vincent Millay.....(verse).....
    (From Collected Poems; 1924)
    FANTASIA MATHEMATICA [Fadiman - 1958]
Evening Primrose by John Collier.................(From The Touch of Nutmeg; 1943)
    OUT OF THIS WORLD [Fast - 1944]
Evolution's End by Robert Arthur...................................TWS  Apr 1941
    ADVENTURES IN TOMORROW [Crossen - 1951]
Ex Machina by Lewis Padgett ps (Henry Kuttner & C. L. Moore).........ASF  Apr 1948
    THE BEST SCIENCE FICTION STORIES: 1949 [Bleiler & Dikty - 1949]
Exalted, The by L. Sprague de Camp..................................ASF  Nov 1940
    THE ASTOUNDING SCIENCE FICTION ANTHOLOGY [J. W. Campbell - 1952]
Excerpts From Encyclopedia Of Galactic Culture — Edited by Edward Wellen.........
    Origins Of Galactic Etiquette........................................Glxy  Oct 1953
    Origins Of Galactic Law..............................................Glxy  Apr 1953
    Origins Of Galactic Slang............................................Glxy  Jul 1952
    Origins Of Galactic Medicine.........................................Glxy  Dec 1953
        ALL ABOUT THE FUTURE [Greenberg - 1955]
Executioner, The by Algis Budrys..................................ASF  Jan 1956
    SPECTRUM  [Amis & Conquest - 1961]
Exile by Everett B. Cole..........................................ASF  Jan 1954
    THE BEST SCIENCE FICTION STORIES AND NOVELS: 1955 [Dikty - 1955]
Exile by Edmond Hamilton..........................................SSF  May 1943
    LOOKING FORWARD [Lesser - 1953]
Exile, The by Alfred Coppel.......................................ASF  Oct 1952
    STORIES FOR TOMORROW [Sloane - 1954]

Exile From Space by Judith Merril.................................FU  Nov 1956
   THE FANTASTIC UNIVERSE OMNIBUS [Santesson - 1960]
Exiled From Earth by Sam Merwin, Jr. .............................TWS  Dec 1940
   ADVENTURES IN TOMORROW [Crossen - 1951]
Exiles, The by Ray Bradbury......................................MMC  9/15/49
   (Originally appeared under title The Mad Wizards Of Mars)
   BEYOND TIME AND SPACE [Derleth - 1950]
Exit by Arthur Wilson Tucker.....................................Ash  Apr 1943
   (Originally appeared under Bob Tucker byline)
   (Story selected by Alden H. Norton)
   EDITOR'S CHOICE IN SCIENCE FICTION [Moskowitz - 1954]
Exit Line by Sam Merwin, Jr. ....................................Stg  Sep 1950
   (Originally appeared under pseudonym Matt Lee)
   POSSIBLE WORLDS OF SCIENCE FICTION [Conklin - 1951]
Expedition by Anthony Boucher....................................TWS  Aug 1943
   THE BEST OF SCIENCE FICTION [Conklin - 1946]
   INVASION FROM MARS [Welles - 1949]
Expedition by Fredric Brown......................................F&SF  Feb 1957
   THE BEST FROM FANTASY & SCIENCE FICTION: 7th SERIES [Boucher - 1958]
   FANTASIA MATHEMATICA [Fadiman - 1958]
Expedition Polychrome by J. A. Winter, M. D. ....................ASF  Jan 1949
   SPACE SERVICE [Norton - 1953]
Expendable by Philip K. Dick.....................................F&SF  Jun 1953
   SCIENCE FICTION SHOWCASE [M. Kornbluth - 1959]
Experiment by Kay Rogers.........................................F&SF  Feb 1953
   THE BEST FROM FANTASY & SCIENCE FICTION: 3rd SERIES [Boucher & McComas-1954]
Experiment Station by Kris Neville...............................Sup  Sep 1950
   (Originally appeared under title The First)
   SCIENCE FICTION ADVENTURES IN MUTATION [Conklin - 1956]
     (Revised for inclusion in this anthology)
Experimental Farm, The by H. G. Wells............................
   (From The Food Of The Gods; 1904)
   SCIENCE IN FICTION [A. E. M. & J. C. Bayliss - 1957]
Exploiters End by James Causey...................................Orb #2  n/d 1954
   BEYOND THE STARS AND OTHER STORIES [Anonymous - 1958]
Expostulation, An by C. S. Lewis..............(verse).............F&SF  Jun 1959
   THE BEST FROM FANTASY & SCIENCE FICTION: 9th SERIES [Mills - 1960]
Exposure by Eric Frank Russell...................................ASF  Jul 1950
   OPERATION FUTURE [Conklin - 1955]
Extending The Holdings by David Grinnell.........................F&SF  Aug 1951
   THE BEST SCIENCE FICTION STORIES: 1952 [Bleiler & Dikty - 1952]
Exterran by Milton Lesser........................................ORIGINAL STORY
   TOMORROW'S UNIVERSE [H. J. Campbell - 1954]
Eye For Iniquity by T. L. Sherred...............................BFF  Jul 1953
   PORTALS OF TOMORROW [Derleth - 1954]
Eye For What, An by Damon Knight.................................Glxy  Mar 1957
   THE WORLD THAT COULDN'T BE AND 8 OTHER NOVELETTES FROM GALAXY [Gold - 1959]
Eyes, The by Henry Hasse.........................................FB #8  n d 1951
   SCIENCE AND SORCERY [Ford - 1953]

Mag.    Year
Fable, A — Anonymous.......(From The Mathematical Gazette Vol 38, 1954 Page 308)
    FANTASIA MATHEMATICA [Fadiman - 1958]
Facts in the Case of M. Valdemar, The by Edgar Allan Poe...........AWR   Dec 1845
    SHOT IN THE DARK [Merril - 1950]
Fall of Knight by A. Bertram Chandler...............................FU    Jun 1958
    THE FANTASTIC UNIVERSE OMNIBUS [Santesson - 1960]
False Dawn by A. Bertram Chandler..................................ASF   Oct 1946
    JOURNEY TO INFINITY [Greenberg - 1951]
Family Resemblance by Alan E. Nourse..............................ASF   Apr 1953
    SCIENCE FICTION ADVENTURES IN MUTATION [Conklin - 1956]
Far Below by Robert Barbour Johnson................................WT    Jul 1939
    (Story selected by Dorothy McIlwraith)
    EDITOR'S CHOICE IN SCIENCE FICTION [Moskowitz - 1954]
Far Centaurus by A. E. Van Vogt...................................ASF   Jan 1944
    STRANGE PORTS OF CALL  [Derleth - 1948]
    MEN AGAINST THE STARS [Greenberg - 1950]
Far From Home by Walter S. Tevis..................................F&SF   Dec 1959
    THE BEST FROM FANTASY & SCIENCE FICTION: 9th SERIES [Mills - 1960]
Far Look, The by Theodore L. Thomas...............................ASF   Aug 1956
    SF: 57 THE YEAR'S GREATEST SCIENCE FICTION AND FANTASY [Merril - 1957]
Farewell To Eden by Theodore Sturgeon.........................ORIGINAL STORY
    INVASION FROM MARS [Welles - 1949]
    THE OUTER REACHES [Derleth - 1951]
Farewell To The Master by Harry Bates.............................ASF   Oct 1940
    ADVENTURES IN TIME AND SPACE [Healy & McComas - 1946]
Farthest Horizon, The by Raymond F. Jones.........................ASF   Apr 1952
    SPACE PIONEERS [Norton - 1954]
    STORIES FOR TOMORROW [Sloane - 1954]
Fascinating Stranger, The by Michael Fessier.....................SEP    5/22/48
    GREAT STORIES OF SCIENCE FICTION [Leinster - 1951]
Fast Falls The Eventide by Eric Frank Russell....................ASF   May 1952
    THE BEST SCIENCE FICTION STORIES: 1953 [Bleiler & Dikty - 1953]
Father-Thing, The by Philip K. Dick..............................F&SF   Dec 1954
    A TREASURY OF GREAT SCIENCE FICTION [Boucher - 1959]
Fear Is A Business by Theodore Sturgeon..........................F&SF   Aug 1956
    A DECADE OF FANTASY & SCIENCE FICTION [Mills - 1960]
Fear Planet, The by Robert Bloch.................................SSS    Feb 1943
    FAR BOUNDARIES [Derleth - 1951]
Fearsome Fable by Bruce Elliot...................................F&SF   Feb 1951
    THE BEST FROM FANTASY & SCIENCE FICTION [Boucher & McComas - 1952]
    FANTASIA MATHEMATICA [Fadiman - 1958]
Feast of Demons, A by William Morrison ps (Joseph Samachson).......Glxy   Mar 1958
    THE FIFTH GALAXY READER [Gold - 1961]
Feedback by Katherine MacLean...................................ASF   Jul 1951
    CROSSROADS IN TIME [Conklin - 1953]
Fellow Who Married The Maxwill Girl, The by Ward Moore...........F&SF   Feb 1960
    THE BEST FROM FANTASY & SCIENCE FICTION: 10th SERIES [Mills - 1961]
    SIXTH ANNUAL OF THE YEAR'S BEST SF [Merril - 1961]

                                                                    Mag.    Year
                                                        .....Glxy   Jul 1954
Felony by James Causey.................................................
     THE BEST SCIENCE FICTION STORIES AND NOVELS: 1955 [Dikty - 1955]
Fessenden's Worlds by Edmond Hamilton.......................WT    Apr 1937
     BEYOND TIME AND SPACE [Derleth - 1950]
Fiction by Allan Grant....................(verse)..................Unk   Feb 1941
     FROM UNKNOWN WORLDS [J. W. Campbell - 1948]
Field Experiment by Chad Oliver.............................ASF    Jan 1955
     THE HIDDEN PLANET [Wollheim - 1959]
Field Study by Peter Phillips.............................Glxy   Apr 1951
     THE GALAXY READER OF SCIENCE FICTION [Gold - 1952]
Figure, The by Edward Grendon..............................ASF    Jul 1947
     A TREASURY OF SCIENCE FICTION [Conklin - 1948]
Final Clearance by Rachel Maddux...........................F&SF   Feb 1956
     THE BEST FROM FANTASY & SCIENCE FICTION: 6th SERIES [Boucher - 1957]
Final Command by A. E. Van Vogt............................Ast    Sep 1936
     THE ROBOT AND THE MAN [Greenberg - 1953]
Final Gentleman by Clifford D. Simak.......................F&SF   Jan 1960
     SIX GREAT SHORT NOVELS OF SCIENCE FICTION [Conklin - 1960]
Finality Unlimited by Donald Wandrei.......................ASF    Nov 1948
     THE OUTER REACHES [Derleth - 1951]
Finest Story In The World, The by Rudyard Kipling.....(From Many Inventions; 1893)
     WORLD OF WONDER [Pratt - 1951]
Finishing Touch, A by A. Bertram Chandler..................NW #16  Jul 1952
     GATEWAY TO TOMORROW [Carnell - 1954]
Fire And The Sword, The by Frank Robinson..................Glxy   Aug 1951
     IMAGINATION UNLIMITED [Bleiler & Dikty - 1952]
Fire Ballons, The by Ray Bradbury.............(See listing "In This Sign...")
Fire-Born, The by Toby Duane ps (W. Paul Ganley)..............ORIGINAL STORY
     SHANADU [Briney - 1953]
Fires Within, The by Arthur C. Clarke......................Fty    Aug 1947
     (Originally appeared under pseudonym E. G. O'Brien)
     THE SCIENCE FICTION GALAXY [Conklin - 1950]
     WORLDS OF TOMORROW [Derleth - 1953]
Firewater by William Tenn ps (Philip Klass)................ASF    Feb 1952
     YEAR'S BEST SCIENCE FICTION NOVELS: 1953 [Bleiler & Dikty - 1953]
First, The by Kris Neville...................(See listing Experiment Station)
First Contact by Murray Leinster ps (Will F. Jenkins)..............ASF   May 194
     THE BEST OF SCIENCE FICTION [Conklin - 1946]
     THE ASTOUNDING SCIENCE FICTION ANTHOLOGY [ J. W. Campbell - 1952]
     STORIES FOR TOMORROW [Sloane - 1954]
First Law by Isaac Asimov..................................FU    Oct 195
     THE FANTASTIC UNIVERSE OMNIBUS [Santesson - 1960]
First Lesson by Mildred Clingerman.........................F&SF   Dec 195
     A DECADE OF FANTASY & SCIENCE FICTION [Mills - 1960]
First Men In The Moon, The by H. G. Wells..................Cpln   Nov 190
     THE PORTABLE NOVELS OF SCIENCE [Wollheim - 1945]
First Stage: Moon by Dick Hetschel.........................If    Dec 195
     THE FIRST WORLD OF IF [Quinn & Wulff - 1957]
Fish Story by Leslie Charteris.............................BB    Nov 195
     GALAXY OF GHOULS [Merril - 1955]
Fishing Season, The by Robert Sheckley.....................TWS    Aug 195
     TERROR IN THE MODERN VEIN [Wollheim - 1955]
Fittest, The by Katherine MacLean..........................WB    Jan 195
     BEYOND HUMAN KEN [Merril - 1952]
5,271,009 by Alfred Bester.................................F&SF   Mar 195
     ASSIGNMENT IN TOMORROW [Pohl - 1954]
Five Years In The Marmalade by Robert W. Krepps...........FA    Jul 19
     (Originally appeared under pseudonym Geoff St. Reynard)
     THE BEST SCIENCE FICTION STORIES: 1950 [Bleiler & Dikty - 1950]

                                                                    Mag.      Year
Flame Midget, The by Frank Belknap Long, Jr. ......................Ast   Dec 1936
    THE BEST OF SCIENCE FICTION [Conklin - 1946]
Flaw by John D. MacDonald....................................Stg   Jan 1949
    THE BEST SCIENCE FICTION STORIES: 1950 [Bleiler & Dikty - 1950]
Flies by Isaac Asimov...........................................F&SF  Jun 1953
    SCIENCE FICTION TERROR TALES [Conklin - 1955]
Flight Into Darkness by Webb Marlowe ps (J. Francis McComas)........Amz   Feb 1943
    ADVENTURES IN TIME AND SPACE [Healy & McComas - 1946]
Flight Of The Dawn Star by Robert Moore Williams...................ASF   Mar 1938
    A TREASURY OF SCIENCE FICTION [Conklin - 1948]
Flight That Failed, The by E. Mayne Hull (Mrs. A. E. Van Vogt)......ASF   Dec 1942
    SCIENCE FICTION ADVENTURES IN DIMENSION [Conklin - 1953]
Flight To Forever by Poul Anderson................................Sup   Nov 1950
    YEAR'S BEST SCIENCE FICTION NOVELS: 1952 [Bleiler & Dikty - 1952]
Flowers For Algernon by Daniel Keyes.............................F&SF  Apr 1959
    THE BEST FROM FANTASY & SCIENCE FICTION: 9th SERIES [Mills - 1960]
    FIFTH ANNUAL THE YEAR'S BEST SF [Merril - 1960]
    BEST SF FOUR SCIENCE FICTION STORIES [Crispin - 1961]
Fly, The by George Langelaan....................................Plby  Jun 1957
    SF: 58 THE YEAR'S GREATEST SCIENCE FICTION AND FANTASY [Merril - 1958]
Fly, The by Arthur Porges......................................F&SF  Sep 1952
    BEYOND HUMAN KEN [Merril - 1952]
    THE BEST SCIENCE FICTION STORIES: 1953 [Bleiler & Dikty - 1953]
Flying Chaucer by Anthony Brode...............(verse)............F&SF  Mar 1956
    THE BEST FROM FANTASY & SCIENCE FICTION: 6th SERIES [Boucher - 1957]
Flying Dutchman by Ward Moore...................................ORIGINAL STORY
    ADVENTURES IN TOMORROW [Crossen - 1951]
Flying High by Eugene Ionesco....................................Mdm   Oct 1957
    SF: 58 THE YEAR'S GREATEST SCIENCE FICTION AND FANTASY [Merril - 1958]
Flying Island, The by Jonathan Swift.....(From The Third Voyage of Gulliver; 1728)
    SCIENCE IN FICTION [A.E.M. & J.C. Bayliss - 1957]
Flying Men, The by Olaf Stapledon.............(From The Last And First Men; 1930)
    BEYOND TIME AND SPACE [Derleth - 1950]
Fondly Fahrenheit by Alfred Bester..............................F&SF  Aug 1954
    THE BEST FROM FANTASY & SCIENCE FICTION:4th SERIES [Boucher - 1955]
Food To All Flesh by Zeena Henderson............................F&SF  Dec 1953
    BEST SF THREE SCIENCE FICTION STORIES [Crispin - 1958]
Footprints by Robert Ernest Gilbert............................FB #8  n/d 1951
    SCIENCE AND SORCERY [Ford - 1953]
For All Practical Purposes by C. Stanley Ogilvy..(Fr Through The Microscope; 1956)
    FANTASIA MATHEMATICA [Fadiman - 1958]
For I Am A Jealous People! by Lester del Rey...................ORIGINAL STORY
    STAR SHORT NOVELS [Pohl - 1954]
For The Public by Bernard I. Kahn...............................ASF   Dec 1946
    SPACE SERVICE [Norton - 1953]
Forever And The Earth by Ray Bradbury...........................PS    Spr 1950
    THE BIG BOOK OF SCIENCE FICTION [Conklin - 1950]
Forgetfulness by Don A. Stuart ps (John W. Campbell, Jr.)...........Ast   Jun 1937
    ADVENTURES IN TIME AND SPACE [Healy & McComas - 1946]
Forget-Me-Not by William F. Temple..............................OW    Sep 1950
    THE BEST SCIENCE FICTION STORIES: 1951 [Bleiler & Dikty - 1951]
Forgiveness Of Tenchu Taen by F. A. Kummer, Jr. .................ASF   Nov 1938
    TRAVELERS OF SPACE [Greenberg - 1952]
Forgotten by P. Schuyler Miller..................................WS    Apr 1933
    (Originally appeared under title The Forgotten Man Of Space)
    STRANGE PORTS OF CALL [Derleth - 1948]

Forgotten Enemy, The by Arthur C. Clarke.........................NW #5 n/d 1949
    STORIES FOR TOMORROW [Sloane - 1954]
Forgotten Man Of Space, The by P. Schuyler Miller..........(See listing Forgotten)
Forgotten World by Edmond Hamilton..............................TWS Win 1946
    THE GIANT ANTHOLOGY OF SCIENCE FICTION [Margulies & Friend - 1954]
Foster, You're Dead by Philip K. Dick...........................ORIGINAL STORY
    STAR SCIENCE FICTION STORIES #3 [Pohl - 1954]
Foundation Of Science Fiction Success, The by Isaac Asimov..(verse).F&SF  Oct 1954
    THE BEST FROM FANTASY & SCIENCE FICTION: 4th SERIES [Boucher - 1955]
Four-Dimensional-Roller-Press, The by Bob Olsen ps (Alfred John Olsen, Jr.)........
                                      Amz  Jun 1927
    EVERY BOY'S BOOK OF SCIENCE FICTION [Wollheim - 1951]
Four In One by Damon Knight....................................Glxy Feb 1953
    THE SECOND GALAXY READER OF SCIENCE FICTION [Gold - 1954]
    BEST SF THREE SCIENCE FICTION STORIES [Crispin - 1958]
Fourth Dimensional Demonstrator, The by Murray Leinster ps (Will F. Jenkins)
                                       Ast  Dec 1935
    THE OTHER WORLDS [Stong - 1944]
Fourth Dynasty, The by R. R. Winterbotham........................Ast  Dec 1936
    THE OMNIBUS OF SCIENCE FICTION [Conklin - 1952]
Fox In The Forest, The by Ray Bradbury...........................Col  5/13/50
    THE BEST SCIENCE FICTION STORIES: 1951 [Bleiler & Dikty - 1951]
Foxholes Of Mars, The by Fritz Leiber, Jr. ....................TWS  Jun 1952
    BEYOND HUMAN KEN [Merril - 1952]
Franchise by Isaac Asimov......................................If  Jul 1955
    THE FIRST WORLD OF IF [Quinn & Wulff - 1957]
Franchise by Kris Neville.....................................ASF  Feb 1951
    STORIES FOR TOMORROW [Sloane - 1954]
Frankenstein — Unlimited by H. A. Highstone...................Ast  Dec 1936
    FAR BOUNDARIES [Derleth - 1951]
Free Flight by P. M. Hubbard.................(verse)..........F&SF  Apr 1956
    THE BEST FROM FANTASY & SCIENCE FICTION: 6th SERIES [Boucher - 1957]
Fresh Guy by E. C. Tubb.......................................SF #29 Jun 1958
    SF: 59 THE YEAR'S GREATEST SCIENCE FICTION AND FANTASY [Merril - 1959]
Friday by John Kippax.........................................NW #80 Feb 1959
    OUT OF THIS WORLD 1 [Williams-Ellis & Owen - 1960]
Friend Of The Family by Richard Wilson.........................ORIGINAL STORY
    STAR SCIENCE FICTION STORIES #2 [Pohl - 1953]
Friend To Alexander, A by James Thurber...(From My Worlds And Welcome To It; 1943)
    TRAVELERS IN TIME [Stern - 1947]
Friendly Demon, The by Daniel Defoe.....................Rpnt — F&SF  Feb 1951
    (Originally printed by J. Roberts; London; 1726)
    THE BEST FROM FANTASY & SCIENCE FICTION [Boucher & McComas - 1952]
Frightened Tree, The by Algis Budrys..........................Glxy  Feb 1953
    (Originally appeared under title Protective Mimicry)
    ASSIGNMENT IN TOMORROW [Pohl - 1954]
Fritzchen by Charles Beaumont.................................Orb #1 n/d 1953
    TERROR IN THE MODERN VEIN [Wollheim - 1955]
From A Private Mad-House by Humphrey Repton...................Var  n/d/a/ 1787
    FAR BOUNDARIES [Derleth - 1951]
From Beyond by H. P. Lovecraft................................WT  Feb 1938
    WORLDS OF TOMORROW [Derleth - 1953]
Fuel For The Future by Jack Hatcher..........................ASF  Mar 1940
    COMING ATTRACTIONS [Greenberg - 1957]
Fulfillment by A. E. Van Vogt.................................ORIGINAL STORY
    NEW TALES OF SPACE AND TIME [Healy - 1951]
Full Circle by Dorothy Cowles Pinkney............(verse).........F&SF  Dec 1956
    THE BEST FROM FANTASY & SCIENCE FICTION: 7th SERIES [Boucher - 1958]
Fun They Had, The by Isaac Asimov.............................NEA  12/1/51
    OPERATION FUTURE [Conklin - 1955]
    JOURNEYS IN SCIENCE FICTION [Loughlin & Popp - 1961]
F Y 1 by James Blish..........................................ORIGINAL STORY
    STAR SCIENCE FICTION STORIES #2 [Pohl - 1953]

# G

Gadget Had A Ghost, The by Murray Leinster ps (Will F. Jenkins)......TWS   Jun 1952
     YEAR'S BEST SCIENCE FICTION NOVELS: 1953 [Bleiler & Dikty - 1953]
Galley Slave by Isaac Asimov........................................Glxy   Dec 1957
     SIX GREAT SHORT SCIENCE FICTION NOVELS [Conklin - 1960]
Game For Blondes, A by John D. MacDonald............................Glxy   Oct 1952
     THE BEST SCIENCE FICTION STORIES: 1953 [Bleiler & Dikty - 1953]
     THE SECOND GALAXY READER OF SCIENCE FICTION [Gold - 1954]
Game Of Rat And Dragon, The by Cordwainer Smith....................Glxy   Oct 1955
     THE BEST SCIENCE FICTION STORIES AND NOVELS: 1956 [Dikty - 1956]
     BEST SF THREE SCIENCE FICTION STORIES [Crispin - 1958]
     THE THIRD GALAXY READER OF SCIENCE FICTION [Gold - 1958]
Game Preserve by Rog Phillips ps (Roger Phillips Graham)..............If   Oct 1957
     SF: 58 THE YEAR'S GREATEST SCIENCE FICTION AND FANTASY [Merril - 1958]
Games by Katherine MacLean.........................................Glxy   Mar 1953
     OPERATION FUTURE [Conklin - 1955]
Gandolphus by Anthony Boucher......................................F&SF   Dec 1956
     A DECADE OF FANTASY & SCIENCE FICTION [Mills - 1960]
Garden In The Forest, The by Robert F. Young.......................ASF   Sep 1953
     OPERATION FUTURE [Conklin - 1955]
Garden Of Fear, The by Robert E. Howard.............................MT    Jul 1934
     THE GARDEN OF FEAR AND OTHER STORIES [Crawford - 1945]
Gardener, The by Margaret St. Clair................................TWS   Oct 1949
     WORLDS OF TOMORROW [Derleth - 1953]
Gateway To Darkness by Fredric Brown................................Sup   Nov 1949
     THE GIANT ANTHOLOGY OF SCIENCE FICTION [Margulies & Friend - 1954]
Gavagan's Bar by L. Sprague de Camp & Fletcher Pratt...............F&SF   Spr 1950
     THE BEST FROM FANTASY & SCIENCE FICTION [Boucher & McComas - 1952]
Genesis by H. Beam Piper...........................................Fut   Nov 1951
     SHADOW OF TOMORROW [Pohl - 1953]
Genius by Poul Anderson............................................ASF   Dec 1948
     THE BEST SCIENCE FICTION STORIES: 1949 [Bleiler & Dikty - 1949]
Genius Of The Species by R. Bretnor.....................ORIGINAL STORY
     9 TALES OF SPACE AND TIME [Healy - 1954]
Gentleman Is An Epwa, The by Carl Jacobi................ORIGINAL STORY
     WORLDS OF TOMORROW [Derleth - 1953]
Gentlemen, Be Seated by Robert A. Heinlein..........................Arg   May 1948
     SHOT IN THE DARK [Merril - 1950]
Gentlest Unpeople, The by Frederik Pohl............................Glxy   Jun 1958
     FOURTH GALAXY READER OF SCIENCE FICTION [Gold - 1959]
Geography For Time Travelers by Willy Ley..........................ASF   Jul 1939
     COMING ATTRACTIONS [Greenberg - 1957]
Get Out Of My Sky by James Blish...................................ASF   Jan 1957
     GET OUT OF SKY [Margulies - 1960]
Ghost, The by A. E. Van Vogt.......................................Unk   Aug 1942
     ZACHERLY'S MIDNIGHT SNACKS [Zacherly - 1960]

Ghost Of Me, The by Anthony Boucher.................................Unk   Jun 1942
    BEYOND THE BARRIERS OF SPACE AND TIME [Merril - 1954]
ghosts by don marquis.....(FROM the lives and times of archy and mehitabel; 1927)
    HUMAN? [Merril - 1954]
Giant In The Earth by Morrison Colladay................................WS   Apr 1933
    THE BEST OF SCIENCE FICTION [Conklin - 1946]
Giant Killer by A. Bertram Chandler....................................ASF   Oct 1945
    WORLDS OF WONDER [Pratt - 1951]
Gift of Gab, The by Jack Vance.........................................ASF   Sep 1955
    BEST SF THREE   SCIENCE FICTION STORIES [Crispin - 1958]
    OUT OF THIS WORLD 2 [Williams-Ellis and Owen - 1961]
Gil Bralter by Jules Verne...............................Rpnt - F&SF   Jul 1958
    (From Le Chemin De France; 1887)   (Translated from French by I. O. Evans)
    THE BEST FROM FANTASY & SCIENCE FICTION: 8th SERIES [Boucher - 1959]
Girl In The Golden Atom, The by Ray Cummings..........................AIS   3/15/19
    THE GIANT ANTHOLOGY OF SCIENCE FICTION [Margulies & Friend - 1954]
Girl With The Hungry Eyes, The by Fritz Leiber, Jr. ...............ORIGINAL STORY
    THE GIRL WITH THE HUNGRY EYES AND OTHER STORIES [Wollheim - 1949]
    TERROR IN THE MODERN VEIN [Wollheim - 1955]
Girls From Earth, The by Frank M. Robinson..........................Glxy   Jan 1952
    THE BEST SCIENCE FICTION STORIES: 1953 [Bleiler & Dikty - 1953]
    STORIES FOR TOMORROW [Sloane - 1954]
Git Along! by L. Sprague de Camp.......................................ASF   Aug 1950
    THE OUTER REACHES [Derleth - 1951]
Glass Eye, The by John Kier Cross..............(From THE OTHER PASSENGER; 1946)
    TIMELESS STORIES FOR TODAY AND TOMORROW [Bradbury - 1952]
Glass of The Future, The by Herman W. Mudgett........(verse).......F&SF   Jan 1955
    THE BEST FROM FANTASY & SCIENCE FICTION: 5th SERIES [Boucher - 1956]
Gleeb For Earth, A by Charles Schafhauser...........................Glxy   May 1953
    THE SECOND GALAXY READER OF SCIENCE FICTION [Gold - 1954]
Gnarly Man, The by L. Spague de Camp..................................Unk   Jun 1939
    HUMAN? [Merril - 1954]
Gnome There Was, A by Lewis Padgett ps (Henry Kuttner and C. L. Moore)...........
    (Originally appeared under Henry Kuttner byline)     Unk   Oct 1941
    BEYOND HUMAN KEN [Merril - 1952]
Gnurrs Come From The Voodvork Out, The by R. Bretnor..............F&SF   Spr 1950
    THE BEST SCIENCE FICTION STORIES: 1951 [Bleiler & Dikty - 1951]
God-Box, The by Howard Wandrei......................................Ast   Apr 1934
    (Originally appeared under pseudonym Howard Von Drey)
    STRANGE PORTS OF CALL [Derleth - 1948]
God and The Machine by Nigel Balchin................................................
    (From Last Recollections of My Uncle Charlie; 1951)
    FANTASIA MATHEMATICA [Fadiman - 1958]
God In A Garden, A by Theodore Sturgeon.............................Unk   Oct 1939
    THE OTHER WORLDS [Stong - 1941]
Goddess In Granite by Robert F. Young...............................F&SF   Sep 1957
    THE BEST FROM FANTASY & SCIENCE FICTION: 7th SERIES [Boucher - 1958]
Going Up! by Dennis Driscoll........................................BLM   May 1957
    (Condensed from article entitled Space Travel)
    SF: 58 THE YEAR'S GREATEST SF AND FANTASY [Merril - 1958]
Gold Standard, The by Leslie Charteris.......(From THE SAINT AND Mr. TEALE; 1933)
    THE SAINT'S CHOICE [Charteris - 1945]
Golden Bough, The by David H. Keller, M. D. ........................MT   Win 1934
    THE GARDEN OF FEAR AND OTHER STORIES [Crawford - 1945]
Golden Egg, The by Theodore Sturgeon................................Unk   Aug 1941
    SCIENCE FICTION THINKING MACHINES [Conklin - 1954]
Golden Helix, The by Theodore Sturgeon..............................TWS   Sum 1954
    THREE TIMES INFINITY [Margulies - 1958]

```
                                                              Mag.     Year
Golden Man, The by Philip K. Dick...................................If   Apr 1954
     BEYOND THE BARRIERS OF SPACE AND TIME [Merril - 1954]
Golden Pyramid, The by Sam Moskowitz................................FU   Nov 1956
     THE FANTASTIC UNIVERSE OMNIBUS [Santesson - 1960]
Goldfish Bowl by Anson MacDonald ps (Robert A. Heinlein)............ASF  Mar 1942
     THE BEST OF SCIENCE FICTION [Conklin - 1946]
Golem, The by Avram Davidson.......................................F&SF  Mar 1955
     THE BEST FROM FANTASY & SCIENCE FICTION: 5th SERIES [Boucher - 1956]
     SF: THE YEAR'S GREATEST SCIENCE FICTION AND FANTASY [Merril - 1956]
Gomez by C. M. Kornbluth..........................................NW #32 Jan 1955
     A TREASURY OF GREAT SCIENCE FICTION [Boucher - 1959]
Gone Away by A. E. Coppard......................(From Fearful Pleasures; 1946)
     TERROR IN THE MODERN VEIN [Wollheim - 1955]
Good-Bye, Ilha! by Laurence Manning..........................ORIGINAL STORY
     BEYOND HUMAN KEN [Merril - 1952]
Good Night, Mr. James by Clifford D. Simak.........................Glxy  Mar 1951
     THE OUTER REACHES [Derleth - 1951]
     THE GALAXY READER OF SCIENCE FICTION [Gold - 1952]
Good Provider, The by Marion Gross.................................F&SF  Sep 1952
     SCIENCE FICTION ADVENTURES IN DIMENSION [Conklin - 1953]
Gorilla Suit by John Shepley.......................................F&SF  May 1958
     THE BEST FROM FANTASY & SCIENCE FICTION: 8th SERIES [Boucher - 1959]
Gostak and The Doshes. The by Miles J. Breuer, M. D. ..............Amz   Mar 1930
     SCIENCE FICTION ADVENTURES IN DIMENSION [Conklin - 1953]
Grandma's Lie Soap by Robert Abernathy.............................FU    Feb 1956
     SF: 57 THE YEAR'S GREATEST SCIENCE FICTION AND FANTASY [Merril - 1957]
Grandpa by James H. Schmitz.......................................ASF   Feb 1955
     PENGUIN SCIENCE FICTION [Aldiss - 1961]
Granny Won't Knit by Theodore Sturgeon.............................Glxy  May 1954
     ALL ABOUT THE FUTURE [Greenberg - 1955]
     FIVE GALAXY SHORT NOVELS [Gold - 1958]
Grantha Sighting, The by Avram Davidson............................F&SF  Apr 1958
     THE BEST FROM FANTASY & SCIENCE FICTION: 8th SERIES [Boucher - 1959]
Gratitude Guaranteed by R. Bretnor and Kris Neville................F&SF  Aug 1953
     PORTALS OF TOMORROW [Derleth - 1954]
Graveyard Rats, The by Henry Kuttner...............................WT    Mar 1936
     THE OTHER WORLDS [Stong - 1941]
Gravity Professor, The by Ray Cummings............................AASW     5/7/21
     EVERY BOY'S BOOK OF SCIENCE FICTION [Wollheim - 1951]
Great Cold, The by Frank Belknap Long, Jr. .......................Ast   Feb 1935
     WORLDS OF TOMORROW [Derleth - 1953]
Great Devlon Mystery, The by Raymond J. Healy.................ORIGINAL STORY
     9 TALES OF SPACE AND TIME [Healy - 1954]
Great Fog, The by H. F. Heard......................................
     (From The Great Fog and Other Weird Tales; 1944)
     A TREASURY OF SCIENCE FICTION [Conklin - 1948]
Great Keinplatz Experiment, The by Sir Arthur Conan Doyle.................
     (Originally published by Rand McNally and Co.; 1895)
     THE BEST OF SCIENCE FICTION [Conklin - 1946]
Great War Syndicate, The by Frank R. Stockton..................OAW  12/22/88
     THE BEST OF SCIENCE FICTION [Conklin - 1946]
Greatest Tertian, The by Anthony Boucher.....................ORIGINAL STORY
     INVADERS OF EARTH [Conklin - 1952]
     THE SCIENCE FICTIONAL SHERLOCK HOLMES [Peterson - 1960]
```

Mag.    Year

Green Cat, The by Cleve Cartmill........................................WB  Jan 1951
   THE OUTER REACHES [Derleth - 1951]
Green Hills of Earth, The by Robert A. Heinlein.....................SEP   2/8/47
   STRANGE PORTS OF CALL [Derleth - 1948]
   INVASION FROM MARS [Welles - 1949]
   MY BEST SCIENCE FICTION STORY [Margulies & Friend - 1949]
Green Splotches by T. S. Stribling.................................Adv   1/3/20
   THE POCKET BOOK OF SCIENCE FICTION [Wollheim - 1943]
Green Thoughts by John Collier.................(From Presenting Moonshine; 1941)
   THE POCKET BOOK OF SCIENCE FICTION [Wollheim - 1943]
Green Torture, The by A. Rowley Hilliard..........................WS  Mar 1931
   FROM OFF THIS WORLD [Margulies & Friend - 1949]
Grenville's Planet by Michael Shaara.............................F&SF  Oct 1952
   BEST SF THREE SCIENCE FICTION STORIES [Crispin - 1958]
Grief of Bagdad by Arthur K. Barnes..............................TWS  Jun 1943
   (Originally appeared under pseudonym Kelvin Kent)
   MY BEST SCIENCE FICTION STORY [Margulies & Friend - 1949]
Guest in the House, A by Frank Belknap Long, Jr. .................ASF  Mar 1946
   STRANGE PORTS OF CALL [Derleth - 1948]
Guilty as Charged by Arthur Porges..........................ORIGINAL STORY
   THE BEST SCIENCE FICTION STORIES AND NOVELS: 1955 [Dikty - 1955]
Guinevere for Everybody by Jack Williamson..................ORIGINAL STORY
   STAR SCIENCE FICTION STORIES #3 [Pohl - 1954]
Gun for Dinosaur, A by L. Sprague de Camp.......................Glxy  Mar 1956
   THE WORLD THAT COULDN'T BE AND 8 OTHER NOVELETS FROM GALAXY [Gold - 1959]
Gun Without a Bang, The by Finn O'Donnevan.......................Glxy  Jun 1958
   THE FOURTH GALAXY READER OF SCIENCE FICTION [Gold - 1959]
Gypsy by Poul Anderson...........................................ASF  Jan 1950
   EVERY BOY'S BOOK OF OUTER SPACE STORIES [Dikty - 1960]

Hair-Raising Adventure by Rosel George Brown.....................ORIGINAL STORY
   STAR SCIENCE FICTION STORIES #5 [Pohl - 1959]
Half a Hoka — Poul Anderson by Gordon R. Dickson.....(From The Program Booklet of
   the 17th World Science Fiction Convention [1959]
   THE SCIENCE FICTIONAL SHERLOCK HOLMES [Peterson - 1960]
Half Pair, The by Bertram Chandler..............................NW #65  Nov 1957
   PENGUIN SCIENCE FICTION [Aldiss - 1961]
Halfling, The by Leigh Brackett (Mrs. Edmond Hamilton).............Ash  Feb 1943
   SHOT IN THE DARK [Merril - 1950]
Hall of Mirrors by Fredric Brown................................Glxy  Dec 1953
   ASSIGNMENT IN TOMORROW [Pohl - 1954]
Hallucination Orbit by J. T. M'Intosh ps (James J. MacGregor).......Glxy  Jan 1952
   GATEWAY TO TOMORROW [Carnell - 1954]
     (Appeared under title The Bliss of Solitude)
   THE SECOND GALAXY READER OF SCIENCE FICTION [Gold - 1954]
   BEST SF FOUR SCIENCE FICTION STORIES [Crispin - 1961]
     (Appeared under title The Bliss of Solitude)
Halo by Hal Clement ps (Harry Clement Stubbs)....................Glxy  Oct 1952
   SHADOW OF TOMORROW [Pohl - 1953]

|  | Mag. | Year |
|---|---|---|

Hand, The by Wessell Hyatt Smitter................................Stry  Feb 1947
   TIMELESS STORIES FOR TODAY AND TOMORROW [Bradbury - 1952]
Handler, The by Damon Knight.....................................Rog  Aug 1960
   FIFTH ANNUAL OF THE YEAR'S BEST SF [Merril - 1960]
Happiest Creature, The by Jack Williamson.................ORIGINAL STORY
   STAR SCIENCE FICTION STORIES #2 [Pohl - 1953]
   STAR OF STARS [Pohl - 1960]
Happy Ending by Henry Kuttner....................................TWS  Aug 1948
   THE BEST SCIENCE FICTION STORIES: 1949 [Bleiler & Dikty - 1949]
Happy Herd, The by Bryce Walton....................................If  Oct 1956
   THE SECOND WORLD OF IF [Quinn & Wulff - 1958]
Hard Luck Diggings by Jack Vance.................................Stg  Jul 1948
   POSSIBLE WORLDS OF SCIENCE FICTION [Conklin - 1951]
Hard Way, The by Alan Barclay...............................NW #21  Jun 1953
   THE BEST FROM NEW WORLDS [Carnell - 1955]
Hardest Bargain, The by Evelyn E. Smith.........................Glxy  Jun 1957
   MIND PARTNER AND 8 OTHER NOVELETS FROM GALAXY [Gold - 1961]
Hated, The by Paul Flehr.......................................Glxy  Jan 1958
   THE FOURTH GALAXY READER OF SCIENCE FICTION [Gold - 1959]
Haunted Corpse, The by Frederik Pohl............................Glxy  Jan 1957
   THE THIRD GALAXY READER OF SCIENCE FICTION [Gold - 1958]
He by H. P. Lovecraft............................................WT  Sep 1926
   TERROR IN THE MODERN VEIN [Wollheim - 1955]
He Didn't Like Cats by L. Ron Hubbard...........................Unk  Feb 1942
   ZACHERLY'S VULTURE STEW [Zacherly - 1960]
He Thought He Saw Electrons Swift by Herbert Dingle...(verse)..(No data available)
   FANTASIA MATHEMATICA [Fadiman - 1958]
He Walked Around the Horses by H. Beam Piper....................ASF  Apr 1948
   WORLD OF WONDER [Pratt - 1951]
   BEST SF THREE SCIENCE FICTION STORIES [Crispin - 1958]
   ASPECTS OF SCIENCE FICTION [Doherty - 1959]
He Was Asking For You by Margery Allingham...(From Wanted: Someone Innocent; 1946)
   SHOT IN THE DARK [Merril - 1950]
He Who Shrank by Henry Hasse....................................Amz  Aug 1936
   ADVENTURES IN TIME AND SPACE [Healy & McComas - 1946]
Head Hunters, The by Ralph Williams.............................ASF  Oct 1951
   THE OMNIBUS OF SCIENCE FICTION [Conklin - 1952]
   STORIES FOR TOMORROW [Sloane - 1954]
Heartburn by Hortense Calisher...............(From In The Absence of Angels; 1951)
   TIMELESS STORIES FOR TODAY AND TOMORROW [Bradbury - 1952]
Heavy Planet by Lee Gregor ps (Milton A. Rothman)...............Ast  Aug 1939
   ADVENTURES IN TIME AND SPACE [Healy & McComas - 1946]
Heirs Apparent by Robert Abernathy.............................F&SF  Jun 1954
   THE BEST FROM FANTASY & SCIENCE FICTION: 4th SERIES [Boucher - 1952]
   THE BEST SCIENCE FICTION STORIES AND NOVELS: 1955 [Dikty - 1955]
Helen O'Loy by Lester del Rey...................................ASF  Dec 1938
   BEYOND HUMAN KEN [Merril - 1952]
   ASSIGNMENT IN TOMORROW [Pohl - 1954]
Help! I am Dr. Morris Goldpepper by Avram Davidson..............Glxy  Jul 1957
   THE THIRD GALAXY READER OF SCIENCE FICTION [Gold - 1958]
Helping Hand by Lester del Rey............................ORIGINAL STORY
   STAR SCIENCE FICTION STORIES #4 [Pohl - 1958]
Helping Hand, The by Poul Anderson..............................ASF  May 1950
   POSSIBLE WORLDS OF SCIENCE FICTION [Conklin - 1951]
Hemingway In Space by Kingsley Amis.............................Pch  12/21/60
   SIXTH ANNUAL OF THE YEAR'S BEST SF [Merril - 1961]

Here Lie We by Fox B. Holden...........................................Stg  Jun 1953
    TALES OF OUTER SPACE [Wollheim - 1954]
Here  There Be Tygers by Ray Bradbury.............................ORIGINAL STORY
    NEW TALES OF SPACE AND TIME [Healy - 1951]
Heredity by Isaac Asimov...............................................Ash  Apr 1941
    BEYOND THE END OF TIME [Pohl - 1952]
Heritage by Robert Abernathy..........................................ASF  Jun 1942
    THE OMNIBUS OF SCIENCE FICTION [Conklin - 1952]
Heritage by Charles L. Harness........................................F&SF  Fal 1950
    TOMORROW'S UNIVERSE [H. J. Campbell - 1954]
Hermit of Saturn's Ring by Neil R. Jones...............................PS  Fal 1940
    FLIGHT INTO SPACE [Wollheim - 1950]
Hermit on Bikini by John Langdon......................................BB  Mar 1953
    PORTALS OF TOMORROW [Derleth - 1954]
Hexer, The by H. W. Guernsey ps (Howard Wandrei)....................Unk  Jun 1939
    FROM UNKNOWN WORLDS [J. W. Campbell - 1948]
Hibited Man, The by L. Sprague de Camp...............................TWS  Oct 1949
    MY BEST SCIENCE FICTION STORY [Margulies & Friend - 1949]
Hickory, Dickory, Kerouac by Richard Gehman.........................Plby  Mar 1958
    (Originally appeared under psuedonym Martin Scott)
    SF: 59 THE YEAR'S GREATEST SCIENCE FICTION AND FANTASY [Merril - 1959]
Hide and Seek by Arthur C. Clarke....................................ASF  Sep 1949
    SPACE, SPACE, SPACE [Sloane - 1953]
    GATEWAY TO TOMORROW [Carnell - 1954]
High Treasure by Alan E. Nourse......................................ASF  Mar 1951
    THE OMNIBUS OF SCIENCE FICTION [Conklin - 1952]
Highway by Robert W. Lowndes.........................................SFQ  Fal 1942
    (Originally appeared under pseudonym Wilfred Owen Morley)
    LOOKING FORWARD [Lesser - 1953]
Hilda by H. B. Hickey ps (Herb Livingston)..........................F&SF  Sep 1952
    OPERATION FUTURE [Conklin - 1952]
Hindsight by Jack Williamson.........................................ASF  May 1940
    THE ASTOUNDING SCIENCE FICTION ANTHOLOGY [J. W. Campbell - 1952]
Historical Note by Murray Leinster ps (Will F. Jenkins).............ASF  Feb 1951
    THE ASTOUNDING SCIENCE FICTION ANTHOLOGY [J. W. Campbell - 1952]
History Lesson by Arthur C. Clarke...................................Stg  May 1949
    THE OMNIBUS OF SCIENCE FICTION [Conklin - 1952]
Hitch In Time, A by James MacCreigh ps (Frederik Pohl)..............TWS  Jun 1947
    SHOT IN THE DARK [Merril - 1950]
Hitch-Hike To Paradise by Geoffrey Whybrow.........(London Observer Prize Story)
    A. D. 2500 [Wilson - 1955]
"Hobbyist" by Eric Frank Russell.....................................ASF  Sep 1947
    THE ASTOUNDING SCIENCE FICTION ANTHOLOGY [J. W. Campbell - 1952]
    BEST SF FOUR SCIENCE FICTION STORIES [Crispin - 1961]
Hobo God by Malcolm Jameson..........................................ASF  Sep 1944
    ALL ABOUT THE FUTURE [Greenberg - 1955]
Hobson's Choice by Alfred Bester.....................................F&SF  Aug 1952
    THE BEST FROM FANTASY & SCIENCE FICTION: 2nd SERIES [Boucher - 1953]
    BEST SF TWO SCIENCE FICTION STORIES [Crispin - 1956]
Hoffer, The by Walter M. Miller, Jr. ................................FU  Sep 1955
    SF: THE YEAR'S GREATEST SCIENCE FICTION AND FANTASY [Merril - 1956]
Hole In The Sky by Irving Cox, Jr. ..............................ORIGINAL STORY
    TIME TO COME [Derleth - 1954]
Holes Around Mars, The by Jerome Bixby..............................Glxy  Jan 1954
    OPERATION FUTURE [Conklin - 1955]
Holiday by Ray Bradbury....................(See listing Vignettes of Tomorrow)

                                                                    Mag.     Year
Holy Grail, The by Tom Purdom................................................ORIGINAL STORY
    STAR SCIENCE FICTION STORIES #6 [Pohl - 1959]
Home There's No Returning by Henry Kuttner & C.L. Moore..(From No Boundaries; 1955)
    SF: THE YEAR'S GREATEST SCIENCE FICTION AND FANTASY [Merril - 1956]
Home is the Hero by E. C. Tubb......................................NW #15  May 1952
    GATEWAY TO TOMORROW [Carnell - 1954]
Homecoming by Ray Bradbury..........................................Mdm   Oct 1946
    GALAXY OF GHOULS [Merril - 1955]
Homeland by Mari Wolf................................................If    Jan 1953
    (Originally appeared under title The Statue)
    STORIES FOR TOMORROW [Sloane - 1954]
Homeless One, The by A. E. Coppard...................(From Fearful Pleasures; 1946)
    TRAVELERS IN TIME [Stern - 1947]
Homing Instincts of Joe Vargo by Stephen Barr......................F&SF  Dec 1959
    SPECTRUM [Amis & Conquest - 1961]
Homo Sol by Isaac Asimov............................................ASF   Sep 1940
    THE OMNIBUS OF SCIENCE FICTION [Conklin - 1952]
Honeymoon In Hell by Fredric Brown..................................Glxy  Nov 1950
    THE GALAXY READER OF SCIENCE FICTION [Gold - 1952]
Honorable Opponent by Clifford D. Simak.............................Glxy  Aug 1956
    THE THIRD GALAXY READER OF SCIENCE FICTION [Gold - 1958]
Hornets of Space by R. F. Starzl....................................WS    Nov 1930
    FROM OFF THIS WORLD [Margulies & Friend - 1949]
Hormones by Fletcher Pratt..........................................ORIGINAL STORY
    STAR SCIENCE FICTION STORIES #2 [Pohl - 1953]
Horror Howce by Margaret St. Clair..................................Glxy  Jul 1956
    THE FOURTH GALAXY READER OF SCIENCE FICTION [Gold - 1959]
Horror Story Shorter by One Letter Than the Shortest Horror Story Ever Written
    by Ron Smith....................................................ORIGINAL STORY
    THE BEST FROM FANTASY & SCIENCE FICTION: 7th SERIES [Boucher - 1958]
Hostess by Isaac Asimov.............................................Glxy  May 1951
    THE GALAXY READER OF SCIENCE FICTION [Gold - 1952]
Hot Argument by Randall Garrett...............(verse)...............F&SF  Feb 1960
    THE FIFTH ANNUAL OF THE YEAR'S BEST SF [Merril - 1960]
Hour After Westerly, The by Robert M. Coates.......................Nykr  11/1/47
    TIMELESS STORIES FOR TODAY AND TOMORROW [Bradbury - 1952]
House Dutiful, The by William Tenn ps (Philip Klass)...............ASF   Apr 1948
    BEYOND HUMAN KEN [Merril - 1952]
House of Ecstasy, The by Ralph Milne Farley........................WT    Apr 1938
    THE OTHER WORLDS [Stong - 1941]
House Where Time Stood Still, The by Seabury Quinn.................WT    Mar 1939
    THE OTHER WORLDS [Stong - 1941]
Housing Problem by Henry Kuttner....................................Chm   Oct 1944
    TIMELESS STORIES FOR TODAY AND TOMORROW [Bradbury - 1952]
Housing Shortage by Harry Walton....................................ASF   Jan 1947
    A TREASURY OF SCIENCE FICTION [Conklin - 1948]
How High on the Ladder by Leo Paige.................................FB #7  n/d 1950
    SCIENCE AND SORCERY [Ford - 1953]
How Near is the Moon? by Judith Merril..............................ORIGINAL STORY
    SF: 58 THE YEAR'S GREATEST SCIENCE FICTION AND FANTASY [Merril - 1958]
How To Count on Your Fingers by Frederik Pohl......................SFS   Sep 1956
    COMING ATTRACTIONS [Greenberg - 1957]
How to Learn Martian by Charles F. Hockett.........................ASF   May 1955
    COMING ATTRACTIONS [Greenberg - 1957]

|                                                                                          | Mag. | Year |
| --- | --- | --- |

How to Think a Science Fiction Story by G. Harry Stine...............ASF  May 1961
   (Excerpt from Science Fiction is too Conservative)
   SIXTH ANNUAL OF THE YEAR'S BEST SF [Merril - 1961]
How-2 by Clifford D. Simak..........................................Glxy  Nov 1954
   THE BEST SCIENCE FICTION STORIES AND NOVELS: 1955 [Dikty - 1955]
   BODYGUARD AND FOUR OTHER SHORT NOVELS FROM GALAXY [Gold - 1960]
Hub, The by Philip MacDonald.......................................F&SF  Aug 1951
   (Originally appeared under title Solitary Confinement)
   THE BEST FROM FANTASY & SCIENCE FICTION [Boucher & McComas - 1952]
Huge Beast by Cleve Cartmill.......................................F&SF  Sum 1950
   THE BEST FROM FANTASY & SCIENCE FICTION [Boucher & McComas - 1952]
Humpty Dumpty Had a Great Fall by Frank Belknap Long................Stg  Nov 1948
   BEYOND TIME AND SPACE [Derleth - 1950]
Hungry Guinea Pig, The by Miles J. Breuer, M. D. ...................Amz  Jan 1930
   SCIENCE FICTION ADVENTURES IN MUTATION [Conklin - 1956]
Hunting Machine by Carol Emshwiller................................SFS  May 1957
   THE BEST SCIENCE FICTION STORIES AND NOVELS: 9th SERIES [Dikty - 1958]
Hunting Season, The by Frank M. Robinson...........................ASF  Nov 1951
   YEAR'S BEST SCIENCE FICTION NOVELS: 1952 [Bleiler & Dikty - 1952]
Hurkle is a Happy Beast, The by Theodore Sturgeon..................F&SF  Fal 1949
   THE SCIENCE FICTION GALAXY [Conklin - 1950]
   THE BEST SCIENCE FICTION STORIES: 1950 [Bleiler & Dikty - 1950]
Hyperpilosity by L. Sprague de Camp................................Ast  Apr 1938
   THE OMNIBUS OF SCIENCE FICTION [Conklin - 1952]
Hypnoglyph, The by John Anthony ps (John Ciardi)...................F&SF  Jul 1953
   PORTALS OF TOMORROW [Derleth - 1954]
   A DECADE OF FANTASY & SCIENCE FICTION [Mills - 1960]

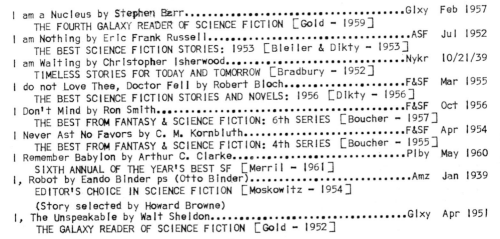

I am a Nucleus by Stephen Barr......................................Glxy  Feb 1957
   THE FOURTH GALAXY READER OF SCIENCE FICTION [Gold - 1959]
I am Nothing by Eric Frank Russell.................................ASF  Jul 1952
   THE BEST SCIENCE FICTION STORIES: 1953 [Bleiler & Dikty - 1953]
I am Waiting by Christopher Isherwood..............................Nykr  10/21/39
   TIMELESS STORIES FOR TODAY AND TOMORROW [Bradbury - 1952]
I do not Love Thee, Doctor Fell by Robert Bloch....................F&SF  Mar 1955
   THE BEST SCIENCE FICTION STORIES AND NOVELS: 1956 [Dikty - 1956]
I Don't Mind by Ron Smith..........................................F&SF  Oct 1956
   THE BEST FROM FANTASY & SCIENCE FICTION: 6th SERIES [Boucher - 1957]
I Never Ast No Favors by C. M. Kornbluth...........................F&SF  Apr 1954
   THE BEST FROM FANTASY & SCIENCE FICTION: 4th SERIES [Boucher - 1955]
I Remember Babylon by Arthur C. Clarke.............................Plby  May 1960
   SIXTH ANNUAL OF THE YEAR'S BEST SF [Merril - 1961]
I, Robot by Eando Binder ps (Otto Binder)..........................Amz  Jan 1939
   EDITOR'S CHOICE IN SCIENCE FICTION [Moskowitz - 1954]
   (Story selected by Howard Browne)
I, The Unspeakable by Walt Sheldon.................................Glxy  Apr 1951
   THE GALAXY READER OF SCIENCE FICTION [Gold - 1952]

|  | Mag. | Year |
|---|---|---|

I Want My Name in the Title by Winona McClintic......(verse)........F&SF  Jul 1956
    THE BEST FROM FANTASY & SCIENCE FICTION: 6th SERIES [Boucher - 1957]
Icarus Montgolfier Wright by Ray Bradbury.............................F&SF  May 1956
    THE BEST FROM FANTASY & SCIENCE FICTION: 6th SERIES [Boucher - 1957]
Idealist by Lester del Rey...........................................ORIGINAL STORY
    STAR SCIENCE FICTION STORIES [Pohl - 1953]
Idealists, The by John W. Campbell, Jr. .............................ORIGINAL STORY
    9 TALES OF SPACE AND TIME [Healy - 1954]
Ideas Die Hard by Isaac Asimov.......................................Glxy  Oct 1957
    THE THIRD GALAXY READER OF SCIENCE FICTION [Gold - 1958]
Idiot Stick by Damon Knight..........................................ORIGINAL STORY
    STAR SCIENCE FICTION STORIES #4 [Pohl - 1958]
Idol of the Flies, The by Jane Rice..................................Unk  Jun 1942
    CHILDREN OF WONDER [Tenn - 1953]
If You was a Maklin by Murray Leinster ps (Will F. Jenkins)........Glxy  Sep 1951
    THE GALAXY READER OF SCIENCE FICTION [Gold - 1952]
Illusionaries, The by Eric Frank Russell.............................PS  Nov 1951
    SPACE PIONEERS [Norton - 1954]
I'm Scared by Jack Finney............................................Col  9/15/51
    TOMORROW, THE STARS [Heinlein - 1952]
Image of the Gods, The by Alan E. Nourse...........................Orb #4  Sep 1954
    PLANET OF DOOM AND OTHER STORIES [Anonymous - 1958]
Imagine: A Proem by Fredric Brown....................................F&SF  May 1955
    (Originally appeared under title Imagine)
    THE BEST FROM FANTASY & SCIENCE FICTION: 5th SERIES [Boucher - 1956]
Immortal, The by Ross Rocklynne......................................Com  Mar 1941
    TOMORROW'S UNIVERSE [H. J. Campbell - 1954]
Immortal Game, The by Poul Anderson..................................F&SF  Feb 1954
    THE BEST FROM FANTASY & SCIENCE FICTION: 4th SERIES [Boucher - 1955]
Immortals, The by James E. Gunn......................................ORIGINAL STORY
    STAR SCIENCE FICTION STORIES #4 [Pohl - 1958]
Implode and Peddle by H. B. Fyfe.....................................ASF  Nov 1951
    SPACE SERVICE [Norton - 1953]
Impossible Highway, The by Oscar J. Friend...........................TWS  Aug 1940
    THE SAINT'S CHOICE [Charteris - 1945]
    GREAT STORIES OF SCIENCE FICTION [Leinster - 1951]
Impossible Voyage Home, The by F. L. Wallace.........................Glxy  Aug 1954
    SCIENCE FICTION ADVENTURES IN MUTATION [Conklin - 1956]
Imposter by Philip K. Dick...........................................Glxy  Jun 1953
    SCIENCE FICTION TERROR TALES [Conklin - 1955]
    BEST SF TWO SCIENCE FICTION STORIES [Crispin - 1956]
    THE END OF THE WORLD [Wollheim - 1956]
Impulse by Eric Frank Russell........................................ASF  Sep 1948
    INVADERS OF EARTH [Conklin - 1952]
"In a Good Cause ── " by Isaac Asimov................................ORIGINAL STORY
    NEW TALES OF SPACE AND TIME [Healy - 1951]
In Hiding by Wilmar H. Shiras........................................ASF  Nov 1948
    THE BEST SCIENCE FICTION STORIES: 1949 [Bleiler & Dikty - 1949]
    GREAT STORIES OF SCIENCE FICTION [Leinster - 1951]
    CHILDREN OF WONDER [Tenn - 1953]
    STORIES FOR TOMORROW [Sloane - 1954]
In Lonely Hands by Harlan Ellison....................................FU  Jan 1959
    THE FANTASTIC UNIVERSE OMNIBUS [Santesson - 1960]
In Memoriam: Fletcher Pratt by James Blish..........(verse).........F&SF  Jan 1957
    THE BEST FROM FANTASY & SCIENCE FICTION: 7th SERIES [Boucher - 1958]

|  |  | Mag. | Year |
|---|---|---|---|

In Memoriam: Henry Kuttner by Karen Anderson.......(verse).........F&SF  May 1958
  THE BEST FROM FANTASY & SCIENCE FICTION: 8th SERIES [Boucher - 1959]
In The Abyss by H. G. Wells...........................................Prn  Aug 1896
  THE POCKET BOOK OF SCIENCE FICTION [Wollheim - 1943]
In The Days of Our Fathers by Winona McClintic.......................MoF  Fal 1949
  THE BEST FROM FANTASY & SCIENCE FICTION [Boucher & McComas - 1952]
In The House, Another by Joseph Whitehill............................F&SF  Apr 1960
  SIXTH ANNUAL OF THE YEAR'S BEST SF [Merril - 1961]
In The Penal Colony by Franz Kafka..................(From The Penal Colony; 1948)
  (Translated by Willa and Edmin Muir)
  TIMELESS STORIES FOR TODAY AND TOMORROW [Bradbury - 1952]
In The Scarlet Star by Jack Williamson...............................Amz  Mar 1933
  EVERY BOY'S BOOK OF SCIENCE FICTION [Wollheim - 1951]
In The Vault by H. P. Lovecraft......................................WT  Apr 1932
  THE OTHER WORLDS [Stong - 1941]
In The World's Dusk by Edmond Hamilton...............................WT  Mar 1936
  THE END OF THE WORLD [Wollheim - 1956]
In The Year 2889 by Jules Verne......................................For  Feb 1889
  THE BIG BOOK OF SCIENCE FICTION [Conklin - 1950]
"In This Sign" by Ray Bradbury.......................................Im  Apr 1951
  LOOKING FORWARD [Lesser - 1953]
  BEST SF SCIENCE FICTION STORIES [Crispin - 1958]
  (Appeared under title The Fire Balloons)
In Value Deceived by H. B. Fyfe......................................ASF  Nov 1950
  POSSIBLE WORLDS OF SCIENCE FICTION [Conklin - 1951]
  STORIES OF SCIENTIFIC IMAGINATION [Gallant - 1954]
  STORIES FOR TOMORROW [Sloane - 1954]
Inanimate Objection by H. Chandler Elliott...........................Glxy  Feb 1954
  SPECTRUM [Amis & Conquest - 1961]
Incident On Calypso by Murray Leinster ps (Will F. Jenkins).........Stg  Fal 1945
  INVASION FROM MARS [Welles - 1949]
Incommunicado by Katherine MacLean...................................ASF  Jun 1950
  SIX GREAT SHORT NOVELS OF SCIENCE FICTION [Conklin - 1960]
Incubation by John D. MacDonald......................................ORIGINAL STORY
  FUTURE TENSE [Crossen - 1953]
Infinity by Rosser Reeves....................(verse).................F&SF  Dec 1960
  THE BEST FROM FANTASY & SCIENCE FICTION: 10th SERIES [Mills - 1961]
Infinity of Guests, An by George Gamow....(From One, Two, Three...Infinity; 1947)
  FANTASIA MATHEMATICA [Fadiman - 1958]
Infinity Zero by Donald Wandrei......................................Ast  Oct 1936
  FAR BOUNDARIES [Derleth - 1951]
Inflexible Logic by Russel Maloney...................................Nykr  2/3/1940
  TIMELESS STORIES FOR TODAY AND TOMORROW [Bradbury - 1952]
  FANTASIA MATHEMATICA [Fadiman - 1958]
Infra-Medians by Sewell Peaslee Wright...............................Ast  Dec 1931
  EVERY BOY'S BOOK OF SCIENCE FICTION [Wollheim - 1951]
Inheritors, The by John Michael and Robert W. Lowndes...............Fut  Oct 1942
  TERROR IN THE MODERN VEIN [Wollheim - 1955]
Inner Worlds, The by William Morrison ps (Joseph Samachson)........F&SF  Apr 1954
  THE BEST SCIENCE FICTION STORIES AND NOVELS: 1955 [Dikty - 1955]
Inquiry Concerning the Curvature of the Earth's Surface and Divers Investigations
  of a Metaphysical Nature, An by Roger Price....................Mncl  Win 1959
  THE FIFTH ANNUAL OF THE YEAR'S BEST SF [Merril - 1960]
Inside Earth by Poul Anderson........................................Glxy  Apr 1951
  THE GALAXY READER OF SCIENCE FICTION [Gold - 1952]

                                                                Mag.     Year
Inside John Barth by William W. Stuart............................Glxy    Jun 1960
    THE FIFTH GALAXY READER [Gold - 1961]
Instinct by Lester del Rey.......................................ASF     Jan 1952
    THE OMNIBUS OF SCIENCE FICTION [Conklin - 1952]
Instructor by Thelwell...............(cartoon)...................Pch     1/18/61
    SIXTH ANNUAL OF THE YEAR'S BEST SF [Merril - 1961]
Interbalance by Katherine MacLean................................F&SF    Oct 1960
    THE BEST FROM FANTASY & SCIENCE FICTION: 10th SERIES [Mills - 1961]
Interloper by Poul Anderson......................................F&SF    Apr 1961
    THE OUTER REACHES [Derleth - 1951]
Interplanetary Copyright by Donald F. Reines..............ORIGINAL STORY
    COMING ATTRACTIONS [Greenberg - 1957]
Interpretation of a Dream by John Collier........................Nykr    5/5/51
    BEYOND THE BARRIERS OF SPACE AND TIME [Merril - 1954]
Interstellar Zoo, The by David Kyle.......................ORIGINAL STORY
    (Special descriptive story accompanying Edd Cartier's pictorial feature "Life
    On Other Worlds")
    TRAVELERS OF SPACE [Greenberg - 1952]
Interview by Bird Ferguson................(verse).................F&SF    Dec 1955
    THE BEST FROM FANTASY & SCIENCE FICTION: 6th SERIES [Boucher - 1957]
Interview With A Lemming by James Thurber...(From My Worlds & Welcome To It; 1943)
    SHOT IN THE DARK [Merril - 1950]
Into Thy Hands by Lester del Rey.................................ASF     Aug 1945
    THE ROBOT AND THE MAN [Greenberg - 1953]
    LOOKING FORWARD [Lesser - 1953]
Into Your Tent I'll Creep by Eric Frank Russell..................ASF     Sep 1957
    THE BEST SCIENCE FICTION STORIES AND NOVELS: 9th SERIES [Dikty - 1958]
Intruder On The Rim by Milton Lesser.................(See listing Operation Zero)
Invariant by John R. Pierce.....................................ASF     Apr 1944
    THE ASTOUNDING SCIENCE FICTION ANTHOLOGY [J. W. Campbell - 1952]
Invasion by Frank Belknap Long...................................Stg     Jul 1950
    FAR BOUNDARIES [Derleth - 1951]
Invasion From Inner Space by Howard Koch..................ORIGINAL STORY
    STAR SCIENCE FICTION STORIES #6 [Pohl - 1959]
Invasion From Mars by Howard Koch............The radio script of the Orson Welles
    broadcast of H. G. Wells' The War Of The Worlds over the Columbia Broadcasting
    System, October 30, 1938.       (Copyright 1940 by Princeton University Press)
    INVASION FROM MARS [Welles - 1949]
    INVADERS OF EARTH [Conklin - 1952]
    THE. TREASURY OF SCIENCE FICTION CLASSICS [Kuebler - 1955]
Invasion of the Planet of Love by George P. Elliott.............F&SF    Jan 1959
    THE BEST FROM FANTASY & SCIENCE FICTION: 9th SERIES [Mills - 1960]
Invisible Boy, The by Ray Bradbury..............................Mdm     Nov 1945
    INVISIBLE MEN [Davenport - 1960]
Invisible Dove Dancer of Strathpheen Island, The by John Collier.................
    (From Presenting Moonshine; 1941)        INVISIBLE MEN [Davenport - 1960]
Invisible Man Murder Case, The by Henry Slesar.................. Fnt     May 1958
    INVISIBLE MEN [Davenport - 1960]
Invisible Prisoner, The by Maurice LeBlanc.....................(No data available)
    INVISIBLE MEN [Davenport - 1960]
Ionian Cycle, The by William Tenn ps (Philip Klass)................TWS    Aug 1949
    TRAVELERS OF SPACE [Greenberg - 1952]
Iron Standard, The by Lewis Padgett ps (Henry Kuttner & C.L. Moore)..ASF  Dec 1945
    MEN AGAINST THE STARS [Greenberg - 1950]
Is There Life on the Moon? by H. Percy Wilkins....................CYE    Jan 1953
    SCIENCE FICTION AND READER'S GUIDE [Barrows - 1954]

|                                                                      | Mag. | Year |
|----------------------------------------------------------------------|------|------|
| Island In the Sky by Manly Wade Wellman.............................. | TWS  | Oct 1941 |
| THE GIANT ANTHOLOGY OF SCIENCE FICTION [Margulies & Friend - 1954]    |      |      |
| Island of Fine Colors by Martin Gardner.............................. | ORIGINAL STORY | |
| FUTURE TENSE [Crossen - 1953]                                         |      |      |
| FANTASIA MATHEMATICA [Fadiman - 1958]                                 |      |      |
| Isolationist by Mack Reynolds........................................ | FA   | Apr 1950 |
| THE BIG BOOK OF SCIENCE FICTION [Conklin - 1950]                      |      |      |
| It Pays To Advertise by Kris Neville................................. | F&SF | Jun 1953 |
| TOMORROW'S UNIVERSE [H. J. Campbell - 1954]                           |      |      |
| It's A Good Life by Jerome Bixby..................................... | ORIGINAL STORY | |
| STAR SCIENCE FICTION STORIES #2 [Pohl - 1952]                         |      |      |
| STAR OF STARS [Pohl - 1960]                                           |      |      |
| BEST SF FOUR SCIENCE FICTION STORIES [Crispin - 1961]                 |      |      |
| It's A Great Big Wonderful Universe by Vance Aandahl................. | F&SF | Nov 1960 |
| THE BEST FROM FANTASY & SCIENCE FICTION: 10th SERIES [Mills - 1961]   |      |      |
| It's All HowwYou Look At It by Isaac Asimov.......(verse).......Fut #39 Oct 1958 |  |  |
| (See listing The Thunder-Thieves)                                    |      |      |
| SF: 59 THE YEAR'S GREATEST SCIENCE-FICTION AND FANTASY [Merril - 1959] |    |      |
| It's Going To Be True! by Burke Fanthway............................. | ORIGINAL STORY | |
| ADVENTURES TO COME [Esenwein - 1937]                                  |      |      |
| It's Great To Be Back by Robert A. Heinlein......................... | SEP  | 7/26/1947 |
| A TREASURY OF SCIENCE FICTION [Conklin - 1948]                        |      |      |
| It's Such A Beautiful Day by Isaac Asimov............................ | ORIGINAL STORY | |
| STAR SCIENCE FICTION STORIES #3 [Pohl - 1954]                         |      |      |
| Ivy War, The by David H. Keller...................................... | Amz  | May 1930 |
| THE BEST OF SCIENCE FICTION [Conklin - 1946]                          |      |      |
| Izzard and the Membrane by Walter M. Miller, Jr. ................... | ASF  | May 1951 |
| YEAR'S BEST SFISNCE FICTION NOVELS: 1952 [Bleiler & Dikty - 1952]     |      |      |

# J

| J. G. by Roger Price..........................(From J. G.: The Upright Ape; 1960) | | |
| SIXTH ANNUAL OF THE YEAR'S BEST SF [Merril - 1961]                    |      |      |
| Jackson Wong's Story by John Bolsover..............(London Observer Prize Story) | | |
| A. D. 2500 [Wilson - 1955]                                            |      |      |
| Jackdaw by Ross Rocklynne............................................ | ASF  | Aug 1942 |
| THE BEST OF SCIENCE FICTION [Conklin - 1946]                          |      |      |
| Jay Score by Eric Frank Russell...................................... | ASF  | May 1941 |
| TOMORROW, THE STARS [Heinlein - 1952]                                 |      |      |
| Jaywalker by Ross Rocklynne......................................... | Glxy | Dec 1950 |
| THE GALAXY READER OF SCIENCE FICTION [Gold - 1952]                    |      |      |
| Jeremy In the Wind by Nigel Kneale....................(From Tomato Cain; 1950) | | |
| TIMELESS STORIES FOR TODAY AND TOMORROW [Bradbury - 1952]             |      |      |
| Jester, The by William Tenn ps (Philip Klass)....................... | TWS  | Aug 1951 |
| SCIENCE FICTION THINKING MACHINES [Conklin - 1954]                    |      |      |
| Jesus Shoes by Allan R. Bosworth..................................... | Unk  | Apr 1942 |
| FROM UNKNOWN WORLDS [J. W. Campbell - 1948]                           |      |      |

|  | Mag. | Year |
|---|---|---|

Jetsam by A. Bertram Chandler.........................................NW #20  Mar 1953
   THE BEST FROM NEW WORLDS [Carnell - 1955]
   MEN ON THE MOON [Wollheim - 1958]
Jezebel by Murray Leinster ps (Will F. Jenkins).......................Stg  Oct 1953
   PORTALS OF TOMORROW [Derleth - 1954]
Jizzle by John Wyndham ps (John Beynon Harris)...............Rpnt - F&SF  Feb 1952
   (Originally appeared in Collier's January 8, 1949 under pseudonym
       John Beynon. Revised for publication in Fantasy & Science Fiction.)
   THE BEST FROM FANTASY & SCIENCE FICTION: 2nd SERIES [Boucher & McComas-1953]
John Jones' Dollar by Harry Stephen Keeler..........................Amz  Apr 1927
   STRANGE PORTS OF CALL [Derleth - 1948]
   FANTASIA MATHEMATICA [Fadiman - 1958]
John The Revelator by Oliver La Farge...............................F&SF  Feb 1951
   THE BEST FROM FANTASY & SCIENCE FICTION [Boucher & McComas - 1952]
John Thomas's Cure by John Leimert..................................Atl  Aug 1945
   THE OMNIBUS OF SCIENCE FICTION [Conklin - 1952]
John W. Campbell Jr.'s Who Goes There by Randall Garrett........................
   (See listings under titles All About "The Thing" and Parodies Tossed.)
John's Other Practice by Winston Marks..............................Im  Jul 1954
   THE BEST SCIENCE FICTION STORIES AND NOVELS: 1955 [Dikty - 1955]
Jon's World by Philip K. Dick....................................ORIGINAL STORY
   TIME TO COME [Derleth - 1954]
Jordan by Zeena Henderson..........................................F&SF  Mar 1959
   A DECADE OF FANTASY & SCIENCE FICTION [Mills - 1960]
Journey, The by Murray Leinster ps (Will F. Jenkins)................ORIGINAL STORY
   STAR SCIENCE FICTION STORIES [Pohl - 1953]
Journey to the Center of the Earth, A by Jules Verne.........................
   (From A Voyage to the Center of the Earth; Hetzel [Paris] 1864)
   JOURNEYS IN SCIENCE FICTION [Loughlin & Popp - 1961]
Journey Work by Dave Dryfoos.......................................If  Jan 1955
   THE FIRST WORLD OF IF [Quinn & Wulff - 1957]
Journey's End by Poul Anderson....................................F&SF  Feb 1957
   THE BEST FROM FANTASY & SCIENCE FICTION: 7th SERIES [Boucher - 1958]
Judas Ram by Sam Merwin, Jr. ......................................Glxy  Dec 1950
   THE GALAXY READER OF SCIENCE FICTION [Gold - 1952]
Judgement Day by L. Sprague de Camp................................ASF  Aug 1955
   THE BEST SCIENCE FICTION STORIES AND NOVELS: 1956 [Dikty - 1956]
Juggernaut by A. E. Van Vogt.......................................ASF  Aug 1944
   A TREASURY OF SCIENCE FICTION [Conklin - 1948]
Jungle, The by Charles Beaumont...................................If  Dec 1954
   THE SECOND WORLD OF IF [Quinn & Wulff - 1958]
Jungle Doctor by Robert F. Young..................................Stg  Fal 1955
   THE BEST SCIENCE FICTION STORIES AND NOVELS: 1956 [Dikty - 1956]
Junior by Robert Abernathy.........................................Glxy  Jan 1956
   SF: THE YEAR'S GREATEST SCIENCE FICTION AND FANTASY [Merril - 1956]
Junkyard by Clifford D. Simak......................................Glxy  May 1953
   THE SECOND GALAXY READER OF SCIENCE FICTION [Gold - 1954]
Jurgen Proves It by Arithmetic by James Branch Cabell..........(From Jurgen; 1919)
   FANTASIA MATHEMATICA [Fadiman - 1958]

# K

Kaleidoscope by Ray Bradbury.........................................TWS   Oct 1949
      THE OMNIBUS OF SCIENCE FICTION [Conklin - 1952]
Keep Out by Fredric Brown...........................................Amz   Mar 1954
      SCIENCE FICTION ADVENTURES IN MUTATION [Conklin ± 1956]
Keeper of the Dream by Charles Beaumont.........................ORIGINAL STORY
      TIME TO COME [Derleth - 1954]
Keyhole by Murray Leinster ps (Will F. Jenkins).....................TWS   Dec 1951
      TOMORROW, THE STARS [Heinlein - 1952]
      CHILDREN OF WONDER [Tenn - 1953]
      MEN ON THE MOON [Wollheim - 1958]
Kill Me With Kindness by Richard Wilson............................Glxy  Jan 1958
      THE FOURTH GALAXY READER OF SCIENCE FICTION [Gold - 1959]
Killdozer! by Theodore Sturgeon.....................................ASF   Nov 1944
      THE BEST OF SCIENCE FICTION [Conklin - 1946]
Kindness by Lester del Rey..........................................ASF   Oct 1954
      THE YEAR AFTER TOMORROW [Del Rey, Matschat and Carmer - 1952]
Kindergarten by Clifford D. Simak..................................Glxy  Jul 1953
      PORTALS OF TOMORROW [Derleth - 1954]
King of the Cats, The by Stephen Vincent Benet......................HBZ   Feb 1929
      OUT OF THIS WORLD [Fast - 1944]
King of the Grey Spaces by Ray Bradbury............................FFM   Dec 1943
      THE SCIENCE FICTION GALAXY [Conklin - 1950]
      EVERY BOY'S BOOK OF SCIENCE FICTION [Wollheim - 1951]
King of Thieves, The by Jack Vance.................................Stg   Jul 1949
      LOOKING FORWARD [Lesser - 1953]
King's Evil by Avram Davidson......................................F&SF  Oct 1956
      THE BEST FROM FANTASY & SCIENCE FICTION: 6th SERIES [Boucher - 1957]
Kleon of the Golden Sun by Ed Earl Repp............................FB #7 n/d 1950
      SCIENCE AND SORCERY [Ford - 1953]
Knitting, The by Margaret Wood....................(London Observer Prize Story)
      A. D. 2500 [Wilson - 1955]
Knock by Fredric Brown.............................................TWS   Dec 1948
      THE BEST SCIENCE FICTION STORIES: 1949 [Bleiler & Dikty - 1949]
      SHOT IN THE DARK [Merril - 1950]

# L

Laboratory by Jerome Bixby..........................................If   Dec 1955
    THE FIRST WORLD OF IF [Quinn & Wulff - 1957]
Lady Who Sailed the Soul, The by Cordwainer Smith....................Glxy  Apr 1960
    MIND PARTNER AND EIGHT OTHER NOVELETS FROM GALAXY [Gold - 1961]
Lagging Profession, The by Leonard Lockhard ps (Theodore L. Thomas)..ASF  Jan 1961
    SIXTH ANNUAL OF THE YEAR'S BEST SF [Merril - 1961]
Lament by a Maker by L. Sprague de Camp.............(verse)..........F&SF  Jan 1955
    THE BEST FROM FANTASY & SCIENCE FICTION: 5th SERIES [Boucher - 1956]
Lancelot Biggs on the Saturn by Nelson S. Bond......................................
    (From Lancelot Biggs: Spaceman; 1950)
    SCIENCE FICTION AND READER'S GUIDE [Barrows - 1954]
Land of No Shadow, The by Carl H. Claudy.........................AmB  Feb 1931
    THE YEAR AFTER TOMORROW [Del Rey, Matschat & Carmer - 1952]
Language For Time Travelers by L. Sprague de Camp...................ASF  Jul 1938
    COMING ATTRACTIONS [Greenberg - 1957]
Lanson Screen, The by Arthur Leo Zagat..............................TWS  Dec 1936
    THE BEST OF SCIENCE FICTION [Conklin - 1946]
Laocoon Complex, The by J. C. Furnas................................Esq  Apr 1937
    TIMELESS STORIES FOR TODAY AND TOMORROW [Bradbury - 1952]
    BEYOND THE BARRIERS OF SPACE AND TIME [Merril - 1954]
Laputa by Jonathan Swift.......................(From Gulliver's Travels; 1726)
    BEYOND TIME AND SPACE [Derleth - 1950]
Large Ant, The by Howard Fast.......................................FU  Feb 1960
    SIXTH ANNUAL OF THE YEAR'S BEST SF [Merril - 1961]
Last American, The by J.A. Mitchell.................................................
    (Originally published by Frederick A. Stokes Co.; 1889)
    FAR BOUNDARIES [Derleth - 1951]
Last Crusade, The by George H. Smith................................If  Feb 1955
    THE FIRST WORLD OF IF [Quinn & Wulff - 1957]
Last Day, The by Richard Matheson...................................Amz  May 1953
    THE BEST SCIENCE FICTION STORIES: 1954 [Bleiler & Dikty - 1954]
Last Day of Summer, The by E. C. Tubb..........................SF #12  Feb 1955
    SF: THE YEAR'S GREATEST SCIENCE FICTION AND FANTASY [Merril - 1956]
Last Days of Shandaker, The by Leigh Brackett (Mrs. Edmond Hamilton)............
                                                               Stg  Apr 1952
    PRIZE SCIENCE FICTION [Wollheim - 1953]
Last Enemy by H. Beam Piper.........................................ASF  Aug 1950
    THE ASTOUNDING SCIENCE FICTION ANTHOLOGY [J. W. Campbell - 1952]
Last Letter, The by Fritz Leiber...................................Glxy  Jun 1958
    THE FIFTH GALAXY READER [Gold - 1961]
Last Magician, The by Bruce Elliot.................................F&SF  Jan 1953
    FANTASIA MATHEMATICA [Fadiman - 1958]
Last Man, The by Charles Beckman, Jr. .........................Orb #5  Nov 1954
    (Originally appeared under title Noah)
    SPACE STATION 42 AND OTHER STORIES [Anonymous - 1958]

|  |  | Mag. | Year |

Last Man, The by Wallace G. West......................................,Amz  Feb 1929
   THE POCKET BOOK OF SCIENCE FICTION [Wollheim - 1943]
Last Martian, The by Fredric Brown...................................Glxy  Oct 1950
   THE BEST SCIENCE FICTION STORIES: 1951 [Bleiler & Dikty - 1951]
   THE GALAXY READER OF SCIENCE FICTION [Gold - 1952]
Last Monster, The by Poul Anderson...................................Sup  Aug 1951
   LOOKING FORWARD [Lesser - 1953]
Last Night Of Summer by Alfred Coppel..............................Orb #4  Sep 1954
   THE END OF THE WORLD [Wollheim - 1956]
   PLANET OF DOOM AND OTHER STORIES [Anonymous - 1958]
Last Objective, The by Paul Carter..................................ASF  Aug 1946
   A TREASURY OF SCIENCE FICTION [Conklin - 1948]
Last of the Masters, The by Philip K. Dick.........................Orb #5  Nov 1954
   SPACE STATION 42 AND OTHER STORIES [Anonymous - 1958]
Last Prophet, The by Mildred Clingerman.............................F&SF  Aug 1955
   THE BEST FROM FANTASY & SCIENCE FICTION: 5th SERIES [Boucher - 1956]
Last Present, The by Will Stanton...................................F&SF  Aug 1956
   THE BEST FROM FANTASY & SCIENCE FICTION: 6th SERIES [Boucher - 1957]
Last Rites by Charles Beaumont.......................................If  Oct 1955
   THE FIRST WORLD OF IF [Quinn & Wulff - 1957]
Last Seance, The by Agatha Christie.................................Gst  n/d/a 1926
   BEYOND THE BARRIERS OF SPACE AND TIME [Merril - 1954]
Last Shall Be First, The by Robert P. Mills........................F&SF  Aug 1958
   A DECADE OF FANTASY & SCIENCE FICTION [Mills - 1960]
Last Terrestrials, The by Olaf Stapledon..........(From Last and First Men; 1930)
   THE TREASURY OF SCIENCE FICTION CLASSICS [Kuebler - 1955]
Last Victory, The by Tom Godwin......................................If  Aug 1957
   THE BEST SCIENCE FICTION STORIES AND NOVELS: 9th SERIES [Dikty - 1958]
Last War, The by Arthur Dekker Savage..............................Orb #2  n/d 1954
   (Originally appeared under title THE BUTTERFLY KISS)
   PLANET OF DOOM AND OTHER STORIES [Anonymous - 1958]
Last Weapon, The by Robert Sheckley............................ORIGINAL STORY
   STAR SCIENCE FICTION STORIES [Pohl - 1952]
Last Woman, The by Thomas S. Gardner.................................WS  Apr 1932
   FROM OFF THIS WORLD [Margulies & Friend - 1949]
Last Word, The by Chad Oliver and Charles Beaumont..................F&SF  Apr 1955
   THE BEST FROM FANTASY & SCIENCE FICTION: 5th SERIES [Boucher - 1956]
Late Night Final by Eric Frank Russell..............................ASF  Dec 1948
   THE ASTOUNDING SCIENCE FICTION ANTHOLOGY [J. W. Campbell - 1952]
Later Than You Think by Fritz Leiber, Jr. ..........................Glxy  Oct 1950
   FAR BOUNDARIES [Derleth - 1951]
Laura by Saki ps (H. H. Munro)..............(From Beast and Super Beasts; 1914)
   OUT OF THIS WORLD [Fast - 1944]
Leech, The by Robert Sheckley.......................................Glxy  Dec 1952
   SCIENCE FICTION TERROR TALES [Conklin - 1955]
Leinbach's Proof by Arthur Schnitzler................................
   (From Flight Into Darkness; S. Fischer - Berlin; 1931)
   FANTASIA MATHEMATICA [Fadiman - 1958]
Let Me Live In a House by Chad Oliver...............................USF  Mar 1954
   SCIENCE FICTION TERROR TALES [Conklin - 1955]
Let Nothing You Dismay by William Sloane.......................ORIGINAL STORY
   STORIES FOR TOMORROW [Sloane - 1954]
Let The Ants Try by James McCreigh ps (Frederik Pohl)...............PS  Win 1949
   BEYOND THE END OF TIME [Pohl - 1952]
Let There Be Light by H. B. Fyfe.....................................If  Nov 1952
   CROSSROADS IN TIME [Conklin - 1953]
   THE FIRST WORLD OF IF [Quinn & Wulff - 1957]

|                                                                                      | Mag. | Year |
|--------------------------------------------------------------------------------------|------|------|

Let's Be Frank by Brian W. Aldiss.................................SF #23 Jun 1957
    SF: 58 THE YEAR'S GREATEST SCIENCE FICTION AND FANTASY [Merril - 1958]
Let's Get Together by Isaac Asimov.....................................Inf Feb 1957
    SF: 58 THE YEAR'S GREATEST SCIENCE FICTION AND FANTASY [Merril - 1958]
Let's Not by Isaac Asimov..............................................BUGJ Dec 1954
    ALL ABOUT THE FUTURE [Greenberg - 1955]
Letters From Laura by Mildred Clingerman...........................F&SF Oct 1954
    A TREASURY OF GREAT SCIENCE FICTION [Boucher - 1959]
Letter From The Stars by A. E. Van Vogt..........................OTWA Jul 1950
    BEYOND THE END OF TIME [Pohl - 1952]
    THE EARTH IN PERIL [Wollheim - 1957]
Letter To a Phoenix by Fredric Brown................................ASF Aug 1949
    JOURNEY TO INFINITY [Greenberg - 1951]
Letter To Ellen by Chan Davis.......................................ASF Jun 1947
    SCIENCE FICTION THINKING MACHINES [Conklin - 1954]
Letter To Tennyson, A — Anonymous.............................No Data available
    FANTASIA MATHEMATICA [Fadiman - 1958]
Letter To the Martians, A by Willy Ley.............................TWS Nov 1940
    (Originally appeared under title Calling All Martians)
    COMING ATTRACTIONS [Greenberg - 1957]
Letters To the Editor by Ron Goulart..............................Plcn Oct 1951
                                 Rpnt — F&SF Apr 1952
    THE BEST FROM FANTASY & SCIENCE FICTION: 2nd SERIES [Boucher & McComas-1952]
Liar! by Isaac Asimov...............................................ASF May 1941
    HUMAN? [Merril - 1954]
Life By Television, A by Jack Arnold...........................ORIGINAL STORY
    ADVENTURES TO COME [Esenwein - 1937]
Life Cycle by Peter Hawkins.........................................NW #9 Spr 1951
    GATEWAY TO TOMORROW [Carnell - 1954]
Life On Other Worlds by Edd Cartier...........................ORIGINAL STORY
    (Special pictorial feature depicting an Interstellar Zoo)
    (See listing The Interstellar Zoo by David Kyle)
    TRAVELERS OF SPACE [Greenberg - 1952]
Life On the Moon by Alexander Samalman..........................TWS Dec 1946
    SHOT IN THE DARK [Merril - 1950]
Life Work Of Professor Muntz, The by Murray Leinster ps (Will F. Jenkins).........
                                           TWS Jun 1949
    THE SCIENCE FICTION GALAXY [Conklin - 1950]
    THE BEST SCIENCE FICTION STORIES: 1950 [Bleiler & Dikty - 1950]
Light, The by Poul Anderson......................................Glxy Mar 1957
    13 GREAT STORIES OF SCIENCE FICTION [Conklin - 1960]
Like A Bird, Like A Fish by H. B. Hickey ps (Herb Livingston).........WB Feb 1951
    WORLDS OF TOMORROW [Derleth - 1953]
Like Gods They Came by Irving Cox, Jr. ...........................AvR Jan 1953
    SPACE, SPACE, SPACE [Sloane - 1953]
Lilies Of Life by Malcolm Jameson.................................ASF Feb 1945
    POSSIBLE WORLDS OF SCIENCE FICTION [Conklin - 1951]
    PLANET OF DOOM AND OTHER STORIES [Anonymous - 1958]
        (Appeared under title Planet Of Doom)
Limiting Factor by Theodore R. Cogswell..........................Glxy Apr 1954
    SCIENCE FICTION ADVENTURES IN MUTATION [Conklin - 1956]
    THE THIRD GALAXY READER OF SCIENCE FICTION [Gold - 1958]
Limiting Factor by Clifford D. Simak..............................Stg Nov 1949
    POSSIBLE WORLDS OF SCIENCE FICTION [Conklin - 1951]
    BEYOND THE STARS AND OTHER STORIES [Anonymous - 1958]
    SPECTRUM [Amis & Conquest - 1961]

|  | Mag. | Year |
|---|---|---|

Line To Tomorrow by Lewis Padgett ps (Henry Kuttner & C.L. Moore).......ASF  Nov 1945
    WORLDS OF TOMORROW [Derleth - 1953]
Link, The by Cleve Cartmill................................................ASF  Aug 1942
    ADVENTURES IN TIME AND SPACE [Healy & McComas - 1946]
Lion's Mouth by Stephen Marlowe ps (Milton Lesser)....................FA  Jun 1952
    LOOKING FORWARD [Lesser - 1953]
Liquid Life by Ralph Milne Farley ps (Roger Sherman Hoar).............TWS  Oct 1936
    THE BEST OF SCIENCE FICTION [Conklin - 1946]
    GREAT STORIES OF SCIENCE FICTION [Leinster - 1951]
Listen by Gordon R. Dickson...............................................F&SF  Aug 1952
    PRIZE SCIENCE FICTION [Wollheim - 1953]
Listen, Children, Listen by Wallace West...............................FU  Nov 1953
    ZACHERLY'S MIDNIGHT SNACKS [Zacherly - 1960]
Listening Child, The by Idris Seabright ps (Margaret St. Clair)........F&SF  Dec 1950
    THE BEST FROM FANTASY & SCIENCE FICTION [Boucher & McComas - 1952]
Literary Corkscrew, The by David H. Keller.............................WS  Mar 1934
    FROM OFF THIS WORLD [Margulies & Friend - 1949]
Little Anton by R. Bretnor................................................ORIGINAL STORY
    NEW TALES OF SPACE AND TIME [Healy - 1951]
Little Black Bag, The by C. M. Kornbluth..............................ASF  Jul 1950
    BEYOND THE END OF TIME [Pohl - 1952]
Little Black Train, The by Manly Wade Wellman.........................F&SF  Aug 1954
    THE BEST FROM FANTASY & SCIENCE FICTION: 4th SERIES [Boucher - 1955]
Little Creeps, The by Walter M. Miller, Jr. ..........................Amz  Dec 1951
    LOOKING FORWARD [Lesser - 1952]
Little Journey, A by Ray Bradbury.....................................Glxy  Aug 1951
    THE GALAXY READER OF SCIENCE FICTION [Gold - 1952]
Little Lost Robot by Isaac Asimov.....................................ASF  Mar 1947
    BEST SF TWO SCIENCE FICTION STORIES [Crispin - 1956]
Little Man On the Subway, The by Isaac Asimov & James MacCreigh ps (Frederik Pohl)...
                                                                     FB #6  n/d 1950
    SCIENCE AND SORCERY [Ford - 1953]
Little Men by Jessamyn West...........................................ORIGINAL STORY
    STAR SHORT NOVELS [Pohl - 1954]
Littlest People, The by Raymond E. Banks.............................Glxy  Mar 1954
    THE BEST SCIENCE FICTION STORIES AND NOVELS: 1955 [Dikty - 1955]
Living Fossil by L. Sprague de Camp..................................ASF  Feb 1939
    A TREASURY OF SCIENCE FICTION [Conklin - 1948]
Living Galaxy, The by Laurence Manning...............................WS  Sep 1934
    THE SCIENCE FICTION GALAXY [Conklin - 1950]
Living Machine, The by David H. Keller...............................WS  May 1935
    EVERY BOY'S BOOK OF SCIENCE FICTION [Wollheim - 1951]
Lobby by Clifford D. Simak...........................................ASF  Apr 1944
    THE BEST OF SCIENCE FICTION [Conklin - 1946]
Locked Out by H. B. Fyfe.............................................ASF  Feb 1940
    MEN AGAINST THE STARS [Greenberg - 1950]
Logic Named Joe, A by Murray Leinster ps (Will F. Jenkins)...........ASF  Mar 1946
    (Originally appeared under byline of Will F. Jenkins)
    SCIENCE FICTION CARNIVAL [Brown & Reynolds - 1953]
Loint Of Paw, A by Isaac Asimov......................................F&SF  Aug 1957
    THE BEST FROM FANTASY & SCIENCE FICTION: 7th SERIES [Boucher - 1958]
Lonely Planet, The by Murray Leinster ps (Will F. Jenkins)...........TWS  Dec 1949
    BEYOND THE END OF TIME [Pohl - 1952]
Long Dawn, The by Noel Loomis........................................Sup  Jan 1950
    THE BIG BOOK OF SCIENCE FICTION [Conklin - 1950]

Mag.    Year

Long Echo, The by Miriam Allen DeFord...............................ORIGINAL STORY
   STAR SCIENCE FICTION STORIES #4 [Pohl - 1958]
Long Remembering, The by Poul Anderson..............................F&SF  Nov 1957
   SCIENCE FICTION SHOWCASE [M. Kornbluth - 1959]
Long View, The by Fletcher Pratt....................................ORIGINAL STORY
   THE PETRIFIED-PLANET [Pratt - 1952]
Long Watch, The by Robert A. Heinlein...............................ALM  Dec 1949
   BEYOND TIME AND SPACE [Derleth - 1950]
Loophole by Arthur C. Clarke........................................ASF  Apr 1946
   A TREASURY OF SCIENCE FICTION [Conklin - 1948]
Lord Mountdrago by W. Somerset Maughm...........(From The Mixture As Before; 1939)
   THE MOONLIGHT TRAVELER [Stern - 1943]
Lord Of A Thousand Suns by Poul Anderson............................PS  Sep 1951
   TALES OF OUTER SPACE [Wollheim - 1954]
Loreli Of the Red Mist by Ray Bradbury & Leigh Brackett  (Mrs. Edmond Hamilton)...
                                                              TWS  Fal 1953
   THREE TIMES INFINITY [Margulies - 1958]
Lost Art by George O. Smith.........................................ASF  Dec 1943
   A TREASURY OF GREAT SCIENCE FICTION [Boucher - 1959]
Lost Chord, The by Sam Moskowitz....................................ORIGINAL STORY
   SCIENCE AND SORCERY [Ford - 1953]
Lost Memory by Peter Phillips.......................................Glxy  May 1952
   GATEWAY TO TOMORROW [Carnell - 1954]
   THE SECOND GALAXY READER OF SCIENCE FICTION [Gold - 1954]
   SCIENCE FICTION TERROR TALES [Conklin - 1955]
Lost Race, The by Murray Leinster ps (Will F. Jenkins)..............TWS  Apr 1949
   MY BEST SCIENCE FICTION STORY [Margulies & Friend - 1949]
Lost Street, The by Carl Jacob' & Clifford D. Simak.................Com  Jul 1941
   (Originally appeared under title The Street That Wasn't There)
   STRANGE PORTS OF CALL [Derleth - 1948]
Lost Years, The by Oscar Lewis......................................
   (Originally published by Alfred A. Knopf, N. Y.; 1951)
   A TREASURY OF GREAT SCIENCE FICTION [Boucher - 1959]
Lot by Ward Moore...................................................F&SF  May 1953
   THE BEST FROM FANTASY & SCIENCE FICTION: 3rd SERIES [Boucher & McComas-1953]
   THE BEST SCIENCE FICTION STORIES: 1954 [Bleiler & Dikty - 1954]
   PENGUIN SCIENCE FICTION [Aldiss - 1961]
Lot's Daughter by Ward Moore........................................F&SF  Oct 1954
   A DECADE OF FANTASY & SCIENCE FICTION [Mills - 1960]
Lotus Eaters, The by Stanley G. Weinbaum............................Ast  Apr 1935
   BEYOND TIME AND SPACE [Derleth - 1950]
   UBERWINDUNG VON RAUM UND ZEIT [Gunther - 1952]
   THE HIDDEN PLANET [Wollheim - 1959]
Love by Richard Wilson..............................................F&SF  Jun 1952
   SHADOW OF TOMORROW [Pohl - 1953]
Love In the Dark by H. L. Gold......................................Sus  Fal 1951
   (Originally appeared under title Love Etheral)
   BEYOND THE END OF TIME [Pohl - 1952]
   INVISIBLE MEN [Davenport - 1960]
Love Of Heaven, The by Theodore Sturgeon............................ASF  Nov 1948
   SCIENCE FICTION ADVENTURES IN MUTATION [Conklin - 1956]
Love Story by Christopher Monig.....................................ORIGINAL STORY
   FUTURE TENSE [Crossen - 1953]
Lover When You're Near Me by Richard Matheson.......................Glxy  May 1952
   THE BEST SCIENCE FICTION STORIES: 1953 [Bleiler & Dikty - 1953]
   THE SECOND GALAXY READER OF SCIENCE FICTION [Gold - 1954]

| | Mag. | Year |
|---|---|---|

Luck Of Ignatz, The by Lester del Rey...............................ASF   Aug 1939
    THE YEAR AFTER TOMORROW [Del Rey, Matschat & Carmer - 1952]
    THE HIDDEN PLANET [Wolheim - 1959]
Luckiest Men In Denv by Simon Eisner................................Glxy   Jun 1952
    SHADOW OF TOMORROW [Pohl - 1953]
Lulugomeena by Gordon R. Dickson....................................Glxy   Jan 1954
    LOOKING FORWARD [Lesser - 1953]
Lunar Escapade by H. B. Fyfe........................................Orb #2   n/d 1954
    PLANET OF DOOM AND OTHER STORIES [Anonymous - 1958]
Lurani by Paul Dennis Lavond ps (Robert W. Lowndes)......(verse).....Unk   Feb 1940
    FROM UNKNOWN WORLDS [J. W. Campbell - 1948]
Lyric For Atom-Splitters by Doris Pitkin Buck...........(verse).....F&SF   May 1957
    THE BEST FROM FANTASY & SCIENCE FICTION: 7th SERIES [Boucher - 1958]
Lysenko Maze, The by David Grinnell.................................F&SF   Jul 1954
    SCIENCE FICTION ADVENTURES IN MUTATION [Conklin - 1956]

# *M*

M 33 In Andromeda by A. E. Van Vogt.................................ASF   Aug 1943
    TOMORROW'S UNIVERSE [H. J. Campbell - 1954]
Machine by John W. Jakes............................................F&SF   Apr 1952
    THE BEST SCIENCE FICTION STORIES: 1953 [Bleiler & Dikty - 1953]
Machine, The by Richard B. Gehman...................................Col   12/14/46
    13 GREAT STORIES OF SCIENCE FICTION [Conklin - 1960]
Machine Made by J. T. M'Intosh ps (James J. MacGregor)............NW #10   Sum 1951
    NO PLACE LIKE EARTH [Carnell - 1952]
Machine Man Of Ardathia, The [L'Homme-Machine D'ardathia] ..........................
    by Francis Flagg ps (George Henry Weiss)........................Amz   Nov 1927
    ESCALES DANS L'INFINI [Gallet - 1954]
Machine Stops, The by E. M. Forster.................................................
    (From The Eternal Moment and Other Stories; 1928)
    THE SCIENCE FICTION GALAXY [Conklin - 1950]
    THE TREASURY OF SCIENCE FICTION CLASSICS [Kuebler - 1955]
Machine, The by Don A. Stuart ps (John W. Campbell, Jr.).............Ast   Feb 1935
    THE BEST OF SCIENCE FICTION [Conklin - 1946]
Machine That Was Lonely, The by Robert Wells.........(London Observer Prize Story)
    A. D. 2500 [Wilson - 1955]
Mad Wizards Of Mars, The by Ray Bradbury.................(See listing The Exiles)
Made In U.S.A. by J. T. M'Intosh ps (James J. MacGregor)............Glxy   Apr 1953
    CROSSROADS IN TIME [Conklin - 1953]
Made To Measure by William Campbell Gault...........................Glxy   Jan 1951
    THE GALAXY READER OF SCIENCE FICTION [Gold - 1952]
Magic City by Nelson S. Bond........................................ASF   Feb 1941
    A TREASURY OF GREAT SCIENCE FICTION [Boucher - 1959]
Make A Prison by Lawrence Block.....................................OSFS   Jan 1959
    THE FIFTH ANNUAL OF THE YEAR'S BEST SF [Merril - 1960]
Maladjusted Classroom, The by H. Nearing, Jr. .....................F&SF   Jun 1953
    THE BEST FROM FANTASY & SCIENCE FICTION: 3rd SERIES [Boucher & McComas-1954]

|                                                                         | Mag. | Year |
|---|---|---|

Malice Aforethought by David Grinnell.............................F&SF  Nov 1952
    BEYOND THE BARRIERS OF SPACE AND TIME [Merril - 1954]
Malignant Marauder by Murray Leinster ps (Will F. Jenkins)..........TWS  Sum 1946
    (Originally appeared under title Dead City)
    THE ULTIMATE INVADER AND OTHER SCIENCE FICTION [Wollheim - 1954]
Man, The by Ray Bradbury.............................................TWS  Feb 1949
    THE BEST SCIENCE FICTION STORIES: 1950 [Bleiler & Dikty - 1950]
Man From Mars, The by P. Schuyler Miller............................WSQ  Sum 1931
    FROM OFF THIS WORLD [Margulies & Friend - 1949]
Man From Outside, The by Jack Williamson............................ASF  Mar 1951
    BEACHHEADS IN SPACE [Derleth - 1952]
    LOOKING FORWARD [Lesser - 1953]
Man In a Quandry by L. J. Stecher, Jr. .............................Glxy  Jul 1958
    THE FOURTH GALAXY READER OF SCIENCE FICTION [Gold - 1959]
Man In Asbestos: An Allegory of the Future by Stephen Leacock...................
    (From Nonsense Novels; 1941)
    ASPECTS OF SCIENCE FICTION [Doherty - 1959]
Man In Space by Daniel Lang.........................................Nykr  11/15/1958
    SF: 59 THE YEAR'S GREATEST SF AND FANTASY [Merril - 1959]
Man in the Black Hat. The by Michael Fessier........................Esq  Feb 1934
    THE OTHER WORLDS [Stong - 1941]
Man In the Earphones, The by Wilbur Schramm................Rpnt-SEP  5/29/1947#
    (From Windwagon Smith and Other Yarns; 1947)
    THE SATURDAY EVENING POST FANTASY STORIES [Fles - 1951]
Man In the Jar by Damon Knight......................................Glxy  Apr 1957
    THE THIRD GALAXY READER OF SCIENCE FICTION [Gold - 1958]
Man In the Moon, The by Henry A. Norton.............................ASF  Feb 1943
    INVADERS OF EARTH [Conklin - 1952]
Man In the Moon, The by Mack Reynolds...............................Amz  Jul 1950
    LOOKING FORWARD [Lesser - 1953]
Man In the Moone, The by Bishop Francis Godwin.................................
    (Originally appeared under pseudonym Domingo Gonsales)
        (Orignally published in London by Joshua Kirton and Thomas Warren; 1638)
    BEYOND TIME AND SPACE [Derleth - 1950]
Man In the Moon Comes Down, A by Berger Copeman...................ORIGINAL STORY
    ADVENTURES TO COME [Esenwein - 1937]
Man In the Sky by Algis Budrys.....................................ASF  Mar 1956
    EVERY BOY'S BOOK OF OUTER SPACE STORIES [Dikty - 1960]
Man Manifold by Peter Young.......................(London Observer Prize Story)
    A. D. 2500 [Wilson - 1955]
Man of Destiny by John Christopher ps (Christopher S. Youd)........Glxy  May 1951
    THE GALAXY READER OF SCIENCE FICTION [Gold - 1952]
    LOOKING FORWARD [Lesser - 1953]
Man of Distinction by Michael Shaara...............................Glxy  Oct 1956
    THE FOURTH GALAXY READER OF SCIENCE FICTION [Gold - 1959]
Man of Parts by H. L. Gold........................................ORIGINAL STORY
    9 TALES OF SPACE AND TIME [Healy - 1954]
Man on Top, The by R. Bretnor..........................................Sch  10/24/1951
                                   Rpnt — F&SF  Sep 1960
    SIXTH ANNUAL OF THE YEAR'S BEST SF [Merril - 1961]
Man Overboard by John Collier......................................F&SF  Mar 1960
    THE BEST FROM FANTASY & SCIENCE FICTION: 10th SERIES [Mills - 1961]
Man Who Always Knew, The by Algis Budrys...........................ASF  Apr 1956
    THE BEST SCIENCE FICTION STORIES AND NOVELS: 1956 [Dikty - 1956]
Man Who Ate The World, The by Frederik Pohl........................Glxy  Nov 1956
    SCIENCE FICTION SHOWCASE [M. Kornbluth - 1959]
Man Who Came Early, The by Poul Anderson...........................F&SF  Jun 1956
    THE BEST FROM FANTASY & SCIENCE FICTION: 6th SERIES [Boucher - 1957]

|                                                                      | Mag. | Year |

Man Who Could Work Miracles, The by H. G. Wells...................ILN  Jul 189●
   THE MOONLIGHT TRAVELER [Stern - 1943]
Man Who Evolved, The by Edmond Hamilton..........................WS  Apr 193
   FROM OFF THIS WORLD [Margulies & Friend - 1949]
Man Who Knew All the Answers, The by Donald Bern.................Amz  Aug 194●
   THE OTHER WORLDS [Stong - 1941]
Man Who Liked Lions, The by John Bernard Daley...................Inf  Oct 195●
   SF: 57 THE YEAR'S GREATEST SCIENCE FICTION & FANTASY [Merril - 1957]
Man Who Lost the Sea, The by Theodore Sturgeon..................F&SF  Oct 195●
   THE BEST FROM FANTASY & SCIENCE FICTION: 9th SERIES [Mills - 1960]
   THE FIFTH ANNUAL OF THE YEAR'S BEST SF [Merril - 1960]
Man Who Missed the Bus, The by Stella Benson ps (Mrs. Jo Anderson)............
   (From The Collected Short Stories of Stella Benson; 1936)
   THE MOONLIGHT TRAVELER [Stern - 1943]
Man Who Rode the Saucer by Kenyon Holmes ps (August Derleth).......ORIGINAL STOR●
   FAR BOUNDARIES [Derleth - 1951]
Man Who Saved the Earth, The by Austin Hall.......................Amz  Apr 192●
   THE BEST OF SCIENCE FICTION [Conklin - 1946]
Man Who Sold Rope to the Gnoles, The by Idris Seabright ps (Margaret St. Clair).
                                                                 F&SF  Oct.195
   BEYOND HUMAN KEN [Merril - 1952]
Man Who Sold the Moon, The by Robert A. Heinlein..............................
   (Originally published by Shasta Publishers; 1950)
   A TREASURY OF GREAT SCIENCE FICTION [Boucher - 1959]
Man With English, The by H. L. Gold............................ORIGINAL STOR●
   STAR SCIENCE FICTION STORIES [Pohl - 1953]
   STAR OF STARS [Pohl - 1960]
Man With the Hour Glass, The by L. A. Eshbach.....................MT  May 193
   THE GARDEN OF FEAR AND OTHER STORIES [Crawford - 1945]
Man With the Strange Head, The by Miles J. Breuer, M. D. ..........Amz  Jan 192
   THE BIG BOOK OF SCIENCE FICTION [Conklin - 1950]
Man Working by Richard Wilson..................................ORIGINAL STOR
   STAR SCIENCE FICTION STORIES #4 [Pohl - 1958]
Manna by Peter Phillips...........................................ASF  Feb 194
   THE BIG BOOK OF SCIENCE FICTION [Conklin - 1950]
Manners of the Age by H. B. Fyfe...............................Glxy  Mar 195●
   THE OMNIBUS OF SCIENCE FICTION [Conklin - 1952]
Mantage by Richard Matheson....................................ORIGINAL STOR
   SCIENCE FICTION SHOWCASE [M. Kornbluth - 1959]
Manuscript Found in a Vacuum by P. M. Hubbard...................Pch  12/17/195
                                                         Rpnt - F&SF  Aug 1953
   THE BEST FROM FANTASY & SCIENCE FICTION: 3rd SERIES [Boucher & McComas-1954
Many Dreams of Earth by Charles E. Fritch..........(See listing Space Station 42
Maracot Deep, The by Arthur Conan Doyle......................................
   (From The Maracot Deep and Other Stories; 1929)
   THE TREASURY OF SCIENCE FICTION CLASSICS [Kuebler - 1955]
Marching Morons, The by Cyril M. Kornbluth......................Glxy  Apr 195
   THE BEST SCIENCE FICTION STORIES: 1952 [Bleiler & Dikty - 1952]
   SHADOW OF TOMORROW [Pohl - 1953]
Margenes, The by Miriam Allen DeFord..............................If  Feb 195
   THE FIRST WORLD OF IF [Quinn & Wulff - 1957]
Margin For Error by Lewis Padgett ps (Henry Kuttner & C.L. Moore)...ASF  Nov 194
   THE BIG BOOK OF SCIENCE FICTION [Conklin - 1950]
Mariana by Fritz Leiber..........................................Fnt  Feb 196●
   THE FIFTH ANNUAL OF THE YEAR'S BEST SF [Merril - 1960]
Mark of the Beast, The by Rudyard Kipling............(From LIFE'S HANDICAP; 1891
   WORLD OF WONDER [Pratt - 1951]

Mars and Miss Pickerell by Ellen MacGregor..........................................
    (From Miss Pickerell Goes To Mars; 1951)
    SCIENCE FICTION AND READER'S GUIDE [Barrows - 1954]
Mars Colonizers by M. J. Breuer.....................................MT   Sum 1935
    THE GARDEN OF FEAR AND OTHER STORIES [Crawford - 1945]
Mars Is Heaven! by Ray Bradbury....................................PS   Fal 1948
    THE BEST SCIENCE FICTION STORIES: 1949 [Bleiler & Dikty - 1949]
    SHOT IN THE DARK [Merril - 1950]
Mars On the Ether by Lord Dunsany..................................Crnt Sep 1937
    STRANGE PORTS OF CALL [Derleth - 1948]
Martian and the Moron, The by Theodore Sturgeon....................WT   Mar 1949
    WORLDS OF TOMORROW [Derleth - 1953]
Martian Crown Jewels, The by Poul Anderson.........................EQMM Feb 1958
                                                        Rpnt — F&SF Apr 1959
    A TREASURY OF GREAT SCIENCE FICTION [Boucher - 1959]
    THE SCIENCE FICTIONAL SHERLOCK HOLMES [Peterson - 1960]
Martian Odyssey, A by Stanley G. Weinbaum..........................WS   Jul 1934
    THE POCKET BOOK OF SCIENCE FICTION [Wollheim - 1943]
    FROM OFF THIS WORLD [Margulies & Friend - 1949]
    ESCALES DANS L'INFINI [Gallet - 1954]  (Appeared as ODYSSEE MARTIENNE)
Martian Shop, The by Howard Fast...................................F&SF Nov 1959
    A DECADE OF FANTASY & SCIENCE FICTION [Mills - 1960]
Martians, The by Olaf Stapledon...................(From Last and First Men; 1930)
    THE TREASURY OF SCIENCE FICTION CLASSICS [Kuebler - 1955]
Martians and the Coys, The by Mack Reynolds........................Im   Jun 1951
    SCIENCE FICTION CARNIVAL [Brown & Reynolds - 1953]
Martyr, The by Poul Anderson.......................................F&SF Mar 1960
    THE BEST FROM FANTASY & SCIENCE FICTION: 10th SERIES [Mills - 1961]
Mary Anonymous by Bryce Walton.....................................PS   Sum 1954
    THE EARTH IN PERIL [Wollheim - 1957]
Mask Of Demeter, The by Martin Pearson ps (Donald A. Wollheim) & Cecil Corwin ps
    (C. M. Kornbluth)..............................................F&SF Jan 1953
    PRIZE SCIENCE FICTION [Wollheim - 1953]
Master Minds of Mars, The by Carl H. Claudy........................AmB  Sep 1931
    (Originally appeared under joint byline Carl H. Claudy and Dr. John C. Paige)
    THE YEAR AFTER TOMORROW [Del Rey, Matschact and Carmer - 1952]
Master of the Asteroid by Clark Ashton Smith.......................WS   Oct 1932
    STRANGE PORTS OF CALL [Derleth - 1948]
Master Race by Richard Ashby.......................................Im   Sep 1951
    SPACE, SPACE, SPACE [Sloane - 1953]
Masquerade by Clifford D. Simak...................(See listing Operation Mercury)
Mathematical Love by Andrew Marvell..............(From The Definition Of Love; 1650)
    FANTASIA MATHEMATICA [Fadiman - 1958]
Mathematical Voodoo, The by H. Nearing, Jr. .......................F&SF Apr 1951
    THE BEST FROM FANTASY & SCIENCE FICTION [Boucher & McComas - 1952]
    FANTASIA MATHEMATICA [Fadiman - 1958]
Mating of the Moons, The by Kenneth O'Hara ps (Bryce Walton)......Orb #2 n/d 1954
    PLANET OF DOOM AND OTHER STORIES [Anonymous - 1958]
Matter Of Energy, A by James Blish.................................F&SF May 1955
    (Excerpt from With Malice To Come - 3 Vignettes)
    THE BEST FROM FANTASY & SCIENCE FICTION: 5th SERIES [Boucher - 1956]
Matter Of Form, A by H. L. Gold....................................ASF  Dec 1938
    THE BIG BOOK OF SCIENCE FICTION [Conklin - 1950]
    ASSIGNMENT IN TOMORROW [Pohl - 1954]
Matter Of Size, A by Harry Bates..................................Ast  Apr 1934
    ADVENTURES IN TIME AND SPACE [Healy & McComas - 1946]

Maturity by Theodore Sturgeon.........................................ASF  Feb 1947
    6 GREAT SHORT NOVELS OF SCIENCE FICTION [Conklin — 1954]
Maturity Night by Frank Belknap Long, Jr. .........................ORIGINAL STORY
    THE GIRL WITH THE HUNGRY EYES AND OTHER STORIES [Wollheim — 1949]
Maybe Just a Little One by R. Bretnor..............................Hpr  Aug 1947
                                 Rpnt — F&SF  Feb 1953
    THE BEST FROM FANTASY & SCIENCE FICTION: 3rd SERIES [Boucher & McComas—1954]
McIlvaine's Star by August Derleth.................................If  Jul 1952
    WORLDS OF TOMORROW [Derleth — 1953]
    PRIZE SCIENCE FICTION [Wollheim — 1953]
Me by Herbert Schenck, Jr. ...............(verse)................F&SF  Aug 1959
    THE BEST FROM FANTASY & SCIENCE FICTION: 9th SERIES [Mills — 1960]
    THE FIFTH ANNUAL OF THE YEAR'S BEST SF [Merril — 1960]
Mechanical Answer, The by John D. MacDonald........................ASF  May 1948
    THE ROBOT AND THE MAN [Greenberg — 1953]
Mechanical Bride, The by Fritz Leiber.............................ORIGINAL STORY
    SCIENCE FICTION THINKING MACHINES [Conklin — 1954]
Mechanical Mice by Maurice G. Hugi ps (Eric Frank Russell)........ASF  Jan 1941
    ADVENTURES IN TIME AND SPACE [Healy & McComas — 1946]
Med Service by Murray Leinster ps (Will F. Jenkins)...............ASF  Aug 1957
    SCIENCE FICTION SHOWCASE [M. Kornbluth — 1959]
Medicine Dancer by Bill Brown.....................................BFF  Nov 1953
    BEYOND THE BARRIERS OF SPACE AND TIME [Merril — 1954]
Meeting Of Relations by John Collier..............................YR  Dec 1941
                                 Rpnt — F&SF  Jan 1959
    A DECADE OF FANTASY & SCIENCE FICTION [Mills — 1960]
Melhem In Ce Klasrum by Dolton Edwards.............................ASF  Sep 1949
    THE ASTOUNDING SCIENCE FICTION ANTHOLOGY [J. W. Campbell — 1952]
Memorial by Theodore Sturgeon.....................................ASF  Apr 1946
    THE OTHER SIDE OF THE MOON [Derleth — 1949]
Memory by Theodore Sturgeon.......................................TWS  Aug 1948
    ADVENTURES IN TOMORROW [Crossen — 1951]
Men Against the Stars by Manly Wade Wellman.......................ASF  Jun 1938
    MEN AGAINST THE STARS [Greenberg — 1950]
    EVERY BOY'S BOOK OF OUTER SPACE STORIES [Dikty — 1960]
Men Are Different by Alan Bloch...................................ORIGINAL STORY
    SCIENCE FICTION THINKING MACHINES [Conklin — 1954]
Men Of Iron by Guy Endore.................(Copyright 1940; Black and White Press)
                                 Rpnt — F&SF  Fal 1949
    A DECADE OF FANTASY & SCIENCE FICTION [Mills — 1960]
Men Of the Ten Books by Jack Vance................................Stg  Mar 1951
    THE BEST SCIENCE FICTION STORIES: 1952 [Bleiler & Dikty — 1952]
    OUT OF THIS WORLD I [Williams-Ellis & Owen — 1960]
Men Who Murdered Mohammed, The by Alfred Bester...................F&SF  Oct 1958
    THE BEST FROM FANTASY & SCIENCE FICTION: 8th SERIES [Boucher — 1959]
Mercurian, The by Frank Belknap Long, Jr. ........................PS  Win 194?
    FLIGHT INTO SPACE [Wollheim — 1950]
Metamorphosis by Franz Kafka......................(From The Metamorphosis; 1937?)
    WORLD OF WONDER [Pratt — 1951]
Metamorphosis of Earth, The by Clark Ashton Smith................WT  Sep 1951
    BEACHHEADS IN SPACE [Derleth — 1954]
Metamorphosite by Eric Frank Russell..............................ASF  Dec 1946
    JOURNEY TO INFINITY [Greenberg — 1951]
    BEACHHEADS IN SPACE [Derleth — 1954]

                                                              Mag.     Year
Meteor by John Beynon Harris...........................................Amz   Mar 1941
    (Originally appeared under title Phony Meteor under byline John Beynon)
    BEACHHEADS IN SPACE [Derleth - 1954]
Meteor by William T. Powers.............................................ASF   Sep 1950
    THE ASTOUNDING SCIENCE FICTION ANTHOLOGY [J. W. Campbell - 1952]
Mewhu's Jet by Theodore Sturgeon........................................ASF   Nov 1946
    THE BIG BOOK OF SCIENCE FICTION [Conklin - 1950]
Mex by Larry M. Harris..................................................FU    Jan 1957
    THE FANTASTIC UNIVERSE OMNIBUS [Santesson - 1960]
Mezzerow Loves Company by F. L. Wallace.................................Glxy  Jun 1956
    THE WORLD THAT COULDN'T BE AND 8 OTHER NOVELETTES FROM GALAXY [Gold - 1959]
Microcosmic God by Theodore Sturgeon....................................ASF   Apr 1941
    THE POCKET BOOK OF SCIENCE FICTION [Wollheim - 1943]
Microscopic Giants, The by Paul Ernst..................................WS    Oct 1936
    FROM OFF THIS WORLD [Margulies & Friend - 1949]
    SCIENCE FICTION TERROR TALES [Conklin - 1955]
Midas Plague, The by Frederik Pohl.....................................Glxy  Apr 1954
    ALL ABOUT THE FUTURE [Greenberg - 1955]
    SPECTRUM [Amis & Conquest - 1961]
Middle of the Week After Next, The by Murray Leinster ps (Will F. Jenkins)........
                                                              TWS     Aug 1952
    SCIENCE FICTION ADVENTURES IN DIMENSION [Conklin - 1953]
    THE BEST SCIENCE FICTION STORIES: 1953 [Bleiler & Dikty - 1953]
    OUT OF THIS WORLD 1 [Ellis & Owen - 1960]
Mile-Long Spaceship, The by Kate Wilhelm...............................ASF   Apr 1957
    THE BEST SCIENCE FICTION STORIES AND NOVELS: 9th SERIES [Dikty - 1958]
Million Year Picnic, The by Ray Bradbury..............................PS    Sum 1946
    STRANGE PORTS OF CALL [Derleth - 1948]
    INVASION FROM MARS [Welles - 1949]
    WORLD OF WONDER [Pratt - 1951]
Millionth Year, The by Martin Pearson ps (Donald A. Wollheim)........SFS   Apr 1943
    ADVENTURES IN THE FAR FUTURE [Wollheim - 1954]
Mimic by Donald A. Wollheim............................................Ash   Dec 1942
    (Originally appeared under pseudonym Martin Pearson)
    TERROR IN THE MODERN VEIN [Wollheim - 1955]
Mimsy Were the Borogoves by Lewis Padgett ps (Henry Kuttner & C. L. Moore)........
                                                              ASF   Feb 1943
    A TREASURY OF SCIENCE FICTION [Conklin - 1948]
    UBERWINDUNG VON RAUM UND ZEIT [Gunther - 1952]
        (Appeared as Erbarmlich War'n Die Burgerbeine)
Mind Partner by Christopher Anvil.....................................Glxy  Aug 1960
    MIND PARTNER AND 8 OTHER NOVELETTES FROM GALAXY [Gold - 1961]
Mindworm, The by Cyril M. Kornbluth....................................WB    Dec 1950
    THE BEST SCIENCE FICTION STORIES: 1951 [Bleiler & Dikty - 1951]
Mine Own Ways by Richard McKenna......................................F&SF  Feb 1960
    THE BEST FROM FANTASY & SCIENCE FICTION: 10th SERIES [Mills - 1961]
    SIXTH ANNUAL OF THE YEAR'S BEST SF [Merril - 1961]
Minimum Man, The by Robert Sheckley...................................Glxy  Jun 1958
    THE FOURTH GALAXY READER OF SCIENCE FICTION [Gold - 1959]
Minimum Sentence by Theodore R. Cogswell..............................Glxy  Aug 1953
    THE SECOND GALAXY READER OF SCIENCE FICTION [Gold - 1954]
Minister Without Portfolio by Mildred Clingerman......................F&SF  Feb 1952
    INVADERS OF EARTH [Conklin - 1952]
    STORIES FOR TOMORROW [Sloane - 1954]
Ministering Angels by C. S. Lewis.....................................F&SF  Jan 1958
    THE BEST FROM FANTASY & SCIENCE FICTION: 8th SERIES [Boucher - 1959]
Miriam by Truman Capote................(From Tree Of Night and Other Stories; 1945)
    CHILDREN OF WONDER [Tenn - 1953]

```
                                                          Mag.    Year
Minority Report by Theodore Sturgeon.........................ASF   Jun 1949
   BEYOND TIME AND SPACE [Derleth - 1950]
Misadventure by Lord Dunsany.................................F&SF  Oct 1954
   THE BEST FROM FANTASY & SCIENCE FICTION: 4th SERIES [Boucher - 1955]
Misbegotten Missionary by Isaac Asimov.......................Glxy  Nov 1950
   TOMORROW, THE STARS [Heinlein - 1952]
Misogynist, The by James E. Gunn............................Glxy .Nov 1952
   SHADOW OF TOMORROW [Pohl - 1953]
   THE SECOND GALAXY READER OF SCIENCE FICTION [Gold - 1954]
Miss Winters and the Wind by Christine Noble Govan..........Tmw   May 1946
   TIMELESS STORIES FOR TODAY AND TOMORROW [Bradbury - 1952]
Missing One's Coach: An Anachromism - Anonymous.............DLM   n/d/a 1838
   FAR BOUNDARIES [Derleth - 1951]
Mission, The by Arthur Sellings....................(London Observer Prize Story)
   A. D. 2500 [Wilson - 1955]
Mist, The by Peter Carter....................................F&SF  Sep 1952
   SCIENCE FICTION ADVENTURES IN DIMENSION [Conklin - 1953]
Mistake Inside by James Blish................................Stg   Mar 1948
   WORLD OF WONDER [Pratt - 1951]
Model of a Judge, The by William Morrison ps (Joseph Samachson).....Glxy  Oct 1953
   THE BEST SCIENCE FICTION STORIES: 1954 [Bleiler & Dikty - 1954]
   THE THIRD GALAXY READER OF SCIENCE FICTION [Gold - 1958]
Mold Of Yancy, The by Philip K. Dick.........................If    Jul 1955
   THE SECOND WORLD OF IF [Quinn & Wulff - 1958]
Moment Without Time by Joel Townsley Rogers..................Stg   Apr 1952
   THE BEST FROM STARTLING STORIES [Mines - 1953]
Momento Homo by Walter M. Miller, Jr. .......................Amz   Mar 1954
   THE BEST SCIENCE FICTION STORIES AND NOVELS: 1955 [Dikty - 1955]
Monster, The by Lester del Rey...............................Arg   Jun 1951
   TOMORROW, THE STARS [Heinlein - 1952]
Monster, The by Gerald Kersh.................................SEP   2/21/48
   THE OTHER SIDE OF THE MOON [Derleth - 1949]
Monster, The by A. E. Van Vogt....................(See listing Resurrection)
Monster From Nowhere, The by Nelson Bond.....................FA    Jul 1939
   THE BEST OF SCIENCE FICTION [Conklin - 1946]
Monster Named Smith, A by James E. Gunn......................If    Jul 1954
   THE SECOND WORLD OF IF [Quinn & Wulff - 1958]
Moon Is Green, The by Fritz Leiber...........................Glxy  Apr 1952
   THE BEST SCIENCE FICTION STORIES: 1953 [Bleiler & Dikty - 1953]
Moon Of Delirium by D. L. James..............................ASF   Jan 1940
   POSSIBLE WORLDS OF SCIENCE FICTION [Conklin - 1951]
Moon Terror, The by A. G. Birch..............................WT    May 1923
   THE MOON TERROR AND OTHER STORIES [Anonymous - 1927]
Moonwalk by H. B. Fyfe.......................................Spc   Nov 1952
   SPACE PIONEERS [Norton - 1954]
   MEN ON THE MOON [Wollheim - 1958]
Mop-Up by Arthur Porges......................................F&SF  Jul 1953
   GALAXY OF GHOULS [Merril - 1955]
More Facts About Robots by Leonard Wolfe..........(verse).........F&SF  Jan 1954
   THE BEST FROM FANTASY & SCIENCE FICTION: 4th SERIES [Boucher - 1955]
Morning Of the Day they Did It, The by E. B. White..............Nykr  2/25/50
   Re: The Second Tree From The Corner; 1950
   A TREASURY OF GREAT SCIENCE FICTION [Boucher - 1959]
Most Maddening Story in the World by Ralph Straus.................
   (From A Second Century of Creepy Stories - Edited by Hugh Walpole; 1937)
   THE MOONLIGHT TRAVELER [Stern - 1943]
Mother by Philip Jose Farmer.................................TWS   Apr 1953
   ASSIGNMENT IN TOMORROW [Pohl - 1954]
Mother and the Decimal Point by Richard Llewellyn...(Fr How Green Was My Valley; 1940)
   FANTASIA MATHEMATICA [Fadiman - 1958]
```

```
                                                              Mag.    Year
Mother Earth by Isaac Asimov.........................................ASF   May 1949
     JOURNEY TO INFINITY [Greenberg - 1951]
     THREE FROM OUT THERE [Margulies - 1959]
Mouse by Fredric Brown...............................................TWS   Jun 1949
     THE BEST SCIENCE FICTION STORIES: 1950 [Bleiler & Dikty - 1950]
Mousetrap by Andre Norton ps (Alice Mary Norton)....................F&SF   Jun 1954
     THE BEST SCIENCE FICTION STORIES AND NOVELS: 1955 [Dikty - 1955]
Moxon's Master by Ambrose Bierce...................(From Can Such Things Be; 1893)
     THE POCKET BOOK OF SCIENCE FICTION [Wollheim - 1943]
     SCIENCE FICTION THINKING MACHINES [Conklin - 1954]
     JOURNEYS IN SCIENCE FICTION [Loughlin & Popp - 1961]
Mr. Arculuris by Conrad Aiken.................(From Among The Last People; 1934)
     THE MOONLIGHT TRAVELER [Stern - 1943]
Mr. Bauer and the Atoms by Fritz Leiber, Jr. .......................WT    Jan 1946
     STRANGE PORTS OF CALL [Derleth - 1948]
Mr. Costello, Hero by Theodore Sturgeon............................Glxy   Dec 1953
     ASSIGNMENT IN TOMORROW [Pohl - 1954]
Mr. Death and the Redheaded Woman by Helen Eustis...................SEP   2/11/50
     (Originally appeared under title The Rider On The Pale Horse)
     TIMELESS STORIES FOR TODAY AND TOMORROW [Bradbury - 1952]
Mr. Kincaid's Pests by J. J. Coupling ps (John R. Pierce)..........F&SF   Aug 1953
     BEYOND THE BARRIERS OF SPACE AND TIME [Merril - 1954]
Mr. Lepescu by Anthony Boucher......................................WT    Sep 1945
     SHOT IN THE DARK [Merril - 1950]
Mr. Mergenthwirker's Lobblies by Nelson S. Bond.....................SM    Nov 1937
     OUT OF THIS WORLD [Fast - 1944]
Mr. Murphy of New York by Thomas McMorrow...........................SEP   3/27/50
     THE BIG BOOK OF SCIENCE FICTION [Conklin - 1950]
Mr. Sakrison's Halt by Mildred Clingerman..........................F&SF   Jan 1956
     THE BEST FROM FANTASY & SCIENCE FICTION: 6th SERIES [Boucher - 1957]
Mr. Stilwell's Stage by Avram Davidson.............................F&SF   Sep 1957
     THE BEST FROM FANTASY & SCIENCE FICTION: 7th SERIES [Boucher - 1958]
Mr. Strenberry's Tale by J. B. Priestly...................(From Four-In-Hand; 1934)
     TRAVELERS IN TIME [Stern - 1947]
     THE TREASURY OF SCIENCE FICTION CLASSICS [Kuebler - 1955]
Mrs. Manifold by Stephen Grendon ps (August Derleth)............ORIGINAL STORY
     THE GIRL WITH THE HUNGRY EYES AND OTHER STORIES [Wollheim - 1949]
Ms. Found In a Chinese Fortune Cookie by C. M. Kornbluth...........F&SF   Jul 1957
     THE BEST FROM FANTASY & SCIENCE FICTION: 7th SERIES [Boucher - 1958]
Multum In Parvo by Jack Sharkey....................................Gent   Dec 1959
     THE FIFTH ANNUAL OF THE YEAR'S BEST SF [Merril - 1960]
Museum Piece by Esther Carlson...............(From Moon Over The Back Fence; 1947)
     WORLD OF WONDER [Pratt - 1951]
Music Master Of Babylon, The by Edgar Pangborn.....................Glxy   Nov 1954
     THE WORLD THAT COULDN'T BE AND 8 OTHER NOVELETTES FROM GALAXY [Gold - 1959]
Music On the Hill, The by Saki ps (H. H. Munro)....................
     (From The Chronicles Of Clovis; 1912)
     THE MOONLIGHT TRAVELER [Stern - 1943]
Mutant's Brother, The by Fritz Leiber, Jr. .........................ASF   Aug 1943
     CROSSROADS IN TIME [Conklin - 1953]
Mute Question, The by Forrest J Ackerman............................OW    Sep 1950
     ADVENTURES IN TOMORROW [Crossen - 1951]
Muted Horn, The by Dorothy Salisbury Davis..........................FU    May 1957
     THE FANTASTIC UNIVERSE OMNIBUS [Santesson - 1960]
Muten by Eric Frank Russell.........................................ASF   Oct 1948
     (Originally appeared under pseudonym Duncan H. Munro)
     SCIENCE FICTION CARNIVAL [Brown & Reynolds - 1953]
My Boy Friend's Name is Jello by Avram Davidson....................F&SF   Jul 1954
     THE BEST FROM FANTASY & SCIENCE FICTION: 4th SERIES [Boucher - 1955]
My Father, The Cat by Henry Slesar..................................FU    Dec 1957
     THE FANTASTIC UNIVERSE OMNIBUS [Santesson - 1960]
My Friend Merton by Julius Fast................................ORIGINAL STORY
     OUT OF THIS WORLD [Fast - 1944]
Mystery Of the Last Guest, The by John Flanders ps (Jean Ray).......WT    Oct 1935
     THE OTHER WORLDS [Stong - 1941]
```

# N

N Day by Philip Latham ps (Robert S. Richardson).....................ASF   Jan 1946
  A TREASURY OF SCIENCE FICTION [Conklin - 1948]
Naked Lady by Mindret Lord.........................................WT   Sep 1934
  THE OTHER WORLDS [Stong - 1941]
Name Your Sympton by Jim Harmon...................................Glxy   Jul 1956
  THE FOURTH GALAXY READER OF SCIENCE FICTION [Gold - 1959]
Naming Of Names, The by Ray Bradbury..............................TWS   Aug 1949
  THE BEST FROM STARTLING STORIES [Mines - 1953]
  SCIENCE AND SORCERY [Ford - 1953]
Narapoia by Alan Nelson..............................Rpnt — F&SF  Apr 1951
  (Originally aprd under title The Origin of Narapoia in What's Doing Apr 1948)
  THE BEST FROM FANTASY & SCIENCE FICTION [Boucher & McComas - 1952]
Natural State by Damon Knight....................................Glxy   Jan 1954
  ALL ABOUT THE FUTURE [Greenberg - 1958]
Near Miss by Henry Kuttner....................................ORIGINAL STORY
  (Copyright 1958 by Dell Publishing Co. & Western Prtg & Lithographing Co.)
  SF: 58 THE YEAR'S GREATEST SF AND FANTASY [Merril - 1958]
Nellthu by Anthony Boucher......................................F&SF   Aug 1955
  THE BEST FROM FANTASY & SCIENCE FICTION: 5th SERIES [Boucher - 1956]
Nerves by Lester del Rey.........................................ASF   Sep 1942
  ADVENTURES IN TIME AND SPACE [Healy & McComas - 1946]
Never Ending Penny, The by Bernard Wolfe........................Plby   Sep 1960
  SIXTH ANNUAL OF THE YEAR'S BEST SF [Merril - 1961]
Never On Mars by John Beynon ps (John Beynon Harris).................FU   Jan 1954
  GATEWAY TO THE STARS [Carnell - 1955]
Never Underestimate... by Theodore Sturgeon.........................If   Jan 1952
  THE OMNIBUS OF SCIENCE FICTION [Conklin - 1952]
New Accelerator, The by H. G. Wells..............................Snd   Dec 1901
  BEYOND TIME AND SPACE [Derleth - 1950]
  INVISIBLE MEN [Davenport - 1960]
New Atlantis, The by Francis Bacon.........(Originally published in London; 1624)
  BEYOND TIME AND SPACE [Derleth - 1950]
New Ballard of Sir Patrick Spens, A by Arthur T. Quiller-Couch..(verse)....n/dta/a
  FANTASIA MATHEMATICA [Fadiman - 1958]
New Lo! by Ron Goulart...........................................F&SF   Jan 1958
  THE BEST FROM FANTASY & SCIENCE FICTION: 8th SERIES [Boucher - 1959]
New Reality, The by Charles L. Harness...........................TWS   Dec 1950
  THE BEST SCIENCE FICTION STORIES: 1951 [Bleiler & Dikty - 1951]
New Ritual by Idris Seabright ps (Margaret St. Clair)..............F&SF   Jan 1953
  THE BEST FROM FANTASY & SCIENCE FICTION: 3rd SERIES [Boucher & McComas-1954]
New Wine, The by John Christopher ps (Christopher S. Youd).......................
  (From The Twenty-Second Century; 1954)
  BEST SF SCIENCE FICTION STORIES [Crispin - 1955]
Next Stop: The Stars by Ray Bradbury.............................................
  (See listing The End Of The Beginning)

                                                                Mag.    Year
Night Flight by Josephine W. Johnson.........................Hpr  Feb 1944
        TIMELESS STORIES FOR TODAY AND TOMORROW [Bradbury - 1952]
Night He Cried, The by Fritz Leiber.......................ORIGINAL STORY
        STAR SCIENCE FICTION STORIES [Pohl - 1953]
        GALAXY OF GHOULS [Merril - 1955]
Night Meeting by Ray Bradbury.................(From The Martian Chronicles; 1950)
        SCIENCE FICTION ADVENTURES IN DIMENSION [Conklin - 1953]
Nightfall by Isaac Asimov...................................ASF  Sep 1951
        ADVENTURES IN TIME AND SPACE [Healy & McComas - 1946]
        THE ASTOUNDING SCIENCE FICTION ANTHOLOGY [J. W. Campbell - 1952]
        UBERWINDUNG VON RAUM UND ZEIT [Gunther - 1952]
           (Appeared under title Einbruch Der Nacht)
        PENGUIN SCIENCE FICTION [Aldiss - 1961]
Nightmare, The by Chan Davis...............................ASF  May 1946
        A TREASURY OF SCIENCE FICTION [Conklin - 1948]
Nightmare Brother by Alan E. Nourse........................ASF  Feb 1953
        SPACE, SPACE, SPACE [Sloane - 1953]
        SCIENCE FICTION TERROR TALES [Conklin - 1955]
Nightmare Blues by Frank Herbert...........................ASF  Jun 1954
        THE BEST SCIENCE FICTION STORIES AND NOVELS: 1955 [Dikty - 1955]
Nightmare For Future Reference: A narrative poem by Stephen Vincent Benet........
        CHILDREN OF WONDER [Tenn - 1953]                     Sch  9/17/38
Nightmare Number Four by Robert Bloch.....(This verse first appeared in a fanzine.
        This is its first professional appearance.)
        SCIENCE FICTION SHOWCASE [M. Kornbluth - 1959 ]
Nightmare Number Three by Stephen Vincent Benet...(verse)..(Fr Burning City; 1936)
        SHOT IN THE DARK [Merril - 1950]
Nightmare With Zeppelins by Frederik Pohl & C. M. Kornbluth........Glxy  Dec 1958
        THE FIFTH GALAXY READER [Gold - 1961]
Nightsound by Algis J. Budrys..............................Stl  Feb 1957
        (Originally appeared under title The Attic Voice)
        THE BEST SCIENCE FICTION STORIES AND NOVELS: 9th SERIES [Dikty - 1958]
Nikita Eisenhower Jones by Robert F. Young.................F&SF  Aug 1960
        THE BEST FROM FANTASY & SCIENCE FICTION: 10th SERIES [Mills - 1961]
Nine Billion Names Of God, The by Arthur C. Clarke.........ORIGINAL STORY
        STAR SCIENCE FICTION STORIES [Pohl - 1953]
        STORIES FOR TOMORROW [Sloane - 1954]
        BEST SF TWO SCIENCE FICTION STORIES [Crispin - 1956]
        ASPECTS OF SCIENCE FICTION [Doherty - 1959]
Nine-Finger Jack by Anthony Boucher........................Esq  May 1951
        THE BEST SCIENCE FICTION STORIES: 1952 [Bleiler & Dikty - 1952]
1980 Overtures by Winona McClintic...........(verse)..........F&SF  Apr 1955
        THE BEST FROM FANTASY & SCIENCE FICTION: 5th SERIES [Boucher - 1956]
No Connection by Isaac Asimov..............................ASF  Jun 1948
        THE BEST SCIENCE FICTION STORIES: 1949 [Bleiler & Dikty - 1949]
No Fire Burns by Avram Davidson............................Plby  Jul 1959
        THE FIFTH ANNUAL OF THE YEAR'S BEST SF [Merril - 1960]
No Land Of Ned by Sherwood Springer........................Stg  Dec 1952
        THE BEST FROM STARTLING STORIES [Mines - 1953]
No Man Pursueth by Ward Moore..............................F&SF  Apr 1956
        THE BEST FROM FANTASY & SCIENCE FICTION: 6th SERIES [Boucher - 1957]
No Matter Where You Go by Joel Townsley Rogers.............F&SF  Feb 1959
        THE BEST FROM FANTASY & SCIENCE FICTION: 9th SERIES [Mills - 1960]
No Moon For Me by Walter M. Miller, Jr. ...................ASF  Sep 1952
        SPACE, SPACE, SPACE [Sloane - 1953]
No More The Stars by Irving E. Cox.........................Orb #4  Sep 1954
        THE SANDS OF MARS AND OTHER STORIES [Anonymous - 1958]
No Morning After by Arthur C. Clarke......................ORIGINAL STORY
        TIME TO COME [Derleth - 1954]
No, No, Not Rogov! by Cordwainer Smith.....................If  Feb 1959
        THE FIFTH ANNUAL OF THE YEAR'S BEST SF [Merril - 1960]
No One Believed Me by Will Thompson........................SEP  4/24/48
        BEYOND THE BARRIERS OF SPACE AND TIME [Merril - 1954]

No Place Like Earth by John Beynon ps (John Beynon Harris)........NW #9  Spr 1951
    (This version incorporates Time To Rest from Arkham Sampler-Winter 1949)
       NO PLACE LIKE EARTH [Carnell - 1952]
       OUT OF THIS WORLD I [Ellis & Owen - 1960]
No Power On Earth by William Whewell..............(verse)....................
    (From An Elementary Treatise on Mechanics; 1819)
       FANTASIA MATHEMATICA [Fadiman - 1958]    (revised version)
No Ships Pass by Lady Eleanor Smith...............................Cas  Apr 1932
       TRAVELERS IN TIME [Stern - 1947]
No-Sided Professor by Martin Gardner..............................Esq  Jan 1947
                                   Rpnt — F&SF  Feb 1951
       THE BEST FROM FANTASY & SCIENCE FICTION [Boucher & McComas - 1952]
       FANTASIA MATHEMATICA [Fadiman - 1958]
No Woman Born by C. L. Moore  (Mrs. Henry Kuttner)................ASF  Dec 1944
       A TREASURY OF SCIENCE FICTION [Conklin - 1946]
       GREAT STORIES OF SCIENCE FICTION [Leinster - 1951]
       BEST SF SCIENCE FICTION STORIES [Crispin - 1955]
Noah by Charles Beckman, Jr. .........................(See listing The Last Man)
Nobody Bothers Gus by Algis Budrys...............................ASF  Nov 1955
    (Originally appeared under psuedonym Paul Janvier)
       SF: THE YEAR'S GREATEST SCIENCE FICTION AND FANTASY [Merril - 1956]
"Nobody Here But —" by Isaac Asimov.............................ORIGINAL STORY
       STAR SCIENCE FICTION STORIES [Pohl - 1953]
Nobody Saw the Ship by Murray Leinster ps (Will F. Jenkins)......Fw/SFS  May 1950
       THE BIG BOOK OF SCIENCE FICTION [Conklin - 1950]
Noise by Jack Vance..............................................Stg  Aug 1952
       THE BEST FROM STARTLING STORIES [Mines - 1953]
Noise In the Night, The by William Hope Hodgson.....................
    (From The House On the Borderland; 1908)
       BEYOND TIME AND SPACE [Derleth - 1950]
Noise Level by Raymond F. Jones..................................ASF  Dec 1952
       STORIES FOR TOMORROW [Sloane - 1954]
None Before Me by Sidney Carroll.................................Csmp  Jul 1949
       TIMELESS STORIES FOR TODAY AND TOMORROW [Bradbury - 1952]
Not A Creature Was Stirring by Dean Evans........................Glxy  Dec 1951
       SHADOW OF TOMORROW [Pohl - 1953]
Not Final! by Isaac Asimov.......................................ASF  Oct 1941
       POSSIBLE WORLDS OF SCIENCE FICTION [Conklin - 1951]
Not Fit For Children by Evelyn E. Smith..........................Glxy  May 1953
       THE SECOND GALAXY READER OF SCIENCE FICTION [Gold - 1954]
Not Fit to be Opened by Roger Flint Young........................ASF  Jan 1950
       THE BEST SCIENCE FICTION STORIES: 1951 [Bleiler & Dikty - 1951]
Not For An Age by Brian W. Aldiss................................Obs  1/9/1955
       A. D. 2500 [Wilson - 1955]
Not Only Dead Men by A. E. Van Vogt..............................ASF  Nov 1942
       INVADERS OF EARTH [Conklin - 1952]
Not With a Bang by Damon Knight..................................F&SF  Spr 1950
       THE BIG BOOK OF SCIENCE FICTION [Conklin - 1950]
Note For the Milkman, A by Sidney Carroll........................TJW  Apr 1950
       TIMELESS STORIES FOR TODAY AND TOMORROW [Bradbury - 1952]
Note On Danger B by Gerald Kersh.................................SEP  4/5/1947
       THE SATURDAY EVENING POST FANTASY STORIES [Fles - 1951]
"Nothing Happens On The Moon" by Paul Ernst......................ASF  Feb 1939
       THE OMNIBUS OF SCIENCE FICTION [Conklin - 1952]
Nothing In the Rules by L. Sprague de Camp.......................Unk  Jul 1939
       FROM UNKNOWN WORLDS [J. W. Campbell - 1948]

Mag.   Year

Nothing Sirius by Fredric Brown.....................................CF   Spr 1944
   MY BEST SCIENCE FICTION STORY [Margulies & Friend - 1949]
Now Let Us Sleep by Avram Davidson.................................Ven   Spr 1957
   SF: 58 THE YEAR'S GREATEST SCIENCE FICTION & FANTASY [Merril - 1958]
Null-P by William Tenn ps (Philip Klass)..........................WB   Jan 1951
   WORLDS OF TOMORROW [Derleth - 1953]
   SPECTRUM [Amis & Conquest - 1961]
Number Nine by Cleve Cartmill.......................................ASF   Feb 1950
   GREAT STORIES OF SCIENCE FICTION [Leinster - 1951]

# O

O Ugly Bird! by Manly Wade Wellman................................F&SF   Dec 1951
   GALAXY OF GHOULS [Merril - 1955]
Obligation, The by Roger Dee ps (Roger D. Aycock)...................Stg   Sep 1952
   ADVENTURES ON OTHER PLANETS [Wollheim - 1955]
Obvious! by Michael Ffolkes..............(cartoon)..................Pch   10/3/1960
   (Originally appeared under title Obvious to the Meaningest Intelligence)
   SIXTH ANNUAL OF THE YEAR'S BEST SF [Merril - 1961]
Obviously Suicide by S. Fowler Wright.............................Sus   Spr 1951
   BEYOND THE END OF TIME [Pohl - 1952]
Oceans Are Wide, The by Frank M. Robinson..........................SS   Apr 1954
   YEAR'S BEST SCIENCE FICTION NOVELS: 1954 [Bleiler & Dikty - 1954]
Odd John by Olaf Stapledon..(Originally published by Methuen & Co. (London);
   THE PORTABLE NOVELS OF SCIENCE [Wollheim - 1948]
Odd Ones, The by Gordon Dickson.....................................If   Feb 1955
   THE SECOND WORLD OF IF [Quinn & Wulff - 1958]
Oddy and Id by Alfred Bester......................................ASF   Aug 1950
   THE BEST SCIENCE FICTION STORIES: 1951 [Bleiler & Dikty - 1951]
Odor of Thought, The by Robert Sheckley.....................ORIGINAL STORY
   STAR SCIENCE FICTION STORIES #2 [Pohl - 1953]
Of Course by Chad Oliver..........................................ASF   May 1954
   THE BEST SCIENCE FICTION STORIES & NOVELS: 1955 [Dikty - 1955]
Of Jovian Build by Oscar J. Friend................................TWS   Oct 1938
   A TREASURY OF SCIENCE FICTION [Conklin - 1948]
Of Missing Persons by Jack Finney...................................GH   Mar 1955
   SF: THE YEAR'S GREATEST SCIENCE FICTION AND FANTASY [Merril - 1956]
Of Those Who Came by George Langdon.............................NW #18   Nov 1952
   GATEWAY TO TOMORROW [Carnell - 1954]
   SPACE POLICE [Norton - 1956]
Of Time and Third Avenue by Alfred Bester........................F&SF   Oct 1951
   THE BEST SCIENCE FICTION STORIES: 1952 [Bleiler & Dikty - 1952]
Off For the Moon by Edwin F. Northup...............(From Zero To Eighty; 1937)
   (Originally appeared under pseudonym Akkad Pseudonman)
   SCIENCE IN FICTION [A. E. M. & J. C. Bayliss - 1957]
Official Record by Fletcher Pratt.................................Spc   Sep 1952
   ASSIGNMENT IN TOMORROW [Pohl - 1954]
Ogre by Clifford D. Simak.........................................ASF   Jan 1949
   ADVENTURES ON OTHER PLANETS [Wollheim - 1955]
Okie by James Blish...............................................ASF   Apr 1950
   STORIES FOR TOMORROW [Sloane - 1954]
Old Faithful by Raymond Z. Gallun.................................ASF   Dec 1943
   IMAGINATION UNLIMITED [Bleiler & Dikty - 1952]
Old Man, The by Holloway Horn.............................................
   (From The Second Omnibus of Crime; 1932 - Edited by Dorothy Sayers)
   TRAVELERS IN TIME [Stern - 1947]
Old Man Henderson by Kris Neville................................F&SF   Jun 1951
   THE BEST FROM FANTASY & SCIENCE FICTION [Boucher & McComas - 1952]

|  | Mag. | Year |
|---|---|---|

Old Man Hundredth by Brian W. Aldiss.............................NW #100  Dec 1960
    SIXTH ANNUAL OF THE YEAR'S BEST SF [Merril - 1961]
Old Order, The by Lester del Rey.................................Mvl  Feb 1951
    SHADOW OF TOMORROW [Pohl - 1953]
Omen, The by Shirley Jackson.................(verse)................F&SF  Mar 1958
    THE BEST FROM FANTASY & SCIENCE FICTION: 8th SERIES [Boucher - 1959]
Omega by Amelia Reynolds Long....................................Amz  Jul 1932
    THE END OF THE WORLD [Wollheim - 1956]
On The Staircase by Katherine Fullerton Gerould......(From Vain Ob ligations; 1914)
    TRAVELERS. IN TIME [Stern - 1947]
Once A Greech by Evelyn E. Smith.................................Glxy  Apr 1957
    THE WORLD THAT COULDN'T BE AND 8 OTHER NOVELETTES FROM GALAXY [Gold - 1959]
$1.98 by Arthur Porges..........................................F&SF  Feb 1953
    THE BEST FROM FANTASY & SCIENCE FICTION: 4th SERIES [Boucher - 1955]
One For The Books by Richard Matheson............................Glxy  Sep 1955
    THE WORLD THAT COULDN'T BE AND 8 OTHER NOVELETTES FROM GALAXY [Gold - 1959]
One Leg Too Many by W. Alexander.................................Amz  Oct 1929
    THE BIG BOOK OF SCIENCE FICTION [Conklin - 1950]
One Ordinary Day, With Peanuts by Shirley Jackson................F&SF  Jan 1955
    THE BEST FROM FANTASY & SCIENCE FICTION [Boucher - 1956]
    SF: 57 THE YEAR'S GREATEST SF & FANTASY [Merril - 1957]
$1,000 A PLATE by Jack McKenty..................................Glxy  Oct 1954
    THE FIFTH GALAXY READER [Gold - 1961]
One Thousand Miles Up by Frank M. Robinson......................SS  Apr 1954
    THE BEST SCIENCE FICTION STORIES & NOVELS: 1955 [Dikty - 1955]
One Way Street by Jerome Bixby..................................Amz  Dec 1953
    THE BEST SCIENCE FICTION STORIES & NOVELS: 1955 [Dikty - 1955]
One Who Waits, The by Ray Bradbury...........(See listing Vignettes of Tomorrow)
Only An Echo by Alan Barclay....................................NW #22  Apr 1954
    GATEWAY TO THE STARS [Carnell - 1955]
Only Thing We Learn, The by C. M. Kornbluth......................Stg  Jul 1949
    THE BIG BOOK OF SCIENCE FICTION [Conklin - 1950]
Ooze by Anthony M. Rud..........................................WT  Mar 1923
    THE MOON TERROR AND OTHER STORIES [Anonymous - 1927]
Open Secret by Lewis Padgett ps (Henry Kuttner & C. L. Moore)........ASF  Apr 1943
    GREAT STORIES OF SCIENCE FICTION [Leinster - 1951]
Open, Sesame by Stephen Grendon ps (August Derleth).................Ark  Win 1949
    FAR BOUNDARIES [Derleth - 1951]
Open Window, The by Saki ps (H. H. Munro).....(From Beasts and Super Beasts; 1914)
    CHILDREN OF WONDER [Tenn - 1953]
Opening Doors by Wilmar H. Shiras...............................ASF  Mar 1949
    THE BEST SCIENCE FICTION STORIES: 1950 [Bleiler & Dikty - 1950]
Opening The Door by Arthur Machen...................(From The Cozy Room; 1936)
    TRAVELERS IN TIME [Stern - 1947]
Operation Zero by Milton Lesser.................................Orb #4  Sep 1954
    (Originally appeared under title Intruder On The Rim)
    THE SANDS OF MARS AND OTHER STORIES [Anonymous - 1958]
Operating Instructions by Robert Sheckley.......................ASF  May 1953
    BEYOND THE BARRIERS OF SPACE AND TIME [Merril - 1954]
Operation Exodus by Lan Wright..................................NW #13  Jan 1952
    GATEWAY TO THE STARS [Carnell - 1955]
Operation Mercury by Clifford D. Simak..........................ASF  Mar 1941
    TALES OF OUTER SPACE [Wollheim - 1954]
Operation Pumice by Raymond Z. Gallun...........................TWS  Apr 1949
    POSSIBLE WORLDS OF SCIENCE FICTION [Conklin - 1951]
    MEN ON THE MOON [Wollheim - 1958]

                                                           Mag.     Year

Operation RSVP by H. Beam Piper...........................................Amz  Jan 1951
    POSSIBLE WORLDS OF SCIENCE FICTION [Conklin - 1951]
Or All The Seas With Oysters by Avram Davidson.....................Glxy  May 1958
    THE FOURTH GALAXY READER OF SCIENCE FICTION [Gold - 1959]
    SF: 59 THE YEAR'S GREATEST SF AND FANTASY [Merril - 1959]
Or Else by Henry Kuttner...............................(From Ahead Of Time; 1953)
    BEST SF SCIENCE FICTION STORIES [Crispin - 1955]
Or The Grasses Grow by Avram Davidson...............................F&SF  Nov 1958
    SCIENCE FICTION SHOWCASE [M. Kornbluth - 1959]
Ordeal Of Professor Klein, The by L. Sprague de Camp................SFA  Oct 1952
    BEACHHEADS IN SPACE [Derleth - 1954]
Origin of Galactic Etiquette ⎞
Origin of Galactic Law      ⎟  by Edward Wellen
Origin of Galactic Slang     ⎟  See listing Excerpts From Encyclopedia Of
Origin of Galactic Medicine ⎠        Galactic Culture
Origin of Narapoia, The by Alan Nelson....................(See listing Narapoia)
Origin of The Species by Karen Anderson..........(verse)...........F&SF  Jun 1958
    THE BEST FROM FANTASY & SCIENCE FICTION: 8th SERIES [Boucher - 1959]
Origin of The Species, The by Katherine MacLean....................ORIGINAL STORY
    CHILDREN OF WONDER [Tenn - 1953]
Original Sin by S. Fowler Wright.................(From The Throne Of Saturn; 1948)
    THE OTHER SIDE OF THE MOON [Derleth - 1949]
Orphans of The Void by Michael Shaara...............................Glxy  Jun 1952
    SHADOW OF TOMORROW [Pohl - 1953]
Other Inaugauration, The by Anthony Boucher.........................F&SF  Mar 1953
    SCIENCE FICTION TERROR TALES [Conklin - 1955]
Other Man, The by Theodore Sturgeon.................................Glxy  Sep 1956
    SF: 57 THE YEAR'S GREATEST SF AND FANTASY [Merril - 1957]
Other Now, The by Murray Leinster ps (Will F. Jenkins).............Glxy  Mar 1951
    THE GALAXY READER OF SCIENCE FICTION [Gold - 1951]
Other People, The by Leigh Brackett  (Mrs. Edmond Hamilton)........Ven  Mar 1957
    (Originally appeared under title The Queer Ones)
    THE BEST SCIENCE FICTION STORIES AND NOVELS: 9th SERIES [Dikty - 1958]
Other Side, The by Walter Kubilius..................................Sup  Apr 1951
    THE BEST SCIENCE FICTION STORIES: 1952 [Bleiler & Dikty - 1952]
Other Side of The Sky, The by Arthur C. Clarke.....................Inf  Sep 1957
    A TREASURY OF GREAT SCIENCE FICTION [Boucher - 1959]
Other Tiger, The by Arthur C. Clarke................................FU  Jul 1953
    PORTALS OF TOMORROW [Derleth - 1954]
Other Tracks by William Sell.......................................ASF  Oct 1938
    SCIENCE FICTION ADVENTURES IN DIMENSION [Conklin - 1953]
Other Wife, The by Jack Finney.....................................SEP  1/30/60
    THE FIFTH ANNUAL OF THE YEAR'S BEST SF [Merril - 1960]
Other World, The by Murray Leinster ps (Will F. Jenkins)...........Stg  Nov 1949
    6 GREAT SHORT NOVELS OF SCIENCE FICTION [Conklin - 1954]
    (Revised for inclusion in this anthology)
Ounce of Prevention, An by Philip Carter...........................F&SF  Sum 1950
    FAR BOUNDARIES [Derleth - 1951]
Our Distant Cousins by Lord Dunsany................................
    (From The Travel Tales of Mr. Joseph Jorkens; 1931)
    THE MOONLIGHT TRAVELER [Stern - 1943]
Our Fair City by Robert A. Heinlein.................................WT  Jan 1949
    BEYOND HUMAN KEN [Merril - 1952]
Out of The Jar by Charles Tanner...................................Sti  Feb 1941
    ZACHERLY'S VULTURE STEW [Zacherly - 1960]

(153)

|  | Mag. | Year |
|---|---|---|

Outer Limit, The by Graham Doar.....................................SEP 12/24/49
    THE BIG BOOK OF SCIENCE FICTION [Conklin - 1950]
Outside by Brian W. Aldiss.......................................NW #31 Jan 1955
    BEST SF TWO SCIENCE FICTION STORIES [Crispin - 1956]
Over The Top by Lester del Rey.....................................ASF Nov 1949
    THE ASTOUNDING SCIENCE FICTION ANTHOLOGY [J. W. Campbell - 1952]
Overdrive by Murray Leinster ps (Will F. Jenkins)...................Stg Jan 1953
    ADVENTURES IN THE FAR FUTURE [Wollheim - 1954]
Overthrow by Cleve Cartmill........................................ASF Nov 1942
    JOURNEY TO INFINITY [Greenberg - 1951]
Overture by Kris Neville......................................ORIGINAL STORY
    9 TALES OF SPACE AND TIME [Healy - 1954]

# P

Pacifist, The by Arthur C. Clarke..................................FU Oct 1956
    THE FANTASTIC UNIVERSE OMNIBUS [Santesson - 1960]
Pact by Winston P. Sanders.......................................F&SF Aug 1959
    THE BEST FROM FANTASY & SCIENCE FICTION: 9th SERIES [Mills - 1960]
Page And Player by Jerome Bixby...................................Stg Aug 1952
    SPACE PIONEERS [Norton - 1954]
Pail of Air, A by Fritz Leiber...................................Glxy Dec 1951
    SPACE PIONEERS [Norton - 1954]
    THE SECOND GALAXY READER OF SCIENCE FICTION [Gold - 1954]
Panel Game by Brian W. Aldiss....................................NW #42 Dec 1955
    ASPECTS OF SCIENCE FICTION [Doherty - 1959]
Pannelled Room, The by August Derleth............................WM Sep 1933
    THE OTHER WORLDS [Stong - 1941]
Paradise II by Robert Sheckley................................ORIGINAL STORY
    TIME TO COME [Derleth - 1954]
Paradox Lost by Fredric Brown.....................................ASF Oct 1943
    SCIENCE FICTION CARNIVAL [Brown & Reynolds - 1953]
Parasite Planet by Stanley G. Weinbaum............................Ast Feb 1935
    FLIGHT INTO SPACE [Wollheim - 1950]
Pardon My Mistake by Fletcher Pratt...............................TWS Dec 1946
    THE OUTER REACHES [Derleth - 1951]
Parodies Tossed..............................(See listings All About The Thing and
    John W. Campbell Jr.'s Who Goes There.)
Pastoral Affair by Charles A. Stearns............................Glxy Feb 1959
    THE FIFTH GALAXY READER [Gold - 1961]
Patient, The by E. Mayne Hull (Mrs. A. E. Van Vogt)...............Unk Oct 1943
    SCIENCE FICTION ADVENTURES IN MUTATION [Conklin - 1956]
Pattern For Penelope, A by Robert F. Young.........................If Nov 1954
    THE FIRST WORLD OF IF [Quinn & Wulff - 1957]
Pattern For Survival by Richard Matheson.........................F&SF May 1955
    THE BEST FROM FANTASY & SCIENCE FICTION: 5th SERIES [Boucher - 1956]

|  | Mag. | Year |
|---|---|---|

Pause, The by August Derleth.........................................ORIGINAL STORY
    TIME TO COME [Derleth - 1954]
Pausodyne by Grant Allen...............................(From Strange Stories; 1884)
    BEYOND TIME AND SPACE [Derleth - 1950]
Pawley's Peepholes by John Wyndham ps (John Beynon Harris)...........Sus  Sum 1951
    BEYOND THE END OF TIME [Pohl - 1952]
      (Appeared under title Operation Peep)
    ESCALES DANS L'INFINI [Gallet - 1954]
      (Appeared under title Tousistes Des Temps Futurs)
Pax Galactica by Ralph Williams.......................................ASF  Nov 1952
    SPACE POLICE [Norton - 1956]
Peacebringer by Ward Moore............................................Amz  Mar 1950
    THE BIG BOOK OF SCIENCE FICTION [Conklin - 1950]
Peaceful Martian, The by J. T. Oliver.................................FB #8  n/d 1951
    SCIENCE AND SORCERY [Ford - 1953]
Peacemaker, The by Alfred Coppel........................................If  Jan 1953
    PRIZE SCIENCE FICTION [Wollheim - 1953]
Peculiar People, A by Betsy Curtis...................................F&SF  Aug 1951
    THE BEST SCIENCE FICTION STORIES: 1952 [Bleiler & Dikty - 1952]
Peddler's Nose, The by Jack Williamson...............................ASF  Apr 1951
    ASSIGNMENT IN TOMORROW [Pohl - 1954]
Pedestrian, The by Ray Bradbury......................................Rptr    8/7/51
    THE BEST SCIENCE FICTION STORIES: 1952 [Bleiler & Dikty - 1952]
    TIMELESS STORIES FOR TODAY AND TOMORROW [Bradbury - 1952]
Pelt by Carol Emshwiller.............................................F&SF  Nov 1958
    SF: 59 THE YEAR'S GREATEST SF AND FANTASY [Merril - 1959]
Pen Pal by Milton Lesser.............................................Glxy  Jul 1951
    INVADERS OF EARTH [Conklin - 1952]
Penelope by Vincent Starrett..........................................WT  May 1923
    THE MOON TERROR AND OTHER STORIES [Anonymous - 1927]
Perfect Answer by L. J. Stecher, Jr. ................................Glxy  Jun 1958
    THE FIFTH GALAXY READER [Gold - 1961]
Perfect Creature by John Wyndham ps (John Beynon Harris)............F&SF  Jan 1953
    SHADOW OF TOMORROW [Pohl - 1953]
Perfect Gentleman, The by R. J. MacGregor...........................Stg  Sep 1952
    THE BEST FROM STARTLING STORIES [Mines - 1953]
Perfect Host, The by Theodore Sturgeon...............................WT  Nov 1948
    BEYOND HUMAN KEN [Merril - 1952]
Perfect Murder by H. L. Gold........................................TWS  Mar 1940
    SCIENCE FICTION ADVENTURES IN DIMENSION [Conklin - 1953]
Perforce To Dream by John Wyndham ps (John Beynon Harris)...........BFF  Jan 1954
    BEYOND THE BARRIERS OF SPACE AND TIME [Merril - 1954]
Peril of The Blue World by Robert Abernathy..........................PS  Win 1942
    FLIGHT INTO SPACE [Wollheim - 1950]
    STORIES OF SCIENTIFIC IMAGINATION [Gallant - 1954]
Period Piece by J. J. Coupling ps (John R. Pierce)..................ASF  Nov 1948
    THE BEST SCIENCE FICTION STORIES: 1949 [Bleiler & Dikty - 1949]
Person From Porlock, The by Raymond F. Jones........................ASF  Aug 1947
    A TREASURY OF SCIENCE FICTION [Conklin - 1948]
Pete Can Fix It by Raymond F. Jones.................................ASF  Feb 1947
    SCIENCE FICTION ADVENTURES IN DIMENSION [Conklin - 1953]
Peter Learns Arithmetic by H.G. Wells...(Fr Joan & Peter [The New Republic]; 1918)
    FANTASIA MATHEMATICA [Fadiman - 1958]
Phalanstery of Thelme, The by Francis Rabelais..............(From Gargantua; 1534)
    BEYOND TIME AND SPACE [Derleth - 1950]

Mag.    Year

Phantas by Oliver Onions............................(From Widdershins; 1911)
  THE MOONLIGHT TRAVELER [Stern - 1943]
  TRAVELERS IN TIME [Stern - 1947]
Phoenix by Clark Ashton Smith....................................ORIGINAL STORY
  TIME TO COME [Derleth - 1954]
Pi Man, The by Alfred Bester.........................................F&SF   Oct 1959
  THE BEST FROM FANTASY & SCIENCE FICTION: 9th SERIES [Mills - 1960]
Pictures Don't Lie by Katherine MacLean...........................Glxy   Aug 1951
  INVADERS OF EARTH [Conklin - 1952]
  BEST SF SCIENCE FICTION STORIES [Crispin - 1955]
  ASPECTS OF SCIENCE FICTION [Doherty - 1959]
Piggy Bank by Henry Kuttner.........................................ASF   Dec 1942
  (Originally appeared under pseudonym Lewis Padgett)
  A TREASURY OF GREAT SCIENCE FICTION [Boucher - 1959]
Pile of Trouble by Henry Kuttner.....................................TWS   Apr 1948
  ZACHERLY'S MIDNIGHT SNACKS [Zacherly - 1960]
Pilgrimage To Earth by Robert Sheckley............................Plby   Sep 1956
  (Originally appeared under title Love, Inc.)
  SPECTRUM [Amis & Conquest - 1961]
Pillar of Fire by Ray Bradbury.......................................PS   Sum 1948
  THE OTHER SIDE OF THE MOON [Derleth - 1949]
  A TREASURY OF GREAT SCIENCE FICTION [Boucher - 1959]
Pillar To Post by John Wyndham ps (John Beynon Harris).............Glxy   Dec 1951
  THE SECOND GALAXY READER OF SCIENCE FICTION [Gold - 1954]
Pillows, The by Margaret St. Clair..................................TWS   Jun 1950
  POSSIBLE WORLDS OF SCIENCE FICTION [Conklin - 1951]
  THE SANDS OF MARS AND OTHER STORIES [Anonymous - 1958]
Pilot And The Bushman, The by Sylvia Jacobs......................Glxy   Aug 1951
  THE GALAXY READER OF SCIENCE FICTION [Gold - 1952]
Piping Death, The by Robert Moore Williams........................Unk   May 1939
  ZACHERLY'S MIDNIGHT SNACKS [Zacherly - 1960]
Pipeline To Pluto by Murray Leinster ps (Will F. Jenkins)...........ASF   Aug 1945
  SCIENCE FICTION TERROR TALES [Conklin - 1955]
Piper's Son, The by Lewis Padgett ps (Henry Kuttner & C. L. Moore)...ASF  Feb 1945
  THE BEST OF SCIENCE FICTION [Conklin - 1946]
  CHILDREN OF WONDER [Tenn - 1953]
Pipes of Pan, The by Lester del Rey.................................Unk   May 1940
  THE OTHER WORLDS [Stong - 1941]
Pirate of The Air by James S. Bradford...........................ORIGINAL STORY
  ADVENTURES TO COME [Esenwein - 1937]
Place of Meeting by Charles Beaumont.............................Orb #2   n/d 1954
  PLANET OF DOOM AND OTHER STORIES [Anonymous - 1954]
Place of The Gods, The by Stephen Vincent Benet............................
  (See listing By The Waters Of Babylon)
Place of The Tigress, The by Isobel Mayne............(London Observer Prize Story)
  A. D. 2500 [Wilson - 1955]
Placet Is A Crazy Place by Fredric Brown...........................ASF   May 1946
  TRAVELERS OF SPACE [Greenberg - 1952]
  BEST SF TWO SCIENCE FICTION STORIES [Crispin - 1956]
  OUT OF THIS WORLD 1 [Williams-Ellis & Owen - 1960]
Plagerist by Peter Phillips.......................................NW #7   Sum 1950
  FUTURE TENSE [Crossen - 1953]
Plague by Murray Leinster ps (Will F. Jenkins)....................ASF   Feb 1944
  THE OMNIBUS OF SCIENCE FICTION [Conklin - 1952]
Plane Geometry by Emma Rounds...............(verse)....(From Creative Youth; 1925)
  FANTASIA MATHEMATICA [Fadiman - 1958]

|  | Mag. | Year |
|---|---|---|

Planet Passage by Donald A. Wollheim.............................FFSF  Oct 1942
   FLIGHT INTO SPACE [Wollheim - 1950]
   STORIES OF SCIENTIFIC IMAGINATION [Gallant - 1954]
Planetoid of Doom, The by Morrison Colladay......................WS  Dec 1932
   THE BIG BOOK OF SCIENCE FICTION [Conklin - 1950]
Planets Must Slay by Frank Belknap Long, Jr. ....................TWS  Apr 1942
   THE SAINT'S CHOICE [Charteris - 1945]
Plant Revolt, The by Edmond Hamilton.............................WT  Apr 1930
   THE EARTH IN PERIL [Wollheim - 1957]
Plants, The by Murray Leinster ps (Will F. Jenkins)..............ASF  Jan 1946
   MEN AGAINST THE STARS [Greenberg - 1950]
Playground, The by Ray Bradbury..................................Esq  Oct 1953
   PORTALS OF TOMORROW [Derleth - 1954]
Pleasant Dreams by Ralph Robin...................................Glxy  Oct 1951
   THE OMNIBUS OF SCIENCE FICTION [Conklin - 1952]
Plenitude by Will Worthington....................................F&SF  Nov 1959
   THE FIFTH ANNUAL OF THE YEAR'S BEST SF [Merril - 1960]
Plum Duff by Peter van Dresser...................................AmB  Dec 1935
   THE YEAR AFTER TOMORROW [Del Rey, Matschat & Carmer - 1952]
Plus X by Eric Frank Russell.....................................ASF  Jun 1956
   FOUR FOR THE FUTURE [Conklin - 1959]
Plutonian Drug, The by Clark Ashton Smith........................Amz  Sep 1934
   THE OUTER REACHES [Derleth - 1951]
Police Operation by H. Beam Piper................................ASF  Jun 1948
   SPACE POLICE [Norton - 1956]
Poor Little Warrior! by Brian W. Aldiss..........................F&SF  Apr 1958
   THE BEST FROM FANTASY & SCIENCE FICTION: 8th SERIES [Boucher - 1959]
   PENGUIN SCIENCE FICTION [Aldiss - 1961]
Portable Phonograph, The by Walter Van Tilburg Clark.............
   (From The Watchful Gods and Other Stories; 1941)
   ADVENTURES IN TOMORROW [Crossen - 1951]
   TIMELESS STORIES FOR TODAY AND TOMORROW [Bradbury - 1952]
Postpaid To Paradise by Robert Arthur............................Arg  6/15/40
                          Rpnt - F&SF  Win 1940
   THE BEST FROM FANTASY & SCIENCE FICTION [Boucher & McComas - 1952]
Postscript to "The Universal Library" by Willy Ley..............ORIGINAL STORY
   FANTASIA MATHEMATICA [Fadiman - 1958]
Potential by Robert Sheckley.....................................ASF  Nov 1953
   PORTALS OF TOMORROW [Derleth - 1954]
Potential Enemy by Mack Reynolds.................................Orb #2  n/d 1954
   BEYOND THE STARS AND OTHER STORIES [Anonymous - 1958]
Pottage by Zeena Henderson......................................F&SF  Sep 1955
   THE BEST FROM FANTASY & SCIENCE FICTION: 5th SERIES [Boucher - 1956]
   SF: THE YEAR'S GREATEST SCIENCE FICTION AND FANTASY [Merril - 1956]
Pound of Cure, A by Lester del Rey..............................ORIGINAL STORY
   STAR SCIENCE FICTION STORIES #2 [Pohl - 1953]
Power, The by Murray Leinster ps (Will F. Jenkins)..............ASF  Sep 1945
   THE OUTER REACHES [Derleth - 1951]
   LOOKING FORWARD [Lesser - 1953]
Prelude To Space by Arthur C. Clarke................(Excerpts)...
   (Originally published by World Editions; 1951)
   SCIENCE IN FICTION [A.E.M. & J. C. Bayliss - 1957]
Present From Joe, A by Eric Frank Russell........................ASF  Feb 1949
   BEST SF SCIENCE FICTION STORIES [Crispin - 1955]
Press Conference by Miriam Allen DeFord.........................ORIGINAL STORY
   STAR SCIENCE FICTION STORIES #6 [Pohl - 1959]
Pressure by Ross Rocklynne.......................................ASF  Jun 1939
   IMAGINATION UNLIMITED [Bleiler & Dikty - 1952]
Pride by Malcolm Jameson.........................................ASF  Sep 1942
   BEYOND HUMAN KEN [Merril - 1952]
Prima Belladonna by J. G. Ballard...............................SF #20  Dec 1956
   SF: 57 THE YEAR'S GREATEST SF & FANTASY [Merril - 1957]

|                                                                          | Mag.   | Year      |
|                                                                          |        |           |

Private Eye by Henry Kuttner............................................ASF    Jan 1949
   THE BEST SCIENCE FICTION STORIES: 1950 [Bleiler & Dikty - 1950]
Private — Keep Out! by Philip MacDonald..............................MoF    Fal 1949
   WORLD OF WONDER [Pratt - 1951]
Prize of Peril, The by Robert Sheckley..............................F&SF    May 1958
   SF: 59 THE YEAR'S GREATEST SF & FANTASY [Merril - 1959]
Problem — (From Talk of The Town; special feature) - Anonymous......Nykr    3/2/57
   FANTASIA MATHEMATICA [Fadiman - 1958]
Problem For Biographers, A by Mindret Lord.........................ORIGINAL STORY
   THE OTHER WORLDS [Stong - 1941]
Problem For Emmy by Robert Sherman Townes...........................Stg    Jun 1952
   SCIENCE FICTION THINKING MACHINES [Conklin - 1954]
Problem On Balak by Roger Dee ps (Roger D. Aycock).................Glxy    Sep 1953
   THE SECOND GALAXY READER OF SCIENCE FICTION [Gold - 1954]
Process, The by A. E. Van Vogt......................................F&SF    Dec 1950
   THE BEST SCIENCE FICTION STORIES: 1951 [Bleiler & Dikty - 1951]
Production Test by Raymond F. Jones..................................ASF    Oct 1949
   LOOKING FORWARD [Lesser - 1953]
Professor Was A Thief, The by L. Ron Hubbard........................ASF    Feb 1940
   MY BEST SCIENCE FICTION STORY [Margulies & Friend - 1949]
Project by Lewis Padgett ps (Henry Kuttner & C. L. Moore)...........ASF    Apr 1947
   OPERATION FUTURE [Conklin - 1955]
Project Nursemaid by Judith Merril..................................F&SF    Oct 1955
   SIX GREAT SHORT NOVELS OF SCIENCE FICTION [Conklin - 1960]
Project — Space Ship by A. E. Van Vogt..............................TWS    Aug 1939
   MY BEST SCIENCE FICTION STORY [Margulies & Friend - 1949]
Proof Positive by Graham Greene.....................................Hpr    Oct 1947
                                          Rpnt — F&SF    Aug 1952
   A DECADE OF FANTASY & SCIENCE FICTION [Mills - 1960]
Propagandist by Murray Leinster ps (Will F. Jenkins)...............ASF    Aug 1947
   POSSIBLE WORLDS OF SCIENCE FICTION [Conklin - 1951]
   STORIES OF SCIENTIFIC IMAGINATION [Gallant - 1954]
Proof by Hal Clement ps (Harry Clement Stubbs).....................ASF    Jun 1942
   POSSIBLE WORLDS OF SCIENCE FICTION [Conklin - 1951]
Proof of The Pudding by Robert Sheckley............................Glxy    Aug 1952
   GALAXY OF GHOULS [Merril - 1955]
Protected Species by H. B. Fyfe.....................................ASF    Mar 1951
   THE ASTOUNDING SCIENCE FICTION ANTHOLOGY [J. W. Campbell - 1952]
Protection by Robert Sheckley......................................Glxy    Apr 1956
   THE THIRD GALAXY READER OF SCIENCE FICTION [Gold - 1958]
Prott by Margaret St. Clair........................................Glxy    Jan 1953
   SCIENCE FICTION TERROR TALES [Conklin - 1955]
   BEST SF SCIENCE FICTION STORIES [Crispin - 1955]
Proud Robot, The by Lewis Padgett ps (Henry Kuttner & C.L. Moore)...ASF    Oct 1943
   ADVENTURES IN TIME AND SPACE [Healy & McComas - 1946]
Psalm by Lester del Rey...................(verse).....................FU    Mar 1960
   SIXTH ANNUAL OF THE YEAR'S BEST SF [Merril - 1961]
Psychomorph, The by E. A. Grosser...................................Unk    Feb 1940
   FROM UNKNOWN WORLDS [J. W. Campbell - 1948]
Public Hating, The by Steve Allen...................................BB    Jan 1955
   SF: THE YEAR'S GREATEST SCIENCE FICTION AND FANTASY [Merril - 1956]
Punishment Without Crime by Ray Bradbury............................OW    Mar 1950
   SCIENCE FICTION TERROR TALES [Conklin - 1955]
Purple Fields, The by Robert Crane.................................ORIGINAL STORY
   STAR SCIENCE FICTION STORIES #2 [Pohl - 1953]
Put Them All Together, They Spell Monster by Ray Russell...........Plby    Oct 1956
   SF: 57 THE YEAR'S GREATEST SF AND FANTASY [Merril - 1957]
Putzi by Ludwig Bemelmans.................................(From The Lottery; 1949)
   TIMELESS STORIES FOR TODAY AND TOMORROW [Bradbury - 1952]
Pythagoras And The Psychoanalyst by Arthur Koestler..(Fr Arrival & Departure; 1943)
   FANTASIA MATHEMATICA [Fadiman - 1958]

# Q

Queen's Astrologer, The by Murray Leinster ps (Will F. Jenkins)......TWS  Oct 1949
    CROSSROADS IN TIME [Conklin - 1953]
Queer Ones, The by Leigh Brackett...................(See listing The Other People)
Quest For Saint Aquin by Anthony Boucher.........................ORIGINAL STORY
    NEW TALES OF SPACE AND TIME [Healy - 1951]
Quest of The Veil by Eugene Deweese..............................ORIGINAL STORY
    SHANADU [Briney - 1953]
Quietus by Ross Rocklynne........................................ASF  Sep 1940
    ADVENTURES IN TIME AND SPACE [Healy & McComas - 1946]
Quis Custodiet...? by Margaret St. Clair..........................Stg  Jul 1948
    THE SCIENCE FICTION GALAXY [Conklin - 1950]
Quit Zoomin' Those Hands Through The Air by Jack Finney..............Col   8/4/51
    OPERATION FUTURE [Conklin - 1955]
    JOURNEYS IN SCIENCE FICTION [Loughlin & Popp - 1961]
Q.U.R. by Anthony Boucher.........................................ASF  Mar 1943
    (Originally published under psuedonym H. H. Holmes)
    ADVENTURES IN TIME AND SPACE [Healy & McComas - 1946]

# R

Rabbits To The Moon by Raymond E. Banks............................F&SF  Jul 1959
    A DECADE OF FANTASY & SCIENCE FICTION [Mills - 1960]
Race With A Dinosaur, A by A. Conan Doyle.............(From The Lost World; 1912)
    SCIENCE IN FICTION [A. E. M. & J. C. Bayliss - 1957]
Radiation Blues by Theodore R. Cogswell.............(song).........ORIGINAL STORY
    SIXTH ANNUAL OF THE YEAR'S BEST SF [Merril - 1961]
Rag Thing, The by David Grinnell..................................F&SF  Oct 1951
    THE OMNIBUS OF SCIENCE FICTION [Conklin - 1952]

Railways Up on Cannis, The by Colin Kapp..........................NW #87  Oct 1959
    OUT OF THIS WORLD 2 [Williams-Ellis & Owen - 1961]
Rainbow Gold, The by Jane Rice....................................F&SF  Dec 1959
    THE BEST FROM FANTASY & SCIENCE FICTION: 10th SERIES [Mills - 1961]
Rainmaker by John Reese...........................................SEP  2/19/1949
    TOMORROW, THE STARS [Heinlein - 1952]
Ralph Wollstonecraft Hedge: A Memoir by Ron Goulart...............F&SF  May 1959
    THE BEST FROM FANTASY & SCIENCE FICTION: 9th SERIES [Mills - 1960]
Ransom by H. B. Fyfe..............................................F&SF  Feb 1952
    THE BEST FROM FANTASY & SCIENCE FICTION: 2nd SERIES [Boucher - 1953]
Rape of the Solar System, The by Leslie F. Stone ps (Mrs. William Silberberg)....
                                                                  Amz  Dec 1934
    FLIGHT INTO SPACE [Wollheim - 1950]
Rat, The by S. Fowler Wright......................................WT  Mar 1929
    THE TREASURY OF SCIENCE FICTION CLASSICS [Kuebler - 1955]
Rat Race by Dorothy and John DeCourcy.............................Stg  Sep 1948
    THE BIG BOOK OF SCIENCE FICTION [Conklin - 1950]
Rat That Could Speak, The by Charles Dickens......................
    (Org aprd in All The Year Around Vol. 3 (Nurse's Stories-September 8, 1860))
    THE BEST FROM FANTASY & SCIENCE FICTION [Boucher & McComas - 1952]
Rats, The by Arthur Porges........................................MnW  Feb 1951
    THE BEST SCIENCE FICTION STORIES: 1952 [Bleiler & Dikty - 1952]
Re-Birth by John Wyndham ps (John Beynon Harris)..................
    (Originally published by Ballantine Books; 1955)
    A TREASURY OF GREAT SCIENCE FICTION FICTION [Boucher - 1959]
Receptive Bosom, The by Edward Shanks.....................(No date available)
    (From a [London] Sunday Times review of H. McKay's The World of Numbers)
    FANTASIA MATHEMATICA [Fadiman - 1958]
Recruiting Station by A. E. Van Vogt..............................ASF  Mar 1942
    THE OMNIBUS OF SCIENCE FICTION [Conklin - 1952]
Red Death of Mars, The by Robert Moore Williams...................ASF  Jul 1940
    MEN AGAINST THE STARS [Greenberg - 1950]
    THE YEAR AFTER TOMORROW [Del Rey, Matschat and Carmer - 1952]
Red Queen's Race, The by Isaac Asimov.............................ASF  Jan 1949
    WORLD OF WONDER [Pratt - 1952]
Red Storm on Jupiter by Frank Belknap Long, Jr. ..................Ast  May 1936
    FLIGHT INTO SPACE [Wollheim - 1950]
Referent by Ray Bradbury..........................................TWS  Oct 1948
    IMAGINATION UNLIMITED [Bleiler & Dikty - 1952]
Refuge, The by Jane Rice..........................................UW  Oct 1943
    FROM UNKNOWN WORLDS [J. W. Campbell - 1948]
Refuge For Tonight by Robert Moore Williams.......................BB  Mar 1949
    THE BEST SCIENCE FICTION STORIES: 1950 [Bleiler & Dikty - 1950]
Relativity — Anonymous............................................(No data available)
    FANTASIA MATHEMATICA [Fadiman - 1958]
Reluctant Heroes, The by Frank M. Robinson........................Glxy  Jan 1951
    THE GALAXY READER OF SCIENCE FICTION [Gold - 1952]
    MEN ON THE MOON [Wollheim - 1958]
    EVERY BOY'S BOOK OF OUTER SPACE STORIES [Dikty - 1960]
Remarkable Case of Davidson's Eyes, The by H. G. Wells............FWB  3/28/1895
    THE BEST OF SCIENCE FICTION [Conklin - 1946]
Remoresful, The by C. M. Kornbluth................................ORIGINAL STORY
    STAR SCIENCE FICTION STORIES #2 [Pohl - 1953]
Repitition by A. E. Van Vogt......................................ASF  Apr 1940
    BEACHHEADS IN SPACE [Derleth - 1952]
Replacement, The by Robert Murray.................................F&SF  Feb 1960
    THE BEST FROM FANTASY & SCIENCE FICTION: 10th SERIES [Mills - 1961]

Mag.    Year

```
                                                         Mag.    Year
Report On The Barnhouse Effect, The by Kurt Vonnegut, Jr. ..........Col   2/11/50
     TOMORROW, THE STARS [Heinlein - 1952]
     JOURNEYS IN SCIENCE FICTION [Loughlin & Popp - 1961]
Report On The Nature of The Lunar Surface by John Bruuner...........ASF   Aug 1960
     SIXTH ANNUAL OF THE YEAR'S BEST SF [Merril - 1961]
Report On The Sexual Behavior of The Extra-Sensory Perceptor by Harmon W. Mudgett
                        (verse)                          F&SF   Aug 1954
     THE BEST FROM FANTASY & SCIENCE FICTION: 4th SERIES [Boucher - 1955]
Republic of The Southern Cross, The by Valery Brussof............................
     (From The Southern Cross and Other Stories; 1919)
     TERROR IN THE MODERN VEIN [Wollheim - 1955]
Requiem by Robert A. Heinlein.....................................ASF   Jan 1940
     ADVENTURES IN TIME AND SPACE [Healy & McComas - 1946]
Rescue by G. C. Edmondson.......................................F&SF   Jun 1957
     THE BEST FROM FANTASY & SCIENCE FICTION: 7th SERIES [Boucher - 1958]
Rescue Party by Arthur C. Clarke................................ASF   May 1946
     A TREASURY OF SCIENCE FICTION [Conklin - 1948]
     BEYOND THE END OF TIME [Pohl - 1952]
     THE END OF THE WORLD [Wollheim - 1956]
Restricted Clientele by Kendall·Foster Crossen.....................TWS   Feb 1951
     ADVENTURES IN TOMORROW [Crossen - 1951]
Resurrection by A. E. Van Vogt....................................ASF   Aug 1948
     THE OTHER SIDE OF THE MOON [Derleth - 1949]
     UBERWINDUNG VON RAUM UND ZEIT [Gunther - 1952]
        (Appeared under title Weiderweckung)
        (Originally appeared under title The Monster)
Retreat From Rigel by Philip K. Dick...............................Orb #2  n/d 1954
        (Originally appeared under title Tony and The Beetles)
     PLANET OF DOOM AND OTHER STORIES [Anonymous - 1958]
Retreat To Mars, The by Leigh Brackett  (Mrs. Edmond Hamilton).......Ash   Nov 1941
     ADVENTURES IN TOMORROW [Crossen - 1951]
Retreat To Mars, The by Cecil B. White.............................Amz   Aug 1927
     THE BEST OF SCIENCE FICTION [Conklin - 1946]
Return, The by H. Beam Piper & John J. McGuire..................(Revised Version)
        (Original version appeared in Astounding Science Fiction; January 1954)
     THE SCIENCE FICTIONAL SHERLOCK HOLMES [Peterson - 1960]
Return of A Legend by Raymond Z. Gallun...........................PS   Mar 1952
     SPACE SERVICE [Norton - 1953]
Return of Andrew Bentley, The by August Derleth & Mack Schorer........Wi   Sep 1933
     THE OTHER WORLDS [Stong - 1941]
Return of The Moon by E. L. Malpass...............................Obs    1/2/55
     A. D. 2500 [Wilson - 1955]
     SF: 57 THE YEAR'S GREATEST SCIENCE FICTION & FANTASY [Merril - 1957]
        (Appeared under title When Grandfather Flew To The Moon)
Reverse Phylogeny by Amelia Reynolds Long..........................Ast   Jun 1937
     SCIENCE FICTION ADVENTURES IN DIMENSION [Conklin - 1953]
Revolt of The Pedestrians, The by David H. Keller, M. D. ...........Amz   Feb 1928
     BEYOND TIME AND SPACE [Derleth - 1950]
Right Thing, The by William Andrew...................(London Observer Prize Story)
     A. D. 2500 [Wilson - 1955]
Ring Around The Redhead by John D. MacDonald.......................Stg   Nov 1948
     SCIENCE FICTION ADVENTURES IN DIMENSION [Conklin - 1953]
River of Riches by Gerald Kersh...................................SEP    3/8/58
     SF: 59 THE YEAR'S GREATEST SF AND FANTASY [Merril - 1959]
Riya's Foundling by Algis Budrys.................................SFS #1  n/d 1953
     HUMAN? [Merril - 1954]
```

Mag.     Year

Road to Nightfall by Robert Silverberg..................................FU    Jul 1958
    THE FANTASTIC UNIVERSE OMNIBUS [Santesson - 1960]
Roads Must Roll, The by Robert A. Heinlein.........................ASF    Jun 1940
    ADVENTURES IN TIME AND SPACE [Healy & McComas - 1946]
    JOURNEYS IN SCIENCE FICTION [Loughlin & Popp - 1961]
Roads of Destiny by O. Henry ps (William Sydney Porter).......................
    (From Roads Of Destiny; 1909)
    THE MOONLIGHT TRAVELER [Stern - 1943]
    WORLD OF WONDER [Pratt - 1952]
Robbie by Isaac Asimov...............................................(From I, Robot; 1950)
    SCIENCE FICTION THINKING MACHINES [Conklin - 1954]
Robinc by H. H. Holmes ps (Anthony Boucher)........................ASF    Sep 1943
    THE ROBOT AND THE MAN [Greenberg - 1953]
Robot Al 76 Goes Astray by Isaac Asimov.............................Amz    Feb 1942
    MY BEST SCIENCE FICTION STORY [Margulies & Friend - 1949]
Robot Who Wanted to Know, The by Felix Boyd........................FU    Mar 1958
    THE FANTASTIC UNIVERSE OMNIBUS [Santesson - 1960]
Robots Don't Bleed by J. W. Groves.................................NW #8    Win 1950
    NO PLACE LIKE EARTH [Carnell - 1952]
    THE BEST FROM NEW WORLDS [Carnell - 1955]
Robots Return by Robert Moore Williams.............................ASF    Sep 1938
    ADVENTURES IN TIME AND SPACE [Healy & McComas - 1946]
    THE ROBOT AND THE MAN [Greenberg - 1953]
Rock Driver by Harry Harrison.......................................WB    Feb 1951
    BEYOND THE END OF TIME [Pohl - 1952]
Rocket to the Sun by Peter van Dresser.............................AmB    Jul 1939
    THE YEAR AFTER TOMORROW [Del Rey, Matschat & Carmer - 1952]
Rocketeers Have Shaggy Ears, The by Keith Bennett..................PS    Spr 1950
    TRAVELERS OF SPACE [Greenberg - 1952]
Rockets Aren't Human by E. C. Tubb................................NW #20    Mar 1953
    THE BEST FROM NEW WORLDS [Carnell - 1955]
Rockets To Where? by Judith Merril...........................ORIGINAL STORY
    SF: 59 THE YEAR'S GREATEST SF AND FANTASY [Merril - 1959]
Rocking-Horse Winner, The by D. H. Lawrence.........(From The Lovely Lady; 1933)
    TRAVELERS IN TIME [Stern - 1947]
    CHILDREN OF WONDER [Tenn - 1953]
Roger Bacon Formula, The by Fletcher Pratt.........................Amz    Jan 1929
    THE BIG BOOK OF SCIENCE FICTION [Conklin - 1950]
Rogue Ship, The by A. E. Van Vogt.................................Sup    Mar 1950
    THE GIANT ANTHOLOGY OF SCIENCE FICTION [Margulies & Friend - 1954]
Rope Enough by John Collier.......................................Nykr    11/18/1939
    HUMAN? [Merril - 1954]
Rotifers, The by Robert Abernathy.................................If    Mar 1953
    THE FIRST WORLD OF IF [Quinn & Wulff - 1955]
Round The Moon by Jules Verne......(Originally published by Hetzel — Paris; 1870)
    THE TREASURY OF SCIENCE FICTION CLASSICS [Kuebler - 1955]
Rousing of Mr. Bradegar, The by H. F. Heard......................................
    (From The Great Fog and Other Weird Tales; 1944)
    TRAVELERS IN TIME [Stern - 1947]
Rover I Will Be, A by Robert Courtney.......................ORIGINAL STORY
    EVERY BOY'S BOOK OF OUTER SPACE STORIES [Dikty - 1960]
Rule Golden by Damon Knight......................................SFAd    May 1954
    SIX GREAT SHORT NOVELS OF SCIENCE FICTION [Gold - 1952]
Rule of Three by Theodore Sturgeon...............................Glxy    Jan 1951
    THE GALAXY READER OF SCIENCE FICTION [Gold - 1952]
Rull, The by A. E. Van Vogt......................................ASF    May 1948
    TRAVELERS OF SPACE [Greenberg - 1952]
    ADVENTURES ON OTHER PLANETS [Wollheim - 1955]

                                                    Mag.    Year
R. U. R. (Rossum's Universal Robots) by Karel Capek.............................
    [A Fantastic Melodrama Copyrighted 1923 by Doubleday, Page and Co.]
    SCIENCE FICTION THINKING MACHINES [Conklin - 1954]
    THE TREASURY OF SCIENCE FICTION CLASSICS [Kuebler - 1955]
Rust by Joseph E. Kelleam............................................ASF   Oct 1939
    THE ROBOT AND THE MAN [Greenberg - 1953]
Rustle Of Wings by Fredric Brown.....................................F&SF  Aug 1953
    PORTALS OF TOMORROW [Derleth - 1954]
Ruum, The by Arthur Porges...........................................F&SF  Oct 1953
    BEST SF SCIENCE FICTION STORIES [Crispin - 1955]
    OUT OF THIS WORLD I [Ellis & Owen - 1960]

# S

Sack, The by William Morrison ps (Joseph Samachson)..................ASF   Sep 1950
    TOMORROW, THE STARS [Heinlein - 1952]
Saint Katy The Virgin by John Steinbeck...............(From The Long Valley; 1938)
    TIMELESS STORIES FOR TODAY AND TOMORROW [Bradbury - 1952]
Sam Hall by Poul Anderson............................................ASF   Sep 1953
    SCIENCE FICTION THINKING MACHINES [Conklin - 1954]
Sam Small's Better Half by Eric Knight..........(From Sam Small Flies Again; 1942)
    THE MOONLIGHT TRAVELER [Stern - 1943]
Sam Small's Tyke by Eric Knight.................(From Sam Small Flies Again; 1942)
    OUT OF THIS WORLD [Fast - 1944]
Sanctuary by Daniel F. Galouye.......................................F&SF  Feb 1954
    THE BEST FROM FANTASY & SCIENCE FICTION: 4th SERIES [Boucher - 1955]
Sandra by George P. Eliott...........................................Epch  Fal 1953
    A TREASURY OF GREAT SCIENCE FICTION [Boucher - 1959]
Sands Of Mars, The by A. E. Van Vogt...............(See listing Enchanted Village)
Sands Of Time, The by P. Schuyler Miller.............................Ast   Apr 1937
    ADVENTURES IN TIME AND SPACE [Healy & McComas - 1946]
Santa Claus Planet, The by Frank M. Robinson.....................ORIGINAL STORY
    THE BEST SCIENCE FICTION STORIES: 1951 [Bleiler & Dikty - 1951]
Satan And Sam Shay by Robert Arthur..................................EM    Aug 1942
    OUT OF THIS WORLD [Fast - 1944]
Satellite Passage by Theodore L. Thomas..............................If    Dec 1958
    SF: 59 THE YEAR'S GREATEST SF & FANTASY [Merril - 1959]
Saturnian Celia by Horace Walpole.........................Rpnt - F&SF  Apr 1957
    (From The Letters Of Horace Walpole by Mrs. Paget Toynbee;
    A DECADE OF FANTASY & SCIENCE FICTION [Mills - 1960]
Saucer Of Lonliness by Theodore Sturgeon.............................Glxy  Feb 1953
    THE SECOND GALAXY READER OF SCIENCE FICTION [Mills - 1960]
Scanners Live In Vain by Cordwainer Smith............................FB #6 n/d 1950
    BEYOND THE END OF TIME [Pohl - 1952]
    SCIENCE AND SORCERY [Ford - 1953]

| | Mag. | Year |
|---|---|---|

Scarab, The by Raymond Z. Gallun............................Ast Aug 1936
  SCIENCE FICTION THINKING MACHINES [Conklin - 1954]
Scarlet Dream by C. L. Moore (Mrs. Henry Kuttner)....................WT May 1934
  FUTURE TENSE [Crossen - 1953]
Scarlet Lunes, The by Stanton A. Coblentz........................FB #6 n/d 1950
  SCIENCE AND SORCERY [Ford - 1953]
Scarlet Plague, The by Jack London..........................ASMM 6/8/13
  OUT OF THIS WORLD [Fast - 1944]
  THE OMNIBUS OF SCIENCE FICTION [Conklin - 1952]
Scene For Saturn by Noel Langley.............................SEP 1/25/47
  THE SATURDAY EVENING POST FANTASY STORIES [Fles - 1951]
Scene Shifter, The by Arthur Sellings......................ORIGINAL STORY
  STAR SCIENCE FICTION STORIES #5 [Pohl - 1959]
Scent For Sarsaparilla, A by Ray Bradbury..................ORIGINAL STORY
  STAR SCIENCE FICTION STORIES [Pohl - 1953]
  STORIES FOR TOMORROW [Sloane - 1954]
Schedule by Harry Walton....................................ASF Jun 1945
  MEN AGAINST THE STARS [Greenberg - 1950]
School For The Unspeakable by Manly Wade Wellman.............WT Sep 1937
  THE OTHER WORLDS [Stong - 1941]
Science-Fiction Book Index, The by Earl Kemp [1954 Listing]...............
  THE BEST SCIENCE FICTION STORIES AND NOVELS: 1955 [Dikty - 1955]
Science-Fiction Book Index, The by Earl Kemp [1955 Listing]...............
  THE BEST SCIENCE FICTION STORIES AND NOVELS: 1956 [Dikty - 1956]
Science-Fiction Book Index, The by Earl Kemp [1956 and 1957 Listing]...........
  THE BEST SCIENCE FICTION STORIES AND NOVELS: 9th SERIES [Dikty - 1958]
Science Fiction Is Too Conservative by G. Harry Stine....................
  (See listing How To Think A Science Fiction Story)
Science Fiction Still Leads Science Fact by Anthony Boucher........NYTM 12/1/57
  SF: 58 THE YEAR'S GREATEST SF & FANTASY [Merril - 1958]
Science Steals A Match by Nelson Richards...................ORIGINAL STORY
  ADVENTURES TO COME [Esenwein - 1937]
Scientist Divides, A by Donald Wandrei..............................Ast Sep 1934
  THE BEST OF SCIENCE FICTION [Conklin - 1946]
Sculptors Of Life by Wallace West...................................ASF Dec 1939
  SCIENCE FICTION THINKING MACHINES [Conklin - 1954]
Sea Change by Thomas N. Scortia.................(See listing The Shores of Night)
Sea Raiders, The by H. G. Wells.........(From The Plattner Story and Others; 1897)
  ASPECTS OF SCIENCE FICTION [Doherty - 1959]
Sealman, The by John Masefield..........................Rpnt — F&SF Jul 1955
  (From Mainsail Haul; 1913)
  A DECADE OF FANTASY & SCIENCE FICTION [Mills - 1960]
Search, The by A. E. Van Vogt......................................ASF Jan 1943
  THE BEST OF SCIENCE FICTION [Conklin - 1946]
Second Chance by Walter Kubilius and Fletcher Pratt................FSM Sep 1952
  SPACE, SPACE, SPACE [Sloane - 1953]
Second Childhood by Clifford D. Simak.............................Glxy Feb 1951
  THE GALAXY READER OF SCIENCE FICTION [Gold - 1952]
  STORIES FOR TOMORROW [Sloane - 1954]
Second Night Of Summer by Joseph H. Schmitz.....................Glxy Dec 1950
  POSSIBLE WORLDS OF SCIENCE FICTION [Conklin - 1951]
Second Variety by Philip K. Dick...................................Spc May 1953
  YEAR'S BEST SCIENCE FICTION NOVELS: 1954 [Bleiler & Dikty - 1954]
Secret by Lee Cahn.................................................ASF Jan 1953
  CROSSROADS IN TIME [Conklin - 1953]

|  | Mag. | Year |
|---|---|---|
| Seeds Of The Dusk by Raymond Z. Gallun...........................ASF | ASF | Jun 1938 |

Seeds Of The Dusk by Raymond Z. Gallun...........................ASF Jun 1938
   ADVENTURES IN TIME AND SPACE [Healy & McComas - 1946]
Seeker Of The Sphinx by Arthur C. Clarke.........................2CB Spr 1951
   YEAR'S BEST SCIENCE FICTION NOVELS: 1952 [Bleiler & Dikty - 1952]
Seekers, The by Robert Moore Williams............................Stg May 1948
   FLIGHT INTO SPACE [Wollheim - 1950]
Seesaw, The by A. E. Van Vogt....................................ASF Jul 1941
   BEYOND TIME AND SPACE [Derleth - 1950]
Self Portrait by Bernard Wolfe...................................Glxy Nov 1951
   THE ROBOT AND THE MAN [Greenberg - 1953]
   THE SECOND GALAXY READER OF SCIENCE FICTION [Gold - 1954]
Sense From Thought Divide by Mark Clifton........................ASF Mar 1955
   SF: THE YEAR'S GREATEST SCIENCE FICTION AND FANTASY [Merril - 1956]
Sentamantalists, The by Murray Leinster ps (Will F. Jenkins).....Glxy Apr 1953
   YEAR'S BEST SCIENCE FICTION NOVELS: 1954 [Bleiler & Dikty - 1954]
Serious Search For Weird Worlds, A by Ray Bradbury...............Life 10/24/60
   SIXTH ANNUAL OF THE YEAR'S BEST SF [Merril - 1961]
Service First by David H. Keller, M. D. .........................AQ Win 1931
   THE OUTER REACHES [Derleth - 1951]
S-F: 1955 [Summation & Honorable Mentions] by Judith Merril.....................
   SF: THE YEAR'S GREATEST SCIENCE FICTION AND FANTASY [Merril - 1956]
Shadow And The Flash, The by Jack London.........................Bkm Jun 1903
   SHOT IN THE DARK [Merril - 1950]
   INVISIBLE MEN [Davenport - 1960]
Shadow — Lay, The by E. D. Fitzpatrick...........(London Observer Prize Story)
   A. D. 2500 [Wilson - 1955]
Shadow Out Of Time, The by H. P. Lovecraft.......................Ast Jun 1936
   THE PORTABLE NOVELS OF SCIENCE [Wollheim - 1945]
Shambleau by C. L. Moore (Mrs. Henry Kuttner)....................WT Nov 1933
   ADVENTURES IN TOMORROW [Crossen - 1951]
   ESCALES DANS L'INFINI [Gallett - 1954]
Shape Of Things, The by Ray Bradbury.............................TWS Feb 1948
   TRAVELERS OF SPACE [Greenberg - 1952]
Shape Of Things To Come, The by Richard Deming...................F&SF Oct 1951
   A TREASURY OF GREAT SCIENCE FICTION [Boucher - 1959]
Share Alike by Jerome Bixby and Joe E. Dean......................BFF Jul 1953
   GALAXY OF GHOULS [Merril - 1955]
   ZACHERLY'S MIDNIGHT SNACKS [Zacherly - 1960]
She Only Goes Out At Night by William Tenn ps (Philip Klass)........FU Oct 1956
   THE FANTASTIC UNIVERSE OMNIBUS [Santesson - 1960]
She Who Laughs by Peter Phillips.................................Glxy Apr 1952
   ASSIGNMENT IN TOMORROW [Pohl - 1954]
Shed, The by E. Everett Evans....................................AvR Jan 1953
   STORIES FOR TOMORROW [Sloane - 1954]
   ZACHERLY'S VULTURE STEW [Zacherly - 1960]
Shepard's Boy by Richard Matheson................................F&SF Mar 1953
   THE BEST FROM FANTASY & SCIENCE FICTION: 3rd SERIES [Boucher & McComas-1953]
Ship From The Stars by Peter Hawkins.............................NW #25 Jul 1954
   THE BEST FROM NEW WORLDS [Carnell - 1955]
Ship Sails At Midnight, The by Fritz Leiber......................FA Sep 1950
   THE OUTER REACHES [Derleth - 1951]
Ship That Turned Aside, The by Green Payton ps (G. Peyton Wertenbaker)...........
   THE BIG BOOK OF SCIENCE FICTION [Conklin - 1950]   Amz Mar 1930
Shipping Clerk by William Morrison ps (Joseph Samachson)..........Glxy Jun 1952
   13 GREAT STORIES OF SCIENCE FICTION [Conklin - 1960]

(165)

Shipshape Home by Richard Matheson........................................Glxy Jul 1952
   THE OMNIBUS OF SCIENCE FICTION [Conklin - 1952]
   TERROR IN THE MODERN VEIN [Wollheim - 1955]
Shock by Henry Kuttner....................................................ASF Mar 1943
   THE OUTER REACHES [Derleth - 1951]
Shock Treatment by J. Francis McComas.......................Rpnt - F&SF Apr 1956
   9 TALES OF SPACE AND TIME [Healy - 1954]   (Original Story)
   A DECADE OF FANTASY & SCIENCE FICTION [Mills - 1960]
Shock Troop by Richard Bolton...............................................If Oct 1956
   THE FIRST WORLD OF IF [Quinn & Wulff - 1957]
Shoddy Lands, The by C. S. Lewis.........................................F&SF Feb 1956
   THE BEST FROM FANTASY & SCIENCE FICTION: 6th SERIES [Boucher - 1957]
Shore Of Tomorrow, The by Chad Oliver.....................................Stg Mar 1953
   TOMORROW'S UNIVERSE [H. J. Campbell - 1954]
Shoreline At Sunset by Ray Bradbury.........(From A Medicine For Melancholy; 1959)
   FIFTH ANNUAL OF THE YEAR'S BEST SF [Merril - 1960]
Shores Of Night, The by Thomas N. Scortia..[Portion entitled Sea Change appeared
   in Astounding Science Fiction; June 1956 - Balance of story was written for
   this anthology.]
   THE BEST SCIENCE FICTION STORIES AND NOVELS: 1956 [Dikty - 1956]
Short-Circuited Probability by Norman L. Knight......................ASF Sep 1941
   THE BEST OF SCIENCE FICTION [Conklin - 1946]
Short In The Chest by Idris Seabright ps (Margaret St. Clair).........FU Jul 1954
   OPERATION FUTURE [Conklin - 1955]
Short Life, The by Francis Donovan.....................................ASF Oct 1955
   BEST SF FOUR SCIENCE FICTION STORIES [Crispin - 1961]
Short Ones, The by Raymond E. Banks....................................F&SF Mar 1955
   THE BEST FROM FANTASY & SCIENCE FICTION: 5th SERIES [Boucher - 1956]
Short-Short Story Of Mankind, The by John Steinbeck.................Plby Apr 1958
   SF: 59 THE YEAR'S GREATEST SF AND FANTASY [Merril - 1959]
   PENGUIN SCIENCE FICTION [Aldiss - 1961]
Shottle Bop by Theodore Sturgeon......................................Unk Feb 1941
   INVISIBLE MEN [Davenport - 1960]
Shout, The by Robert Graves.....................................Rpnt - F&SF Apr 1952
   (Originally published by Elkins Mathews & Mariot, Ltd.: London; 1929)
   THE BEST FROM FANTASY & SCIENCE FICTION: 2nd SERIES [Boucher & McComas-1952]
Sierra Sam by Ralph Dighton..................Associated Press Release 1/10/60
   FIFTH ANNUAL OF THE YEAR'S BEST SF [Merril - 1960]
Sigh For Cybernetics, A by Felica Lamport..........(verse).........Hpr Jan 1961
   SIXTH ANNUAL OF THE YEAR'S BEST SF [Merril - 1961]
Silence, The by Bernard McLaughlin.....................................Sti Jun 1941
   TERROR IN THE MODERN VEIN [Wollheim - 1955]
Silence, Please! by Arthur C. Clarke................................SF #2 Win 1950
   13 GREAT STORIES OF SCIENCE FICTION [Conklin - 1960]
Silent Brother by Algis Budrys........................................ASF Feb 1956
   (Originally appeared under pseudonym Paul Janvier)
   SF: 57 THE YEAR'S GREATEST SF AND FANTASY [Merril - 1957]
Silent, Upon Two Peaks by Herman W. Mudgett.........(verse).......F&SF Jul 1955
   THE BEST FROM FANTASY & SCIENCE FICTION: 5th SERIES [Boucher - 1956]
Silk And The Song, The by Charles L. Fontenay......................F&SF Jul 1956
   THE BEST FROM FANTASY & SCIENCE FICTION: 6th SERIES [Boucher - 1957]
Silly Season, The by C. M. Kornbluth................................F&SF Fal 1950
   TOMORROW, THE STARS [Heinlein - 1952]
   THE EARTH IN PERIL [Wollheim - 1957]
Silver Mirror, The by Arthur Conan Doyle............(From Tales Of Long Ago; 1925)
   TRAVELERS IN TIME [Stern - 1947]

```
                                                              Mag.    Year
Simworthy's Circus by Larry Shaw...................................WB   Dec 1950
     SCIENCE FICTION CARNIVAL [Brown & Reynolds - 1953]
Singing Bell, The by Isaac Asimov...............................F&SF   Jan 1955
     THE BEST FROM FANTASY & SCIENCE FICTION: 5th SERIES [Boucher - 1956]
Sister Planet by Poul Anderson....................................SSF   May 1959
     GET OUT OF MY SKY [Margulies - 1960]
Sitting Duck by Oliver Saari......................................ASF   Jun 1952
     EVERY BOY'S BOOK OF OUTER SPACE STORIES [Dikty - 1960]
Six Hundred Fathoms by Norman Leslie....................ORIGINAL STORY
     ADVENTURES TO COME [Esenwein - 1937]
Skag With the Queer Head by Murray Leinster ps (Will F. Jenkins).....MSF   Aug 1951
     SCIENCE FICTION ADVENTURES IN MUTATION [Conklin - 1954]
Skills Of Xanadu, The by Theodore Sturgeon.......................Glxy   Jul 1956
     13 GREAT STORIES OF SCIENCE FICTION [Conklin - 1954]
Skirmish by Clifford D. Simak....................................Amz   Dec 1950
     SCIENCE FICTION THINKING MACHINES [Conklin - 1954]
     PENGUIN SCIENCE FICTION [Aldiss - 1961]
          (Appeared under title Bathe Your Bearings In Blood)
Sky People, The by Poul Anderson.................................F&SF   Mar 1959
     A DECADE OF FANTASY & SCIENCE FICTION [Mills - 1960]
Sky Was Full of Ships, The by Theodore Sturgeon...................TWS   Jun 1947
     SHOT IN THE DARK [Merril - 1950]
Sly Bungerhop, The by William Morrison ps (Joseph Samachson)........Glxy   Sep 1957
     MIND PARTNER AND 8 OTHER NOVELETTES FROM GALAXY [Gold - 1961]
Small Assasin by Ray Bradbury.....................................DM   Nov 1946
     CHILDREN OF WONDER [Tenn - 1953]
Small World of M-75, The by Ed M. Clinton, Jr. ...................If   Jul 1954
     SCIENCE FICTION ADVENTURES IN MUTATION [Conklin - 1956]
     THE FIRST WORLD OF IF [Quinn & Wulff - 1957]
Smile, The by Ray Bradbury.......................................Fnt   Sum 1952
     WORLDS OF TOMORROW   Derleth - 1953]
Smile of the Sphinx, The [Le Sourire Du Sphinx] by Wm. F. Temple....ToW   Aug 1938
     ESCALES DANS L'INFINI [Gallet - 1954]
Smoke Ghost by Fritz Leiber, Jr. ................................UW   Oct 1941
     HUMAN? [Merril - 1954]
Snowball Effect, The Katherine MacLean...........................Glxy   Sep 1952
     THE SECOND GALAXY READER OF SCIENCE FICTION [Gold - 1954]
     PENGUIN SCIENCE FICTION [Aldiss - 1961]
Snuffles by R. A. Lafferty.......................................Glxy   Dec 1960
     MIND PARTNER AND EIGHT OTHER NOVELETTES FROM GALAXY [Gold - 1961]
Snulbug by Anthony Boucher................................Rpnt — F&SF   May 1953
     (Originally appeared in Unknown Worlds; December 1941)
     THE BEST FROM FANTASY & SCIENCE FICTION: 3rd SERIES [Boucher & McComas-1953]
So Proudly We Hail by Judith Merril.....................ORIGINAL STORY
     STAR SCIENCE FICTION STORIES [Pohl - 1953]
Soap Opera by Alan Nelson.......................................F&SF   Apr 1953
     13 GREAT STORIES OF SCIENCE FICTION [Conklin - 1960]
Soaring Statue, The by L. Sprague de Camp...............ORIGINAL STORY
     TOMORROW'S UNIVERSE [H. J. Campbell - 1954]
Socrates by John Christopher ps (Christopher S. Youd)..............Glxy   Mar 1951
     BEYOND HUMAN KEN [Merril - 1952]
     STORIES FOR TOMORROW [Sloane - 1954]
Socrates And The Slave by Plato...................(Translated by Benjamin Jowett)
     (From The Meno Of Plato; Oxford University Press: 1892)
     FANTASIA MATHEMATICA [Fadiman - 1958]
Solar Plexus by James Blish.......................................Ash   Sep 1941
     BEYOND HUMAN KEN [Merril - 1952]
Soldier Boy by Michael Shaara...................................Glxy   Jul 1953
     SCIENCE FICTION THINKING MACHINES [Conklin - 1954]
```

|  | Mag. | Year |
|---|---|---|

Sole Solution by Eric Frank Russell........................................FU Apr 1956
  PENGUIN SCIENCE FICTION [Aldiss - 1961]
Solitary Confinement by Philip MacDonald......................(See listing The Hub)
Solution Unsatisfactory by Anson MacDonald ps (Robert A. Heinlein)...ASF May 1941
  THE BEST OF SCIENCE FICTION [Conklin - 1946]
Some Facts About Robots by Leonard Wolf..........(verse)............F&SF Jul 1954
  THE BEST FROM FANTASY & SCIENCE FICTION: 4th SERIES [Boucher - 1953]
Something by Allen Drury.......................................F&SF Oct 1960
  THE BEST FROM FANTASY & SCIENCE FICTION: 10th SERIES [Mills - 1961]
Something Bright by Zeena Henderson...............................Glxy Feb 1960
  SIXTH ANNUAL OF THE YEAR'S BEST SF [Merril - 1961]
Something From Above by Donald Wandrei............................WT Dec 1930
  THE OTHER SIDE OF THE MOON [Derleth - 1949]
Something Invented Me by R. C. Phelan............................Rptr 10/13/60
  SIXTH ANNUAL OF THE YEAR'S BEST SF [Merril - 1961]
Somnium by Johannes Kepler............(English translation by Everett F. Bleiler)
  (Posthoumously published in Latin: Frankfurt; 1634)
  BEYOND TIME AND SPACE [Derleth - 1950]
Son Of Two Worlds by Edmond Hamilton............................TWS Aug 1941
  THREE FROM OUT THERE [Margulies - 1959]
Song Of The Pewee, The by Stephen Grendon ps (August Derleth)........Ark Aut 1949
  FAR BOUNDARIES [Derleth - 1951]
Song Of The Slaves, The by Manly Wade Wellman......................WT Mar 1940
  THE OTHER WORLDS [Stong - 1941]
Soothsayer, The by Kem Bennett....................................F&SF Aug 1952
  THE BEST FROM FANTASY & SCIENCE FICTION: 2nd SERIES [Boucher & McComas-1953]
Sorcerer's Apprentice, The by Malcolm Jameson.....................ASF Dec 1941
  OPERATION FUTURE [Conklin - 1955]
Sorry, Right Number by Richard Matheson...........................Bynd Nov 1953
  ZACHERLY'S MIDNIGHT SNACKS [Zacherly - 1960]
Soul Mate by Lee Sutton...........................................F&SF Jun 1959
  THE BEST FROM FANTASY & SCIENCE FICTION: 9th SERIES [Mills - 1960]
Sound Machine, The by Roald Dahl..................................Nykr 9/17/49
  TIMELESS STORIES FOR TODAY AND TOMORROW [Bradbury - 1952]
Sound Of Bugles, The by Robert Moore Williams.....................Stg Mar 1949
  ADVENTURES ON OTHER PLANETS [Wollheim - 1954]
Sound Of Thunder, A by Ray Bradbury.........(From Golden Apples Of The Sun; 1953)
  ASPECTS OF SCIENCE FICTION [Doherty - 1959]
Sound Sweep, The by J. G. Ballard.................................SF #39 Feb 1960
  FIFTH ANNUAL OF THE YEAR'S BEST SF [Merril - 1960]
Space by John Buchan..............................................LvA 6/17/11
  BEYOND TIME AND SPACE [Derleth - 1950]
Space Burial by Brian W. Aldiss............(verse)............F&SF Jul 1959
  THE BEST FROM FANTASY & SCIENCE FICTION: 9th SERIES [Mills - 1960]
Space Fix by R. S. Richardson....................................ASF Mar 1943
  COMING ATTRACTIONS [Greenberg - 1957]
Space Rating by John Berryman.....................................ASF Oct 1939
  (Originally appeared under title Beyond The Stars)
  POSSIBLE WORLDS OF SCIENCE FICTION [Conklin - 1951]
  BEYOND THE STARS AND OTHER STORIES [Anonymous - 1958]
    (Appeared under title Beyond The Stars)
Space Station No. 1 by Manly Wade Wellman.........................Arg 10/10/36
  MY BEST SCIENCE FICTION STORY [Margulies & Friend - 1949]
  ESCALES DANS L'INFINI [Gallet - 1954]
    (Appeared under title Station Interplanetaire No. 1)

|  | Mag. | Year |
|---|---|---|

Space Station 42 by Charles E. Fritch..........................Orb #5  Nov 1954
    (Originally appeared under title Many Dreams Of Earth)
    SPACE STATION 42 AND OTHER STORIES [Anonymous - 1958]
Space-Time For Springers by Fritz Leiber......................ORIGINAL STORY
    STAR SCIENCE FICTION STORIES #4 [Pohl - 1958]
    SF: 59 THE YEAR'S GREATEST SF AND FANTASY [Merril - 1959]
    STAR OF STARS [Pohl - 1960]
Space War by Willy Ley........................................ASF  Aug 1939
    COMING ATTRACTIONS [Greenberg - 1957]
Space War Tactics by Malcolm Jameson..........................ASF  Aug 1939
    COMING ATTRACTIONS [Greenberg - 1957]
Sparkie's Fall by Gavin Hyde..................................ORIGINAL STORY
    STAR SCIENCE FICTION STORIES #5 [Pohl - 1959]
    STAR OF STARS [Pohl - 1960]
Spawn Of The Stars by Charles W. Diffin.......................Ast  Feb 1930
    THE BEST OF SCIENCE FICTION [Conklin - 1946]
Special Delivery by Damon Knight..............................Glxy  Apr 1954
    OPERATION FUTURE [Conklin - 1955]
Specialist by Robert Sheckley.................................Glxy  May 1953
    THE SECOND GALAXY READER OF SCIENCE FICTION [Gold - 1954]
Spectator Sport by John D. MacDonald..........................TWS  Feb 1950
    THE OMNIBUS OF SCIENCE FICTION [Conklin - 1952]
Specter General, The by Theodore R. Cogswell..................ASF  Jun 1952
    SPACE SERVICE [Norton - 1953]
Spiro by Eric Frank Russell...................................WT  Mar 1947
    THE OTHER SIDE OF THE MOON [Derleth - 1949]
Spokesman For Terra by Hugh Raymond ps (John Michael).........Sti  Jun 1941
    SHOT IN THE DARK [Merril - 1950]
Sportsman's Difficulty by Doris Pitkin Buck..........(verse).......F&SF  Mar 1959
    THE BEST FROM FANTASY & SCIENCE FICTION: 9th SERIES [Mills - 1960]
Special Flight by John Berryman...............................ASF  May 1939
    SPECTRUM [Amis & Conquest - 1961]
Spud And Cochise by Oliver La Farge...................Rpnt — F&SF  Dec 1957
    (Originally appeared in Forum: January 1936)
    A DECADE OF FANTASY & SCIENCE FICTION [Mills - 1960]
Spud Failure Definite by Noel Peart..................London Observer Prize Story
    A. D. 2500 [Wilson - 1955]
Sputnik: One Reason Why We Lost by G. Harry Stine.............F&SF  Jan 1958
    SF: 58 THE YEAR'S GREATEST SF AND FANTASY [Merril - 1958]
Srl Ad by Richard Matheson....................................F&SF  Apr 1952
    SCIENCE FICTION CARNIVAL [Brown & Reynolds - 1953]
Stair Trick by Mildred Clingerman.............................F&SF  Aug 1952
    THE BEST FROM FANTASY & SCIENCE FICTION: 2nd SERIES [Boucher & McComas-1953]
Star, The by David H. Keller..................................ORIGINAL STORY
    BEACHHEADS IN SPACE [Derleth - 1954]
Star, The by H. G. Wells......................................Grp  Xmas 1897
    THE OTHER SIDE OF THE MOON [Derleth - 1949]
    SHOT IN THE DARK [Merril - 1950]
    THE TREASURY OF SCIENCE FICTION CLASSICS [Kuebler - 1955]
    THE EARTH IN PERIL [Wollheim - 1957]
    SCIENCE IN FICTION [A.E.M. & J.C. Bayliss - 1957]
Star Bright by Mark Clifton...................................Glxy  Jul 1952
    PRIZE SCIENCE FICTION [Wollheim - 1953]
    THE SECOND GALAXY READER OF SCIENCE FICTION [Gold - 1954]
Star Bright by Jack Williamson................................Arg  11/29/39
    MY BEST SCIENCE FICTION STORY [Margulies & Friend - 1949]

```
                                                                Mag.    Year
Star Ducks, The by Bill Brown..........................................F&SF  Fal 1950
     THE BEST SCIENCE FICTION STORIES: 1951 [Bleiler & Dikty - 1951]
     SCIENCE FICTION AND READER'S GUIDE [Barrows - 1954]
Star Dummy, The by Anthony Boucher....................................Fnt  Fal 1952
     THE OMNIBUS OF SCIENCE FICTION [Conklin - 1952]
Star Gypsies, The by William Lindsay Gresham.........................F&SF  Jul 1953
     THE BEST FROM FANTASY & SCIENCE FICTION: 3rd SERIES [Boucher & McComas-1954]
Star Light, Star Bright by Alfred Bester.............................F&SF  Jul 1953
     THE BEST FROM FANTASY & SCIENCE FICTION: 3rd SERIES [Boucher & McComas-1954]
Star-Lined by H. B. Fyfe.............................................ASF  Feb 1952
     SPACE SERVICE [Norton - 1953]
Star Mouse, The by Fredric Brown......................................PS  Spr 1942
     ADVENTURES IN TIME AND SPACE [Healy & McComas - 1946]
     INVASION FROM MARS [Welles - 1949]
Star of Wonder by Julian May.........................................TWS  Feb 1953
     EVERY BOY'S BOOK OF OUTER SPACE STORIES [Dikty - 1960]
Starbride by Anthony Boucher.........................................TWS  Dec 1951
     STORIES FOR TOMORROW [Sloane - 1954]
Stardust by Chad Oliver..............................................ASF  Jul 1952
     ADVENTURES IN THE FAR FUTURE [Wollheim - 1954]
Stars Are the Styx, The by Theodore Sturgeon........................Glxy  Oct 1950
     THE GALAXY READER OF SCIENCE FICTION [Gold - 1952]
Stars My Destination, The by Alfred Bester..........................Glxy  Oct 1956
     A TREASURY OF GREAT SCIENCE FICTION [Boucher - 1959]
Statue, The by Mari Wolf...............................(See listing Homeland)
Status Quondam by P. Schuyler Miller...........................ORIGINAL STORY
     NEW TALES OF SPACE AND TIME [Healy - 1951]
Steel Brother by Gordon R. Dickson...................................ASF  Feb 1952
     SPACE SERVICE [Norton - 1953]
Stentorii Luggage, The by Neal Barrett, Jr. ........................Glxy  Oct 1960
     MIND PARTNER AND 8 OTHER NOVELETS FROM GALAXY [Gold - 1961]
Stepson of Space by Raymond Z. Gallun................................Ash  Apr 1940
     BEYOND THE END OF TIME [Pohl - 1952]
Stickeney and the Critic by Mildred Clingerman......................F&SF  Feb 1952
     PORTALS OF TOMORROW [Derleth - 1954]
Still Waters by Lester del Rey....................................NW #78  Dec 1958
     OUT OF THIS WORLD 2 [Williams-Ellis & Owen - 1961]
Stitch in Time by J. T. McIntosh ps (James J. MacGregor)..........SF #5  Aut 1952
     GATEWAY TO THE STARS [Carnell - 1955]
Stolen Centuries by Otis Adelbert Kline.............................TWS  Jun 1939
     (Story selected by Oscar J. Friend)            Rpnt - FSQ  Sep 1953
     EDITOR'S CHOICE IN SCIENCE FICTION [Moskowitz - 1954]
Stone and a Spear, A by Raymond F. Jones............................Glxy  Dec 1950
     THE OMNIBUS OF SCIENCE FICTION [Conklin - 1952]
Storm Warning by Donald A. Wollheim.................................FFSF  Oct 1942
     (Originally appeared under pseudonym Millard Verne Gordon)
     INVADERS OF EARTH [Conklin - 1952]
Story of a Panic by E. M. Forster....(From Collected Tales of E.M. Forster; 1947)
     CHILDREN OF WONDER [Tenn - 1953]
Strange Case of John Kingman, The by Murray Leinster ps (Will F. Jenkins).......
     THE BEST SCIENCE FICTION STORIES: 1949 [Bleiler & Dikty-1949] ASF  May 1948
     GREAT STORIES OF SCIENCE FICTION [Wollheim - 1955]
Strange Case of Lemuel Jenkins, The by Philip M. Fisher, Jr. .......AIS 7/26/1919
     TERROR IN THE MODERN VEIN [Wollheim - 1955]
Strange Drug of Dr. Caber, The by Lord Dunsany..............................
     (From The Fourth Book of Jorkens; 1948)
     THE OTHER SIDE OF THE MOON [Derleth - 1949]
Strange Harvest by Donald Wandrei...................................WT  May 1953
     WORLDS OF TOMORROW [Derleth - 1953]
```

|  | Mag. | Year |
|---|---|---|

Strange Playfellow by Isaac Asimov.....................................Sup  Sep 1940
    SHOT IN THE DARK [Merril - 1950]
Stranger From Space by Gene Lees.....................................SF #7  Mar 1954
    GATEWAY TO THE STARS [Carnell - 1955]
Stranger Station by Damon Knight.....................................F&SF  Dec 1956
    SF: 57 THE YEAR'S GREATEST SF AND FANTASY [Merril - 1957]
Strawberry Window, The by Ray Bradbury...........................ORIGINAL STORY
    STAR SCIENCE FICTION STORIES #3 [Pohl - 1958]
Street That Wasn't There, The by Clifford D. Simak and Carl Jacobi...............
    (See listing The Lost Street)
Student Body by F. L. Wallace........................................Glxy  Mar 1953
    CROSSROADS IN TIME [Conklin - 1953]
    THE SECOND GALAXY READER OF SCIENCE FICTION [Gold - 1954]
Stutterer, The by R. R. Merliss......................................ASF  Apr 1955
    SF: THE YEAR'S GREATEST SF AND FANTASY [Merril - 1956]
Sub-Standard Sardines, The by Jack Vance.............................Stg  Jan 1949
    SPACE POLICE [Norton - 1956]
Sublime Virgil, The by Chester D. Cuthbert...........................WS  Feb 1934
    (Story selected by Hugo Gernsback)
    EDITOR'S CHOICE IN SCIENCE FICTION [Moskowitz - 1954]
Subterfuge by Ray Bradbury...........................................Ash  Apr 1943
    ASSIGNMENT IN TOMORROW [Pohl - 1954]
Suburban Frontiers by Roger Flint Young..............................ASF  Feb 1950
    SCIENCE FICTION ADVENTURES IN DIMENSION [Conklin - 1953]
Subway Named Mobius, A by A. J. Deutsch..............................ASF  Dec 1950
    THE OMNIBUS OF SCIENCE FICTION [Conklin - 1952]
    FANTASIA MATHEMATICA [Fadiman - 1958]
    BEST SF FOUR SCIENCE FICTION STORIES [Crispin - 1961]
Such Interesting Neighbors by Jack Finney............................Col  1/6/51
    BEYOND THE END OF TIME [Pohl - 1952]
Summer Wear by L. Sprague de Camp....................................Stg  Mar 1950
    THE BEST SCIENCE FICTION STORIES: 1951 [Bleiler & Dikty - 1951]
Summons, The by Don Evans............................................Unk  Jun 1939
    FROM UNKNOWN WORLDS [J. W. Campbell - 1948]
Sun Maker, The by Jack Williamson....................................TWS  Jun 1940
    THE GIANT ANTHOLOGY OF SCIENCE FICTION [Margulies & Friend - 1954]
Sunward by Stanton A. Coblentz.......................................TWS  Apr 1940
    FLIGHT INTO SPACE [Wollheim - 1950]
Superiority by Arthur C. Clarke......................................F&SF  Aug 1951
    WORLDS OF TOMORROW [Derleth - 1953]
    FANTASIA MATHEMATICA [Fadiman - 1958]
Supremacy Of Uruguay, The by E. B. White.............................Nykr  11/25/33
    WORLDS OF TOMORROW [Derleth --1953]
Surface Tension by James Blish.......................................Glxy  Aug 1952
    YEAR'S BEST SCIENCE FICTION NOVELS: 1953 [Bleiler & Dikty - 1953]
    SIX GREAT SHORT NOVELS OF SCIENCE FICTION [Conklin - 1954]
        (Revised for inclusion in this anthology)
    THE SECOND GALAXY READER OF SCIENCE FICTION [Gold - 1954]
Survival by John Beynon ps (John Beynon Harris)......................TWS  Feb 1952
    NO PLACE LIKE EARTH [Carnell - 1952]
    THE BEST SCIENCE FICTION STORIES: 1953 [Bleiler & Dikty - 1953]
Survival by Carlyn Coffin.................(verse)................F&SF  Jun 1955
    THE BEST FROM FANTASY & SCIENCE FICTION: 5th SERIES [Boucher - 1956]
Survival Ship by Judith Merril.......................................WB  Jan 1951
    TOMORROW, THE STARS [Heinlein - 1952]

(171)

|  | Mag. | Year |
|---|---|---|

Susceptability by John D. MacDonald...............................Glxy  Jan 1951
   THE GALAXY READER OF SCIENCE FICTION [Gold - 1952]
Swenson, Dispatcher by R. DeWitt Miller...........................Glxy  Apr 1956
   THE BEST SCIENCE FICTION STORIES AND NOVELS: 1956 [Dikty - 1956]
Sword Of Peace by Ward Moore...........................(See listing Peacebringer)
Sword Of Tomorrow by Henry Kuttner...................................TWS  Fal 1945
   THE GIANT ANTHOLOGY OF SCIENCE FICTION [Margulies & Friend - 1954]
Swordsman Of Varnis, The by Clive Jackson.............................OW  Sep 1950
   SCIENCE FICTION CARNIVAL [Brown & Reynolds - 1953]
Symbiosis by Will F. Jenkins.........................................Col  1/14/47
   THE OTHER SIDE OF THE MOON [Derleth - 1949]
   GREAT STORIES OF SCIENCE FICTION [Leinster - 1951]
   STORIES OF SCIENTIFIC IMAGINATION [Gallant - 1954]
Symbiotica by Eric Frank Russell....................................ASF  Oct 1943
   ADVENTURES IN TIME AND SPACE [Healy & McComas - 1946]
Syndrone Johnny by Charles Dye......................................Glxy  Jul 1951
   THE GALAXY READER OF SCIENCE FICTION [Gold - 1952]

# T

Taipan, The by W. Somerset Maugham...............(From On A Chinese Screen; 1922)
   TRAVELERS IN TIME [Stern - 1947]
Take A Deep Breath by Roger Thorne..................................Tgr  n/da 1956
   SF: 57 THE YEAR'S GREATEST SF AND FANTASY [Merril - 1957]
Take A Seat by Eric Frank Russell...................................Stg  May 1952
   HUMAN? [Merril - 1954]
Take Wooden Indians by Avram Davidson...............................Glxy  Jun 1959
   THE FIFTH GALAXY READER [Gold - 1961]
Tale Of A Chemist — Anonymous...........(From The Story-Teller; or Table-Book of
   Popular Literature; 1843: Edited by Robert Bell)
   FAR BOUNDARIES [Derleth - 1951]
Tale Of Negative Gravity, A by Frank R. Stockton.....(From A Borrowed Month; 1887)
   BEYOND TIME AND SPACE [Derleth - 1950]
   JOURNEYS IN SCIENCE FICTION [Loughlin & Popp - 1961]
Tale Of The Ragged Mountain, A by Edgar Allen Poe...................GLB  Apr 1844
   THE BEST OF SCIENCE FICTION [Conklin - 1946]
Tale Of The Thirteenth Floor, A by Ogden Nash......................F&SF  Jul 1955
   A DECADE OF FANTASY & SCIENCE FICTION [Mills - 1960]
Talent by Theodore Sturgeon........................................Bynd  Sep 1953
   ZACHERLY'S MIDNIGHT SNACKS [Zacherly - 1960]
Tangle Hold by F. L. Wallace.......................................Glxy  Jun 1953
   FIVE GALAXY SHORT NOVELS [Gold - 1958]
Tea Tray In The Sky by Evelyn E. Smith.............................Glxy  Sep 1952
   THE SECOND GALAXY READER OF SCIENCE FICTION [Gold - 1954]

|  | Mag. | Year |
|---|---|---|

Teacher From Mars, The by Eando Binder ps (Otto Binder)...............TWS  Feb 1941
    MY BEST SCIENCE FICTION STORY [Margulies & Friend - 1949]
Technical Advisor by Chad Oliver.....................................F&SF  Feb 1953
    CROSSROADS IN TIME [Conklin - 1953]
Technical Slip by John Beynon ps (John Beynon Harris)..................Im  Dec 1950
    OPERATION FUTURE [Conklin - 1955]
Technological Retreat by G. C. Edmondson............................F&SF  May 1956
    13 GREAT STORIES OF SCIENCE FICTION [Conklin - 1960]
Teething Ring by James Causey.......................................Glxy  Jan 1953
    THE SECOND GALAXY READER OF SCIENCE FICTION [Gold - 1954]
Temporal Transgressor, The by Frank Belknap Long, Jr. ...............ASF  Aug 1944
    THE ULTIMATE INVADER AND OTHER SCIENCE FICTION [Woolheim - 1954]
Temptation Of Harringay, The by H. G. Wells.........................................
    (From The Stolen Bacillus and Other Incidents; 1920)
    HUMAN? [Merril - 1954]
Ten-Story Jigsaw by Brian W. Aldiss...............................Neb #26  Jan 1958
    SF: 59 THE YEAR'S GREATEST SF AND FANTASY [Merril - 1959]
Tepondicon by Carl Jacobi..............................................PS  Win 1946
    FAR BOUNDARIES [Derleth - 1951]
Terminal Quest by Poul Anderson.......................................Sup  Aug 1951
    CHILDREN OF WONDER [Tenn - 1953]
Terrible Answer, The by Paul Gallico..................................SEP  1/17/50
    THE SATURDAY EVENING POST FANTASY STORIES [Fles - 1951]
Terrible Sense, The by Calvin Peregoy ps (Thomas Calvert McClary)....ASF  Aug 1938
    THE BEST OF SCIENCE FICTION [Conklin - 1946]
Terror Out Of Space by Leigh Brackett  (Mrs. Edmond Hamilton)........PS  Sum 1944
    THE HIDDEN PLANET [Wollheim - 1959]
Test, The by Richard Matheson.......................................F&SF  Nov 1954
    THE BEST FROM FANTASY & SCIENCE FICTION: 4th SERIES [Boucher - 1955]
Test Piece by Eric Frank Russell......................................OW  Mar 1951
    THE OMNIBUS OF SCIENCE FICTION [Conklin - 1952]
Testament Of Andros by James Blish...................................FSF  Jan 1953
    PORTALS OF TOMORROW [Derleth - 1954]
Thang by Martin Gardner...............................................Cmt  Fal 1948
    THE BEST SCIENCE FICTION STORIES: 1949 [Bleiler & Dikty - 1949]
That Low by Theodore Sturgeon........................................FFM  Oct 1948
    SCIENCE FICTION SHOWCASE [M. Kornbluth - 1959]
That Only A Mother by Judith Merril..................................ASF  Jun 1948
    WORLD OF WONDER [Pratt - 1951]    CHILDREN OF WONDER [Tenn - 1953]
That Share of Glory by C. M. Kornbluth .............................Glxy  Jan 1951
    SPACE SERVICE [Norton - 1953]
    EVERY BOY'S BOOK OF OUTER SPACE STORIES [Dikty - 1960]
"The Hatchery" by Aldous Huxley.......................(From Brave New World; 1932)
    CHILDREN OF WONDER [Tenn - 1953]
"The Year's Draw Nigh" by Lester del Rey.............................ASF  Oct 1951
    BEACHHEADS IN SPACE [Derleth - 1954]
Theory Of Rocketry by C. M. Kornbluth...............................F&SF  Jul 1958
    THE BEST FROM FANTASY & SCIENCE FICTION: 8th SERIES [Boucher - 1959]
There Once Was A Breathy Baboon by Sir Arthur Eddington.(verse).(No dta available)
    FANTASIA MATHEMATICA [Fadiman - 1958]
There Shall Be Darkness by C. L. Moore  (Mrs. Henry Kuttner)........ASF  Feb 1942
    JOURNEY TO INFINITY [Greenberg - 1951]

There Shall Be No Darkness by James Blish...........................TWS  Apr 1950
    WITCHES THREE [Pratt - 1952]
    ZACHERLY'S VULTURE STEW [Zacherly - 1960]
There Was A Young Fellow Named Fisk — Anonymous...(verse).....(No data available)
    FANTASIA MATHEMATICA [Fadiman - 1958]
There Was A Young Man From Trinity —— Anonymous....(verse)....(No data available)
    FANTASIA MATHEMATICA [Fadiman - 1958]
There Was An Old Man Who Said, "Do" — Anonymous....(verse)....(No data available)
    FANTASIA MATHEMATICA [Fadiman - 1958]
There Will Come Soft Rains by Ray Bradbury.........................Col    5/6/50
    ADVENTURES IN TOMORROW [Crossen - 1951]
    BEYOND THE END OF TIME [Pohl - 1952]
They by Robert A. Heinlein.........................................Unk  Apr 1941
    WORLD OF WONDER [Pratt - 1951]
    SCIENCE FICTION TERROR TALES [Conklin - 1955]
    TERROR IN THE MODERN VEIN [Wollheim - 1955]
They Bite by Anthony Boucher......................................Unk  Aug 1943
    ZACHERLY'S VULTURE STEW [Zacherly - 1960]
Thing by Ivan Janvier ps (Algis Budrys)..............................FU  Mar 1955
    THE BEST SCIENCE FICTION STORIES AND NOVELS: 1956 [Dikty - 1956]
Thing From Outside, The by George Allan England....................S&I  Apr 1923
    STRANGE PORTS OF CALL [Derleth - 1948]
Thing In The Attic, The by James Blish...............................If  Jul 1954
    THE SECOND WORLD OF IF [Quinn & Wulff - 1958]
Thing In The Pond, The by Paul Ernst...............................Ast  Jun 1934
    MY BEST SCIENCE FICTION STORY [Margulies & Friend - 1949]
Thing In The Woods, The by Fletcher Pratt and B. F. Ruby...........Amz  Feb 1935
    THE OMNIBUS OF SCIENCE FICTION [Conklin - 1952]
Thing Of Custom, A by L. Sprague de Camp.............................FU  Jan 1957
    THE FANTASTIC UNIVERSE OMNIBUS [Santesson - 1960]
Thing On Outer Shoal, The by P. Schuyler Miller....................ASF  Sep 1947
    THE OTHER SIDE OF THE MOON [Derleth - 1949]
Things Of Distinction by Kendall Foster Crossen....................Stg  Mar 1952
    FUTURE TENSE [Crossen - 1953]
Things Pass By by Murray Leinster ps (Will F. Jenkins)..............TWS  Sum 1945
    THE GIANT ANTHOLOGY OF SCIENCE FICTION [Margulies & Friend - 1954]
    THE EARTH IN PERIL [Wollheim - 1957]
Thinker And The Thought, The by August Derleth....(See listing Thinkers, Mark VII)
Thinkers, The by Walt Kelly.........(cartoon)............Hall Syndicate  1/29/61
    SIXTH ANNUAL OF THE YEAR'S BEST SF [Merril - 1961]
Thinkers, Mark VII by August Derleth..............................Orb #4  Sep 1954
    (Originally appeared under title The Thinker and The Thought)
    THE SANDS OF MARS AND OTHER STORIES [Anonymous - 1958]
Thiotimoline And The Space Age by Isaac Asimov.....................ASF  Oct 1960
    SIXTH ANNUAL OF THE YEAR'S BEST SF [Merril - 1961]
Third From The Sun by Richard Matheson............................Glxy  Oct 1950
    THE GALAXY READER OF SCIENCE FICTION [Gold - 1952]
Third Level, The by Jack Finney....................................Col  10/7/50
                                            Rpnt - F&SF  Oct 1952
    THE BEST FROM FANTASY & SCIENCE FICTION: 2nd SERIES [Boucher & McComas -1953]
Thirsty God by Margaret St. Clair..................................F&SF  Mar 1953
    CROSSROADS IN TIME [Conklin - 1953]
Thirty Second Of May, The by Paul Ernst............................Ast  Apr 1935
    THE BEST OF SCIENCE FICTION [Conklin - 1946]

|  | Mag. | Year |

Thirty Seconds — Thirty Days by Arthur C. Clarke.....................TWS  Dec 1949
    NO PLACE LIKE EARTH [Carnell - 1952]
    (Appeared under title Breaking Strain)
    THE BEST FROM STARTLING STORIES [Mines - 1953]
    OUT OF THIS WORLD I [Williams-Ellis & Owen - 1960]
This Earth Of Majesty by Arthur C. Clarke.........................F&SF  Jul 1955
    THE BEST FROM FANTASY & SCIENCE FICTION: 5th SERIES [Boucher - 1956]
This Is The Land by Nelson Bond.......................................BB  Apr 1951
    THE OUTER REACHES [Derleth - 1951]
This One's On Me by Eric Frank Russell.............................NSF  Aug 1953
    SCIENCE FICTION ADVENTURES IN MUTATION [Conklin - 1956]
This Side Up by Raymond E. Banks...................................Glxy  Jul 1954
    THE FIFTH GALAXY READER [Gold - 1961]
This Star Shall Be Free by Murray Leinster ps (Will F. Jenkins)......Sup  Nov 1949
    INVADERS OF EARTH [Conklin - 1952]
Thou Good And Faithful by K. Houston Brunner.....................ASF  Mar 1953
    (Originally appeared under pseudonym John Loxsmith)
    SPACE PIONEERS [Norton - 1954]
Though Dreamers Die by Lester del Rey.............................ASF  Oct 1939
    THE ROBOT AND THE MAN [Greenberg - 1953]
Thousandth-And-Second-Tale-Of-Scherazade, The by Edgar Allen Poe.....GLB  Feb 1843
    BEYOND TIME AND SPACE [Derleth - 1950]
Three Brothers, The by William Moy Russell.........................Obs  12/26/54
    A. D. 2500 [Wilson - 1955]
Three Lines Of Old French [Trois Lignes De Vieux Francais] by A. Merritt........
                                                              Arg  8/9/19
    ESCALES DANS L'INFINI [Gallet - 1954]
Threepenny Piece, The by James Stephens..............(From Here Are Ladies; 1913)
                                              Rpnt — F&SF  Jun 1951
    THE BEST FROM FANTASY & SCIENCE FICTION [Boucher & McComas - 1952]
Threes (To Be Sung by Niels Bohr) by John Atherton.......(verse)....Nykr  3/2/57
    FANTASIA MATHEMATICA [Fadiman - 1958]
Through Channels by Richard Matheson...............................F&SF  Apr 1951
    SCIENCE FICTION TERROR TALES [Conklin - 1955]
Through The Purple Cloud by Jack Williamson.........................WS  May 1931
    FROM OFF THIS WORLD [Margulies & Friend - 1949]
Through Time And Space With Ferdinand Feghott [VII] by Grendel Briarton ps
    R. Bretnor.....................................................F&SF  Mar 1958
    THE BEST FROM FANTASY & SCIENCE FICTION: 8th SERIES [Boucher - 1959]
Through Time And Space With Ferdinand Feghott [VIII] by Grendel Briarton ps
    R. Bretnor.....................................................F&SF  Aug 1958
    THE BEST FROM FANTASY & SCIENCE FICTION: 8th SERIES [Boucher - 1959]
Through Time And Space With Ferdinand Feghott [X] by Grendel Briarton ps
    R. Bretnor.....................................................F&SF  Jan 1959
    THE BEST FROM FANTASY & SCIENCE FICTION: 9th SERIES [Mills - 1960]
Through Time And Space With Ferdinand Feghott [XI] by Grendel Briarton ps
    R. Bretnor.....................................................F&SF  Feb 1959
    THE BEST FROM FANTASY & SCIENCE FICTION: 9th SERIES [Mills - 1960]
Through Time And Space With Ferdinand Feghott [XII] by Grendel Briarton ps
    R. Bretnor.....................................................F&SF  Mar 1959
    THE BEST FROM FANTASY & SCIENCE FICTION: 9th SERIES [Mills - 1960]
Through Time And Space With Ferdinand Feghott [XIII]by Grendel Briarton ps
    R. Bretnor.....................................................F&SF  Apr 1959
    THE BEST FROM FANTASY & SCIENCE FICTION: 9th SERIES [Mills - 1960]
Through Time And Space With Ferdinand Feghott [XIV] by Grendel Briarton ps
    R. Bretnor.....................................................F&SF  May 1959
    THE BEST FROM FANTASY & SCIENCE FICTION: 9th SERIES [Mills - 1960]

                                                          Mag.    Year

Through Time And Space With Ferdinand Feghott [XV] by Grendel Briarton ps
R. Bretnor.....................................................F&SF  Jun 1959
   THE BEST FROM FANTASY & SCIENCE FICTION: 9th SERIES [Mills - 1960]
Throwback by Miriam Allen deFord.................................Stg  Oct 1952
   FUTURE TENSE [Crossen - 1953]
Thunder And Roses by Theodore Sturgeon...........................ASF  Nov 1947
   STRANGE PORTS OF CALL [Derleth - 1948]
   MY BEST SCIENCE FICTION STORY [Margulies & Friend - 1949]
   THE ASTOUNDING SCIENCE FICTION ANTHOLOGY [J. W. Campbell - 1952]
Thunder-Thieves, The by Isaac Asimov........................ORIGINAL STORY
   Note: This article contains a verse that originally appeared in Future Science
      Fiction #39 (October 1958) under the title It's All How You Look At It.
   SF: 59 THE YEAR'S GREATEST SF AND FANTASY [Merril - 1959]
Thus I Refute Beelzy by John Collier.............(From The Touch Of Nutmeg; 1943)
   OUT OF THIS WORLD [Fast - 1944]
Ticket To Anywhere by Damon Knight...............................Glxy  Apr 1952
   SCIENCE FICTION SHOWCASE [M. Kornbluth - 1959]
Ticking His Life Away by T. D. Hamm (Mrs. T. E. Dikty)..........ORIGINAL STORY
   TOMORROW'S UNIVERSE [H. J. Campbell - 1954]
Tiger By The Tail by Alan E. Nourse..............................Glxy  Nov 1951
   SCIENCE FICTION ADVENTURES IN DIMENSION [Conklin - 1953]
   THE SECOND GALAXY READER OF SCIENCE FICTION [Gold - 1954]
Time And Time Again by H. Beam Piper.............................ASF  Apr 1947
   A TREASURY OF SCIENCE FICTION [Conklin - 1948]
   UBERWINDUNG VON RAUM UND ZEIT [Gunther - 1952]
      (Appeared under title Zeit Und Weider Zelt)
Time Decelerator, The by A. Macfadyen, Jr. ......................Ast  Jul 1936
   CROSSROADS IN TIME [Conklin - 1953]
Time In The Round by Fritz Leiber................................Glxy  May 1957
   THE THIRD GALAXY READER OF SCIENCE FICTION [Gold - 1958]
Time Is The Traitor by Alfred Bester.............................F&SF  Sep 1953
   THE BEST SCIENCE FICTION STORIES: 1954 [Bleiler & Dikty - 1954]
Time Locker by Lewis Padgett ps (Henry Kuttner & C. L. Moore)........ASF  Jan 1943
   ADVENTURES IN TIME AND SPACE [Healy & McComas - 1946]
Time Machine, The by H. G. Wells.................................NwR  Jan 1895
   TRAVELERS IN TIME [Stern - 1947]
   THE TREASURY OF SCIENCE FICTION CLASSICS [Kuebler - 1954]
Time To Rest by John Beynon Harris...............................Ark  Win 1949
   FAR BOUNDARIES [Derleth - 1951]
Time Travel And The Law by C. M. Kornbluth......................ORIGINAL STORY
   COMING ATTRACTIONS [Greenberg - 1957]
Time-Travel Happens! by A. M. Phillips...........................Unk  Dec 1939
   ADVENTURES IN TIME AND SPACE [Healy & McComas - 1946]
Timeless Ones, The by Eric Frank Russell.........................SFQ  Nov 1952
   PRIZE SCIENCE FICTION [Wollheim - 1953]
Tinkler, The by Poul Anderson....................................WB  Feb 1951
   WORLDS OF TOMORROW [Derleth - 1955]
Tiny And The Monster by Theodore Sturgeon........................ASF  May 1947
   INVADERS OF EARTH [Conklin - 1952]
Title Fight by William Campbell Gault............................FU  Dec 1956
   THE FANTASTIC UNIVERSE OMNIBUS [Santesson - 1960]
To A Ripe Old Age by Wilson Tucker...............................F&SF  Dec 1952
   SHADOW OF TOMORROW [Pohl - 1953]
To Fell A Tree by Robert F. Young................................F&SF  Jul 1959
   A DECADE OF FANTASY & SCIENCE FICTION [Mills - 1960]
To Follow Knowledge by Frank Belknap Long, Jr. ..................ASF  Dec 1942
   SCIENCE FICTION ADVENTURES IN DIMENSION [Conklin - 1953]

o Give Them Beauty For Ashes by Winona McClintic......(verse)......F&SF  Sep 1959
    THE BEST FROM FANTASY & SCIENCE FICTION: 9th SERIES [Mills - 1960]
o Here And The Easel by Theodore Sturgeon.........................ORIGINAL STORY
    STAR SHORT NOVELS [Pohl - 1954]
o People A New World by Nelson Bond.............................BB  Nov 1950
    BEACHHEADS IN SPACE [Derleth - 1954]
o Serve Man by Damon Knight.....................................Glxy  Nov 1950
    THE BEST SCIENCE FICTION STORIES: 1951 [Bleiler & Dikty - 1951]
o Think That Two And Two Are Four by A. E. Housman...............................
    (From The Collected Poems of A. E. Housman; 1940)
    FANTASIA MATHEMATICA [Fadiman - 1958]
obermory by Saki ps (H. H. Munro).............................(No data available)
    JOURNEYS IN SCIENCE FICTION [Loughlin & Popp - 1961]
olliver's Travels by Frank Fenton & Joseph Petracca.............ORIGINAL STORY
    NEW TALES OF SPACE AND TIME [Healy - 1951]
omorrow's Children by Poul Anderson & F. N. Waldrop.............ASF  Mar 1947
    A TREASURY OF SCIENCE FICTION [Conklin - 1948]
omorrow's Gift by Edmund Cooper................................ORIGINAL STORY
    STAR SCIENCE FICTION STORIES #4 [Pohl - 1958]
ongue Of Beast by Carl H. Claudy.............................AmB  May 1939
    THE YEAR AFTER TOMORROW [Del Rey, Matschat & Carmer - 1952]
ony And The Beetles by Philip K. Dick...........(See listing Retreat From Rigel)
oo Far by Fredric Brown.......................................F&SF  Sep 1955
    THE BEST FROM FANTASY & SCIENCE FICTION: 5th SERIES [Boucher - 1956]
ools by Clifford D. Simak.....................................ASF  Jul 1942
    A TREASURY OF SCIENCE FICTION [Conklin - 1948]
ools Of The Trade by Raymond F. Jones.........................ASF  Nov 1950
    SPACE, SPACE, SPACE [Sloane - 1953]
ooth, The by G. Gordon Dewey..................................F&SF  Aug 1952
    THE BEST FROM FANTASY & SCIENCE FICTION: 2nd SERIES [Boucher & McComas-1953]
op Secret by David Grinnell..................................Sir  Jul 1949
    INVADERS OF EARTH [Conklin - 1952]
ough Old Man by L. Ron Hubbard................................Stg  Nov 1950
    SPACE POLICE [Norton - 1956]
Tourist Trade, The by Bob Tucker..............................WB  Jan 1951
    TOMORROW, THE STARS [Heinlein - 1952]
    THE BEST SCIENCE FICTION STORIES: 1952 [Bleiler & Dikty - 1952]
Track 12 by J. G. Ballard....................................NW #70  Apr 1958
    PENGUIN SCIENCE FICTION [Aldiss - 1961]
Trail Blazer by Raymond Z. Gallun.............................FSM  Fal 1951
    SPACE PIONEERS [Norton - 1954]
Trail To The Stars by Capt. Burr W. Leyson....................BLM  Feb 1950
    SCIENCE FICTION AND READER'S GUIDE [Barrows - 1954]
Transfer Point by Anthony Boucher.............................Glxy  Nov 1950
    ADVENTURES IN TOMORROW [Crossen - 1951]
    SHADOW OF TOMORROW [Pohl - 1953]
Transience by Arthur C. Clarke................................Stg  Jul 1949
    LOOKING FORWARD [Lesser - 1953]
Transition — From Fantasy To Science by Arthur C. Clarke.......................
    (From The Making Of A Moon; 1957)
    SF: 58 THE YEAR'S GREATEST SF & FANTASY [Merril - 1958]
Traveler In Time, A by August Derleth.................(See listing Century Jumper)
Tree Men Of Potu, The by Lewis Holberg.........................................
    (From A Journey To The World Under-Ground; Prussia: 1741)
    BEYOND TIME AND SPACE [Derleth - 1950]
Trends by Isaac Asimov........................................ASF  Jul 1939
    MEN AGAINST THE STARS [Greenberg - 1950]

Mag.    Year

Trick Or Two, A by John Novotny............................F&SF   Jul 1957
   A DECADE OF FANTASY & SCIENCE FICTION [Mills - 1960]
Trespass! by Poul Anderson & Gordon R. Dickson....................FSQ   Spr 1950
   THE BEST SCIENCE FICTION STORIES: 1951 [Bleiler & Dikty - 1951]
Tricky Tonnage by Malcolm Jameson.................................ASF   Dec 1944
   THE BEST OF SCIENCE FICTION [Conklin - 1946]
Triffid, The by John Wyndham ps (John Beynon Harris)......................
   (From The Day Of The Triffids; 1951)
   SCIENCE IN FICTION [A.E.M. & J.C. Bayliss - 1957]
Triflin' Man by Walter M. Miller, Jr. ...........................FU    Jan 1955
   GALAXY OF GHOULS [Merril - 1955]
Trigger Tide by Wyman Guin.......................................ASF   Oct 1950
   THE OMNIBUS OF SCIENCE FICTION [Conklin - 1952]
Triggerman by J. F. Bone.........................................ASF   Dec 1958
   SF: 59 THE YEAR'S GREATEST SF AND FANTASY [Merril - 1959]
   JOURNEYS IN SCIENCE FICTION [Loughlin & Popp - 1961]
Trip One by Edward Grendon.......................................ASF   Jul 1949
   SPACE, SPACE, SPACE [Sloane - 1953]
Triplanetary by E. E. Smith..........................(See listing Atlantis)
Trophy by Henry Kuttner..........................................TWS   Win 1944
   (Originally appeared under pseudonym Scott Morgan)
   THE SAINT'S CHOICE [Charteris - 1945]
Trouble On Tantalus by P. Schuyler Miller........................ASF   Feb 1941
   TRAVELERS OF SPACE [Greenberg - 1952]
Trouble With Emily, The by James M. White.....................NW #77  Nov 1958
   OUT OF THIS WORLD TWO [Williams-Ellis & Owen - 1961]
Trouble With Water by H. L. Gold.................................Unk   Mar 1939
   FROM UNKNOWN WORLDS [J. W. Campbell - 1948]
True History, A by Lucian......................(Written about 165 A. D.)
   BEYOND TIME AND SPACE [Derleth - 1950]
Truth About Pyecraft, The by H. G. Wells........................Snd   Apr 1903
   SCIENCE FICTION AND READER'S GUIDE [Barrows - 1954]
Truth Is A Plague by David Wright O'Brien........................Amz   Feb 1940
   THE OTHER WORLDS [Stong - 1941]
Tunesmith, The by Lloyd Biggle, Jr. .............................If    Aug 1957
   THE BEST SCIENCE FICTION STORIES AND NOVELS: 9th SERIES [Dikty - 1958]
Twenty-Five Miles Aloft by Raymond Watson.................ORIGINAL STORY
   ADVENTURES TO COME [Esenwein - 1937]
2066: Election Day by Michael Shaara.............................ASF   Dec 1956
   THE BEST SCIENCE FICTION STORIES AND NOVELS: 9th SERIES [Dikty - 1958]
Twilight by Don A. Stuart ps (John W. Campbell, Jr.)............Ast   Nov 1934
   THE POCKET BOOK OF SCIENCE FICTION [Wollheim - 1943]
Twilight Years, The by Kirk & Garen Drussai.....................If    Jun 1955
   THE FIRST WORLD OF IF [Quinn & Wulff - 1957]
Twinkle, Twinkle, Little Star by Ralph Barton............(verse)..........
   (From Science In Rhyme and Without Reason; 1924)
   FANTASIA MATHEMATICA [Fadiman - 1958]
Twin's Wail by Elizabeth Mann Borgese.....................ORIGINAL STORY
   STAR SCIENCE FICTION STORIES #6 [Pohl - 1959]
   STAR OF STARS [Pohl - 1960]
Two Face by Frank Belknap Long..................................WT    Mar 1950
   THE BEST SCIENCE FICTION STORIES: 1951 [Bleiler & Dikty - 1951]
Two Shadows, The by William F. Temple...........................Stg   Mar 1951
   THE BEST SCIENCE FICTION STORIES: 1952 [Bleiler & Dikty - 1952]
   NO PLACE LIKE EARTH [Carnell - 1952]
Twonky, The by Lewis Padgett ps (Henry Kuttner & C. L. Moore)........ASF   Sep 1942
   ADVENTURES IN TIME AND SPACE [Healy & McComas - 1946]

# U

Ugly Sister by Jan Struther ps (Joyce Maxtone Graham)................LM   Dec 1935
                                                   Rpnt — F&SF   Feb 1952
   THE BEST FROM FANTASY & SCIENCE FICTION: 2nd SERIES [Boucher & McComas-1953]
Ullr Uprising by H. Beam Piper.............................................ORIGINAL STORY
   THE PETRIFIED PLANET [Pratt - 1952]
Ultima Thule by Eric Frank Russell.......................................ASF   Oct 1951
   LOOKING FORWARD [Lesser - 1953]
Ultimate Catalyst, The by John Taine ps (Eric Temple Bell)...........TWS   Jun 1929
   THE BEST OF SCIENCE FICTION [Conklin - 1946]
   MY BEST SCIENCE FICTION STORY [Margulies & Friend - 1949]
Ultimate Egoist by Theodore Sturgeon....................................Unk   Feb 1941
   (Originally appeared under pseudonym E. Hunter Waldo)
   HUMAN? [Merril - 1954]
Ultimate Invader, The by Eric Frank Russell...........................PS   Jan 1953
   (Originally appeared under title Design For Great Day)
   THE ULTIMATE INVADER AND OTHER SCIENCE FICTION [Wollheim - 1954]
Ultimate Metal, The by Nat Schachner....................................Ast   Feb 1935
   THE BEST OF SCIENCE FICTION [Conklin - 1946]
Un-Man by Poul Anderson...................................................ASF   Jan 1953
   ALL ABOUT THE FUTURE [Greenberg - 1955]
Una by John Wyndham ps (John Beynon Harris).....(See listing The Perfect Creature)
Unchartered Isle, The by Clark Ashton Smith..........................WT   Nov 1950
   MY BEST SCIENCE FICTION STORY [Margulies & Friend - 1949]
Underground Movement by Kris Neville...................................F&SF   Jun 1952
   BEYOND HUMAN KEN [Merril - 1952]
Unfortunate Passage by E. C. Tubb.....................................SF #7   Mar 1954
   GATEWAY TO THE STARS [Carnell - 1955]
Unfortunate Topologist, The by Cyril Kornbluth.....................F&SF   Jul 1957
   (Originally appeared under pseudonym S. D. Gottesman)
   FANTASIA MATHEMATICA [Fadiman - 1958]
Unhuman Sacrifice by Katherine MacLean..............................ASF   Nov 1958
   SPECTRUM [Amis & Conquest - 1961]
Unite And Conquer by Theodore Sturgeon.............................ASF   Oct 1948
   JOURNEY TO INFINITY [Greenberg - 1951]
Universal Library, The by Kurd Lasswitz...............(From Seifenblasen; 1903)
   (Translated by Willy Ley)    FANTASIA MATHEMATICA [Fadiman - 1958]
Universal Panacea, The by Howard Schoenfeld.......(See listing Built Up Logically)
Universe by Robert A. Heinlein.........................................ASF   May 1941
   THE BEST OF SCIENCE FICTION [Conklin - 1946]
University by Peter Phillips...........................................Glxy   Apr 1953
   THE SECOND GALAXY READER OF SCIENCE FICTION [Gold - 1954]
Unknown Quality by Peter Phillips.....................................NW #5   n/d 1949
   NO PLACE LIKE EARTH [Carnell - 1952]
   THE BEST FROM NEW WORLDS [Carnell - 1955]

|  | Mag. | Year |
|---|---|---|

Unready To Wear by Kurt Vonnegut, Jr. ..............................Glxy  Apr 1953
    THE SECOND GALAXY READER OF SCIENCE FICTION [Gold - 1954]
Untimely Toper, The by L. Sprague de Camp & Fletcher Pratt..........F&SF  Jul 1953
    THE BEST FROM FANTASY & SCIENCE FICTION: 3rd SERIES [Boucher & McComas -1954]
Unto The Fourth Generation by Isaac Asimov..........................F&SF  Apr 1959
    A DECADE OF FANTASY & SCIENCE FICTION [Mills - 1960]
Unwelcome Tenant by Roger Dee ps (Roger D. Aycock)..................PS  Sum 1950
    BEYOND HUMAN KEN [Merril - 1952]
Up-To-Date Sorcerer, The by Isaac Asimov............................F&SF  Jul 1958
    THE BEST FROM FANTASY & SCIENCE FICTION: 8th SERIES [Boucher - 1959]
Upper Level Road, The by Warner Van Lorne ps (F. Orlin Tremaine).....Ast  Aug 1935
    THE BEST OF SCIENCE FICTION [Conklin - 1946]
Uses Of Mathematics by Samuel Butler................(verse).....................
    (From Hudibras, First Part, Canto I; 1663)
    FANTASIA MATHEMATICA [Fadiman - 1958]
Utopia by Sir Thomas More..........(Written about 1516: published in English; 1551)
    BEYOND TIME AND SPACE [Derleth - 1950]

V-2; Rocket Cargo Ship by Willy Ley.................................ASF  May 1945
    ADVENTURES IN TIME AND SPACE [Healy & McComas - 1946]
Valley Of Dreams by Stanley G. Weinbaum.............................WS  Nov 1934
    FROM OFF THIS WORLD [Margulies & Friend - 1949]
Vampire's Saga, A by Norman Belkin...............(verse).........F&SF  May 1959
    THE BEST FROM FANTASY & SCIENCE FICTION: 9th SERIES [Mills - 1960]
Vandy, Vandy by Manly Wade Wellman.................................F&SF  Mar 1953
    THE BEST FROM FANTASY & SCIENCE FICTION: 3rd SERIES [Boucher & McComas-1954]
Vanishing American, The by Charles Beaumont........................F&SF  Aug 1955
    THE BEST FROM FANTASY & SCIENCE FICTION: 5th SERIES [Boucher - 1956]
    INVISIBLE MEN [Davenport - 1960]
Vault Of The Beast by A. E. Van Vogt...............................ASF  Aug 1940
    THE OTHER SIDE OF THE MOON [Derleth - 1949]
    THE ASTOUNDING SCIENCE FICTION ANTHOLOGY [J. W. Campbell - 1952]
Yelled Island by Emmet McDowell....................................ASF  Jan 1946
    SCIENCE FICTION ADVENTURES IN MUTATION [Conklin - 1956]
Veldt, The by Ray Bradbury.........................................SEP  9/23/50
    BEYOND THE BARRIERS OF SPACE AND TIME [Merril - 1954]
Velvet Glove, The by Harry Harrison................................FU  Nov 1956
    THE FANTASTIC UNIVERSE OMNIBUS [Santesson - 1960]
Venture To The Moon by Arthur C. Clarke............................F&SF  Dec 1956
    THE BEST FROM FANTASY & SCIENCE FICTION: 7th SERIES [Boucher - 1958]
Venturer Of The Martian Mimic by Eric Frank Russell............(See listing Spiro)
Venus And The Rabbitt by E. M. Fitzpatrick...........(London Observer Prize Story)
    A. D. 2500 [Wilson - 1955]
Venus And The Seven Sexes by William Tenn ps (Philip Klass)........Original Story
    THE GIRL WITH THE HUNGRY EYES AND OTHER STORIES [Wollheim - 1949]
    SCIENCE FICTION CARNIVAL [Brown & Reynolds - 1953]

|  | Mag. | Year |
|---|---|---|

Venus Is A Man's World by William Tenn ps (Philip Klass)............Glxy   Jul 1951
   THE GALAXY READER OF SCIENCE FICTION [Gold - 1952]
Victory Unintentional by Isaac Asimov..............................Sup   Aug 1942
   INVASION FROM MARS [Welles - 1949]
   LOOKING FORWARD [Lesser - 1953]
View From A Hill, A by M. R. James.................................................
   (From A Warning To The Curious And Other Stories; 1926)
   TRAVELERS IN TIME [Stern - 1947]
Vignettes Of Tomorrow by Ray Bradbury.............................................
   One Who Waits, The.............................................Ark   Sum 1949
   Holiday.......................................................Ark   Oct 1949
      FAR BOUNDARIES [Derleth - 1951]
Vilbar Party, The by Evelyn E. Smith..............................Glxy   Jan 1955
   THE THIRD GALAXY READER OF SCIENCE FICTION [Gold - 1958]
Vintage Season by Lawrence O'Donnell ps (Henry Kuttner & C.L. Moore).ASF   Sep 1946
   A TREASURY OF SCIENCE FICTION [Conklin - 1948]
Virtuoso by Robert Goldstone......................................F&SF   Feb 1953
   SCIENCE FICTION THINKING MACHINES [Conklin - 1954]
Vision Of Judgement, A by H. G. Wells..(Fr The Time Machine & Other Stories; 1895)
   OUT OF THIS WORLD [Fast - 1944]
Visit To A Small Planet by Gore Vidal....(a play)...(Copyright 1955 by Gore Vidal)
   JOURNEYS IN SCIENCE FICTION [Loughlin & Popp - 1961]
Visiting Yokel by Cleve Cartmill..................................TWS   Aug 1943
   MY BEST SCIENCE FICTION STORY [Margulies & Friend - 1949]
Vocation by George O. Smith.......................................ASF   Apr 1945
   CROSSROADS IN TIME [Conklin - 1953]
Voice From The Gallery by Catherine Brownlow.........(London Observer Prize Story)
   A. D. 2500 [Wilson - 1955]
Voice In The Earphones, The by Wilbur Schramm................Rpnt - SEP   5/29/47
   (From Windwagon Smith and Other Yarns; 1947)
   THE SATURDAY EVENING POST FANTASY STORIES [Fles - 1951]
Voice In The Lobster, The by Henry Kuttner........................TWS   Feb 1950
   ADVENTURES IN TOMORROW [Crossen - 1951]
Voices From The Cliff by John Martin Leahy........................WT   May 1925
   SCIENCE AND SORCERY [Ford - 1953]
Voices In The Dust by Gerald Kersh................................SEP   8/13/47
   SHOT IN THE DARK [Merril - 1950]
Volpa by Wyman Guin...............................................Glxy   May 1956
   THE THIRD GALAXY READER OF SCIENCE FICTION [Gold - 1958]
   13 GREAT STORIES OF SCIENCE FICTION [Conklin - 1960]
Voyage That Lasted Six Hundred Years, The by Don Wilcox.............Amz   Oct 1940
   LOOKING FORWARD [Lesser - 1953]
Voyage To Sfanmoe, A by Clark Ashton Smith.........................WT   Aug 1931
   BEYOND TIME AND SPACE [Derleth - 1950]

# W

Wabbler, The by Murray Leinster ps (Will F. Jenkins)................ASF   Oct 1942
   BEYOND HUMAN KEN [Merril - 1952]
   BEST SF THREE SCIENCE FICTION STORIES [Crispin - 1958]
Wages Of Synergy, The by Theodore Sturgeon........................Stg   Aug 1953
   THE BEST FROM STARTLING STORIES [Mines - 1953]

| | Mag. | Year |
|---|---|---|

Wait, The by Kit Reed.............................................F&SF Apr 1958
  THE BEST FROM FANTASY & SCIENCE FICTION: 8th SERIES [Boucher - 1959]
Waker Dreams, The by Richard Matheson............................Glxy Jul 1951
  THE GALAXY READER OF SCIENCE FICTION [Gold - 1952]
Waldo by Robert A. Heinlein......................................ASF Aug 1942
  (Originally appeared under pseudonym Anson MacDonald)
  A TREASURY OF GREAT SCIENCE FICTION [Boucher - 1959]
Walk in the Dark, A by Arthur C. Clarke..........................TWS Aug 1950
  POSSIBLE WORLDS OF SCIENCE FICTION [Conklin - 1951]
Walk Like A Mountain by Manly Wade Wellman.......................F&SF Jun 1955
  A DECADE OF FANTASY & SCIENCE FICTION [Mills - 1960]
Walkabout by Stephen Earl............................(London Observer Prize Story)
  A. D. 2500 [Wilson - 1955]
Wall Around the World, The by Theodore R. Cogswell...............BFF Sep 1953
  BEYOND THE BARRIERS OF SPACE AND TIME [Merril - 1954]
Wall of Darkness by Arthur C. Clarke.............................Sup Jul 1949
  (Story selected by Eljer Jakobsson)
  EDITOR'S CHOICE IN SCIENCE FICTION [Moskowitz - 1954]
Wall of Fire, The by Jack Kirkland...............................BB Jul 1932
  (Story selected by Donald Kennicott)
  EDITOR'S CHOICE IN SCIENCE FICTION [Moskowitz - 1954]
Wanderer of Time by John Russell Fearn...........................Stg Sum 1934
  MY BEST SCIENCE FICTION STORY [Margulies & Friend - 1949]
Wanted — An Enemy — by Fritz Leiber, Jr. ........................ASF Feb 1945
  BEYOND TIME AND SPACE [Derleth - 1950]
War Against the Moon, The by Andre Maurois.........................................
  (From The Next Chapter: The War Against the Moon; 1928)
  THE OMNIBUS OF SCIENCE FICTION [Conklin - 1952]
War Is Over, The by Algis Budrys................................ASF Feb 1957
  13 GREAT STORIES OF SCIENCE FICTION [Conklin - 1960]
Warm by Robert Sheckley..........................................Glxy Jun 1953
  THE SECOND GALAXY READER OF SCIENCE FICTION [Gold - 1954]
Warning, The by Peter Phillips...................................F&SF Sep 1953
  BEYOND THE BARRIERS OF SPACE AND TIME [Merril - 1954]
Watchbird by Robert Sheckley.....................................Glxy Feb 1953
  SHADOW OF TOMORROW [Pohl - 1953]
Watchers, The by Anthony Brode.............(verse)................F&SF Apr 1958
  THE BEST FROM FANTASY & SCIENCE FICTION: 8th SERIES [Boucher - 1959]
Watchers, The by R. H. Deutsch ...............................Original Story
  SCIENCE AND SORCERY [Ford - 1953]
Watershed by James Blish.........................................If May 1955
  THE FIRST WORLD OF IF [Quinn & Wulff - 1957]
Waveries, The by Fredric Brown...................................ASF Jan 1945
  INVADERS OF EARTH [Conklin - 1952]
Way of Escape by William F. Temple...............................TWS Jun 1948
  SCIENCE FICTION ADVENTURES IN DIMENSION [Conklin - 1953]
Way of Life, A by Robert Bloch...................................FU Oct 1956
  THE FANTASTIC UNIVERSE OMNIBUS [Santesson - 1960]
We Don't Want Any Trouble by James H. Schmitz...................Glxy Jun 1953
  ASSIGNMENT IN TOMORROW [Pohl - 1954]
We Kill People by Lewis Padgett ps (Henry Kuttner & C.L. Moore)......ASF Mar 1946
  LOOKING FORWARD [Lesser - 1953]
We Never Mention Aunt Nora by Paul Flehr.........................Glxy Jul 1958
  THE FIFTH GALAXY READER [Gold - 1961]
We The People by Ward Moore......................................SFQ May 1952
  FUTURE TENSE [Crossen - 1953]

(182)

|  | Mag. | Year |
|---|---|---|

Weapon, The by Fredric Brown.........................................ASF Apr 1951
    THE OMNIBUS OF SCIENCE FICTION [Conklin - 1952]
Weapon Shop, The by A. E. Van Vogt.................................ASF Dec 1942
    ADVENTURES IN TIME AND SPACE [Healy & McComas - 1946]
Weapon Shops Of Isher, The by A. E. Van Vogt.........................
    (Originally published by Greenberg: Publishers; 1951)
    A TREASURY OF GREAT SCIENCE FICTION [Boucher - 1959]
Weissenbroch Spectacles, The by L. Sprague de Camp & Fletcher Pratt.F&SF Nov 1954
    INVISIBLE MEN [Davenport - 1960]
Well-Oiled Machine, The by H. B. Fyfe...............................F&SF Dec 1950
    SCIENCE-FICTION CARNIVAL [Brown & Reynolds - 1953]
What Dead Men Tell by Theodore Sturgeon.............................ASF Nov 1949
    IMAGINATION UNLIMITED [Bleiler & Dikty - 1952]
"What Do You Mean...Human?" by John W. Campbell, Jr. ...............ASF Sep 1959
    FIFTH ANNUAL OF THE YEAR'S BEST SF [Merril - 1960]
What Does Up by Alfred Coppel, Jr. .................................FB #6 n/d 1950
    SCIENCE AND SORCERY [Ford - 1953]
What Have I Done? by Mark Clifton...................................ASF May 1952
    BEYOND HUMAN KEN [Merril - 1952]
What If... by Isaac Asimov..........................................Fnt Sum 1952
    SCIENCE FICTION ADVENTURES IN DIMENSION [Conklin - 1953]
What Now, Little Man? by Mark Clifton...............................F&SF Dec 1959
    FIFTH ANNUAL OF THE YEAR'S BEST SF [Merril - 1960]
What Rough Beast? by Damon Knight...................................F&SF Feb 1959
    THE BEST FROM FANTASY & SCIENCE FICTION: 9th SERIES [Mills - 1960]
"What So Proudly We Hail..." by Day Keene...........................Im Dec 1950
    SCIENCE FICTION ADVENTURES IN DIMENSION [Conklin - 1953]
What The Left Hand Was Doing by Darrell T. Langart..................ASF Feb 1960
    FIFTH ANNUAL OF THE YEAR'S BEST SF [Merril - 1960]
What Thin Partitions by Mark Clifton & Alex Apostolides.............ASF Sep 1953
    EDITOR'S CHOICE IN SCIENCE FICTION [Moskowitz - 1954]
    (Story selected by J. W. Campbell, Jr.)
    THE BEST SCIENCE FICTION STORIES: 1954 [Bleiler & Dikty - 1954]
What Time Is It? by Richard M. Elam, Jr. ...........................
    (From Teen-Age Science Fiction Stories; 1952)
    SCIENCE FICTION AND READER'S GUIDE [Barrows - 1954]
What You Need by Lewis Padgett ps (Henry Kuttner & C.L. Moore).......ASF Oct 1945
    THE OMNIBUS OF SCIENCE FICTION [Conklin - 1952]
What Was It? by Fitz-James O'Brien..................................Hpr Mar 1859
    INVISIBLE MEN [Davenport - 1960]
Whatever Counts by Frederik Pohl....................................Glxy Jun 1959
    BODYGUARD AND FOUR OTHER SHORT NOVELS FROM GALAXY [Gold - 1960]
Whatever Happened To Corporal Cuckoo? by Gerald Kersh..............
    (From The Brighten Monster; 1953)
    STAR SCIENCE FICTION STORIES #3 [Pohl - 1954]
    STAR OF STARS [Pohl - 1960]
What's He Doing In There? by Fritz Leiber...........................Glxy Dec 1957
    THE FOURTH GALAXY READER OF SCIENCE FICTION [Gold - 1959]
What's It Like Out There? by Edmond Hamilton........................Stg Dec 1952
    THE BEST FROM STARTLING STORIES [Mines - 1953]
Wheel of Time, The by Robert Arthur.................................Sup Mar 1950
    SCIENCE FICTION CARNIVAL [Brown & Reynolds - 1953]
Wheelbarrow Boy, The by Richard Parker..............................Lpt Oct 1950
    GALAXY OF GHOULS [Merril - 1955]
When Grandfather Flew To The Moon by E. L. Malpass.................
    (See listing Return To The Moon)

                                                            Mag.    Year
When Shadows Fall by L. Ron Hubbard.................................Stg  Jul 1948
    MEN AGAINST THE STARS [Greenberg - 1950]
When The Bough Breaks by Lewis Padgett ps (Henry Kuttner & C. L. Moore)...........
                                                            ASF  Nov 1944
    BEYOND TIME AND SPACE [Derleth - 1950]
    THE ASTOUNDING SCIENCE FICTION ANTHOLOGY [J. W. Campbell - 1952]
When The Earth Lived by Henry Kuttner...............................TWS  Oct 1937
    FROM OFF THIS WORLD [Margulies & Friend - 1949]
When The Green Star Waned by Nictzin Dyalhis.........................WT   Apr 1925
    BEYOND TIME AND SPACE [Derleth - 1950]
When The People Fell by Cordwainer Smith.............................Glxy Apr 1959
    THE FIFTH GALAXY READER [Gold - 1961]
When You're Smiling by Theodore Sturgeon.............................Glxy Jan 1955
    BEST SF TWO SCIENCE FICTION STORIES [Crispin - 1956]
When Worlds Collide by Edwin Balmer & Philip Wylie.........(excerpts).............
    (Originally published by Frederick A. Stokes Co.; 1932)
    THE TREASURY OF SCIENCE FICTION CLASSICS [Kuebler - 1954]
Where Do We Go From Here? by Willy Ley...............................ORIGINAL STORY
    SF: 58 THE YEAR'S GREATEST SCIENCE FICTION & FANTASY [Merril - 1958]
Wherever You May Be by James E. Gunn................................Glxy May 1953
    FIVE GALAXY SHORT NOVELS [Gold - 1958]
Where To? by Robert A. Heinlein.....................................Glxy Feb 1952
    ALL ABOUT THE FUTURE [Greenberg - 1955]
Whispering Gallery, The by William F. Temple........................FU   Nov 1953
    ZACHERLY'S MIDNIGHT SNACKS [Zacherly - 1960]
White Army, The by Daniel Dressler..................................Amz  Sep 1929
    EVERY BOY'S BOOK OF SCIENCE FICTION [Wollheim - 1951]
    STORIES OF SCIENTIFIC IMAGINATION [Gallant - 1954]
White Pinnacle, The by Carl Jacobi.................................ORIGINAL STORY
    TIME TO COME [Derleth - 1954]
Who? by Theodore Sturgeon.......................(See listing Bulkhead)
Who Dreams Of Ivy by Will Worthington...............................F&SF Nov 1960
    THE BEST FROM FANTASY & SCIENCE FICTION: 10th SERIES [Mills - 1961]
Who Goes There? by Don A. Stuart ps (John W. Campbell, Jr.)..........ASF  Aug 1938
    ADVENTURES IN TIME AND SPACE [Healy & McComas - 1956]
    UBDERWINDUNG VON RAUM UND ZEIT [Gunther - 1952]
    (Appeared as Wer Da? under John W. Campbell, Jr. byline)
Who Is Charles Avison? by Edison Marshall...........................Arg  Apr 1916
    SHOT IN THE DARK [Merril - 1950]
Who Knows His Brother by Graham Doar................................Stg  Feb 1952
    HUMAN? [Merril - 1954]
"Who Shall I Say Is Calling?" by August Derleth....................F&SF Aug 1952
    HUMAN? [Merril - 1954]
Who's Cribbing? by Jack Lewis......................................Stg  Jan 1953
    THE BEST FROM STARTLING STORIES [Mines - 1953]
[Widget], The [Wadgett], and Boff, The by Theodore Sturgeon.....F&SF Nov 1955
    A TREASURY OF GREAT SCIENCE FICTION [Boucher - 1959]
Wild Surmise, A by Henry Kuttner & C. L. Moore....................ORIGINAL STORY
    STAR SCIENCE FICTION STORIES [Pohl - 1953]
Wild Wood, The by Mildred Clingerman................................F&SF Jan 1957
    THE BEST FROM FANTASY & SCIENCE FICTION: 7th SERIES [Boucher - 1958]
Wilderness by Zeena Henderson......................................F&SF Jan 1957
    SF: 58 THE YEAR'S GREATEST SCIENCE FICTION AND FANTASY [Merril - 1958]
Wilderness, The by Ray Bradbury....................................Phl  4/6/52
    STORIES FOR TOMORROW [Sloane - 1954]

|  | Mag. | Year |
|---|---|---|
| Will, The by Walter M. Miller, Jr. .....................................Fnt | Feb 1954 |
| THE BEST SCIENCE FICTION STORIES & NOVELS: 1955 [Dikty - 1955] | | |
| Will You Wait? by Alfred Bester.............................................F&SF | Mar 1959 |
| A DECADE OF FANTASY & SCIENCE FICTION [Mills - 1960] | | |
| "Will You Walk A Little Faster?" by William Tenn ps (Philip Klass)...MSF | Nov 1951 |
| INVADERS OF EARTH [Conklin - 1952] | | |
| William Wilson by Edgar Allan Poe.......................................Gft | n/d 1840 |
| THE MOONLIGHT TRAVELER [Stern - 1943] | | |
| Willow Tree, The by Jane Rice..........................................F&SF | Feb 1959 |
| THE BEST FROM FANTASY & SCIENCE FICTION: 9th SERIES [Mills - 1960] | | |
| Win The World by Chad Oliver...........................................Stg | Feb 1952 |
| LOOKING FORWARD [Lesser - 1953] | | |
| Wind Between the Worlds, The by Lester del Rey......................Glxy | Mar 1951 |
| ADVENTURES IN THE FAR FUTURE [Wollheim - 1955] | | |
| Wind Is Rising, A by Finn O'Donnevan....................................Glxy | Jul 1957 |
| THE THIRD GALAXY READER OF SCIENCE FICTION [Gold - 1958] | | |
| Wines Of Earth, The by Idris Seabright ps (Margaret St. Clair)......F&SF | Sep 1957 |
| THE BEST FROM FANTASY & SCIENCE FICTION: 7th SERIES [Boucher - 1958] | | |
| Wingless Victory by H. F. Heard.....(From The Great Fog & Other Weird Tales; 1944) | | |
| BEYOND TIME AND SPACE [Derleth - 1950] | | |
| Wings Across The Cosmos by Polton Cross ps (John Russell Fearn)......TWS | Jun 1938 |
| A TREASURY OF SCIENCE FICTION [Conklin - 1948] | | |
| Wings of Night, The by Lester del Rey.................................ASF | Mar 1942 |
| THE BIG BOOK OF SCIENCE FICTION [Conklin - 1950] | | |
| Winner Lose All by Jack Vance........................................Glxy | Dec 1951 |
| THE OMNIBUS OF SCIENCE FICTION [Conklin - 1952] | | |
| Winner Take All by Ross Rocklynne....................................ORIGINAL STORY |
| TIME TO COME [Derleth - 1954] | | |
| "Wireless" by Rudyard Kipling.........................................SM | Aug 1902 |
| THE MOONLIGHT TRAVELER [Stern - 1943] | | |
| JOURNEYS IN SCIENCE FICTION [Loughlin & Popp - 1961] | | |
| Witch, The by A. E. Van Vogt..........................................Unk | Feb 1943 |
| ZACHERLY'S VULTURE STEW [Zacherly - 1960] | | |
| Witch War by Richard Matheson..........................................Stg | Jul 1951 |
| THE BEST SCIENCE FICTION STORIES: 1952 [Bleiler & Dikty - 1952] | | |
| Witches of Karres, The by James L. Schmitz...........................ASF | Dec 1949 |
| THE ASTOUNDING SCIENCE FICTION ANTHOLOGY [J. W. Campbell - 1952] | | |
| With Flaming Swords by Cleve Cartmill.................................ASF | Sep 1942 |
| A TREASURY OF SCIENCE FICTION [Conklin - 1948] | | |
| With Folded Hands by Jack Williamson..................................ASF | Jul 1947 |
| A TREASURY OF SCIENCE FICTION [Conklin - 1948] | | |
| With Malice To Come by James Blish................(See listing A Matter Of Energy) | | |
| With Redfern on Capella XII by Charles Satterfield...................Glxy | Nov 1955 |
| MIND PARTNER AND EIGHT OTHER NOVELETTES FROM GALAXY [Gold - 1961] | | |
| Within the Pyramid by R. DeWitt Miller...............................Ast | Mar 1937 |
| ADVENTURES IN TIME AND SPACE [Healy & McComas - 1946] | | |
| Witnesses, The by William Sanson.......(From Fireman Flower & Other Stories; 1944) | | |
| TIMELESS STORIES FOR TODAY AND TOMORROW [Bradbury - 1952] | | |
| Wolf Pack by Walter M. Miller, Jr. ....................................Fnt | Oct 1953 |
| BEYOND THE BARRIERS OF SPACE AND TIME [Merril - 1954] | | |
| Wolves Don't Cry by Bruce Elliot......................................F&SF | Apr 1954 |
| GALAXY OF GHOULS [Merril - 1955] | | |
| Woman In Grey, The by Walker G. Everett..............................WT | Jun 1935 |
| THE OTHER WORLDS [Stong - 1941] | | |
| Woman's Place by Mark Clifton.........................................Glxy | May 1955 |
| THE WORLD THAT COULDN'T BE AND EIGHT OTHER NOVELETTES FROM GALAXY [Gold-1959] | | |
| Wonder Child by Joseph Shallit........................................Fnt | Feb 1953 |
| THE BEST SCIENCE FICTION STORIES: 1954 [Bleiler & Dikty - 1954] | | |

Mag.    Year

Wonder Horse, The by George Byram........................................Atl  Aug 1957
    SF: 58 THE YEAR'S GREATEST SCIENCE FICTION AND FANTASY [Merril - 1958]
Woods Grow Darker, The by Leah Bodine Drake..........(verse)........F&SF  Nov 1955
    THE BEST FROM FANTASY & SCIENCE FICTION: 6th SERIES [Boucher - 1957]
Word, The by Mildred Clingerman.........................................F&SF  Nov 1953
    PORTALS OF TOMORROW [Derleth - 1954]
Words of Guru, The by C. M. Kornbluth..................................Sti  Jun 1941
    CHILDREN OF WONDER [Tenn - 1953]
Work of Art, A by James Blish..........................................SFS  Jul 1956
    SCIENCE FICTION SHOWCASE [M. Kornbluth - 1959]
World of Wulkins, The by Frank Belknap Long, Jr. .....................TWS  Apr 1948
    THE OTHER SIDE OF THE MOON [Derleth - 1949]
World That Couldn't Be, The by Clifford D. Simak....................Glxy  Jan 1958
    THE WORLD THAT COULDN'T BE AND 8 OTHER NOVELETTES FROM GALAXY [Gold - 1959]
World Without, The by Benson Herbert....................................WS  Feb 1931
    FROM OFF THIS WORLD [Margulies & Friend - 1949]
World Without Children by Damon Knight...............................Glxy  Dec 1951
    FIVE GALAXY SHORT NOVELS [Gold - 1958]
Worm, The by David H. Keller..........................................Amz  Mar 1929
    STRANGE PORTS OF CALL [Derleth - 1948]
Worrywart by Clifford D. Simak.......................................Glxy  Sep 1953
    OPERATION FUTURE [Conklin - 1955]
    BEST SF TWO SCIENCE FICTION STORIES [Crispin - 1956]

# X - Y

X + L by Edgar Allan Poe......................................(No data available)
    FANTASIA MATHEMATICA [Fadiman - 1958]
XI Effect, The by Philip Latham ps (Robert S. Richardson)............ASF  Jan 1950
    IMAGINATION UNLIMITED [Bleiler & Dikty - 1952]
    BEST SF SCIENCE FICTION STORIES [Crispin - 1955]
Yankee Exodus by Ruth M. Goldsmith...................................F&SF  Jul 1953
    THE BEST SCIENCE FICTION STORIES: 1954 [Bleiler & Dikty - 1954]
Year of the Jackpot, The by Robert A. Heinlein.....................Glxy  Mar 1952
    SHADOW OF TOMORROW [Pohl - 1953]
    THE SECOND GALAXY READER OF SCIENCE FICTION [Gold - 1954]
    THE END OF THE WORLD [Wollheim - 1956]
Year's S-F, The by Judith Merril...............(Summation and honorable mentions)
    SF: 57 THE YEAR'S GREATEST SCIENCE FICTION & FANTASY [Merril - 1957]
    SF: 58 THE YEAR'S GREATEST SCIENCE FICTION & FANTASY [Merril - 1958]
    SF: 59 THE YEAR'S GREATEST SF & FANTASY [Merril - 1959]
Yellow Pill, The by Rog Phillips ps (Roger Phillips Graham).........ASF  Oct 1958
    SF: 59 THE YEAR'S GREATEST SF AND FANTASY [Merril - 1959]
    BEST SF FOUR SCIENCE FICTION STORIES [Crispin - 1961]
Yes, But... by Anthony Brode.........................................F&SF  Sep 1957
    THE BEST FROM FANTASY & SCIENCE FICTION: 7th SERIES [Boucher - 1958]
Yesterday Was Monday by Theodore Sturgeon.............................Unk  Jun 1941
    FROM UNKNOWN WORLDS [J. W. Campbell - 1948]
    SCIENCE FICTION ADVENTURES IN DIMENSION [Conklin - 1953]

                                                                     Mag.     Year

Yet What Are All... by Lewis Carroll ps (Charles Lutwidge Dodgson)....(verse).....
   (No data available)
   FANTASIA MATHEMATICA [Fadiman - 1958]
Ylla by Ray Bradbury.........................(From The Martian Chronicles; 1950)
   THE OUTER REACHES [Derleth - 1951]
You Can't Say That by Cleve Cartmill................................ORIGINAL STORY
   NEW TALES OF SPACE AND TIME [Healy - 1951]
You Cheated Us by Tom Godwin.........................................FU  Oct 1955
   THE BEST SCIENCE FICTION STORIES AND NOVELS: 1956 [Dikty - 1956]
You Know Wille by Theodore R. Cogswell..............................F&SF  May 1957
   SF: 58 THE YEAR'S GREATEST SCIENCE FICTION & FANTASY [Merril - 1958]
Young Archimedes by Aldous Huxley....................(From Young Archimedes; 1924)
   FANTASIA MATHEMATICA [Fadiman - 1958]
You're Another by Damon Knight......................................F&SF  Jun 1955
   THE BEST FROM FANTASY & SCIENCE FICTION: 5th SERIES [Boucher - 1956]

# Z

Z by Charles L. Fontenay.............................................If  Jun 1956
   THE SECOND WORLD OF IF [Quinn & Wulff - 1958]
Zen by Jerome Bixby.................................................Glxy  Oct 1952
   CROSSROADS IN TIME [Conklin - 1953]
Zeritsky's Law by Ann Warren Griffith..............................Glxy  Nov 1951
   THE OMNIBUS OF SCIENCE FICTION [Conklin - 1952]
Zero Hour by Ray Bradbury............................................PS  Fal 1947
   INVASION FROM MARS [Welles - 1949]
   MY BEST SCIENCE FICTION STORY [Margulies & Friend - 1949]
   BEST SF TWO SCIENCE FICTION STORIES [Crispin - 1956]
   ASPECTS OF SCIENCE FICTION [Doherty - 1959]

# Miscellaneous

∞ by Sir Arthur Eddington...................(From New Pathways of Science; 1935)
   FANTASIA MATHEMATICA [Fadiman - 1958]

# Alphabetical Author Listing

## A

AANDAHL, VANCE  (1)                                          Mag.    Year
  It's a Great Big Wonderful Universe...........................F&SF   Nov 1960
    THE BEST FROM FANTASY & SCIENCE FICTION: 10th SERIES [Mills - 1961]
ABERNATHY, ROBERT  (9)
  Axolotl......................................................F&SF   Jan 1954
    THE BEST SCIENCE FICTION STORIES & NOVELS: 1954 [Bleiler & Dikty - 1954]
  Canal Builders, The..........................................ASF    Jan 1945
    EVERY BOY'S BOOK OF OUTER SPACE STORIES [Dikty - 1960]
  Grandma's Lie Soap...........................................FU     Feb 1956
    SF: THE YEAR'S GREATEST SCIENCE FICTION & FANTASY [Merril - 1956]
  Heirs Apparent...............................................F&SF   Jun 1954
    THE BEST FROM FANTASY & SCIENCE FICTION: 4th SERIES [Boucher - 1952]
    THE BEST SCIENCE FICTION STORIES & NOVELS: 1955 [Dikty - 1955]
  Heritage.....................................................ASF    Jun 1942
    THE OMNIBUS OF SCIENCE FICTION [Conklin - 1952]
  Junior.......................................................Glxy   Jan 1956
    SF: THE YEAR'S GREATEST SCIENCE FICTION & FANTASY [Merril - 1956]
  Peril of the Blue World......................................PS     Win 1942
    FLIGHT INTO SPACE [Wollheim - 1950]
    STORIES OF SCIENTIFIC IMAGINATION [Gallant - 1954]
  Rotifers, The................................................If     Mar 1953
    THE FIRST WORLD OF IF [Quinn & Wulff - 1957]
ACKERMAN, FORREST J  (1)
  Mute Question, The...........................................OW     Sep 1950
    ADVENTURES IN TOMORROW [Crossen - 1951]
AIKEN, CONRAD  (1)
  Mr. Arcularis................................(From Among The Last People; 1934)
    THE MOONLIGHT TRAVELER [Stern - 1943]
ALDISS, BRIAN W.  (10)
  But Who Can Replace A Man?...................................Inf    Jun 1958
    OUT OF THIS WORLD 2 [Williams-Ellis & Owen - 1961]
  Dumb Show....................................................Neb #19 Dec 1956
    ASPECTS OF SCIENCE FICTION [Doherty - 1959]
  Let's Be Frank...............................................SF #23  Jun 1957
    SF: 58 THE YEAR'S GREATEST SCIENCE FICTION & FANTASY [Merril - 1958]
  Not For An Age...............................................Obs    1/9/55
    A. D. 2500 [Wilson - 1955]
  Old Man Hundredth............................................NW #100 Dec 1960
    SIXTH ANNUAL OF THE YEAR'S BEST SF [Merril - 1961]
  Outside......................................................NW #31  Jan 1955
    BEST SF TWO SCIENCE FICTION STORIES [Crispin - 1956]
  Panel Game...................................................NW #42  Dec 1955
    ASPECTS OF SCIENCE FICTION [Doherty - 1959]
  Poor Little Warrior..........................................F&SF   Apr 1958
    THE BEST FROM FANTASY & SCIENCE FICTION: 8th SERIES [Boucher - 1959]
    PENGUIN SCIENCE FICTION [Aldiss - 1961]

ALDISS, BRIAN W. [Cont'd]                                          Mag.    Year
   Space Burial.....................(verse)....................F&SF   Jul 1959
      THE BEST FROM FANTASY & SCIENCE FICTION: 9th SERIES [Mills - 1960]
   Ten-Story Jigsaw...........................................Neb #26  Jan 1958
      SF: 59 THE YEAR'S GREATEST SF AND FANTASY [Merril - 1959]
ALEXANDER, W.  (1)
   One Leg Too Many...........................................Amz   Oct 1929
      THE BIG BOOK OF SCIENCE FICTION [Conklin - 1950]
ALLEN, GRANT  (1)
   Pausodyne......................................(From Strange Stories; 1884)
      BEYOND TIME AND SPACE [Derleth - 1950]
ALLEN, STEVE  (1)
   Public Hating, The.........................................BB   Jan 1955
      SF: THE YEAR'S GREATEST SCIENCE FICTION AND FANTASY [Merril - 1956]
ALLINGHAM, MARGERY  (1)
   He Was Asking For You...............(From Wanted: Someone Innocent; 1946)
      SHOT IN THE DARK [Merril - 1950]
AMIS, KINGSLEY  (1)
   Hemingway In Space.........................................Plby  12/21/60
      SIXTH ANNUAL OF THE YEAR'S BEST SF [Merril - 1961]
AMUNDSON, GRACE  (1)
   Child Who Believed, The....................................SEP   12/16/50
      THE SATURDAY EVENING POST FANTASY STORIES [Fles - 1951]
ANDERSON, KAREN  (2)  (Mrs. Poul Anderson)
   In Memoriam: Henry Kuttner.................................F&SF  May 1958
      THE BEST FROM FANTASY & SCIENCE FICTION: 8th SERIES [Boucher - 1959]
   Origin of the Species.................(verse)...............F&SF  Jun 1958
      THE BEST FROM FANTASY & SCIENCE FICTION: 8th SERIES [Boucher - 1959]
ANDERSON, POUL  (29)
   Backwardness...............................................F&SF  Mar 1958
      THE BEST FROM FANTASY & SCIENCE FICTION: 8th SERIES [Boucher - 1959]
   Barbarian, The.............................................F&SF  May 1956
      THE BEST FROM FANTASY & SCIENCE FICTION: 6th SERIES [Boucher - 1957]
   Brain Wave...................(Originally published by Ballantine Books; 1954)
      A TREASURY OF GREAT SCIENCE FICTION [Boucher - 1959]
   Butch......................................................ORIGINAL STORY
      TIME TO COME [Derleth - 1954]
   Call Me Joe................................................ASF   Apr 1957
      THE BEST SCIENCE FICTION STORIES & NOVELS: 9th SERIES [Dikty - 1958]
   Chapter Ends, The..........................................DSF   Jan 1954
      ADVENTURES IN THE FAR FUTURE [Wollheim - 1954]
   Double-Dyed Villians, The..................................ASF   Sep 1949
      TRAVELERS OF SPACE [Greenberg - 1952]
   Enough Rope................................................ASF   Jul 1953
      FOUR FOR THE FUTURE [Conklin - 1959]
   Flight To Forever..........................................Sup   Nov 1950
      THE YEAR'S BEST SCIENCE FICTION NOVELS: 1952 [Bleiler & Dikty - 1952]
   Genius.....................................................ASF   Dec 1948
      THE BEST SCIENCE FICTION STORIES: 1949 [Bleiler & Dikty - 1949]
   Gypsy......................................................ASF   Jan 1950
      EVERY BOY'S BOOK OF OUTER SPACE STORIES [Dikty - 1960]
   Helping Hand, The..........................................ASF   May 1950
      POSSIBLE WORLDS OF SCIENCE FICTION [Conklin - 1951]
   Immortal Crime, The........................................F&SF  Feb 1954
      THE BEST FROM FANTASY & SCIENCE FICTION: 4th SERIES [Boucher - 1955]

ANDERSON, POUL [Cont'd]                                              Mag.    Year
  Inside Earth.........................................................Glxy  Apr 1951
      THE GALAXY READER OF SCIENCE FICTION [Gold - 1952]
  Interloper...........................................................F&SF  Apr 1951
      THE OUTER REACHES [Derleth - 1951]
  Journey's End........................................................F&SF  Feb 1957
      THE BEST FROM FANTASY & SCIENCE FICTION: 7th SERIES [Boucher - 1958]
  Last Monster, The.....................................................Sup  Aug 1951
      LOOKING FORWARD [Lesser - 1953]
  Light, The...........................................................Glxy  Mar 1957
      13 GREAT STORIES OF SCIENCE FICTION [Conklin - 1960]
  Long Remembering, The................................................F&SF  Nov 1957
      SCIENCE FICTION SHOWCASE [M. Kornbluth - 1959]
  Man Who Came Early, The..............................................F&SF  Jun 1956
      THE BEST FROM FANTASY & SCIENCE FICTION: 6th SERIES [Boucher - 1957]
  Martian Crown Jewels, The.............................................EQM  Feb 1958
      A TREASURY OF GREAT SCIENCE FICTION [Boucher - 1959]
      THE SCIENCE-FICTIONAL SHERLOCK HOLMES [Peterson - 1960]
  Martyr, The..........................................................F&SF  Mar 1960
      THE BEST FROM FANTASY & SCIENCE FICTION: 10th SERIES [Mills - 1961]
  Sam Hall..............................................................ASF  Aug 1953
      SCIENCE FICTION THINKING MACHINES [Conklin - 1954]
  Sister Planet.........................................................SSF  May 1959
      GET OUT OF MY SKY [Margulies - 1960]
  Sky People, The......................................................F&SF  Mar 1959
      A DECADE OF FANTASY & SCIENCE FICTION [Mills - 1960]
  Terminal Quest........................................................Sup  Aug 1951
      CHILDREN OF WONDER [Tenn - 1953]
  Un-Man................................................................ASF  Jan 1953
      ALL ABOUT THE FUTURE [Greenberg - 1955]
  w/Gordon R. Dickson
  Trespass..............................................................FSQ  Spr 1950
      THE BEST SCIENCE FICTION STORIES: 1951 [Bleiler & Dikty - 1951]
  w/F. N. Waldrop
  Tomorrow's Children...................................................ASF  Mar 1947
      A TREASURY OF SCIENCE FICTION [Conklin - 1948]
ANDREW, WILLIAM (1)
  Right Thing, The.........................................(Observer Prize Story)
      A. D. 2500 [Wilson - 1955]
ANONYMOUS
  Fable, A...............(From The Mathematical Gazette: Vol. 38, 1954, Page
      FANTASIA MATHEMATICA [Fadiman - 1958]
  Letter To Tennyson, A.......(From The Mathematical Gazette: No data available)
      FANTASIA MATHEMATICA [Fadiman - 1958]
  Missing One's Coach: An Anachromism...................................DLM  n/d 1838
      FAR BOUNDARIES [Derleth - 1951]
  Problem — (From Talk Of The Town - special feature)...........Nykr    3/2/57
      FANTASIA MATHEMATICA [Fadiman - 1958]
  Relativity..................(verse)........................(No data available)
      FANTASIA MATHEMATICA [Fadiman - 1958]
  Tale Of a Chemist...........(From The Story Teller: or, Table Book of Popular
      Literature; Edited by Robert Bell: 1843)
      FAR BOUNDARIES [Derleth - 1951]
  There Was a Young Fellow Named Fisk........(verse).........(No data available)
      FANTASIA MATHEMATICA [Fadiman - 1958]

ANONYMOUS [Cont'd]                                           Mag.    Year
    There Was A Young Man From Trinity........(verse)..........(No data available)
        FANTASIA MATHEMATICA [Fadiman - 1958]
    There Was An Old Man Who Said "DO".........(verse).........(No data available)
        FANTASIA MATHEMATICA [Fadiman - 1958]
ANTHONY, JOHN ps (John Ciardi)  (1)
    Hypnoglyph, The................................................F&SF   Jul 1953
        PORTALS OF TOMORROW [Derleth - 1954]
        A DECADE OF FANTASY & SCIENCE FICTION [Mills - 1960]
ANVIL, CHRISTOPHER  (1)
    Mind Partner...................................................Glxy  Aug 1960
        MIND PARTNER & 8 OTHER NOVELETTES FROM GALAXY [Gold - 1961]
APOSTOLIDES, ALEX  (3)
    w/ Mark Clifton
            Civilized............................................Glxy  Aug 1953
                (Originally appeared under title We're Civilized)
                PORTALS OF TOMORROW [Derleth - 1954]
            Crazy Joey...........................................ASF   Aug 1953
                BEYOND THE BARRIERS OF SPACE AND TIME [Merril - 1954]
            What Thin Partitions.................................ASF   Sep 1953
                EDITOR'S CHOICE IN SCIENCE FICTION [Moskowitz - 1954]
                    (Story selected by John W. Campbell, Jr.)
                THE BEST SCIENCE FICTION STORIES: 1954 [Bleiler & Dikty - 1954]
ARNOLD, JACK  (1)
    Life By Television, A..........................................ORIGINAL STORY
        ADVENTURES TO COME [Esenwein - 1937]
ARR, STEPHEN  ps (Stephen A. Rynas)  (1)
    Chain of Command..............................................Glxy  May 1954
        SCIENCE FICTION ADVENTURES IN MUTATION [Conklin - 1956]
ARTHUR, ROBERT  (4)
    Evolution's End...............................................TWS   Apr 1941
        ADVENTURES IN TOMORROW [Crossen - 1951]
    Postpaid To Paradise.....................................Rpnt — F&SF  Win 1950
        (Originally appeared under title Postmarked For Paradise in Argosy 6/15/40)
        THE BEST FROM FANTASY & SCIENCE FICTION [Boucher & McComas - 1952]
    Satan and Sam Shay............................................Elks  Aug 1942
        OUT OF THIS WORLD [Fast - 1944]
    Wheel of Time, The............................................Sup   Mar 1950
        SCIENCE-FICTION CARNIVAL [Brown & Reynolds - 1953]
ASHBY, RICHARD  (1)
    Master Race....................................................Im   Sep 1951
        SPACE, SPACE, SPACE [Sloane - 1953]
ASIMOV, ISAAC   (47)
    Belief........................................................ASF   Oct 1953
        BEYOND THE BARRIERS OF SPACE AND TIME [Merril - 1954]
    Blind Alley...................................................ASF   Mar 1945
        THE BEST OF SCIENCE FICTION [Conklin - 1946]
    "Breeds There A Man...?".......................................ASF   Jun 1951
        BEACHHEADS IN SPACE [Derleth - 1954]
    Bridle and Saddle.............................................ASF   Jun 1942
        MEN AGAINST THE STARS [Greenberg - 1950]
    C-Chute.......................................................Glxy  Oct 1951
        SHADOW OF TOMORROW [Pohl - 1953]
        THE SECOND GALAXY READER OF SCIENCE FICTION [Gold - 1954]

ASIMOV, ISAAC [Cont'd]                                                    Mag.    Year
    Christmas On Ganymede.......................................Stg  Jan 1942
        ADVENTURES IN TOMORROW [Crossen - 1951]
    Death Sentence.............................................ASF  Jun 1942
        THE OUTER REACHES [Derleth - 1951]
    Dreaming Is a Private Thing................................F&SF  Dec 1955
        SF: THE YEAR'S GREATEST SCIENCE FICTION AND FANTASY [Merril - 1956]
    Dreamworld................................................F&SF  Nov 1955
        THE BEST FROM FANTASY & SCIENCE FICTION: 5th SERIES [Boucher - 1956]
    Each An Explorer..........................................Fut #30  n/d 1956
        SF: 57 THE YEAR'S GREATEST SCIENCE FICTION & FANTASY [Merril - 1957]
    First Law.................................................FU  Oct 1956
        THE FANTASTIC UNIVERSE OMNIBUS [Santesson - 1960]
    Flies.....................................................F&SF  Jun 1953
        SCIENCE FICTION TERROR TALES [Conklin - 1955]
    Foundation Of Science Fiction Success, The..........(verse).....F&SF  Oct 1954
        THE BEST FROM FANTASY & SCIENCE FICTION: 4th SERIES [Boucher - 1955]
    Franchise.................................................If  Jul 1955
        THE FIRST WORLD OF IF [Quinn & Wulff - 1957]
    Fun They Had, The.........................................NEA  12/1/51
        OPERATION FUTURE [Conklin - 1955]
    Galley Slave..............................................Glxy  Dec 1957
        SIX GREAT SHORT SCIENCE FICTION NOVELS [Conklin - 1960]
    Heredity..................................................Ash  Apr 1941
        BEYOND THE END OF TIME [Pohl - 1952]
    Homo Sol..................................................ASF  Sep 1940
        THE OMNIBUS OF SCIENCE FICTION [Conklin - 1952]
    Hostess...................................................Glxy  May 1951
        THE GALAXY READER OF SCIENCE FICTION [Gold - 1952]
    Ideas Die Hard............................................Glxy  Oct 1957
        THE THIRD GALAXY READER OF SCIENCE FICTION [Gold - 1958]
    "In A Good Cause — ".....................................ORIGINAL STORY
        NEW TALES OF SPACE AND TIME [Healy - 1951]
    It's All How You Look At It.............(verse).............Fut #39  Oct 1958
        SF: 59 THE YEAR'S GREATEST SCIENCE FICTION & FANTASY [Merril - 1959]
    It's Such A Beautiful Day.................................ORIGINAL STORY
        STAR SCIENCE FICTION STORIES #3 [Pohl - 1954]
    Let's Get Together........................................Inf  Feb 1957
        SF: 58 THE YEAR'S GREATEST SCIENCE FICTION AND FANTASY [Merril - 1958]
    Let's Not.................................................BGJ  Dec 1954
        ALL ABOUT THE FUTURE [Greenberg - 1955]
    Liar!.....................................................ASF  May 1941
        HUMAN? [Merril - 1954]
    Little Lost Robot.........................................ASF  Mar 1947
        BEST SF TWO SCIENCE FICTION STORIES [Crispin - 1956]
    Loint Of Paw, A...........................................F&SF  Aug 1957
        THE BEST FROM FANTASY & SCIENCE FICTION: 7th SERIES [Boucher - 1958]
    Misbegotten Missionary....................................Glxy  Nov 1950
        TOMORROW, THE STARS [Heinlein - 1952]
    Mother Earth..............................................ASF  May 1949
        JOURNEY TO INFINITY [Greenberg - 1951]
        THREE FROM OUT THERE [Margulies - 1959]

ASIMOV, ISAAC [Cont'd]

Mag.    Year

Nightfall...................................................................ASF   Sep 1941
    ADVENTURES IN TIME AND SPACE [Healy & McComas - 1946]
    THE ASTOUNDING SCIENCE FICTION ANTHOLOGY [J. W. Campbell - 1952]
    UBERWINDUNG VON RAUM UND ZEIT [Gunther - 1952]
    PENGUIN SCIENCE FICTION [Aldiss - 1961]
No Connection...............................................................ASF   Jun 1948
    THE BEST SCIENCE FICTION STORIES: 1949 [Bleiler & Dikty - 1949]
"Nobody Here But — "........................................................ORIGINAL STORY
    STAR SCIENCE FICTION STORIES [Pohl - 1953]
Not Final!..................................................................ASF   Oct 1941
    POSSIBLE WORLDS OF SCIENCE FICTION [Conklin - 1951]
Pause, The..................................................................ORIGINAL STORY
    TIME TO COME [Derleth - 1954]
Robbie......................................................................(From I, Robot; 1950)
    (Revised version of Strange Playfellow)
    SCIENCE FICTION THINKING MACHINES [Conklin - 1954]
Robot AL 76 Goes Astray.....................................................Amz   Feb 1942
    MY BEST SCIENCE FICTION STORY [Margulies & Friend - 1949]
Singing Bell, The...........................................................F&SF  Jan 1955
    THE BEST FROM FANTASY & SCIENCE FICTION: 5th SERIES [Boucher - 1956]
Strange Playfellow..........................................................Sup   Sep 1940
    SHOT IN THE DARK [Merril - 1950]
Thiotimoline and the Space Age..............................................ASF   Oct 1960
    SIXTH ANNUAL OF THE YEAR'S BEST SF [Merril - 1961]
Thunder-Thieves, The........................................................ORIGINAL STORY
    Note: This article contains a verse that originally appeared in Future
        Science Fiction #39 (October 1958) under the title It's All How You
        Look At It.
    SF: 59 THE YEAR'S GREATEST SF AND FANTASY [Merril - 1959]
Trends......................................................................ASF   Jul 1939
    MEN AGAINST THE STARS [Greenberg - 1950]
Unto the Fourth Generation..................................................F&SF  Apr 1959
    A DECADE OF FANTASY & SCIENCE FICTION [Mills - 1960]
Up-To-Date-Sorcerer, The....................................................F&SF  Jul 1958
    THE BEST FROM FANTASY & SCIENCE FICTION: 8th SERIES [Boucher - 1959]
Victory Unintentional.......................................................Sup   Aug 1942
    LOOKING FORWARD [Lesser - 1953]
    INVASION FROM MARS [Welles - 1949]
What If.....................................................................Fnt   Sum 1952
    SCIENCE FICTION ADVENTURES IN DIMENSION [Conklin - 1953]
w/ James MacCreigh ps (Frederik Pohl)
    Little Man on the Subway, The...........................................FB #6  n/d 1950
        SCIENCE AND SORCERY [Ford - 1953]

ATHERTON, JOHN

Threes (To Be Sung by Niels Bohr)..............(verse)..........Nykr   3/2/57
    FANTASIA MATHEMATICA [Fadiman - 1958]

**B**

BACON, FRANCIS (I)

New Atlantis, The.......................(Originally published in London; 1624)
    BEYOND TIME AND SPACE [Derleth - 1950]

Mag.    Year

BADE, WILLIAM L.   (1) .....................................................Glxy   Oct 1951
    Ambition.........................................................
        SCIENCE FICTION ADVENTURES IN DIMENSION [Conklin - 1953]

BALCHIN, NIGEL   (1)
    God and the Machine........(From Last Recollections of My Uncle Charles; 1951)
        FANTASIA MATHEMATICA [Fadiman - 1958]

BALLARD, J. G.   (3) .....................................................SF #20  Dec 1956
    Prima Belladonna................................................
        SF: 57 THE YEAR'S GREATEST SF AND FANTASY [Merril - 1957]
    Sound Sweep, The................................................SF #39  Feb 1960
        THE FIFTH ANNUAL OF THE YEAR'S BEST SF [Merril - 1960]
    Track 12........................................................NW #70  Apr 1958
        PENGUIN SCIENCE FICTION [Aldiss - 1961]

BALMER, EDWIN
    w/Philip Wylie
        When Worlds Collide....................(excerpts)...................
            (Originally published by Frederick A. Stokes Co.; 1932)
        THE TREASURY OF SCIENCE FICTION CLASSICS [Kuebler - 1954]

BANGS, JOHN KENDRICK   (1)
    Disputed Authorship, A...................(From A Houseboat On The Styx; 1895)
        OUT OF THIS WORLD [Fast - 1944]

BANKS, RAYMOND E.   (5) .....................................................F&SF   Jan 1954
    Christmas Trombone...............................................
        THE BEST SCIENCE FICTION STORIES AND NOVELS: 1955 [Dikty - 1955]
    Littlest People, The............................................Glxy   Mar 1954
        THE BEST SCIENCE FICTION STORIES AND NOVELS: 1955 [Dikty - 1955]
    Rabbitts To the Moon............................................F&SF   Jul 1959
        A DECADE OF FANTASY & SCIENCE FICTION [Mills - 1960]
    Short Ones, The.................................................F&SF   Mar 1955
        THE BEST FROM FANTASY & SCIENCE FICTION: 5th SERIES [Boucher - 1956]
    This Side Up....................................................Glxy   Apr 1954
        THE FIFTH GALAXY READER [Gold - 1961]

BARCLAY, ALAN   (2) .....................................................NW #21   Jun 1953
    Hard Way, The...................................................
        THE BEST FROM NEW WORLDS [Carnell - 1955]
    Only An Echo....................................................NW #22   Apr 1954
        GATEWAY TO THE STARS [Carnell - 1955]

BARING, MAURICE   (1)
    Alternative, The.......(From Half A Minute's Silence and Other Stories;  1925)
        TRAVELERS IN TIME [Stern - 1947]

BARNES, ARTHUR K.   (1) .....................................................TWS   Jun 1943
    Grief of Bagdad.................................................
        (Originally appeared under pseudonym Kelvin Kent)
    MY BEST SCIENCE FICTION STORY [Margulies & Friend - 1949]

BARR, STEPHEN   (2) .....................................................F&SF   Dec 1959
    Homing Instincts of Joe Vargo..................................
        SPECTRUM [Amis & Conquest - 1961]
    I Am A Nucleus.................................................Glxy   Feb 1957
        THE FOURTH GALAXY READER OF SCIENCE FICTION [Gold - 1959]

BARRETT, NEAL JR.   (1) .....................................................Glxy   Oct 1960
    Stentoril Luggage, The.........................................
        MIND PARTNER AND 8 OTHER NOVELETTES FROM GALAXY [Gold - 1961]

BARTON, RALPH (1)
    Twinkel, Twinkel, Little Star.................(verse)....................... Mag.   Year
    (From Science In Rhyme and Without Reason; 1924)
        FANTASIA MATHEMATICA [Fadiman - 1958]
BATES, HARRY (4)
    Alas, All Thinking!.......................................................Ast  Jun 1935
        THE OTHER WORLDS [Stong - 1941]
        IMAGINATION UNLIMITED [Bleiler & Dikty - 1952]
    Death of a Sensitive......................................................SF+  May 1953
        EDITOR'S CHOICE IN SCIENCE FICTION [Moskowitz - 1954]
    (Story selected by Sam Moskowitz)
    Farewell To the Master....................................................ASF  Oct 1940
        ADVENTURES IN TIME AND SPACE [Healy & McComas - 1946]
    Matter of Size, A.........................................................Ast  Apr 1934
        ADVENTURES IN TIME AND SPACE [Healy & McComas - 1946]
BEARD, JAMES H. (1)
    Dawn of Reason, The...................(verse)....................Unk  Oct 1939
        FROM UNKNOWN WORLDS [J. W. Campbell - 1948]
BEAUMONT, CHARLES (9)
    Beautiful Woman, The.......................................................If  Sep 1952
    (Originally appeared under title The Beautiful People)
        PRIZE SCIENCE FICTION [Wollheim - 1953]
    Fritzchen..............................................................Orb #1  n/d 1953
        TERROR IN THE MODERN VEIN [Wollheim - 1955]
    Jungle, The................................................................If  Dec 1954
        THE SECOND WORLD OF IF [Quinn & Wulff - 1958]
    Keeper of the Dream...........................................ORIGINAL STORY
        TIME TO COME [Derleth - 1954]
    Last Rites.................................................................If  Oct 1955
        THE FIRST WORLD OF IF [Quinn & Wulff - 1957]
    Place of Meeting.......................................................Orb #2  n/d 1954
        PLANET OF DOOM AND OTHER STORIES [Anonymous - 1954]
    Vanishing American, The.................................................F&SF  Aug 1955
        THE BEST FROM FANTASY & SCIENCE FICTION: 5th SERIES [Boucher - 1956]
        INVISIBLE MEN [Davenport - 1960]
    w/ Chad Oliver
        Last Word, The......................................................F&SF  Apr 1955
        THE BEST FROM FANTASY & SCIENCE FICTION: 5th SERIES [Boucher - 1956]
BECKMAN, CHARLES JR. (1)
    Last Man, The..........................................................Orb #5  Nov 1954
    (Originally appeared under title Noah)
        SPACE STATION 42 AND OTHER STORIES [Anonymous - 1958]
BEERBOHM, MAX (1)
    Enoch Soames..............................................(From Seven Men; 1919)
        THE MOONLIGHT TRAVELER [Stern - 1943]
        TRAVELERS IN TIME [Stern - 1947]
BELKIN, NORMAN (1)
    Vampire's Saga, A...................(verse)....................F&SF May 1959
        THE BEST FROM FANTASY & SCIENCE FICTION: 9th SERIES [Mills - 1960]
BELLAMY, EDWARD (1)
    Blindman's World, The........(From The Blindman's World & Other Stories; 1898)
        BEYOND TIME AND SPACE [Derleth - 1950]
BEMELMANS, LUDWIG (1)
    Putzi...................................................(From Small Beer; 1939)
        TIMELESS STORIES FOR TODAY AND TOMORROW [Bradbury - 1952]

Mag.    Year

BENEDICT, MYRLE (1)
Sit By the Fire.............................................FU  May 1958
    THE FANTASTIC UNIVERSE OMNIBUS [Santesson - 1960]

BENET, STEPHEN VINCENT (6)
Angel Was A Yankee, The....................................McI  Oct 1940
    BEYOND HUMAN KEN [Merril - 1952]
By The Waters of Babylon...................................SEP  7/31/37
    (Originally appeared under title The Place of the Gods)
    POCKET BOOK OF SCIENCE FICTION [Wollheim - 1943]
Curfew Tolls, The..........................................SEP  10/5/35
    THE MOONLIGHT TRAVELER [Stern - 1943]
King of the Cats, The......................................HBzr  Feb 1929
    OUT OF THIS WORLD [Fast - 1944]
Nightmare For Future Reference: A Narrative Poem...........Sch  9/17/38
    CHILDREN OF WONDER [Tenn - 1953]
Nightmare Number Three........(verse).............(From Burning City; 1936)
    SHOT IN THE DARK [Merril - 1950]

BENNETT, KEITH (1)
Rocketeers Have Shaggy Ears, The...........................PS  Spr 1950
    TRAVELERS OF SPACE [Greenberg - 1952]

BENNETT, KEM (2)
Different Purpose, A.......................................F&SF  Nov 1958
    THE BEST FROM FANTASY & SCIENCE FICTION: 9th SERIES [Mills - 1960]
Soothsayer, The............................................F&SF  Aug 1952
    THE BEST FROM F&SF: 2nd SERIES [Boucher & McComas - 1953]

BENSON, STELLA ps (Mrs. Jo Anderson) (1)
Man Who Missed the Bus, The...(From Collected Stories of Stella Benson; 1936)
    THE MOONLIGHT TRAVELER [Stern - 1943]

BERESFORD, JOHN D. (1)
Appearance Of Man, The....................(From Signs and Wonders; 1921)
    THE OTHER SIDE OF THE MOON [Derleth - 1949]

BERN, DONALD (1)
Man Who Knew All the Answers, The..........................Amz  Aug 1940
    THE OTHER WORLDS [Stong - 1941]

BERRYMAN, JOHN (3)
Berom......................................................ASF  Jan 1951
    IMAGINATION UNLIMITED [Bleiler & Dikty - 1952]
Space Rating...............................................ASF  Oct 1939
    (Originally appeared under title Beyond the Stars)
    POSSIBLE WORLDS OF SCIENCE FICTION [Conklin - 1951]
    BEYOND THE STARS AND OTHER STORIES [Anonymous - 1958]
        (Appeared under title Beyond the Stars)
Special Flight.............................................ASF  May 1939
    SPECTRUM [Amis & Conquest - 1961]

BESTER, ALFRED (13)
Adam and No Eve............................................ASF  Sep 1941
    ADVENTURES IN TIME AND SPACE [Healy & McComas - 1946]
Disappearing Act..........................................ORIGINAL STORY
    STAR SCIENCE FICTION STORIES #2 [Pohl - 1953]
    STAR OF STARS [Pohl - 1960]
5,271,000.................................................F&SF  Mar 1954
    ASSIGNMENT IN TOMORROW [Crossen - 1951]
Fondly Fahrenheit.........................................F&SF  Aug 1954
    THE BEST FROM FANTASY & SCIENCE FICTION: 4th SERIES [Boucher - 1955]

BESTER, ALFRED [Cont'd]                                          Mag.     Year
  Hobson's Choice.............................................F&SF  Aug 1952
     THE BEST FROM F&SF: 2nd SERIES [Boucher & McComas - 1953]
  Men Who Murdered Mohammed, The..............................F&SF  Oct 1958
     THE BEST FROM FANTASY & SCIENCE FICTION: 8th SERIES [Boucher - 1959]
  Oddy And Id.................................................ASF   Aug 1950
     (Originally appeared under title The Devil's Invention)
     THE BEST SCIENCE FICTION STORIES: 1951 [Bleiler & Dikty - 1951]
  Of Time And Third Avenue....................................F&SF  Oct 1951
     THE BEST SCIENCE FICTION STORIES: 1952 [Bleiler & Dikty - 1952]
  Pi Man, The.................................................F&SF  Oct 1959
     THE BEST FROM FANTASY & SCIENCE FICTION: 9th SERIES [Mills - 1960]
  Star Light, Star Bright.....................................F&SF  Jul 1953
     THE BEST FROM FANTASY & SCI. FIC.: 3rd SERIES [Boucher & McComas-1954]
  Stars My Destination, The...................................Glxy  Oct 1956
     A TREASURY OF GREAT SCIENCE FICTION [Boucher - 1959]
  Time Is the Traitor.........................................F&SF  Sep 1953
     THE BEST SCIENCE FICTION STORIES: 1954 [Bleiler & Dikty - 1954]
  Will You Wait?..............................................F&SF  Mar 1959
     A DECADE OF FANTASY & SCIENCE FICTION [Mills - 1960]
BEYNON, JOHN ps (John Beynon Harris) (3)
  (See listings of John Beynon Harris and John Wyndham)
  Never On Mars...............................................FU    Jan 1954
     GATEWAY TO THE STARS [Carnell - 1955]
  No Place Like Earth.........................................NW #9  Spr 1951
     (Incorporating Time To Rest from Arkham Sampler Winter 1949)
     NO PLACE LIKE EARTH [Carnell - 1952]
     OUT OF THIS WORLD I [Ellis & Owen - 1960]
  Technical Slip..............................................Im    Dec 1950
     OPERATION FUTURE [Conklin - 1955]
BIERCE, AMBROSE (2)
  Damned Thing, The...........................(From Can Such Things Be?; 1893)
     THE TREASURY OF SCIENCE FICTION CLASSICS [Kuebler - 1954]
  Moxon's Master..............................(From Can Such Things Be?; 1893)
     THE POCKET BOOK OF SCIENCE FICTION [Wollheim - 1943]
     SCIENCE FICTION THINKING MACHINES [Conklin - 1954]
     JOURNEYS IN SCIENCE FICTION [Loughlin & Popp - 1961]
BIGGLE, LLOYD JR. (1)
  Tunesmith, The..............................................If    Aug 1957
     THE BEST SCIENCE FICTION STORIES & NOVELS: 9th SERIES [Dikty - 1958]
BINDER, EANDO ps (Otto Binder) (4)
  Adam Link's Vengeance.......................................Amz   Feb 1940
     THE OTHER WORLDS [Stong - 1941]
  Conquest Of Life............................................TWS   Aug 1937
     FROM OFF THIS WORLD [Margulies & Friend - 1949]
  I, Robot....................................................Amz   Jan 1939
     EDITOR'S CHOICE IN SCIENCE FICTION [Moskowitz - 1954]
     (Story selected by Howard Browne)
  Teacher From Mars, The......................................TWS   Feb 1941
     MY BEST SCIENCE FICTION STORY [Margulies & Friend - 1949]
BIRCH, A. G. (1)
  Moon Terror, The............................................WT    May 1923
     THE MOON TERROR [Anonymous - 1927]

                                                              Mag.    Year
BIXBY, JEROME (8)
    Angels In the Jets.........................................FA  Fal 1952
        ASSIGNMENT IN TOMORROW [Crossen - 1951]
    Holes Around Mars, The....................................Glxy  Jan 1954
        OPERATION FUTURE [Conklin - 1955]
    It's A Good Life..........................................ORIGINAL STORY
        STAR SCIENCE FICTION STORIES #2 [Pohl - 1953]
        STAR OF STARS [Pohl - 1960]
        BEST SF FOUR SCIENCE FICTION STORIES [Crispin - 1961].....If  Dec 1955
    Laboratory................................................Amz  Jan 1954
        THE FIRST WORLD OF IF [Quinn & Wulff - 1957]
    One Way Street............................................Stg  Aug 1952
        THE BEST SCIENCE FICTION STORIES AND NOVELS: 1955 [Dikty - 1955]
    Page and Player...........................................Glxy  Oct 1952
        SPACE PIONEERS [Norton - 1954]
    Zen.......................................................
        CROSSROADS IN TIME [Conklin - 1953]

    w/Joe E. Dean.............................................BFF  Jul 1953
        Share Alike..........................................
            GALAXY OF GHOULS [Merril - 1955]
            ZACHERLY'S MIDNIGHT SNACKS [Zacherly - 1960]

BLACKWOOD, ALGERNON (1)
    Elsewhere and Otherwise...................................(From Shocks; 1936)
        TRAVELERS IN TIME [Stern - 1947]

BLEILER, EVERETT F. (Translator)
    (See listing Somnium by Johannes Keppler).

BLISH, JAMES (18)
    Battle of the Unborn......................................Fw/SF  May 1950
        SCIENCE FICTION ADVENTURES IN MUTATION [Conklin - 1956]
    Beanstalk.................................................ORIGINAL STORY
        FUTURE TENSE [Crossen - 1953]
    Beep......................................................Glxy  Feb 1954
        STORIES FOR TOMORROW [Sloane - 1954]
        SPACE POLICE [Norton - 1956]
    Case Of Conscience, A.....................................If  Sep 1953
        BEST SF SCIENCE FICTION STORIES [Crispin - 1955]
    Common Time...............................................SFQ  Aug 1953
        SHADOW OF TOMORROW [Pohl - 1953]
    F Y I.....................................................ORIGINAL STORY
        STAR SCIENCE FICTION STORIES #2 [Pohl - 1953]
    Get Out of My Sky.........................................ASF  Jan 1957
        GET OUT OF MY SKY [Margulies - 1960]
    In Memoriam: Fletcher Pratt.............(verse)...........F&SF  Jan 1957
        THE BEST FROM FANTASY & SCIENCE FICTION: 7th SERIES [Boucher - 1958]
    Matter of Energy, A.......................................F&SF  May 1953
        (Excerpt from With Malice To Come — 3 vignettes)
            THE BEST FROM FANTASY & SCIENCE FICTION: 5th SER. [Boucher - 1956]
    Mistake Inside............................................Stg  Mar 194
        WORLD OF WONDER [Pratt - 1951]
    Okie......................................................ASF  Apr 195
        STORIES FOR TOMORROW [Sloane - 1954]
    Portals of Andros.........................................FSF  Jan 195
        PORTALS OF TOMORROW [Derleth - 1954]
    Solar Plexus..............................................Ash  Sep 194
        BEYOND HUMAN KEN [Merril - 1952]

BLISH, JAMES [Cont'd]                                          Mag.    Year
    Surface Tension....................................................Glxy  Aug 1952
        YEAR'S BEST SCIENCE FICTION NOVELS: 1953 [Bleiler & Dikty - 1953]
        6 GREAT SHORT NOVELS OF SCIENCE FICTION [Conklin - 1954]
            (Revised for inclusion in this anthology)
        THE SECOND GALAXY READER OF SCIENCE FICTION [Gold - 1954]
    There Shall Be No Darkness.........................................TWS   Apr 1950
        WITCHES THREE [Pratt - 1952]
        ZACHERLY'S VULTURE STEW [Zacherly - 1960]
    Thing in the Attic, The............................................If    Jul 1954
        THE SECOND WORLD OF IF [Quinn & Wulff - 1958]
    Watershed..........................................................If    Mar 1955
        THE FIRST WORLD OF IF [Quinn & Wulff - 1957]
    Work of Art, A.....................................................SFS   Jul 1956
        SCIENCE FICTION SHOWCASE [M. Kornbluth - 1959]
BLOCH, ALAN  (1)
    Men Are Different..................................................ORIGINAL STORY
        SCIENCE FICTION THINKING MACHINES [Conklin - 1954]
BLOCH, ROBERT  (8)
    Almost Human.......................................................FA    Jun 1943
        (Originally appeared under pseudonym Tarleton Fiske)
        MY BEST SCIENCE FICTION STORY [Margulies & Friend - 1949]
    Cloak, The.........................................................Unk   May 1939
        FROM UNKNOWN WORLDS [J. W. Campbell - 1948]
    Daybroke...........................................................Str   Jan 1958
        STAR OF STARS [Pohl - 1960]
    Dream Makers, The..................................................BFF   Sep 1953
        TERROR IN THE MODERN VEIN [Wollheim - 1955]
    Fear Planet, The...................................................SSS   Feb 1943
        FAR BOUNDARIES [Derleth - 1951]
    I Do Not Love Thee, Doctor Fell....................................F&SF  Mar 1955
        THE BEST SCIENCE FICTION STORIES AND NOVELS: 1956 [Dikty - 1956]
    Nightmare Number Four........(This verse first appeared in a fanzine.  This is
        its first professional appearance.)
            SCIENCE FICTION SHOWCASE [M. Kornbluth - 1959]
    Way of Life, A.....................................................FU    Oct 1956
        THE FANTASTIC UNIVERSE OMNIBUS [Santesson - 1960]
BLOCK, LAWRENCE  (1)
    Make A Prison......................................................OSFS  Jan 1959
        THE FIFTH ANNUAL OF THE YEAR'S BEST SF [Merril - 1960]
BOLSOVER, JOHN  (1)
    JACKSON WONG'S STORY.....................................(Observer Prize Story)
        A. D. 2500 [Wilson - 1955]
BOND, NELSON  (12)
    Abduction of Abner Green, The......................................BB    Jun 1941
        SCIENCE FICTION CARNIVAL [Brown & Reynolds - 1953]
    And Lo! The Bird...................................................BB    Sep 1950
        FAR BOUNDARIES [Derleth - 1951]
    Castaway, The......................................................PS    Win 1940
        (Originally appeared under pseudonym George Danzell)
            INVASION FROM MARS [Welles - 1949]
    Conquerors' Isle...................................................BB    Jun 1946
        THE OTHER SIDE OF THE MOON [Derleth - 1949]
        WORLD OF WONDER [Pratt - 1951]
        STORIES OF SCIENTIFIC IMAGINATION [Gallant - 1954]
    Cunning of the Beast...............................................BB    Nov 1942
        (Originally appeared under title Another World Begins)
            STRANGE PORTS OF CALL [Derleth - 1948]

BOND, NELSON [Cont'd]                                    Mag.    Year
   Day We Celebrate, The..........................................ASF  Jan 1941
      POSSIBLE WORLDS OF SCIENCE FICTION [Conklin - 1951]
   Lancelot Biggs On the Saturn.............(From Lancelot Biggs: Spaceman; 1950)
      SCIENCE FICTION AND READER'S GUIDE [Barrows - 1954]
   Magic City.....................................................ASF  Feb 1941
      A TREASURY OF GREAT SCIENCE FICTION [Boucher - 1959]
   Monster From Nowhere, The......................................FA  Jul 1939
      THE BEST OF SCIENCE FICTION [Conklin - 1946]
   Mr. Mergenthwirker's Lobblies..................................SM  Nov 1937
      OUT OF THIS WORLD [Fast - 1944]
   This Is the Land...............................................BB  Apr 1951
      THE OUTER REACHES [Derleth - 1951]
   To People A New World..........................................BB  Nov 1950
      BEACHHEADS IN SPACE [Derleth - 1954]
BONE, J. F.  (1)
   Triggerman.....................................................ASF  Dec 1958
      SF: 59 THE YEAR'S GREATEST SF AND FANTASY [Merril - 1959]
      JOURNEYS IN SCIENCE FICTION [Loughlin & Popp - 1961]
BORGESE, ELIZABETH MANN  (1)
   Twin's Wail................................................ORIGINAL STORY
      STAR SCIENCE FICTION STORIES #6 [Pohl - 1959]
      STAR OF STARS [Pohl - 1960]
BOSWORTH, ALLAN R.  (1)
   Jesus Shoes....................................................Unk  Apr 1942
      FROM UNKNOWN WORLDS [J. W. Campbell - 1948]
BOUCHER, ANTHONY  (24)    See also pseudonym H. H. Holmes
   Ambassadors, The...............................................Stg  Jun 1952
      FUTURE TENSE [Crossen - 1953]
      GALAXY OF GHOULS [Merril - 1955]
   Anomaly of the Empty Man, The..................................F&SF  Apr 1952
      THE SCIENCE FICTIONAL SHERLOCK HOLMES [Peterson - 1960]
   Balaam.....................................................ORIGINAL STORY
      9 TALES OF SPACE AND TIME [Healy - 1954]
      BEST SF FOUR SCIENCE FICTION STORIES [Crispin - 1961]
   Barrier, The...................................................ASF  Sep 1942
      6 GREAT SHORT NOVELS OF SCIENCE FICTION [Conklin - 1954]
        (Revised for inclusion in this anthology)
   Bite, They.....................................................Unk  Aug 1943
      ZACHERLY'S VULTURE STEW [Zacherly - 1960]
   Chronokinesis of Jonathan Hull, The............................ASF  Jun 1946
      GREAT STORIES OF SCIENCE FICTION [Leinster - 1951]
   Compleat Werewolf, The.........................................Unk  Apr 1942
      FROM UNKNOWN WORLDS [J. W. Campbell - 1948]
      BEYOND HUMAN KEN [Merril - 1952]
   Conquest...................................................ORIGINAL STORY
      STAR SCIENCE FICTION STORIES #2 [Pohl - 1953]
   Expedition.....................................................TWS  Aug 1943
      THE BEST OF SCIENCE FICTION [Conklin - 1946]
      INVASION FROM MARS [Welles - 1949]
   Gandolphus.....................................................F&SF  Dec 1956
      A DECADE OF FANTASY & SCIENCE FICTION [Mills - 1960]
   Ghost of Me, The...............................................Unk  Jun 1942
      BEYOND THE BARRIERS OF SPACE AND TIME [Merril - 1954]

BOUCHER, ANTHONY [Cont'd]                                            Mag.    Year
    Greatest Tertian, The.............................................ORIGINAL STORY
        INVADERS OF EARTH [Conklin - 1952]
        THE SCIENCE FICTIONAL SHERLOCK HOLMES [Peterson - 1960]
    Mr. Lepescu......................................................WT    Sep 1945
        SHOT IN THE DARK [Merril - 1950]
    Nellthu..........................................................F&SF  Aug 1955
        THE BEST FROM FANTASY & SCIENCE FICTION: 5th SERIES [Boucher - 1956]
    Nine-Finger Jack.................................................Esq   May 1951
        THE BEST SCIENCE FICTION STORIES: 1952 [Bleiler & Dikty - 1952]
    Other Inauguaration, The.........................................F&SF  Mar 1953
        SCIENCE FICTION TERROR TALES [Conklin - 1955]
    Quest For Saint Aquin............................................ORIGINAL STORY
        NEW TALES OF SPACE AND TIME [Healy - 1951]
    Q.U.R. ..........................................................ASF   Mar 1943
        ADVENTURES IN TIME AND SPACE [Healy & McComas - 1946]
    Science Fiction Still Leads Science Fact.........................NYTM  12/1/57
        SF: 58 THE YEAR'S GREATEST SF AND FANTASY [Merril - 1958]
    Snulbug......................................................Rpnt — F&SF  May 1953
        THE BEST FROM FANTASY & SCI. FIC.: 3rd Series [Boucher & McComas - 1954]
                                    Originally appeared in Unk   Dec 1941
    Starbride........................................................TWS   Dec 1951
        STORIES FOR TOMORROW [Sloane - 1954]
    Star Dummy, The..................................................Fnt   Fal 1952
        THE OMNIBUS OF SCIENCE FICTION [Conklin - 1952]
    They Bite........................................................Unk   Aug 1943
        ZACHERLY'S VULTURE STEW [Zacherly - 1960]
    Transfer Point...................................................Glxy  Nov 1950
        ADVENTURES IN TOMORROW [Crossen - 1951]
        SHADOW OF TOMORROW [Pohl - 1953]
BOWEN, ELIZABETH (I
    Cherry Soul, The.............................................Rpnt — F&SF  Apr 1952
        (From Ivy Gripped The Steps; 1941)
            THE BEST FROM F&SF: 2nd SERIES [Boucher & McComas - 1953]
BOYD, FELIX (I)
    Robot Who Wanted To Know, The....................................FU    Mar 1958
        THE FANTASTIC UNIVERSE OMNIBUS [Santesson - 1960]
BRACKETT, LEIGH (7) (Mrs. Edmond Hamilton)
    Enchantress Of Venus.............................................PS    Fal 1949
        THE GIANT ANTHOLOGY OF SCIENCE FICTION [Margulies & Friend - 1949]
    Halfling, The....................................................Ash   Feb 1943
        SHOT IN THE DARK [Merril - 1950]
    Last Days Of Shandaker, The......................................Stg   Apr 1952
        PRIZE SCIENCE FICTION [Wollheim - 1953]
    Other People, The................................................Ven   Mar 1957
        (Originally appeared under title The Queer Ones)
            THE BEST SCIENCE FICTION STORIES & NOVELS: 9th SERIES [Dikty-1958]
    Retreat To the Stars.............................................Ash   Nov 1941
        ADVENTURES IN TOMORROW [Crossen - 1951]
    Terror Out of Space..............................................PS    Sum 1944
        THE HIDDEN PLANET [Wollheim - 1959]

    w/ Ray Bradbury

        Loreli of The Red Mist.......................................TWS   Fal 1953
            THREE TIMES INFINITY [Margulies - 1958]
BRADBURY, RAY (45)
    All Summer In A Day..............................................F&SF  Feb 1954
        THE BEST FROM FANTASY & SCIENCE FICTION: 4th SERIES [Boucher - 1955]

BRADBURY, RAY [Cont'd]                                           Mag.    Year
  ...And the Moon Be Still as Bright... .........................TWS   Jun 1948
    THE BEST SCIENCE FICTION STORIES: 1949 [Bleiler & Dikty - 1949]
  Asleep In Armageddon.........................................PS   Win 1948
    POSSIBLE WORLDS OF SCIENCE FICTION [Conklin - 1951]
    BEYOND THE STARS AND OTHER STORIES [Anonymous - 1958]
  Crowd, The.....................................................WT   May 1943
    TERROR IN THE MODERN VEIN [Wollheim - 1955]
  Dwellers In Silence............................................PS   Spr 1949
    THE BEST SCIENCE FICTION STORIES: 1950 [Bleiler & Dikty - 1950]
  Earth Men, The................................................TWS   Aug 1948
    THE OTHER SIDE OF THE MOON [Derleth - 1949]
  End of the Beginning, The.....................................MMC   10/27/56
    (Originally appeared under title Next Stop: The Stars)
    SCIENCE FICTION SHOWCASE [M. Kornbluth - 1959]
  Exiles, The...................................................MMC   9/15/49
    (Originally appeared under title The Mad Wizards of Mars)
    BEYOND TIME AND SPACE [Derleth - 1950]
  Forever And the Earth..........................................PS   Spr 1950
    THE BIG BOOK OF SCIENCE FICTION [Conklin - 1950]
  Fox In the Forest, The........................................Col   5/13/50
    THE BEST SCIENCE FICTION STORIES: 1951 [Bleiler & Dikty - 1951]
  Here There Be Tygers.....................................ORIGINAL STORY
    NEW TALES OF SPACE AND TIME [Healy - 1951]
  Homecoming, The...............................................Mdm   Oct 1946
    GALAXY OF GHOULS [Merril - 1955]
  Icarus Montgolfier Wright....................................F&SF   May 1956
    THE BEST FROM FANTASY & SCIENCE FICTION: 6th SERIES [Boucher - 1957]
  In This Sign...................................................Im   Apr 1951
    LOOKING FORWARD [Lesser - 1953]
    BEST SF SCIENCE FICTION STORIES [Crispin - 1958]
    (Appeared under title The Fire Ballons)
  Invisible Boy, The............................................Mdm   Nov 1945
    INVISIBLE MEN [Davenport - 1960]
  Kaleidoscope.................................................TWS   Oct 1949
    THE OMNIBUS OF SCIENCE FICTION [Conklin - 1952]
  King of the Grey Spaces......................................FFM   Dec 1943
    THE SCIENCE FICTION GALAXY [Conklin - 1950]
    EVERY BOY'S BOOK OF SCIENCE FICTION [Wollheim - 1951]
  Little Journey, A............................................Glxy   Aug 1951
    THE GALAXY READER OF SCIENCE FICTION [Gold - 1952]
  Man, The....................................................TWS   Feb 1949
    THE BEST SCIENCE FICTION STORIES: 1950 [Bleiler & Dikty - 1950]
  Mars Is Heaven!...............................................PS   Fal 1948
    THE BEST SCIENCE FICTION STORIES: 1949 [Bleiler & Dikty - 1949]
    SHOT IN THE DARK [Merril - 1950]
  Million Year Picnic, The......................................PS   Sum 1946
    STRANGE PORTS OF CALL [Derleth - 1948]
    INVASION FROM MARS [Welles - 1949]
    WORLD OF WONDER [Pratt - 1951]
  Naming Of Names..............................................TWS   Aug 1949
    THE BEST FROM STARTLING STORIES [Mines - 1953]
    SCIENCE AND SORCERY [Ford - 1953]
  Night Meeting.............................(From The Martian Chronicles; 1950)
    SCIENCE FICTION ADVENTURES IN DIMENSION [Conklin - 1953]
  Pedestrians, The.............................................Rptr   8/7/51
    THE BEST SCIENCE FICTION STORIES: 1952 [Bleiler & Dikty - 1952]
    TIMELESS STORIES FOR TODAY AND TOMORROW [Bradbury - 1952]

BRADBURY, RAY [Cont'd]                                         Mag.    Year
  Pillar of Fire.........................................PS   Sum 1948
      THE OTHER SIDE OF THE MOON [Derleth - 1949]
      A TREASURY OF GREAT SCIENCE FICTION [Boucher - 1959]
  Playground, The........................................Esq   Oct 1953
      PORTALS OF TOMORROW [Derleth - 1954]
  Punishment Without Crime...............................OW   Mar 1950
      SCIENCE FICTION TERROR TALES [Conklin - 1955]
  Referent...............................................TWS   Oct 1948
      (Originally appeared under house pseudonym Brett Sterling)
        IMAGINATION UNLIMITED [Bleiler & Dikty - 1952]
  Scent of Sarsaparilla..................................ORIGINAL STORY
      STAR SCIENCE FICTION STORIES [Pohl - 1953]
      STORIES FOR TOMORROW [Sloane - 1954]
  Serious Searh For Weird Worlds, A......................Life   10/24/60
      SIXTH ANNUAL OF THE YEAR'S BEST SF [Merril - 1961]
  Shape of Things, The...................................TWS   Feb 1948
      TRAVELERS OF SPACE [Greenberg - 1952]
  Shoreline At Sunset....................(From A Medicine For Melancholy; 1959)
      FIFTH ANNUAL OF THE YEAR'S BEST SF [Merril - 1960]
  Small Assasin..........................................DM   Nov 1946
      CHILDREN OF WONDER [Tenn - 1953]
  Smile, The.............................................Fnt   Sum 1952
      WORLDS OF TOMORROW [Derleth - 1955]
  Sound of Thunder, A....................(From Golden Apples of the Sun; 1953)
      ASPECTS OF SCIENCE FICTION [Doherty - 1959]
  Strawberry Window, The.................................ORIGINAL STORY
      STAR SCIENCE FICTION STORIES #3 [Pohl - 1954]
  Subterfuge.............................................Ash   Apr 1943
      ASSIGNMENT IN TOMORROW [Pohl - 1954]
  There Will Come Soft Rains.............................Col   5/6/50
      ADVENTURES IN TOMORROW [Crossen - 1951]
      BEYOND THE END OF TIME [Pohl - 1952]
  Veldt, The.............................................SEP   9/23/50
      (Originally appeared under title The World The Children Made)
        BEYOND THE BARRIERS OF SPACE AND TIME [Merril - 1954]
  Vignettes Of Tomorrow
      One Who Waits, The.................................Ark   Sum 1949
      Holiday............................................Ark   Oct 1949
        FAR BOUNDARIES [Derleth - 1951]
  Wilderness, The........................................Phl   4/6/52
      STORIES FOR TOMORROW [Sloane - 1954]
  Ylla...................................(From The Martian Chronicles; 1950)
      THE OUTER REACHES [Derleth - 1951]
  Zero Hour..............................................PS   Fal 1947
      INVASION FROM MARS [Welles - 1949]
      MY BEST SCIENCE FICTION STORY [Margulies & Friend - 1949]
      BEST SF TWO SCIENCE FICTION STORIES [Crispin - 1956]
  w/ Leigh Brackett
      Loreli of the Red Mist.............................TWS   Fal 1953
        THREE TIMES INFINITY [Margulies - 1958]
BRADFORD, JAMES S.  (1)
  Pirate of the Air......................................ORIGINAL STORY
      ADVENTURES TO COME [Esenwein - 1937]

BRETNOR, R.   (7)     (See also pseudonym Grendel Briarton)
   Door Step, The....................................................ASF  Nov 1956
      SF: 57 THE YEAR'S GREATEST SF AND FANTASY [Merril - 1957]
   Genius of the Species........................................ORIGINAL STORY
      NINE TALES OF SPACE AND TIME [Healy - 1954]
   Gnurrs Come From the Voodvork Out, The...........................F&SF  Spr 1951
      THE BEST SCIENCE FICTION STORIES: 1951 [Bleiler & Dikty - 1951]
   Little Anton................................................ORIGINAL STORY
      NEW TALES OF SPACE AND TIME [Healy - 1951]
   Man On Top, The..................................................Sch  10/24/1951
                                                                   F&SF  Sep 1960
      SIXTH ANNUAL OF THE YEAR'S BEST SF [Merril - 1961]
   Maybe Just A Little One..........................................Hpr  Aug 1947
                                                        Rpnt - F&SF  Feb 1953
      THE BEST FROM FANTASY & SCIENCE FICTION: 3rd SER [Boucher & McComas-1954]
   w/ Kris Neville
      Gratitude Guaranteed.........................................F&SF  Aug 1953
         PORTALS OF TOMORROW [Derleth - 1954]
BREUER, MILES J.  M. D.   (7)
   Appendix and the Spectacles, The.................................Amz  Dec 1928
      THE SCIENCE FICTION GALAXY [Conklin - 1950]
   Captured Cross-Section, The......................................Amz  Feb 1929
      FANTASIA MATHEMATICA [Fadiman - 1958]
   Gostak and the Doshes, The.......................................Amz  Mar 1930
      SCIENCE FICTION ADVENTURES IN DIMENSION [Conklin - 1953]
   Hungry Guinea Pig, The...........................................Amz  Jan 1930
      SCIENCE FICTION ADVENTURES IN MUTATION [Conklin - 1956]
   Man with the Strange Head, The...................................Amz  Jan 1927
      THE BIG BOOK OF SCIENCE FICTION [Conklin - 1950]
   Mars Colonizes....................................................MT  Sum 1935
      THE GARDEN OF FEAR AND OTHER STORIES [Crawford - 1945]
   w/ Clare Winger Harris
      Baby on Neptune, A...........................................Amz  Dec 1929
         FLIGHT INTO SPACE [Wollheim - 1950]
BRIARTON, GRENDEL ps (R. Bretnor)   (8)
   Through Time and Space with Ferdinand Feghott (VII)............F&SF  Mar 1958
      THE BEST FROM FANTASY & SCIENCE FICTION: 8th SERIES [Boucher - 1959]
   Through Time and Space with Ferdinand Feghott (VIII)..........F&SF  Aug 1958
      THE BEST FROM FANTASY & SCIENCE FICTION: 8th SERIES [Boucher - 1959]
   Through Time and Space with Ferdinand Feghott (X).............F&SF  Jan 1959
      THE BEST FROM FANTASY & SCIENCE FICTION: 9th SERIES [Mills - 1960]
   Through Time and Space with Ferdinand Feghott (XI)............F&SF  Feb 1959
      THE BEST FROM FANTASY & SCIENCE FICTION: 9th SERIES [Mills - 1960]
   Through Time and Space with Ferdinand Feghott (XII)...........F&SF  Mar 1959
      THE BEST FROM FANTASY & SCIENCE FICTION: 9th SERIES [Mills - 1960]
   Through Time and Space with Ferdinand Feghott (XIII)..........F&SF  Apr 1959
      THE BEST FROM FANTASY & SCIENCE FICTION: 9th SERIES [Mills - 1960]
   Through Time and Space with Ferdinand Feghott (XIV)...........F&SF  May 1959
      THE BEST FROM FANTASY & SCIENCE FICTION: 9th SERIES [Mills - 1960]
   Through Time and Space with Ferdinand Feghott (XV)............F&SF  Jun 1959
      THE BEST FROM FANTASY & SCIENCE FICTION: 9th SERIES [Mills - 1960]
BRODE, ANTHONY   (5)
   Better Bet, The.....................(verse)..................F&SF  Feb 1958
      THE BEST FROM FANTASY & SCIENCE FICTION: 8th SERIES [Boucher - 1959]
   Call Me Mister......................(verse)..................F&SF  Feb 1959
      THE BEST FROM FANTASY & SCIENCE FICTION: 9th SERIES [Mills - 1960]

BRODE, ANTHONY [Cont'd]                                        Mag.    Year
  Flying Chaucer.....................(verse)....................F&SF  Mar 1956
     THE BEST FROM FANTASY & SCIENCE FICTION: 6th SERIES [Boucher - 1957]
  Watchers, The.....................(verse)....................F&SF  Apr 1958
     THE BEST FROM FANTASY & SCIENCE FICTION: 8th SERIES [Boucher - 1959]
  Yes, But... .................................................F&SF  Sep 1957
     THE BEST FROM FANTASY & SCIENCE FICTION: 7th SERIES [Boucher - 1958]
BROUGHTON, RHODA  (1)
  Behold It Was A Dream....................(From Tales For Christmas Eve; 1873)
     BEYOND THE BARRIERS OF SPACE AND TIME [Merril - 1954]
BROWN, BILL  (2)
  Medicine Dancer..............................................BFF   Nov 1953
     BEYOND THE BARRIERS OF SPACE AND TIME [Merril - 1954]
  Star Ducks, The..............................................F&SF  Fal 1950
     THE BEST SCIENCE FICTION STORIES: 1951 [Bleiler & Dikty - 1951]
     SCIENCE FICTION AND READER'S GUIDE [Barrows - 1954]
BROWN, FREDRIC  (25)
  Abominable...................................................Dude  Mar 1960
     SIXTH ANNUAL OF THE YEAR'S BEST SF [Merril - 1961]
  Answer, The..............................(From Angels and Spaceships; 1954)
     BEST SF THREE SCIENCE FICTION STORIES [Crispin - 1958]
  Arena........................................................ASF   Jun 1944
     THE BIG BOOK OF SCIENCE FICTION [Conklin - 1950]
     SCIENCE FICTION TERROR TALES [Conklin - 1955]
  Blood........................................................F&SF  Feb 1955
     GALAXY OF GHOULS [Merril - 1955]
  Daymare......................................................TWS   Fal 1943
     THE SAINT'S CHOICE [Charteris - 1945]
  Etaoin Shrdlu................................................Unk   Feb 1942
     WORLD OF WONDER [Pratt - 1951]
  Expedition...................................................F&SF  Feb 1957
     THE BEST FROM FANTASY & SCIENCE FICTION: 7th SERIES [Boucher - 1958]
     FANTASIA MATHEMATICA [Fadiman - 1958]
  Gateway To Darkness..........................................Sup   Nov 1949
     THE GIANT ANTHOLOGY OF SCIENCE FICTION [Margulies & Friend - 1949]
  Hall of Mirrors..............................................Glxy  Dec 1953
     ASSIGNMENT IN TOMORROW [Pohl - 1954]
  Honeymoon In Hell............................................Glxy  Nov 1950
     THE GALAXY READER OF SCIENCE FICTION [Gold - 1952]
  Imagine: A Proem.............................................F&SF  May 1955
     (Originally appeared under title Imagine)
     THE BEST FROM FANTASY & SCIENCE FICTION: 5th SERIES [Boucher - 1956]
  Keep Out.....................................................Amz   Mar 1954
     SCIENCE FICTION ADVENTURES IN MUTATION [Conklin - 1956]
  Knock........................................................TWS   Dec 1948
     THE BEST SCIENCE FICTION STORIES: 1949 [Bleiler & Dikty - 1951].
     SHOT IN THE DARK [Merril - 1950]
  Last Martian, The............................................Glxy  Oct 1950
     THE BEST SCIENCE FICTION STORIES: 1951 [Bleiler & Dikty - 1951]
     THE GALAXY READER OF SCIENCE FICTION [Gold - 1952]
  Letter To A Phoenix..........................................ASF   Aug 1949
     JOURNEY TO INFINITY [Greenberg - 1951]
  Mouse........................................................TWS   Jun 1949
     THE BEST SCIENCE FICTION STORIES: 1950 [Bleiler & Dikty - 1950]
  Nothing Sirius...............................................CF    Spr 1944
     MY BEST SCIENCE FICTION STORY [Margulies & Friend - 1949]
  Paradox Lost.................................................ASF   Oct 1949
     SCIENCE-FICTION CARNIVAL [Brown & Reynolds - 1953]

(205)

BROWN, FREDRIC [Cont'd]                                        Mag.    Year
    Placet Is A Crazy Place.....................................ASF   May 1946
        TRAVELERS OF SPACE [Greenberg - 1952]
        BEST SF TWO SCIENCE FICTION STORIES [Crispin - 1956]
        OUT OF THIS WORLD I [Williams-Ellis & Owen - 1960]
    Rustle of Wings............................................F&SF   Aug 1953
        PORTALS OF TOMORROW [Derleth - 1954]
    Star Mouse, The.............................................PS    Spr 1942
        ADVENTURES IN TIME AND SPACE [Healy & McComas - 1946]
        INVASION FROM MARS [Welles - 1949]
    Too Far...................................................F&SF    Sep 1955
        THE BEST FROM FANTASY & SCIENCE FICTION: 5th SERIES [Boucher - 1956]
    Waveries, The..............................................ASF    Jan 1945
        INVADERS OF EARTH [Conklin - 1952]
    Weapon, The................................................ASF    Apr 1951
        THE OMNIBUS OF SCIENCE FICTION [Conklin - 1950]
    w/ Mack Reynolds
        Dark Interlude.........................................Glxy   Jan 1951
            THE GALAXY READER OF SCIENCE FICTION [Gold - 1952]
            THE BEST SCIENCE FICTION STORIES: 1952 [Bleiler & Dikty - 1952]
BROWN, ROSEL GEORGE  (2)
    David's Daddy..............................................Fnt    Jun 1960
        SIXTH ANNUAL OF THE YEAR'S BEST SF [Merril - 1961]
    Hair-Raising Adventure............................ORIGINAL STORY
        STAR SCIENCE FICTION STORIES #5 [Pohl - 1959]
BROWNING, JOHN S. ps (Robert Moore Williams)  (1)  See Robert Moore Williams
    Burning Bright.............................................ASF    Jul 1948
        THE ROBOT AND THE MAN [Greenberg - 1953]
BROWNLOW, CATHERINE  (1)
    Voice From the Gallery............................Observer Prize Story
        A. D. 2500 [Wilson - 1955]
BRUNNER, JOHN  (1)
    Report on the Nature of the Lunar Surface..................ASF    Aug 1960
        SIXTH ANNUAL OF THE YEAR'S BEST SF [Merril - 1961]
BRUNNER, K. HOUSTON  (1)
    Thou Good and Faithful.....................................ASF    Mar 1953
        (Originally appeared under pseudonym John Loxmith)
        SPACE PIONEERS [Norton - 1954]
BRUSSOF, VALERY  (1)
    Republic of the Southern Cross...(Fr The Southern Cross & Other Stories; 1919)
        TERROR IN THE MODERN VEIN [Woolheim - 1955]
BUCHAN, JOHN  (1)
    Space......................................................LvA    6/17/11
        BEYOND TIME AND SPACE [Derleth - 1950]
BUCK, DORIS PITKIN  (3)
    Classical Query Composed While Shampooing.......(verse).........F&SF   Jul 1959
        THE BEST FROM FANTASY & SCIENCE FICTION: 9th SERIES [Mills - 1960]
    Epithalamium.....................(verse)................F&SF   Jan 1958
        THE BEST FROM FANTASY & SCIENCE FICTION: 8th SERIES [Boucher - 1959]
    Sportsman's Difficulty................(verse)................F&SF   Mar 1959
        THE BEST FROM FANTASY & SCIENCE FICTION: 9th SERIES [Mills - 1960]

BUDRYS, ALGIS J.  (13)  (See also pseudonym Ivan Janvier)          Mag.     Year
  Chain Reaction...................................................ASF   Apr 1957
      (Originally appeared under pseudonym John A. Sentry)
      SIX GREAT SHORT NOVELS OF SCIENCE FICTION [Conklin - 1960]
  Congruent People  The...........................................ORIGINAL STORY
      STAR SCIENCE FICTION STORIES #2 [Pohl - 1953]
  Edge of the Sea, The.............................................Ven   Mar 1958
      SF: 58 THE YEAR'S GREATEST SF AND FANTASY [Merril - 1958]
  End of Summer, The..............................................ASF   Nov 1954
      PENGUIN SCIENCE FICTION [Aldiss - 1961]
  Executioner, The................................................ASF   Jan 1956
      SPECTRUM [Amis & Conquest - 1961]
  Frightened Tree, The............................................Glxy  Feb 1953
      (Originally appeared under title Protective Mimicry)
      ASSIGNMENT IN TOMORROW [Pohl - 1954]
  Man in the Sky..................................................ASF   Mar 1956
      EVERY BOY'S BOOK OF OUTER SPACE STORIES [Dikty - 1960]
  Man Who Always Knew, The........................................ASF   Apr 1956
      THE BEST SCIENCE FICTION STORIES AND NOVELS: 1956 [Dikty - 1956]
  Nightsound.......................................................Stl  Feb 1957
      (Originally appeared under title The Attic Voice)
      THE BEST SCIENCE FICTION STORIES & NOVELS: 9th SERIES [Dikty - 1958]
  Nobody Bothers Gus..............................................ASF   Nov 1955
      (Originally appeared under pseudonym Paul Janvier)
      SF: THE YEAR'S GREATEST SCIENCE FICTION AND FANTASY [Merril - 1956]
  Riya's Foundling................................................ORIGINAL STORY
      STAR SCIENCE FICTION STORIES [Pohl - 1953]
      HUMAN? [Merril - 1954]
  Silent Brother..................................................ASF   Feb 1956
      (Originally appeared under pseudonym Paul Janvier)
      SF: 57 THE YEAR'S GREATEST SF AND FANTASY [Merril - 1957]
  War Is Over, The................................................ASF   Feb 1957
      13 GREAT STORIES OF SCIENCE FICTION [Conklin - 1960]
BULFINCH, THOMAS  (1)
  Deadalus....................................(From The Age of Fable; 1855)
      JOURNEYS IN SCIENCE FICTION [Loughlin & Popp - 1961]
BURKS, ARTHUR J.  (1)
  Escape Into Yesterday...........................................ORIGINAL STORY
      SCIENCE AND SORCERY [Ford - 1953]
BURRAGE, A. M.  (1)
  Between the Minute and the Hour...............(From Some Ghost Stories; 1927)
      TRAVELERS IN TIME [Stern - 1947]
BUTLER, SAMUEL  (1)
  Uses Of Mathematics...................(verse)...............................
      (From Hudibras, First Part, Canto I; 1663)
      FANTASIA MATHEMATICA [Fadiman - 1958]
BYRAM, GEORGE  (1)
  Wonder Horse, The...............................................Atl.  Aug 1957
      SF: 58 THE YEAR'S GREATEST SF AND FANTASY [Merril - 1958]

# C

CABELL, JAMES BRANCH  (1)                                    Mag.    Year
    Jurgen Proves It By Arithmetic.............................(From Jurgen; 1919)
        FANTASIA MATHEMATICA [Fadiman - 1958]
CAHN, LEE  (1)
    Secret....................................................ASF   Jan 1953
        CROSSROADS IN TIME [Conklin - 1953]
CALISHER, HORTENSE  (1)
    Heartburn.................................(From In The Absence Of Angels; 1951)
        TIMELESS STORIES FOR TODAY AND TOMORROW [Bradbury - 1952]
CAMPANELLA, GIOVANNI DOMENICO  (1)
    City of the Sun, The..................(Written 1623; published in Paris 1634)
        BEYOND TIME AND SPACE [Derleth - 1950]
CAMPBELL, JOHN W. JR.  (3) (See also pseudonym Don A. Stuart)
    Blindness.................................................Ast   Mar 1935
        (Originally appeared under pseudonym Don A. Stuart)
            MY BEST SCIENCE FICTION STORY [Margulies & Friend - 1949]
    Idealists, The..........................................ORIGINAL STORY
        9 TALES OF SPACE AND TIME [Healy - 1954]
    "What Do You Mean...Human?".............................ASF   Sep 1959
        FIFTH ANNUAL OF THE YEAR'S BEST SF [Merril - 1960]
CANTINE, HOLLEY  (1)
    Double, Double, Toil and Trouble........................F&SF   Jan 1960
        THE BEST FROM FANTASY & SCIENCE FICTION: 10th SERIES [Mills - 1961]
        SIXTH ANNUAL OF THE YEAR'S BEST SF [Merril - 1961]
CAPEK, KAREL  (2)
    Death of Archimedes, The.....................(From Apocryphal Stories; 1949)
        FANTASIA MATHEMATICA [Fadiman - 1958]
    R.U.R. [Rossum's Universal Robots] ....................................
        (A fantastic melodrama copyright 1923 by Doubleday Page and Co.)
            SCIENCE FICTION THINKING MACHINES [Conklin - 1954]
            THE TREASURY OF SCIENCE FICTION CLASSICS [Kuebler - 1955]
CAPOTE, TRUMAN  (1)
    Miriam.......................(From Tree of Night and Other Stories;  1945)
        CHILDREN OF WONDER [Tenn - 1953]
CARLSON, ESTHER  (1)
    Museum Piece........................(From Moon over the Back Fence; 1947)
        WORLD OF WONDER [Pratt - 1951]
CARR, ROBERT S.  (1)
    Easter Eggs...............................................SEP   9/24/49
        THE BEST SCIENCE FICTION STORIES: 1950 [Bleiler & Dikty - 1950]
CARROLL, LEWIS  ps (Charles Lutwidge Dodgson)  (2)
    Eternity: A Nightmare.............................................
        (From Sylvie and Bruno Concluded; Chapter XVI; 1893)
        FANTASIA MATHEMATICA [Fadiman - 1958]
    Yet What Are All................(verse)..................(No data available)
        FANTASIA MATHEMATICA [Fadiman - 1958]

CARROLL, SIDNEY  (2)                                              Mag.    Year
  None Before Me.....................................................Cmpn  Jul 1949
    TIMELESS STORIES FOR TODAY AND TOMORROW [Bradbury - 1952]
  Note For the Milkman, A............................................TdW   Apr 1950
    TIMELESS STORIES FOR TODAY AND TOMORROW [Bradbury - 1952]
CARTER, PAUL  (1)
  Last Objective, The................................................ASF   Aug 1946
    A TREASURY OF SCIENCE FICTION [Conklin - 1948]
CARTER, PETER  (1)
  Mist, The..........................................................F&SF  Sep 1952
    SCIENCE FICTION ADVENTURES IN DIMENSION [Conklin - 1953]
CARTER, PHILIP  (1)
  Ounce of Prevention, An............................................F&SF  Sum 1950
    FAR BOUNDARIES [Derleth - 1951]
CARTIER, EDD  (1)
  Life On Other Worlds..........(Illustrated Feature).............ORIGINAL STORY
    (Accompanies David Kyle's story The Interstellar Zoo)
        TRAVELERS OF SPACE [Greenberg - 1952]
CARTMILL, CLEVE  (9)
  Deadline...........................................................ASF   Mar 1944
    THE BEST OF SCIENCE FICTION [Conklin - 1946]
  Green Cat, The.....................................................WB    Jan 1951
    THE OUTER REACHES [Derleth - 1951]
  Huge Beast.........................................................F&SF  Sum 1950
    THE BEST FROM FANTASY & SCIENCE FICTION [Boucher & McComas - 1952]
  Link, The..........................................................ASF   Aug 1942
    ADVENTURES IN TIME AND SPACE [Healy & McComas - 1946]
  Number Nine........................................................ASF   Feb 1950
    GREAT STORIES OF SCIENCE FICTION [Leinster - 1951]
  Overthrow..........................................................ASF   Nov 1942
    JOURNEY TO INFINITY [Greenberg - 1951]
  Visiting Yokel.....................................................TWS   Aug 1943
    MY BEST SCIENCE FICTION STORY [Margulies & Friend - 1949]
  With Flaming Hands.................................................ASF   Sep 1942
    A TREASURY OF SCIENCE FICTION [Conklin - 1948]
  You Can't Say That.............................................ORIGINAL STORY
    NEW TALES OF SPACE AND TIME [Healy - 1951]
CAUSEY, JAMES  (3)
  Exploiters End.................................................Orb #2  n/d 1954
    BEYOND THE STARS AND OTHER STORIES [Anonymous - 1958]
  Felony.............................................................Glxy  Jul 1954
    THE BEST SCIENCE FICTION STORIES AND NOVELS: 1955 [Dikty - 1955]
  Teething Ring......................................................Glxy  Jan 1953
    THE SECOND GALAXY READER OF SCIENCE FICTION [Gold - 1954]
CHAMBERS, ROBERT W.  (1)
  Demoisells D'Ys.............................(From The King In Yellow; 1895)
    (Story selected by Mary Gnaedinger)         Rpnt- FFM  Nov 1942
        EDITOR'S CHOICE IN SCIENCE FICTION [Moskowitz - 1954]
CHANDLER, A. BERTRAM  (8)
  Cage, The..........................................................F&SF  Jun 1957
    THE BEST FROM FANTASY & SCIENCE FICTION: 8th SERIES [Boucher - 1958]
  Castaway...........................................................WT    Nov 1947
    NO PLACE LIKE EARTH [Carnell-1952] (Aprd under pseud George Whitley)
    SCIENCE FICTION ADVENTURES IN DIMENSION [Conklin - 1953]

CHANDLER, A. BERTRAM [Cont'd]                                    Mag.    Year
  Fall of Knight.............................................FU   Jun 1958
      THE FANTASTIC UNIVERSE OMNIBUS [Santesson - 1960]
  False Dawn................................................ASF  Oct 1946
      JOURNEY TO INFINITY [Greenberg - 1951]
  Finishing Touch, A........................................NW #16  Jul 1952
      GATEWAY TO TOMORROW [Carnell - 1954]
  Giant Killer..............................................ASF  Oct 1945
      WORLD OF WONDER [Pratt - 1951]
  Half Pair, The............................................NW #65  Nov 1957
      PENGUIN SCIENCE FICTION [Aldiss - 1961]
  Jetsam....................................................NW #20  Mar 1953
      THE BEST FROM NEW WORLDS [Carnell - 1955]
      MEN ON THE MOON [Wollheim - 1958]
CHARTERIS, LESLIE  (2)
  Fish Story................................................BB   Nov 1953
      GALAXY OF GHOULS [Merril - 1955]
  Gold Standard, The.....................(From The Saint and Mr. Teale; 1933)
      THE SAINT'S CHOICE [Charteris - 1945]
CHEEVER, JOHN  (1)
  Enormous Radio, The.......................................Nykr    5/17/47
      TIMELESS STORIES FOR TODAY AND TOMORROW [Bradbury - 1952]
CHRISTIE, AGATHA  (1)
  Last Seance, The..........................................n/d/a/  1926
      BEYOND THE BARRIERS OF SPACE AND TIME [Merril - 1954]
CHRISTOPHER, JOHN ps (Christopher S. Youd)  (6)
  Balance...................................................NW #9   Spr 1951
      THE BEST SCIENCE FICTION STORIES: 1952 [Bleiler & Dikty - 1952]
      NO PLACE LIKE EARTH [Carnell - 1952]
  Conspiracy................................................Auth #53  Jan 1955
      GATEWAY TO THE STARS [Carnell - 1955]
  Drop, The.................................................Glxy  Mar 1953
      GATEWAY TO TOMORROW [Carnell - 1954]
  Man of Destiny............................................Glxy  May 1951
      THE GALAXY READER OF SCIENCE FICTION [Gold - 1952]
      LOOKING FORWARD [Lesser - 1953]
  New Wine, The....................(From The Twenty-Second Century; 1954)
      BEST SF SCIENCE FICTION STORIES [Crispin - 1955]
  Socrates..................................................Glxy  Mar 1951
      BEYOND HUMAN KEN [Merril - 1952]
      STORIES FOR TOMORROW [Sloane - 1954]
CLARK, WALTER VAN TILBURG  (1)
  Portable Phonograph, The......(From The Watchful Gods and Other Stories; 1941)
      ADVENTURES IN TOMORROW [Crossen - 1951]
      TIMELESS STORIES FOR TODAY AND TOMORROW [Bradbury - 1952]
CLARKE, ARTHUR C.  (24)
  All the Time In the World.................................Stg  Jul 1952
      PRIZE SCIENCE FICTION [Wollheim - 1953]
  Breaking Strain...........................................TWS  Dec 1949
      (Originally appeared under title Thirty Seconds - Thirty Days)
      NO PLACE LIKE EARTH [Carnell - 1952]
      THE BEST FROM STARTLING STORIES [Mines - 1953]
          (Appeared under title Thirty Seconds - Thirty Days)
      OUT OF THIS WORLD 1 [Williams-Ellis & Owen - 1960]
          (Appeared under title Thirty Seconds - Thirty Days)

CLAUDY, CARL H.  (3)                                          Mag.    Year
    Land of No Shadow, The.......................................AmB  Feb 1931
        THE YEAR AFTER TOMORROW [Del Rey, Matschat & Carmer - 1953]
    Master Minds of Mars, The...................................AmB  Sep 1931
        THE YEAR AFTER TOMORROW [Del Rey, Matschat & Carmer - 1953]
        (Originally appeared under joint byline Carl H. Claudy & Dr. John C. Paige)
    Tongue of Beast.............................................AmB  May 1939
        THE YEAR AFTER TOMORROW [Del Rey, Matschat & Carmer - 1953]
CLEMENT, HAL ps (Harry Clement Stubbs)  (7)
    Answer......................................................ASF  Apr 1947
        SCIENCE FICTION THINKING MACHINES [Conklin - 1954]
    Assumption Unjustified......................................ASF  Oct 1946
        CROSSROADS IN TIME [Conklin - 1953]
    Attitude....................................................ASF  Sep 1943
        TRAVELERS OF SPACE [Greenberg - 1952]
    Cold Front..................................................ASF  Jul 1946
        MEN AGAINST THE STARS [Greenberg - 1950]
    Critical Factor....................................ORIGINAL STORY
        STAR SCIENCE FICTION STORIES #2 [Pohl - 1953]
    Halo.......................................................Glxy  Oct 1952
        SHADOW OF TOMORROW [Pohl - 1953]
    Proof......................................................ASF  Jun 1942
        POSSIBLE WORLDS OF SCIENCE FICTION [Conklin - 1951]
CLIFTON, MARK  (10)
    Clerical Error..............................................ASF  Feb 1956
        THE BEST SCIENCE FICTION STORIES AND NOVELS: 1956 [Dikty - 1956]
    Conqueror, The..............................................ASF  Aug 1952
        THE OMNIBUS OF SCIENCE FICTION [Conklin - 1952]
        THE BEST SCIENCE FICTION STORIES: 1953 [Bleiler & Dikty - 1953]
    Sense From Thought..........................................ASF  Mar 1955
        SF THE YEAR'S GREATEST SCIENCE FICTION AND FANTASY [Merril - 1956]
    Star Bright................................................Glxy  Jul 1952
        PRIZE SCIENCE FICTION [Wollheim - 1953]
        THE SECOND GALAXY READER OF SCIENCE FICTION [Gold - 1954]
    What Have I Done?...........................................ASF  May 1952
        BEYOND HUMAN KEN [Merril - 1952]
    What Now, Little Man?......................................F&SF  Dec 1959
        FIFTH ANNUAL OF THE YEAR'S BEST SF [Merril - 1960]
    Woman's Place..............................................Glxy  May 1955
        THE WORLD THAT COULDN'T BE AND 8 OTHER NOVELETTES FROM GALAXY [Gold-1959]
    w/ Alex Apostolides
        Civilized..............................................Glxy  Aug 1953
            (Originally appeared under title We're Civilized)
            PORTALS OF TOMORROW [Derleth - 1954]
        Crazy Joe..............................................ASF  Aug 1953
            BEYOND THE BARRIERS OF SPACE AND TIME [Merril - 1954]
        What Thin Partitions...................................ASF  Sep 1953
            EDITOR'S CHOICE IN SCIENCE FICTION [Moskowitz - 1954]
            (Story selected by John W. Campbell, Jr.)
            THE BEST SCIENCE FICTION STORIES: 1954 [Bleiler & Dikty - 1954]
CLINGERMAN, MILDRED  (10)
    Birds Can't Count.........................................F&SF  Feb 1955
        THE BEST FROM FANTASY & SCIENCE FICTION: 5th SERIES [Boucher - 1956]
        SF: THE YEAR'S GREATEST SCIENCE FICTION AND FANTASY [Merril - 1956]
    First Lesson..............................................F&SF  Dec 1956
        A DECADE OF FANTASY & SCIENCE FICTION [Mills - 1960]

CLINGERMAN, MILDRED [Cont'd]                                     Mag.    Year
  Last Prophet, The.................................................F&SF  Aug 1955
    THE BEST FROM FANTASY & SCIENCE FICTION: 5th SERIES [Boucher - 1956]
  Letters From Laura...............................................F&SF  Oct 1954
    A TREASURY OF GREAT SCIENCE FICTION [Boucher - 1959]
  Minister Without Portfolio.......................................F&SF  Feb 1952
    INVADERS OF EARTH [Conklin - 1952]
    STORIES FOR TOMORROW [Sloane - 1954]
  Mr. Sakrison's Halt..............................................F&SF  Jan 1956
    THE BEST FROM FANTASY & SCIENCE FICTION: 6th SERIES [Boucher - 1957]
  Stair Trick......................................................F&SF  Aug 1952
    THE BEST FROM FANTASY & SCIENCE FICTION: 2nd SER [Boucher & McComas-1953]
  Stickeney and the Critic.........................................F&SF  Feb 1953
    PORTALS OF TOMORROW [Derleth - 1954]
  Wild Wood, The...................................................F&SF  Jan 1957
    THE BEST FROM FANTASY & SCIENCE FICTION: 7th SERIES [Boucher - 1958]
  Word, The........................................................F&SF  Nov 1953
    PORTALS OF TOMORROW [Derleth - 1954]

CLINTON, ED M., JR.  (1)
  Small World of M-75, The.........................................If  Jul 1954
    SCIENCE FICTION ADVENTURES IN MUTATION [Conklin - 1956]
    THE FIRST WORLD OF IF [Quinn & Wulff - 1957]

CLOETE, STUART  (1)
  Blast, The......................................................Col  4/12/47
    6 GREAT SHORT NOVELS OF SCIENCE FICTION [Conklin - 1954]
      (Revised for inclusion in this anthology)

CLOUGH, ROY L., JR. (1)
  Bait............................................................ASF  Jun 1951
    SPACE POLICE [Norton - 1956]

COATES, ROBERT M.  (1)
  Hour After Westerly, The.......................................Nykr  11/1/47
    TIMELESS STORIES FOR TODAY AND TOMORROW [Bradbury - 1952]

COBLENTZ, STANTON A.  (2)
  Scarlet Lunes, The..............................................FB #6  n/d 1950
    SCIENCE AND SORCERY [Ford - 1953]
  Sunward.........................................................TWS  Apr 1940
    FLIGHT INTO SPACE [Wollheim - 1950]

COFFIN, CARLYN  (1)
  Survival.........................(verse).........................F&SF  Jun 1955
    THE BEST FROM FANTASY & SCIENCE FICTION: 5th SERIES [Boucher - 1956]

COGSWELL, THEODORE R.  (7)
  Blowup Blues.....................(Song).................ORIGINAL STORY
    SIXTH ANNUAL OF THE YEAR'S BEST SF [Merril - 1961]
  Limiting Factor................................................Glxy  Apr 1954
    SCIENCE FICTION ADVENTURES IN MUTATION [Conklin - 1956]
    THE THIRD GALAXY READER OF SCIENCE FICTION [Gold - 1958]
  Minimum Sentence...............................................Glxy  Aug 1953
    THE SECOND GALAXY READER OF SCIENCE FICTION [Gold - 1954]
  Radiation Blues..................(Song).................ORIGINAL STORY
    SIXTH ANNUAL OF THE YEAR'S BEST SF [Merril - 1961]
  Spector General, The...........................................ASF  Jun 1952
    SPACE SERVICE [Norton - 1953]
  Wall Around the World, The.....................................BFF  Sep 1953
    BEYOND THE BARRIERS OF SPACE AND TIME [Merril - 1954]
  You Know Willie................................................F&SF  May 1957
    SF: 58 THE YEAR'S GREATEST SF AND FANTASY [Merril - 1958]

CLARKE, ARTHUR C. [Cont'd]                         Mag.    Year

Deep Range, The.................................................ORIGINAL STORY
   STAR SCIENCE FICTION STORIES #3 [Pohl - 1954]
Fires Within, The.....................................................Fty  Aug 1947
   (Originally appeared under pseudonym E. G. O'Brien)
      THE SCIENCE FICTION GALAXY [Conklin - 1950]
      WORLDS OF TOMORROW [Derleth - 1955]
Forgotten Enemy, The..............................................NW #5  n/d 1949
   SPACE, SPACE, SPACE [Sloane - 1953]
   GATEWAY TO TOMORROW [Carnell - 1954]
History Lesson.......................................................Stg  May 1949
   THE OMNIBUS OF SCIENCE FICTION [Conklin - 1952]
I Remember Babylon..................................................Plby  May 1960
   SIXTH ANNUAL OF THE YEAR'S BEST SF [Merril - 1961]
Loophole.............................................................ASF  Apr 1946
   A TREASURY OF SCIENCE FICTION [Conklin - 1948]
Nine Billion Names of God, The..................................ORIGINAL STORY
   STAR SCIENCE FICTION STORIES [Pohl - 1953]
   STORIES FOR TOMORROW [Sloane - 1954]
   BEST SF TWO SCIENCE FICTION STORIES [Crispin - 1956]
   ASPECTS OF SCIENCE FICTION [Doherty - 1959]
No Morning After................................................ORIGINAL STORY
   TIME TO COME [Derleth - 1954]
Other Side of the Sky, The...........................................Inf  Sep 1957
   A TREASURY OF GREAT SCIENCE FICTION [Boucher - 1959]
Other Tiger, The......................................................FU  Jul 1953
   PORTALS OF TOMORROW [Derleth - 1954]
Pacifist, The.........................................................FU  Oct 1956
   THE FANTASTIC UNIVERSE OMNIBUS [Santesson - 1960]
Prelude to Space....(excerpts)........(Org published by World Editions;  1951)
   SCIENCE IN FICTION [A.E.M. & J. C. Bayliss - 1957]
Rescue Party, The....................................................ASF  May 1946
   A TREASURY OF SCIENCE FICTION [Conklin - 1948]
   BEYOND THE END OF TIME [Pohl - 1952]
   THE END OF THE WORLD [Wollheim - 1956]
Seeker of the Sphinx.................................................2CB  Spr 1951
   YEAR'S BEST SCIENCE FICTION NOVELS: 1952 [Bleiler & Dikty - 1952]
Silence, Please!....................................................SF #2  Win 1950
   13 GREAT STORIES OF SCIENCE FICTION [Conklin - 1960]
Superiority........................................................F&SF  Aug 1951
   WORLDS OF TOMORROW [Derleth - 1953]
   FANTASIA MATHEMATICA [Fadiman - 1958]
This Earth of Majesty..............................................F&SF  Jul 1955
   THE BEST FROM FANTASY & SCIENCE FICTION: 5th SERIES [Boucher - 1956]
Transience..........................................................Stg  Jul 1949
   LOOKING FORWARD [Lesser - 1953]
Transition —— From Fantasy to Science.....................................
   (From The Making of a Moon; 1957)
   SF: 58 THE YEAR'S GREATEST SF AND FANTASY [Merril - 1958]
Venture to the Moon.................................................F&SF  Dec 1956
   THE BEST FROM FANTASY & SCIENCE FICTION: 7th SERIES [Boucher - 1958]
Walk In the Dark, A.................................................TWS  Aug 1950
   POSSIBLE WORLDS OF SCIENCE FICTION [Conklin - 1951]
Wall of Darkness, The...............................................Sup  Jul 1949
   (Story selected by Eljer Jakobsson)
      EDITOR'S CHOICE IN SCIENCE FICTION [Moskowitz - 1954]

COLE, EVERETT B.   (1)                                    Mag.      Year
    Exile.................................................................ASF   Jan 1954
        THE BEST SCIENCE FICTION STORIES AND NOVELS: 1955 [Dikty - 1955]
COLLADAY, MORRISON   (2)
    Giant In the Earth............................................WS   Apr 1933
        THE BEST OF SCIENCE FICTION [Conklin - 1946]
    Planetoid of Doom, The........................................WS   Dec 1932
        THE BIG BOOK OF SCIENCE FICTION [Conklin - 1950]
COLLIER, JOHN   (7)
    Evening Primrose...............................(From The Touch of Nutmeg; 1943)
        OUT OF THIS WORLD [Fast - 1944]
    Green Thoughts.................................(From Presenting Moonshine; 1941)
        THE POCKET BOOK OF SCIENCE FICTION [Wollheim - 1943]
    Interpretation of a Dream.....................................Nykr     5/5/51
        BEYOND THE BARRIERS OF SPACE AND TIME [Merril - 1954]
    Invisible Dove Dancer of Strathpheen Island, The............................
        (From Presenting Moonshine; 1941)
            INVISIBLE MEN [Davenport - 1960]
    Man Overboard.................................................F&SF   Mar 1960
        THE BEST FROM FANTASY & SCIENCE FICTION: 10th SERIES [Mills - 1961]
    Meeting of Relations .....................................Rpnt — F&SF   Jan 1959
        A DECADE OF FANTASY & SCIENCE FICTION [Mills-1960] Org aprd YR   Dec 1941
    Rope Enough...................................................Nykr   11/18/39
        HUMAN? [Merril - 1954]
CONDIT, TOM   (1)
    w/Katherine MacLean
        Trouble With Treaties.................................ORIGINAL STORY
            STAR SCIENCE FICTION STORIES #5 [Pohl - 1959]
COOPER, EDMUND   (1)
    Tomorrow's Gift...........................................ORIGINAL STORY
        STAR SCIENCE FICTION STORIES #4 [Pohl - 1958]
COPEMAN, BERGER   (2)
    Dawn Attack...............................................ORIGINAL STORY
        ADVENTURES TO COME [Esenwein - 1937]
    Man in the Moon Comes Down, A.............................ORIGINAL STORY
        ADVENTURES TO COME [Esenwein - 1937]
COPPARD, A. E.   (3)
    Adam and Eve and Pinch Me..............(From Adam And Eve And Pinch Me; 1921)
        THE MOONLIGHT TRAVELER [Stern - 1943]
    Gone Away....................................(From Fearful Pleasures; 1946)
        TERROR IN THE MODERN VEIN [Wollheim - 1955]
    Homeless One, The............................(From Fearful Pleasures; 1946)
        TRAVELERS IN TIME [Stern - 1947]
COPPEL, ALFRED   (5)
    Dreamer, The..................................................F&SF   Apr 1952
        THE BEST SCIENCE FICTION STORIES: 1953 [Bleiler & Dikty - 1953]
    Exile, The....................................................ASF   Oct 1952
        STORIES FOR TOMORROW [Sloane - 1954]
    Last Night of Summer.......................................Orb #4   Sep 1954
        THE END OF THE WORLD [Wollheim - 1956]
        PLANET OF DOOM AND OTHER STORIES [Anonymous - 1958]
    Peacemaker, The..............................................If   Jan 1953
        PRIZE SCIENCE FICTION [Wollheim - 1953]
    What Goes Up................................................FB #6   n/d 1950
        SCIENCE AND SORCERY [Ford - 1953]

CORREY, LEE ps (G. Harry Stine)  (1)
  "...And A Star To Steer By..."......................................ASF  Jun 1953
    EVERY BOY'S BOOK OF OUTER SPACE STORIES [Dikty - 1960]
CORWIN, CECIL ps (C. M. Kornbluth)  (1)
  w/ Martin Pearson ps (Donald A. Wollheim)
    Mask of Demeter, The...........................................F&SF  Jan 1953
    PRIZE SCIENCE FICTION [Wollheim - 1953]
COTTRELL, C. L.  (1)
  Danger! Child At Large.....................................ORIGINAL STORY
    STAR SCIENCE FICTION STORIES #6 [Pohl - 1959]
COUPLING, J. J. ps (John R. Pierce)  (2)    See John R. Pierce
  Mr. Kincaid's Pests...........................................F&SF  Aug 1953
    BEYOND THE BARRIERS OF SPACE AND TIME [Merril - 1954]
  Period Piece..................................................ASF  Nov 1948
    THE BEST SCIENCE FICTION STORIES: 1949 [Bleiler & Dikty - 1949]
COURTNEY, ROBERT  (1)
  Rover I Will Be, A.........................................................
    EVERY BOY'S BOOK OF OUTER SPACE STORIES [Dikty - 1960]
COWIE, GEORGE R.  (1)
  Demobilization..............................................Vtx  n/d 1947
    SCIENCE AND SORCERY [Ford - 1953]
COX, ARTHUR J.  (1)
  Blight, The...............................................ORIGINAL STORY
    TIME TO COME [Derleth - 1954]
COX, IRVING (E., JR.)  (3)
  Hole In the Sky...........................................ORIGINAL STORY
    TIME TO COME [Derleth - 1954]
  Like Gods They Came...........................................AvR  Jan 1953
    SPACE, SPACE, SPACE [Sloane - 1953]
  No More the Stars...........................................Orb #4  Sep 1954
    THE SANDS OF MARS AND OTHER STORIES [Anonymous - 1958]
CRANE, ROBERT  (1)
  Purple Fields, The........................................ORIGINAL STORY
    STAR SCIENCE FICTION STORIES #2 [Pohl - 1953]
CROSS, JOHN KIER  (1)
  Glass Eye, The.................................(From The Other Passenger; 1946)
    TIMELESS STORIES FOR TODAY AND TOMORROW [Bradbury - 1952]
CROSS, POLTON ps (John Russell Fearn)  (1) (See John Russell Fearn)
  Wings Across the Cosmos.......................................TWS  Jun 1938
    A TREASURY OF SCIENCE FICTION [Conklin - 1948]
CROSSEN, KENDALL FOSTER  (5)
  Ambassadors From Venus, The....................................PS  Mar 1951
    BEACHHEADS IN SPACE [Derleth - 1954]
  Assignment In Aldebaran.......................................TWS  Feb 1953
    THE YEAR'S BEST SCIENCE FICTION NOVELS: 1954 [Bleiler & Dikty - 1954]
  Closed Door, The.............................................Amz  Sep 1953
    SPACE POLICE [Norton - 1956]
  Restricted Clientele.........................................TWS  Feb 1951
    ADVENTURES IN TOMORROW [Crossen - 1951]
  Things of Distinction........................................Stg  Mar 1952
    FUTURE TENSE [Crossen - 1953]
CUMMINGS, RAY  (2)
  Girl in the Golden Atom, The...................................ASM  3/15/19
    THE GIANT ANTHOLOGY OF SCIENCE FICTION [Margulies & Friend - 1954]
  Gravity Professor, The.......................................AASW  5/7/21
    EVERY BOY'S BOOK OF SCIENCE FICTION [Wollheim - 1951]
CURTIS, BETSY  (1)
  Peculiar People, A...........................................F&SF  Aug 1951
    THE BEST SCIENCE FICTION STORIES: 1952 [Bleiler & Dikty - 1952]
CUTHBERT, CHESTER D.  (1)
  Sublime Virgil, The...........................................WS  Feb 1934
    EDITOR'S CHOICE IN SCI. FIC. [Moskowitz-1954] (Selected by Hugo Gernsback)

# D

DAHL, ROALD (1)                                              Mag.      Year
  Sound Machine, The......................................Nykr    9/17/49
     TIMELESS STORIES FOR TODAY AND TOMORROW [Bradbury - 1952]
DALEY, JOHN BERNARD (1)
  Man Who Liked Lions, The................................Inf   Oct 1956
     SF: 57 THE YEAR'S GREATEST SF AND FANTASY [Merril - 1957]
DANCEY, MAX (1)
  w/ G. Gordon Dewey
    Collectors, The......................................Amz   Jul 1953
      THE BEST SCIENCE FICTION STORIES: 1954 [Bleiler & Dikty - 1954]
DAVIDSON, AVRAM (15)
  Apres Nous.............................................F&SF   Mar 1960
     THE BEST FROM FANTASY & SCIENCE FICTION: 10th SERIES [Mills - 1961]
  Bounty Hunter, The.....................................FU    Mar 1958
     THE FANTASTIC UNIVERSE OMNIBUS [Santesson - 1960]
  Certificate, The.......................................F&SF   Mar 1959
     A DECADE OF FANTASY & SCIENCE FICTION [Mills - 1960]
  Dagon..................................................F&SF   Oct 1959
     THE BEST FROM FANTASY & SCIENCE FICTION: 9th SERIES [Mills - 1960]
  Golem, The.............................................F&SF   Mar 1955
     THE BEST FROM FANTASY & SCIENCE FICTION: 5th SERIES [Boucher - 1956]
     SF: THE YEAR'S GREATEST SCIENCE FICTION AND FANTASY [Merril - 1956]
  Grantha Sighting, The..................................F&SF   Apr 1958
     THE BEST FROM FANTASY & SCIENCE FICTION: 8th SERIES [Boucher - 1959]
  Help! I Am Dr. Morris Goldpepper.......................Glxy   Jul 1957
     THE THIRD GALAXY READER OF SCIENCE FICTION [Gold - 1958]
  King's Evil............................................F&SF   Oct 1956
     THE BEST FROM FANTASY & SCIENCE FICTION: 6th SERIES [Boucher - 1957]
  Mr. Stilwell's Stage...................................F&SF   Sep 1957
     THE BEST FROM FANTASY & SCIENCE FICTION: 7th SERIES [Boucher - 1958]
  My Boy Friend's Name is Jello..........................F&SF   Jul 1954
     THE BEST FROM FANTASY & SCIENCE FICTION: 4th SERIES [Boucher - 1955]
  No Fire Burns..........................................Plby   Jul 1959
     FIFTH ANNUAL OF THE YEAR'S BEST SF [Merril - 1960]
  Now Let Us Sleep......................................Ven   Sep 1957
     SF: 58 THE YEAR'S GREATEST SF & FANTASY [Merril - 1958]
  Or All the Seas With Oysters...........................Glxy   May 1958
     THE FOURTH GALAXY READER OF SCIENCE FICTION [Gold - 1959]
     SF: 59 THE YEAR'S GREATEST SF AND FANTASY [Merril - 1959]
  Or The Grasses Grow....................................F&SF   Nov 1958
     SCIENCE FICTION SHOWCASE [M. Kornbluth - 1959]
  Take Wooden Indians....................................Glxy   Jun 1959
     THE FIFTH GALAXY READER [Gold - 1961]
DAVIS, CHAN (3)
  Adrift On the Policy Level.............................ORIGINAL STORY
     STAR SCIENCE FICTION STORIES #5 [Pohl - 1959]
  Letter to Ellen........................................ASF   May 1946
     SCIENCE FICTION THINKING MACHINES [Conklin - 1954]
  Nightmare, The.........................................ASF   May 1946
     A TREASURY OF SCIENCE FICTION [Conklin - 1948]

DAVIS, DOROTHY SALISBURY  (1)                                            Mag.    Year
  Muted Horn, The...........................................................FU  May 1957
      THE FANTASTIC UNIVERSE OMNIBUS [Santesson - 1960]
DE CAMP, L. SPRAGUE  (20)
  Blue Giraffe, The........................................................ASF  Aug 1949
      ADVENTURES IN TIME AND SPACE [Healy & McComas - 1946]
      WORLD OF WONDER [Pratt - 1951]
      ESCALES DANS L'INFINI [Gallet - 1954]
  Employment...............................................................ASF  May 1949
      (Originally appeared under psuedonym Lyman R. Lyon)
      IMAGINATION UNLIMITED [Bleiler & Dikty - 1952]
  Exalted, The............................................................ASF  Nov 1940
      THE ASTOUNDING SCIENCE FICTION ANTHOLOGY [J. W. Campbell - 1952]
  Git Along!..............................................................ASF  Aug 1950
      THE OUTER REACHES [Derleth - 1951]
  Gnarly Man, The.........................................................Unk  Jun 1939
      HUMAN? [Merril - 1951]
  Hibited Man.............................................................TWS  Oct 1949
      MY BEST SCIENCE FICTION STORY [Margulies & Friend - 1949]
  Hyperpilosity...........................................................ASF  Apr 1938
      THE OMNIBUS OF SCIENCE FICTION [Conklin - 1952]
  Judgement Day...........................................................ASF  Aug 1955
      THE BEST SCIENCE FICTION STORIES AND NOVELS: 1956 [Dikty - 1956]
  Lament By A Maker.................(verse)................................F&SF  Jan 1955
      THE BEST FROM FANTASY & SCIENCE FICTION: 5th SERIES [Boucher - 1956]
  Language For Time Travelers.............................................ASF  Jul 1938
      COMING ATTRACTIONS [Greenberg - 1957]
  Living Fossil...........................................................ASF  Feb 1939
      A TREASURY OF SCIENCE FICTION [Conklin - 1948]
  Nothing In the Rules....................................................Unk  Jul 1939
      FROM UNKNOWN WORLDS [J. W. Campbell - 1948]
  Ordeal of Professor Klein, The..........................................SFA  Oct 1952
      BEACHHEADS IN SPACE [Derleth - 1954]
  Soaring Statue, The.........................................ORIGINAL STORY
      TOMORROW'S UNIVERSE [H. J. Campbell - 1954]
  Summer Wear.............................................................Stg  May 1950
      THE BEST SCIENCE FICTION STORIES: 1951 [Bleiler & Dikty - 1951]
  Thing of Custom, A......................................................FU  Jan 1957
      THE FANTASTIC UNIVERSE OMNIBUS [Santesson - 1960]
  w/ Fletcher Pratt
    Black Ball, The......................................................F&SF  Oct 1952
      THE BEST FROM FANTASY & SCIENCE FICTION: 2nd SERIES
               [Boucher & McComas - 1953]
    Gavagan's Bar........................................................F&SF  Spr 1950
      THE BEST FROM FANTASY & SCIENCE FICTION [Boucher & McComas - 1952]
    Untimely Toper, The..................................................F&SF  Jul 1953
      THE BEST FROM FANTASY & SCIENCE FICTION: 3rd SERIES
               [Boucher & McComas - 1954]
    Weissenbroch Spectacles, The.........................................F&SF  Nov 1954
      INVISIBLE MEN [Davenport - 1960]
DE COURCY, JOHN & DOROTHY  (1)
  Rat Race................................................................Stg  Sep 1948
      THE BIG BOOK OF SCIENCE FICTION [Conklin - 1950]
DE LA MARE, WALTER  (1)
  All Hallows................................................(From The Connoisseur; 1926)
      THE MOONLIGHT TRAVELER [Stern - 1943]

(217)

DEAN, JOE E. (I)                                                          Mag.    Year
   w/ Jerome Bixby
      Share Alike..................................................BFF   Jul 1953
            GALAXY OF GHOULS [Merril - 1955]
            ZACHERLY'S MIDNIGHT SNACKS [Zacherly - 1960]
DEE, ROGER ps (Roger D. Aycock)  (3)
   Obligation, The.................................................Stg   Sep 1952
            ADVENTURES ON OTHER PLANETS [Wollheim - 1955]
   Problem On Balak...............................................Glxy   Sep 1953
            THE SECOND GALAXY READER OF SCIENCE FICTION [Gold - 1954]
   Unwelcome Tenant................................................PS    Sum 1950
            BEYOND HUMAN KEN [Merril - 1952]
DEFOE, DANIEL  (I)
   Friendly Demon, The.........................................Rpnt — F&SF  Feb 1951
            (Originally printed by J. Roberts: London; 1726)
            THE BEST FROM FANTASY & SCIENCE FICTION [Boucher & McComas - 1952]
DeFORD, MIRIAM ALLEN  (5)
   Eel, The.......................................................Glxy   Apr 1958
            THE FIFTH GALAXY READER [Gold - 1961]
   Long Echo, The.......................................ORIGINAL STORY
            STAR SCIENCE FICTION STORIES #4 [Pohl - 1958]
   Margenes, The....................................................If   Feb 1956
            THE FIRST WORLD OF IF [Quinn & Wulff - 1957]
   Press Conference.....................................ORIGINAL STORY
            STAR SCIENCE FICTION STORIES #6 [Pohl - 1959]
   Throwback......................................................Stg    Oct 1952
            FUTURE TENSE [Crossen - 1953]
DEKKER, THOMAS  (I)
   Circle and the Square, The....................(verse)..................
            (From The Honest Whore, Part II Act I, Scene 3; 1650)
            FANTASIA MATHEMATICA [Fadiman - 1958]
DEL REY, LESTER  (25)      (See listing Philip St. John)
   Alien.................................................ORIGINAL STORY
            STAR SCIENCE FICTION STORIES #3 [Pohl - 1954]
   ...And It Comes Out Here.......................................Glxy   Feb 1951
            SCIENCE FICTION ADVENTURES IN DIMENSION [Conklin - 1953]
   Dark Mission...................................................ASF    Sep 1942
            ADVENTURES IN TIME AND SPACE [Healy & McComas - 1946]
   Day Is Done....................................................ASF    May 1939
            OPERATION FUTURE [Conklin - 1955]
   Dead Ringer....................................................Glxy   Nov 1956
            THE THIRD GALAXY READER OF SCIENCE FICTION [Gold - 1958]
   For I Am A Jealous People!...........................ORIGINAL STORY
            STAR SHORT NOVELS [Pohl - 1954]
   Helen O'Loy....................................................ASF    Dec 1938
            BEYOND HUMAN KEN [Merril - 1952]
            ASSIGNMENT IN TOMORROW [Pohl - 1954]
   Helping Hand.........................................ORIGINAL STORY
            STAR SCIENCE FICTION STORIES #4 [Pohl - 1958]
   Idealist.............................................ORIGINAL STORY
            STAR SCIENCE FICTION STORIES [Pohl - 1953]
   Instinct.......................................................ASF    Jan 1952
            THE OMNIBUS OF SCIENCE FICTION [Conklin - 1952]
   Into Thy Hands.................................................ASF    Aug 1945
            THE ROBOT AND THE MAN [Greenberg - 1953]
            LOOKING FORWARD [Lesser - 1953]

DEL REY, LESTER [Cont'd]          Mag.    Year
  Kindness.....................................................ASF   Oct 1944
     THE YEAR AFTER TOMORROW [Del Rey, Matschat & Carmer - 1952]
  Luck Of Ignatz, The..........................................ASF   Aug 1939
     THE YEAR AFTER TOMORROW [Del Rey, Matschat & Carmer - 1952]
     THE HIDDEN PLANET [Wollheim - 1959]
  Monster, The.................................................Arg   Jun 1951
     TOMORROW, THE STARS [Heinlein - 1952]
  Nerves.......................................................ASF   Sep 1942
     ADVENTURES IN TIME AND SPACE [Healy & McComas - 1946]
  Old Order, The...............................................MSF   Feb 1951
     (Originally appeared under title The New Gods Lead)
       SHADOW OF TOMORROW [Pohl - 1953]
  Over The Top.................................................ASF   Nov 1949
     THE ASTOUNDING SCIENCE FICTION ANTHOLOGY [J. W. Campbell - 1952]
  Pipes of Pan, The............................................Unk   May 1940
     THE OTHER WORLDS [Stong - 1941]
  Pound of Cure, A....................................ORIGINAL STORY
     STAR SCIENCE FICTION STORIES #2 [Pohl - 1953]
  Psalm......................(verse).............................FU   Mar 1960
     SIXTH ANNUAL OF THE YEAR'S BEST SF [Merril - 1961]
  Still Waters, The.........................................NW #78   Dec 1958
     OUT OF THIS WORLD 2 [Williams-Ellis & Owen - 1961]
  Though Dreamers Die..........................................ASF   Feb 1944
     THE ROBOT AND THE MAN [Greenberg - 1953]
  Wind Between the Worlds, The................................Glxy   Mar 1951
     ADVENTURES IN THE FAR FUTURE [Wollheim - 1954]
  Wings of Night, The..........................................ASF   Mar 1942
     THE BIG BOOK OF SCIENCE FICTION [Conklin - 1950]
  "Year's Draw Nigh, The"......................................ASF   Oct 1951
     BEACHHEADS IN SPACE [Derleth - 1954]

DELL, DUDLEY ps (H. L. Gold (1)
  Biography Project, The......................................Glxy   Sep 1951
     THE GALAXY READER OF SCIENCE FICTION [Gold - 1952]

DEMING, RICHARD (1)
  Shape of Things fo Come, The................................F&SF   Oct 1951
     A TREASURY OF GREAT SCIENCE FICTION [Boucher - 1959]

DERLETH, AUGUST (8)
  Century Jumper.............................................Orb #2   n/d 1954
     (Originally appeared under title A Traveler In Time)
       BEYOND THE STARS AND OTHER STORIES [Anonymous - 1958]
  McIlvaine's Star..............................................If   Jul 1952
     WORLDS OF TOMORROW [Derleth   1953]
     PRIZE SCIENCE FICTION [Wollheim - 1953]
  Pannelled Room, The...........................................WM   Sep 1933
     THE OTHER WORLDS [Stong - 1941]
  Thinkers, Mark VII.........................................Orb #4   Sep 1954
     (Originally appeared under title The Thinker and the Thought)
       THE SANDS OF MARS AND OTHER STORIES [Anonymous - 1958]
  "Who Shall I Say Is Calling?"................................F&SF   Aug 1952
     HUMAN? [Merril - 1954]
  w/ Mack Reynolds
    Adventure of the Ball of Nostradamus, The.................F&SF   Jul 1955
       THE SCIENCE FICTIONAL SHERLOCK HOLMES [Peterson - 1960]
    Adventure of the Snitch In Time, The......................F&SF   Jul 1953
       THE SCIENCE FICTIONAL SHERLOCK HOLMES [Peterson - 1960]
  w/ Mack Schorer
    Return of Andrew Bentley, The..............................WT   Sep 1933
       THE OTHER WORLDS [Stong - 1941]

DEUTSCH, A. J.   (1)
    Subway Named Mobius, A.........................................ASF    Dec '950
        THE OMNIBUS OF SCIENCE FICTION [Conklin - 1952]
        FANTASIA MATHEMATICA [Fadiman - 1958]
        BEST SF FOUR SCIENCE FICTION STORIES [Crispin - 1961]

DEUTSCH, R. H.   (1)
    Watchers, The.................................................ORIGINAL STORY
        SCIENCE AND SORCERY [Ford - 1953]

DEWEESE, EUGENE   (1)
    Quest of the Veil............................................ORIGINAL STORY
        SHANADU [Briney - 1953]

DEWEY, G. GORDON   (2)
    Tooth, The...................................................F&SF    Aug 1952
        THE BEST FROM FANTASY & SCIENCE FICTION: 2nd SER [Boucher & McComas-1953]
    w/ Max Dancey
    Collectors, The..............................................Amz    Jul 1953
        THE BEST SCIENCE FICTION STORIES: 1954 [Bleiler & Dikty - 1954]

DICK, PHILIP K.   (11)
    Adjustment Team..............................................Orb #4   Sep 1954
        THE SANDS OF MARS AND OTHER STORIES [Anonymous - 1958]
    Captive Market...............................................If    Apr 1955
        THE FIRST WORLD OF IF [Quinn & Wulff - 1957]
    Expendable...................................................F&SF    Jun 1955
        SCIENCE FICTION SHOWCASE [M. Kornbluth - 1959]
    Father-Thing, The............................................F&SF    Dec 1954
        A TREASURY OF GREAT SCIENCE FICTION [Boucher - 1959]
    Foster, You're Dead..........................................ORIGINAL STORY
        STAR SCIENCE FICTION STORIES #3 [Pohl - 1953]
    Imposter.....................................................Glxy    Jun 1953
        SCIENCE FICTION TERROR TALES [Conklin - 1955]
        BEST SF TWO SCIENCE FICTION STORIES [Crispin - 1956]
        THE END OF THE WORLD [Wollheim - 1956]
    Jon's World..................................................ORIGINAL STORY
        TIME TO COME [Derleth - 1954]
    Last of the Masters, The.....................................Orb #5   Nov 1954
        SPACE STATION 42 AND OTHER STORIES [Anonymous - 1958]
    Mold of Yancy, The...........................................If    Jul 1955
        THE SECOND WORLD OF IF [Quinn & Wulff - 1958]
    Retreat From Rigel...........................................Orb #2   n/d 1954
        (Originally appeared under title Tony and the Beetles)
        PLANET OF DOOM AND OTHER STORIES [Anonymous - 1958]
    Second Variety...............................................Spc    May 1953
        THE YEAR'S BEST SCIENCE FICTION NOVELS: 1954 [Bleiler & Dikty - 1954]

DICKENS, CHARLES   (1)
    Rat That Could Speak, The.........................Rpnt — F&SF    Aug 1951
        (Originally appeared in All The Year Around — Volume III,
        Nurse's Stories; September 8, 1860)
        THE BEST FROM FANTASY & SCIENCE FICTION [Boucher & McComas - 1952]

DICKSON, GORDON R.   (9)
    Ballard of the Shoshonu.............(song).....................ORIGINAL STORY
        SIXTH ANNUAL OF THE YEAR'S BEST SF [Merril - 1961]
    Black Charlie................................................Glxy    Apr 1954
        THE FIFTH GALAXY READER [Gold - 1961]

DICKSON, GORDON R. [Cont'd]                                          Mag.    Year
   Dreamsman, The.................................................ORIGINAL STORY
      STAR SCIENCE FICTION STORIES #6 [Pohl - 1959]
      FIFTH ANNUAL OF THE YEAR'S BEST SF [Merril - 1960]
   Half A Hoka — Poul Anderson..................(From The Program Booklet of the
      17th World Science Fiction Convention; 1959)
      THE SCIENCE FICTIONAL SHERLOCK HOLMES [Peterson - 1960]
   Listen.........................................................F&SF    Aug 1952
      PRIZE SCIENCE FICTION [Wollheim - 1953]
   Lulugomeena....................................................Glxy    Jan 1954
      LOOKING FORWARD [Lesser - 1953]
   Odd Ones, The..................................................If      Feb 1955
      THE SECOND WORLD OF IF [Quinn & Wulff - 1958]
   Steel Brother..................................................ASF     Feb 1952
      SPACE SERVICE [Norton - 1953]
   w/ Poul Anderson
      Trespass!...................................................FSQ     Spr 1950
         THE BEST SCIENCE FICTION STORIES: 1951 [Bleiler & Dikty - 1951]
DIFFIN, CHARLES W.  (1)
   Spawn of the Stars............................................Ast     Feb 1930
      THE BEST OF SCIENCE FICTION [Conklin - 1946]
DIGHTON, RALPH  (1)
   Sierra Sam....................................................AP      1/10/60
      FIFTH ANNUAL OF THE YEAR'S BEST SF [Merril - 1960]
DINGLE, HERBERT  (1)
   He Thought He Saw Electrons Swift........(verse)..........(No data available)
      FANTASIA MATHEMATICA [Fadiman - 1958]
DOAR, GRAHAM  (2)
   Outer Limit, The..............................................SEP     12/24/49
      THE BIG BOOK OF SCIENCE FICTION [Conklin - 1950]
   Who Knows His Brother.........................................Stg     Feb 1952
      HUMAN? [Merril - 1954]
DONOVAN, FRANCIS  (1)
   Short Life, The...............................................ASF     Oct 1955
      BEST SF FOUR SCIENCE FICTION STORIES [Crispin - 1961]
DOYLE, ARTHUR CONAN  (5)
   Disintergration Machine, The......(From The Maracot Deep & Other Stories; 1929)
      JOURNEYS IN SCIENCE FICTION [Loughlin & Popp - 1961]
   Great Keinplatz Experiment, The...(Org published by Rand McNally & Co.;  1895)
      THE BEST OF SCIENCE FICTION [Conklin - 1946]
   Maracot Deep, The................(From The Maracot Deep & Other Stories; 1929)
      THE TREASURY OF SCIENCE FICTION CLASSICS [Kuebler - 1955]
   Race With A Dinosaur, A..............................(From The Lost World; 1912)
      SCIENCE IN FICTION [A.E.M. & J.C. Bayliss - 1957]
   Silver Mirror, The........................(From Tales of Long Ago; 1925)
      TRAVELERS IN TIME [Stern - 1947]
DRAKE, LEAH BODINE  (1)
   Woods Grow Darker, The........................................F&SF    Nov 1955
      THE BEST FROM FANTASY & SCIENCE FICTION: 6th SERIES [Boucher - 1957]
DRESSLER, DR. DANIEL  (1)
   White Army, The...............................................Amz     Sep 1929
      EVERY BOY'S BOOK OF SCIENCE FICTION [Wollheim - 1951]
      STORIES OF SCIENTIFIC IMAGINATION [Gallant - 1954]

DRISCOLL, DENNIS (1)
                           Mag.  Year
  Going Up!....(Condensed from article entitled "Space Travel")....BLM May 1957
     SF: 58 THE YEAR'S GREATEST SF & FANTASY [Merril - 1958]
DRUSSAI, KIRK & GAREN (1)
  Twilight Years, The.............................................If Jun 1955
     THE FIRST WORLD OF IF [Quinn & Wulff - 1957]
DRURY, ALLEN (1)
  Something.....................................................F&SF Oct 1960
     THE BEST FROM FANTASY & SCIENCE FICTION: 10th SERIES [Mills - 1961]
DRYFOOS, DAVE (2)
  Bridge Crossing.............................................Glxy May 1951
     BEYOND THE END OF TIME [Pohl - 1952]
  Journey Work...................................................If Jan 1955
     THE FIRST WORLD OF IF [Quinn & Wulff - 1957]
DUANE, ANDREW ps (Robert C. Briney) (1)
  w/ Brian J. McNaughton
  Black Tower, The.........................................ORIGINAL STORY
     SHANADU [Briney - 1953]
DUANE, TOBY ps (W. Paul Ganley) (1)
  Fire-Born, The..........................................ORIGINAL STORY
     SHANADU [Briney - 1953]
DUNSANY, LORD (5)
  Club Secretary........................(From Jorkens Remembers Africa; 1934)
     OUT OF THIS WORLD [Fast - 1944]
  Mars On the Ether.........................................Cnt Sep 1937
     STRANGE PORTS OF CALL [Derleth - 1948]
  Misadventure.............................................F&SF Oct 1954
     THE BEST FROM FANTASY & SCIENCE FICTION: 4th SERIES [Boucher - 1955]
  Our Distant Cousins.........(From The Travel Tales of Mr. Joseph Jorkens; 1931)
     THE MOONLIGHT TRAVELER [Stern - 1943]
  Strange Drug of Dr. Caber, The........(From The Fourth Book of Jorkens; 1948)
     THE OTHER SIDE OF THE MOON [Derleth - 1949]
DYALHIS, NICTZIN (1)
  When the Green Star Waned.................................WT Apr 1925
     BEYOND TIME AND SPACE [Derleth - 1950]
DYE, CHARLES (1)
  Syndrone Johnny...........................................Glxy Jul 1951
     THE GALAXY READER OF SCIENCE FICTION [Gold - 1952]

**E**

EARL, STEPHEN (1)
  Walkabout...........................................London Observer Prize Stor
     A. D. 2500 [Wilson - 1955]
EDDINGTON, SIR ARTHUR (2)
  There Once Was A Breathy Baboon.........(verse)............(No data available
     FANTASIA MATHEMATICA [Fadiman - 1958]

EDDINGTON, SIR ARTHUR [Cont'd]                                        Mag.    Year
   ∞.........................................(From New Pathways of Science; 1935)
      FANTASIA MATHEMATICA [Fadiman - 1958]
EDMONDSON, G. C.  (2)
   Rescue..................................................................F&SF  Jun 1957
      THE BEST FROM FANTASY & SCIENCE FICTION: 7th SERIES [Boucher - 1958]
   Technological Retreat..................................................F&SF  May 1956
      13 GREAT STORIES OF SCIENCE FICTION [Conklin - 1960]
EDWARDS, DOLTON  (1)
   Meihem In Ce Klasrum...................................................ASF  Sep 1946
      THE ASTOUNDING SCIENCE FICTION ANTHOLOGY [J. W. Campbell - 1952]
EDWARDS, KELLY  (1)
   Counterspy.............................................................ASF  Dec 1953
      BEST SF THREE SCIENCE FICTION STORIES [Crispin - 1958]
EISNER, SIMON  (1)
   Luckiest Man In Denv...................................................Glxy  Jun 1952
      SHADOW OF TOMORROW [Pohl - 1953]
ELAM, RICHARD M., JR.  (2)
   Adventures On Mars.....................................................Stp  Dec 1952
      SCIENCE FICTION AND READER'S GUIDE [Barrows - 1954]
   What Time Is It?..................(From Teen-Age Science Fiction Stories; 1952)
      SCIENCE FICTION AND READER'S GUIDE [Barrows - 1954]
ELLANBY, BOYD ps (William C. & Lyle G. Boyd)  (1)
   Category Phoenix.......................................................Glxy  May 1952
      YEAR'S BEST SCIENCE FICTION NOVELS: 1953 [Bleiler & Dikty - 1953]
ELLIOT, BRUCE  (5)
   Battle of the S...S, The...............................................ORIGINAL STORY
      FUTURE TENSE [Crossen - 1953]
   Devil Was Sick, The....................................................F&SF  Apr 1951
      ADVENTURES IN TOMORROW [Crossen - 1951]
   Fearsome Fable.........................................................F&SF  Feb 1951
      THE BEST FROM FANTASY & SCIENCE FICTION [Boucher & McComas - 1952]
      FANTASIA MATHEMATICA [Fadiman - 1958]
   Last Magician, The.....................................................F&SF  Jan 1953
      FANTASIA MATHEMATICA [Fadiman - 1958]
   Wolves Don't Cry.......................................................F&SF  Apr 1954
      GALAXY OF GHOULS [Merril - 1955]
ELLIOT, ROSE BEDRICK  (1)
   Baby Killers...........................................................ORIGINAL STORY
      FUTURE TENSE [Crossen - 1953]
ELLIOTT, GEORGE P.  (2)
   Invasion of the Planet of Love.........................................F&SF  Jan 1959
      THE BEST FROM FANTASY & SCIENCE FICTION: 9th SERIES [Mills - 1960]
   Sandra.................................................................Epch  Fal 1953
      A TREASURY OF GREAT SCIENCE FICTION [Boucher - 1959]
ELLIOTT, H. CHANDLER  (1)
   Inanimate Objection....................................................Glxy  Feb 1954
      SPECTRUM [Amis & Conquest - 1961]
ELLISON, HARLAN  (1)
   In Lonely Hands........................................................FU  Jan 1959
      THE FANTASTIC UNIVERSE OMNIBUS [Santesson - 1960]
EMMETT, ELIZABETH  (1)
   Enchantment............................................................SEP  10/1/60
      SIXTH ANNUAL OF THE YEAR'S BEST SF [Merril - 1961]

EMSHWILLER, CAROL  (3)                                              Mag.    Year
    Day at the Beach.................................................F&SF  Aug 1959
        FIFTH ANNUAL OF THE YEAR'S BEST SF [Merril - 1960]
    Hunting Machine.................................................SFS   May 1957
        THE BEST SCIENCE FICTION STORIES AND NOVELS: 9th SERIES [Dikty - 1958]
    Pelt............................................................F&SF  Aug 1959
        SF: 59 THE YEAR'S GREATEST SF AND FANTASY [Merril - 1959]
ENGLAND, GEORGE ALLAN  (1)
    Thing From Outside, The........................................S&I   Apr 1923
        STRANGE PORTS OF CALL [Derleth - 1948]
ERNST, PAUL  (5)
    Escape.........................................................WT    Jul 1938
        THE OTHER WORLDS [Stong - 1941]
    Microscopic Giants, The........................................TWS   Oct 1936
        FROM OFF THIS WORLD [Margulies & Friend - 1949]
        SCIENCE FICTION TERROR TALES [Conklin - 1955]
    "Nothing Happens On the Moon"..................................ASF   Feb 1939
        THE OMNIBUS OF SCIENCE FICTION [Conklin - 1952]
    Thing in the Pond, The.........................................Ast   Jun 1934
        MY BEST SCIENCE FICTION STORY [Margulies & Friend - 1949]
    32nd Of May, The...............................................Ast   Apr 1935
        THE BEST OF SCIENCE FICTION [Conklin - 1946]
ESHBACH, L. A.  (1)
    Man With the Hour Glass, The...................................MT    May 1934
        THE GARDEN OF FEAR AND OTHER STORIES [Crawford - 1945]
EUSTIS, HELEN  (1)
    Mr. Death and the Redheaded Woman..............................SEP   2/11/50
        (Originally appeared under title The Rider on the Pale Horse)
        TIMELESS STORIES FOR TODAY AND TOMORROW [Bradbury - 1952]
EVANS, DEAN  (1)
    Not a Creature Was Stirring....................................Glxy  Dec 1951
        SHADOW OF TOMORROW [Pohl - 1953]
EVANS, DON  (1)
    Summons, The...................................................Unk   Jun 1939
        FROM UNKNOWN WORLDS [J. W. Campbell - 1948]
EVANS, E. EVERETT  (1)
    Shed, The......................................................AvR   Jan 1953
        STORIES FOR TOMORROW [Sloane - 1954]
        ZACHERLY'S VULTURE STEW [Zacherly - 1960]
EVERETT, WALTER G.  (1)
    Woman in Grey, The.............................................WT    Jun 1931
        THE OTHER WORLDS [Stong - 1941]
EVANS, I. O.  (1)  (Translator)
    Gil Bralter by Jules Verne..........................(Translated From French
        (From Le Chemin De France; 1887)
                                                        Rpnt - F&SF  Jul 1958
        THE BEST FROM FANTASY & SCIENCE FICTION: 8th SERIES [Boucher - 1959]

# F

FARLEY, RALPH MILNE ps (Roger Sherman Hoar)  (2)  Mag.  Year
  House of Ecstasy, The.....................................................WT  Apr 1938
    THE OTHER WORLDS [Stong - 1941]
  Liquid Life................................................................TWS  Oct 1936
    THE BEST OF SCIENCE FICTION [Conklin - 1946]
    GREAT STORIES OF SCIENCE FICTION [Leinster - 1951]
FAIRMAN, PAUL W.  (1)
  Brother Beyond the Void....................................................FA  Mar 1952
    WORLDS OF TOMORROW [Derleth - 1953]
FARMER, PHILIP JOSE  (2)
  Attitudes..................................................................F&SF  Oct 1953
    THE BEST FROM FANTASY & SCIENCE FICTION: 3rd SERIES [Boucher & McComas-
    1954]
  Mother.....................................................................TWS  Apr 1953
    ASSIGNMENT IN TOMORROW [Pohl - 1954]
FARNSWORTH, MONA  (1)
  All Roads.......................  ..........................................Unk  Aug 1940
    EDITOR'S CHOICE IN SCIENCE FICTION [Moskowitz - 1954]
      (Story selected by John W. Campbell, Jr.)
FAST, HOWARD  (2)
  Large Ant, The.............................................................FU  Feb 1960
    SIXTH ANNUAL OF THE YEAR'S BEST SF [Merril - 1961]
  Martian Shop, The..........................................................F&SF  Nov 1959
    A DECADE OF FANTASY & SCIENCE FICTION [Mills - 1960]
FAST, JULIUS  (1)
  My Friend Merton...........................................................ORIGINAL STORY
    OUT OF THIS WORLD [Fast - 1944]
FEARN, JOHN RUSSELL  (1)  See also pseudonym Polton Cross)
  Wanderer of Time...........................................................Stg  Sum 1934
    (Originally appeared under psuedonym Polton Cross)
    MY BEST SCIENCE FICTION STORY [Margulies & Friend - 1949]
FENNEL, ERIK  (1)
  Doughnut Jockey............................................................BB  May 1948
    THE BEST SCIENCE FICTION STORIES: 1949 [Bleiler & Dikty - 1949]
FENTON, FRANK  (2)
  Chicken Or the Egghead, The................................................ORIGINAL STORY
    9 TALES OF SPACE AND TIME [Healy - 1954]
  w/ Joseph Petracca
    Tolliver's Travels.....................................................ORIGINAL STORY
      NEW TALES OF SPACE AND TIME [Healy - 1951]
FERGUSON, BIRD  (1)
  Interview.....................(verse)........................................F&SF  Dec 1955
    THE BEST FROM FANTASY & SCIENCE FICTION: 6th SERIES [Boucher - 1957]
FESSIER, MICHAEL  (2)
  Fascinating Stranger, The..................................................SEP  5/22/48
    GREAT STORIES OF SCIENCE FICTION [Leinster - 1951]

FESSIER, MICHAEL [Cont'd]                                    Mag.   Year
    Man In the Black Hat, The..........................................Esq  Feb 1934
        THE OTHER WORLDS [Stong - 1941]
FFOLKES, MICHAEL (1)
    Obvious!....................(cartoon)..........................Pch   10/3/60
        (Org aprd under title Obvious To the Meaningest Intelligence)
        SIXTH ANNUAL OF THE YEAR'S BEST SF [Merril - 1961]
FINK, DAVID HAROLD M. D.  (1)
    Compound 3.......................................................ORIGINAL STORY
        9 TALES OF SPACE AND TIME [Healy - 1954]
FINNEY, JACK  (6)
    I'm Scared......................................................Col   9/15/51
        TOMORROW, THE STARS [Heinlein - 1952]
    Of Missing Persons..............................................GH  Mar 1955
        SF: THE YEAR'S GREATEST SCIENCE FICTION AND FANTASY [Merril - 1956]
    Other Wife, The................................................SEP  1/30/60
        FIFTH ANNUAL OF THE YEAR'S BEST SF [Merril - 1960]
    Quit Zoomin' Those Hands Through The Air........................Col   8/4/51
        OPERATION FUTURE [Conklin - 1955]
        JOURNEYS IN SCIENCE FICTION [Loughlin & Popp - 1961]
    Such Interesting Neighbors......................................Col   1/6/51
        BEYOND THE END OF TIME [Pohl - 1952]
    Third Level, The.........................................Rprt — F&SF  Oct 1952
        THE BEST FROM FANTASY & SCI. FIC.: 2nd SER [Boucher & McComas - 1953]
                                                   Org aprd in Col   10/7/50

FISHER, PHILIP M., JR.  (1)
    Strange Case of Lemuel Jenkins, The.............................Als   7/26/19
        TERROR IN THE MODERN VEIN [Wollheim - 1955]
FITZPATRICK, E. D.  (1)
    Shadow — Lay, The...............................London Observer Prize Story
        A. D. 2500 [Wilson - 1955]
FITZPATRICK, E. M.  (1)
    Venus and the Rabbitt..........................London Observer Prize Story
        A. D. 2500 [Wilson - 1955]
FITZGERALD, F. SCOTT  (2)
    Curious Case of Benjamin Button, The........(From Tales of the Jazz Age; 1920)
        TRAVELERS IN TIME [Stern - 1947]
        THE TREASURY OF SCIENCE FICTION CLASSICS [Kuebler - 1955]
    Diamond As Big As the Ritz, The............(From Tales of the Jazz Age; 1920)
        THE MOONLIGHT TRAVELER [Stern - 1943]
FLAGG, FRANCIS ps (George Henry Weiss)  (1)
    Machine Man of Ardathia, The....................................Amz  Nov 1927
        ESCALES DANS L'INFINI [Gallett - 1954]
FLANDERS, JOHN ps (Jean Ray)  (1)
    Mystery of the Last Guest, The..................................WT  Oct 1935
        THE OTHER WORLDS [Stong - 1941]
FLEHR, PAUL  (1)
    Hated, The......................................................Glxy  Jan 1958
        THE FOURTH GALAXY READER OF SCIENCE FICTION [Gold - 1959]
FONTENAY, CHARLES L.  (3)
    Disqualified....................................................IF  Sep 1954
        THE FIRST WORLD OF IF [Quinn & Wulff - 1957]

                              226

FORSTER, E. M.  (3)
                                                               Mag.    Year
    Celestial Omnibus, The....(From The Celestial Omnibus and Other Stories; 1923)
        THE MOONLIGHT TRAVELER [Stern - 1943]
    Machine Stops, The..........(From The Eternal Moment and Other Stories; 1928)
        SCIENCE FICTION GALAXY [Conklin - 1950]
        THE TREASURY OF SCIENCE FICTION CLASSICS [Kuebler - 1955]
    Story of a Panic..........(From The Celestial Omnibus and Other Stories; 1923)
        CHILDREN OF WONDER [Tenn - 1953]
FRANTHWAY, BURKE  (1)
    It's Going To Be True!...........................................ORIGINAL STORY
        ADVENTURES TO COME [Esenwein - 1937]
FREEMAN, R. AUSTIN  (1)
    Bronze Parrott, The...................(From The Great Portrait Mystery; 1924)
        SHOT IN THE DARK [Merril - 1950]
FRIBORG, ALBERT COMPTON  (1)
    Careless Love.........................................................F&SF  Jul 1954
        THE BEST FROM FANTASY & SCIENCE FICTION: 4th SERIES [Boucher - 1955]
        THE BEST SCIENCE FICTION STORIES AND NOVELS: 1955 [Dikty - 1955]
FRIEDMAN, STUART  (1)
    Beautiful, Beautiful, Beautiful!....................................FSFS  Mar 1952
        WORLDS OF TOMORROW [Derleth - 1953]
FRIEND, OSCAR J.  (2)
    Impossible Highway, The.............................................TWS  Aug 1940
        GREAT STORIES OF SCIENCE FICTION [Leinster - 1951]
    Of Jovian Build.....................................................TWS  Oct 1938
        A TREASURY OF SCIENCE FICTION [Conklin - 1948]
FRITCH, CHARLES E.  (1)
    Space Station 42..................................................Orb #5  Nov 1954
        (Originally appeared under title Many Dreams of Earth)
            SPACE STATION 42 AND OTHER STORIES [Anonymous - 1958]
FURNAS, J. C.  (1)
    Laocoon Complex.....................................................Esq  Apr 1937
        TIMELESS STORIES FOR TODAY AND TOMORROW [Bradbury - 1952]
        BEYOND THE BARRIERS OF SPACE AND TIME [Merril - 1954]
FYFE, H. B.  (12)
    Afterthought......................................................Fw/SFS  Jan 1951
        BEYOND HUMAN KEN [Merril - 1952]
    Bureau of Slick Tricks..............................................ASF  Dec 1948
        TRAVELERS OF SPACE [Greenberg - 1952]
    Implode and Peddle..................................................ASF  Nov 1951
        SPACE SERVICE [Norton - 1953]
    In Value Deceived...................................................ASF  Nov 1950
        POSSIBLE WORLDS OF SCIENCE FICTION [Conklin - 1951]
        STORIES FOR TOMORROW [Sloane - 1954]
        STORIES OF SCIENTIFIC IMAGINATION [Gallant - 1954]
    Let There Be Light...................................................If  Nov 1952
        CROSSROADS IN TIME [Conklin - 1953]
        THE FIRST WORLD OF IF [Quinn & Wulff - 1957]
    Locked Out..........................................................ASF  Feb 1940
        MEN AGAINST THE STARS [Greenberg - 1950]
    Manners of the Age..................................................Glxy  Mar 1952
        THE OMNIBUS OF SCIENCE FICTION [Conklin - 1952]
    Moonwalk............................................................Spc  Nov 1952
        SPACE PIONEERS [Norton - 1954]
        MEN ON THE MOON [Wollheim - 1958]

FYFE, HORACE B. [Cont'd]                                          Mag.    Year
   Protected Species.........................................................ASF   Mar 1951
      THE ASTOUNDING SCIENCE FICTION ANTHOLOGY [J. W. Campbell — 1952]
   Ransom....................................................................F&SF  Dec 1952
      THE BEST FROM FANTASY & SCIENCE FICTION: 2nd SER. [Boucher & McComas — 1953
   Star-Lined...............................................................ASF   Feb 1952
      SPACE SERVICE [Norton — 1953]
   Well Oiled Machine, The...................................................F&SF  Dec 1950
      SCIENCE FICTION CARNIVAL [Brown & Reynolds — 1953]

# *G*

GALLERY, REAR ADMIRAL D.V., USN  (1)
   Enemy Planet, The........................................................SEP   9/30/50
      THE SATURDAY EVENING POST FANTASY STORIES [Fles — 1951]
GALLICO, PAUL  (1)
   Terrible Answer, The.....................................................SEP   1/17/50
      THE SATURDAY EVENING POST FANTASY STORIES· [Fles — 1951]
GALLUN, RAYMOND Z.  (10)
   Asteroid of Fear.........................................................PS    Mar 1951
      SPACE PIONEERS [Norton — 1954]
   Beast of the Void, A.....................................................Ast   Sep 1936
      ESCALES DANS L'INFINI [Gallet — 1954]
   Davy Jones' Ambassador...................................................Ast   Dec 1935
      THE BEST OF SCIENCE FICTION [Conklin — 1946]
   Old Faithful.............................................................Ast   Dec 1934
      IMAGINATION UNLIMITED [Bleiler & Dikty — 1952]
   Operation Pumice.........................................................TWS   Apr 1949
      POSSIBLE WORLDS OF SCIENCE FICTION [Conklin — 1951]
      MEN ON THE MOON [Wollheim — 1958]
   Return of a Legend.......................................................PS    Mar 1952
      SPACE SERVICE [Norton — 1955]
   Scarab, The..............................................................Ast   Aug 1936
      SCIENCE FICTION THINKING MACHINES [Conklin — 1954]
   Seeds of the Dusk........................................................ASF   Jun 1938
      ADVENTURES IN TIME AND SPACE [Healy & McComas — 1946]
   Stepson of Space.........................................................Ash   Apr 1940
      BEYOND THE END OF TIME [Pohl — 1952]
   Trail Blazer.............................................................FSM   Fal 1951
      SPACE PIONEERS [Norton — 1954]
GALOUYE, DANIEL F.  (3)
   City of Force, The.......................................................Glxy  Apr 1959
      BODYGUARD AND FOUR  OTHER SHORT NOVELS FROM GALAXY [Gold — 1960]
   Diplomatic Coop..........................................................ORIGINAL STORY
      STAR SCIENCE FICTION STORIES #5 [Pohl — 1959]
   Sanctuary................................................................F&SF  Feb 1954
      THE BEST FROM FANTASY & SCIENCE FICTION: 4th SERIES [Boucher — 1955

GAMOW, GEORGE  (1)                                                  Mag.    Year
    Infinity of Guests, An..................(From One, Two, Three...Infinity; 1947)
        FANTASIA MATHEMATICA [Fadiman - 1958]
GARDNER, MARTIN  (3)
    Island of Fine Colors.........................................,...ORIGINAL STORY
        FUTURE TENSE [Crossen - 1953]
        FANTASIA MATHEMATICA [Fadiman - 1958]
    No-Sided Professor.....................................Rpnt - F&SF  Feb 1951
        THE BEST FROM FANTASY & SCIENCE FICTION[Boucher & McComas- 1952]
        FANTASIA MATHEMATICA [Fadiman - 1958]       Org aprd in Esq  Jan 1947
    Thang.................................................................Cmt  Fal 1948
        THE BEST SCIENCE FICTION STORIES: 1949 [Bleiler & Dikty - 1949]
GARDNER, THOMAS S.  (1)
    Last Woman, The..................................................WS  Apr 1932
        FROM OFF THIS WORLD [Margulies & Friend - 1949]
GARRETT, RANDALL  (3)
    All About the Thing...................(parody)....................SFS  May 1956
        (Originally appeared as a feature under  general title PARODIES TOSSED.
        This parody appeared under title JOHN W. CAMPBELL JR.'S WHO GOES THERE?)
            SF: 57 THE YEAR'S GREATEST SF AND FANTASY [Merril - 1957]
    Blaze of Glory.....................(verse)....................F&SF  Dec 1955
        THE BEST FROM FANTASY & SCIENCE FICTION: 6th SERIES [Boucher - 1957]
    Hot Argument....................(verse)....................F&SF  Feb 1960
        FIFTH ANNUAL OF THE YEAR'S BEST SF [Merril - 1960]
GAULT, WILLIAM CAMPBELL  (2)
    Made To Measure......................................................Glxy  Jan 1951
        THE GALAXY READER OF SCIENCE FICTION [Gold - 1952]
    Title Fight...........................................................FU  Dec 1956
        THE FANTASTIC UNIVERSE OMNIBUS [Santesson - 1960]
GEHMAN, RICHARD (B.)  (2)
    Hickory, Dickory, Kerouac......................................Plby  Mar 1958
        (Originally appeared under pseudonym Martin Scott)
            SF: 59 THE YEAR'S GREATEST SCIENCE FICTION & FANTASY [Merril - 1959]
    Machine, The.......................................................Col  12/14/46
        13 GREAT STORIES OF SCIENCE FICTION [Conklin - 1960]
GEIER, CHESTER S.  (1)
    Environment........................................................ASF  May 1944
        THE OMNIBUS OF SCIENCE FICTION [Conklin - 1952]
GEROULD, KATHERINE FULLERTON  (1)
    On the Staircase...........................(From Vain Obligations; 1914)
        TRAVELERS IN TIME [Stern - 1947]
GIESY, J. U.  (1)
    Blind Man's Buff..................................................AIS  1/24/20
        ESCALES DANS L'INFINI [Gallet - 1954]
GILBERT, ROBERT ERNEST  (1)
    Footprints.......................................................FB #8  n/d 1951
        SCIENCE AND SORCERY [Ford - 1953]
GODWIN, BISHOP FRANCIS  (1)
    Man In the Moone, The..............................................
        (Originally appeared under pseudonym Domingo Gonsales)
        (Originally published in London by Joshua Kirton & Thomas Warren; 1638)
            BEYOND TIME AND SPACE [Derleth - 1950]

(229)

Mag.    Year

GODWIN, TOM  (3)
  Cold Equations, The........................................................ASF  Aug 1954
      THE BEST SCIENCE FICTION STORIES AND NOVELS: 1955 [Dikty - 1955]
      BEST SF THREE SCIENCE FICTION STORIES [Crispin - 1958]
      BEYOND THE STARS AND OTHER STORIES [Anonymous - 1958]
      ASPECTS OF SCIENCE FICTION [Doherty - 1959].............................If  Aug 1957
  Last Victory.............................................................
      THE BEST SCIENCE FICTION STORIES AND NOVELS: 9th SERIES [Dikty - 1958]
  You Cheated Us..........................................................FU  Oct 1955
      THE BEST SCIENCE FICTION STORIES AND NOVELS: 1956 [Dikty - 1956]

GOLD, H. L.  (7)   (See also pseudonym Dudley Dell)
  Love In the Dark........................................................Sus  Fal 1951
      (Originally appeared under title Love Etheral)
          BEYOND THE END OF TIME [Pohl - 1952]
          INVISIBLE MEN [Davenport - 1960]
  Man With English, The..................................................ORIGINAL STORY
      STAR SCIENCE FICTION STORIES [Pohl - 1953]
      STAR OF STARS [Pohl - 1960]
  Matter of Form, A......................................................ASF  Dec 1938
      THE BIG BOOK OF SCIENCE FICTION [Conklin - 1950]
      ASSIGNMENT IN TOMORROW [Pohl - 1954]
  Perfect Murder.........................................................TWS  Mar 1940
      SCIENCE FICTION ADVENTURES IN DIMENSION [Conklin - 1953]
  Trouble With Water.....................................................Unk  Mar 1939
      FROM UNKNOWN WORLDS [J. W. Campbell - 1948]

  w/ Robert W. Krepps
      Enormous Room, The...............................................Amz  Nov 1953
          THE YEAR'S BEST SCIENCE FICTION NOVELS: 1954 [Bleiler & Dikty - 1954]

GOLDSMITH, RUTH M.  (1)
  Yankee Exodus..........................................................F&SF  Jul 1953
      THE BEST SCIENCE FICTION STORIES: 1954 [Bleiler & Dikty - 1954]

GOLDSTONE, ROBERT  (1)
  Virtuoso...............................................................F&SF  Feb 1954
      SCIENCE FICTION THINKING MACHINES [Conklin - 1954]

GOODWIN, JOHN B.L.  (1)
  Cocoon, The............................................................Stry  Sep 1946
      TIMELESS STORIES FOR TODAY AND TOMORROW [Bradbury - 1952]

GOULART, RON  (3)
  Letters To the Editor...............................................Rpnt-F&SF  Apr 1952
      THE BEST FROM FANTASY & SCIENCE FICTION: 2nd SER. [Boucher & McComas-1953]
                                          Org aprd in  Plcn  Oct 1951
  New Lot, A.............................................................F&SF  Jan 1958
      THE BEST FROM FANTASY & SCIENCE FICTION: 8th SERIES [Boucher - 1959]
  Ralph Wollstonecraft Hedge: A Memoir...................................F&SF  May 1959
      THE BEST FROM FANTASY & SCIENCE FICTION: 9th SERIES [Mills - 1960]

GOVAN, CHRISTINE NOBLE  (1)
  Miss Winters and the Wind.............................................Tmw  May 1946
      TIMELESS STORIES FOR TODAY AND TOMORROW [Bradbury - 1952]

GRANT, ALLAN  (1)
  Fiction.........................................(verse)................Unk  Feb 1941
      FROM UNKNOWN WORLDS [J. W. Campbell - 1948]

GRAVES, ROBERT  (1)
  Shout, The.......(Originally published by Elkins Mathews & Marlot, Ltd.; 1929)
      THE BEST FROM F&SF: 2nd SERIES [Boucher & McComas-1953] Rpnt-F&SF  Apr 1952

(230)

GRAY, WILL H.  (1)                                              Mag.     Year
   Bees From Borneo, The.....................................Amz   Feb 1931
        THE OMNIBUS OF SCIENCE FICTiON [Conklin - 1952]
GREENE, GRAHAM  (2)
   End of the Party, The...........................(From Nineteen Stories; 1947)
        CHILDREN OF WONDER [Tenn - 1953]
   Proof Positive........................................Rpnt - F&SF   Aug 1952
        A DECADE OF FANTASY & SCIENCE FICTION [Mills-1960]
GREGOR, LEE ps (Milton A. Rothman)  (1)
   Heavy Planet...........................................Ast   Aug 1939
        ADVENTURES IN TIME AND SPACE [Healy & McComas - 1946]
GRENDON, EDWARD  (3)
   Crisis.................................................ASF   Jun 1951
        INVADERS OF EARTH [Conklin - 1952]
   Figure, The............................................ASF   Jul 1947
        A TREASURY OF SCIENCE FICTION [Conklin - 1948]
   Trip One...............................................ASF   Jul 1949
        SPACE, SPACE, SPACE [Sloane - 1953]
GRENDON, STEPHEN ps (August Derleth)  (3)
   Mrs. Manifold..................................................ORIGINAL STORY
        THE GIRL WITH THE HUNGRY EYES AND OTHER STORIES [Wollheim - 1949]
   Open, Sesame...........................................Ark   Win 1949
        FAR BOUNDARIES [Derleth - 1951]
   Song of the Pewee, The.................................Ark   Aut 1949
        FAR BOUNDARIES [Derleth - 1951]
GRESHAM, WILLIAM LINDSAY  (1)
   Star Gypsies, The......................................F&SF   Jul 1953
        THE BEST FROM FANTASY & SCIENCE FICTION: 3rd SER. [Boucher & McComas-1954]
GRIFFITH, ANN WARREN  (2)
   Captive Audience.......................................F&SF   Aug 1953
        THE BEST FROM FANTASY & SCIENCE FICTION: 3rd SER [Boucher & McComas-1954]
   Zeritsky's Law.........................................Glxy   Nov 1951
        THE OMNIBUS OF SCIENCE FICTION [Conklin - 1952]
GRIMM, CHRISTOPHER  (1)
   Bodyguard..............................................Glxy   Feb 1956
        BODYGUARD AND FOUR OTHER SHORT NOVELS FROM GALAXY [Gold - 1960]
GRINNELL, DAVID  (5)
   Extending the Holdings.................................F&SF   Apr 1951
        THE BEST SCIENCE FICTION STORIES: 1952 [Bleiler & Dikty - 1952]
   Lysenko Maze, The......................................F&SF   Jul 1954
        SCIENCE FICTION ADVENTURES IN MUTATION [Conklin - 1956]
   Malice Aforethought....................................F&SF   Nov 1952
        BEYOND THE BARRIERS OF SPACE AND TIME [Merril - 1954]
   Rag Thing, The.........................................F&SF   Oct 1951
        THE OMNIBUS OF SCIENCE FICTION [Conklin - 1952]
        TERROR IN THE MODERN VEIN [Wollheim - 1955]
   Top Secret.............................................Sir   Jul 1949
        INVADERS OF EARTH [Conklin - 1952]
GROSS, MARION  (1)
   Good Provider, The.....................................F&SF   Sep 1952
        SCIENCE FICTION ADVENTURES IN DIMENSION [Conklin - 1953]
GROSSER, E. A.  (1)
   Psychomorph, The.......................................Unk   Feb 1940
        FROM UNKNOWN WORLDS [J. W. Campbell - 1948]

GROVES, J. W.  (1)                                                    Mag.    Year
    Robots Don't Bleed.................................................NW #8   Win 1950
        NO PLACE LIKE EARTH [Carnell - 1952]
        THE BEST FROM NEW WORLDS [Carnell - 1955]
GRUNERT, KARL
    Enemies of Space..............................(Originally published in 1907)
        (Translated from German by Willy Ley)
            INVADERS OF EARTH [Conklin - 1952]
GUERNSEY, H. W. ps (Howard Wandrei)  (1)
    Hexer, The....................................................Unk    Jun 1939
        FROM UNKNOWN WORLDS [J. W. Campbell - 1948]
GUIN, WYMAN  (3)
    Beyond Bedlam.................................................Glxy   Aug 1951
        THE GALAXY READER OF SCIENCE FICTION [Gold - 1952]
    Trigger Tide.................................................ASF    Oct 1950
        (Originally appeared under pseudonym Norman Menasco)
            THE OMNIBUS OF SCIENCE FICTION [Conklin - 1952]
    Volpa........................................................Glxy   May 1956
        THE THIRD GALAXY READER OF SCIENCE FICTION [Gold - 1958]
        13 GREAT STORIES OF SCIENCE FICTION [Conklin - 1960]
GUNN, JAMES E.  (5)
    Cave of Night, The...........................................Glxy   Feb 1955
        SF: THE YEAR'S GREATEST SCIENCE FICTION AND FANTASY [Merril - 1956]
    Immortals, The.......................................ORIGINAL STORY
        STAR SCIENCE FICTION STORIES #4 [Pohl - 1958]
    Misogynist, The..............................................Glxy   Nov 1952
        SHADOW OF TOMORROW [Pohl - 1953]
        THE SECOND GALAXY READER OF SCIENCE FICTION [Gold - 1954]
    Monster Named Smith, A.......................................If     Jul 1954
        THE SECOND WORLD OF IF [Quinn & Wulff - 1958]
    Whereever You May Be.........................................Glxy   May 1953
        FIVE GALAXY SHORT NOVELS [Gold - 1958]

HALL, AUSTIN  (1)
    Man Who Saved The Earth, The.................................Amz    Apr 1926
        THE BEST OF SCIENCE FICTION [Conklin - 1946]
HAMILTON, EDMOND  (11)
    Conquest of Two Worlds, A....................................WS     Feb 1932
        EVERY BOY'S BOOK OF SCIENCE FICTION [Wollheim - 1951]
    Dead Planet, The.............................................Stg    Spr 1946
        WORLD OF TOMORROW [Derleth - 1953]
    Exile........................................................Sup    May 1943
        LOOKING FORWARD [Lesser - 1953]
    Fessenden's Worlds...........................................WT     Apr 1937
        BEYOND TIME AND SPACE [Derleth - 1950]

HAMILTON, EDMOND [Cont'd]                                    Mag.    Year
   Forgotten World...........................................TWS   Win 1946
      THE GIANT ANTHOLOGY OF SCIENCE FICTION [Margulies & Friend - 1954]
   In the World's Dusk.......................................WT    Mar 1936
      THE END OF THE WORLD [Wollheim - 1956]
   Inn Outside the World, The................................WT    Jul 1945
      MY BEST SCIENCE FICTION STORY [Margulies & Friend - 1949]
   Man Who Evolved, The......................................WS    Apr 1931
      FROM OFF THIS WORLD [Margulies & Friend - 1949]
   Plant Revolt, The.........................................WT    Apr 1930
      THE EARTH IN PERIL [Wollheim - 1957]
   Son of Two Worlds.........................................TWS   Aug 1941
      THREE FROM OUT THERE [Margulies - 1959]
   What's It Like Out There?.................................Stg   Dec 1952
      THE BEST FROM STARTLING STORIES [Mines - 1953]
HAMM, T. ·D.  (Mrs. T. E. Dikty)  (1)
   Ticking His Life Away.................................ORIGINAL STORY
      TOMORROW'S UNIVERSE [H. J. Campbell - 1954]
HARDY, G. H.  (1)
   Bertrand Russell's Dream..............(From A Mathematician's Apology; 1948 )
      FANTASIA MATHEMATICA [Fadiman - 1958]
HARMON, JIM  (1)
   Name Your Sympton.......................................Glxy  Jul 1956
      THE FOURTH GALAXY READER OF SCIENCE FICTION [Gold - 1959]
HARNESS, CHARLES L.  (3)
   Child By Chronos.........................................F&SF   Jun 1953
      THE BEST FROM FANTASY & SCIENCE FICTION: 3rd SER [Boucher & McComas-1954]
   Heritage................................................F&SF   Fal 1950
      TOMORROW'S UNIVERSE [H. J. Campbell - 1954]
   New Reality, The........................................TWS   Dec 1950
      THE BEST SCIENCE FICTION STORIES: 1951 [Bleiler & Dikty - 1951]
HARRIS, CLARE WINGER  (1)
   w/ Miles J. Breuer, M. D.
      Baby On Neptune, A....................................Amz   Dec 1929
         FLIGHT INTO SPACE [Wollheim - 1950]
HARRIS, JOHN BEYNON  (2)  (See listings John Beynon and John Wyndham)
   Meteor...................................................Amz   Mar 1941
      (Originally appeared as Phony Meteor under John Beynon byline)
         BEACHHEADS IN SPACE [Derleth - 1954]
   Time To Rest............................................Ark   Win 1949
      (Originally appeared under John Beynon byline)
         FAR BOUNDARIES [Derleth - 1951]
HARRIS, LARRY M.  (1)
   Mex.....................................................FU    Jan 1957
      THE FANTASTIC UNIVERSE OMNIBUS [Santesson - 1960]
HARRISON, HARRY  (2)
   Rock Driver.............................................WB #3  Feb 1951
      BEYOND THE END OF TIME [Pohl - 1952]
   Velvet Glove, The.......................................FU    Nov 1956
      THE FANTASTIC UNIVERSE OMNIBUS [Santesson - 1960]
HARVEY, W. F.  (1)
   August Heat...........(From The Beast With Five Fingers And Other Tales; 1928)
      TRAVELERS IN TIME [Stern - 1947]

(233)

Mag.    Year

HASSE, HENRY  (2)
  Eyes, The.................................................FB #8  n/d 1951
    SCIENCE AND SORCERY [Ford - 1953]
  He Who Shrank............................................Amz  Aug 1936
    ADVENTURES IN TIME AND SPACE [Healy & McComas - 1946]
HASTINGS, CHRISTEL  (1)
  Black Cats...................(verse).....................Unk  Dec 1940
    FROM UNKNOWN WORLDS [J. W. Campbell - 1948]
HATCHER, JACK  (1)
  Fuel For the Future......................................ASF  Mar 1940
    COMING ATTRACTIONS [Greenberg - 1957]
HAWKINS, PETER  (3)
  Circus...................................................SF #5  Aut 1952
    GATEWAY TO THE STARS [Carnell - 1955]
  Life Cycle...............................................NW #9  Spr 1951
    GATEWAY TO TOMORROW [Carnell - 1954]
  Ship From the Stars......................................NW #25  Jul 1954
    THE BEST FROM NEW WORLDS [Carnell - 1955]
HAWTHORNE, NATHANIEL  (1)
  Birthmark, The...................(From Mosses From An Old Manse; 1846)
    JOURNEYS IN SCIENCE FICTION [Loughlin & Popp - 1961]
HEALY, RAYMOND J.  (1)
  Great Devon Mystery, The.........................ORIGINAL STORY
    9 TALES OF SPACE AND TIME [Healy - 1954]
HEARD, H. F.  (6)
  B + M — Planet 4.................................ORIGINAL STORY
    NEW TALES OF SPACE AND TIME [Healy - 1951]
  Collector, The...........................................F&SF  Aug 1951
    THE BEST FROM FANTASY & SCIENCE FICTION [Boucher & McComas - 1952]
  Cyclops..........................................ORIGINAL STORY
    FUTURE TENSE [Crossen - 1953]
  Great Fog, The...............(From The Great Fog and Other Weird Tales; 1944)
    A TREASURY OF SCIENCE FICTION [Conklin - 1946]
  Rousing of Mr. Bradegar, The....(From The Great Fog & Other Weird Tales; 1944)
    TRAVELERS IN TIME [Stern - 1947]
  Wingless Victory.............(From The Great Fog and Other Weird Tales; 1944)
    BEYOND TIME AND SPACE [Derleth - 1950]
HEINLEIN, ROBERT A.  (20) (See also listings Anson MacDonald and Lyle Monroe)
  "All You Zombies".......................................F&SF  Mar 1959
    THE BEST FROM FANTASY & SCIENCE FICTION: 9th SERIES [Mills - 1960]
  " — And He Built A Crooked House — "....................ASF  Feb 1941
    THE POCKET BOOK OF SCIENCE FICTION [Wollheim - 1943]
    FANTASIA MATHEMATICA [Fadiman - 1958]
  Black Pits of Luna.......................................SEP  1/10/48
    POSSIBLE WORLDS OF SCIENCE FICTION [Conklin - 1951]
    SCIENCE FICTION AND READER'S GUIDE [Barrows - 1954]
    STORIES OF SCIENTIFIC IMAGINATION [Gallant - 1954]
  Blowups Happen...........................................ASF  Sep 1940
    THE BEST OF SCIENCE FICTION [Conklin - 1946]
    THE ASTOUNDING SCIENCE FICTION ANTHOLOGY [J. W. Campbell - 1952]
    BEST SF TWO SCIENCE FICTION STORIES [Crispin - 1956]
  Coventry.................................................ASF  Jul 1940
    6 GREAT SHORT NOVELS OF SCIENCE FICTION [Conklin - 1954]
    (Revised for inclusion in this anthology)
  Destination Moon.........................................SS  Sep 1950
    THREE TIMES INFINITY [Margulies - 1958]

(234)

HEINLEIN, ROBERT A. [Cont'd]                                    Mag.    Year
    Gentlemen, Be Seated...............................................Arg   May 1948
        SHOT IN THE DARK [Merril - 1950]
    Green Hills of Earth, The.........................................SEP    2/8/47
        STRANGE PORTS OF CALL [Derleth - 1948]
        INVASION FROM MARS [Welles - 1949]
        MY BEST SCIENCE FICTION STORY [Margulies & Friend - 1949]
    It's Great To Be Back.............................................SEP    7/26/47
        A TREASURY OF SCIENCE FICTION [Conklin - 1948]
    Long Watch, The...................................................ALM   Dec 1949
        BEYOND TIME AND SPACE [Derleth - 1950]
    Man Who Sold the Moon, The...(Originally published by Shasta Publishers; 1950)
        A TREASURY OF GREAT SCIENCE FICTION [Boucher - 1959]
    Our Fair City.....................................................WT    Jan 1949
        BEYOND HUMAN KEN [Merril - 1952]
    Requiem...........................................................ASF   Jan 1940
        ADVENTURES IN TIME AND SPACE [Healy & McComas - 1946]
    Roads Must Roll, The..............................................ASF   Jun 1940
        ADVENTURES IN TIME AND SPACE [Healy & McComas - 1946]
        JOURNEYS IN SCIENCE FICTION [Loughlin & Popp - 1961]
    They..............................................................Unk   Apr 1941
        WORLD OF WONDER [Pratt - 1952]
        SCIENCE FICTION TERROR TALES [Conklin - 1955]
        TERROR IN THE MODERN VEIN [Wollheim - 1955]
    Universe..........................................................ASF   May 1941
        THE BEST OF SCIENCE FICTION [Conklin - 1946]
    Waldo.............................................................ASF   Aug 1942
        (Originally appeared under pseudonym Anson MacDonald)
        A TREASURY OF GREAT SCIENCE FICTION [Boucher - 1959]
    Where To?.........................................................Glxy  Feb 1952
        ALL ABOUT THE FUTURE [Greenberg - 1955]
    Year of the Jackpot, The..........................................Glxy  Mar 1952
        SHADOW OF TOMORROW [Pohl - 1953]
        THE SECOND GALAXY READER OF SCIENCE FICTION [Gold - 1954]
        THE END OF THE WORLD [Wollheim - 1956]
    w/ Elma Wentz
        Beyond Doubt..................................................ASF   Apr 1941
            (Originally appeared under pseudonym Lyle Monroe)
            BEYOND THE END OF TIME [Pohl - 1952]
HENDERSON, ZEENA (9)
    Anything Box......................................................F&SF  Oct 1956
        SF: 57 THE YEAR'S GREATEST SF AND FANTASY [Merril - 1957]
    Ararat............................................................F&SF  Oct 1952
        THE BEST SCIENCE FICTION STORIES: 1953 [Bleiler & Dikty - 1953]
    Captivity.........................................................F&SF  Jun 1958
        THE BEST FROM FANTASY & SCIENCE FICTION: 8th SERIES [Boucher - 1959]
    Come On, Wagon!...................................................F&SF  Dec 1951
        THE BEST FROM FANTASY & SCIENCE FICTION: 2nd SER [Boucher & McComas-1953]
    Food To All Flesh.................................................F&SF  Dec 1953
        BEST SF THREE SCIENCE FICTION STORIES [Crispin - 1958]
    Jordan............................................................F&SF  Mar 1959
        A DECADE OF FANTASY & SCIENCE FICTION [Mills - 1960]
    Pottage...........................................................F&SF  Sep 1955
        THE BEST FROM FANTASY & SCIENCE FICTION: 5th SERIES [Boucher - 1956]
        SF: THE YEAR'S GREATEST SCIENCE FICTION AND FANTASY [Merril - 1956]
    Something Bright..................................................Glxy  Feb 1960
        SIXTH ANNUAL OF THE YEAR'S BEST SF [Merril - 1961]
    Wilderness........................................................F&SF  Jan 1957
        SF: 58 THE YEAR'S GREATEST SF AND FANTASY [Merril - 1958]

HENNEBERG, CHARLES  (I)                                           Mag.    Year
    Blind Pilot, The...............................(Translated by Damon Knight)
        THE BEST FROM FANTASY & SCIENCE FICTION: 10th SERIES [Mills - 1961]
                                                              F&SF  Jan 1960
HENRY, O. ps (William Sydney Porter)  (I)
    Roads of Destiny............................(From Roads of Destiny; 1909)
        THE MOONLIGHT TRAVELER [Stern - 1943]
        WORLD OF WONDER [Pratt - 1952]
HERBERT, BENSON  (I)
    World Without, The...........................................WS  Feb 1931
        FROM OFF THIS WORLD [Margulies & Friend - 1949]
HERBERT, FRANK  (I)
    Nightmare Blues.............................................ASF  Jun 1954
        THE BEST SCIENCE FICTION STORIES AND NOVELS: 1955 [Dikty - 1955]
HETSCHEL, DICK  (I)
    First Stage: Moon............................................If  Dec 1954
        THE FIRST WORLD OF IF [Quinn & Wulff - 1957]
HICKEY, H. B. ps (Herb Livingston)  (2)
    Hilda.....................................................F&SF  Sep 1952
        OPERATION FUTURE [Conklin - 1955]
    Like A Bird, Like A Fish.....................................WB  Feb 1951
        WORLDS OF TOMORROW [Derleth - 1953]
HIGHSTONE, H. A.  (I)
    Frankenstein - Unlimited....................................Ast  Dec 1936
        FAR BOUNDARIES [Derleth - 1951]
HILLIARD, A. ROWLEY  (2)
    Death From the Stars.........................................WS  Oct 1931
        THE SCIENCE FICTION GALAXY [Merril - 1950]
    Green Torture, The...........................................WS  Mar 1931
        FROM OFF THIS WORLD [Margulies & Friend - 1949]
HILTON-YOUNG, W.  (I)
    Choice, The.................................................Pch   3/19/52
        THE OMNIBUS OF SCIENCE FICTION [Conklin - 1952]
HOCKETT, CHARLES F.  (I)
    How to Learn Martian.......................................ASF  May 1955
        COMING ATTRACTIONS [Greenberg - 1957]
HODGSON, WILLIAM HOPE  (I)
    Derelict, The............................(From Men of Deep Waters; 1914)
        THE SCIENCE FICTION GALAXY [Conklin - 1950]
HOLBERG, LEWIS [Baron Ludwig Holberg]  (I)
    Tree Men of Potu, The.........(From A Journey to the World Under-Ground; 1741)
        BEYOND TIME AND SPACE [Derleth - 1950]
HOLDEN, FOX B.  (I)
    Here Lie We...............................................Stg  Jun 1953
        TALES OF OUTER SPACE [Wollheim - 1954]
HOLMES, H. H. ps (Anthony Boucher)  (I)
    Robinic....................................................ASF  Sep 1943
        THE ROBOT AND THE MAN [Greenberg - 1953]
HOLMES, KENYON ps (August Derleth)  (I)
    Man Who Rode the Saucer.................................ORIGINAL STORY
        FAR BOUNDARIES [Derleth - 1951]
HORN, HOLLOWAY  (I)
    Old Man, The...(Fr The Second Omnibus of Crime-1932; Edited by Dorothy Sayers)
        TRAVELERS IN TIME [Stern - 1947]

HOUSEMAN, A. E.  (1)                                         Mag.   Year
    To Think That Two and Two Are Four.................(verse)..................
        (From The Collected Poems of A. E. Housman; 1940)
            FANTASIA MATHEMATICA [Fadiman - 1958]
HOWARD, ROBERT E.  (1)
    Garden of Fear, The...................................................MT   Jul 1934
        THE GARDEN OF FEAR AND OTHER STORIES [Crawford - 1945]
HROLDA, JEAN  (1)
    Eight Mistresses, The................................................Esq  Aug 1937
        TIMELESS STORIES FOR TODAY AND TOMORROW [Bradbury - 1952]
HUBBARD, L. RON  (5)
    Behind the Black Nebula..............................................ASF    Jan 1942
        (Originally appeared under title The Invaders)
            TALES OF OUTER SPACE [Wollheim - 1954]
    He Didn't Like Cats..................................................Unk   Feb 1942
        ZACHERLY'S VULTURE STEW [Zacherly - 1960]
    Professor Was A Thief, The...........................................ASF   Feb 1940
        MY BEST SCIENCE FICTION STORY [Margulies & Friend - 1949]
    Tough Old Man........................................................Stg   Nov 1950
        SPACE POLICE [Norton - 1956]
    When Shadows Fall....................................................Stg   Jul 1948
        MEN AGAINST THE STARS [Greenberg - 1950]
HUBBARD, P. M.  (3)
    Botany Bay...........................................................F&SF  Feb 1955
        THE BEST FROM FANTASY & SCIENCE FICTION 5th SERIES [Boucher - 1956]
    Free Flight..........................................................F&SF  Apr 1956
        THE BEST FROM FANTASY & SCIENCE FICTION: 6th SERIES [Boucher - 1957]
    Manuscript Found In a Vacuum.............................Rpnt — F&SF  Aug 1953
        THE BEST FROM FANTASY & SCIENCE FICTION: 3rd SER [Boucher & McComas-1954]
                                        Org apprd in Pch  12/17/52
HUGI, MAURICE G. ps (Eric Frank Russell)  (1)
    Mechanical Mice......................................................ASF   Jan 1941
        ADVENTURES IN TIME AND SPACE [Healy & McComas - 1946]
HULL, E. MAYNE  (Mrs. A. E. Van Vogt)  (3)
    Competition..........................................................ASF   Jun 1943
        MEN AGAINST THE STARS [Greenberg - 1950]
    Flight that Failed, The..............................................ASF   Dec 1942
        SCIENCE FICTION ADVENTURES IN DIMENSION [Conklin - 1953]
    Patient, The.........................................................Unk   Oct 1943
        SCIENCE FICTION ADVENTURES IN MUTATION [Conklin - 1956]
HUXLEY, ALDOUS  (3)
    Brave New World...................(Excerpts)..................................
        (Originally published by Doubleday Doran and Co.; 1932)
            THE TREASURY OF SCIENCE FICTION CLASSICS [Kuebler - 1955]
    "The Hatchery".................................(From Brave New World; 1932)
        CHILDREN OF WONDER [Tenn - 1953]
    Young Archimedes.........................(From Young Archimedes; 1924)
        FANTASIA MATHEMATICA [Fadiman - 1958]
HUXLEY, JULIAN  (1)
    Tissue Culture King, The.............................................Amz   Aug 1927
        THE BEST OF SCIENCE FICTION [Conklin - 1946]
HYDE, GAVIN  (1)
    Sparkie's Fall.......................................................ORIGINAL STORY
        STAR SCIENCE FICTION STORIES #5 [Pohl - 1959]
        STAR OF STARS [Pohl - 1960]

# I

IONESCO, EUGENE  (1)                                                              Mag.    Year
   Flying High..................................................Mdm  Oct 1957
        SF: 58 THE YEAR'S GREATEST SF AND FANTASY [Merril - 1958]
IRWIN, MARGARET E.  (1)
   Earlier Service, The............................Rpnt — F&SF  Dec 1951
        (From Madame Fears The Dark: Seven Stories and a Play; 1935)
            THE BEST FROM F&SF: 2nd SERIES [Boucher & McComas - 1953]
ISHERWOOD, CHRISTOPHER  (1)
   I Am Waiting....................................................Nykr  10/21/39
        TIMELESS STORIES FOR TODAY AND TOMORROW [Bradbury - 1952]

# J

JACKSON, SHIRLEY  (4)                                                      F&SF  Mar 1954
   Bulletin......................................................F&SF  Mar 1954
        THE BEST FROM FANTASY & SCIENCE FICTION: 4th SERIES [Boucher - 1955]
   Demon Lover, The............................(From The Lottery; 1949)
        TIMELESS STORIES FOR TODAY AND TOMORROW [Bradbury - 1952]
   Omen, The....................................................F&SF  Jan 1955
        SF: THE YEAR'S GREATEST SCIENCE FICTION AND FANTASY [Merril - 1956]
        THE BEST FROM FANTASY & SCIENCE FICTION: 8th SERIES [Boucher - 1959]
   One Ordinary Day, With Peanuts...............................F&SF  Jan 1955
        THE BEST FROM FANTASY & SCIENCE FICTION: 5th SERIES [Boucher - 1956]
        SF: 57 THE YEAR'S GREATEST SF AND FANTASY [Merril - 1957]
JACOBI, CARL  (4)
   Gentleman Is An Epwa, The..............................ORIGINAL STORY
        WORLDS OF TOMORROW [Derleth - 1953]
   Tepondicon...................................................PS  Win 1946
        FAR BOUNDARIES [Derleth - 1951]
   White Pinnacle, The...................................ORIGINAL STORY
        TIME TO COME [Derleth - 1954]
   w/ Clifford D. Simak
      Lost Street, The..........................................CS  Jul 1941
           (Originally appeared under title The Street That Wasn't There)
                STRANGE PORTS OF CALL [Derleth - 1948]
JACOBS, SYLVIA  (1)
   Pilot and the Bushman, The..................................Glxy  Aug 1951
        THE GALAXY READER OF SCIENCE FICTION [Gold - 1952]
JAFFRAY, NORMAN R.  (1)
   Cowboy Lament..........................(verse)................F&SF  Jan 1954
        THE BEST FROM FANTASY & SCIENCE FICTION: 4th SERIES [Boucher - 1955]
JAKES, JOHN W.  (1)
   Machine......................................................F&SF  Apr 1952
        THE BEST SCIENCE FICTION STORIES: 1953 [Bleiler & Dikty - 1953]

```
JAMES, D. L.  (1)                                              Mag.    Year
    Moon of Delirium.............................................ASF   Jan 1940
        POSSIBLE WORLDS OF SCIENCE FICTION [Conklin - 1951]
JAMES, E. R.  (1)
    Emergency Working............................................NW #17  Sep 1952
        GATEWAY TO TOMORROW [Carnell - 1954]
JAMES, M. R.  (1)
    View from the Hill, The......................................
        (From A Warning to the Curious and Other Ghost Stories; 1926)
        TRAVELERS IN TIME [Stern - 1947]
JAMES, PHILIP  (1)
    Carillion of Skulls..........................................Unk   Feb 1941
        ZACHERLY'S MIDNIGHT SNACKS [Zacherly - 1960]
JAMESON, MALCOLM  (11)
    Alien Envoy..................................................ASF   Nov 1944
    THE ULTIMATE INVADER AND OTHER SCIENCE FICTION [Wollheim - 1954]
    Blind Alley..................................................Unk   Jun 1943
        GREAT STORIES OF SCIENCE FICTION [Leinster - 1951]
    Blind Man's Buff.............................................ASF   Oct 1944
        IMAGINATION UNLIMITED [Bleiler & Dikty - 1952]
        EVERY BOY'S BOOK OF OUTER SPACE STORIES [Dikty - 1960]
    Bullard Reflects.............................................ASF   Dec 1941
        A TREASURY OF GREAT SCIENCE FICTION [Boucher - 1959]
    Children of the "Betsy-B."...................................ASF   Mar 1939
        A TREASURY OF SCIENCE FICTION [Conklin - 1948]
    Hobo God....................................................ASF   Sep 1944
        ALL ABOUT THE FUTURE [Greenberg - 1955]
    Lilies of Life..............................................ASF   Feb 1945
        POSSIBLE WORLDS OF SCIENCE FICTION [Conklin - 1951]
        PLANET OF DOOM AND OTHER STORIES [Anonymous - 1958]
            (Appeared under title Planet of Doom)
    Pride.......................................................ASF   Sep 1942
        BEYOND HUMAN KEN [Merril - 1952]
    Sorcerer's Apprentice, The..................................ASF   Dec 1941
        OPERATION FUTURE [Conklin - 1955]
    Space War Tactics...........................................ASF   Aug 1939
        COMING ATTRACTIONS [Greenberg - 1955]
    Tricky Tonnage..............................................ASF   Dec 1944
        THE BEST OF SCIENCE FICTION [Conklin - 1946]
JANVIER, IVAN ps (Algis Budrys)  (1)
    Thing.......................................................FU   Mar 1955
        THE BEST SCIENCE FICTION STORIES AND NOVELS: 1956 [Dikty - 1956]
JENKINS, WILL F.  (2)      (See also pseudonym Murray Leinster)
    Doomsday Deferred...........................................SEP  9/24/1949
        THE BEST SCIENCE FICTION STORIES: 1950 [Bleiler & Dikty - 1950]
        THE SATURDAY EVENING POST FANTASY STORIES [Fles - 1951]
    Symbiosis...................................................Col  1/14/1947
        THE OTHER SIDE OF THE MOON [Derleth - 1949]
        GREAT STORIES OF SCIENCE FICTION [Leinster - 1951]
        STORIES OF SCIENTIFIC IMAGINATION [Gallant - 1954]
JESSELL, JOHN ps (Stanley G. Weinbaum)  (1)
    Adaptive Ultimate, The......................................Ast   Nov 1935
        THE OTHER WORLDS [Stong - 1941]
JOHNSON, JOSEPHINE W.  (1)
    Night Flight................................................Hpr   Feb 1944
        TIMELESS STORIES FOR TODAY AND TOMORROW [Bradbury - 1952]
```

JOHNSON, ROBERT BARBOUR  (1)                                    Mag.    Year
    Far Below.................................................WT   Jul 1939
        EDITOR'S CHOICE IN SCIENCE FICTION [Moskowitz - 1954]
            (Story selected by Dorothy McIlwraith)
JONES, ALICE ELEANOR  (1)
    Created He Them.........................................F&SF   Jun 1955
        THE BEST FROM FANTASY & SCIENCE FICTION: 5th SERIES [Boucher - 1956]
JONES, NEIL R.  (1)
    Hermit of Saturn's Ring...................................PS   Fal 1940
        FLIGHT INTO SPACE [Woolheim - 1950]
JONES, RAYMOND F.  (9)
    Colonists, The............................................If   Jun 1954
        THE SECOND WORLD OF IF [Quinn & Wulff - 1958]
    Correspondence Course....................................ASF   Apr 1945
        ADVENTURES IN TIME AND SPACE [Healy & McComas - 1946]
    Farthest Horizon, The....................................ASF   Apr 1952
        SPACE PIONEERS [Norton - 1954]
        STORIES FOR TOMORROW [Sloane - 1954]
    Noise Level..............................................ASF   Dec 1952
        STORIES FOR TOMORROW [Sloane - 1954]
    Person From Porlock, The.................................ASF   Aug 1947
        A TREASURY OF SCIENCE FICTION [Conklin - 1948]
    Pete Can Fix It..........................................ASF   Feb 1947
        SCIENCE FICTION ADVENTURES IN DIMENSION [Conklin - 1953]
    Production Test..........................................ASF   Oct 1949
        LOOKING FORWARD [Lesser - 1953]
    Stone and a Spear, A....................................GIxy   Dec 1950
        THE OMNIBUS OF SCIENCE FICTION [Conklin - 1952]
    Tools of the Trade.......................................ASF   Nov 1950
        SPACE, SPACE, SPACE [Sloane - 1953]
JOWETT, BENJAMIN  (1)  (Translator)
    Socrates and the Slave by Plato..........................................
        (From The Meno of Plato; Oxford University Press: 1896)
            FANTASIA MATHEMATICA [Fadiman - 1958]

**K**

KAEMPFFERT, WALDEMAR  (1)
    Diminishing Draft, The...................................AIs     2/9/18
        THE BIG BOOK OF SCIENCE FICTION [Conklin - 1950]
KAFKA, FRANZ  (3)
    Burrow, The.............................(From The Great Wall of China; 1946)
        TERROR IN THE MODERN VEIN [Woolheim - 1955]
    In the Penal Colony.......................(From The Penal Colony; 1948)
        TIMELESS STORIES FOR TODAY AND TOMORROW [Bradbury - 1952]
    Metamorphosis.............................(From The Metamorphosis; 1937)
        WORLD OF WONDER [Pratt - 1952]
KAHN, BERNARD I.  (2)
    Command..................................................ASF   Jan 1947
        SPACE SERVICE [Norton - 1953]

KAHN, BERNARD I. [Cont'd]                                 Mag.      Year
  For the Public.........................................................ASF   Dec 1946
      SPACE SERVICE [Norton - 1953]
KANIN, GARSON (I)
  Damnedest Thing, The...................................................Esq   Feb 1956
      SF: 57 THE YEAR'S GREATEST SF AND FANTASY [Merril - 1957]
KAPP, COLIN (I)
  Railways Up On Cannis, The.............................................NW #87 Oct 1959
      OUT OF THIS WORLD 2 [Williams-Ellis & Owen - 196!]
KELLEAM, JOSEPH E. (2)
  Eagles Gather, The.....................................................ASF   Apr 1942
      CROSSROADS IN TIME [Conklin - 1953]
  Rust...................................................................ASF   Oct 1939
      THE ROBOT AND THE MAN [Greenberg - 1953]
KEELER, HARRY STEPHEN (I)
  John Jones' Dollar.....................................................Amz   Apr 1927
      STRANGE PORTS OF CALL [Derleth - 1948]
      FANTASIA MATHEMTICA [Fadiman - 1958]
KEENE, DAY (I)
  "What So Proudly We Hail..."...........................................Im    Dec 1950
      SCIENCE FICTION ADVENTURES IN DIMENSION [Conklin - 1953]
KELLER, DAVID H., M. D. (9)
  Doorbell, The..........................................................WS    Jun 1934
      THE OMNIBUS OF SCIENCE FICTION [Conklin - 1952]
  Golden Bough, The......................................................MT    Win 1934
      THE GARDEN OF FEAR AND OTHER STORIES [Crawford - 1945]
  Ivy War, The...........................................................Amz   May 1930
      THE BEST OF SCIENCE FICTION [Conklin - 1946]
  Literary Corkscrew, The................................................WS    Mar 1934
      FROM OFF THIS WORLD [Margulies & Friend - 1949]
  Living Machine, The....................................................WS    May 1935
      EVERY BOY'S BOOK OF SCIENCE FICTION [Wollheim - 1951]
  Revolt of the Pedestrians, The.........................................Amz   Feb 1928
      BEYOND TIME AND SPACE [Derleth - 1950]
  Service First..........................................................AQ    Win 1931
      THE OUTER REACHES [Derleth - 1951]
  Star, The..............................................................ORIGINAL STORY
      BEACHHEADS IN SPACE [Derleth - 1954]
  Worm, The..............................................................Amz   Mar 1929
      STRANGE PORTS OF CALL [Derleth - 1948]
KELLY, WALT (I)
  Thinkers, The...............(cartoon)................Hall Syndicate   1/29/61
      SIXTH ANNUAL OF THE YEAR'S BEST SF [Merril - 1961]
KEMP, EARL (3)
  Science-Fiction Book Index, The [1954 Listing].............................
      THE BEST SCIENCE FICTION STORIES AND NOVELS: 1955 [Dikty - 1955]
  Science-Fiction Book Index, The [1955 Listing].............................
      THE BEST SCIENCE FICTION STORIES AND NOVELS: 1956 [Dikty - 1956]
  Science-Fiction Book Index, The [1956 and 1957 Listing]
      THE BEST SCIENCE FICTION STORIES AND NOVELS: 9th SERIES [Dikty - 1958]
KEPPLER, JOHANNES (I)
  Somnium..........................(English translation by Everett F. Bleiler)
      (Originally published in Latin; Frankfurt: 1634)
          BEYOND TIME AND SPACE [Derleth - 1950]

KENT, KELVIN (1) (See also listings Henry Kuttner & Lewis Padgett) Mag.    Year
    Comedy of Eras, The................................................TWS  Sep 1940
        THE OTHER WORLDS [Stong - 1941]
KENT, RUSSELL (1)
    Cruise of the S-900, The........................................ORIGINAL STORY
        ADVENTURES TO COME [Esenwein - 1937]
KERSH, GERALD (6)
    Copper Dahlia, The...........(From The Brighton Monster & Other Stories; 1953)
        BEST SF TWO SCIENCE FICTION STORIES [Crispin - 1956]
    Monster, The...................................................SEP    2/21/48
        THE OTHER SIDE OF THE MOON [Derleth - 1949]
    Note On Danger B..............................................SEP    4/5/47
        THE SATURDAY EVENING POST FANTASY STORIES [Fles - 1951]
    River of Riches...............................................SEP    3/8/58
        SF: 59 THE YEAR'S GREATEST SF AND FANTASY [Merril - 1959]
    Voices in the Dust............................................SEP    9/13/47
        SHOT IN THE DARK [Merril - 1950]
    Whatever Happened To Corporal Cuckoo?.........................................
        (From The Brighton Monster and Other Stories; 1953)
            STAR SCIENCE FICTION STORIES #3 [Pohl - 1954]
            STAR OF STARS [Pohl - 1960]
KEYES, DANIEL (2)
    Crazy Maro...................................................F&SF  Apr 1960
        THE BEST FROM FANTASY & SCIENCE FICTION: 10th SERIES [Mills - 1961]
    Flowers For Algernon.........................................F&SF  Apr 1959
        THE BEST FROM FANTASY & SCIENCE FICTION: 9th SERIES [Mills - 1960]
        FIFTH ANNUAL OF THE YEAR'S BEST SF [Merril - 1960]
        BEST SF FOUR SCIENCE FICTION STORIES [Crispin - 1961]
KING, MARSHALL (1)
    Beach Scene..................................................Glxy  Oct 1960
        SIXTH ANNUAL OF THE YEAR'S BEST SF [Merril - 1961]
KIPLING, RUDYARD (4)
    Easy As A.B.C. ..............................................LM  Apr 1912
        THE SCIENCE FICTION GALAXY [Conklin - 1950]
    Finest Story in the World, The...............(From Many Inventions; 1893)
        TRAVELERS IN TIME [Stern - 1947]
        WORLD OF WONDER [Pratt - 1951]
    Mark of the Beast, The.......................(From Life's Handicap; 1891)
        WORLD OF WONDER [Pratt - 1951]
    "Wireless".....................................................SM  Aug 1902
        THE MOONLIGHT TRAVELER [Stern - 1943]
        JOURNEYS IN SCIENCE FICTION [Loughlin & Popp - 1961]
KIPPAX, JOHN (2)
    Dusty Death, The............................................NW #77  Nov 1958
        OUT OF THIS WORLD 2 [Williams-Ellis & Owen - 1961]
    Friday......................................................NW #80  Feb 1959
        OUT OF THIS WORLD 1 [Williams-Ellis & Owen - 1960]
KIRKLAND, JACK (1)
    Wall of Fire, The...........................................BB  Jul 1932
        EDITOR'S CHOICE IN SCIENCE FICTION [Moskowitz - 1954]
        (Story selected by Donald Kennicott)
KLINE, OTIS ADELBERT (1) ·
    Stolen Centuries.............................................TWS  Jun 1939
        EDITOR'S CHOICE IN SCIENCE FICTION [Moskowitz - 1954]
        (Story selected by Oscar J. Friend)        Rpnt - FFM  Sep 1953

KNEALE, NIGEL  (I)                                      Mag.    Year
   Jeremy In the Wind...............................(From Tomato Cain; 1950)
      TIMELESS STORIES FOR TODAY AND TOMORROW [Bradbury - 1952]
KNIGHT, DAMON  (23)
   Analogues, The.............................................ASF   Jan 1952
      13 GREAT STORIES OF SCIENCE FICTION [Conklin - 1960]
   Ask Me Anything............................................Glxy  May 1951
      THE GALAXY READER OF SCIENCE FICTION [Gold - 1952]
   Cabin Boy..................................................Glxy  Sep 1951
      THE GALAXY READER OF SCIENCE FICTION [Gold - 1952]
   Catch That Martian.........................................Glxy  Mar 1952
      THE OMNIBUS OF SCIENCE FICTION [Conklin - 1952]
   Country of the Kind, The...................................F&SF  Feb 1956
      SF: THE YEAR'S GREATEST SCIENCE FICTION AND FANTASY [Merril - 1956]
   Don't Live In the Past.....................................Glxy  Jun 1951
      THE GALAXY READER OF SCIENCE FICTION [Gold - 1952]
   Double Meaning.............................................Stg   Jan 1953
      THREE FROM OUT THERE [Margulies - 1959]
   Eye For What?, An..........................................Glxy  Mar 1957
      THE WORLD THAT COULDN'T BE AND 8 OTHER NOVELETTES FROM GALAXY [Gold-1959]
   Four In One................................................Glxy  Feb 1953
      THE SECOND GALAXY READER OF SCIENCE FICTION [Gold - 1954]
      BEST SF THREE SCIENCE FICTION STORIES [Crispin - 1958]
   Handler, The...............................................Rogue Aug 1960
      FIFTH ANNUAL OF THE YEAR'S BEST SF [Merril - 1960]
   Idiot Stick.............................................ORIGINAL STORY
      STAR SCIENCE FICTION STORIES #4 [Pohl - 1958]
   Man In the Jar.............................................Glxy  Apr 1957
      THE THIRD GALAXY READER OF SCIENCE FICTION [Gold - 1958]
   Natural State..............................................Glxy  Jan 1954
      ALL ABOUT THE FUTURE [Greenberg - 1955]
   Not With A Bang............................................F&SF  Spr 1950
      THE BIG BOOK OF SCIENCE FICTION [Conklin - 1950]
   Rule Golden................................................SFAd  May 1954
      SIX GREAT SHORT NOVELS OF SCIENCE FICTION [Conklin - 1960]
   Special Delivery...........................................Glxy  Apr 1954
      OPERATION FUTURE [Conklin - 1955]
   Stranger Station...........................................F&SF  Dec 1956
      SF: 57 THE YEAR'S GREATEST SF AND FANTASY [Merril - 1957]
   Ticket To Anywhere.........................................Glxy  Apr 1952
      SCIENCE FICTION SHOWCASE [M. Kornbluth - 1959]
   To Serve Man...............................................Glxy  Nov 1950
      THE BEST SCIENCE FICTION STORIES: 1951 [Bleiler & Dikty - 1951]
   What Rough Beast?..........................................F&SF  Feb 1959
      THE BEST FROM FANTASY & SCIENCE FICTION: 9th SERIES [Mills - 1960]
   World Without Children.....................................Glxy  Dec 1951
      FIVE GALAXY SHORT NOVELS [Gold - 1958]
   You're Another.............................................F&SF  Jun 1955
      THE BEST FROM FANTASY & SCIENCE FICTION: 5th SERIES [Boucher - 1956]
   Translation From French

      Blind Pilot, The by Charles Henneberg...............F&SF  Jan 1960
         THE BEST FROM FANTASY & SCIENCE FICTION: 10th SERIES [Mills - 1961]

KNIGHT, DAVID C. (1)                                                    Mag.    Year
   Amazing Mrs. Mimms, The...........................................FU  Aug 1958
     THE FANTASTIC UNIVERSE OMNIBUS [Santesson - 1960]
KNIGHT, ERIC (2)
   Sam Small's Better Half....................(From Sam Small Flies Again; 1942)
     THE MOONLIGHT TRAVELER [Stern - 1943]
   Sam Small's Tyke...........................(From Sam Small Flies Again; 1942)
     OUT OF THIS WORLD [Fast - 1944]
KNIGHT, NORMAN L. (2)
   Crisis In Utopia..................................................ASF  Jul 1940
     FIVE SCIENCE FICTION NOVELS [Greenberg - 1952]
   Short-Circuited Probability.......................................ASF  Sep 1941
     THE BEST OF SCIENCE FICTION [Conklin - 1946]
KOCH, HOWARD (2)
   Invasion From Mars..........The radio script of the Orson Welles broadcast of
     H. G. Wells' "The War of the Worlds" over the Columbia Broadcasting
     System, October 30, 1938.    (Copyright 1940 Princeton University Press)
        INVASION FROM MARS [Welles - 1949]
        INVADERS OF EARTH [Conklin - 1952]
        THE TREASURY OF SCIENCE FICTION CLASSICS [Kuebler - 1955]
   Invasion From Inner Space.....................................ORIGINAL STORY
     STAR SCIENCE FICTION STORIES #6 [Pohl - 1959]
KOESTLER, ARTHUR (1)
   Pythagoras and the Psychoanalyst............(From Arrival and Departure; 1943)
     FANTASIA MATHEMATICA [Fadiman - 1958]
KORNBLUTH, C. M. (20)    (See also listing Cecil Corwin)
   Advent On Channel Twelve, The.................................ORIGINAL STORY
     STAR SCIENCE FICTION STORIES #4 [Pohl - 1958]
   Adventurer, The...................................................Spc  May 1953
     ASSIGNMENT IN TOMORROW [Pohl - 1954]
   Altar At Midnight, The...........................................Glxy Mar 1952
     BEST SF TWO SCIENCE FICTION STORIES [Crispin - 1956]
   Cosmic Expense Account, The......................................F&SF Jan 1956
     THE BEST FROM FANTASY & SCIENCE FICTION: 6th SERIES [Boucher - 1957]
     SF: 57 THE YEAR'S GREATEST SF AND FANTASY [Merril - 1957]
   Dominoes.....................................................ORIGINAL STORY
     STAR SCIENCE FICTION STORIES [Pohl - 1953]
   Gomez............................................................NW #32 Jan 1955
     A TREASURY OF GREAT SCIENCE FICTION [Boucher - 1959]
   I Never Ast No Favors............................................F&SF Apr 1954
     THE BEST FROM FANTASY & SCIENCE FICTION: 4th SERIES [Boucher - 1955]
   Little Black Bag, The............................................ASF  Jul 1950
     BEYOND THE END OF TIME [Pohl - 1952]
   Marching Morons, The.............................................Glxy Apr 1951
     THE BEST SCIENCE FICTION STORIES: 1952 [Bleiler & Dikty - 1952]
     STORIES FOR TOMORROW [Sloane - 1954]
   Mindworm, The....................................................WB  Dec 1950
     THE BEST SCIENCE FICTION STORIES: 1951 [Bleiler & Dikty - 1951]
   Ms. Found In a Chinese Fortune Cookie............................F&SF Jul 1957
     THE BEST FROM FANTASY & SCIENCE FICTION: 7th SERIES [Boucher - 1958]
   Only Thing We Learn, The.........................................Stg  Jul 1949
     THE BIG BOOK OF SCIENCE FICTION [Conklin - 1950]
   Remorseful, The..............................................ORIGINAL STORY
     STAR SCIENCE FICTION STORIES #2 [Pohl - 1953]
   Silly Season, The................................................F&SF Fal 1950
     TOMORROW, THE STARS [Heinlein - 1952]
     THE EARTH IN PERIL [Wollheim - 1957]

KORNBLUTH, C. M. [Cont'd]                                          Mag.    Year
    That Share of Glory..............................................ASF    Jan 1952
        SPACE SERVICE [Norton - 1953]
        EVERY BOY'S BOOK OF OUTER SPACE STORIES [Dikty - 1960]
    Theory of Rocketry..............................................F&SF    Jul 1958
        THE BEST FROM FANTASY & SCIENCE FICTION: 8th SERIES [Boucher - 1959]
    Time Travel and the Law.......................................ORIGINAL STORY
        COMING ATTRACTIONS [Greenberg - 1957]
    Unfortunate Topologist, The.....................................F&SF    Jul 1957
        (Originally appeared under pseudonym S. D. Gottesman)
        FANTASIA MATHEMATICA [Fadiman - 1958]
    Words of Guru, The...............................................Sti    Jun 1941
        (Originally appeared under pseudonym Kenneth Falconer)
        CHILDREN OF WONDER [Tenn - 1953]
w/ Frederik Pohl
    Nightmare with Zeppelins.......................................Glxy    Dec 1958
        THE FIFTH GALAXY READER [Gold - 1961]
KREPPS, ROBERT W.   (2)
    Five Years in the Marmalade.......................................FA    Jul 1949
        (Originally appeared under pseudonym Geoff St. Reynard)
        THE BEST SCIENCE FICTION STORIES: 1950 [Bleiler & Dikty - 1950]
    w/ H. L. Gold
    Enormous Room, The..............................................Amz    Nov 1953
        YEAR'S BEST SCIENCE FICTION NOVELS: 1954 [Bleiler & Dikty - 1954]
KRUSE, CLIFTON B.   (1)
    Dr. Lu-Mie......................................................Ast    Jul 1934
        EVERY BOY'S BOOK OF SCIENCE FICTION [Wollheim - 1951]
KUBILIUS, WALTER   (2)
    Other Side, The.................................................SSS    Apr 1951
        THE BEST SCIENCE FICTION STORIES: 1952 [Bleiler & Dikty - 1952]
    w/ Fletcher Pratt
    Second Chance...................................................FSM    Sep 1952
        SPACE, SPACE, SPACE [Sloane - 1953]
KUMMER, F. A. JR.   (1)
    Forgiveness of Tenchu Taen, The.................................ASF    Nov 1938
        TRAVELERS OF SPACE [Greenberg - 1952]
KUTTNER, HENRY   (21)       (See also listings Kelvin Kent and Lewis Padgett)
    Absalom.........................................................Stg    Fal 1946
        TOMORROW, THE STARS [Heinlein - 1952]
    Call Him Demon..................................................TWS    Fal 1946
        (Originally appeared under pseudonym Keith Hammond)
        STRANGE PORTS OF CALL [Derleth - 1948]
    Children's Hour, The............................................ASF    Mar 1944
        (Originally appeared under pseudonym Lawrence O'Donnell)
        FOUR FOR THE FUTURE [Conklin - 1959]
        A TREASURY OF GREAT SCIENCE FICTION [Boucher - 1959]
    Cold War.......................................................TWS    Oct 1949
        SCIENCE FICTION ADVENTURES IN MUTATION [Conklin - 1956]
    Cross of Centuries, A.......................................ORIGINAL STORY
        STAR SCIENCE FICTION STORIES #4 [Pohl - 1958]
        STAR OF STARS [Pohl - 1960]
    Devil We Know, The..............................................Unk    Aug 1941
        FROM UNKNOWN WORLDS [Campbell - 1948]
    Don't Look Now..................................................Stg    Mar 1948
        MY BEST SCIENCE FICTION STORY [Margulies & Friend - 1949]
    Dream's End.....................................................Stg    Jul 1947
        FUTURE TENSE [Crossen - 1953]

KUTTNER, HENRY [Cont'd]                                             Mag.    Year
    Ego Machine, The.................................................Spc  May 1952
        SCIENCE FICTION CARNIVAL [Brown & Reynolds - 1953]
    Graveyard Rats, The..............................................WT   Mar 1936
        THE OTHER WORLDS [Stong - 1941]
    Happy Ending....................................................TWS   Aug 1948
        THE BEST SCIENCE FICTION STORIES: 1949 [Bleiler & Dikty - 1949]
    Housing Problem.................................................Chm   Oct 1944
        TIMELESS STORIES FOR TODAY AND TOMORROW [Bradbury - 1952]
    Near Miss.............................................................ORIGINAL STORY
        (Copyright 1958 by the Dell Publishing Co. & Western Prtg & Litho. Co.)
            SF: 58 THE YEAR'S GREATEST SF AND FANTASY [Merril - 1958]
    Or Else...................................................(From Ahead of Time; 1953)
        BEST SF SCIENCE FICTION STORIES [Crispin - 1955]
    Piggy Bank......................................................ASF   Dec 1942
        (Originally appeared under pseudonym Lewis Padgett)
        A TREASURY OF GREAT SCIENCE FICTION [Boucher - 1959]
    Pile of Trouble.................................................TWS   Apr 1948
        ZACHERLY'S MIDNIGHT SNACKS [Zacherly - 1960]
    Private Eye.....................................................ASF   Jan 1949
        (Originally appeared under pseudonym Lewis Padgett)
        THE BEST SCIENCE FICTION STORIES: 1950 [Bleiler & Dikty - 1950]
    Shock...........................................................ASF   Mar 1943
        (Originally appeared under pseudonym Lewis Padgett)
        THE OUTER REACHES [Derleth - 1951]
    Sword of Tomorrow...............................................TWS   Fal 1945
        THE GIANT ANTHOLOGY OF SCIENCE FICTION [Margulies & Friend - 1954]
    Trophy..........................................................TWS   Win 1944
        (Originally appeared under pseudonym Scott Morgan)
        THE SAINT'S CHOICE [Charteris - 1945]
    w/ C. L. Moore  (Mrs. Henry Kuttner)
        Home There's No Returning......................(From No Boundaries; 1955)
            SF: THE YEAR'S GREATEST SCIENCE FICTION & FANTASY [Merril - 1956]

# L

LA FARGE, OLIVER  (2)
    John the Revelator...........................................F&SF   Feb 1951
        THE BEST FROM FANTASY & SCIENCE FICTION [Boucher & McComas - 1952]
    Spud and Cochise......................................Rpnt - F&SF   Dec 1957
        A DECADE OF FANTASY & SCIENCE FICTION [Mills - 1960]     For   Jan 1936
LAFFERTY, R. A.  (1)
    Snuffles.....................................................Glxy   Dec 1960
        MIND PARTNER AND 8 OTHER NOVELETTES FROM GALAXY [Gold - 1961]
LAMPORT, FELICA  (1)
    Sigh For Cybernetics, A..............(verse)..................Hpr   Jan 1961
        SIXTH ANNUAL OF THE YEAR'S BEST SF [Merril - 1961]
LANG, ALLEN K.  (1)
    Eel by the Tail, An...........................................Im   Apr 1951
        INVADERS OF EARTH [Conklin - 1952]

```
LANG, DANIEL  (I)                                                    Mag.     Year
   Man In Space.........................................................Nykr  11/15/58
         SF: 59 THE YEAR'S GREATEST SF AND FANTASY [Merril - 1959]
LANGART, DARREL T.   (I)
   What the Left Hand Was Doing........................................ASF   Feb 1960
         FIFTH ANNUAL OF THE YEAR'S BEST SF [Merril - 1960]
LANGDON, GEORGE  (I)
   Of Those Who Came...................................................NW #18  Nov 1952
         GATEWAY TO TOMORROW [Carnell - 1954]
         SPACE POLICE [Norton - 1956]
LATHAM, PHILIP ps (Robert S. Richardson)  (2)
   N Day...............................................................ASF   Jan 1946
         A TREASURY OF SCIENCE FICTION [Conklin - 1948]
   Xi Effect, The......................................................ASF   Jan 1950
         IMAGINATION UNLIMITED [Bleiler & Dikty - 1952]
         BEST SF SCIENCE FICTION STORIES [Crispin - 1955]
LAVOND, PAUL DENNIS ps  (Robert W. Lowndes)
   Lurani................................(verse).......................Unk   Feb 1940
         FROM UNKNOWN WORLDS [J. W. Campbell - 1948]
LAWRENCE, D. H.   (I)
   Rocking-Horse Winner, The.........................(From The Lovely Lady; 1933)
         CHILDREN OF WONDER [Tenn - 1953]
LEACOCK, STEPHEN  (I)
   Man In Asbestos: An Allegory of the Future........(From Nonsense Novels; 1941)
         ASPECTS OF SCIENCE FICTION [Doherty - 1959]
LEAHY, JOHN MARTIN  (I)
   Voices From the Cliff...............................................WT    May 1925
         SCIENCE AND SORCERY [Ford - 1953]
LeBLANC, MAURICE  (I)
   Invisible Prisoner, The............................................(No data available)
         INVISIBLE MEN [Davenport - 1960]
LEES, GENE  (I)
   Stranger From Space.................................................SF #7  Mar 1954
         GATEWAY TO THE STARS [Carnell - 1955]
LEIBER, FRITZ (JR.)  (29)
   Appointment In Tomorrow.............................................Glxy   Jul 1951
         TOMORROW, THE STARS [Heinlein - 1952]
             (Appeared under title Poor Superman)
         THE BEST SCIENCE FICTION STORIES: 1952 [Bleiler & Dikty - 1952]
   Bad Day For Sales, A................................................Glxy   Jul 1953
         SHADOW OF TOMORROW [Pohl - 1953]
         THE SECOND GALAXY READER OF SCIENCE FICTION [Gold - 1954]
         THE BEST SCIENCE FICTION STORIES: 1954 [Bleiler & Dikty - 1954]
   Big Holiday, The....................................................F&SF   Jan 1953
         THE BEST SCIENCE FICTION STORIES: 1954 [Bleiler & Dikty - 1954]
   Big Trek, The.......................................................F&SF   Oct 1957
         THE BEST FROM FANTASY & SCIENCE FICTION: 7th SERIES [Boucher - 1958]
   Business of Killing.................................................ASF   Sep 1944
         SCIENCE FICTION ADVENTURES IN DIMENSION [Conklin - 1953]
         GALAXY OF GHOULS [Merril - 1955]
   Coming Attractions..................................................Glxy   Nov 1950
         THE BEST SCIENCE FICTION STORIES: 1951 [Bleiler & Dikty - 1951]
         THE GALAXY READER OF SCIENCE FICTION [Gold - 1952]
   Conjure Wife........................................................Unk   Apr 1943
         WITCHES THREE [Pratt - 1952]
```

(247)

```
LEIBER, FRITZ (JR.) [Cont'd]                                            Mag.   Year
    Deskful of Girls, A.........................................F&SF Apr 1958
        THE BEST FROM FANTASY & SCIENCE FICTION: 8th SERIES [Boucher - 1959]
    Destiny Times Three.........................................ASF  Apr 1945
        FIVE SCIENCE FICTION NOVELS [Greenberg - 1952]
    Enchanted Forest, The.......................................ASF  Oct 1950
        WORLDS OF TOMORROW [Derleth - 1953]
    Foxholes of Mars, The.......................................TWS  Jun 1952
        BEYOND HUMAN KEN [Merril - 1952]
    Girl With the Hungry Eyes, The..............................ORIGINAL STORY
        THE GIRL WITH THE HUNGRY EYES AND OTHER STORIES [Wollheim - 1949]
        TERROR IN THE MODERN VEIN [Wollheim - 1955]
    Last Letter, The............................................Glxy Jun 1958
        THE FIFTH GALAXY READER [Gold - 1961]
    Later Than You Think........................................Glxy Oct 1950
        FAR BOUNDARIES [Derleth - 1951]
    Mariana.....................................................Fnt  Feb 1960
        FIFTH ANNUAL OF THE YEAR'S BEST SF [Merril - 1960]
    Mechanical Bride, The.......................................ORIGINAL STORY
        SCIENCE FICTION THINKING MACHINES [Conklin - 1954]
    Moon Is Green, The..........................................Glxy Apr 1952
        THE BEST SCIENCE FICTION STORIES: 1953 [Bleiler & Dikty - 1953]
    Mr. Bauer and the Atoms.....................................WT   Jan 1946
        STRANGE PORTS OF CALL [Derleth - 1948]
    Mutant's Brother, The.......................................ASF  Aug 1943
        CROSSROADS IN TIME [Conklin - 1953]
    Night He Cried, The.........................................ORIGINAL STORY
        STAR SCIENCE FICTION STORIES [Pohl - 1953]
    Pail of Air, A..............................................Glxy Dec 1951
        SPACE PIONEERS [Norton - 1954]
        THE SECOND GALAXY READER OF SCIENCE FICTION [Gold - 1954]
    Sanity......................................................ASF  Apr 1944
        THE BIG BOOK OF SCIENCE FICTION [Conklin - 1950]
    Ship Sails at Midnight, The.................................FA   Sep 1950
        THE OUTER REACHES [Derleth - 1951]
    Smoke Ghost.................................................Unk  Oct 1941
        HUMAN? [Merril - 1954]
    Space-Time For Springers....................................ORIGINAL STORY
        STAR SCIENCE FICTION STORIES #4 [Pohl - 1958]
        SF: 59 THE YEAR'S GREATEST SF AND FANTASY [Merril - 1959]
        STAR OF STARS [Pohl - 1960]
    Taboo.......................................................ASF  Feb 1944
        JOURNEY TO INFINITY [Greenberg - 1951]
    Time In the Round...........................................Glxy May 1957
        THE THIRD GALAXY READER OF SCIENCE FICTION [Gold - 1958]
    Wanted-An Enemy.............................................ASF  Feb 1945
        BEYOND TIME AND SPACE [Derleth - 1950]
    What's He Doing In There?...................................Glxy Dec 1957
        THE FOURTH GALAXY READER OF SCIENCE FICTION [Gold - 1959]
LEIMERT, JOHN (1)
    John Thomas's Cure..........................................Atl  Aug 1945
        THE OMNIBUS OF SCIENCE FICTION [Conklin - 1952]
LEINSTER, MURRAY ps (Will F. Jenkins) (38)   (See also listing Will F. Jenkins)
    Assignment On Pasik.........................................TWS  Feb 1949
        ADVENTURES ON OTHER PLANETS [Wollheim - 1954]
```

LEINSTER, MURRAY [Cont'd]                                      Mag.    Year
    Cure For A Ylith................................................Stg  Nov 1949
        OPERATION FUTURE [Conklin - 1955]
    Day of the Deepies, The........................................FFM  Oct 1947
        SHOT IN THE DARK [Merril - 1950]
    De Profundis...................................................TWS  Win 1945
        FAR BOUNDARIES [Derleth - 1951]
    Devil of East Lupton, The......................................TWS  Aug 1948
        (Originally appeared under title The Devil of East Lupton Vermont under
            byline William Fitzgerald)
                THE OTHER SIDE OF THE MOON [Derleth - 1949]
    Ethical Equations, The.........................................ASF  Jun 1945
        A TREASURY OF SCIENCE FICTION [Conklin - 1948]
    First Contact..................................................ASF  May 1945
            THE BEST OF SCIENCE FICTION [Conklin - 1946]
            THE ASTOUNDING SCIENCE FICTION ANTHOLOGY [J. W. Campbell - 1952]
            STORIES FOR TOMORROW [Sloane - 1954]
    Fourth Dimensional Demonstrator, The...........................Ast  Dec 1935
        THE OTHER WORLDS [Stong - 1941]
    Gadget Had A Ghost, The........................................TWS  Jun 1952
        THE YEAR'S BEST SCIENCE FICTION NOVELS: 1952 [Bleiler & Dikty - 1952]
    Historical Note................................................ASF  Feb 1951
        THE ASTOUNDING SCIENCE FICTION ANTHOLOGY [J. W. Campbell - 1952]
    If You Was A Maklin............................................Glxy Sep 1951
        THE GALAXY READER OF SCIENCE FICTION [Gold - 1952]
    Incident On Calypso............................................Stg  Fai 1945
        INVASION FROM MARS [Welles - 1949]
    Jezebel........................................................Stg  Oct 1953
        PORTALS OF TOMORROW [Derleth - 1954]
    Journey, The...................................................ORIGINAL STORY
        STAR SCIENCE FICTION STORIES [Pohl - 1953]
    Keyhole........................................................TWS  Dec 1951
        TOMORROW, THE STARS [Heinlein - 1952]
        CHILDREN OF WONDER [Tenn - 1953]
        MEN ON THE MOON [Wollheim - 1958]
    Life-Work of Professor Muntz, The..............................TWS  Jun 1949
        THE SCIENCE FICTION GALAXY [Conklin - 1950]
        THE BEST SCIENCE FICTION STORIES: 1950 [Bleiler & Dikty - 1950]
    Logic Named Joe, A.............................................ASF  Mar 1946
        (Originally appeared under byline Will F. Jenkins)
            SCIENCE FICTION CARNIVAL [Brown & Reynolds - 1953]
    Lonely Planet, The.............................................TWS  Dec 1949
        BEYOND THE END OF TIME [Pohl - 1952]
    Lost Race, The.................................................TWS  Apr 1949
        MY BEST SCIENCE FICTION STORY [Margulies & Friend - 1949]
    Malignant Marauder.............................................TWS  Sum 1946
        (Originally appeared under title Dead City)
            THE ULTIMATE INVADER AND OTHER STORIES [Wollheim - 1954]
    Med Service....................................................ASF  Aug 1957
        SCIENCE FICTION SHOWCASE [M. Kornbluth - 1959]
    Middle of the Week After Next, The by Murray Leinster ps (Will F. Jenkins)....
                                                                   TWS  Aug 1952
            SCIENCE FICTION ADVENTURES IN DIMENSION [Conklin - 1953]
            THE BEST SCIENCE FICTION STORIES: 1953 [Bleiler & Dikty - 1953]
            OUT OF THIS WORLD I [Williams-Ellis & Owen - 1960]

LEINSTER, MURRAY [Cont'd]                                     Mag.    Year
    Nobody Saw The Ship..............................................FSFS   Jun 1950
        THE BIG BOOK OF SCIENCE FICTION [Conklin - 1950]
    Other Now, The...................................................Glxy   Mar 1951
        THE GALAXY READER OF SCIENCE FICTION [Gold - 1952]
    Other World, The.................................................Stg    Nov 1949
        SIX GREAT SHORT NOVELS OF SCIENCE FICTION [Conklin - 1954]
            (Revised for inclusion in this anthology)
    Over Drive.......................................................Stg    Jan 1953
        ADVENTURES IN THE FAR FUTURE [Wollheim - 1954]
    Pipeline To Pluto................................................ASF    Aug 1945
        SCIENCE FICTION TERROR TALES [Conklin - 1955]
    Plague...........................................................ASF    Feb 1944
        THE OMNIBUS OF SCIENCE FICTION [Conklin - 1952]
    Plants, The......................................................ASF    Jan 1946
        MEN AGAINST THE STARS [Greenberg - 1950]
    Power, The.......................................................ASF    Sep 1945
        THE OUTER REACHES [Derleth - 1951]
        LOOKING FORWARD [Lesser - 1953]
    Propagandist.....................................................ASF    Aug 1947
        POSSIBLE WORLDS OF SCIENCE FICTION [Conklin - 1951]
        STORIES OF SCIENTIFIC IMAGINATION [Gallant - 1954]
    Queen's Astrologer, The..........................................TWS    Oct 1949
        CROSSROADS IN TIME [Conklin - 1953]
    Sentamentalists, The.............................................Glxy   Apr 1953
        THE YEAR'S BEST SCIENCE FICTION NOVELS: 1954 [Bleiler & Dikty - 1954]
    Skag With the Queer Head.........................................MSF    Aug 1951
        SCIENCE FICTION ADVENTURES IN MUTATION [Conklin - 1956]
    Strange Case of John Kingman, The................................ASF    May 1948
        THE BEST SCIENCE FICTION STORIES: 1949 [Bleiler & Dikty - 1949]
        GREAT STORIES OF SCIENCE FICTION [Leinster - 1951]
    Things Pass By...................................................TWS    Sum 1945
        THE GIANT ANTHOLOGY OF SCIENCE FICTION [Margulies & Friend - 1954]
        THE EARTH IN PERIL [Wollheim - 1957]
    This Star Shall Be Free..........................................Sup    Nov 1949
        INVADERS OF EARTH [Conklin - 1952]
    Wabbler, The.....................................................ASF    Oct 1942
        BEYOND HUMAN KEN [Merril - 1952]
        BEST SF THREE SCIENCE FICTION STORIES [Crispin - 1958]
LESLIE, NORMAN   (1)
    Six Hundred Fathoms..............................................ORIGINAL STORY
        ADVENTURES TO COME [Esenwein - 1937]
LESSER, MILTON   (5)  See also listing Stephen Marlowe
    Black Eyes and the Daily Grind...................................If     Mar 1952
        STORIES FOR TOMORROW [Sloane - 1954]
    Cold Night For Dying, A..........................................If     Dec 1954
        THE FIRST WORLD OF IF [Quinn & Wulff - 1957]
    Exterran.........................................................ORIGINAL STORY
        TOMORROW'S UNIVERSE [H. J. Campbell - 1954]
    Operation Zero...................................................Orb #4  Sep 1954
        (Originally appeared under title Intruder on the Rim)
            THE SANDS OF MARS AND OTHER STORIES [Anonymous - 1958]
    Pen Pal..........................................................Glxy   Jul 1951
        INVADERS OF EARTH [Conklin - 1952]

LEWIS, C. S.   (4)                                                            Mag.    Year
    Adventure In a Space Ship, An.............(From Out of the Silent Planet; 1938)
        SCIENCE IN FICTION [A.E.M. & J.C. Bayliss - 1957]
    Expostulation, An..................(verse).....................F&SF   Jun 1959
        THE BEST FROM FANTASY & SCIENCE FICTION: 9th SERIES [Mills - 1960]
    Ministering Angels............................................F&SF   Jan 1958
        THE BEST FROM FANTASY & SCIENCE FICTION: 8th SERIES [Boucher - 1959]
    Shoddy Lands, The.............................................F&SF   Feb 1956
        THE BEST FROM FANTASY & SCIENCE FICTION: 6th SERIES [Boucher - 1957]
LEWIS, JACK   (1)
    Who's Cribbing?...............................................Stg    Jan 1953
        THE BEST FROM STARTLING STORIES [Mines - 1953]
LEWIS, OSCAR   (1)
    Lost Years, The...............(Originally published by Alfred A. Knopf; 1951)
        A TREASURY OF GREAT SCIENCE FICTION [Boucher - 1959]
LEY, WILLY   (7)
    Geography For Time Travelers..................................ASF    Jul 1939
        COMING ATTRACTIONS [Greenberg - 1957]
    Letter to the Martians, A.....................................TWS    Nov 1940
        (Originally appeared under title Calling All Martians)
        COMING ATTRACTIONS [Greenberg - 1957]
    Space War.....................................................ASF    Aug 1939
        COMING ATTRACTIONS [Greenberg - 1957]
    Where Do We Go From Here?.............................ORIGINAL STORY
        SF: 58 THE YEAR'S GREATEST SF AND FANTASY [Merril - 1958]
    Translation from German
            Enemies of Space by Karl Grunert..........(Originally published in 1907)
                INVADERS OF EARTH [Conklin - 1952]
            Universal Library, The by Kurd Lasswitz....(Originally published in 1901)
                FANTASIA MATHEMATICA [Fadiman - 1958]
            Postscript to "The Universal Library" by Willy Ley.........ORIGINAL STORY
                FANTASIA MATHEMATICA [Fadiman - 1958]
LEYSON, CAPTAIN BURR W.   (1)
    Trail to the Stars............................................BLM    Feb 1950
        SCIENCE FICTION AND READER'S GUIDE [Barrows - 1954]
LLEWELLYN, RICHARD   (1)
    Mother and the Decimal Point.............(From How Green Was My Valley; 1940)
        FANTASIA MATHEMATICA [Fadiman - 1958]
LINDSAY, VACHEL   (1)
    Euclid.....................(From The Congo and other Poems; 1914)
        FANTASIA MATHEMATICA [Fadiman - 1958]
LOCKE, ROBERT DONALD   (2)
    Dark Nuptial..................................................TWS    Feb 1953
        THE BEST FROM STARTLING STORIES [Mines - 1953]
    Demotion......................................................ASF    Sep 1952
        PRIZE SCIENCE FICTION [Wollheim - 1953]
LOCKHARD, LEONARD ps (Theodore L. Thomas)   (1)
    Lagging Profession, The.......................................ASF    Jan 1961
        SIXTH ANNUAL OF THE YEAR'S BEST SF [Merril - 1961]
LONDON, JACK   (2)
    Scarlet Plague, The...........................................ASMM   6/8/13
        OUT OF THIS WORLD [Fast - 1944]
        THE OMNIBUS OF SCIENCE FICTION [Conklin - 1952]

Mag.    Year

LONDON, JACK [Cont'd]
  Shadow and the Flash, The.......................................Bkm  Jun 1903
      SHOT IN THE DARK [Merril - 1950]
      INVISIBLE MEN [Davenport - 1960]
LONG, AMELIA REYNOLDS  (2)
  Omega.........................................................Amz  Jul 1932
      THE END OF THE WORLD [Wollheim - 1956]
  Reverse Phylogemy.............................................ASF  Jun 1937
      SCIENCE FICTION ADVENTURES IN DIMENSION [Conklin - 1953]
LONG, FRANK BELKNAP (JR.)  (17)
  And Someday To Mars...........................................TWS  Feb 1952
      EDITOR'S CHOICE IN SCIENCE FICTION [Moskowitz - 1954]
        (Story selected by Samuel Mines)
  Cones.........................................................Ast  Feb 1936
      POSSIBLE WORLDS OF SCIENCE FICTION [Conklin - 1951]
  Critters, The.................................................ASF  Nov 1945
      THE OUTER REACHES [Derleth - 1951]
  Flame Midget, The.............................................Ast  Dec 1936
      THE BEST OF SCIENCE FICTION [Conklin - 1946]
  Great Cold, The...............................................Ast  Feb 1935
      WORLDS OF TOMORROW [Derleth - 1953]
  Guest In the House, A.........................................ASF  Mar 1946
      STRANGE PORTS OF CALL [Derleth - 1948]
  House of Rising Winds, The....................................Stg  Mar 1948
      MY BEST SCIENCE FICTION STORY [Margulies & Friend - 1949]
  Humpty Dumpty Had a Great Fall................................Stg  Nov 1948
      BEYOND TIME AND SPACE [Derleth - 1950]
  Invasion......................................................Stg  Jul 1950
      FAR BOUNDARIES [Derleth - 1951]
  Maturity Night.........................................ORIGINAL STORY
      THE GIRL WITH THE HUNGRY EYES AND OTHER STORIES [Wollheim - 1947]
  Mercurian, The................................................PS  Win 1941
      FLIGHT INTO SPACE [Wollheim - 1950]
  Planets Must Slay.............................................TWS  Apr 1942
      THE SAINT'S CHOICE [Charteris - 1945]
  Red Storm on Jupiter..........................................Ast  May 1936
      FLIGHT INTO SPACE [Wollheim - 1950]
  Temporal Transgressor, The....................................ASF  Aug 1944
      (Originally appeared under title Bridgehead)
      THE ULTIMATE INVADER AND OTHER SCIENCE FICTION [Wollheim - 1954]
  To Follow Knowedge............................................ASF  Dec 1942
      SCIENCE FICTION ADVENTURES IN DIMENSION [Conklin - 1953]
  Two Face......................................................WT  Mar 1950
      THE BEST SCIENCE FICTION STORIES: 1951 [Bleiler & Dikty - 1951]
  World of Wulkins, The.........................................TWS  Apr 1948
      STRANGE PORTS OF CALL [Derleth - 1948]
LOOMIS, NOEL  (1)
  Long Dawn, The................................................Sup  Jan 1950
      THE BIG BOOK OF SCIENCE FICTION [Conklin - 1950]
LORD, MINDRET  (3)
  Dr. Jacobus Meliflore's Last Patient.........................F&SF  Nov 1953
      ZACHERLY'S VULTURE STEW [Zacherly - 1960]
  Naked Lady....................................................WT  Sep 1934
      THE OTHER WORLDS [Stong - 1941]
  Problem For Biographers, A.............................ORIGINAL STORY
      THE OTHER WORLDS [Stong - 1941]

LOVECRAFT, H. P.   (8)                                                  Mag.    Year
    At the Mountains of Madness...........................................Ast   Apr 1936
        STRANGE PORTS OF CALL [Derleth - 1948]
    Beyond the Wall of Sleep..............................................WT    Mar 1938
        THE OTHER SIDE OF THE MOON [Derleth - 1949]
    Celephais.............................................................MT    May 1934
        THE GARDEN OF FEAR AND OTHER STORIES [Crawford - 1945]
    Colour Out of Space, The..............................................Amz   Sep 1927
        THE OMNIBUS OF SCIENCE FICTION [Conklin - 1952]
    From Beyond...........................................................WT    Feb 1938
        WORLDS OF TOMORROW [Derleth - 1953]
    He....................................................................WT    Sep 1926
        TERROR IN THE MODERN VEIN [Wollheim - 1955]
    In the Vault..........................................................WT    Apr 1932
        THE OTHER WORLDS [Stong - 1941]
    Shadow Out of Time, The...............................................Ast   Jun 1936
        THE PORTABLE NOVELS OF SCIENCE [Wollheim - 1945]
LOWNDES, ROBERT W.   (2)    (See also listing Paul Dennis Lavond)
    Highway...............................................................SFQ   Fal 1942
        (Originally appeared under pseudonym Wilfred Owen Morley)
            LOOKING FORWARD [Lesser - 1953]
    w/ John Michael
        Inheritors, The...................................................Fut   Oct 1942
            TERROR IN THE MODERN VEIN [Wollheim - 1955]
LUCIEN   (2)
    Ancient Gulliver, An............(From A True History; Written about 165 A. D.)
        SCIENCE IN FICTION [A.E.M. & J. C. Bayliss - 1957]
    True History, A.....................................(Written about 165 A. D.)
        BEYOND TIME AND SPACE [Derleth - 1950]
LUDWIG, EDWARD W.   (1)
    Drivers, The..........................................................If    Mar 1956
        THE FIRST WORLD OF IF [Quinn & Wulff - 1957]

MacCORMAC, JOHN   (1)
    Enchanted Weekend, The................................................Unk   Oct 1939
        FROM UNKNOWN WORLDS [J. W. Campbell - 1948]
MacCREIGH, JAMES  ps (Frederik Pohl)   (3)    (See listing Frederik Pohl)
    Hitch In Time, A......................................................TWS   Jun 1947
        SHOT IN THE DARK [Merril - 1950]
    Let the Ants Try......................................................PS    Win 1949
        BEYOND THE END OF TIME [Pohl - 1952]
    w/ Isaac Asimov
        Little Man on the Subway, The.....................................FB #6 n/d 1950
            SCIENCE AND SORCERY [Ford - 1953]
MacDONALD, ANSON  ps (Robert A. Heinlein)   (3)
    (See also listing Robert A. Heinlein)

MacDONALD, ANSON [Cont'd]                                           Mag.    Year
  By His Bootstraps...................................................ASF  Oct 1941
        ADVENTURES IN TIME AND SPACE [Healy & McComas - 1946]
        THE GIANT ANTHOLOGY OF SCIENCE FICTION [Margulies & Friend - 1954]
          (Appeared under Robert A. Heinlein byline)
        SPECTRUM [Amis & Conquest - 1961].......................ASF  Mar 1942
  Goldfish Bowl......................................................ASF  Mar 1942
        THE BEST OF SCIENCE FICTION [Conklin - 1946]
  Solution Unsatisfactory...........................................ASF  May 1941
        THE BEST OF SCIENCE FICTION [Conklin - 1946]
MacDONALD, JOHN D.  (13)                                            WB   Dec 1950
  Big Contest, The...................................................WB   Dec 1950
        HUMAN? [Merril - 1954]
  Child is Crying, A.................................................TWS  Dec 1948
        THE SCIENCE FICTION GALAXY [Conklin - 1950]
  Common Denominator................................................Glxy Jul 1951
        THE GALAXY READER OF SCIENCE FICTION [Gold - 1952]
  Dance of a New World..............................................ASF  Sep 1948
        JOURNEY TO INFINITY [Greenberg - 1951]
  Flaw..............................................................Stg  Jan 1949
        THE BEST SCIENCE FICTION STORIES: 1949 [Bleiler & Dikty - 1949]
  Game For Blondes, A...............................................Glxy Oct 1952
        THE BEST SCIENCE FICTION STORIES: 1953 [Bleiler & Dikty - 1953]
        THE SECOND GALAXY READER OF SCIENCE FICTION [Gold - 1954]
  Hunted, The.......................................................Sup  Jul 1949
        BEYOND THE END OF TIME [Pohl - 1952]
  Incubation...............................................ORIGINAL STORY
        FUTURE TENSE [Crossen - 1953]
  Mechanical Answer, The............................................ASF  May 1948
        THE ROBOT AND THE MAN [Greenberg - 1953]
  Miniature, The....................................................Sup  Sep 1949
        THE BIG BOOK OF SCIENCE FICTION [Conklin - 1950]
          (Originally appeared under pseudonym Peter Reed)
  Ring Around the Redhead...........................................Stg  Nov 1948
        SCIENCE FICTION ADVENTURES IN DIMENSION [Conklin - 1953]
  Spectator Sport...................................................TWS  Feb 1950
        THE OMNIBUS OF SCIENCE FICTION [Conklin - 1952]
  Susceptibility....................................................Glxy Jan 1951
        THE GALAXY READER OF SCIENCE FICTION [Gold - 1952]
MacDONALD, PHILIP  (2)                                              F&SF Aug 1951
  Hub, The..........................................................F&SF Aug 1951
        (Originally appeared under title Solitary Confinement)
        THE BEST FROM FANTASY & SCIENCE FICTION [Boucher & McComas - 1952]
  Private-Keep Out!.................................................MoF  Fal 1949
        WORLD OF WONDER [Pratt - 1952]
MacFADYEN, A. JR. (1)
  Time Decelerator, The.............................................Ast  Jul 1936
        CROSSROADS IN TIME [Conklin - 1953]
MacFARLANE, WALLACE  (1)
  Dead End..........................................................Glxy Jan 1952
        SCIENCE FICTION THINKING MACHINES [Conklin - 1954]
MacGREGOR, ELLEN  (1)
  Mars and Miss Pickerell..............(From Miss Pickerell Goes To Mars; 1951)
        SCIENCE FICTION AND READER'S GUIDE [Barrows - 1954]

```
MacGREGOR, R. J.  (I)                                                      Mag.    Year
    Perfect Gentleman, The.................................................Stg  Sep 1952
        THE BEST FROM STARTLING STORIES [Mines - 1953]
MACHEN, ARTHUR  (I)
    Opening the Door.............................(From The Cozy Room;  1936)
        TRAVELERS IN TIME [Stern - 1947]
MacLEAN, KATHERINE  (12)
    And Be Merry.........................................................ASF  Feb 1950
        THE OMNIBUS OF SCIENCE FICTION [Conklin - 1952]
    Contagion............................................................Glxy Oct 1950
        POSSIBLE WORLDS OF SCIENCE FICTION [Conklin - 1951]
        THE BEST SCIENCE FICTION STORIES [Bleiler & Dikty - 1951]
    Defense Mechanism....................................................ASF  Oct 1949
        THE BIG BOOK OF SCIENCE FICTION [Conklin - 1950]
        BEYOND THE BARRIERS OF SPACE AND TIME [Merril - 1954]
    Feedback.............................................................ASF  Jul 1951
        CROSSROADS IN TIME [Conklin - 1953]
    Fittest, The.........................................................WB   Jan 1951
        BEYOND HUMAN KEN [Merril - 1952]
    Games................................................................Glxy Mar 1953
        OPERATION FUTURE [Conklin - 1955]
    Incommunicado........................................................ASF  Jun 1950
        SIX GREAT SHORT NOVELS OF SCIENCE FICTION [Conklin - 1960]
    Interbalance.........................................................F&SF Oct 1960
        THE BEST FROM FANTASY & SCIENCE FICTION: 10th SERIES [Mills - 1961]
    Origin of the Species, The...................................ORIGINAL STORY
        CHILDREN OF WONDER [Tenn - 1953]
    Pictures Don't Lie...................................................Glxy Aug 1951
        INVADERS OF EARTH [Conklin - 1952]
        BEST SF SCIENCE FICTION STORIES [Crispin - 1955]
    Snowball Effect, The.................................................Glxy Sep 1952
        THE SECOND GALAXY READER OF SCIENCE FICTION [Gold - 1954]
        PENGUIN SCIENCE FICTION [Aldiss - 1961]
    Unhuman Sacrifice....................................................ASF  Nov 1958
        SPECTRUM [Amis & Conquest - 1961]
MADDUX, RACHEL  (I)
    Final Clearance......................................................F&SF Feb 1956
        THE BEST FROM FANTASY & SCIENCE FICTION: 6th SERIES [Boucher - 1957]
MALONEY, RUSSELL  (I)
    Inflexible Logic.....................................................Nykr   2/3/40
        TIMELESS STORIES FOR TODAY AND TOMORROW [Bradbury - 1952]
MALPASS, E. L.  (I)
    Return of the Moon...................................................Obs    1/2/55
        A. D. 2500 [Wilson - 1955]
        SF: 57 THE YEAR'S GREATEST SCIENCE FICTION & FANTASY [Merril - 1957]
            (Appeared under title When Grandfather Flew to the Moon)
MANNING, LAURENCE  (2)
    Good-Bye, Ilha!..............................................ORIGINAL STORY
        BEYOND HUMAN KEN [Merril - 1952]
    Living Galaxy, The...................................................WS   Sep 1934
        THE SCIENCE FICTION GALAXY [Conklin - 1950]
MARKS, WINSTON K.  (2)
    Call Me Adam.........................................................F&SF Feb 1954
        OPERATION FUTURE [Conklin - 1955]
    John's Other Practice................................................Im   Jul 1954
        THE BEST SCIENCE FICTION STORIES AND NOVELS: 1955 [Dikty - 1955]
```

MARLOWE, STEPHEN ps (Milton Lesser)  (1)                          Mag.    Year
    (See also listing Milton Lesser)
    Lion's Mouth................................................FA  Jun 1952
        LOOKING FORWARD [Lesser - 1953]
MARLOWE, WEBB ps (J. Francis McComas)  (1)  (See listing J. Francis McComas)
    Flight Into Darkness.......................................Amz Feb 1943
        ADVENTURES IN TIME AND SPACE [Healy & McComas - 1946]
MARQUIS, DON  (1)
    ghosts.................(FROM the lives and times of archy and mehitabel; 1927)
        HUMAN? [Merril - 1954]
MARSH, WILLARD  (1)
    Ethicators, The............................................If  Aug 1955
        SF: THE YEAR'S GREATEST SCIENCE FICTION AND FANTASY [Merril - 1956]
MARSHALL, EDISON TESLA  (1)
    Who Is Charles Avison?.....................................Arg Apr 1916
        SHOT IN THE DARK [Merril - 1950]
MARVELL, ANDREW  (1)
    Mathematical Love....................(From The Definition of Love; 1650)
        FANTASIA MATHEMATICA [Fadiman - 1958]
MASEFIELD, JOHN  (1)
    Sealman, The.............................(From Mainsail Haul; 1913)
        A DECADE OF FANTASY & SCIENCE FICTION [Mills - 1960] Rpnt-F&SF  Jul 1955
MASON, A. E. W.  (1)
    Clock, The....................(From The Four Corners of the World; 1917)
        TRAVELERS IN TIME [Stern - 1947]
MATHESON, RICHARD  (16)
    Born of Man and Woman......................................F&SF  Sum 1950
        THE BEST SCIENCE FICTION STORIES: 1951 [Bleiler & Dikty - 1951]
        CHILDREN OF WONDER [Tenn - 1953]
    Dance of the Dead..........................................ORIGINAL STORY
        STAR SCIENCE FICTION STORIES #3 [Pohl - 1954]
        STAR OF STARS [Pohl - 1960]
    Last Day, The..............................................Amz May 1953
        THE BEST SCIENCE FICTION STORIES: 1954 [Bleiler & Dikty - 1954]
    Lover When You're Near Me..................................Glxy  May 1952
        THE BEST SCIENCE FICTION STORIES: 1953 [Bleiler & Dikty - 1953]
        THE SECOND GALAXY READER OF SCIENCE FICTION [Gold - 1954]
    Mantage....................................................ORIGINAL STORY
        SCIENCE FICTION SHOWCASE [M. Kornbluth - 1959]
    One For the Books..........................................Glxy Sep 1955
        THE WORLD THAT COULDN'T BE & 8 OTHER NOVELETTES FROM GALAXY [Gold -1959]
    Pattern For Survival.......................................F&SF  May 1955
        THE BEST FROM FANTASY & SCIENCE FICTION: 5th SERIES [Boucher - 1956]
    Shipshape Home.............................................Glxy Jul 1952
        THE OMNIBUS OF SCIENCE FICTION [Conklin - 1952]
        TERROR IN THE MODERN VEIN [Wollheim - 1955]
    Sorry, Right Number........................................Bynd Nov 1953
        ZACHERLY'S MIDNIGHT SNACKS [Zacherly - 1960]
    Srl Ad.....................................................F&SF Apr 1952
        SCIENCE FICTION CARNIVAL [Brown & Reynolds - 1953]
    Test, The..................................................F&SF Nov 1954
        THE BEST FROM FANTASY & SCIENCE FICTION: 4th SERIES [Boucher - 1955]
    Third From the Sun.........................................Glxy Oct 1950
        THE GALAXY READER OF SCIENCE FICTION [Gold - 1952]
    Through Channels...........................................F&SF Apr 1951
        SCIENCE FICTION TERROR TALES [Conklin - 1955]

MATHESON, RICHARD [Cont'd]                                    Mag.   Year
    Touch of Grapefruit, A.........................................ORIGINAL STORY
        STAR SCIENCE FICTION STORIES #5 [Pohl - 1959]
    Waker Dreams, The..............................................Glxy Jul 1951
        THE GALAXY READER OF SCIENCE FICTION [Gold - 1952]
    Witch War......................................................Stg  Jul 1951
        THE BEST SCIENCE FICTION STORIES: 1952 [Bleiler & Dikty - 1952]
MAUGHAM, W. SOMERSET  (2)
    Lord Mountdrago.....................(From THE MIXTURE AS BEFORE; 1939)
        THE MOONLIGHT TRAVELER [Stern - 1943]
    Taipan, The.........................(From ON A CHINESE SCREEN; 1922)
        TRAVELERS IN TIME [Stern - 1947]
MAUROIS, ANDRE  (1)
    War Against the Moon, The.........................London Observer Prize Story
        (From The Next Chapter: The War Against The Moon; 1928)
        THE OMNIBUS OF SCIENCE FICTION [Conklin - 1952]
MAY, JULIAN C.  (2)
    Dune Roller....................................................ASF  Dec 1951
        IMAGINATION UNLIMITED [Bleiler & Dikty - 1952]
        STORIES FOR TOMORROW [Sloane - 1954]
    Star of Wonder.................................................TWS  Feb 1953
        EVERY BOY'S BOOK OF OUTER SPACE STORIES [Dikty - 1960]
MAYNE, ISOBEL  (1)
    Place of the Tigress, The.........................London Observer Prize Story
        A. D. 2500 [Wilson - 1955]
McCLINTIC, WINONA  (7)
    Anti-Climax, The...................(verse).....................F&SF Jul 1956
        THE BEST FROM FANTASY & SCIENCE FICTION: 6th SERIES [Boucher - 1957]
    Bright Destruction.................(verse).....................F&SF Jun 1956
        THE BEST FROM FANTASY & SCIENCE FICTION: 6th SERIES [Boucher - 1957]
    Doctrine of Original Design, The...........(verse)............F&SF Mar 1955
        THE BEST FROM FANTASY & SCIENCE FICTION: 5th SERIES [Boucher - 1956]
    I Want My Name in the Title............(verse)................F&SF Jul 1956
        THE BEST FROM FANTASY & SCIENCE FICTION: 6th SERIES [Boucher - 1957]
    In the Days of Our Fathers....................................MoF  Fal 1949
        THE BEST FROM FANTASY & SCIENCE FICTION [Boucher & McComas - 1952]
    1980 Overtures.......................(verse)..................F&SF Apr 1955
        THE BEST FROM FANTASY & SCIENCE FICTION: 5th SERIES [Boucher - 1956]
    To Give Them Beauty for Ashes...........(verse)...............F&SF Sep 1959
        THE BEST FROM FANTASY & SCIENCE FICTION: 9th SERIES [Mills - 1960]
McCLUSKY, THORP  (1)
    Considerate Hosts, The........................................WT   Dec 1939
        THE OTHER WORLDS [Stong - 1941]
McCOMAS, J. FRANCIS  (2)        (See also listing Webb Marlowe)
    Brave New World...............................................F&SF Sep 1954
        THE BEST FROM FANTASY & SCIENCE FICTION: 4th SERIES [Boucher - 1955]
    Shock Treatment...........................................Rpnt — F&SF Apr 1956
        9 TALES OF SPACE AND TIME [Healy - 1954]  (Original Story)
        A DECADE OF FANTASY & SCIENCE FICTION [Mills - 1960]
McDOWELL, EMMET  (1)
    Veiled Island.................................................ASF  Jan 1946
        SCIENCE FICTION ADVENTURES IN MUTATION [Conklin - 1956]
McGUIRE, JOHN J.  w/ H. Beam Piper  (1)
    Return, The...................................................ASF  Jan 1954
        THE SCIENCE FICTIONAL SHERLOCK HOLMES [Peterson - 1960]
        (Revised for inclusion in this anthology)

McINTOSH, J. T. ps (James J. MacGregor)   (6)                          Mag.    Year
    (Alternate spelling: J. T. M'Intosh)
  Broken Record, The.....................................NW #17  Sep 1952
        THE BEST FROM NEW WORLDS [Carnell - 1955]
  Hallucination Orbit...................................Glxy  Jan 1952
        GATEWAY TO TOMORROW [Carnell - 1954]
            (Appeared under title The Bliss of Solitude)
        THE SECOND GALAXY READER OF SCIENCE FICTION [Gold - 1954]
        BEST SF FOUR SCIENCE FICTION STORIES [Crispin - 1961]
            (Appeared under title The Bliss of Solitude)
  Machine Made..........................................NW #10  Sum 1951
        NO PLACE LIKE EARTH [Carnell - 1952]
        OUT OF THIS WORLD 2 [Williams-Ellis & Owen - 1961]
  Made In U. S. A. .....................................Glxy  Apr 1953
        CROSSROADS IN TIME [Conklin - 1953]
  One In Three Hundred..................................F&SF  Feb 1953
        THE BEST SCIENCE FICTION STORIES: 1954 [Bleiler & Dikty - 1954]
  Stitch In Time........................................SF #5  Aut 1952
        GATEWAY TO THE STARS [Carnell - 1955]

McKENNA, R.(ichard) M.   (2)                                    F&SF  Sep 1958
  Casey Agonistes.......................................
        THE BEST FROM FANTASY & SCIENCE FICTION: 9th SERIES [Mills - 1960]
  Mine Own Ways.........................................F&SF  Feb 1960
        THE BEST FROM FANTASY & SCIENCE FICTION: 10th SERIES [Mills - 1961]
        SIXTH ANNUAL OF THE YEAR'S BEST SF [Merril - 1961]

McKENTY, JACK   (1)                                             Glxy  Oct 1954
  $1,000 A Plate........................................
        THE FIFTH GALAXY READER [Gold - 1961]

McLAUGHLIN, DEAN   (1)                                          ASF  Jul 1960
  Brotherhood of Keepers, The...........................
        SIXTH ANNUAL OF THE YEAR'S BEST SF [Merril - 1961]

McLAUGHLIN, BERNARD   (1)                                       Sti  Jun 1941
  Silence, The..........................................
        TERROR IN THE MODERN VEIN [Wollheim - 1955]

McMORROW, THOMAS   (1)                                          SEP   3/27/30
  Mr. Murphy of New York................................
        THE BIG BOOK OF SCIENCE FICTION [Conklin - 1950]

McNAUGHTON, BRIAN J.   (1)
  w/ Andrew Duane ps (Robert E. Briney)                        ORIGINAL STORY
        Black Tower, The................................
            SHANADU [Briney - 1953]

MERCIER, LOUIS SEBASTIAN   (1)
  Early Time-Traveler, An..............(From Journal of the Year 2440; 1795)
        SCIENCE IN FICTION [A. E. M. & J. C. Bayliss - 1957]

MERLISS, R. R.   (1)                                            ASF  Apr 1955
  Stutterer, The........................................
        SF: THE YEAR'S GREATEST SCIENCE FICTION AND FANTASY [Merril - 1956]

MERRIL, JUDITH   (15)                                           F w/SFS  Aug 1950
  Barrier of Dread......................................
        JOURNEY TO INFINITY [Greenberg - 1951]
  Daughters of Earth....................................ORIGINAL STORY
        THE PETRIFIED PLANET [Pratt - 1952]
  Dead Center...........................................F&SF  Nov 1954
        A TREASURY OF GREAT SCIENCE FICTION [Boucher - 1959]
  Death is the Penalty..................................ASF  Jan 1949
        BEYOND THE END OF TIME [Pohl - 1952]

MERRIL, JUDITH [Cont'd]                                          Mag.    Year
  Exile From Space......................................................FU  Nov 1956
      THE FANTASTIC UNIVERSE OMNIBUS [Santesson - 1960]
  How Near is the Moon?.............................................ORIGINAL STORY
      SF: 58 THE YEAR'S GREATEST SF AND FANTASY [Merril - 1958]
  Project Nursemaid...............................................F&SF  Oct 1955
      SIX GREAT SHORT NOVELS OF SCIENCE FICTION [Conklin - 1960]*
  Rockets To Where?................................................ORIGINAL STORY
      SF: 59 THE YEAR'S GREATEST SF AND FANTASY [Merril - 1959]
  S-F: 1955.................................(Summation and honorable mentions)
      SF: THE YEAR'S GREATEST SCIENCE FICTION AND FANTASY [Merril - 1956]
  So Proudly We Hail...............................................ORIGINAL STORY
      STAR SCIENCE FICTION STORIES [Pohl - 1953]
  Survival Ship.........................................................WB  Jan 1951
      TOMORROW, THE STARS [Heinlein - 1952]
  That Only A Mother....................................................ASF  Jun 1948
      WORLD OF WONDER [Pratt - 1952]
      CHILDREN OF WONDER [Tenn - 1953]
  Year's S-F, The...........................(Summation and honorable mentions)
      SF: 57 THE YEAR'S GREATEST SF & FANTASY [Merril - 1957]
      SF: 58 THE YEAR'S GREATEST SF & FANTASY [Merril - 1958]
      SF: 59 THE YEAR'S GREATEST SF & FANTASY [Merril - 1959]
MERRITT, A. (1)
  Three Lines of Old French.............................................Arg  10/10/36
      ESCALES DANS L'INFINI [Gallet - 1954]
MERWIN, SAM JR. (4)
  Carriers, The........................................................TWS  Feb 1949
      MY BEST SCIENCE FICTION STORY [Margulies & Friend - 1949]
  Exiled From Earth....................................................TWS  Dec 1940
      ADVENTURES IN TOMORROW [Crossen - 1951]
  Exit Line............................................................Stg  Sep 1950
      (Originally published under pseudonym Matt Lee)
      POSSIBLE WORLDS OF SCIENCE FICTION [Conklin - 1951]
  Judas Ram...........................................................Glxy  Dec 1950
      THE GALAXY READER OF SCIENCE FICTION [Gold - 1952]
MIDDLETON, RICHARD  (1)
  Shepard's Boy......................................................F&SF  Mar 1953
      THE BEST FROM FANTASY & SCIENCE FICTION: 3rd SER [Boucher & McComas-1953]
MILLAY, EDNA ST. VINCENT  (1)
  Euclid Alone Has Looked On Beauty Bare...........(verse)....................
      (From Collected Poems; 1924)
          FANTASIA MATHEMATICA [Fadiman - 1958]
MILLER, LION  (1)
  Available Data on the Warp Reaction, The........................F&SF  Sep 1953
      BEST SF THREE SCIENCE FICTION STORIES [Crispin - 1958]
      13 GREAT STORIES OF SCIENCE FICTION [Conklin - 1960]
MILLER, P. SCHUYLER  (10)
  As Never Was.........................................................ASF  Jan 1944
      ADVENTURES IN TIME AND SPACE [Healy & McComas - 1946]
  Cave, The............................................................ASF  Jan 1943
      CROSSROADS IN TIME [Conklin - 1953]
  Chrysalis, The.......................................................Ast  Apr 1936
      A TREASURY OF SCIENCE FICTION [Conklin - 1948]
  Day Dream.......................................................ORIGINAL STORY
      THE GIRL WITH THE HUNGRY EYES AND OTHER STORIES [Wollheim - 1949]

|  | Mag. | Year |
|---|---|---|

MILLER, P. SCHUYLER [Cont'd]

Forgotten.............................................WS Apr 1933
   (Originally appeared under title The Forgotten Man of Space)
     STRANGE PORTS OF CALL [Derleth - 1948]
Man From Mars, The...................................WSQ Sum 1931
   FROM OFF THIS WORLD [Margulies & Friend - 1949]
Sands of Time, The...................................Ast Apr 1937
   ADVENTURES IN TIME AND SPACE [Healy & McComas - 1946]
Status Quondam...................................ORIGINAL STORY
   NEW TALES OF SPACE AND TIME [Healy - 1951]
Thing On Outer Shoal, The............................ASF Sep 1947
   THE OTHER SIDE OF THE MOON [Derleth - 1949]
Trouble On Tantalus..................................ASF Feb 1941
   TRAVELERS OF SPACE [Greenberg - 1952]

MILLER, R. DE WITT (2)

Swenson, Dispatcher..................................Glxy Apr 1956
   THE BEST SCIENCE FICTION STORIES AND NOVELS: 1956 [Dikty - 1956]
Within The Pyramid...................................Ast Mar 1937
   ADVENTURES IN TIME AND SPACE [Healy & McComas - 1946]

MILLER, WALTER M. JR. (15)

Big Hunger, The......................................ASF Oct 1952
   PRIZE SCIENCE FICTION [Wollheim - 1953]
Blood Bank...........................................ASF Jun 1952
   ALL ABOUT THE FUTURE [Greenberg - 1955]
Canticle For Leibowitz, A............................F&SF Apr 1955
   THE BEST FROM FANTASY & SCIENCE FICTION: 4th SERIES [Boucher - 1956]
   THE BEST SCIENCE FICTION STORIES AND NOVELS: 1956 [Dikty - 1956]
Command Performance..................................Glxy Nov 1952
   THE BEST SCIENCE FICTION STORIES: 1953 [Bleiler & Dikty - 1953]
   THE SECOND GALAXY READER OF SCIENCE FICTION [Gold - 1954]
   PENGUIN SCIENCE FICTION [Aldiss - 1961]
Conditionally Human..................................Glxy Feb 1952
   YEAR'S BEST SCIENCE FICTION NOVELS: 1953 [Bleiler & Dikty - 1953]
Crucifixus Etiam.....................................ASF Feb 1953
   HUMAN? [Merril - 1954]
   THE BEST SCIENCE FICTION STORIES: 1954 [Bleiler & Dikty - 1954]
Dumb Waiter..........................................ASF Apr 1953
   SCIENCE FICTION THINKING MACHINES [Conklin - 1954]
Hoffer, The..........................................FU Sep 1955
   SF: THE YEAR'S GREATEST SCIENCE FICTION AND FANTASY [Merril - 1956]
Izzard and the Membrane..............................ASF May 1951
   YEAR'S BEST SCIENCE FICTION NOVELS: 1952 [Bleiler & Dikty - 1952]
Little Creeps, The...................................Amz Dec 1951
   LOOKING FORWARD [Lesser - 1953]
Momento Homo.........................................Amz Mar 1954
   THE BEST SCIENCE FICTION STORIES AND NOVELS: 1955 [Dikty - 1955]
No Moon For Me.......................................ASF Sep 1952
   SPACE, SPACE, SPACE [Sloane - 1953]
Triflin' Man.........................................FU Jan 1955
   A GALAXY OF GHOULS [Merril - 1955]
Will, The............................................Fnt Feb 1954
   THE BEST SCIENCE FICTION STORIES AND NOVELS: 1955 [Dikty - 1955]
Wolf Pack............................................Fnt Oct 1953
   BEYOND THE BARRIERS OF SPACE AND TIME [Merril - 1954]

MILLS, ROBERT P.   (1)
    Last Shall Be First, The..........................................F&SF  Aug 1958
        A DECADE OF FANTASY & SCIENCE FICTION [Mills - 1960]
MITCHELL, J. A.   (1)
    Last American, The.....(Originally published by Frederick A. Stokes Co.; 1889)
        FAR BOUNDARIES [Derleth - 1951]
MITCHELL, EDWARD PAGE   (1)
    Tachypomp, The............................................................SM  n/d/a 1873
        FANTASIA MATHEMATICA [Fadiman - 1958]
MONIG, CHRISTOPHER   (1)
    Love Story................................................................ORIGINAL STORY
        FUTURE TENSE [Crossen - 1953]
MONROE, LYLE ps (Robert A. Heinlein)  (1)  See listing Robert A. Heinlein
    Columbus Was A Dope......................................................Stg  May 1947
       (Originally published under byline Robert A. Heinlein)
        TRAVELERS OF SPACE [Greenberg - 1952]
MOORE, C. L.  (Mrs. Henry Kuttner)   (6)
  (See listings Lawrence O'Donnell and Lewis Padgett)
    No Woman Born............................................................ASF  Dec 1944
        A TREASURY OF SCIENCE FICTION [Conklin - 1948]
        GREAT STORIES OF SCIENCE FICTION [Leinster - 1951]
        BEST SF SCIENCE FICTION STORIES [Crispin - 1955]
    Scarlet Dream............................................................WT  May 1934
        FUTURE TENSE [Crossen - 1953]
    Shambleau................................................................WT  Nov 1933
        ADVENTURES IN TOMORROW [Crossen - 1951]
        ESCALES DANS L'INFINI [Gallet - 1954]
    There Shall Be Darkness..................................................ASF  Feb 1942
        JOURNEY TO INFINITY [Greenberg - 1951]
  w/ Henry Kuttner
    Home There's No Returning.......................(From No Boundaries; 1955)
        SF: THE YEAR'S GREATEST SCIENCE FICTION & FANTASY [Merril - 1956]
    Wild Surmise.............................................................ORIGINAL STORY
        STAR SCIENCE FICTION STORIES [Pohl - 1953]
MOORE, WARD   (9)
    Adjustment...............................................................F&SF  May 1957
        THE BEST FROM FANTASY & SCIENCE FICTION: 7th SERIES [Boucher - 1958]
    Dominions Beyond.........................................................SEP  8/28/54
        THE BEST SCIENCE FICTION STORIES AND NOVELS: 1955 [Dikty - 1955]
    Fellow Who Married the Maxwill Girl, The.................................F&SF  Feb 1960
        THE BEST FROM FANTASY & SCIENCE FICTION: 10th SERIES [Mills - 1961]
        SIXTH ANNUAL OF THE YEAR'S BEST SF [Merril - 1961]
    Flying Dutchman..........................................................ORIGINAL STORY
        ADVENTURES IN TOMORROW [Crossen - 1951]
    Lot.....................................................................F&SF  May 1953
        THE BEST FROM FANTASY & SCIENCE FICTION: 3rd SER [Boucher & McComas-1953]
        THE BEST SCIENCE FICTION STORIES: 1954 [Bleiler & Dikty - 1954]
        PENGUIN SCIENCE FICTION [Aldiss - 1961]
    Lot's Daughter..........................................................F&SF  Oct 1954
        A DECADE OF FANTASY & SCIENCE FICTION [Mills - 1960]
    No Man Pursueth.........................................................F&SF  Apr 1956
        THE BEST FROM FANTASY & SCIENCE FICTION: 6th SERIES [Boucher - 1957]
    Peacebringer............................................................Amz  Mar 1950
       (Originally appeared under title Sword Of Peace)
        THE BIG BOOK OF SCIENCE FICTION [Conklin - 1950]
    We The People...........................................................SFQ  May 1952
        FUTURE TENSE [Crossen - 1953]

MORE, SIR THOMAS  (1)                                                    Mag.    Year
    Utopia.......................(Written about 1516; published in English: 1551)
        BEYOND TIME AND SPACE [Derleth - 1950]
MORLEY, CHRISTOPHER  (1)
    Circle, The....................(verse).................(No data available)
        FANTASIA MATHEMATICA [Fadiman - 1958]
MORRIS, GOUVERNEUR  (1)
    Back There In the Grass.....................(From It and Other Stories; 1922)
        WORLD OF WONDER [Pratt - 1952]
MORRISON, D. A. C.  (1)
    Another Antigone.............................London Observer Prize  Story
        A. D. 2500 [Wilson - 1955]
MORRISON, WILLIAM ps (Joseph Samachson)  (7)
    Country Doctor..............................................ORIGINAL STORY
        STAR SCIENCE FICTION STORIES [Pohl - 1953]
        STAR OF STARS [Pohl - 1960]
    Feast of Demons, A.........................................Glxy  Mar 1958
        THE FIFTH GALAXY READER [Gold - 1961]
    Inner Worlds, The..........................................F&SF  Apr 1954
        THE BEST SCIENCE FICTION STORIES AND NOVELS: 1955 [Dikty - 1955]
    Model of a Judge, The......................................Glxy  Oct 1953
        THE BEST SCIENCE FICTION STORIES: 1954 [Bleiler & Dikty - 1954]
        THE THIRD GALAXY READER OF SCIENCE FICTION [Gold - 1958]
    Sack, The..................................................ASF  Sep 1950
        TOMORROW, THE STARS [Heinlein - 1952]
    Shipping Clerk.............................................Glxy  Jun 1952
        13 GREAT STORIES OF SCIENCE FICTION [Conklin - 1960]
    Sly Bungerhop, The.........................................Glxy  Sep 1957
        THE MIND PARTNER AND 8 OTHER NOVELETTES FROM GALAXY [Gold - 1961]
MOSKOWITZ, SAM  (1)
    Lost Chord, The............................................ORIGINAL STORY
        SCIENCE AND SORCERY [Ford - 1953]
MUDGETT, HERMAN W.  (3)
    Glass of the Future, The...............(verse).................F&SF  Jan 1955
        THE BEST FROM FANTASY & SCIENCE FICTION: 5th SERIES [Boucher - 1956]
    Report on the Sexual Behavior of the Extra-Sensory Perceptor.....(verse)......
                                                                F&SF  Aug 1954
        THE BEST FROM FANTASY & SCIENCE FICTION: 4th SERIES [Boucher - 1955]
    Silent, Upon Two Peaks.....................................F&SF  Jul 1955
        THE BEST FROM FANTASY & SCIENCE FICTION: 5th SERIES [Boucher - 1956]
MURRAY, ROBERT  (1)
    Replacement, The...........................................F&SF  Feb 1960
        THE BEST FROM FANTASY & SCIENCE FICTION: 10th SERIES [Mills - 1961]

NASH, OGDEN  (1)
    Tale of the Thirteenth Floor, A............................F&SF  Jul 1955
        A DECADE OF FANTASY & SCIENCE FICTION [Mills - 1960]
NATHAN, ROBERT  (1)
    Digging the Weans..........................................Hpr  Nov 1956
        SF: 57 THE YEAR'S GREATEST SF AND FANTASY [Merril - 1957]

NEARING, H. JR. (4)                                                Mag.    Year

Cerebrative Psittacoid, The...........................................F&SF  Aug 1953
    BEST SF SCIENCE FICTION STORIES [Crispin - 1955]
Hyperspherical Basketball, The.......................................F&SF  Dec 1951
    THE BEST FROM FANTASY & SCIENCE FICTION: 2nd SER [Boucher & McComas— 1953]
Maladjusted Classroom, The...........................................F&SF  Jun 1953
    THE BEST FROM FANTASY & SCIENCE FICTION: 3rd SER [Boucher & McComas-1954]
Mathematical Voodoo, The...........................................  F&SF  Apr 1951
    THE BEST FROM FANTASY & SCIENCE FICTION [Boucher & McComas - 1952]
    FANTASIA MATHEMATICA [Fadiman - 1958]
NELSON, ALAN (2)
Narapoia..................................................Rpnt - F&SF  Apr 1951
    THE BEST FROM F&SF [Boucher & McComas - 1952]   Org aprd - Wdg  Apr 1948
    (Originally appeared under title The Origin of Narapoia)
Soap Opera.........................................................F&SF  Apr 1953
    13 GREAT STORIES OF SCIENCE FICTION [Conklin - 1960]
NEVILLE, KRIS (10)
Bettyann...........................................................ORIGINAL STORY
    NEW TALES OF SPACE AND TIME [Healy - 1951]
    STORIES FOR TOMORROW [Sloane - 1954]
Cold War.............................................................ASF  Oct 1949
    THE ASTOUNDING SCIENCE FICTION ANTHOLOGY [J. W. Campbell - 1952]
Experiment Station...................................................Sup  Sep 1950
    (Originally appeared under title The First)
    SCIENCE FICTION ADVENTURES IN MUTATION [Conklin - 1956]
    (Revised for inclusion in this anthology)
Franchise...........................................................ASF  Feb 1951
    STORIES FOR TOMORROW [Sloane - 1954]
Hold Back Tomorrow...................................................Im   Sep 1951
    IMAGINATION UNLIMITED [Bleiler & Dikty - 1952]
It Pays To Advertise................................................F&SF  Jun 1953
    TOMORROW'S UNIVERSE [H. J. Campbell - 1954]
Old Man Henderson...................................................F&SF  Jun 1951
    THE BEST FROM FANTASY & SCIENCE FICTION [Boucher & McComas - 1952]
Overture...........................................................ORIGINAL STORY
    9 TALES OF SPACE AND TIME [Healy - 1951]
Underground Movement................................................F&SF  Jun 1952
    BEYOND HUMAN KEN [Merril - 1952]
w/ R. Bretnor
    Attitude Guaranteed.............................................F&SF  Aug 1953
        PORTALS OF TOMORROW [Derleth - 1954]
NORBET, W. ps (Dr. Norbett Weiner) (1)
Brain, The..........................................................TEN  Apr 1952
    (Originally appeared under byline Dr. Norbett Weiner)
    CROSSROADS IN TIME [Conklin - 1953]
NORTHUP, EDWIN F. (1)
Off For the Moon.............................................(From Zero To Eighty; 1937)
    (Originally appeared under pseudonym Akkad Pseudonman)
    SCIENCE IN FICTION [A.E.M. & J. C. Bayliss - 1957]
NORTON, ANDRE ps (Alice Mary Norton) (1)
Mousetrap...........................................................F&SF  Jun 1954
    THE BEST SCIENCE FICTION STORIES AND NOVELS: 1955 [Dikty - 1955]
NORTON, HENRY A. (1)
Man In the Moon, The................................................ASF  Feb 1943
    INVADERS OF EARTH [Conklin - 1952]
NOURSE, ALAN·E. (6)
Brightside Crossing.................................................Glxy  Jan 1956
    THE WORLD THAT COULDN'T BE AND 8 OTHER NOVELETTES FROM GALAXY [Gold-1959]

NOURSE, ALAN E. [Cont'd]                                     Mag.    Year
  Family Resemblance.........................................ASF  Apr 1953
      SCIENCE FICTION ADVENTURES IN MUTATION [Conklin - 1956]
  High Threshold........................................ASF  Mar 1951
      THE OMNIBUS OF SCIENCE FICTION [Conklin - 1952]
  Image of the Gods, The..............................Orb #4  Sep 1954
      PLANET OF DOOM AND OTHER STORIES [Anonymous - 1958]
  Nightmare Brother....................................ASF  Feb 1953
      SPACE, SPACE, SPACE [Sloane - 1953]
      SCIENCE FICTION TERROR TALES [Conklin - 1955]
  Tiger By the Tail...................................Glxy  Nov 1951
      SCIENCE FICTION ADVENTURES IN DIMENSION [Conklin - 1953]
      THE SECOND GALAXY READER OF SCIENCE FICTION [Gold - 1954]
NOVOTNY, JOHN (1)
  Trick Or Two, A...................................F&SF  Jul 1957
      A DECADE OF FANTASY & SCIENCE FICTION [Mills - 1960]

# O

OBOLER, ARCH (1)
  And Adam Begot.............(From This Freedom: Thirteen New Radio Plays; 1942)
      OUT OF THIS WORLD [Fast - 1944]
O'BRIEN, DAVID WRIGHT (1)
  Truth Is A Plague....................................Amz  Feb 1940
      THE OTHER WORLDS [Stong - 1941]
O'BRIEN, FITZ-JAMES (1)
  What Was It?........................................Hpr  Mar 1859
      INVISIBLE MEN [Davenport - 1960]
O'DONNEVAN, FINN (2)
  Gun Without A Bang, The.............................Glxy  Jun 1958
      THE FOURTH GALAXY READER OF SCIENCE FICTION [Gold - 1959]
  Wind Is Rising, A..................................Glxy  Jul 1957
      THE THIRD GALAXY READER OF SCIENCE FICTION [Gold - 1958]
O'DONNELL, LAWRENCE ps (C. L. Moore) (2)
  See listings C. L. Moore and Lewis Padgett)
    Clash By Night....................................ASF  Mar 1943
      THE ASTOUNDING SCIENCE FICTION ANTHOLOGY [J. W. Campbell - 1952]
    Vintage Season..................................ASF  Sep 1946
      A TREASURY OF SCIENCE FICTION [Conklin - 1948]
OGILVY, C. STANLEY (1)
  For All Practical Purposes.............(From Through The Microscope; 1956)
      FANTASIA MATHEMATICA [Fadiman - 1958]
O'HARA, KENNETH ps (Bryce Walton) (1)  See listing Bryce Walton
  Mating of the Moons, The............................Orb #2  n/d 1954
      PLANET OF DOOM AND OTHER STORIES [Anonymous - 1958]
OLIVER, CHAD (15)
  Ant and the Eye, The...............................ASF  Apr 1953
      STORIES FOR TOMORROW [Sloane - 1954]

OLIVER, CHAD [Cont'd]                                               Mag.    Year
    Any More At Home Like You?...............................ORIGINAL STORY
        STAR SCIENCE FICTION STORIES #3 [Pohl - 1954]
    Between the Thunder and the Sun..........................F&SF   May 1957
        THE BEST FROM FANTASY & SCIENCE FICTION: 7th SERIES [Boucher - 1958]
    Blood's A Rover...........................................ASF    May 1952
        OPERATION FUTURE [Conklin - 1955]
    Boy Next Door, The........................................F&SF   Jun 1951
        HUMAN? [Merril - 1954]
    Controlled Experiment.....................................Orb #5 Nov 1954
        SPACE STATION 42 AND OTHER STORIES [Anonymous - 1958]
    Didn't He Ramble..........................................F&SF   Apr 1957
        THE BEST SCIENCE FICTION STORIES AND NOVELS: 9th SERIES [Dikty - 1958]
    Field Experiment..........................................ASF    Jan 1955
        THE HIDDEN PLANET [Woolheim - 1959]
    Let Me Live In a House....................................USF    Mar 1954
        SCIENCE FICTION TERROR TALES [Conklin - 1955]
    Of Course.................................................ASF    May 1954
        THE BEST SCIENCE FICTION STORIES AND NOVELS: 1955 [Dikty - 1955]
    Shore of Tomorrow, The....................................Stg    Mar 1953
        TOMORROW'S UNIVERSE [H. J. Campbell - 1954]
    Stardust..................................................ASF    Jul 1952
        ADVENTURES IN THE FAR FUTURE [Woolheim - 1954]
    Technical Advisor.........................................F&SF   Feb 1953
        CROSSROADS IN TIME [Conklin - 1953]
    Win the World.............................................Stg    Feb 1952
        LOOKING FORWARD [Lesser - 1953]
    w/ Charles Beaumont
        Last Word, The........................................F&SF   Apr 1955
            THE BEST FROM FANTASY & SCIENCE FICTION: 5th SERIES [Boucher - 1956]
OLIVER, J. T.  (1)
    Peaceful Martian, The.....................................FB #8  n/d 1951
        SCIENCE AND SORCERY [Ford - 1953]
OLSEN, BOB ps (Alfred John Olsen, Jr.)  (1)
    Four-Dimensional-Roller-Press, The........................Amz    Jun 1927
        EVERY BOY'S BOOK OF SCIENCE FICTION [Woolheim - 1951]
ONIONS, OLIVER  (1)
    Phantas...........................................(From Widdershins; 1911)
        THE MOONLIGHT TRAVELER [Stern - 1943]
        TRAVELERS IN TIME [Stern - 1947]
OSBORNE, ROBERTSON  (1)
    Action On Azura...........................................PS     Fal 1949
        THE BIG BOOK OF SCIENCE FICTION [Conklin - 1950]
            (Appeared under title Contact, Inc.)
        TRAVELERS OF SPACE [Greenberg - 1952]

PADGETT, LEWIS ps (Henry Kuttner & C. L. Moore)  (19)
    (See listings Henry Kuttner and C. L. Moore)
            Cure, The.........................................ASF    May 1946
                THE OTHER SIDE OF THE MOON [Derleth - 1949]

PADGETT, LEWIS [Cont'd]                                          Mag.    Year
    Dark Angel, The.........................................................Stg  Mar 1946
        (Originally appeared under byline Henry Kuttner)
            SHOT IN THE DARK [Merril - 1950]
    Deadlock................................................................ASF  Aug 1942
        THE ROBOT AND THE MAN [Greenberg - 1953]
    Endowment Policy........................................................ASF  Aug 1943
        SCIENCE FICTION ADVENTURES IN DIMENSION [Conklin - 1949]
    Ex Machina.............................................................ASF  Apr 1948
        THE BEST SCIENCE FICTION STORIES: 1949 [Bleiler & Dikty - 1949]
    Gnome There Was, A......................................................UW  Oct 1941
        (Originally appeared under byline Henry Kuttner)
            BEYOND HUMAN KEN [Merril - 1952]
    Iron Standard, The......................................................ASF  Dec 1945
        MEN AGAINST THE STARS [Greenberg - 1950]
    Line To Tomorrow........................................................ASF  Nov 1945
        WORLDS OF TOMORROW [Derleth - 1953]
    Margin For Error........................................................ASF  Nov 1947
        THE BIG BOOK OF SCIENCE FICTION [Conklin - 1950]
    Mimsy Were the Borogoves................................................ASF  Feb 1943
        A TREASURY OF SCIENCE FICTION [Conklin - 1948]
        UBERWINDUNG VON RAUM UND ZEIT [Gunther - 1952]
    Open Secret............................................................ASF  Apr 1943
        GREAT STORIES OF SCIENCE FICTION [Leinster - 1951]
    Piper's Son, The.......................................................ASF  Feb 1945
        THE BEST OF SCIENCE FICTION [Conklin - 1946]
        CHILDREN OF WONDER [Tenn - 1953]
    Project................................................................ASF  Apr 1947
        OPERATION FUTURE [Conklin - 1955]
    Proud Robot, The.......................................................ASF  Oct 1943
        ADVENTURES IN TIME AND SPACE [Healy & McComas - 1946]
    Time Locker............................................................ASF  Jan 1943
        ADVENTURES IN TIME AND SPACE [Healy & McComas - 1946]
    Twonky, The............................................................ASF  Sep 1942
        ADVENTURES IN TIME AND SPACE [Healy & McComas - 1946]
    We Kill People.........................................................ASF  Mar 1946
        LOOKING FORWARD [Lesser - 1953]
    What You Need..........................................................ASF  Oct 1945
        THE OMNIBUS OF SCIENCE FICTION [Conklin - 1952]
    When the Bough Breaks..................................................ASF  Nov 1944
        BEYOND TIME AND SPACE [Derleth - 1950]
        THE ASTOUNDING SCIENCE FICTION ANTHOLOGY [J. W. Campbell - 1952]
PAGE, NORVELL W.  (1)
    But Without Horns......................................................Unk  Jun 1940
        FIVE SCIENCE FICTION NOVELS [Greenberg - 1952]
PAIGE, LEO  (1)
    How High On the Ladder?.............................................FB #7  n/d 1950
        SCIENCE AND SORCERY [Ford - 1953]
PANGBORN, EDGAR   (2)
    Angel's Egg............................................................ASF  Jun 1951
        INVADERS OF EARTH [Conklin - 1952]
        BEST SF TWO SCIENCE FICTION STORIES [Crispin - 1956]
    Music Master of Babylon...............................................Glxy  Nov 1954
        THE WORLD THAT COULDN'T BE AND 8 OTHER NOVELETTES FROM GALAXY [Gold-1959]
PARKER, RICHARD  (1)
    Wheelbarrow Boy, The...................................................Lpt  Oct 1950
        A GALAXY OF GHOULS [Merril - 1955]

PAYTON, GREEN ps (G. Peyton Wertenbaker) (1)                          Mag.    Year
  Ship That Turned Aside, The...........................................Amz  Mar 1930
      (Originally appeared under byline G. P. Wertenbaker)
        THE BIG BOOK OF SCIENCE FICTION [Conklin - 1950]
PEARSON, MARTIN ps (Donald A. Wollheim) (4) See listing Donald A. Woolheim
  Ajax of Ajax.....................................................Fw/SF  Aug 1942
      FLIGHT INTO SPACE [Woolheim - 1950]
  Embassy, The.....................................................ASF  Mar 1942
      A TREASURY OF SCIENCE FICTION [Conklin - 1948]
      BEYOND THE END OF TIME [Pohl - 1952]
  Millionth Year, The..............................................SFS  Apr 1943
      ADVENTURES IN THE FAR FUTURE [Woolheim - 1954]
  w/ Cecil Corwin ps (C. M. Kornbluth)
    Mask of Demeter, The.........................................F&SF  Jan 1953
        PRIZE SCIENCE FICTION [Woolheim - 1953]
PEART, NOEL (1)
  Spud Failure Definite............................London Observer Prize Story
      A. D. 2500 [Wilson - 1955]
PEREGOY, CALVIN ps (Thomas Calvert McClary) (1)
  Terrible Sense, The..............................................ASF  Aug 1938
      THE BEST OF SCIENCE FICTION [Conklin - 1946]
PETRACCA, JOSEPH (1)
  w/ Frank Fenton
    Tolliver's Travels.......................................ORIGINAL STORY
        NEW TALES OF SPACE AND TIME [Healy - 1951]
PHELAN, R. C. (1)
  Something Invented Me.......................................Rptr  10/13/60
      SIXTH ANNUAL OF THE YEAR'S BEST SF [Merril - 1961]
PHILLIPS, A. M. (2)
  Death of the Moon, The...........................................Amz  Feb 1929
      FLIGHT INTO SPACE [Woolheim - 1950]
  Time-Travel Happens!.............................................Unk  Dec 1939
      ADVENTURES IN TIME AND SPACE [Healy & McComas - 1946]
PHILLIPS, PETER (12)
  At No Extra Cost................................................MSF  Aug 1951
      THE BEST SCIENCE FICTION STORIES: 1952 [Bleiler & Dikty - 1952]
  C/o Mr. Makepeace...............................................F&SF  Feb 1954
      OPERATION FUTURE [Conklin - 1955]
  Counter Charm...................................................Snt  Spr 1951
      THE OMNIBUS OF SCIENCE FICTION [Conklin - 1952]
  Dreams Are Sacred...............................................ASF  Sep 1948
      IMAGINATION UNLIMITED [Bleiler & Dikty - 1952]
  Field Study.....................................................Glxy  Apr 1951
      THE GALAXY READER OF SCIENCE FICTION [Gold - 1952]
  Lost Memory.....................................................Glxy  May 1952
      GATEWAY TO TOMORROW [Carnell - 1954]
      THE SECOND GALAXY READER OF SCIENCE FICTION [Gold - 1954]
      SCIENCE FICTION TERROR TALES [Conklin - 1955]
  Manna...........................................................ASF  Feb 1949
      THE BIG BOOK OF SCIENCE FICTION [Conklin - 1950]
  Plagerist.......................................................NW #7  Sum 1950
      FUTURE TENSE [Crossen - 1953]
  She Who Laughs..................................................Glxy  Apr 1952
      ASSIGNMENT IN TOMORROW [Pohl - 1954]
  University.......................................................Glxy  Apr 1953
      THE SECOND GALAXY READER OF SCIENCE FICTION [Gold - 1954]
  Unknown Quantity.......................... ....................NW #5  n/d 1949
      NO PLACE LIKE EARTH [Carnell - 1952]
      THE BEST FROM NEW WORLDS [Carnell - 1955]
  Warning, The....................................................F&SF  Sep 1953
      BEYOND THE BARRIERS OF SPACE AND TIME [Merril - 1954]

```
PHILLIPS, ROG ps (Roger Phillips Graham)  (2)                    Mag      Year
   Game Preserve.........................................................If   Oct 1957
        SF: 58 THE YEAR'S GREATEST SF AND FANTASY [Merril - 1958]
   Yellow Pill, The......................................................ASF  Oct 1958
        SF: 59 THE YEAR'S GREATEST SF AND FANTASY [Merril - 1959]
        BEST SF FOUR SCIENCE FICTION STORIES [Crispin - 1961]
PIERCE, JOHN R.  (1)    See listing J. J. Coupling
   Invariant............................................................ASF   Apr 1944
        THE ASTOUNDING SCIENCE FICTION ANTHOLOGY [J. W. Campbell - 1952]
PINKNEY, DOROTHY COWLES  (1)
   Full Circle..........................................................F&SF  Dec 1956
        THE BEST FROM FANTASY & SCIENCE FICTION: 7th SERIES [Boucher - 1958]
PIPER, H. BEAM  (7)
   Genesis..............................................................Fw/SFS  Dec 1951
        SHADOW OF TOMORROW [Pohl - 1953]
   He Walked Around the Horses..........................................ASF   Apr 1948
        WORLD OF WONDER [Pratt - 1951]
        BEST SF THREE SCIENCE FICTION STORIES [Crispin - 1958]
   Last Enemy...........................................................ASF   Aug 1950
        THE ASTOUNDING SCIENCE FICTION ANTHOLOGY [J. W. Campbell - 1952]
   Operation RSVP.......................................................Amz   Jan 1951
        WORLD OF WONDER [Pratt - 1951]
   Police Operation.....................................................ASF   Jun 1948
        SPACE POLICE [Norton - 1956]
   Time and Time Again..................................................ASF   Apr 1947
        A TREASURY OF SCIENCE FICTION [Conklin - 1948]
        UBERWINDUNG VON RAUM UND ZEIT [Gunther - 1952]
   Ullr Uprising......................................................ORIGINAL STORY
        THE PETRIFIED PLANET [Pratt - 1952]
PLATO  (1)
   Atlantis....................................................(Written about 370 B.C.)
        BEYOND TIME AND SPACE [Derleth - 1950]
POE, EDGAR ALLAN  (7)
   Conversation Between Eiros and Charmion, The.........................BGM   Dec 1839
        THE TREASURY OF SCIENCE FICTION CLASSICS [Kuebler - 1955]
   Descent Into the Maelstrom, A........................................GLGM  May 1841
        JOURNEYS IN SCIENCE FICTION [Loughlin & Popp - 1961]
   Facts In the Case of M. Valdemar, The................................AWR   Dec 1845
        SHOT IN THE DARK [Merril - 1950]
   Tale of the Ragged Mountain, A.......................................GLB   Apr 1844
        THE BEST OF SCIENCE FICTION [Conklin - 1946]
   Thousandth-and-Second-Tale of Scherazade, The........................GLB   Feb 1843
        BEYOND TIME AND SPACE [Derleth - 1950]
   William Wilson.......................................................Gft   n/d 1840
        THE MOONLIGHT TRAVELER [Stern - 1943]
   X + L.......................................................(No data available)
        FANTASIA MATHEMATICA [Fadiman - 1958]
POHL, FREDERIK  (8)       See listing James MacCreigh
   Bitterest Pill, The..................................................Glxy  Apr 1959
        THE FIFTH GALAXY READER [Gold - 1961]
   Census Takers, The...................................................F&SF  Feb 1956
        THE BEST FROM FANTASY & SCIENCE FICTION: 6th SERIES [Boucher - 1957]
   Gentlest People, The.................................................Glxy  Jun 1958
        THE FOURTH GALAXY READER OF SCIENCE FICTION [Gold - 1959]
   Haunted Corpse, The..................................................Glxy  Jan 1957
        THE THIRD GALAXY READER OF SCIENCE FICTION [Gold - 1958]
```

```
POHL, FREDERIK [Cont'd]                                        Mag.    Year
   How To Count On Your Fingers.........................SFS   Sep 1956
       COMING ATTRACTIONS [Greenberg - 1957]
   Man Who Ate the World, The...........................Glxy  Nov 1956
       SCIENCE FICTION SHOWCASE [M. Kornbluth - 1959]
   Midas Plague, The....................................Glxy  Apr 1954
       ALL ABOUT THE FUTURE [Greenberg - 1955]
       SPECTRUM [Amis & Conquest - 1961]
   Whatever Counts......................................Glxy  Jun 1959
       BODYGUARD AND FOUR OTHER SHORT NOVELS FROM GALAXY [Gold - 1960]
PORGES, ARTHUR  (7)
   Devil and Simon Flagg, The...........................F&SF  Aug 1954
       FANTASIA MATHEMATICA [Fadiman - 1958]
   Fly, The.............................................F&SF  Sep 1952
       BEYOND HUMAN KEN [Merril - 1952]
       THE BEST SCIENCE FICTION STORIES: 1953 [Bleiler & Dikty - 1953]
   Guilty As Charged....................................ORIGINAL STORY
       THE BEST SCIENCE FICTION STORIES AND NOVELS: 1955 [Dikty - 1955]
   Mop-Up...............................................F&SF  Jul 1953
       GALAXY OF GHOULS [Merril - 1955]
   $1.98................................................F&SF  May 1954
       THE BEST FROM FANTASY & SCIENCE FICTION: 4th SERIES [Boucher - 1955]
   Rats, The............................................MnW   Feb 1951
       THE BEST SCIENCE FICTION STORIES: 1952 [Bleiler & Dikty - 1952]
   Ruum, The............................................F&SF  Oct 1953
       BEST SF SCIENCE FICTION STORIES [Crispin - 1955]
       OUT OF THIS WORLD I [Williams-Ellis & Owen - 1960]
POWERS, WILLIAM T.  (2)
   Allegory.............................................ASF   Apr 1953
       13 GREAT STORIES OF SCIENCE FICTION [Conklin - 1960]
   Meteor...............................................ASF   Sep 1950
       THE ASTOUNDING SCIENCE FICTION ANTHOLOGY [J. W. Campbell - 1952]
PRATT, FLETCHER  (12)
   Blue Star, The.......................................ORIGINAL STORY
       WITCHES THREE [Pratt - 1952]
   Doctor Grimshaw's Sanitarium.........................Amz   May 1934
       MY BEST SCIENCE FICTION STORY [Margulies & Friend - 1949]
   Hormones.............................................ORIGINAL STORY
       STAR SCIENCE FICTION STORIES #2 [Pohl - 1953]
   Long View, The.......................................ORIGINAL STORY
       THE PETRIFIED PLANET [Pratt - 1952]
   Official Record......................................Spc   Sep 1952
       ASSIGNMENT IN TOMORROW [Pohl - 1954]
   Pardon My Mistake....................................TWS   Dec 1946
       THE OUTER REACHES [Derleth - 1951]
   Roger Bacon Formula, The.............................Amz   Jan 1929
       (Originally appeared under joint byline Irvin Lester & Fletcher Pratt)
       THE BIG BOOK OF SCIENCE FICTION [Conklin - 1950]
            (Revised for inclusion in this anthology)
   w/ L. Sprague de Camp
       Black Ball, The..................................F&SF  Oct 1952
           THE BEST FROM FANTASY & SCIENCE FICTION: 2nd SER [Boucher & McComas
                                                                        1953]
       Gavigan's Bar....................................F&SF  Spr 1950
           THE BEST FROM FANTASY & SCIENCE FICTION [Boucher & McComas - 1952]
       Untimely Toper, The..............................F&SF  Jul 1953
           THE BEST FROM F&SF: 3rd SERIES [Boucher & McComas - 1954]
   w/ Walter Kubilius
       Second Chance....................................FSM   Sep 1952
           SPACE, SPACE, SPACE [Sloane - 1953]
```

PRATT, FLETCHER [Cont'd]                                              Mag.    Year
     w/ B. F. Ruby
         Thing In the Woods, The..............................................Amz  Feb 1935
              THE OMNIBUS OF SCIENCE FICTION [Conklin - 1952]
PRESSLIE, ROBERT  (1)
     Another Word For Man.............................................NW #78  Dec 1958
              OUT OF THIS WORLD 2 [Williams-Ellis & Owen - 1961]
PRICE, ROGER  (1)
     Inquiry Concerning the Curvature of the Earth's Surface and Divers  Investiga-
              tions of a Metaphysical Nature, An.........................Mncl  Win 1959
              THE FIFTH ANNUAL OF THE YEAR'S BEST SF [Merril - 1960]
PRIESTLY, J. B.  (2)
     Demon King, The................................(From My Best Thriller; 1934)
              A GALAXY OF GHOULS [Merril - 1955]
     Mr. Strenberry's Tale............................(From Four-In-Hand; 1934)
              TRAVELERS IN TIME [Stern - 1947]
              THE TREASURY OF SCIENCE FICTION CLASSICS [Kuebler - 1955]
PURDOM, TOM  (1)
     Holy Grail, The..................................... ..............ORIGINAL STORY
              STAR SCIENCE FICTION STORIES #6 [Pohl - 1959]


# Q


QUILLER-COUCH, ARTHUR T.  (1)
     New Ballard of Sir Patrick Spens, A........(verse)..........(No data available)
              FANTASIA MATHEMATICA [Fadiman - 1958]
QUINN, SEABURY  (1)
     House Where Time Stood Still, The...............................WT  Mar 1939
              THE OTHER WORLDS [Stong - 1941]


# R


RABELAIS, FRANCIS  (1)
     Phalanstery of Thelme, The.............................(From Gargantua; 1534)
              BEYOND TIME AND SPACE [Derleth - 1950]
RAYMOND, HUGH ps (John Michael)  (1)
     Spokesman For Terra.............................................Sti  Jun 1941
              SHOT IN THE DARK [Merril - 1950]
READY, W. B.  (1)
     Devlin..............................................................F&SF  Apr 1953
              THE BEST FROM FANTASY & SCIENCE FICTION: 3rd SER. [Boucher & McComas-1954]
REESE, JOHN  (1)
     Rainmaker..........................................................SEP  2/19/49
              TOMORROW, THE STARS [Heinlein - 1952]
REEVES, ROSSER  (1)
     Infinity.........................(verse)......................F&SF  Dec 1960
              THE BEST FROM FANTASY & SCIENCE FICTION: 10th SERIES [Mills - 1961]

REINES, DONALD F.  (1)                                              Mag.    Year
    Interplanetary Copyright.........................................ORIGINAL STORY
        COMING ATTRACTIONS [Greenberg - 1957]
REPP, ED EARL  (1)
    Kleon of the Golden Sun...........................................FB #7  n/d 1950
        SCIENCE AND SORCERY [Ford - 1953]
REPTON, HUMPHREY  (1)
    From A Private Mad-House..........................................Var  n/d/a 1787
        FAR BOUNDARIES [Derleth - 1951]
REYNOLDS, MACK  (10)
    And Thou Beside Me................................................F&SF   Apr 1954
        SCIENCE FICTION ADVENTURES IN MUTATION [Conklin - 1956]
    Business, As Usual, The...........................................F&SF   Jun 1952
        WORLDS OF TOMORROW [Derleth - 1953]
    Compounded Interest...............................................F&SF   Aug 1956
        SF: 57 THE YEAR'S GREATEST SF AND FANTASY [Merril - 1957]
    Discord Makers, The...............................................OTWA   Jul 1950
        INVADERS OF EARTH [Conklin - 1952]
    D.P. From Tomorrow................................................OSF   Fal 1953
        PORTALS OF TOMORROW [Derleth - 1954]
    Isolationist......................................................FA   Apr 1950
        THE BIG BOOK OF SCIENCE FICTION [Conklin - 1950]
    Man in the Moon, The..............................................Amz   Jul 1950
        LOOKING FORWARD [Lesser - 1953]
    Martians and the Coys, The........................................Im   Jun 1951
        SCIENCE FICTION CARNIVAL [Brown & Reynolds - 1953]
    Potential Enemy...................................................Orb #2  n/d 1954
        BEYOND THE STARS AND OTHER STORIES [Anonymous - 1958]
    w/ Fredric Brown
        Dark Interlude................................................Glxy   Jan 1951
            THE GALAXY READER OF SCIENCE FICTION [Gold - 1952]
            THE BEST SCIENCE FICTION STORIES: 1952 [Bleiler & Dikty - 1952]
RICE, JANE  (4)
    Idol of the Flies, The............................................UW   Jun 1942
        CHILDREN OF WONDER [Tenn - 1953]
    Rainbow Gold, The.................................................F&SF   Dec 1959
        THE BEST FROM FANTASY & SCIENCE FICTION: 10th SERIES [Mills - 1961]
    Refugee, The......................................................UW   Oct 1943
        FROM UNKNOWN WORLDS [J. W. Campbell - 1952]
    Willow Tree, The..................................................F&SF   Feb 1959
        THE BEST FROM FANTASY & SCIENCE FICTION: 9th SERIES [Mills - 1960]
RICHARDS, NELSON  (1)
    Science Steals a Match............................................ORIGINAL STORY
        ADVENTURES TO COME [Esenwein - 1937]
RICHARDSON, R. S.  (1)    See listing Philip Latham
    Space Fix.........................................................ASF   Mar 1943
        COMING ATTRACTIONS [Greenberg - 1957]
RICHTER, CONRAD  (1)
    Doctor Hanray's Second Chance.....................................SEP   1/10/50
        THE SATURDAY EVENING POST FANTASY STORIES [Fles - 1951]
RIKER, ANTHONY  (1)
    Between Two Worlds................................................Orb #5  Nov 1954
        (Originally appeared under title Aunt Elsie's Stairway)
        SPACE STATION 42 AND OTHER STORIES [Anonymous - 1958]

271

RILEY, FRANK (1)                                                Mag.   Year
     Cyber and Justice Holmes.................................................If   Mar 1955
          THE BEST SCIENCE FICTION STORIES AND NOVELS: 1956 [Dikty - 1956]
          THE FIRST WORLD OF IF [Quinn & Wulff - 1957]
ROBERTS, MORLEY (1)
     Anticipator, The.....(From THE KEEPERS OF THE WATERS AND OTHER STORIES; 1898)
          TRAVELERS IN TIME [Stern - 1947]
ROBERTSON, MORGAN (1)
     Battle of the Monsters, The.....................................................
          (From Where Angels Fear to Tread and Other Tales of the Sea; 1899)
          BEYOND TIME AND SPACE [Derleth - 1950]
ROBIN, RALPH (2)
     Budding Explorer...............................................F&SF   Sep 1952
          THE BEST FROM FANTASY & SCIENCE FICTION: 2nd SER [Boucher & McComas-1953]
     Pleasant Dreams................................................Glxy   Oct 195?
          THE OMNIBUS OF SCIENCE FICTION [Conklin - 1952]
ROBINSON, FRANK M.  (8)
     Dream Street...................................................ImT   Mar 1955
          THE BEST SCIENCE FICTION STORIES AND NOVELS: 1956 [Dikty - 1956]
     Fire and the Sword, The........................................Glxy   Aug 1951
          IMAGINATION UNLIMITED [Bleiler & Dikty - 1952]
     Girls From the Earth, The......................................Glxy   Jan 1952
          THE BEST SCIENCE FICTION STORIES: 1953 [Bleiler & Dikty - 1953]
          STORIES FOR TOMORROW [Sloane - 1954]
     Hunting Season, The............................................ASF   Nov 1951
          YEAR'S BEST SCIENCE FICTION NOVELS: 1952 [Bleiler & Dikty - 1952]
     Oceans Are Wide, The...........................................SS   Apr 1954
          YEAR'S BEST SCIENCE FICTION NOVELS: 1954 [Bleiler & Dikty - 1954]
     One Thousand Miles Up..........................................SS   Apr 1954
          THE BEST SCIENCE FICTION STORIES AND NOVELS: 1955 [Dikty - 1955]
     Reluctant Heroes, The..........................................Glxy   Jan 1951
          THE GALAXY READER OF SCIENCE FICTION [Gold - 1952]
          MEN ON THE MOON [Wollheim - 1958]
     Santa Claus Planet, The........................................ORIGINAL STORY
          THE BEST SCIENCE FICTION STORIES: 1951 [Bleiler & Dikty - 1951]
ROCKLYNNE, ROSS  (7)
     Backfire.......................................................ASF   Jan 1943
          THE OMNIBUS OF SCIENCE FICTION [Conklin - 1952]
     Immortal, The..................................................Com   Mar 1941
          TOMORROW'S UNIVERSE [H. J. Campbell - 1954]
     Jackdaw........................................................ASF   Aug 1942
          THE BEST OF SCIENCE FICTION [Conklin - 1946]
     Jaywalker......................................................Glxy   Dec 1950
          THE GALAXY READER OF SCIENCE FICTION [Gold - 1952]
     Pressure.......................................................ASF   Jun 1939
          IMAGINATION UNLIMITED [Bleiler & Dikty - 1952]
     Quietus........................................................ASF   Sep 1940
          ADVENTURES IN TIME AND SPACE [Healy & McComas - 1946]
     Winner Take All................................................ORIGINAL STORY
          TIME TO COME [Derleth - 1954]
ROGERS, JOEL TOWNSLEY  (3)
     Beyond Space and Time..........................................Sup   Sep 1950
          A TREASURY OF GREAT SCIENCE FICTION [Boucher - 1959]
     Moment Without Time............................................Stg   Apr 1952
          THE BEST FROM STARTLING STORIES [Mines - 1953]
     No Matter Where You Go.........................................F&SF   Feb 1959
          THE BEST FROM FANTASY & SCIENCE FICTION: 9th SERIES [Mills - 1960]

```
ROGERS, KAY  (1)                                                    Mag.    Year
    Experiment.............................................F&SF  Feb 1953
         THE BEST FROM F&SF: 3rd SERIES [Boucher & McComas - 1954]
ROUNDS, EMMA  (1)
    Plane Geometry...............(verse)............(From Creative Youth; 1925)
         FANTASIA MATHEMATICA [Fadiman - 1958]
RUBY, B. F.  (1)
    w/ Fletcher Pratt
       Thing In the Woods, The.................................Amz  Feb 1935
         THE OMNIBUS OF SCIENCE FICTION [Conklin - 1952]
RUD, ANTHONY M.  (1)
    Ooze...................................................WT  Mar 1923
         THE MOON TERROR AND OTHER STORIES [Anonymous - 1927]
RUSSELL, ERIC FRANK  (26)    See listing Maurice G. Hugi
    And Then There Were None...............................ASF  Jun 1951
         YEAR'S BEST SCIENCE FICTION NOVELS: 1952 [Bleiler & Dikty - 1952]
         STORIES FOR TOMORROW [Sloane - 1954]
    Boomerang..............................................FU   Sep 1953
         SCIENCE FICTION THINKING MACHINES [Conklin - 1954]
    Dear Devil.............................................OW   May 1950
         THE BIG BOOK OF SCIENCE FICTION [Conklin - 1950]
         SPACE, SPACE, SPACE [Sloane - 1953]
    Exposure...............................................ASF  Jul 1950
         OPERATION FUTURE [Conklin - 1955]
    Fast Falls the Eventide................................ASF  May 1952
         THE BEST SCIENCE FICTION STORIES: 1953 [Bleiler & Dikty - 1953]
    Glass Eye, The.........................................ASF  Mar 1949
         BEYOND HUMAN KEN [Merril - 1952]
    "Hobbyist".............................................ASF  Sep 1947
         THE ASTOUNDING SCIENCE FICTION ANTHOLOGY [J. W. Campbell - 1952]
         BEST SF FOUR SCIENCE FICTION STORIES [Crispin - 1961]
    I Am Nothing...........................................ASF  Jul 1952
         THE BEST SCIENCE FICTION STORIES: 1953 [Bleiler & Dikty - 1953]
    Illusionaries, The.....................................PS   Nov 1951
         SPACE PIONEERS [Norton - 1954]
    Impulse................................................ASF  Sep 1938
         INVADERS OF EARTH [Conklin - 1952]
    Into Your Tent I'll Creep..............................ASF  Sep 1957
         THE BEST SCIENCE FICTION STORIES AND NOVELS: 9th SERIES [Dikty - 1958]
    Jay Score..............................................ASF  May 1941
         TOMORROW, THE STARS [Heinlein - 1952]
    Late Night Final.......................................ASF  Dec 1948
         THE ASTOUNDING SCIENCE FICTION ANTHOLOGY [J. W. Campbell - 1952]
    Metamorphosite.........................................ASF  Dec 1946
         JOURNEY TO INFINITY [Greenberg - 1951]
         BEACHHEADS IN SPACE [Derleth - 1954]
    Muten..................................................ASF  Oct 1948
         (Originally appeared under pseudonym Duncan H. Munro)
            SCIENCE FICTION CARNIVAL [Brown & Reynolds - 1953]
    Plus X.................................................ASF  Jun 1956
         FOUR FOR THE FUTURE [Conklin - 1959]
    Present From Joe, A.....................................ImT  Mar 1955
         THE BEST SCIENCE FICTION STORIES AND NOVELS: 1956 [Dikty - 1956]
    Sole Solution..........................................FU   Apr 1956
         PENGUIN SCIENCE FICTION [Aldiss - 1961]
```

RUSSELL, ERIC FRANK  [Cont'd]                                          Mag.    Year
    Spiro..........................................................WT   Mar 1947
        (Originally appeared under title Venturer of the Martian Mimich)
        THE OTHER SIDE OF THE MOON [Derleth - 1949]
    Symbiotica.....................................................ASF  Oct 1943
        ADVENTURES IN TIME AND SPACE [Healy & McComas - 1946]
    Take a Seat....................................................Stg  May 1952
        HUMAN? [Merril - 1954]
    Test Piece.....................................................OW   Mar 1951
        THE OMNIBUS OF SCIENCE FICTION [Conklin - 1952]
    This One's On Me................................................NSF  Aug 1953
        SCIENCE FICTION ADVENTURES IN MUTATION [Conklin - 1956]
    Timeless Ones, The.............................................SFQ  Nov 1952
        PRIZE SCIENCE FICTION [Wollheim - 1953]
    Ultima Thule...................................................ASF  Oct 1951
        LOOKING FORWARD [Lesser - 1953]
    Ultimate Invader, The..........................................PS   Jan 1953
        (Originally appeared under title Design For Great Day)
        THE ULTIMATE INVADER AND OTHER SCIENCE FICTION [Wollheim - 1954]
RUSSELL, WILLIAM MOY  (1)
    Three Brothers, The............................................Obs  12/26/1954
        A. D. 2500 [Wilson - 1955]
RYMER, G. A.  (1)
    Atavists, The...........................................London Observer Prize Story
        A. D. 2500 [Wilson - 1955]


*S*


SAARI, OLIVER  (1)
    Sitting Duck...................................................ASF  Jun 1952
        VERY BOY'S BOOK OF OUTER SPACE STORIES [Dikty - 1960]
ST. CLAIR, MARGARET  (8)          (See listing Idris Seabright)
    Age of Prophecy, The...........................................Fw/SFS Mar 1951
        SCIENCE FICTION ADVENTURES IN MUTATION [Conklin - 1956]
    Child of Void..................................................Sup  Nov 1949
        INVADERS OF EARTH [Conklin - 1952]
    Gardener, The..................................................TWS  Oct 1949
        WORLDS OF TOMORROW [Derleth - 1953]
    Horror Howce...................................................Glxy Jul 1956
        THE FOURTH GALAXY READER OF SCIENCE FICTION [Gold - 1959]
    Pillows, The...................................................TWS  Jun 1950
        POSSIBLE WORLDS OF SCIENCE FICTION [Conklin - 1951]
        THE SANDS OF MARS AND OTHER STORIES [Anonymous - 1958]
    Prott..........................................................Glxy Jan 1953
        SCIENCE FICTION TERROR TALES [Conklin - 1955]
        BEST SF SCIENCE FICTION STORIES [Crispin - 1955]
    Quis Custodlet...?.............................................Stg  Jul 1948
        THE SCIENCE FICTION GALAXY [Conklin - 1950]
    Thirsty God....................................................F&SF Mar 1953
        (Originally appeared under psuedonym Idris Seabright)
        CROSSROADS IN TIME [Conklin - 1953]
ST. JOHN, PHILIP ps (Lester del Rey)  (1)     (See listing Lester del Rey)
    Anything.......................................................Unk  Oct 1939
        FROM UNKNOWN WORLDS [J. W. Campbell - 1948]

SAKI ps (H. H. Munro)  (4)                                   Mag.   Year
   Laura.........................................(From Beasts and Super Beasts; 1914)
      OUT OF THIS WORLD [Fast - 1944]
   Music On the Hill, The..................(From The Chronicles of Clovis; 1912)
      THE MOONLIGHT TRAVELER [Stern - 1943]
   Open Window, The.......................(From Beasts and Super Beasts; 1914)
      CHILDREN OF WONDER [Tenn - 1953]
   Tobermory..............................................(No data available)
      JOURNEYS IN SCIENCE FICTION [Loughlin & Popp - 1961]
SAMALMAN, ALEXANDER  (1)
   Life On the Moon....................................................TWS  Dec 1946
      SHOT IN THE DARK [Merril - 1950]
SAMBROT, WILLIAM  (1)
   Creature of the Snows............................................SEP  10/29/60
      SIXTH ANNUAL OF THE YEAR'S BEST SF [Merril - 1961]
SANDBURG, CARL  (1)
   Arithmetic.........................................(From Complete Poems; 1950)
      FANTASIA MATHEMATICA [Fadiman - 1958]
SANDERS, WINSTON P.  (1)
   Pact.........................................................F&SF  Aug 1959
      THE BEST FROM FANTASY & SCIENCE FICTION: 9th SERIES [Mills - 1960]
SANSOM, WILLIAM  (1)
   Witnesses, The...................(From Fireman Flower and Other Stories; 1944)
      TIMELESS STORIES FOR TODAY AND TOMORROW [Bradbury - 1952]
SATTERFIELD, CHARLES  (1)
   With Redfern On Capella XII.................................Glxy  Nov 1955
      MIND PARTNER AND 8 OTHER NOVELETTES FROM GALAXY [Gold - 1961]
SAVAGE, ARTHUR DEKKER  (1)
   Last War, The.............................................Orb #2  n/d 1954
      (Originally appeared under title The Butterfly Kiss)
      PLANET OF DOOM AND OTHER STORIES [Anonymous - 1958]
SCHACHNER, NAT  (1)
   Ultimate Metal, The.........................................Ast  Feb 1935
      THE BEST OF SCIENCE FICTION [Conklin - 1946]
SCHAFHAUSER, CHARLES  (1)
   Gleeb For Earth, A.........................................Glxy  May 1953
      THE SECOND GALAXY READER OF SCIENCE FICTION [Gold - 1954]
SCHENCK, HERBERT JR.  (1)
   Ed Lear Wasn't So Crazy....................................F&SF  Jun 1960
      SIXTH ANNUAL OF THE YEAR'S BEST SF [Merril - 1961]
SCHMITZ, JAMES H.  (7)
   Agent of Vega.............................................ASF   Jun 1949
      SPACE POLICE [Norton - 1956]
   Caretaker................................................Glxy  Jul 1953
      THE SECOND GALAXY READER OF SCIENCE FICTION [Gold - 1954]
   End of the Line, The.....................................ASF   Jul 1951
      SPACE PIONEERS [Norton - 1954]
   Grandpa..................................................ASF   Feb 1955
      PENGUIN SCIENCE FICTION [Aldiss - 1961]
   Second Night of Summer...................................Glxy  Dec 1950
      POSSIBLE WORLDS OF SCIENCE FICTION [Conklin - 1951]
   We Don't Want Any Trouble................................Glxy  Jun 1953
      ASSIGNMENT IN TOMORROW [Pohl - 1954]
   Witches of Karres, The...................................ASF   Dec 1949
      THE ASTOUNDING SCIENCE FICTION ANTHOLOGY [J. W. Campbell - 1952]

SCHNIRRING, MARY-ALICE  (1)                                                    Mag.    Year
      Child's Play...................................................WT  Mar 1942
            CHILDREN OF WONDER [Tenn - 1953]
SCHNITZLER, ARTHUR  (1)
      Leinbach's Proof.............................(From Flight Into Darkness; 1931)
            FANTASIA MATHEMATICA [Fadiman - 1958]
SCHOENFELD, HOWARD  (1)
      Built Up Logically..................................Rpnt — F&SF  Fal 1950
            (Originally appeared under title The Universal Panacea In Retort Win 1949)
            THE BEST FROM FANTASY & SCIENCE FICTION [Boucher & McComas - 1952]
SCHORER, MACK  (1)
      w/ August Derleth

            Return of Andrew Bentley, The..........................WT  Sep 1933
                  THE OTHER WORLDS [Stong - 1941]
SCHRAMM, WILBUR  (1)
      Voice In the Earphones, The.......(From Windwagon Smith and Other Yarns; 1947)
            THE SATURDAY EVENING POST FANTASY STORIES [Fles - 1951] Rpnt–SEP 5/29/47
SCORTIA, THOMAS N.  (3)
      Alien Night.............................................SFad  Aug 1957
            GET OUT OF MY SKY [Margulies - 1960]
      Bomb In the Bathtub, The..............................Glxy  Feb 1957
            THE FOURTH GALAXY READER OF SCIENCE FICTION [Gold - 1959]
      Shores of Night, The...............................ORIGINAL STORY
            (Portion entitled Sea Change appeared in ASF June 1956. Balance of  story
                  written for this anthology.)
            THE BEST SCIENCE FICTION STORIES AND NOVELS: 1956 [Dikty - 1956]
SEABRIGHT, IDRIS ps (Margaret St. Clair) (10)  See listing Margaret St. Clair
      Altruists, The.........................................F&SF  Nov 1953
            PORTALS OF TOMORROW [Derleth - 1954]
      Brightness Falls From the Air..........................F&SF  Apr 1951
            THE BEST SCIENCE FICTION STORIES: 1952 [Bleiler & Dikty - 1952]
      Causes, The............................................F&SF  Jun 1952
            A DECADE OF FANTASY & SCIENCE FICTION [Mills - 1960]
      Egg a Month From All Over, An..........................F&SF  Oct 1952
            HUMAN? [Merril - 1954]
      Hole In the Moon, The..................................F&SF  Feb 1952
            THE BEST FROM F&SF: 2nd SERIES [Boucher & McComas - 1953]
      Listening Child, The...................................F&SF  Dec 1950
            THE BEST FROM FANTASY & SCIENCE FICTION [Boucher & McComas - 1952]
      Man Who Sold Rope to the Gnoles, The...................F&SF  Oct 1951
            BEYOND HUMAN KEN [Merril - 1952]
      New Ritual.............................................F&SF  Jan 1953
            THE BEST FROM F&SF: 3rd SERIES [Boucher & McComas - 1954]
      Short In the Chest.......................................FU  Jul 1954
            OPERATION FUTURE [Conklin - 1955]
      Wines of Earth, The....................................F&SF  Sep 1957
            THE BEST FROM FANTASY & SCIENCE FICTION: 7th SERIES [Boucher - 1958]
SEAMARK ps (Austin J. Hall)  (1)
      Avenging Ray, The.........(excerpts)...........(Originally published in 1930)
            SCIENCE IN FICTION [A.E.M. & J.C. Bayliss - 1957]
SELL, WILLIAM  (1)
      Other Tracks...........................................ASF  Oct 1938
            SCIENCE FICTION ADVENTURES IN DIMENSION [Conklin - 1953]
SELLINGS, ARTHUR  (3)
      Blank Form.............................................Glxy  Jul 1958
            THE FOURTH GALAXY READER OF SCIENCE FICTION [Gold - 1959]

SELLINGS, ARTHUR [Cont'd]                                   Mag.   Year
    Mission, The.........................................London Observer Prize Story
       A. D. 2500 [Wilson - 1955]
    Scene Shifter, The.................................................ORIGINAL STORY
       STAR SCIENCE FICTION STORIES #5 [Pohl - 1959]
SERVISS, GARRETT P.  (I)
    Edison's Conquest of Mars.......................................NYEJ  1/12/98
       THE TREASURY OF SCIENCE FICTION CLASSICS [Kuebler - 1955]
SHAARA, MICHAEL  (5)
    Grenville's Planet..............................................F&SF  Oct 1952
       BEST SF THREE SCIENCE FICTION STORIES [Crispin - 1958]
    Man of Distinction.............................................Glxy  Oct 1956
       THE FOURTH GALAXY READER OF SCIENCE FICTION [Gold - 1959]
    Orphans of the Void............................................Glxy  Jun 1952
       SHADOW OF TOMORROW [Pohl - 1953]
    Soldier Boy....................................................Glxy  Jul 1953
       SCIENCE FICTION THINKING MACHINES [Conklin - 1954]
    2066: Election Day.............................................ASF  Dec 1956
       THE BEST SCIENCE FICTION STORIES AND NOVELS: 9th SERIES [Dikty - 1958]
SHALLIT, JOSEPH  (I)
    Wonder Child...................................................Fnt  Feb 1953
       THE BEST SCIENCE FICTION STORIES: 1954 [Bleiler & Dikty - 1954]
SHANKS, EDWARD  (I)
    Receptive Bosom, The..........................................(No date available)
      (From A [London] Sunday Times review of H. McKay's The World of Numbers)
       FANTASIA MATHEMATICA [Fadiman - 1958]
SHARKEY, JACK  (I)
    Multum In Parvo...............................................Gent  Dec 1959
       THE FIFTH ANNUAL OF THE YEAR'S BEST SF [Merril - 1960]
SHARP, D. D.  (I)
    Eternal Man, The..............................................SWS  Aug 1929
       A TREASURY OF SCIENCE FICTION [Conklin - 1948]
       FROM OFF THIS WORLD [Margulies & Friend - 1949]
SHAW, LARRY  (I)
    Simworthy's Circus............................................WB  Dec 1950
       SCIENCE-FICTION CARNIVAL [Brown & Reynolds - 1953]
SHECKLEY, ROBERT  (17)
    Accountant, The...............................................F&SF  Jul 1954
       THE BEST FROM FANTASY & SCIENCE FICTION: 4th SERIES [Boucher - 1955]
    Battle, The...................................................If  Sep 1954
       THE FIRST WORLD OF IF [Quinn & Wulff - 1957]
    Fishing Season, The...........................................TWS  Aug 1953
       TERROR IN THE MODERN VEIN [Wollheim - 1955]
    Last Weapon, The..............................................ORIGINAL STORY
       STAR SCIENCE FICTION STORIES [Pohl - 1953]
    Leech, The....................................................Glxy  Dec 1952
       SCIENCE FICTION TERROR TALES [Conklin - 1955]
    Minimum Man, The..............................................Glxy  Jun 1958
       THE FOURTH GALAXY READER OF SCIENCE FICTION [Gold - 1959]
    Odor of Thought, The..........................................ORIGINAL STORY
       STAR SCIENCE FICTION STORIES #2 [Pohl - 1953]
    Operation Instructions........................................ASF  May 1953
       BEYOND THE BARRIERS OF SPACE AND TIME [Merril - 1954]
    Paradise II...................................................ORIGINAL STORY
       TIME TO COME [Derleth - 1954]
    Pilgrimage to Earth...........................................Plby  Sep 1956
       SPECTRUM [Amis & Conquest-1961]  (Org aprd under title Love, Inc.)

```
SHECKLEY, ROBERT [Cont'd]                                       Mag.    Year
   Potential................................................ASF    Nov 1953
      PORTALS OF TOMORROW [Derleth - 1954]
   Prize of Peril, The......................................F&SF   May 1958
      SF: 59 THE YEAR'S GREATEST SF AND FANTASY [Merril - 1959]
   Proof of the Pudding.....................................Glxy   Aug 1952
      A GALAXY OF GHOULS [Merril - 1955]
   Protection...............................................Glxy   Apr 1956
      THE THIRD GALAXY READER OF SCIENCE FICTION [Gold - 1958]
   Specialist...............................................Glxy   May 1953
      THE SECOND GALAXY READER OF SCIENCE FICTION [Gold - 1954]
   Warm.....................................................Glxy   Jun 1953
      THE SECOND GALAXY READER OF SCIENCE FICTION [Gold - 1954]
   Watchbird................................................Glxy   Feb 1953
      SHADOW OF TOMORROW [Pohl - 1953]
SHELDON, WALT (2)
   Chore for a Spaceman.....................................TWS    Dec 1950
      SPACE SERVICE [Norton - 1953]
   I, The Unspeakable.......................................Glxy   Apr 1951
      THE GALAXY READER OF SCIENCE FICTION [Gold - 1952]
SHELTON, JERRY (1)
   Culture..................................................ASF    Sep 1944
      THE BIG BOOK OF SCIENCE FICTION [Conklin - 1950]
SHEPLEY, JOHN (1)
   Gorilla Suit.............................................F&SF   May 1958
      THE BEST FROM FANTASY & SCIENCE FICTION: 8th SERIES [Boucher - 1959]
SHERRED, T. L. (2)
   E For Effort.............................................ASF    May 1947
      THE BIG BOOK OF SCIENCE FICTION [Conklin - 1950]
      THE ASTOUNDING SCIENCE FICTION ANTHOLOGY [J. W. Campbell - 1952]
   Eye for Iniquity.........................................BFF    Jul 1953
      PORTALS OF TOMORROW [Derleth - 1954]
SHIRAS, WILMAR H. (2)
   In Hiding................................................ASF    Nov 1948
      THE BEST SCIENCE FICTION STORIES: 1949 [Bleiler & Dikty - 1949]
      GREAT STORIES OF SCIENCE FICTION [Leinster - 1951]
      CHILDREN OF WONDER [Tenn - 1953]
      STORIES FOR TOMORROW [Sloane - 1954]
   Opening Doors............................................ASF    Mar 1949
      THE BEST SCIENCE FICTION STORIES: 1950 [Bleiler & Dikty - 1950]
SILVERBERG, ROBERT (3)
   Company Store...................................ORIGINAL STORY
      STAR SCIENCE FICTION STORIES #5 [Pohl - 1959]
   Double Dare..............................................Glxy   Nov 1956
      THE FIFTH GALAXY READER [Gold - 1961]
   Road to Nightfall........................................FU     Jul 1958
      THE FANTASTIC UNIVERSE OMNIBUS [Santesson - 1960]
SILVERSTEIN, SHEL (1)
   Distortion, The..................(cartoon)....................Plby   May 1960
      SIXTH ANNUAL OF THE YEAR'S BEST SF [Merril - 1961]
SIMAK, CLIFFORD D. (24)
   Answers, The.............................................FSF    Mar 1953
      (Originally appeared under title And The Truth Shall Make You Free)
      STORIES FOR TOMORROW [Sloane - 1954]
   Asteroid of Gold, The....................................WS     Nov 1932
      EVERY BOY'S BOOK OF SCIENCE FICTION [Wollheim - 1951]
```

Beachhead...............................................................FA   Jul 1951
     BEACHHEADS IN SPACE [Derleth - 1954]
Contraption.............................................................ORIGINAL STORY
     STAR SCIENCE FICTION STORIES [Pohl - 1953]
Courtesy................................................................ASF  Aug 1951
     SPACE, SPACE, SPACE [Sloane - 1953]
     CROSSROADS IN TIME [Conklin - 1953]
Death in the House, A...................................................Glxy  Oct 1959
     FIFTH ANNUAL OF THE YEAR'S BEST SF [Merril - 1960]
Desertion...............................................................ASF  Nov 1944
     THE BIG BOOK OF SCIENCE FICTION [Conklin - 1950]
     UBERWINDUNG VON RAUM UND ZEIT [Gunther - 1952]
     A GALAXY OF GHOULS [Merril - 1955]
Eternity Lost...........................................................ASF  Jul 1949
     THE BEST SCIENCE FICTION STORIES: 1950 [Bliler & Dikty - 1950]
     THE ASTOUNDING SCIENCE FICTION ANTHOLOGY [J. W. Campbell - 1952]
Final Gentleman.........................................................F&SF Jan 1960
     SIX GREAT SHORT NOVELS OF SCIENCE FICTION [Conklin - 1960]
Good Night, Mr. James...................................................Glxy  Mar 1951
     THE OUTER REACHES [Derleth - 1951]
     THE GALAXY READER OF SCIENCE FICTION [Gold - 1952]
Honorable Opponent......................................................Glxy  Aug 1956
     THE THIRD GALAXY READER OF SCIENCE FICTION [Gold - 1958]
How-2...................................................................Glxy  Nov 1954
     THE BEST SCIENCE FICTION STORIES & NOVELS: 1955 [Dikty - 1955]
     BODYGUARD AND FOUR OTHER SHORT NOVELS FROM GALAXY [Gold - 1960]
Junkyard................................................................Glxy  Mar 1953
     THE SECOND GALAXY READER OF SCIENCE FICTION [Gold - 1954]
Kindergarten............................................................Glxy  Jul 1953
     PORTALS OF TOMORROW [Derleth - 1954]
Limiting Factor.........................................................Stg  Nov 1949
     POSSIBLE WORLDS OF SCIENCE FICTION [Conklin - 1951]
     BEYOND THE STARS AND OTHER STORIES [Anonymous - 1958]
     SPECTRUM [Amis & Conquest - 1961]
Lobby...................................................................ASF  Apr 1944
     THE BEST OF SCIENCE FICTION [Conklin - 1946]
Ogre....................................................................ASF  Jan 1949
     ADVENTURES ON OTHER PLANETS [Wollheim - 1954]
Operation Mercury.......................................................ASF  Mar 1941
     (Originally appeared under title Masquerade)
     TALES OF OUTER SPACE [Wollheim - 1954]
Second Childhood........................................................Glxy  Feb 1951
     THE GALAXY READER OF SCIENCE FICTION [Gold - 1952]
     STORIES FOR TOMORROW [Sloane - 1954]
Skirmish................................................................Amz  Dec 1950
     (Originally appeared under title Bathe Your Bearings in Blood)
     SCIENCE FICTION THINKING MACHINES [Conklin - 1954]
     PENGUIN SCIENCE FICTION [Aldiss - 1961]
Tools...................................................................ASF  Jul 1942
     A TREASURY OF SCIENCE FICTION [Conklin - 1948]
World That Couldn't be, The.............................................Glxy  Jan 1958
     THE WORLD THAT COULDN'T BE & 8 OTHER NOVELETTES FROM GALAXY [Gold-1959]
Worrywart...............................................................Glxy  Sep 1953
     OPERATION FUTURE [Conklin - 1952]
     BEST SF TWO SCIENCE FICTION STORIES [Crispin - 1956]
w/ Carl Jacobi
     Lost Street, The..................................................Com  Jul 1941
         (Originally appeared under title The Street That Wasn't There)
         STRANGE PORTS OF CALL [Derleth - 1948]

```
SLESAR, HENRY  (2)                                                        Mag.    Year
    Invisible Man Murder Case, The...............................Fnt  May 1958
        INVISIBLE MEN [Davenport - 1960]
    My Father, The Cat...........................................FU  Dec 1957
        THE FANTASTIC UNIVERSE OMNIBUS [Santesson - 1960]
SLOANE, WILLIAM  (1)
    Let Nothing You Dismay.....................................ORIGINAL STORY
        STORIES FOR TOMORROW [Sloane - 1954]
SMITH, CLARK ASHTON  (8)
    Beyond the Singing Flame, The.................................WS  Nov 1931
        FROM OFF THIS WORLD [Margulies & Friend - 1949]
    City of the Singing Flame, The...............................WS  Jul 1931
        THE OTHER SIDE OF THE MOON [Derleth - 1949]
        FROM OFF THIS WORLD [Margulies & Friend - 1949]
    Master of the Asteroid.......................................WS  Oct 1932
        STRANGE PORTS OF CALL [Derleth - 1948]
    Metamorphosis of Earth, The..................................WT  Sep 1951
        BEACHHEADS IN SPACE [Derleth - 1954]
    Phoenix....................................................ORIGINAL STORY
        TIME TO COME [Derleth - 1954]
    Plutonian Drug, The.........................................Amz  Sep 1934
        THE OUTER REACHES [Derleth - 1951]
    Unchartered Isle, The........................................WT  Nov 1930
        MY BEST SCIENCE FICTION STORY [Margulies & Friend - 1949]
    Voyage To Sfanomoe, A........................................WT  Aug 1931
        BEYOND TIME AND SPACE [Derleth - 1950]
SMITH, CORDWAINER  (6)
    Angerhelm..................................................ORIGINAL STORY
        STAR SCIENCE FICTION STORIES #6 [Pohl - 1959]
    Game of Rat and Dragon, The.................................Glxy  Oct 1955
        THE BEST SCIENCE FICTION STORIES AND NOVELS: 1956 [Dikty - 1956]
        BEST SF THREE SCIENCE FICTION STORIES [Crispin - 1958]
        THE THIRD GALAXY READER OF SCIENCE FICTION [Gold - 1958]
    Lady Who Sailed the Soul, The...............................Glxy  Apr 1960
        MIND PARTNER AND 8 OTHER NOVELETTES FROM GALAXY [Gold - 1961]
    No, No, Not Rogov!............................................If  Feb 1959
        FIFTH ANNUAL OF THE YEAR'S BEST SF [Merril - 1960]
    Scanners Live In Vain......................................FB #6  n/d 1950
        BEYOND THE END OF TIME [Pohl - 1952]
        SCIENCE AND SORCERY [Ford - 1953]
    When the People Fell........................................Glxy  Apr 1959
        THE FIFTH GALAXY READER [Gold - 1961]
SMITH, E. E.  (1)
    Atlantis...............................(Excerpts from Triplanetary; 1950)
        JOURNEY TO INFINITY [Greenberg - 1951]
SMITH, EVELYN E.  (6)
      D
      a
    Baxbr......................................................ORIGINAL STORY
      b        TIME TO COME [Derleth - 1954]
      r        BEST SF FOUR SCIENCE FICTION STORIES [Crispin - 1961]
               JOURNEYS IN SCIENCE FICTION [Loughlin & Popp - 1961]
    Hardest Bargain, The........................................Glxy  Jun 1957
        MIND PARTNER AND 8 OTHER NOVELETTES FROM GALAXY [Gold - 1961]
    Not Fit For Children........................................Glxy  May 1953
        THE SECOND GALAXY READER OF SCIENCE FICTION [Gold - 1954]
    Once A Greech...............................................Glxy  Apr 1957
        THE WORLD THAT COULDN'T BE & 8 OTHER NOVELETTES FROM GALAXY [Gold - 1959]
```

```
SMITH, EVELYN E. [Cont'd]                                    Mag.    Year
    Tea Tray In the Sky.................................Glxy  Sep 1952
        THE SECOND GALAXY READER OF SCIENCE FICTION [Gold - 1954]
    Vilbar Party, The..................................Glxy  Jan 1955
        THE THIRD GALAXY READER OF SCIENCE FICTION [Gold - 1958]
SMITH, GEORGE H.  (1)
    Last Crusade, The.....................................If  Feb 1955
        THE FIRST WORLD OF IF [Quinn & Wulff - 1957]
SMITH, GEORGE O.  (3)
    Cosmic Jackpot, The.................................TWS  Oct 1948
        SCIENCE FICTION CARNIVAL [Brown & Reynolds - 1953]
    Lost Art..........................................ASF  Dec 1943
        A TREASURY OF GREAT SCIENCE FICTION [Boucher - 1959]
    Vocation..........................................ASF  Apr 1945
        CROSSROADS IN TIME [Conklin - 1953]
SMITH, LADY ELEANOR  (1)
    No Ships Pass......................................Cas  Apr 1932
        TRAVELERS IN TIME [Stern - 1947]
SMITH, RON  (2)
    Horror Story Shorter By One Letter Than the Shortest Horror Story Ever Written
        THE BEST FROM F&SF: 7th SERIES [Boucher - 1958]    ORIGINAL STORY
    I Don't Mind......................................F&SF  Oct 1956
        THE BEST FROM FANTASY & SCIENCE FICTION: 6th SERIES [Boucher - 1957]
SMITTER, WESSEL HYATT  (1)
    Hand, The.........................................Stry  Feb 1947
        TIMELESS STORIES FOR TODAY AND TOMORROW [Bradbury - 1952]
SPRINGER, SHERWOOD  (2)
    Epitaph Near Moonport..................(verse)...........F&SF  Jul 1954
        THE BEST FROM FANTASY & SCIENCE FICTION: 4th SERIES [Boucher - 1955]
    No Land of Ned.....................................Stg  Dec 1952
        THE BEST FROM STARTLING STORIES [Mines - 1953]
STANGLAND, A. G.  (1)
    Ancient Brain, The.................................SWS  Oct 1929
        FROM OFF THIS WORLD [Margulies & Friend - 1949]
STANTON, WILL  (3)
    Barney............................................F&SF  Feb 1951
        THE BEST FROM FANTASY & SCIENCE FICTION [Boucher & McComas - 1952]
    Dodger Fan........................................F&SF  Jun 1957
        THE BEST FROM FANTASY & SCIENCE FICTION: 7th SERIES [Boucher - 1958]
    Last Present, The.................................F&SF  Aug 1956
        THE BEST FROM FANTASY & SCIENCE FICTION: 6th SERIES [Boucher - 1957]
STAPLEDON, OLAF  (4)
    Flying Men, The....................(From The Last and First Men; 1930)
        BEYOND TIME AND SPACE [Derleth - 1950]
    Last Terrestrials, The.............(From The Last and First Men; 1930)
        THE TREASURY OF SCIENCE FICTION CLASSICS [Kuebler - 1955]
    Martians, The......................(From The Last and First Men; 1930)
        THE TREASURY OF SCIENCE FICTION CLASSICS [Kuebler - 1955]
    Odd John.................(Originally published by Methuen and Co.; 1935)....
        THE PORTABLE NOVELS OF SCIENCE [Derleth - 1950]
STARRETT, VINCENT  (1)
    Penelope...........................................WT  May 1923
        THE MOON TERROR AND OTHER STORIES [Anonymous - 1927]
STARZL, R. F.  (1)
    Hornets of Space...................................WS  Nov 1930
        FROM OFF THIS WORLD [Margulies & Friend - 1949]
```

STEARNS, CHARLES A.   (1)                                                                      Mag.     Year
  Pastoral Affair.............................................Glxy  Feb 1959
       THE FIFTH GALAXY READER [Gold - 1961]
STECHER, L. J. JR.   (2)
  Man in a Quandry..........................................Glxy   Jul 1958
       THE FOURTH GALAXY READER OF SCIENCE FICTION [Gold - 1959]
  Perfect Answer............................................Glxy   Jun 1958
       THE FIFTH GALAXY READER [Gold - 1961]
STEINBECK, JOHN   (2)
  Saint Katy The Virgin.........................(From THE LONG VALLEY; 1938)
       TIMELESS STORIES FOR TODAY AND TOMORROW [Bradbury - 1952]
  Short-Short Story of Mankind, The............................Plby  Apr 1958
       SF: 59 THE YEAR'S GREATEST SF AND FANTASY [Merril - 1959]
       PENGUIN SCIENCE FICTION [Aldiss - 1961]
STEPHENS, JAMES   (3)
  Desire.........................................(From ETCHED IN MOONLIGHT; 1928)
       THE MOONLIGHT TRAVELER [Stern - 1943]
  Etched In Moonlight............................(From ETCHED IN MOONLIGHT; 1928)
       TRAVELERS IN TIME [Stern - 1947]
  Threepenny Piece, The.........................(From HERE ARE LADIES;  1913)
       THE BEST FROM F&SF [Boucher & McComas - 1952]     Rpnt - F&SF  Jun 1951
STEVENSON, ROBERT LOUIS   (1)
  Bottle imp, The.............................................B&W   Mar 1891
       THE MOONLIGHT TRAVELER [Stern - 1943]
STINE, G. HARRY   (2)
  How to Think a Science Fiction Story........................ASF   May 1961
       (Excerpts from Science Fiction is too Conservative)
       SIXTH ANNUAL OF THE YEAR'S BEST SF [Merril - 1961]
  Sputnik: One Reason Why We Lost.............................F&SF   Jan 1958
       SF: 58 THE YEAR'S GREATEST SF AND FANTASY [Merril - 1958]
STOCKTON, FRANK R.   (2)
  Great War Syndicate, The....................................OAW   12/22/1888
       THE BEST OF SCIENCE FICTION [Conklin - 1946]
  Tale of Negative Gravity, A...................(From A BORROWED MONTH; 1887)
       BEYOND TIME AND SPACE [Derleth - 1950]
       JOURNEYS IN SCIENCE FICTION [Loughlin & Popp - 1961]
STONE, LESLIE F. ps (Mrs. William Silberberg)   (2)
  Conquest of Gola, The.......................................WS   Apr 1931
       THE BEST OF SCIENCE FICTION [Conklin - 1946]
  Rape of the Solar System, The...............................Amz  Dec 1934
       FLIGHT INTO SPACE [Wollheim - 1950]
STONES, JONATHAN   (1)
  Alpha in Omega.................................(London Observer Prize Story )
       A. D. 2500 [Wilson - 1955]
STRAUS, RALPH   (1)
  Most Maddening Story in the World, The.......................
       (From A Second Century of Creepy Stories-Edited by Hugh Walpole; 1937)
       THE MOONLIGHT TRAVELER [Stern - 1943]
STRIBLING, T. S.   (1)
  Green Splotches.............................................Adv   1/3/1920
       THE POCKET BOOK OF SCIENCE FICTION [Wollheim - 1943]
STRUTHER, JAN ps (Mrs. Joyce Maxtone Graham)   (1)
  Cobbler, Cobbler, Mend my Shoe..............................11/9/1929
       THE MOONLIGHT TRAVELER [Stern - 1943]
STUART, DON A. ps (John W. Campbell, Jr) (1) (See listing John W. Campbell, Jr)
  Atomic Power...............................................Ast  Dec 1934
       THE BEST OF SCIENCE FICTION [Conklin - 1946]

STUART, WILLIAM W.  (I)             Mag. Year
  Inside John Barth.......................................Glxy Jun 1961
STURGEON, THEODORE  (49)
  And Now the News........................................F&SF Dec 1956
    THE BEST FROM FANTASY & SCIENCE FICTION: 6th SERIES [Boucher - 1957]
  Baby Is Three...........................................Glxy Oct 1952
    CHILDREN OF WONDER [Tenn - 1953]
  Bulkhead................................................Glxy Mar 1955
    (Originally appeared under title WHO?)
    SF: THE YEAR'S GREATEST SCIENCE FICTION AND FANTASY [Merril - 1956]
  Chromium Helmet, The....................................ASF Jun 1946
    GREAT STORIES OF SCIENCE FICTION [Leinster - 1951]
  Claustrophile, The......................................Glxy Aug 1956
    FOUR FOR THE FUTURE [Conklin - 1959]
  Clinic, The.............................................ORIGINAL STORY
    STAR SCIENCE FICTION STORIES #2 [Pohl - 1953]
  Comedian's Children, The................................VSF May 1958
    SF: 59 THE YEAR'S GREATEST SF AND FANTASY [Merril - 1959]
  Completely Automatic....................................ASF Feb 1941
    POSSIBLE WORLDS OF SCIENCE FICTION [Conklin - 1951]
  Derm Fool...............................................Unk Mar 1940
    CROSSROADS IN TIME [Conklin - 1953]
  Education of Drusilla Strange, The......................Glxy Mar 1954
    OPERATION FUTURE [Conklin - 1955]
  Farewell To Eden........................................ORIGINAL STORY
    INVASION FROM MARS [Welles - 1949]
    THE OUTER REACHES [Derleth - 1951]
  Fear Is A Business......................................F&SF Aug 1956
    A DECADE OF FANTASY & SCIENCE FICTION [Mills - 1960]
  God In A Garden, A......................................Unk Oct 1939
    THE OTHER WORLDS [Stong - 1941]
  Golden Egg, The.........................................Unk Aug 1941
    SCIENCE FICTION THINKING MACHINES [Conklin - 1954]
  Golden Helix, The.......................................TWS Sum 1954
    THREE TIMES INFINITY [Margulies - 1958]
  Granny Won't Knit.......................................Glxy Mar 1954
    ALL ABOUT THE FUTURE [Greenberg - 1955]
    FIVE GALAXY SHORT NOVELS [Gold - 1958]
  Hurkle Is a Happy Beast, The............................MoF Fal 1949
    THE SCIENCE FICTION GALAXY [Conklin - 1950]
    THE BEST SCIENCE FICTION STORIES: 1950 [Bleiler & Dikty - 1950]
  Killdozer!..............................................ASF Nov 1944
    THE BEST OF SCIENCE FICTION [Conklin - 1946]
  Love of Heaven, The.....................................ASF Nov 1948
    SCIENCE FICTION ADVENTURES IN MUTATION [Conklin - 1956]
  Man Who Lost the Sea, The...............................F&SF Oct 1959
    THE BEST FROM FANTASY & SCIENCE FICTION: 9th SERIES [Mills - 1960]
    FIFTH ANNUAL OF THE YEAR'S BEST SF [Merril - 1960]
  Martian and the Moron, The..............................WT Mar 1949
    WORLDS OF TOMORROW [Derleth - 1953]
  Maturity................................................ASF Feb 1947
    6 GREAT SHORT NOVELS OF SCIENCE FICTION [Conklin - 1954]
     (Revised for inclusion in this anthology)
  Memorial...............................................ASF Apr 1946
    THE OTHER SIDE OF THE MOON [Derleth - 1949]
    SCIENCE FICTION TERROR TALES [Conklin - 1955]
  Memory.................................................TWS Aug 1948
    ADVENTURES IN TOMORROW [Crossen - 1951]
  Mewhu's Jet............................................ASF Nov 1946
    THE BIG BOOK OF SCIENCE FICTION [Conklin - 1950]

STURGEON, THEODORE [Cont'd]                                     Mag.     Year

    Microcosmic God.............................................ASF     Apr 1941
        THE POCKET BOOK OF SCIENCE FICTION [Wollheim - 1943]
    Minority Report.............................................ASF     Jun 1949
        BEYOND TIME AND SPACE [Derleth - 1950]
    Mr. Costello, Hero..........................................Glxy    Dec 1953
        ASSIGNMENT IN TOMORROW [Pohl - 1954]
    Never Underestimate.........................................If      Jan 1952
        THE OMNIBUS OF SCIENCE FICTION [Conklin - 1952]
    Other Man, The..............................................Glxy    Sep 1956
        SF: 57 THE YEAR'S GREATEST SF AND FANTASY [Merril - 1957]
    Perfect Host, The...........................................WT      Nov 1948
        BEYOND HUMAN KEN [Merril - 1952]
    Rule of Three...............................................Glxy    Jan 1951
        THE GALAXY READER OF SCIENCE FICTION [Gold - 1952]
    Saucer of Lonliness.........................................Glxy    Feb 1953
        THE SECOND GALAXY READER OF SCIENCE FICTION [Gold - 1954]
    Shottle Bop.................................................Unk     Feb 1941
        INVISIBLE MEN [Davenport - 1960]
    Sky Was Full of Ships, The..................................TWS     Jun 1947
        SHOT IN THE DARK [Merril - 1950]
    Stars Are the Styx, The.....................................Glxy    Oct 1950
        THE GALAXY READER OF SCIENCE FICTION [Gold - 1952]
    Talent......................................................Bynd    Sep 1953
        ZACHERLY'S MIDNIGHT SNACKS [Zacherly - 1960]
    That Low....................................................FFM     Oct 1948
        SCIENCE FICTION SHOWCASE [M. Kornbluth - 1959]
    Thunder and Roses...........................................ASF     Nov 1947
        STRANGE PORTS OF CALL [Derleth - 1948]
        MY BEST SCIENCE FICTION STORY [Margulies & Friend - 1949]
        THE ASTOUNDING SCIENCE FICTION ANTHOLOGY [Campbell - 1952]
    Tiny and the Monster........................................ASF     May 1947
        INVADERS OF EARTH [Conklin - 1952]
    To Here and Easel......................................ORIGINAL STORY
        STAR SHORT NOVELS [Pohl - 1954]
    Ultimate Egoist.............................................Unk     Feb 1941
        (Originally appeared under pseudonym E. Hunter Waldo)
            HUMAN? [Merril - 1954]
    Unite and Conquer...........................................ASF     Oct 1948
        JOURNEY TO INFINITY [Greenberg - 1951]
    Wages of Synergy, The.......................................Stg     Aug 1953
        THE BEST FROM STARTLING STORIES [Mines - 1953]
    Way of Thinking, A..........................................Amz     Nov 1953
        GALAXY OF GHOULS [Merril - 1955]
    What Dead Men Tell..........................................ASF     Nov 1949
        IMAGINATION UNLIMITED [Bleiler & Dikty - 1952]
    When You're Smiling.........................................Glxy    Jan 1955
        BEST SF TWO SCIENCE FICTION STORIES [Crispin - 1956]
    [Widget], The [Wadgett], and Boff, The......................F&SF    Nov 1955
        A TREASURY OF GREAT SCIENCE FICTION [Boucher - 1959]
    Yesterday Was Monday........................................Unk     Jun 1941
        FROM UNKNOWN WORLDS [J. W. Campbell - 1948]
        SCIENCE FICTION ADVENTURES IN DIMENSION [Conklin - 1953]

SUTHERLAND, HERB (1)
    Blond Kid, The...............................London Observer Prize Story
        A. D. 2500 [Wilson - 1955]
SUTTON, LEE (1)
    Soul Mate...................................................F&SF    Jun 1959
        THE BEST FROM FANTASY & SCIENCE FICTION: 9th SERIES [Mills - 1960]

SWAIN, VIRGINIA  (1)                                                    Mag.    Year
    Aunt Cassie...............................................................ORIGINAL STORY
         THE OTHER WORLDS [Stong - 1941]
SWIFT, JONATHAN  (2)
    Flying Island, The...................(From The Third Voyage of Gulliver; 1728)
         SCIENCE IN FICTION [A.E.M. & J.C. Bayliss - 1957]
    Laputa.........................................(From Gulliver's Travels; 1726)
         BEYOND TIME AND SPACE [Derleth - 1950]

# T

TAINE, JOHN ps (Eric Temple Bell)  (2)
    Before The Dawn................(Copyright 1934 by The Williams and Wilkins Co)
         THE PORTABLE NOVELS OF SCIENCE [Wollheim - 1945]
    Ultimate Catalyst, The..................................................TWS    Jun 1939
         THE BEST OF SCIENCE FICTION [Conklin - 1946]
         MY BEST SCIENCE FICTION STORY [Margulies & Friend - 1949]
TANNER, CHARLES  (1)
    Out of the Jar...........................................................Sti    Feb 1941
         ZACHERLY'S VULTURE STEW [Zacherly - 1960]
TEMPLE, WILLARD  (1)
    Eternal Duffer, The......................................................SEP    5/18/46
         THE SATURDAY EVENING POST FANTASY STORIES [Fles - 1951]
TEMPLE, WILLIAM F.  (7)
    Counter-Transference.....................................................TWS    Apr 1952
         THE BEST SCIENCE FICTION STORIES: 1953 [Bleiler & Dikty - 1953]
    Date To Remember, A......................................................TWS    Aug 1949
         INVADERS OF EARTH [Conklin - 1952]
    Forget-Me-Not............................................................OW     Sep 1950
         THE BEST SCIENCE FICTION STORIES: 1951 [Bleiler & Dikty - 1951]
    Smile of the Sphinx, The.................................................TOW    Aut 1938
         ESCALES DANS L'INFINI [Gallet - 1954]
    Two Shadows, The.........................................................Stg    Mar 1951
         THE BEST SCIENCE FICTION STORIES: 1952 [Bleiler & Dikty - 1952]
         NO PLACE LIKE EARTH [Carnell - 1952]
    Way of Escape............................................................TWS    Jun 1948
         SCIENCE FICTION ADVENTURES IN DIMENSION [Conklin - 1953]
    Whispering Gallery, The..................................................FU     Nov 1953
         ZACHERLY'S MIDNIGHT SNACKS [Zacherly - 1960]
TENN, WILLIAM ps (Philip Klass)  (17)
    Alexander The Bait.......................................................ASF    May 1946
         THE OMNIBUS OF SCIENCE FICTION [Conklin - 1952]
    Betelgeuse Bridge........................................................Glxy   Apr 1951
         TOMORROW. THE STARS [Heinlein - 1952]
         THE GALAXY READER OF SCIENCE FICTION [Gold - 1952]
    Brooklyn Project.........................................................PS     Fal 1948
         SHOT IN THE DARK [Merril - 1950]
    Child's Play.............................................................ASF    Mar 1947
         A TREASURY OF SCIENCE FICTION [Conklin - 1948]
         WORLD OF WONDER [Pratt - 1951]
         THE ASTOUNDING SCIENCE FICTION ANTHOLOGY [J. W. Campbell - 1952]
         A GALAXY OF GHOULS [Merril - 1955]

TENN, WILLIAM [Cont'd]                                              Mag.    Year
   Deserter, The...........................................ORIGINAL STORY
        STAR SCIENCE FICTION STORIES [Pohl - 1953]
   Eastward Ho!.................................................F&SF  Oct 1958
        THE BEST FROM FANTASY & SCIENCE FICTION: 9th SERIES [Mills - 1960]
   Errand Boy.....................................................ASF  Jun 1947
        CHILDREN OF WONDER [Tenn - 1953]
   Firewater......................................................ASF  Feb 1952
        YEAR'S BEST SCIENCE FICTION NOVELS: 1953 [Bleiler & Dikty - 1953]
   Generation of Noah............................................Sus  Spr 1951
        THE BEST SCIENCE FICTION STORIES: 1952 [Bleiler & Dikty - 1952]
   House Dutiful, The.............................................ASF  Apr 1948
        BEYOND HUMAN KEN [Merril - 1952]
   Ionian Cycle, The.............................................TWS  Aug 1949
        TRAVELERS OF SPACE [Greenberg - 1952]
   Jester, The...................................................TWS  Aug 1951
        SCIENCE FICTION THINKING MACHINES [Conklin - 1954]
   Null-P.........................................................WB  Jan 1951
        WORLDS OF TOMORROW [Derleth - 1953]
        SPECTRUM [Amis & Conquest - 1961]
   She Only Goes Out At Night.....................................FU  Oct 1956
        THE FANTASTIC UNIVERSE OMNIBUS [Santesson - 1960]
   Venus and the Seven Sexes..............................ORIGINAL STORY
        THE GIRL WITH THE HUNGRY EYES AND OTHER STORIES [Wollheim - 1949]
        SCIENCE FICTION CARNIVAL [Brown & Reynolds - 1953]
   Venus Is A Man's World.......................................Glxy  Jul 1951
        THE GALAXY READER OF SCIENCE FICTION [Gold - 1952]
   "Will You Walk A Little Faster?"..............................MSF  Nov 1951
        INVADERS OF EARTH [Conklin - 1952]
TEVIS, WALTER S.  (1)
   Far From Home................................................F&SF  Dec 1959
        THE BEST FROM FANTASY & SCIENCE FICTION: 9th SERIES [Mills  1960]
THELWELL  (1)
   Instructor...................(cartoon).......................Pch   1/18/61
        SIXTH ANNUAL OF THE YEAR'S BEST SF [Merril - 1961]
THOMAS, THEODORE L.  (2)
   Far Look, The.................................................ASF  Aug 1956
        SF: 57 THE YEAR'S GREATEST SF AND FANTASY [Merril - 1957]
   Satellite Passage.............................................If  Dec 1958
        SF: 59 THE YEAR'S GREATEST SF AND FANTASY [Merril - 1959]
THOMPSON, WILL  (1)
   No One Believed Me............................................SEP  4/24/48
        BEYOND THE BARRIERS OF SPACE AND TIME [Merril - 1954]
THORNE, ROGER  (1)
   Take a Deep Breath..........................................Tiger  n/d/a 1956
        SF: 57 THE YEAR'S GREATEST SF AND FANTASY [Merril - 1957]
THURBER, JAMES  (2)
   Friend To Alexander, A.............(From My Worlds and Welcome To It; 1943)
        TRAVELERS IN TIME [Stern - 1947]
   Interview With a Lemming...........(From My Worlds and Welcome To It; 1943)
        SHOT IN THE DARK [Merril - 1950]
TOWNES, ROBERT SHERMAN  (1)
   Problem For Emmy..............................................Stg  Jun 1952
        SCIENCE FICTION THINKING MACHINES [Conklin - 1954]
TUBB, E. C.  (5)
   Fresh Guy...................................................SF #29  Jun 1958
        SF: 59 THE YEAR'S GREATEST SF AND FANTASY [Merril - 1959]

(286)

TUBB, E. C. [Cont'd]                     Mag.     Year
   Home is the Hero..........................................NW #15   May 1952
       GATEWAY TO TOMORROW [Carnell - 1954]
   Last Day of Summer, The..................................SF #12   Feb 1955
       SF: THE YEAR'S GREATEST SCIENCE FICTION AND FANTASY [Merril - 1956]
   Rockets Aren't Human.....................................NW #20   Mar 1953
       THE BEST FROM NEW WORLDS [Carnell - 1955]
   Unfortunate Passage......................................SF #7    Mar 1954
       GATEWAY TO THE STARS [Carnell - 1955]
TUCKER, [ARTHUR] WILSON "BOB" (3)
   Exit.....................................................Ash      Apr 1943
       EDITOR'S CHOICE IN SCIENCE FICTION [Moskowitz - 1954]
       (Story selected by Alden H. Norton)
   To a Ripe Old Age........................................F&SF    Dec 1952
       SHADOW OF TOMORROW [Pohl - 1953]
   Tourist Trade, The.......................................WB       Jan 1951
       THE BEST SCIENCE FICTION STORIES: 1952 [Bleiler & Dikty - 1952]
       TOMORROW, THE STARS [Heinlein - 1952]
TUCKER, REV. LOUIS, D. D. (1)
   Cubic City, The..........................................SWS     Sep 1929
       FROM OFF THIS WORLD [Margulies & Friend - 1949]
TWAIN, MARK ps (Samuel L. Clemens) (1)
   Connecticut Yankee In King Arthur's Court, A..............(Condensed Version)
       (Originally published by Harper and Bros.; 1889)
       STORIES OF SCIENTIFIC IMAGINATION [Gallant - 1954]

# V

VAN DRESSER, PETER (3)
   By Virtue of Circumference...............................AmB    Nov 1937
       THE YEAR AFTER TOMORROW [Del Rey, Matschat & Carmer - 1952]
   Plum Duff................................................AmB    Dec 1935
       THE YEAR AFTER TOMORROW [Del Rey, Matschat & Carmer - 1952]
   Rocket To the Sun........................................AmB    Jul 1939
       THE YEAR AFTER TOMORROW [Del Rey, Matschat & Carmer - 1952]
VAN LORNE, WARNER ps (F. Orlin Tremaine) (1)
   Upper Level Road, The....................................Ast    Aug 1935
       THE BEST OF SCIENCE FICTION [Conklin - 1946]
VAN VOGT, A. E. (28)
   Asylum...................................................ASF    May 1942
       ADVENTURES IN TIME AND SPACE [Healy & McComas - 1946]
   Automaton................................................OW     Sep 1950
       ADVENTURES IN TOMORROW [Crossen - 1951]
   Black Destroyer..........................................ASF    Jul 1939
       ADVENTURES IN TIME AND SPACE [Healy & McComas - 1946]
   Chronicler, The..........................................ASF    Nov 1946
       FIVE SCIENCE FICTION NOVELS [Greenberg - 1952]
   Co-Operate-Or Else!......................................ASF    Apr 1942
       THE OUTER REACHES [Derleth - 1951]
   Dear Pen Pal.............................................Ark    Aut 1949
       FAR BOUNDARIES [Derleth - 1951]
   Dormant..................................................Stg    Nov 1948
       THE BEST FROM STARTLING STORIES [Mines - 1953]
       BEST SF SCIENCE FICTION STORIES [Crispin - 1955]

```
VAN VOGT, A. E. [Cont'd]                                                    Mag.    Year
  Enchanted Village.........................................................OW   Jul 1950
      POSSIBLE WORLDS OF SCIENCE FICTION [Conklin - 1951]
      THE SANDS OF MARS AND OTHER STORIES [Anonymous - 1958]
          (Appeared under title The Sands of Mars)
  Far Centaurus............................................................ASF   Jan 1944
      STRANGE PORTS OF CALL [Derleth - 1948]
      MEN AGAINST THE STARS [Greenberg - 1950]
  Final Command...........................................................ASF   Nov 1949
      THE ROBOT AND THE MAN [Greenberg - 1953]
  Fulfillment.....................................................ORIGINAL STORY
      NEW TALES OF SPACE AND TIME [Healy - 1951]
  Ghost, The..............................................................Unk   Aug 1942
      ZACHERLY'S MIDNIGHT SNACKS [Zacherly - 1960]
  Juggernaut..............................................................ASF   Aug 1944
      A TREASURY OF SCIENCE FICTION [Conklin - 1948]
  Letter From the Stars..................................................OTWA   Jul 1950
      BEYOND THE END OF TIME [Pohl - 1952]
      THE EARTH IN PERIL [Wollheim -.1957]
  M 33 In Andromeda.......................................................ASF   Aug 1942
      TOMORROW'S UNIVERSE [H. J. Campbell - 1954]
  Not Only Dead Men.......................................................ASF   Nov 1942
      INVADERS OF EARTH [Conklin - 1952]
  Process, The...........................................................F&SF   Dec 1950
      THE BEST SCIENCE FICTION STORIES: 1951 [Bleiler & Dikty - 1951]
  Project — Space Ship....................................................TWS   Aug 1939
      MY BEST SCIENCE FICTION STORY [Margulies & Friend - 1949]
  Recruiting Station......................................................ASF   Mar 1942
      THE OMNIBUS OF SCIENCE FICTION [Conklin - 1952]
  Repitition..............................................................ASF   Apr 1940
      BEACHHEADS IN SPACE [Derleth - 1954]
  Resurrection............................................................ASF   Aug 1948
      THE OTHER SIDE OF THE MOON [Derleth - 1949]
      UBERWINDUNG VON RAUM UND ZEIT [Gunther - 1952]
          (Originally appeared under title The Monster)
  Rogue Ship..............................................................Sup   Mar 1950
      THE GIANT ANTHOLOGY OF SCIENCE FICTION [Margulies & Friend - 1954]
  Rull, The...............................................................ASF   May 1948
      TRAVELERS OF SPACE [Greenberg - 1952]
      ADVENTURES ON OTHER PLANETS [Wollheim - 1954]
  Search, The.............................................................ASF   Jan 1943
      THE BEST OF SCIENCE FICTION [Conklin - 1941]
  Seesaw, The.............................................................ASF   Jul 1941
      BEYOND TIME AND SPACE [Derleth - 1950]
  Vault of the Beast......................................................ASF   Aug 1940
      THE OTHER SIDE OF THE MOON [Derleth - 1949]
      THE ASTOUNDING SCIENCE FICTION ANTHOLOGY [ J. W. Campbell - 1952]
  Weapon Shops of Isher, The...(Originally published by Greenberg:Publishers 1951
      A TREASURY OF GREAT SCIENCE FICTION [Boucher - 1959]
  Witch, The..............................................................Unk   Feb 1943
      ZACHERLY'S VULTURE STEW [Zacherly - 1960]
VANCE, JACK  (10)
  Devil On Salvation Bluff, The..................................ORIGINAL STORY
      STAR SCIENCE FICTION STORIES #3 [Pohl - 1954]
  D P!..................................................................ASF&F   Apr 1953
      THE BEST SCIENCE FICTION STORIES: 1954 [Bleiler & Dikty - 1954]
  Dreamer, The..........................................................Orb #5  Nov 1954
      (Originally appeared under title The Enchanted Village)
      SPACE STATION 42 AND OTHER STORIES [Anonymous - 1958]
```

VANCE, JACK [Cont'd]                                          Mag.    Year
    Gift of Gab, The......................................ASF    Sep 1955
        BEST SF THREE SCIENCE FICTION STORIES [Crispin - 1958]
        OUT OF THIS WORLD 2 [Williams-Ellis & Owen - 1961]
    Hard-Luck Diggings....................................Stg    Jul 1948
        POSSIBLE WORLDS OF SCIENCE FICTION [Conklin - 1951]
    King of Thieves, The..................................Stg    Jul 1949
        LOOKING FORWARD [Lesser - 1953]
    Men of the Ten Books..................................Stg    Mar 1951
        THE BEST SCIENCE FICTION STORIES: 1952 [Bleiler & Dikty - 1952]
    Noise.................................................Stg    Aug 1952
        THE BEST FROM STARTLING STORIES [Mines - 1953]
    Sub-Standard Sardines, The............................Stg    Jan 1949
        SPACE POLICE [Norton - 1956]
    Winner Lose All.......................................Glxy   Dec 1951
        THE OMNIBUS OF SCIENCE FICTION [Conklin - 1952]
VERNE, JULES  (6)
    Captain Nemo's Thunderbolt...........(From 20,000 Leagues Under The Sea; 1873)
        SCIENCE IN FICTION [A.E.M. & J. C. Bayliss - 1957]
    Dr. Ox's Experiment......(From Doctor Ox's Experiment and Other Stories; 1874)
        BEYOND TIME AND SPACE [Derleth - 1950]
    Gil Bralter..............................(From Le Chemin De France; 1887)
        (Translated from the French by I. O. Evans)        F&SF   Jul 1958
            THE BEST FROM FANTASY & SCIENCE FICTION: 8th SERIES [Boucher-1959]
    In the Year 2889......................................For    Feb 1889
        THE BIG BOOK OF SCIENCE FICTION [Conklin - 1950]
    Journey To the Center of the Earth, A.................
        (From A Voyage To the Center of the Earth; 1864)
            JOURNEYS IN SCIENCE FICTION [Loughlin & Popp - 1961]
    Round the Moon...............(Originally published by Hetzel: Paris; 1870 )
        THE TREASURY OF SCIENCE FICTION CLASSICS [Kuebler - 1955]
VIDAL, GORE  (1)
    Visit To A Small Planet.....(A play)...........(Copyright 1955 by Gore Vidal)
        JOURNEYS IN SCIENCE FICTION [Loughlin & Popp - 1961]
VONNEGUT, KURT JR.  (3)
    Big Trip Up Yonder, The...............................Glxy   Jan 1954
        Assignment In Tomorrow [Pohl - 1954]
    Report On the Barnhouse Effect, The...................Col    2/11/50
        TOMORROW, THE STARS [Heinlein - 1952]
        JOURNEYS IN SCIENCE FICTION [Loughlin & Popp - 1961]
    Unready To Wear.......................................Glxy   Apr 1953
        THE SECOND GALAXY READER OF SCIENCE FICTION [Gold - 1954]

WALDROP, F. N.  (1)
    w/ Poul Anderson
        Tomorrow's Children...............................ASF    Mar 1947
            A TREASURY OF SCIENCE FICTION [Conklin - 1948]
WALLACE, F. L.  (6)
    Delay In Transit......................................Glxy   Sep 1952
        BODYGUARD AND FOUR OTHER SHORT NOVELS FROM GALAXY [Gold - 1960]
    End As A World........................................Glxy   Sep 1955
        THE THIRD GALAXY READER OF SCIENCE FICTION [Gold - 1958]

WALLACE, F. L. [Cont'd]                                           Mag.    Year
  Impossible Voyage Home, The........................................Glxy  Aug 1954
      SCIENCE FICTION ADVENTURES IN MUTATION [Conklin - 1956]
  Mezzerow Loves Company.............................................Glxy  Jun 1956
      THE WORLD THAT COULDN'T BE AND 8 OTHER NOVELETTES FROM GALAXY [Gold-1959]
  Student Body.......................................................Glxy  Mar 1953
      CROSSROADS IN TIME [Conklin - 1953]
      THE SECOND GALAXY READER OF SCIENCE FICTION [Gold - 1954]
  Tangle Hold........................................................Glxy  Jun 1953
      FIVE GALAXY SHORT NOVELS [Gold - 1958]

WALPOLE, HORACE  (1)
  Saturnian Celia...............................................Rpnt — F&SF  Apr 1957
      (From The Letters of Horace Walpole by Mrs. Paget Toynbee; 1903)
          A DECADE OF FANTASY & SCIENCE FICTION [Mills - 1960]

WALSH, BUTHRAM  (1)
  Case of Omega Smith, The.........................London Observer Prize Story
      A. D. 2500 [Wilson - 1955]

WALTON, BRYCE  (2)
  Happy Herd, The....................................................If    Oct 1956
      THE SECOND WORLD OF IF [Quinn & Wulff - 1958]
  Mary Anonymous.....................................................PS    Sum 1954
      THE EARTH IN PERIL [Wollheim - 1957]

WALTON, HARRY  (3)
  Episode On Dhee Minor..............................................ASF   Oct 1939
      TRAVELERS OF SPACE [Greenberg - 1952]
  Housing Shortage...................................................ASF   Jan 1947
      A TREASURY OF SCIENCE FICTION [Conklin - 1948]
  Schedule...........................................................ASF   Jun 1945
      MEN AGAINST THE STARS [Greenberg - 1950]

WANDREI, DONALD  (8)
  Blinding Shadows, The..............................................Ast   May 1934
      BEACHHEADS IN SPACE [Derleth - 1954]
  Colossus...........................................................Ast   Jan 1934
      BEYOND TIME AND SPACE [Derleth - 1950]
  Crystal Bullet, The................................................WT    Mar 1941
      STRANGE PORTS OF CALL [Derleth - 1948]
  Finality Unlimited.................................................Ast   Sep 1936
      THE OUTER REACHES [Derleth - 1951]
  Infinity Zero......................................................Ast   Oct 1936
      FAR BOUNDARIES [Derleth - 1951]
  Scientist Divides, A...............................................Ast   Sep 1934
      THE BEST OF SCIENCE FICTION [Conklin - 1946]
  Something From Above...............................................WT    Dec 1930
      THE OTHER SIDE OF THE MOON [Derleth - 1949]
  Strange Harvest....................................................WT    May 1953
      WORLDS OF TOMORROW [Derleth - 1953]

WANDREI, HOWARD  (1)           (See listing H. W. Guernsey)
  God-Box, The.......................................................Ast   Apr 1934
      STRANGE PORTS OF CALL [Derleth - 1948]
          (Originally appeared under pseudonym Howard Von Drey)

WATSON, RAYMOND  (1)
  Twenty-Five Miles Aloft......................................ORIGINAL STORY
      ADVENTURES TO COME [Esenwein - 1937]

WEINBAUM, STANLEY G.  (4)       See listing John Jessel
  Lotus Eaters, The..................................................Ast   Apr 1935
      BEYOND TIME AND SPACE [Derleth - 1950]
      UBERWINDUNG VON RAUM UND ZEIT [Gunther - 1952]
      THE HIDDEN PLANET [Wollheim - 1959]

WEINBAUM, STANLEY G. [Cont'd]                                    Mag.    Year
    Martian Odyssey, A....................................WS   Jul 1934
        THE POCKET BOOK OF SCIENCE FICTION [Wollheim - 1943]
        FROM OFF THIS WORLD [Margulies & Friend - 1949]
        ESCALES DANS L'INFINI [Gallet - 1954]
    Parasite Planet.......................................Ast  Feb 1935
        FLIGHT INTO SPACE [Wollheim - 1950]
    Valley of Dreams......................................WS   Nov 1934
        FROM OFF THIS WORLD [Margulies & Friend - 1949]
WELLMAN, MANLY WADE   (12)
    Come Into My Parlor...................................ORIGINAL STORY
        THE GIRL WITH THE HUNGRY EYES AND OTHER STORIES [Wollheim - 1949]
    Desrick on Yandro, The................................F&SF  Jun 1952
        THE BEST FROM FANTASY & SCIENCE FICTION: 2nd SER [Boucher & McComas-1953]
    Devil is Not Mocked, The..............................Unk  Jun 1943
        ZACHERLY'S VULTURE STEW [Zacherly - 1960]
    Island in the Sky.....................................TWS  Oct 1941
        THE GIANT ANTHOLOGY OF SCIENCE FICTION [Margulies & Friend - 1954]
    Little Black Train, The...............................F&SF  Aug 1954
        THE BEST FROM FANTASY & SCIENCE FICTION: 4th SERIES [Boucher - 1955]
    Men Against the Stars.................................ASF  Jun 1938
        MEN AGAINST THE STARS [Greenberg - 1950]
        EVERY BOY'S BOOK OF OUTER SPACE STORIES [Dikty - 1960]
    O Ugly Bird!..........................................F&SF  Dec 1951
        A GALAXY OF GHOULS [Merril - 1955]
    School for the Unspeakable............................WT   Sep 1937
        THE OTHER WORLDS [Stong - 1941]
    Song of the Slaves, The...............................WT   Mar 1940
        THE OTHER WORLDS [Stong - 1941]
    Space Station No. 1...................................Arg  10/10/1936
        MY BEST SCIENCE FICTION STORY [Margulies & Friend - 1949]
        ESCALES DANS L'INFINI [Gallet - 1954]
    Vandy, Vandy..........................................F&SF  Mar 1953
        THE BEST FROM FANTASY & SCIENCE FICTION: 3rd SER [Boucher & McComas-1954]
    Walk Like a Mountain..................................F&SF  Jun 1955
        A DECADE OF FANTASY & SCIENCE FICTION [Mills - 1960]
WELLEN, EDWARD   (4)
    Excerpts From Encyclopedia of Galactic Culture
        Origins of Galactic Etiquette....................Glxy  Oct 1953
        Origins of Galactic Law..........................Glxy  Apr 1953
        Origins of Galactic Medicine.....................Glxy  Dec 1953
        Origins of Galactic Slang........................Glxy  Jul 1952
            ALL ABOUT THE FUTURE [Greenberg - 1955]
WELLS, H. G.   (15)
    Aepyornis Island......................................PMB  Xmas 1894
        JOURNEYS IN SCIENCE FICTION [Loughlin & Popp - 1961]
    Croquet Player, The...................(From THE CROQUET PLAYER; 1936)
        TERROR IN THE MODERN VEIN [Wollheim - 1955]
    Crystal Egg, The......................................NW   May 1897
        STRANGE PORTS OF CALL [Derleth - 1948]
    First Men in the Moon, The............................Cpln  Nov 1900
        THE PORTABLE NOVELS OF SCIENCE [Wollheim - 1945]
    In the Abyss..........................................Prn  Aug 1896
        THE POCKET BOOK OF SCIENCE FICTION [Wollheim - 1943]
    Man Who Could Work Miracles, The......................ILN  Jul 1898
        THE MOONLIGHT TRAVELER [Stern - 1943]
    New Accelerator, The..................................Snd  Dec 1901
        BEYOND TIME AND SPACE [Derleth - 1950]
    Peter Learns Arithmetic.........(From JOAN & PETER [The New Republic]; 1918)
        FANTASIA MATHEMATICA [Fadiman - 1958]

```
WELLS, H. G. [Cont'd]                                            Mag.   Year
    Remarkable Case of Davidson's Eyes, The.....................PMB  3/28/95
        THE BEST OF SCIENCE FICTION [Conklin - 1946]
    Sea Raiders, The....................(From The Plattner Story and Others; 1897)
        ASPECTS OF SCIENCE FICTION [Doherty - 1959]
    Star, The..............................................................Grp Xmas 1897
        THE OTHER SIDE OF THE MOON [Derleth - 1949]
        SHOT IN THE DARK [Merril - 1950]
        THE TREASURY OF SCIENCE FICTION CLASSICS [Kuebler - 1955]
        THE EARTH IN PERIL [Wolheim - 1957]
        SCIENCE IN FICTION [A.E.M. & J.C. Bayliss - 1957]
    Temptation of Harringay, The.......................................................
        (From The Stolen Bacillus and Other Incidents; 1920)
        HUMAN? [Merril - 1954]
    Time Machine, The............................................NW  Jan 1895
        TRAVELERS IN TIME [Stern - 1947]
        THE TREASURY OF SCIENCE FICTION CLASSICS [Kuebler - 1955]
    Truth About Pyecraft, The....................................Snd  Apr 1903
        SCIENCE FICTION AND READER'S GUIDE [Barrows - 1954]
    Vision of Judgement, A.........(From The Time Machine and Other Stories; 1895)
        OUT OF THIS WORLD [Fast - 1944]

WELLS, ROBERT (I)
    Machine That Was Lonely, The...................London Observer Prize Story
        A. D. 2500 [Wilson - 1955]

WENTZ, ELMA
    w/ Robert A. Heinlein
        Beyond Doubt.........................................................Ash  Apr 1941
            (Originally aprd under byline Lyle Monroe and Elma Wentz)
            BEYOND THE END OF TIME [Pohl - 1952]

WEST, JESSAMYN (I)
    Little Men...................................................ORIGINAL STORY
        STAR SHORT NOVELS [Pohl - 1954]

WEST, WALLACE (4)
    En Route To Pluto...........................................Ast  Aug 1936
        THE BEST OF SCIENCE FICTION [Conklin - 1946]
    Last Man, The...............................................Amz  Feb 1929
        THE POCKET BOOK OF SCIENCE FICTION [Wollheim - 1943]
    Listen, Children, Listen....................................FU  Nov 1953
        ZACHERLY'S MIDNIGHT SNACKS [Zacherly - 1960]
    Sculptors of Life...........................................ASF  Dec 1939
        SCIENCE FICTION THINKING MACHINES [Conklin - 1954]

WHEWELL, DR. WILLIAM (I)
    No Power On Earth......................................No data available
        FANTASIA MATHEMATICA [Fadiman - 1958]

WHITE, CECIL B. (I)
    Retreat To Mars, The........................................Amz  Aug 1927
        THE BEST OF SCIENCE FICTION [Conklin - 1946]

WHITE, JAMES [M.] (4)
    Assisted Passage............................................NW #19  Jan 1953
        GATEWAY TO THE STARS [Carnell - 1955]
    Conspirators, The...........................................NW #24  Jun 1954
        SCIENCE FICTION ADVENTURES IN MUTATION [Conklin - 1956]
    Crossfire...................................................NW #21  Jun 1953
        THE BEST FROM NEW WORLDS [Carnell - 1955]
    Trouble With Emily, The.....................................NW #77  Nov 1958
        OUT OF THIS WORLD 2 [Williams-Ellis & Owen - 1961]
```

WHITE, E. B.  (2)                                                      Mag.    Year
    Morning of the Day They Did It, The.........................Nykr   2/12/50
        Re: The Second Tree From the Corner ; 1950
            A TREASURY OF GREAT SCIENCE FICTION [Boucher - 1959]
    Supremacy of Uruguay, The.................................Nykr   11/25/33
        TIMELESS STORIES FOR TODAY AND TOMORROW [Bradbury - 1952]
WHITEHILL, JOSEPH  (1)
    In the House, Another.....................................F&SF   Apr 1960
        SIXTH ANNUAL OF THE YEAR'S BEST SF [Merril - 1961]
WHYBROW, GEOFFREY  (1)
    Hitchhike To Paradise..........................London Observer Prize Story
        A. D. 2500 [Wilson - 1955]
WILCOX, DON  (1)
    Voyage That Lasted Six Hundred Years, The.....................Amz   Oct 1940
        LOOKING FORWARD [Lesser - 1953]
WILDE, NIALL  (1)
    Divvil With the Women, A..................................F&SF   Jan 1960
        THE BEST FROM FANTASY & SCIENCE FICTION: 10th SERIES [Mills - 1961]
WILDE, OSCAR  (1)
    Canterville Ghost, The....................................C&SR   3/2/87
        OUT OF THIS WORLD [Fast - 1944]
WILHELM, KATE  (1)
    Mile-Long Spaceship, The..................................ASF   Apr 1957
        THE BEST SCIENCE FICTION STORIES AND NOVELS: 9th SERIES [Dikty - 1958]
WILKINS, H. PERCY  (1)
    Is There Life On the Moon?................................CYE   Jan 1953
        SCIENCE FICTION AND READER'S GUIDE [Barrows - 1954]
WILLIAMS, JAY  (1)
    Asa Rule, The.............................................F&SF   Jun 1956
        THE BEST FROM FANTASY & SCIENCE FICTION: 6th SERIES [Boucher - 1957]
WILLIAMS, RALPH  (4)
    Doorway In the Sky........................................ASF   Jan 1954
        (Originally appeared under title Bertha)
            TALES OF OUTER SPACE [Wollheim - 1954]
    Emergency Landing.........................................ASF   Jul 1940
        THE BIG BOOK OF SCIENCE FICTION [Conklin - 1950]
    Head Hunters, The.........................................ASF   Oct 1951
        THE OMNIBUS OF SCIENCE FICTION [Conklin - 1952]
        STORIES FOR TOMORROW [Sloane - 1954]
    Pax Galactica............................................ASF   Nov 1952
        SPACE POLICE [Norton - 1956]
WILLIAMS, ROBERT MOORE  (8)     (See listing John S. Browning)
    Castaway..................................................ASF   Feb 1951
        INVADERS OF EARTH [Conklin - 1952]
    Flight of the Dawn Star...................................ASF   Mar 1938
        A TREASURY OF SCIENCE FICTION [Conklin - 1948]
    Piping Death, The.........................................Unk   May 1939
        ZACHERLY'S MIDNIGHT SNACKS [Zacherly - 1960]
    Red Death of Mars, The....................................ASF   Jul 1940
        MEN AGAINST THE STARS [Greenberg - 1950]
        THE YEAR AFTER TOMORROW [Del Rey, Matschat & Carmer - 1952]
    Refuge For Tonight........................................BB   Mar 1949
        THE BEST SCIENCE FICTION STORIES: 1949 [Bleiler & Dikty - 1949]
    Robots Return.............................................ASF   Sep 1938
        ADVENTURES IN TIME AND SPACE [Healy & McComas - 1946]
        THE ROBOT AND THE MAN [Greenberg - 1953]
    Seekers, The..............................................Stg   May 1948
        FLIGHT INTO SPACE [Wollheim - 1950]

```
                                                                Mag.    Year
WILLIAMS, ROBERT MOORE [Cont'd]                              .Stg  Mar 1949
    Sound of Bugles, The.........................................
        ADVENTURES ON OTHER PLANETS [Wollheim - 1954]
WILLIAMSON, IAN  (1)                                         .NW #8  Win 1950
    Chemical Plant...........................................
        NO PLACE LIKE EARTH [Carnell - 1952]
        OUT OF THIS WORLD I [Williams-Ellis & Owen - 1960]
WILLIAMSON, JACK  (13)                                       .ASF  Jan 1942
    Breakdown................................................
        JOURNEY TO INFINITY [Greenberg - 1951]
    Cold Green-Eye, The                                      .Fnt  Mar 1953
        SCIENCE FICTION SHOWCASE [M. Kornbluth - 1959]
    Crucible of Power, The...................................  .ASF  Feb 1939
        FIVE SCIENCE FICTION NOVELS [Greenberg - 1952]
    Guinevere For Everybody..................................  .ORIGINAL STORY
        STAR SCIENCE FICTION STORIES #3 [Pohl - 1953]
    Happiest Creature, The...................................  .ORIGINAL STORY
        STAR SCIENCE FICTION STORIES #2 [Pohl - 1953]
        STAR OF STARS [Pohl - 1960]
    Hindsight................................................  .ASF  May 1940
        THE ASTOUNDING SCIENCE FICTION ANTHOLOGY [J. W. Campbell - 1952]
    In the Scarlet Star                                       .Amz  Mar 1933
        EVERY BOY'S BOOK OF SCIENCE FICTION [Wollheim - 1951]
    Man From Outside, The....................................  .ASF  Mar 1951
        BEACHHEADS IN SPACE [Derleth - 1951]
        LOOKING FORWARD [Lesser - 1953]
    Peddler's Nose, The......................................  .ASF  Apr 1951
        ASSIGNMENT IN TOMORROW [Pohl - 1954]
    Star Bright..............................................  .Arg  11/25/39
        MY BEST SCIENCE FICTION STORY [Margulies & Friend - 1949]
    Sun Maker, The...........................................  .TWS  Jun 1940
        THE GIANT ANTHOLOGY OF SCIENCE FICTION [Margulies & Friend - 1954]
    Through the Purple Cloud.................................  .WS  May 1931
        FROM OFF THIS WORLD [Margulies & Friend - 1949]
    With Folded Hands........................................  .ASF  Jul 1947
        A TREASURY OF SCIENCE FICTION [Conklin - 1948]
WILSON, RICHARD  (5)                                          .Glxy  May 1954
    Back To Julie............................................
        ASSIGNMENT IN TOMORROW [Pohl - 1954]
    Friend of the Family.....................................  .ORIGINAL STORY
        STAR SCIENCE FICTION STORIES #2 [Pohl - 1953]
    Kill Me With Kindness....................................  .Glxy  Jan 1958
        THE FOURTH GALAXY READER OF SCIENCE FICTION [Gold - 1959]
    Love.....................................................  .F&SF  Jun 1952
        SHADOW OF TOMORROW [Pohl - 1953]
    Man Working..............................................  .ORIGINAL STORY
        STAR SCIENCE FICTION STORIES #4 [Pohl - 1958]
WINTER, J. A.  MD  (1)                                        .ASF  Jan 1949
    Expedition Polychrome....................................
        SPACE SERVICE [Norton - 1953]
WINTERBOTHAM, R. R.  (1)                                      .Ast  Dec 1936
    Fourth Dynasty, The......................................
        THE OMNIBUS OF SCIENCE FICTION [Conklin - 1952]
WOLF, LEONARD  (2)                                            .F&SF  Jan 195
    More Facts About Robots...................(verse)........
        THE BEST FROM FANTASY & SCIENCE FICTION: 4th SERIES [Boucher - 1955]
    Some Facts About Robots...................(verse)........  .F&SF  Jul 195
        THE BEST FROM FANTASY & SCIENCE FICTION: 4th SERIES [Boucher - 1955]
```

WOLF, MARI  (1)                                                      Mag.    Year
   Homeland...............................................................If   Jan 1953
         (Originally appeared under title The Statue)
               STORIES FOR TOMORROW [Sloane - 1954]
WOLFE, BERNARD  (2)
   Never Ending Penny, The.............................................Plby  Sep 1960
         SIXTH ANNUAL OF THE YEAR'S BEST SF [Merril - 1961]
   Self Portrait.......................................................Glxy  Nov 1951
         THE ROBOT AND THE MAN [Greenberg - 1953]
         THE SECOND GALAXY READER OF SCIENCE FICTION [Gold - 1954]
WOLLHEIM, DONALD A.  (5)     (See listing Martin Pearson)
   Bones................................................................Sti  Feb 1941
         ZACHERLY'S VULTURE STEW [Zacherly - 1960]
   Disguise..............................................................OW  Feb 1953
         STORIES FOR TOMORROW [Sloane - 1954]
   Mimic................................................................Ash  Dec 1942
         (Originally appeared under pseudonym Martin Pearson)
               TERROR IN THE MODERN VEIN [Wollheim - 1955]
   Planet Passage......................................................FFSF  Oct 1942
         (Originally appeared under pseudonym Martin Pearson)
               FLIGHT INTO SPACE [Wollheim - 1950]
               STORIES OF SCIENTIFIC IMAGINATION [Gallant - 1954]
   Storm Warning.......................................................FFSF  Oct 1942
         (Originally appeared under pseudonym Millard Verne Gordon)
               INVADERS OF EARTH [Conklin - 1952]
WOOD, MARGARET  (1)
   Knitting, The.............................London Observer Prize Story
         A. D. 2500 [Wilson - 1955]
WORTHINGTON, WILL  (2)
   Plenitude...........................................................F&SF  Nov 1959
         FIFTH ANNUAL OF THE YEAR'S BEST SF [Merril - 1960]
   Who Dreams of Ivy...................................................F&SF  Nov 1960
         THE BEST FROM FANTASY & SCIENCE FICTION: 10th SERIES [Mills - 1961]
WRIGHT, FARNSWORTH  (1)
   Adventure in the Fourth Dimension, An................................WT  Oct 1923
         THE MOON TERROR AND OTHER STORIES [Anonymous - 1927]
WRIGHT, LAN  (1)
   Operation Exodus................................................NW #13  Jan 1952
         GATEWAY TO THE STARS [Carnell - 1955]
WRIGHT, S. FOWLER  (6)
   Automata.............................................................WT  Sep 1929
         SCIENCE FICTION THINKING MACHINES [Conklin - 1954]
   Better Choice, The......................................ORIGINAL STORY
         SCIENCE FICTION ADVENTURES IN MUTATION [Conklin - 1956]
   Brain.................................(From The New Gods Lead; 1932)
         ADVENTURES IN TIME AND SPACE [Healy & McComas - 1946]
   Obviously Suicide...................................................Sus  Sum 1951
         BEYOND THE END OF TIME [Pohl - 1952]
   Original Sin..............................(From The Throne of Saturn; 1949)
         THE OTHER SIDE OF THE MOON [Derleth - 1949]
   Rat, The.............................................................WT  Mar 1929
         THE TREASURY OF SCIENCE FICTION CLASSICS [Kuebler - 1955]
WRIGHT, SEWELL PEASLEE  (1)
   Infra-Medians, The..................................................Ast  Dec 1931
         EVERY BOY'S BOOK OF SCIENCE FICTION [Wollheim - 1951]

(295)

WYLIE, PHILIP (2)                                                      Mag.    Year
    Blunder.............................................................Col  2/12/1946
          STRANGE PORTS OF CALL [Derleth - 1948]
          SHOT IN THE DARK [Merril - 1950]
w/ Edwin Balmer
    When Worlds Collide.................(excerpts)..........................
          (Originally published by Frederick A. Stokes Co.; 1932)
          THE TREASURY OF SCIENCE FICTION CLASSICS [Kuebler - 1955]
WYNDHAM, JOHN ps (John Beynon Harris) (10)
              (See listings John Beynon and John Beynon Harris)
    And the Walls Came Tumbling Down..................................Stg  May 1951
          BEACHHEADS IN SPACE [Derleth - 1954]
    Chronoclasm, The.................................................ORIGINAL STORY
          STAR SCIENCE FICTION STORIES [Pohl - 1953]
    Compassion Circuit.................................................FU   Dec 1954
          13 GREAT STORIES OF SCIENCE FICTION [Conklin - 1960]
    Dumb Martian......................................................Glxy  Jul 1953
          GATEWAY TO TOMORROW [Carnell - 1954]
          BEST SF SCIENCE FICTION STORIES [Crispin - 1955]
Jizzle.................................................................F&SF  Feb 1952
    (Revised for publication in Fantasy & Science Fiction)
    (Original version appeared in Collier's January 8, 1949 under John Beynon
     byline)
    THE BEST FROM FANTASY & SCIENCE FICTION: 2nd SER [Boucher & McComas-1953]
Operation Peep........................................................Sus  Sum 1951
    BEYOND THE END OF TIME [Pohl - 1952]
    ESCALES DANS L'INFINI [Gallet - 1954]*
        *(Appeared under title Tousistes Des Temps Futurs)
              (Pawley's Peepholes)
Perfect Creature......................................................F&SF  Jan 1953
    SHADOW OF TOMORROW [Pohl - 1953]
    BEST SF TWO SCIENCE FICTION STORIES [Crispin - 1956]*
        *(Appeared under title Una)
Perforce To Dream.....................................................BFF   Jan 1954
    BEYOND THE BARRIERS OF SPACE AND TIME [Merril - 1954]
Pillar to Pose........................................................Glxy  Dec 1951
    THE SECOND GALAXY READER OF SCIENCE FICTION [Gold - 1954]
Re-Birth.......................(Originally published by Ballantine Books; 1955)
    A TREASURY OF GREAT SCIENCE FICTION [Boucher  1959]

# y

YOUD, CHRISTOPHER S.  (1)          (See listing John Christopher)
    Christmas Tree......................................................ASF  Feb 1949
          TRAVELERS OF SPACE [Greenberg - 1952]
YOUNG, PETER (1)
    Man Manifold...............................London Observer Prize Story
          A. D. 2500 [Wilson - 1955]

YOUNG, ROBERT F.  (7)                                          Mag.    Year
    Chrome Pastures.....................................................If   Apr 1956
        THE SECOND WORLD OF IF [Quinn & Wulff - 1958]
    Garden in the Forest, The.........................................ASF  Sep 1953
        OPERATION FUTURE [Conklin - 1955]
    Goddess in Granite...............................................F&SF  Sep 1957
        THE BEST FROM FANTASY & SCIENCE FICTION: 7th SERIES [Boucher - 1958]
    Jungle Doctor.....................................................Stg  Fal 1955
        THE BEST SCIENCE FICTION STORIES AND NOVELS: 1956 [Dikty - 1956]
    Nikita Eisenhower Jones..........................................F&SF  Aug 1960
        THE BEST FROM FANTASY & SCIENCE FICTION: 10th SERIES [Mills - 1961]
    Pattern for Penelope, A............................................If  Nov 1954
        THE FIRST WORLD OF IF [Quinn & Wulff - 1957]
    To Fell A Tree...................................................F&SF  Jul 1959
        A DECADE OF FANTASY & SCIENCE FICTION [Mills - 1960]
YOUNG, ROGER FLINT  (2)
    Not to be Opened.................................................ASF  Jan 1950
        THE BEST SCIENCE FICTION STORIES: 1951 [Bleiler & Dikty - 1951]
    Suburban Frontiers..............................................ASF  Feb 1950
        SCIENCE FICTION ADVENTURES IN DIMENSION [Conklin - 1953]

# Z

ZAGAT, ARTHUR LEO  (1)
    Lanson Screen, The..............................................TWS  Dec 1936
        THE BEST OF SCIENCE FICTION [Conklin - 1946]
ZIRUL, ARTHUR  (1)
    Beautiful Things, The............................. ...............FU  May 1958
        SF: 59 THE YEAR'S GREATEST SF AND FANTASY [Merril - 1959]

# *Listing by Editors*

ALDISS, BRIAN                                    Mag.    Year

   MORE PENGUIN SCIENCE FICTION
   12 stories   236 pages   3/6   (.50¢)   1963  Penguin Books Ltd.  (England)

| | | |
|---|---|---|
| The Monkey Wrench by Gordon R. Dickson | ASF | Aug 1951 |
| The First Men by Howard Fast | F&SF | Feb 1960 |
| Counterfeit by Alan E. Nourse | TWS | Aug 1952 |
| The Greater Thing by Tom Godwin | ASF | Feb 1954 |
| Built Up Logically by Howard Schoenfeld | Retort | Win 1949 |
|    (Originally appeared under title The Universal Tancea) | | |
| The Liberation of Earth by William Tenn ps (Philip Klass) | FSF | May 1953 |
| An Alien Agony by Harry Harrison | NW #122 | Sep 1962 |
|    (Originally appeared under title The Streets of Ashkalon) | | |
| The Tunnel Under the World by Frederik Pohl | Glxy | Jan 1955 |
| The Store of the Worlds by Robert Sheckley | Plby | Sep 1959 |
|    (Originally appeared under title World of Heart's Desire) | | |
| Jokester by Isaac Asimov | Inf | Dec 1956 |
| Pyramid by Robert Abernathy | ASF | Jul 1954 |
| The Forgotten Enemy by Arthur C. Clarke | NW #5 | n/d 1949 |

AMIS, KINGSLEY & ROBERT CONQUEST

   SPECTRUM II                Victor Gollancz, Ltd.  London, England
   8 stories   271 pages   18/  ($2.50)   September 6, 1962

| | | |
|---|---|---|
| Beyond Bedlam by Wyman Guin | Glxy | Aug 1951 |
| Bridge by James Blish | ASF | Feb 1952 |
| There is a Tide by Brian W. Aldiss | NW #44 | Feb 1956 |
| Second Variety by Philip K. Dick | Spc | May 1953 |
| The Feeling of Power by Isaac Asimov | If | Feb 1958 |
| Sense From Thought Divide by Mark Clifton | ASF | Mar 1955 |
| Resurrection by A. E. Van Vogt | ASF | Aug 1948 |
| Vintage Season by Henry Kuttner | ASF | Sep 1946 |
|    (Originally appeared under pseudonym Lawrence O'Donnell) | | |

   SPECTRUM III               Victor Gollancz, Ltd.  London, England
   8 stories   272 pages   18/  ($2.50)   September 12, 1963

| | | |
|---|---|---|
| Killdozer by Theodore Sturgeon | ASF | Nov 1944 |
| The Voices of Time by J. G. Ballard | NW #99 | Nov 1960 |
| Call Me Joe by Poul Anderson | ASF | Apr 1957 |
| We Would See a Sign by Mark Rose | ORIGINAL STORY | |
| Dreams Are Sacred by Peter Phillips | ASF | Sep 1948 |
| Exploration Team by Murray Leinster ps (Will F. Jenkins) | ASF | Mar 1956 |
| Fondly Fahrenheit by Alfred Bester | F&SF | Aug 1954 |
| The Sentinel by Arthur C. Clarke | 10SF | Spr 1951 |
|    (Originally appeared under title Sentinel of Eternity) | | |

ANONYMOUS

   BEYOND [Compiled by Thomas A. Dardis ~ Staff Editor of Berkley Books]
   9 stories   160 pages   F712   .50¢   January 3, 1963  Berkley Books; N. Y., N.Y.

         ALL STORIES FROM BEYOND FANTASY FICTION

| | |
|---|---|
| The Watchful Poker Chip by Ray Bradbury | March 1954 |
| The Ghost Maker by Frederik Pohl | January 1954 |

BEYOND [Continued]

| | Mag. | Year |
|---|---|---|
| Can Such Beauty Be? by Jerome Bixby | September | 1954 |
| The Real People by Algis Budrys | November | 1953 |
| The Beautiful Brew by James E. Gunn | September | 1954 |
| I'd Give a Dollar by Winston Marks | May | 1954 |
| The Root and the Ring by Wyman Guin | September | 1954 |
| Double Whammy by Fredric Brown | September | 1954 |
| Talent by Theodore Sturgeon | September | 1954 |

EDITOR'S NOTE:  The two Soviet Science Fiction collections listed below  were officially released by the Foreign Languages Publishing House prior to 1962.  Due to lack of data they were not included in our main listing.  As information, limited due to obvious reasons, was obtained afterwards we decided to  include  them in this supplement in order to keep our Checklist accurate.  No data is available as to the original source of publication on the stories listed.

THE HEART OF THE SERPENT    Foreign Languages Publishing House; Moscow, USSR
6 stories  266 pages  .95¢  (Published in 1961)

U. S. Edition:  MORE SOVIET SCIENCE FICTION    (Introduction by Isaac Asimov)
5 stories  190 pages  AS295V  .95¢  July 1962   Collier Books; N. Y., N. Y.

Translated from Russian by R. Prokofieva  (both editions)

| | |
|---|---|
| The Heart of the Serpent by Ivan Yefremov | (No data available) |
| Siema by Anatoly Dnieprov | " " " |
| The Trial of Tantalus by Victor Saparin | " " " |
| Stone from the Stars by Valentine Zhuravieva | " " " |
| Six Matches by Arkady and Boris Strugatsky | " " " |

A VISITOR FROM OUTER SPACE   Foreign Languages Publishing House; Moscow, USSR
6 stories  202 pages  .95¢  (No publishing data available)

U. S. Edition:  SOVIET SCIENCE FICTION    (Introduction by Isaac Asimov)
6 stories  189 pages  AS279V  .95¢  August 1962  Collier Books; N. Y., N. Y.

Translated from Russian by Violet L. Dutt  (both editions)

| | |
|---|---|
| Hoity-Toity by Alexander Belayev | (No data available) |
| Spontaneous Reflex by Arkady and Boris Strugatsky | " " " |
| A Visitor from Outer Space by Alexander Kazantsev | " " " |
| The Martian by Alexander Kazantsev | " " " |
| Infra Draconis by Georgy Gurevich | " " " |
| Professor Bern's Awakening by Vladimir Savchenko | " " " |

ASIMOV, ISAAC
    THE HUGO WINNERS            Doubleday & Co., Inc.; Garden City, N. Y.
    9 stories  313 pages  $4.50  September 7, 1962

1955: 13th CONVENTION, CLEVELAND

| | | |
|---|---|---|
| The Darfsteller by Walter M. Miller, Jr. | ASF | Jan 1955 |
| Allamagoosa by Eric Frank Russell | ASF | May 1955 |

1956: 14th CONVENTION, NEW YORK

| | | |
|---|---|---|
| Exploration Team by Murray Leinster ps (Will F. Jenkins) | ASF | May 1956 |
| The Star by Arthur C. Clarke | Inf | Nov 1955 |

1958: 16th CONVENTION, LOS ANGELES

THE HUGO WINNERS [Continued]                                    Mag.      Year

   Or All the Seas with Oysters by Avram Davidson            Glxy   May 1958

1959:  17th CONVENTION, DETROIT

   The Big Front Yard by Clifford D. Simak                  ASF    Oct 1958
   The Hell-Bound Train by Robert Bloch                     F&SF   Sep 1958

1960:  18th CONVENTION, PITTSBURGH

   Flowers for Algernon by Daniel Keyes                     F&SF   Apr 1959

1961:  19th CONVENTION, SEATTLE

   The Longest Voyage by Poul Anderson                      ASF    Dec 1960

  w/ Groff Conklin

    FIFTY SHORT SCIENCE FICTION TALES        Collier Books; New York, N. Y.
    50 stories, 2 verses  287 pages  AS516  .95¢    February 1963

Ballade of an Artificial Satellite by Poul Anderson    (verse)   F&SF   Oct 1958
The Fun They Had by Isaac Asimov                                 NEA    12/1/51
Men are Different by Alan Bloch
   (From Science Fiction Thinking Machines; Groff Conklin - 1954)
The Ambassadors by Anthony Boucher                               Stg    Jun 1952
The Weapon by Fredric Brown                                      ASF    Apr 1951
Random Sample by T. P. Caravan                                   F&SF   Apr 1953
Oscar by Cleve Cartmill                                          Unk    Feb 1941
The Mist by Peter Cartur                                         F&SF   Sep 1952
Teething Ring by James Causey                                    Glxy   Jan 1953
The Haunted Space Suit by Arthur C. Clarke                       TW     5/11/58
Stair Trick by Mildred Clingerman                                F&SF   Aug 1952
Unwelcome Tenant by Roger Dee ps (Roger D. Aycock)               PS     Sum 1950
The Mathematicians by Arthur Feldman                             Amz    Nov 1953
The Third Level by Jack Finney                                   Col    10/2/50
Beautiful, Beautiful, Beautiful! by Stuart Friedman             Fut    Mar 1952
The Figure by Edward Grendon                                     ASF    Jul 1947
The Rag Thing by David Grinnell                                  F&SF   Oct 1951
The Good Provider by Marion Gross                                F&SF   Sep 1952
Columbus Was a Dope by Robert A. Heinlein                        Stg    May 1947
Texas Week by Albert Hernhunter                                  FU     Jan 1954
Hilda by H. B. Hickey ps (Herb Livingston)                       F&SF   Sep 1952
The Choice by W. Hilton-Young                                    Pch    3/19/52
Not With a Bang by Damon Knight                                  F&SF   Spr 1950
The Altar at Midnight by C. M. Kornbluth                         Glxy   Mar 1952
A Bad Day for Sales by Fritz Leiber                              Glxy   Jul 1953
Who's Cribbing? by Jack Lewis                                    Stg    Jan 1953
Spectator Sport by John D. MacDonald                             TWS    Feb 1950
The Cricket Ball by Avro Manhattan                               F&SF   Oct 1955
Double-Take by Winston K. Marks                                  SFAd   Dec 1953
   (Originally appeared under pseudonym Ken Winney)
Prolog by John P. McKnight                                       F&SF   Aug 1951
The Available Data on the Worp Reaction by Lion Miller           F&SF   Sep 1953
Narapoia by Alan Nelson                                          Wdg    Apr 1948
   (Originally appeared under title The Origin of Naropoia)
Tiger By the Tail by Alan E. Nourse                              Glxy   Nov 1951
Counter Charm by Peter Phillips                                  Sint   Spr 1951
The Fly by Arthur Porges                                         F&SF   Sep 1952

FIFTY SHORT SCIENCE FICTION TALES [Continued]                    Mag.    Year
The Business, As Usual by Mack Reynolds                          F&SF  Jun 1952
Two Weeks in August by Frank M. Robinson                        Glxy  Feb 1951
See? by Edward G. Robles, Jr.                                    Glxy  Jun 1954
Appointment at Noon by Eric Frank Russell                        Amz  Mar 1954
We Don't Want Any Trouble by James H. Schmitz                   Glxy  Jun 1953
Built Down Logically by Howard Schoenfeld                      Retort  Win 1949
      (Originally appeared under title The Universal Tancea)
An Egg a Month From All Over by Idris Seabright ps (Margaret St. Clair)
                                                                F&SF  Oct 1952
The Perfect Woman by Robert Sheckley                            F&SF  Oct 1952
The Hunters by Walt Sheldon                                      Amz  Dec 1958
The Martian and the Magician by Evelyn E. Smith                  Stg  Mar 1952
Barney by Will Stanton                                          F&SF  Nov 1952
Talent by Theodore Sturgeon                                     Bynd  Sep 1953
Project Hush by William Tenn ps (Philip Klass)                  Glxy  Feb 1954
The Great Judge by A. E. Van Vogt                              FB #3  n/d 1948
Emergency Landing by Ralph Williams                              ASF  Jul 1940
Obviously Suicide by S. Fowler Wright                            Sus  Spr 1951
Six Haiku by Karen Handerson                  (verse)           F&SF  Jul 1962

BENSON, D. R.

      THE UNKNOWN                         Pyramid Books; New York, N. Y.
      11 stories  192 pages  R-851  .50¢  April 17, 1963
                    ALL STORIES FROM UNKNOWN WORLDS
The Misguided Halo by Henry Kuttner                            August  1939
Prescience by Nelson S. Bond                                   October 1941
Yesterday Was Monday by Theodore Sturgeon                         June 1941
The Gnarly Man by L. Sprague de Camp                              June 1939
The Bleak Shore by Fritz Leiber                              November 1940
Trouble With Water by H. L. Gold                                 March 1939
Double and Redoubled by Malcolm Jameson                      February 1941
When It Was Moonlight by Manly Wade Wellman                   February 1940
Mr. Jinx by Robert Arthur                                      August 1941
Snulbug by Anthony Boucher                                   December 1941

CAMPBELL, JOHN W.

      ANALOG I                    Doubleday & Co., Inc.; Garden City, N. Y.
      8 stories  219 pages  $3.95  February 8, 1963
                 ALL STORIES FROM ANALOG SCIENCE FICTION AND FACT

Monument by Lloyd Biggle, Jr.                                     June 1961
The Plague by Teddy Keller                                    February 1961
Remember the Alamo by T. R. Fehrenbach                        December 1961
      (Originally appeared under byline R. R. Fehrenbach)
The Hunch by Christopher Anvil                                    July 1961
Barnacle Bull by Winston P. Sanders                         September 1960
Join Our Gang? by Sterling E. Lanier                              May 1961
Sleight of Wit by Gordon R. Dickson                          December 1961
Prologue to an Analogue by Leigh Richmond                         June 1961


      PROLOGUE TO ANALOG          Doubleday & Co., Inc.; Garden City, N. Y.
      10 stories  308 pages  $3.95  January 12, 1962


              ALL STORIES FROM ASTOUNDING SCIENCE FICTION

PROLOGUE TO ANALOG [Continued]                                      Mag.    Year

Belief by Isaac Asimov                                          October  1963
Pandora's Planet by Christopher Anvil                         September  1956
Sound Decision by Randall Garrett & Robert Silverberg          October  1956
Omnilingual by H. Beam Piper                                  February  1957
Triggerman by J. F. Bone                                      December  1958
A Filbert is a Nut by Rick Raphael                           November  1959
Business As Usual, During Alterations by Ralph Williams          July  1958
Pushbutton War by Joseph P. Martino                           August  1960
We Didn't Do Anything Wrong, Hardly by Roger Kuykendall          May  1959
Minor Ingredient by Eric Frank Russell                         March  1956


CONKLIN, GROFF
    GREAT SCIENCE FICTION BY SCIENTISTS          Collier Books; New York, N. Y.
    16 stories  313 pages  A5218  .95¢      June 1962

What If...by Isaac Asimov                                      Fnt   Sum 1952
The Ultimate Catalyst by Eric Frank Russell                   TWS   Jun 1939
    (Originally appeared under John Taine byline)
The Gostak and the Doshes by Miles J. Breuer, M. D.           Amz   Mar 1930
Summertime in Icarus by Arthur C. Clarke                      Vog   Jun 1960
    (Org aprd under title The Hottest Piece of Real Estate in the Solar System)
The Neutrino Bomb by Ralph C. Cooper                         LASLN    7/13/61
Last Year's Grave Undug by Chan Davis                        ORIGINAL STORY
The Gold Makers by J. B. S. Haldane          (From The Inequality of Man; 1932)
The Tissue Culture King by Julian Huxley                      Amz   Aug 1927
A Martian Adventure by Willy Ley                              ASF   Feb 1937
    (Org aprd under title At the Perhilion under pseudonym Robert Willey)
Learning Theory by James McConnell                            If    Dec 1957
The Mother of Necessity by Chad Oliver        (From Another Kind; 1955)
John Sze's Future by John R. Pierce                          ORIGINAL STORY
Kid Anderson by Robert S. Richardson                         Spc   Spr 1956
    (Originally appeared under pseudonym Philip Latham)
Pilot Lights of the Apocalypse by Dr. Louis N. Riderenow     Ftn   Jan 1946
Report on Grand Central Terminal by Leo Szilard              UCM   n/d/a 1952
The Brain by Norbert Weiner                                   TEN   Apr 1952
    (Originally appeared under pseudonym W. Norbert)

    GREAT STORIES OF SPACE TRAVEL     Tempo Books-Grosset & Dunlap; N. Y., N.Y.
    11 stories  256 pages  T-39  .50¢      July 1963

                         THE SOLAR SYSTEM
The Wings of Night by Lester del Rey                         ASF   Mar 1942
The Holes Around Mars by Jerome Bixby                        Glxy  Jan 1954
Kaleidoscope by Ray Bradbury                                 TWS   Oct 1949
I'll Build Your Dream Castle by Jack Vance                   ASF   Sep 1947

...AND BEYOND THE SOLAR SYSTEM

Far Centaurus by A. E. Van Vogt                              ASF   Jan 1944
Propagandist by Murray Leinster ps (Will F. Jenkins)        Glxy  Jan 1954
Cabin Boy by Damon Knight                                    Glxy  Sep 1951
A Walk in the Dark by Arthur C. Clarke                       TWS   Aug 1950
Blind Alley by Isaac Asimov                                  ASF   Mar 1945
The Helping Hand by Poul Anderson                            ASF   May 1950
Allamagoosa by Eric Frank Russell                            ASF   May 1955

| 17 X INFINITY | Dell Books; New York, N. Y. | | Mag. | Year |
|---|---|---|---|---|

17 stories, 1 verse  272 pages  #7746  .50¢  August 15, 1963

| | | |
|---|---|---|
| The Simian Problem by Hollis Alpert | F&SF | Jul 1960 |
| Strikebreaker by Isaac Asimov | SFS | Jan 1957 |
| Come Into My Cellar by Ray Bradbury | Glxy | Oct 1962 |
| Ms Fnd In a Lbry by Hal Draper | F&SF | Dec 1961 |
| Cato The Martian by Howard Fast | F&SF | Jun 1960 |
| The Spaceman Cometh by Henry Gregor Felsen | F&SF | Apr 1956 |
| The Machine Stops by E. M. Forster | | |
| (From The Eternal Moment and Other Stories; 1928) | | |
| Frances Harkins by Richard Goggin | F&SF | Dec 1952 |
| The Day They Got Boston by Herbert Gold | F&SF | Sep 1961 |
| A-W-F Unlimited by Frank Herbert | Glxy | Jun 1961 |
| As Easy as A.B.C. by Rudyard Kipling | LM | Mar 1912 |
| MacDonough's Song by Rudyard Kipling | MpIn | Mar 1912 |
| Silenzia by Alan Nelson | F&SF | Sep 1953 |
| What to do Until the Analyst Comes by Frederik Pohl | Im | Feb 1956 |
| (Originally appeared under title Everybody's Happy But Me!) | | |
| Short in the Chest by Idris Seabright ps (Margaret St. Clair) | FU | Jul 1954 |
| The Last of the Spode by Evelyn Smith | F&SF | Jun 1953 |
| Never Underestimate by Theodore Sturgeon | If | Jan 1952 |
| Brooklyn Project by William Tenn ps (Philip Klass) | PS | Fal 1948 |

12 GREAT CLASSICS OF SCIENCE FICTION    Gold Medal Books; Greenwich, Conn.
12 stories  192 pages  d1366  .50¢  December 1963

| | | |
|---|---|---|
| Due Process by Algis Budrys | ASF | Dec 1960 |
| Earthmen Bearing Gifts by Fredric Brown | Glxy | Jun 1960 |
| Things by Zeena Henderson | F&SF | Jul 1960 |
| The Top by George Sumner Albee | F&SF | Aug 1962 |
| My Object All Sublime by Poul Anderson | Glxy | Jun 1961 |
| Human Man's Burden by Robert Sheckley | Glxy | Sep 1956 |
| On The Fourth Planet by J. F. Bone | Glxy | Apr 1963 |
| The Ballard of Lost C'Mell by Cordwainer Smith | Glxy | Oct 1962 |
| Thirty Days Had September by Robert F. Young | F&SF | Oct 1957 |
| The C ge by Bertram Chandler | F&SF | Jun 1957 |
| Star-Crossed Lover by William W. Stuart | Glxy | Apr 1962 |
| Immortality...For Some by J. T. McIntosh ps (James J. MacGregor) | ASF | Mar 1960 |

WORLDS OF WHEN    Pyramid Books; New York, N. Y.
5 stories  159 pages  F-733  .40¢  May 15, 1962

| | | |
|---|---|---|
| Transfusion by Chad Oliver | ASF | Jun 1959 |
| Bullet With His Name by Fritz Leiber | Glxy | Jul 1958 |
| Death and the Senator by Arthur C. Clarke | ASF | May 1961 |
| Farmer by Mack Reynolds | Glxy | Jun 1961 |
| Rations of Tantalus by Margaret St. Clair | FU | Jul 1954 |

w/ Noah D. Fabricant, M. D.
GREAT SCIENCE FICTION ABOUT DOCTORS    Collier Books; New York, N. Y.
18 stories  412 pages  AS 518  .95¢  April 1963

| | | |
|---|---|---|
| The Man Without an Appetite by Miles J. Breuer, M. D. | BV | n/d/a 1916 |
| Out of the Cradle, Endlessly Orbiting by Arthur C. Clarke | Dude | Mar 1959 |
| (Originally appeared under title Out of the Cradle) | | |
| The Brothers by Clifton L. Dance, Jr. M. D. | F&SF | Jun 1952 |
| The Great Keinplatz Experiment by Sir Arthur Conan Doyle | | |
| (Originally published by Rand McNally; 1895) | | |

Compound B by David Harold Fink, M. D.
   (From 9 Tales of Space and Time; Raymond J. Healy - 1954)
Rappaccini's Daughter by Nathaniel Hawthorne ......................... DR  Dec 1844
The Psychophonic Nurse by David H. Keller, M. D. ..................... Amz  Nov 1928
The Little Black Bag by C. M. Kornbluth ............................. ASF  Jul 1950
Ribbon in the Sky by Murray Leinster ps (Will F. Jenkins) .......... ASF  Jun 1957
Mate in Two Moves by Winston K. Marks ............................... Glxy May 1954
Bedside Manner by William Morrison ps (Joseph Samachson) ............ Glxy May 1954
The Shopdropper by Alan Nelson ..................................... F&SF Jan 1955
Family Resemblance by A an E. Nourse, M. D. ........................ ASF  Apr 1953
The Facts in the Case of M. Valdemar by Edgar Allan Poe ............ AWR  Dec 1845
Emergency Operation by Arthur Porges ............................... F&SF May 1956
A Matter of Ethics by J. R. Shango ................................ F&SF Nov 1954
Bolden's Pets by F. L. Wallace .................................... Glxy Oct 1955
Expedition Mercy by J. A. Winter, M. D. .......................... ASF  Nov 1948

CRISPIN, EDMUND ps (R. B. Montgomery)
   BEST SF FIVE SCIENCE FICTION STORIES     Faber & Faber Ltd.; London, England
   11 stories  256 pages  18/ ($2.50)  June 28, 1963

On Handling the Data by Henry I. Hirshfield & G. M. Mateyko ........ ASF  Sep 1959
   (Originally appeared under byline M. I. Mayfield)
Noise Level by Raymond F. Jones .................................. ASF  Dec 1952
Green Thumb by Clifford D. Simak ................................. Glxy Jul 1954
The Quest for Saint Aquin by Anthony Boucher
   (From New Tales of Space and Time; Raymond J. Healy - 1951)
The Monsters by Robert Sheckley .................................. F&SF Mar 1953
Who Can Replace a Man? by Brian W. Aldiss ........................ Inf  Jun 1958
   (Originally appeared under title But Who Can Replace a Man?)
The Prisoner by Christopher Anvil ............................... ASF  Feb 1956
The Star by Arthur C. Clarke .................................... Inf  Nov 1955
Consider Her Ways by John Wyndham ps (John Beynon Harris)
   (From Sometime Never; 1957)
The Martyr by Poul Anderson ..................................... F&SF Mar 1960
Later Than You Think by Fritz Leiber ............................ Glxy Oct 1950

DAVIDSON, AVRAM
   THE BEST FROM FANTASY & SCIENCE FICTION: 12th SERIES     May 5, 1963
   15 stories  225 pages  $3.95  Doubleday & Co., Inc.; Garden City, N. Y.
        ALL STORIES FROM FANTASY & SCIENCE FICTION

Test by Theodore L. Thomas ...................................... April   1962
Please Stand By by Ron Goulart .................................. January 1962
Who's In Charge Here? by James Blish ........................... May     1962
Three for the Stars by Joseph Dickinson ........................ April   1962
When Lilacs Last in the Dooryard Bloomed by Vance Aandahl ...... May     1962
Landscape with Sphinxes by Karen Anderson ..................... November 1962
My Dear Emily by Joanna Russ .................................. July    1962
The Gumdrop King by Will Stanton .............................. August  1962
The Golden Horn by Edgar Pangborn ............................ February 1962
The Singular Events which Occured in the Hovel on the Alley off of
   Eye Street by Avram Davidson .............................. February 1962
A Kind of Artistry by Brian W. Aldiss ........................ October  1962
Two's a Crowd by Sasha Gillen ................................ July    1962
The Man without a Planet by Kate Wilhelm ..................... July    1962
The Garden of Time by J. G. Ballard ......................... February 1962
Hop-Friend by Terry Carr .................................... November 1962

DeGRAEFF, ALLEN                                          Mag.    Year
    HUMAN AND OTHER BEINGS                    Collier Books; New York, N. Y.
    16 stories  319 pages  As567  .95¢       June 1963

Dark Interlude by Fredric Brown & Mack Reynolds            Glxy   Jan 1951
Love by Richard Wilson                                     F&SF   Jun 1952
Honor by Richard Wilson                                    SFQ    Feb 1956
Double Dome by Raymond E. Banks                            Glxy   May 1957
Way in the Middle of the Air by Ray Bradbury               OW     Jul 1950
The Other Foot by Ray Bradbury                             NwS    Mar 1951
The Vilbar Party by Evelyn E. Smith                        Glxy   Jan 1955
Made in U. S. A. by J. T. McIntosh ps (James J. MacGregor) Glxy   Apr 1953
The NRACP by George P. Elliott                             HdR    Aut 1949
The Big Stink by Theodore R. Cogswell                      If     Jul 1954
Down Among the Dead Men by William Tenn ps (Philip Klass)  Glxy   Jun 1954
All the Colors of the Rainbow by Leigh Brackett  (Mrs. Edmond Hamilton)
                                                           VSF    Nov 1957
The World of Myrion Flowers by Frederik Pohl & C. M. Kornbluth   F&SF   Oct 1961
My Lady Green Sleeves by Frederik Pohl                     Glxy   Feb 1957
Holdout by Robert Sheckley                                 F&SF   Dec 1957
Test Piece by Eric Frank Russell                           OW     Mar 1951

DIXON, RICHARD
    DESTINATION: AMALTHEIA       Foreign Languages Publishing House; Moscow, USSR
    7 stories  420 pages  $1.00  (Published in 1963)

            Translated from Russian by Leonid Kolesnikov

The Astronaut by Valentina Zhuravlyova                 (No data available)
Over the Abyss by Alexander Belayev                    "    "      "
The Maxwell Equations by Anatoly Dnieprov              "    "      "
The Valley of the Four Crosses by Igor Zabelin         "    "      "
The Golub-Yavan by Kirill Stanyukovich                 "    "      "
Flying Flowers by Mikhail Vasilyev                     "    "      "
Destination: Amaltheia by Arkaday & Boris Strugatsky   "    "      "

FADIMAN, CLIFTON

    THE MATHEMATICAL MAGPIE               Simon & Schuster; New York, N. Y.
    114 selections  300 pages  $4.95     July 1962

Cartoon [untitled] by Abner Dean            (From What Am I Doing Here?; 1947)

I    A SET OF IMAGINARIES

Cartoon [untitled] by Alan Dunn                            SRL    3/12/55
The Feeling of Power by Isaac Asimov                       If     Feb 1958
The Law by Robert M. Coates                                Nykr   11/29/47
The Appendix and the Spectacles by Miles J. Breuer, M. D.  Amz    Dec 1928
Paul Bunyon Versus the Conveyor Belt by William Hazlett Upson  FTM  n/d 1949
The Pacifist by Arthur C. Clarke                           FU     Oct 1956
The Hermeneutical Doughnut by H. Nearing, Jr.
    (From The Sinister Researches of C. P. Ransom; 1954)
Star, Bright by Mark Clifton                               Glxy   Jul 1952
F Y I by James Blish..(From Star Science Fiction Stories #2; Frederik Pohl; 1953)
The Vanishing Man by Richard Hughes          (From A Moment in Time; 1926)
The Nine Billion Names of God by Arthur C. Clarke
    (From Star Science Fiction Stories; Frederik Pohl - 1953)

II    COMIC SECTIONS

Three Mathematical Diversions by Raymond Queneau
    1.  An Exercise in Style: Mathematical
    2.  On the Aerodynamic Properties of Addition
    3.  The Geometrical Disappearance of Dino
            (From Exercises in Style; 1958)
                (Translated from French by Barbara Wright)
The Wonderful World of Figures by Corey Ford
    (From Corey Ford's Guide to Thinking; 1961)
A, B, and C — The Human Element in Mathematics by Stephen Leacock
    (From Literary Lapses; 1912)
B. C. by Johnny Hart              (cartoon)                 NYHT    8/13/61
A Note on the Einstein Theory by Max Beerbohm    (From Mainly on the Air; 1946)
The Achievment of H. T. Wensel by H. Allen Smith            SRL     5/21/60
Needed: Feminine Math by Parke Cummings        (From The Fly in the Martini; 1961)
Culver City Arithmetic Exercise Paper — Anonymous          Nykr    2/25/61
Cartoon [untitled] by Alfred Frueh                         Nykr    4/19/58
    [Two ] Extracts by Mark Twain ps (Samuel L. Clemens)       (No data available)
Mathematics for Golfers by Stephen Leacock         (From Literary Lapses; 1922)
The Mathematician's Nightmare: The Vision of Professor Squarepoint
    by Bertrand Russell              (From Nightmares of Eminent Persons; 1955)
Milo and the Mathemagician by Norton Juster    (From The Phantom Tollbroth; 1961)

III    IRREGULAR FIGURES

Cartoon by Saul Steinberg (Tid Alligator Walking Line) (From The Labyrinth; 1960)
Sixteen Stones by Samuel Beckett                       (From Molloy; 1955)
    (Translated from French by Patrick Bowles)
O'Brien's Table by J. L. Synge          (From Science: Sense and Nonsense; 1951)
The Purse of Fortunatus by Lewis Carroll ps (Charles Lutwidge Dodgson)
    (From Sylvie and Bruno; 1889)
Cartoon by Saul Steinberg    (Titled Man In Cube)          Nykr    9/10/60
The Symbolic Logic of Murder by John Reese                 EQMM    Oct 1960

IV    SIMPLE HARMONIC MOTIONS

Cartoon [untitled] by James Frankfort                      Vlg     10/12/61
The Square of the Hypotenuse    (song)     (From The Film: MERRY ANDREW;    1958)
    Music by Saul Chapling — Lyrics by Johnny Mercer
The Ta Ta                   (Song)              (From Bogey Beasts; 1962)
    Music by Joseph Charles Holbrooke — Jingles by Sidney H. Sime

V    DIVIDENDS AND REMAINDERS

Cartoon by Saul Steinberg    (Titled Question Mark on a Seesaw)    Nykr    7/23/60
Apothems [5] by George Christopher Lichtenberg
    (From The Lichtenberg Reader; Franz H. Mautner & Henry Hatfield-1959)
Apothems [4] by Stanislaw Jerzy Lec               (From Unkempt Thoughts; 1962)
    (Translated from Polish by Jack Galazka)
Apothems [3] by G. Polya                  (From How to Solve It; 1945)
Apothem by Lewis Carroll ps (Charles Lutwidge Dodgson)
    (From Alice's Adventures in Wonderland; 1896)
Apothem by Jules Renard               (From Histories Naturellies; n/d/a)
Apothem by George Orwell ps (Eric Blair)       (From Animal Farm; 1945)
Apothem by Geothe                         (No data available)
Apothem by Winston Churchill              (No data available)

Apothem by J. B. Mencken                    (From DE CHARIATANERIA ERUDITORUM; 1715 )
Apothem by August De Morgan                 (From A BUDGET OF PARADOXES; 1872)
Apothem by Etienne Donnot De Condillac              (No data available)
Apothem by Bill Mortlock                    (From LAWYER, HEAL THYSELF; 1959)
Apothem — Anonymous                                 (No data available)

A Subset of Anecdotes

    Euler, Diderot, Algebra and God by Augustus De Morgan
        (From A Budget of Paradoxes; 1872)
    Paradise Lost at Cambridge by Thomas Jefferson Hogg        (No data available)
    With Apologies to Boyal by George Gamow
        (From One, Two, Three...Infinity; 1947)
    Extinction by Subtraction by W. W. R. Ball                 (No data available)
    $\pi$ and the Actuary by W. W. R. Ball                     (No data available)
    That Mason-Dixon Line by Simon Newcomb                     (No data available)
    Mathematics Chez Madame Mariette by Elliot Paul
        (From The Last Time I Saw Paris; 1942)
    The Devil a Mathematician Would be by A. J. Lohwater       (No data available)

A Little Nursery Mathematics

    Verse — Anonymous
        (From The Lore and Language of Schoolchildren by Iona & Peter Opie; 1959)
    Verse by Frederik Winsor          (From THE SPACE CHILD'S MOTHER GOOSE; 1958)
    Riddle — Anonymous
        (From The Oxford Dictionary of Nursery Rhymes by Iona & Peter Opie; 1951)
    [Three] Verses (untitled) by Frederick Winsor
        (From The Space Child's Mother Goose; 1958)
    [Three] Verses (untitled) by L. A. Graham
        (From Ingenious Mathematical Problems and Methods; 1959)

A Quadrinominal of Poems

    To a Missing Member of a Family Group of Terms in an Algebraical Formula
        by J. J. Sylvester                          (No data available)
    Portrait of a Mathematician by Christopher Morley      (verse)
        (From The Ballard of New York, New York and Other Poems: 1930-1950; 1950)
    The Dunciad: (An Heroic Poem in Three Books) by Alexander Pope  (excerpts)
                                                 DP  5/18/1728
    Geometry by Wm. Wordsworth  (Fr THE PRELUDE; OR GROWTH OF A POET'S MIND; 1805)

Surd and Absurd

    Me by Hilbert Schenck, Jr.              (verse)              F&SF  Aug 1959
    Cartoon [untitled] by Leo Demare               Man's Magazine n/d/a 1958
    Song of the Screw — Anonymous           (verse)          (No data available)
    The Modern Hiawatha — Anonymous         (verse)          (No data available)
    The Love of the Triangles by John Hookham Frere & George Canning (verse)
    The Mathematician in Love by W.J.M. Rankins (verse)(Fr SONGS AND FABLES; 1874)
    $E = MC^2$ by Morris Bishop        (verse)      (From A BOWL OF BISHOP; 1954)
    Engineer's Yell — Anonymous             (verse)          (No data available)
        Rhymes by Algebra
        Verse [untitled] by Dr. William Whewell
            (From Handy-Book of Literary Curiosities by W. S. Walsh; 1925)
        Verse [untitled] by Stephen Barr
            (Original variation of the William Whewell verse)
        Note on $\dot\theta$ $\varnothing$ and $\psi$ by Michael Roberts      NS  3/23/1935

A Song Against Circles by R. P. Lister                (verse)      Nykr   5/13/61
Wockyjabber by Hilbert Schenck, Jr.                   (verse)      F&SF   May 1960
Einstein: A Parody in the Manner of Edw-n Markh-m by Louis Untermeyer   (verse)
   (From Collected Parodies; 1926)
Tending to Infinity by J. L. Synge    (verse)      From Kandelman's Krim; 1957)
The Superlative Degree by Earnest Elmo Calkins       (verse)      SRL    5/16/59
The Magic Box by W. R. Baker                                      Hpr    Apr 1928
The Kiss Precise by Frederick Soddy                              Ntr    6/20/36
The Kiss Precise (Generalized) by Thorold Gosset      (verse)     Ntr    1/9/37
The Hexlet by Frederick Soddy                (verse)              Ntr    12/5/36
Short Cuts to Success by Ronald A. Knox                          Slp    Nov 1917

     Group of Limericks

         The Young Lady Named Bright by A. H. Reginald Buller, F. R. S.   (verse)
                                                            (No data available)
         There Was an Old Man Who Said, "Do..." — Anonymous     (verse)
                                                            (No data available)
         Cartoon [untitled] by Paul Peter Porges           ALM  Jul 1955
         The Young Man of Sid Sussex by Arthur C. Hilton    (verse)
            (From What Cheer; Edited by David McCord - 1945)
         Pun in Orbit by Hilbert Schenck, Jr.      (verse)   ORIGINAL VERSE
         A Mathematician Confided — Anonymous    (verse)   (No data available)
         A Mathematician Named Klein — Anonymous   (verse)  (No data available)

Three Random Points

     The Map of England and the Absolute by George Santayana)
        (From Character and Opinion in the United States; 1920)
     Cupid with an Adding Machine by Charles D. Rice                 TW    9/18/60
     The Miniver Problem by Jan Struther ps (Mrs. Joyce Maxtone Graham)
        (From Mrs. Miniver; 1940)
     The Miniver Problem  (solution)  by L. A. Graham
        (From Ingenious Problems and Methods; 1959)


HAY, GEORGE
     HELL HATH FURY                       Neville Spearman, Ltd.; London, England
     7 stories  240 pages  15/      October 25, 1963
                      ALL STORIES FROM UNKNOWN WORLDS
Hell Hath Fury by Cleve Cartmill                              August 1942
The Bleak Shore by Fritz Leiber, Jr.                        November 1940
The Frog by P. Schuyler Miller                               October 1942
The Refugee by Jane Rice                                     October 1943
The Devil's Rescue by L. Ron Hubbard                         October 1940
The Cloak by Robert Bloch                                        May 1939
The Extra Bricklayer by A. M. Phillips                     September 1940


HOWARD, IVAN
     ESCAPE TO EARTH                          Belmont Books; New York, N.Y.
     6 stories  173 pages  L92-571  .50¢  September 1963
Escape to Earth by Manly Banister                             SFQ   Nov 1957
We Are Alone by Robert Sheckley                               FSF   Nov 1952
Doomsday's Color-Press by Raymond F. Jones                    FSF   Nov 1952
A Big Man with the Girls by James MacCreigh ps (Frederik Pohl) & Judith Merril
                                                              FSF   Mar 1953

Temple of Despair by M. C. Pease                                DSF     Oct 1953
"If the Court Pleases" by Noel Loomis                           BSF     Jun 1953

    NOVELETS OF SCIENCE FICTION            Belmont Books; New York, N. Y.
    8 stories   173 pages   L92-567  .50¢   July 1963

Ultrasonic God by L. Sprague de Camp                           Fw/SFS  Jul 1951
The Chapter Ends by Poul Anderson                              DSF     Jan 1954
"A" As In Android by Milton Lesser                             Fw/SFS  May 1951
...And the Truth Shall Make You Free by Clifford D. Simak      FSF     Mar  953
Night-Fear by Frank Belknap Long                               DSF     Oct 1953
I Am Tomorrow by Lester del Rey                                DSF     Dec 1952
Testament of Andros by James Blish                             FSF     Jan 1953
The Possessed by Arthur C. Clarke                              DSF     Mar 1953

    RARE SCIENCE FICTION                   Belmont Books; New York, N. Y.
    8 stories   173 pages   L92-557  .50¢   January 1963

Let's Have Fun by L. Sprague de Camp                           SFQ     May 1957
Do It Yourself by Milton Lesser                                FSF #33 Sum 1957
In Human Hands by Algis Budrys                                 SFS #2  n/d 1954
Protective Camouflage by Charles V. De Vet                     SFS     May 1955
Asylum by Alice Bullock                                        FSF     Aug 1954
Quick Freeze by Robert Silverberg                             SFQ     May 1957
Luck, Inc. by Jim Harmon                                       SFS     Nov 1959
Ripeness by M. C. Pease                                        SFS     Jun 1955

    6 AND THE SILENT SCREAM                Belmont Books; New York, N. Y.
    6 stories   173 pages   L92-564  .50¢   May 1963

Vulcan's Hammer by Philip K. Dick                             FSF #29 n/d 1956
Riddle of the Deadly Paradise by Frank Belknap Long          SFS     Nov 1958
The Ear-Friend by R. E. Banks                                 SFS     Mar 1955
Peace on Earth by Irving Cox, Jr.                            FSF     Jun 1954
Ask a Foolish Question by Robert Sheckley                    SFS #1  n/d 1953
Children of Fortune by D. A. Jourdan                         SFQ     Feb 1957

    WAY OUT                                Belmont Books; New York, N. Y.
    7 stories   173 pages   L92-575  .50¢   December 1963

Ennui by Milton Lesser                                        DSF     Dec 1952
Knowledge is Power by H. B. Fyfe                              DSF     Dec 1952
Snail's Pace by Algis Budrys                                  DSF     Oct 1953
"X" For "Expendable" by William C. Bailey                     DSF     Dec 1952
Blood Lands by Alfred Coppell                                 DSF     Dec 1952
Blunder Enlightening by Dave Dryfoos                          DSF     Dec 1952
Honorable Enemies by Poul Anderson                           Fw/SFS  May 1951

    Editor's Note:  Although this collection was published without any byline, we
        were advised by the publishers that Ivan Howard edited this anthology.
    THE WEIRD ONES                         Belmont Books; New York, N. Y.
    7 stories   173 pages   L92-541  .50¢   July 1962

Small Lord by Frederik Pohl                                   SFQ     Feb 1957
Sentiment, Inc. by Poul Anderson                             SFS #1  n/d 1953
Name Your Tiger by Milton Lesser                             SFQ     May 1957
Iron Man by Eando Binder ps (Otto Binder)                    FSF #28 n/d 1955
The Haunted Ones by Mack Reynolds                            SFS     Nov 1959
Hail to the Chief by Sam Sackett                             SFS     Jun 1954
Impractical Joke by L. Sprague de Camp                       FSF #29 n/d 1956

KEYES, NOEL ps (David Keightley)                                          Mag.    Year
    CONTACT                              Paperback Library, Inc.; New York, N. Y.
    12 stories   176 pages   52-211   .50¢        May 1963

MAN THE DISCOVERER
    First Contact by Murray Leinster ps (Will F. Jenkins)          ASF    May 1945
    Intelligence Test by Harry Walton                              SF+    Jun 1953
    The Large Ant by Howard Fast                                   FU     Feb 1960
    What's He Doing In There? by Fritz Leiber                      Glxy   Dec 1957
    Chemical Plant by Ian Williamson                               NW #18 Dec 1950
    Limiting Factor by Clifford D. Simak                           Stg    Nov 1949
    The Fire Balloons by Ray Bradbury                              Im     Apr 1951
        (Originally appeared under title "In This Sign...")

MAN THE DISCOVERED
    Invasion From Mars by Howard Koch       (The radio script of the Orson Welles
        broadcast of H. G. Wells' "The War of the Worlds" over the Columbia Broad-
        casting System; October 30, 1938)   (Copyright 1940 Princeton Univ. Press)
    The Gentle Vultures by Isaac Asimov                            SSF    Dec 1957
    Knock by Fredric Brown                                         TWS    Dec 1948
    Specialist by Robert Sheckley                                  Glxy   May 1953
    Lost Memory by Peter Phillips                                  Glxy   May 1952

KNIGHT, DAMON
    A CENTURY OF SCIENCE FICTION              Simon & Schuster; New York, N.Y.
    26 stories   352 pages   $4.95      May 1962

    ROBOTS
    The Ideal by Stanley G. Weinbaum          (Excerpts)           WS     Sep 1935
    Moxon's Master by Ambrose Bierce          (From Can Such Things Be; 1893)
    Reason by Isaac Asimov                                         ASF    Sep 1941
    But Who Can Replace a Man? by Brian Aldiss                     Inf    Jun 1958

II  TIME TRAVEL
    The Time Machine by H. G. Wells           (Excerpts)           NwR    Jan 1895
    Of Time and Third Avenue by Alfred Bester                      F&SF   Oct 1951
    Sail On! Sail On! by Philip Jose Farmer                        Stg    Dec 1952
    Worlds of the Imperium by Keith Laumer    (Excerpts)           Fnt    Feb 1961
    The Business, As Usual by Mack Reynolds                        F&SF   Jun 1952

III SPACE
    What's It Like Out There? by Edmond Hamilton                   Stg    Dec 1952
    Sky Lift by Robert A. Heinlein                                 Im     Nov 1953
    The Star by Arthur C. Clarke                                   Inf    Nov 1955

IV  OTHER WORLDS AND PEOPLE
    The Crystal Egg by H. G. Wells                                 NwR    May 1897
    The Wind People by Marion Zimmer Bradley                       If     Feb 1959
    Unhuman Sacrifice by Katherine MacLean                         ASF    Nov 1958

V   ALIENS AMONG US
    What Was It? by Fitz-James O'Brien                             Hpr    Mar 1859
    The First Days of May by Claude Velliott                       Fctn   May 1960
        (Translated from French by Damon Knight)
    Day of Succession by Theodore L. Thomas                        ASF    Aug 1959
    Angel's Egg by Edgar Pangborn                                  Glxy   Jun 1951

VI    SUPERMAN

   Another World by J. H. Rosny Aine ps (Honore Boex)          RvP  n/d/a1895
   ◾    (Translated from French by Damon Knight)
   Odd John by Olaf Stapledon                    (Excerpts)
      (Originally published by Methuen and Co.; 1935)
   Call Me Joe by Poul Anderson                               ASF   Apr 1957

VII   MARVELOUS INVENTIONS

   From The London Times of 1904 by Mark Twain ps (Samuel L. Clemens)
                                                             Cny   Nov 1898
   Twenty Thousand Leagues under the Sea by Jules Verne      (Excerpts)
      (Originally published by G. M. Smith; 1873)
   You Are With It! by Will Stanton                          F&SF  Dec 1961
   Cease Fire by Frank Herbert                               ASF   Jan 1958

   FIRST FLIGHT: Maiden Voyages in Space and Time      September 1963
   10 stories  160 pages  #72-672  .50¢           Lancer Books; New York, N. Y.

The Isolinguals by L. Sprague de Camp                        ASF   Sep 1937
The Faithful by Lester del Rey                               ASF   Apr 1938
Black Destroyer by A. E. Van Vogt                            ASF   Jul 1939
Life-Line by Robert A. Heinlein                              ASF   Aug 1939
Ether Breather by Theodore Sturgeon                          ASF   Sep 1939
Loophole by Arthur C. Clarke                                 ASF   Apr 1946
Tomorrow's Children by Poul Anderson                         ASF   Mar 1947
   (Originally appeared under byline Poul Anderson & F. N. Waldrop)
That Only a Mother by Judith Merril                          ASF   Jun 1948
Walk to the World by Algis Budrys                            Spc   Nov 1952
T by Brian W. Aldiss                                         Neb #18 Nov 1956

MARGULIES, LEO

   THREE IN ONE                            Pyramid Books; New York, N. Y.
   3 stories  144 pages  F-899  .40¢  August 15, 1963

There Is No Defense by Theodore Sturgeon                     ASF   Feb 1948
Galactic Chest by Clifford D. Simak                          OSFS  Sep 1956
West Wind by Murray Leinster ps (Will F. Jenkins)           ASF   Mar 1948

MERRIL, JUDITH

   SEVENTH ANNUAL OF THE YEAR'S BEST SF      Simon & Schuster; New York, N. Y.
   32 selections  399 pages  $4.50         December 10, 1962

Oneiromachia by Conrad Aiken              (verse)           Atl   Oct 1961
A Passage from the Stars by Kaatje Hurlbut                  SEP   5/13/61
Among the Dangs by George P. Elliott                        Esq   Jun 1958
Immediately Yours by Robert Beverly Hale                    Mdm   Nov 1961
Parky by David Rome                                         SF #48 Aug 1961
The Fastest Gun Dead by Julian F. Grow                      If    Mar 1961
All the Tea in China by R. Bretnor                          F&SF  May 1961
The Portobello Road by Murial Spark          (From The Go-Away Bird; 1958)
Ottmar Balleau X 2 by George Bamber                         Rog   Mar 1961
The Dandelion Girl by Robert F. Young                       SEP   4/1/61
Nightmare in Time by Frederic Brown                         Dude n/d/a 1961
Looking Backward by Jules Feiffer            (cartoon)      HS    12/10/61

Three Prologues and an Episode by John Dos Passos                  Adt   Spr 1961
It Becomes Necessary by Ward Moore                                 Gent  n/d/a1961
        (Originally appeared under title The Cold Peace)
My Trial as a War Criminal by Leo Szilard                          UCLR  Aut 1949
A Prize for Edie by J. F. Bone                                     ASF   Apr 1961
Freedom by Mack Reynolds                                           ASF   Feb 1961
High Barbary by Lawrence Durrell                                   Mdm   Sep 1961
The Quaker Cannon by Frederik Pohl & C. M. Kornbluth              ASF   Aug 1961
Quake, Quake, Quake by Paul Dehn and Edward Gorey        (verse)
        (From Quake, Quake, Quake; 1961)
Judas Bomb by Kit Reed                                            F&SF  Apr 1961
The Tunnel Ahead by Alice Glaser                                 F&SF  Nov 1961
Extraterrestrial Trilogue on Terran Self-Destruction by Sheri S. Eberhart
                (verse)                                            Glxy  Aug 1961
The Countdown by John Haase                                        Nykr  10/7/61
The Beat Cluster by Fritz Leiber                                  Glxy  Oct 1961
In Tomorrow's Little Black Bag by James Blish                      ORIGINAL STORY
The Ship Who Sang by Anne McCaffrey                               F&SF  Apr 1961
A Planet Named Shayol by Cordwainer Smith                        Glxy  Oct 1961
The Asteroids, 2194 by John Wyndham ps (John Beynon Harris)      Amz   Jan 1961
        (Originally appeared under title The Emptiness of Space; NW #100 November 1960)
The Long Night by Ray Russell   (Org aprd as The Exploits of Orgo)  Rog  Apr 1961
To an Astronaut Dying Young by Maxine W. Kumin                     Atl   Dec 1961
Books by Anthony Boucher                           (Special Original Feature)

        8th ANNUAL OF THE YEAR'S BEST SF        Simon & Schuster; New York, N. Y.
        29 stories  392 pages  $4.50  December 6, 1963

The Unsafe Deposit Box by Gerald Kersh                            SEP   4/14/62
Seven-Day Terror by R. A. Lafferty                                If    Mar 1962
The Toy Shop by Harry Harrison                                    ASF   Apr 1962
The Face in the Photo by Jack Finney
        (From I Love Galesburg in the Springtime; 1962)
The Circuit Riders by R. C. FitzPatrick                           ASF   Apr 1962
Such Stuff by John Brunner                                       F&SF  Mar 1962
The Man Who Made Friends with Electricity by Fritz Leiber        F&SF  Mar 1962
Kings Who Die by Poul Anderson                                    If    Mar 1962
The Unfortunate Mr. Morky by Vance Aandahl                       F&SF  Oct 1962
Christmas Treason by James White                                 F&SF  Jan 1962
A Miracle of Rare Device by Ray Bradbury                          Plby  Jan 1962
All the Sounds of Fear by Harlan Ellison          (From Ellison Wonderland; 1962)
One of those Days by William F. Nolan                            F&SF  May 1962
The Day Rembrandt Went Public by Arnold M. Auerbach               Hpr   Jul 1962
Ms. Found in a Bus by Russell Baker                      N.Y. Times n/d/a 1962
The Insane Ones by J. G. Ballard                                  Amz   Jan 1962
Leprechaun by William Sambrot                                     Escp n/d/a 1962
Change of Heart by George Whitley ps (A. Bertram Chandler)        Fnt   May 1962
Angela's Satyr by Brian Cleeve                                    SEP   11/3/62
Puppet Show by Fredric Brown                                      Plby  Nov 1962
Hang, Head, Vandal by Mark Clifton                                Amz   Apr 1962

MARS PROBE: REPORT IN TRIPLICATE

Earthlings Go Home! by Mack Reynolds                              Rog   Aug 1962
The Martian Star-Gazers by Frederik Pohl                         Glxy  Feb 1962
        (Originally appeared under pseudonym Ernst Mason)
Planetary Effulgence by Bertrand Russell         (From Fact and Fiction; 1961)
Deadly Game by Edward Wellen                                      If    May 1962
Subcommittee by Zeene Henderson                                  F&SF  Jul 1962
The Piebold Hippogriff by Karen Anderson                          Fnt   May 1962
Home from the Shore by Gordon R. Dickson                         Glxy  Feb 1963
Books by Anthony Boucher                           (Special Original Feature)

MILLS, ROBERT P.                                                    Mag.    Year
    THE WORLDS OF SCIENCE FICTION                    Dial Press; New York, N. Y.
    16 stories  349 pages  $4.95  June 28, 1963

The First Men by Howard Fast                                    F&SF  Feb 1960
A Work of Art by James Blish                                    SFS   Jul 1956
    (Originally appeared under title Art Work)
Evening Primrose by John Collier              (From Presenting Moonshine; 1941)
Momento Homo by Walter M. Miller, Jr.                           Amz   Mar 1954
A Miracle of Rare Device by Ray Bradbury                        Plby  Jan 1962
"All You Zombies — " by Robert A. Heinlein                      F&SF  Mar 1959
Faq by George P. Elliott                                        HdR   Spr 1952
Babal II by Damon Knight                                        Bynd  Jul 1953
A Saucer of Lonliness by Theodore Sturgeon                      Glxy  Feb 1953
Night Piece by Poul Anderson                                    F&SF  Jul 1961
The Strange Girl by Mark Van Doren              (From Collected Stories; 1962)
The Quest for Saint Aquin by Anthony Boucher
    (From NEW TALES OF SPACE AND TIME; Raymond J. Healy — 1951)
The War in the Air by R. V. Cassill                             Epch n/d/a 1962
The Ugly Little Boy by Isaac Asimov                             Glxy  Sep 1958
    (Originally appeared under title Lastborn)

Epilogue

    My Private World of Science Fiction by Alfred Bester        Original Story


MOSKOWITZ, SAM
    THE COMING OF THE ROBOTS                    Collier Books; New York, N. Y.
    10 stories  254 pages  AS548  .95¢  February 1963

I, Robot by Eando Binder ps (Otto Binder)                       Amz   Jan 1939
Helen O'Loy by Lester del Rey                                   ASF   Dec 1938
The Lost Machine by John Wyndham ps (John Beynon Harris)
    (Originally appeared under byline John Beynon Harris)
Runaround by Isaac Asimov                                       ASF   Mar 1942
Earth for Inspiration by Clifford D. Simak                      TWS   Apr 1941
Lost Memory by Peter Phillips                                   Glxy  May 1952
Rex by Harl Vincent ps (Harl Vincent Schoepflin)               ASF   Jun 1934
True Confession by F. Orlin Tremaine                            TWS   Feb 1940
Derelict by Raymond Z. Gallun                                   ASF   Oct 1935
Misfit by Michael Fischer                                       SF+   Dec 1953

    EXPLORING OTHER WORLDS                       Collier Books; New York, N. Y.
    8 stories  256 pages  AS551  .95¢  February 1963

The Mad Moon by Stanley G. Weinbaum                             ASF   Dec 1935
Garden in the Void by Poul Anderson                             Glxy  May 1952
At the Center of Gravity by Ross Rocklynne                      ASF   Jun 1936
Something Green by Fredric Brown
    (From Space on My Hands; 1951)
The Dead Planet by Edmond Hamilton                              Stg   Spr 1946
The Radiant Enemies by R. F. Starzl                             Arg   2/10/34
Via Asteroid by Eando Binder ps (Otto Binder)                   TWS   Feb 1938
    (Originally appeared under pseudonym Gordon A. Giles)
Man of the Stars by Sam Moskowitz                               PS    Win 1941

POHL, FREDERIK                                                      Mag.    Year
    THE EXPERT DREAMERS        Doubleday and Co., Inc.; Garden City, N. Y.
    16 stories  248 pages  $3.95  October 12, 1962

At the End of the Orbit by Arthur C. Clarke                         If   Nov 1961
On the Feasibility of Coal-Driven Power Stations by O. R. Frisch    SA   Mar 1956
A Feast of Demons by William Morrison ps (Joseph Samachson)        Glxy  Mar 1958
The Heart on the Other Side by George Gamow                      ORIGINAL STORY
Lenny by Isaac Asimov                                              Inf   Jan 1958
The Singers by W. Grey Walter          (From The Curve of the Snowflake; 1956)
The Invasion by Robert Willey ps (Willy Ley)                      Sup   Sep 1940
To Explain Mrs. Thompson by Philip Latham ps (Robert S. Richardson) ASF  Nov 1951
Adrift on the Policy Level by Chan Davis)
    (From Star Science Fiction Stories #5; Frederik Pohl; 1959)
The Black Cloud by Fred Hoyle                    (From The Black Cloud; 1957)
Chain Reaction by Boyd Ellanby ps (Lyle & William C. Boyd)        Glxy  Sep 1956
The Miracle of the Broom Closet by W. Norbet ps (Norbert Weiner)   TEN  Apr 1952
Heavy Planet by Lee Gregor ps (Milton A. Rothman)                 ASF   Aug 1939
The Test Stand by Lee Correy ps (G. Harry Stine)                  ASF   Mar 1955
Amateur in Chancery by George O. Smith                            Glxy  Oct 1961
The Mark Gable Foundation by Leo Szilard   (From The Voice of the Dolphins; 1961)

    TIME WAITS FOR WINTHROP AND FOUR OTHER SHORT NOVELS FROM GALAXY
    5 stories  336 pages  $3.95  November 9, 1962   Doubleday; Garden City, N.Y.

             ALL STORIES FROM GALAXY SCIENCE FICTION

Time Waits for Winthrop by William Tenn ps (Philip Klass)           August 1957
Accidental Flight by F. L. Wallace                                  April 1952
To Marry Medusa by Theodore Sturgeon                               August 1958
Natural State by Damon Knight                                      January 1954
Galley Slave by Isaac Asimov                                       December 1957

SERLING, ROD
    ROD SERLING'S TRIPLE W: WITCHES, WARLOCKS AND WEREWOLVES
    12 stories  181 pages  J2623  .40¢  May 1963    Bantam Books; New York, N. Y.

The Amulet by Gordon R. Dickson                                    F&SF  Apr 1959
The Story of Sidi Norman — Anonymous                          (No data available)
The Final Ingredient by Jack Sharkey                              F&SF  Aug 1960
Blind Alley by Malcolm Jameson                                    Unk   Jun 1943
Young Goodman Brown by Nathaniel Hawthorne                         NEM   Apr 1835
The Chestnut Beads by Jane Roberts                                F&SF  Oct 1957
Hatchery of Dreams by Fritz Leiber                                Fnt   Nov 1961
The Mark of the Beast by Rudyard Kipling          (From Life's Handicap; 1891)
And Not Quite Human by Joe L. Hensley                             Bynd  Sep 1953
Wolves Don't Cry by Bruce Elliott                                 F&SF  Apr 1954
The Black Retriever by Charles G. Finney                          F&SF  Oct 1958
Witch Trials and the Law by Charles Mackay     (article)    (Excerpts)
    (From Extraordinary Popular Delusions and the Madness of Crowds; 1841)
SHAW, LARRY T.
    GREAT SCIENCE FICTION ADVENTURES        Lancer Books, Inc.; New York, N. Y.
    4 stories  174 pages  .50¢  October 1963

             ALL STORIES FROM SCIENCE FICTION ADVENTURES

The Starcombers by Edmond Hamilton                                December 1956
The Man from the Big Dark by John Brunner                         June 1958
The World Otalmi Made by Harry Harrison                           June 1958
Hunt the Space Witch by Robert Silverberg                         January 1958

    (Originally appeared under pseudonym Ivar Jorgenson)

SISSONS, MICHAEL                                      Mag.    Year
    ASLEEP IN ARMAGEDDON              Panther Books; London, England
    10 stories  189 pages  #1379  2/6 (.35¢)    June 1962
Asleep In Armageddon by Ray Bradbury                    PS   Win 1948
The Weapon by Fredric Brown                            ASF   Apr 1951
Not Final! by Isaac Asimov                             ASF   Oct 1941
Home There's No Returning by C. L. Moore        (From No Boundaries; 1955)
    (Originally appeared under joint byline Henry Kuttner & C. L. Moore)
This Star Shall Be Free by Murray Leinster ps (Will F. Jenkins)   Sup  Nov 1949
The Scarlet Plague by Jack London                     ASMM   9/13/13
Enchanted Village by A. E. Van Vogt                     OW   Jul 1950
Crucifixius Etiam by Walter M. Miller, Jr.             ASF   Feb 1953
Being by Richard Matheson                               If   Aug 1954
Camouflage by Henry Kuttner                            ASF   Sep 1945
    (Originally appeared under pseudonym Lewis Padgett)

WILLIAMS-ELLIS, AMABEL & MABLY OWEN
    OUT OF THIS WORLD 3            Blackie & Son, Ltd.; London, England
    8 stories  175 pages  12/6  ($1.75)  May 1962
Sands Our Abode by Francis G. Rayer                  NW #84   Jun 1959
Round Trip to Esidrap by Lloyd Biggle, Jr.              If   Nov 1960
    (Originally appeared under title Esidarap of Pirt Dnuor)
Living Space by Isaac Asimov                           SFS   May 1956
The Apprentice by James White                        NW #99   Nov 1960
    D
    a
Baxb  by Evelyn E. Smith          (From Time To Come; August Derleth - 1954)
    b
    r
Dumb Martian by John Wyndham ps (John Beynon Harris)   Glxy  Jul 1952
Who's There by Arthur C. Clarke                      NW #77   Nov 1958
Ararat by Zeena Henderson                             F&SF   Oct 1952

WOLLHEIM, DONALD A.
    MORE ADVENTURES ON OTHER PLANETS     Ace Books, Inc.; New York, N. Y.
    6 stories  190 pages  F-178  .40¢     January 1963
Child of the Sun by Leigh Brackett                      PS   Spr 1942
Sunrise on Mercury by Robert Silverberg                SFS   May 1957
By the Name of Man by John Brunner                   Neb #17   Jul 1956
The Red Death of Mars by Robert Moore Williams         ASF   Jul 1940
The Planet of Doubt by Stanley G. Weinbaum             ASF   Oct 1935
Tiger by the Tail by Poul Anderson                      PS   Jan 1951

# Listing by Story Titles

# A

|  | Mag. | Year |
|---|---|---|

"A" as in Android by Milton Lesser.........................Fw/SFS   May 1951
   NOVELETS OF SCIENCE FICTION [Howard - 1963]
A, B, and C — The Human Element in Mathematics by Stephen Leacock..............
   (From Literary Lapses; 1912)
   THE MATHEMATICAL MAGPIE [Fadiman - 1962]
Abominable Mr. Gunn, The by Robert Graves..........(From Five Pens in Hand; 1955)
   THE MATHEMATICAL MAGPIE [Fadiman - 1962]
Achievment of H. T. Wensel, The by H. Allen Smith..................SRL    5/21/60
   THE MATHEMATICAL MAGPIE [Fadiman - 1962]
Accidental Flight by F. L. Wallace...............................Glxy   Apr 1952
   TIME WAITS FOR WINTHROP & FOUR OTHER SHORT NOVELS FROM GALAXY [Pohl - 1962]
*Adrift on the Policy Level by Chan Davis.......................................
   (From Star Science Fiction Stories #5; Frederik Pohl - 1959)
   THE EXPERT DREAMERS [Pohl - 1962]
All the Tea in China by R. Bretnor...............................F&SF   May 1961
   7th ANNUAL OF THE YEAR'S BEST SF [Merril - 1962]
Alien Agony, An by Harry Harrison..............................NW #122  Sep 1962
   (Originally appeared under title The Streets of Ashkalon)
   MORE PENGUIN SCIENCE FICTION [Aldiss - 1963]
All the Colors of the Rainbow by Leigh Brackett               VSF    Nov 1957
   HUMAN AND OTHER BEINGS [DeGraeff - 1963]
All the Sounds of Fear by Harlan Ellison..........(From Ellison Wonderland; 1962)
   8th ANNUAL OF THE YEAR'S BEST SF [Merril - 1963]
*"All You Zombies — " by Robert A. Heinlein......................F&SF   Mar 1959
   THE WORLDS OF SCIENCE FICTION [Mills - 1963]
Allamagoosa by Eric Frank Russell...............................ASF    May 1955
   THE HUGO WINNERS [Asimov - 1962]
   GREAT STORIES OF SPACE TRAVEL [Conklin - 1963]
*Altar at Midnight, The by C. M. Kornbluth......................Glxy   Mar 1952
   FIFTY SHORT SCIENCE FICTION TALES [Asimov & Conklin - 1963]
Amateur in Chancery by George O. Smith                        Glxy   Oct 1961
   THE EXPERT DREAMERS [Pohl - 1962]
*Ambassadors, The by Anthony Boucher............................Stg    Jun 1952
   FIFTY SHORT SCIENCE FICTION TALES [Asimov & Conklin - 1963]
Among the Dangs by George P. Elliott............................Esq    Jun 1958
   7th ANNUAL OF THE YEAR'S BEST SF [Merril - 1962]
Amulet, The by Gordon R. Dickson................................F&SF   Apr 1959
   ROD SERLING'S TRIPLE W: WITCHES, WARLOCKS AND WEREWOLVES [Serling - 1963]
And Not Quite Human by Joe L. Hensley...........................Bynd   Sep 1953
   ROD SERLING'S TRIPLE W: WITCHES, WARLOCKS AND WEREWOLVES [Serling - 1963]
*And the Truth Shall Make You Free by Clifford D. Simak.........FSF    Mar 1952
   NOVELETS OF SCIENCE FICTION [Howard - 1963]
Another World by J. H. Rosny Aine ps (Honore Boex)..................RP   n/d/a 1895
   A CENTURY OF SCIENCE FICTION [Knight - 1962]
      (Translated from French by Damon Knight)
Angela's Satyr by Brian Cleeve...............................SEP    11/3/62
   8th ANNUAL OF THE YEAR'S BEST SF [Merril - 1963]
*Angel's Egg by Edgar Pangborn................................Glxy   Jun 1951
   A CENTURY OF SCIENCE FICTION [Knight - 1962]
Apothem [untitled] — Anonymous..........................(No data available)
   THE MATHEMATICAL MAGPIE [Fadiman - 1962]
Apothem [untitled] by Lewis Caroll ps (Charles Lutwidge Dodgson)..............
   (From Alice's Adventures in Wonderland; 1866)
   THE MATHEMATICAL MAGPIE [Fadiman - 1962]

Apothem [untitled] by Winston Churchill......................(No data available)
    THE MATHEMATICAL MAGPIE [Fadiman - 1962]
Apothem [untitled] by Etienne Bonnot De Condillac...........(No data available)
    THE MATHEMATICAL MAGPIE [Fadiman - 1962]
Apothem [untitled] by Augustus De Morgan.....(From A Budget of Paradoxes; 1872)
    THE MATHEMATICAL MAGPIE [Fadiman - 1962]
Apothem [untitled] by Goethe................................(No data available)
    THE MATHEMATICAL MAGPIE [Fadiman - 1962]
Apothems (Four) [untitled] by Stanislaw Jerzy Lec..(Fr Unkmpt Thoughts; 1962)
    (Translated from Polish by Jack Galazka)
    THE MATHEMATICAL MAGPIE [Fadiman - 1962]
Apothems (Five) [untitled] by George Christopher Lichtenburg..................
    (From The Lichtenburg Reader-Edited by Franz H. Mautner & Henry Hatfield-1959)
    THE MATHEMATICAL MAGPIE [Fadiman - 1962]
Apothem [untitled] by J. B. Mencken....(From De Charlataneria Eruditorum; 1715)
    THE MATHEMATICAL MAGPIE [Fadiman - 1962]
Apothem [untitled] by Bill Mortlock...........(From Lawyer, Heal Thyself; 1959)
    THE MATHEMATICAL MAGPIE [Fadiman - 1962]
Apothem [untitled] by George Orwell ps (Eric Blair).....(From Animal Farm; 1945)
    THE MATHEMATICAL MAGPIE [Fadiman - 1962]
Apothems (Three) [untitled] by G. Polya...........(From How to Solve It; 1945)
    THE MATHEMATICAL MAGPIE [Fadiman - 1962]
Apothem [untitled] by Jules Renard...........(From Histoires Naturalles; n/d/a)
    THE MATHEMATICAL MAGPIE [Fadiman - 1962]
*Appendix and the Spectacles, The by Miles J. Breuer................Amz  Dec 1928
    THE MATHEMATICAL MAGPIE [Fadiman - 1962]
Appointment at Noon by Eric Frank Russell.........................Amz  Mar 1952
    FIFTY SHORT SCIENCE FICTION TALES [Asimov & Conklin - 1963]
Apprentice, The by James White....................................NW #99  Nov 1960
    OUT OF THIS WORLD 3 [Williams-Ellis & Owen - 1962]
*Ararat by Zeena Henderson.........................................F&SF  Oct 1952
    OUT OF THIS WORLD 3 [Williams-Ellis & Owen - 1962]
Armageddon by Fredric Brown.......................................UW  Aug 1941
    THE UNKNOWN [Benson - 1963]
Art Work by James Blish................................(See listing A Work of Art)
*As Easy as A.B.C. by Rudyard Kipling.............................LM  Mar 1912
    17 X INFINITY [Conklin - 1963]
Ask a Foolish Question by Robert Sheckley........................SFS #1  n/d 1953
    6 AND THE SILENT SCREAM [Howard - 1963]
*Asleep In Armageddon by Ray Bradbury.............................PS  Win 1948
    ASLEEP IN ARMAGEDDON [Sissons - 1962]
Asteroids, 2194, The by John Wyndham ps (John Beynon Harris)...Rpnt-Amz  Jan 1961
    (Originally aprd under title The Emptiness of Space; NW #100 November 1960)
    7th ANNUAL OF THE YEAR'S BEST SF [Merril - 1962]
Astronaut, The by Valentina Zhuravlyova.......................(No data available)
    DESTINATION: AMALTHEIA [Dixon - 1963]
        (Translated from Russian by Leonid Kolesnkov)
Asylum by Alice Bullock...........................................FSF  Aug 1954
    RARE SCIENCE FICTION [Howard - 1963]
At the Center of Gravity by Ross Rocklynne.......................ASF  Jan 1936
    EXPLORING OTHER WORLDS [Moskowitz - 1963]
At the End of the Orbit by Arthur C. Clarke.......................If  Nov 1961
    THE EXPERT DREAMERS [Pohl - 1962]
At the Perhilion by Robert Willey..........(See A Martian Adventure by Willy Ley)
*Available Data on the Worp Reaction, The by Lion Miller..........F&SF  Sep 1953
    FIFTY SHORT SCIENCE FICTION TALES [Asimov & Conklin - 1963]

|  | Mag. | Year |
|---|---|---|
| A-W-F Unlimited by Frank Herbert........................................Glxy | Glxy | Jun 1961 |

17 X INFINITY [Conklin - 1963]

**B**

B. C. by Johnny Hart..................(cartoon)....................NYHT  8/13/61
   THE MATHEMATICAL MAGPIE [Fadiman - 1962]
Babel II by Damon Knight.............................................Bynd  Jul 1953
   THE WORLDS OF SCIENCE FICTION [Mills - 1963]
*Bad Day for Sales, A by Fritz Leiber...............................Glxy  Jul 1953
   FIFTY SHORT SCIENCE FICTION TALES [Asimov & Conklin - 1963]
Ballade of an Artificial Satellite by Poul Anderson....(verse).....F&SF  Oct 1958
   FIFTY SHORT SCIENCE FICTION TALES [Asimov & Conklin - 1963]
Barnacle Bull by Winston P. Sanders.................................ASF  Sep 1960
   ANALOG I [J. W. Campbell - 1963]
*Barney by Will Stanton.............................................F&SF  Feb 1951
   FIFTY SHORT SCIENCE FICTION TALES [Asimov & Conklin - 1963]
Beat Cluster, The by Fritz Leiber...................................Glxy  Oct 1961
   7th ANNUAL OF THE YEAR'S BEST SF [Merril - 1962]
*Beautiful, Beautiful, Beautiful! by Stuart Friedman................Fut  Mar 1952
   FIFTY SHORT SCIENCE FICTION TALES [Asimov & Conklin - 1963]
Beautiful Brew, The by James E. Gunn...............................Bynd  Sep 1954
   BEYOND [Anonymous - 1963]
Bedside Manner by William Morrison ps (Joseph Samachson)...........Glxy  May 1954
   GREAT SCIENCE FICTION ABOUT DOCTORS [Conklin & Fabricant - 1963]
Being by Richard Matheson...........................................If  Aug 1954
   ASLEEP IN ARMAGEDDON [Sissons - 1962]
*Belief by Isaac Asimov.............................................ASF  Oct 1953
   PROLOGUE TO ANALOG [J. W. Campbell - 1962]
*Beyond Bedlam by Wyman Guin.......................................Glxy  Aug 1951
   SPECTRUM II [Amis & Conquest - 1962]
Big Front Yard, The by Clifford D. Simak...........................ASF  Oct 1958
   THE HUGO WINNERS [Asimov - 1962]
Big Man with the Girls, A by James MacCreigh ps (Frederik Pohl) & Judith Merril..
                                                                   FSF  Mar 1953
   ESCAPE TO EARTH [Howard - 1963]
Big Stink, The by Theodore R. Cogswell.............................If  Jul 1954
   HUMAN AND OTHER BEINGS [DeGraeff - 1963]
Black Cloud, The........................................(From The Black Cloud; 1957)
   THE EXPERT DREAMERS [Pohl - 1962]
*Black Destroyer by A. E. Van Vogt................................ASF  Jul 1939
   FIRST FLIGHT: Maiden Voyages in Space and Time [Knight - 1963]
Black Retriever, The by Charles G. Finney.........................F&SF  Oct 1958
   ROD SERLING'S TRIPLE W: WITCHES, WARLOCKS AND WEREWOLVES [Serling - 1963]
*Bleak Shore, The by Fritz Leiber.................................UW  Nov 1940
   HELL HATH FURY [Hay - 1963]
*Blind Alley by Isaac Asimov......................................ASF  Mar 1945
   GREAT STORIES OF SPACE TRAVEL [Conklin - 1963]
*Blind Alley by Malcolm Jameson...................................UW  Jun 1943
   ROD SERLING'S TRIPLE W: WITCHES, WARLOCKS AND WEREWOLVES [Serling - 1963]
Blood Lines by Alfred Coppel......................................DSF  Dec 1952
   WAY OUT [Howard - 1963]
Blunder Enlightening by Dave Dryfoos..............................DSF  Dec 1952
   WAY OUT [Howard - 1963]
Bolden's Pets by F. L. Wallace....................................Glxy  Oct 1955
   GREAT SCIENCE FICTION ABOUT DOCTORS [Conklin & Fabricant - 1963]

|  |  | Mag. | Year |
|---|---|---|---|
| Books by Anthony Boucher......................................(Special Original Feature) | | | |
|     7th ANNUAL OF THE YEAR'S BEST SF [Merril - 1962] | | | |
|     8th ANNUAL OF THE YEAR'S BEST SF [Merril - 1963] | | | |
| *Brain, The by W. Norbet ps (Dr. Norbett Weiner).....................TEN | | | Apr 1952 |

Books by Anthony Boucher......................................(Special Original Feature)
    7th ANNUAL OF THE YEAR'S BEST SF [Merril - 1962]
    8th ANNUAL OF THE YEAR'S BEST SF [Merril - 1963]
*Brain, The by W. Norbet ps (Dr. Norbett Weiner).....................TEN   Apr 1952
    GREAT SCIENCE FICTION BY SCIENTISTS [Conklin - 1962]
Bridge by James Blish...............................................ASF   Feb 1952
    SPECTRUM II [Amis & Conquest - 1962]
*Brooklyn Project by William Tenn ps (Philip Klass)..................PS    Fal 1948
    17 X INFINITY [Conklin - 1963]
Brothers, The by Clifton L. Dance, Jr. M. D. .......................F&SF   Jun 1952
    GREAT SCIENCE FICTION ABOUT DOCTORS [Conklin & Fabricant - 1963]
*Built Up Logically by Howard Schoenfeld           Retort   Win 1949
    (Originally appeared under title Built Down Logically)
    FIFTY SHORT SCIENCE FICTION TALES [Asimov & Conklin - 1963]
        (Appeared under title Built Down Logically)
    MORE PENGUIN SCIENCE FICTION [Aldiss - 1963]
Bullet With His Name by Fritz Leiber................................Glxy   Jul 1958
    WORLDS OF WHEN [Conklin - 1962]
Business as Usual, During Alterations by Ralph Williams.............ASF   Jul 1958
    PROLOGUE TO ANALOG [J. W. Campbell - 1962]
*Business, As Usual, The by Mack Reynolds...........................F&SF   Jun 1952
    A CENTURY OF SCIENCE FICTION [Knight - 1962]
    FIFTY SHORT SCIENCE FICTION TALES [Asimov & Conklin - 1963]
*But Who Can Replace a Man? by Brian Aldiss.........................Inf   Jun 1958
    A CENTURY OF SCIENCE FICTION [Knight - 1962]
By the Name of Man by John Brunner..................................Neb #17   Jul 1956
    MORE ADVENTURES ON OTHER PLANETS [Wollheim - 1963]

# C

*Cabin Boy by Damon Knight..........................................Glxy   Sep 1951
    GREAT STORIES OF SPACE TRAVEL [Conklin - 1963]
*Cage, The by A. Bertram Chandler...................................F&SF   Jun 1957
    12 GREAT CLASSICS OF SCIENCE FICTION. [Conklin - 1963]
*Call Me Joe by Poul Anderson.......................................ASF   Apr 1957
    A CENTURY OF SCIENCE FICTION [Knight - 1962]
    SPECTRUM III [Amis & Conquest - 1963]
Camouflage by Henry Kuttner.........................................ASF   Sep 1945
    (Originally appeared under pseudonym Lewis Padgett)
    ASLEEP IN ARMAGEDDON [Sissons - 1962]
Can Such Beauty Be? by Jerome Bixby.................................Bynd   Sep 1953
    BEYOND [Anonymous - 1963]
Cartoon [untitled] by Abner Dean..............(From What Am I Doing Here?; 1947)
    THE MATHEMATICAL MAGPIE [Fadiman - 1962]
Cartoon [untitled] by Leo Demare.......................Man's Magazine n/d/a 1958
    THE MATHEMATICAL MAGPIE [Fadiman - 1962]
Cartoon [untitled] by Alan Dunn.....................................SRL   3/12/55
    THE MATHEMATICAL MAGPIE [Fadiman - 1962]
Cartoon [untitled] by James Frankfort...............................Vlg   10/12/61
    THE MATHEMATICAL MAGPIE [Fadiman - 1962]
Cartoon [untitled] by Alfred Frueh..................................Nykr   4/19/58
    THE MATHEMATICAL MAGPIE [Fadiman - 1962]
Cartoon [untitled] by Peter Paul Porges.............................ALM   Jul 1955
    THE MATHEMATICAL MAGPIE [Fadiman - 1962]
Cartoon by Saul Steinberg (Tld Alligator Walking Line)(From The Labyrinth; 1960)
    THE MATHEMATICAL MAGPIE [Fadiman - 1962]
Cartoon by Saul Steinberg (Titled Man in Cube)..................... Nykr   9/10/60
    THE MATHEMATICAL MAGPIE [Fadiman - 1962]

|  |  | Mag. | Year |
|---|---|---|---|
| Cartoon by Saul Steinberg   (Titled Question Mark on a Seesaw) |  | Nykr | 7/23/60 |
| THE MATHEMATICAL MAGPIE [Fadiman - 1962] |  |  |  |
| Cato The Martian by Howard Fast............................... | F&SF | Jun 1960 |
| 17 X INFINITY [Conklin - 1963] |  |  |
| Cease Fire by Frank Herbert.................................. | ASF | Jan 1958 |
| A CENTURY OF SCIENCE FICTION [Knight - 1962] |  |  |
| Chain Reaction by Boyd Ellanby ps (Lyle G. & William C. Boyd)......Glxy | Sep 1956 |
| THE EXPERT DREAMERS [Pohl - 1962] |  |  |
| Change of Heart by George Whitley ps (A. Bertram Chandler).........Fnt | May 1962 |
| 8th ANNUAL OF THE YEAR'S BEST SF [Merril - 1963] |  |  |
| *Chapter Ends, The by Poul Anderson................................DSF | Jan 1954 |
| NOVELETS OF SCIENCE FICTION [Howard - 1963] |  |  |
| *Chemical Plant by Ian Williamson.................................NW #8 | Dec 1950 |
| CONTACT [Keyes - 1963] |  |  |
| Chestnut Beads, The by Jane Roberts.............................F&SF | Oct 1957 |
| ROD SERLING'S TRIPLE W: WITCHES, WARLOCKS AND WEREWOLVES [Serling - 1963] |  |  |
| Child of the Sun by Leigh Brackett...............................PS | Spr 1942 |
| MORE ADVENTURES ON OTHER PLANETS [Wollheim - 1963] |  |  |
| Children of Fortune by D. A. Jourdan............................SFQ | Feb 1957 |
| 6 AND THE SILENT SCREAM [Howard - 1963] |  |  |
| *Choice, The by W. Hilton-Young...................................Pch | 3/19/52 |
| FIFTY SHORT SCIENCE FICTION TALES [Asimov & Conklin - 1963] |  |  |
| Christmas Treason by James White................................F&SF | Jan 1962 |
| 8th ANNUAL OF THE YEAR'S BEST SF [Merril - 1963] |  |  |
| Circuit Riders, The by R. C. FitzPatrick........................ASF | Apr 1962 |
| 8th ANNUAL OF THE YEAR'S BEST SF [Merril - 1963] |  |  |
| Cloak, The by Robert Bloch......................................UW | May 1939 |
| HELL HATH FURY [Hay - 1963] |  |  |
| Coconuts by Bem Ames Williams...................................SEP | 10/9/26 |
| THE MATHEMATICAL MAGPIE [Fadiman - 1962] |  |  |
| *Columbus Was a Dope by Robert A. Heinlein.......................Stg | May 1947 |
| FIFTY SHORT SCIENCE FICTION TALES [Asimov & Conklin - 1963] |  |  |
| Come Into My Cellar by Ray Bradbury.............................Glxy | Oct 1962 |
| 17 X INFINITY [Conklin - 1963] |  |  |
| *Compound B by David Harold Fink, M. D. ........................... |  |  |
| (From NEW TALES OF SPACE AND TIME; Raymond J. Healy - 1954) |  |  |
| GREAT SCIENCE FICTION ABOUT DOCTORS [Conklin & Fabricant - 1963] |  |  |
| Consider Her Ways by John Wyndham ps (John Beynon Harris)...................... |  |  |
| (From Sometime Never; 1956) |  |  |
| BEST SF FIVE SCIENCE FICTION STORIES [Crispin - 1963] |  |  |
| Countdown, The by John Hasse...................................Nykr | 10/7/61 |
| 7th ANNUAL OF THE YEAR'S BEST SF [Merril - 1962] |  |  |
| *Counter Charm by Peter Phillips.................................Slnt | Spr 1951 |
| FIFTY SHORT SCIENCE FICTION TALES [Asimov & Conklin - 1963] |  |  |
| Counterfeit by Alan E. Nourse...................................TWS | Aug 1952 |
| MORE PENGUIN SCIENCE FICTION [Aldiss - 1963] |  |  |
| Cricket Ball, The by Avro Manhattan............................F&SF | Oct 1955 |
| FIFTY SHORT SCIENCE FICTION TALES [Asimov & Conklin - 1963] |  |  |
| *Crucifixus Etiam by Walter M. Miller, Jr. ......................ASF | Feb 1953 |
| ASLEEP IN ARMAGEDDON [Sissons - 1962] |  |  |
| *Crystal Egg, The by H. G. Wells.................................NR | May 1897 |
| A CENTURY OF SCIENCE FICTION [Knight - 1962] |  |  |
| Culver City Arithmetic Exercise Paper - Anonymous.................Nykr | 2/25/61 |
| THE MATHEMATICAL MAGPIE [Fadiman - 1962] |  |  |

|  |  | Mag. | Year |
| Cupid With an Adding Machine by Charles D. Rice | ................... | TW | 9/18/60 |

THE MATHEMATICAL MAGPIE [Fadiman - 1962]

**D**

Dandelion Girl, The by Robert F. Young.................................SEP    4/1/61
   7th ANNUAL OF THE YEAR'S BEST SF [Merril - 1962]
Darfsteller, The by Walter M. Miller, Jr. ..........................ASF   Jan 1955
   THE HUGO WINNERS [Asimov - 1962]
*Dark Interlude by Fredric Brown and Mack Reynolds.................Glxy   Jan 1951
   HUMAN AND OTHER BEINGS [DeGraeff - 1963]
   D
   a
*Baxbr by Evelyn E. Smith...............(From Time To Come; August Derleth-1954)
   b
   r
   OUT OF THIS WORLD 3 [Williams-Ellis & Owen - 1962]
Day of Succession by Theodore L. Thomas............................ASF   Aug 1959
   A CENTURY OF SCIENCE FICTION [Knight - 1962]
Day Rembrandt Went Public, The by Arnold M. Auerbach...............Hpr   Jul 1962
   8th ANNUAL OF THE YEAR'S BEST SF [Merril - 1963]
Day They Got Boston, The by Herbert Gold..........................F&SF   Sep 1961
   17 X INFINITY [Conklin - 1963]
*Dead Planet, The by Edmond Hamilton...............................Stg   Spr 1946
   EXPLORING OTHER WORLDS [Moskowitz - 1963]
Deadly Game by Edward Wellen........................................If   May 1962
   8th ANNUAL OF THE YEAR'S BEST SF [Merril - 1963]
Death and the Senator by Arthur C. Clarke..........................ASF   May 1961
   WORLDS OF WHEN [Conklin - 1962]
Derelict by Raymond Z. Gallun......................................ASF   Oct 1935
   THE COMING OF THE ROBOTS [Moskowitz - 1963]
Destination: Amaltheia by Arkady and Boris Strugatsky.........(No data available)
   DESTINATION: AMALTHEIA [Dixon - 1963]
      (Translated from Russian by Leonid Kolesnikov)
Devil a Mathematician Would Be, The by A. J. Lohwater.........(No data available)
   THE MATHEMATICAL MAGPIE [Fadiman - 1962]
Devil's Rescue, The by L. Ron Hubbard..............................UW   Oct 1940
   HELL HATH FURY [Hay - 1963]
Do It Yourself by Milton Lesser..................................FSF #33   Sum 1957
   RARE SCIENCE FICTION [Howard - 1963]
Doomsday's Color-Press by Raymond F. Jones.........................FSF   Nov 1952
   ESCAPE TO EARTH [Howard - 1963]
Double and Redoubled by Malcolm Jameson............................UW   Feb 1941
   THE UNKNOWN [Benson - 1963]
Double Dome by Raymond E. Banks...................................Glxy   May 1957
   HUMAN AND OTHER BEINGS [DeGraeff - 1963]
Double-Take by Winston K. Marks...................................SFAd   Dec 1953
   (Originally appeared under pseudonym Ken Winney)
   FIFTY SHORT SCIENCE FICTION TALES [Asimov & Conklin - 1963]
Double Whammy by Fredric Brown....................................Bynd   Sep 1954
   BEYOND [Anonymous - 1963]
Down Among the Dead Men by William Tenn ps (Philip Klass).........Glxy   Jun 1954
   HUMAN AND OTHER BEINGS [DeGraeff - 1963]
*Dreams Are Sacred by Peter Phillips...............................ASF   Sep 1948
   SPECTRUM III [Amis & Conquest - 1963]
Due Process by Algis Budrys........................................ASF   Dec 1960
   12 GREAT CLASSICS OF SCIENCE FICTION [Conklin - 1963]

*Dumb Martian by John Wyndham ps (John Beynon Harris)..............Glxy  Jul 1952
     OUT OF THIS WORLD 3 [Williams-Ellis & Owen - 1962]
Dunciad, The (An Heroic Poem in 3 books) by Alexander Pope.......(Excerpts)......
                                                                  DP   5/18/1728
     THE MATHEMATICAL MAGPIE [Fadiman - 1962]

# E

E = MC$^2$ by Morris Bishop...........(verse).........(From A Bowl of Bishop; 1954 )
     THE MATHEMATICAL MAGPIE [Fadiman - 1962]
Ear-Friend by R. E. Banks....................................................SFS  Mar 1955
     6 AND THE SILENT SCREAM [Howard - 1963]
Earth for Inspiration by Clifford D. Simak...........................TWS  Apr 1941
     THE COMING OF THE ROBOTS [Moskowitz - 1963]
Earthlings Go Home! by Mack Reynolds.................................Rog  Aug 1962
     8th ANNUAL OF THE YEAR'S BEST SF [Merril - 1963]
Earthman Bearing Gifts by Fredric Brown.............................Glxy  Jun 1960
     12 GREAT CLASSICS OF SCIENCE FICTION [Conklin - 1963]
*Egg a Month From all Over, An by Idris Seabright ps (Margaret St. Clair)
                                                                  F&SF  Oct 1952
     FIFTY SHORT SCIENCE FICTION TALES [Asimov & Conklin - 1963]
Einstein: A Parody in the Manner of Edw-n Markh-m by Louis Untermeyer...(verse)..
     (From Collected Parodies; 1926)
     THE MATHEMATICAL MAGPIE [Fadiman - 1962]
*Emergency Landing by Ralph Williams................................ASF  Jul 1940
     FIFTY SHORT SCIENCE FICTION TALES [Asimov & Conklin - 1963]
Emergency Operation by Arthur Porges................................F&SF  May 1956
     GREAT SCIENCE FICTION ABOUT DOCTORS [Conklin & Fabricant - 1963]
Emptiness of Space, The by John Wyndham.........(See listing The Asteroids; 2194)
*Enchanted Village by A. E. Van Vogt...............................OW  Jul 1950
     ASLEEP IN ARMAGEDDON [Sissons - 1962]
Engineer's Yell — Anonymous...............(verse)
     THE MATHEMATICAL MAGPIE [Fadiman - 1962]
Ennui by Milton Lesser.............................................DSF  Dec 1952
     WAY OUT [Howard - 1963]
Escape to Earth by Manly Banister..................................SFQ  Nov 1957
     ESCAPE TO EARTH [Howard - 1963]
Esidarap Ot Pirt Dnuor by Lloyd Biggle, Jr...(See listing Round Trip To Esidarap)
Ether Breather by Theodore Sturgeon................................ASF  Sep 1939
     FIRST FLIGHT: Maiden Voyages in Space and Time [Knight - 1963]
Euclid and the Bright Boy by J.L. Synge....(From Science: Sense & Nonsense; 1951)
     THE MATHEMATICAL MAGPIE [Fadiman - 1962]
Euler, Diderot, Algebra, and God by Augustus de Morgan......................
     (From A Budget of Paradoxes; 1872)
     THE MATHEMATICAL MAGPIE [Fadiman - 1962]
*Evening Primrose by John Collier..............(From Presenting Moonshine; 1941)
     THE WORLDS OF SCIENCE FICTION [Mills - 1963]
Everybody's Happy But Me by Frederik Pohl...................................
     (See listing What To Do Until the Analyst Comes)
Exercise in Style: Mathematical, An by Raymond Queneau.....................
     (From Exercises In Style; 1958)
          (Translated from French by Barbara Wright)
     THE MATHEMATICAL MAGPIE [Fadiman - 1962]
Expedition Mercy by J. A. Winter, M. D. ...........................ASF  Nov 1948
     GREAT SCIENCE FICTION ABOUT DOCTORS [Conklin & Fabricant - 1963]

Exploration Team by Murray Leinster ps (Will F. Jenkins)............ASF  Mar 1956
    THE HUGO WINNERS [Asimov - 1962]
    SPECTRUM III [Amis & Conquest - 1963]
Extinction by Subtraction by W. W. R. Ball
    THE MATHEMATICAL MAGPIE [Fadiman - 1962]
Extra Bricklayer, The by A. M. Phillips..............................UW  Sep 1940
    HELL HATH FURY [Hay - 1963]
Extraterrestrial Trilogue on Terran Self-Destruction by Sheri S. Eberhart........
                  (verse)               Glxy  Aug 1961
    7th ANNUAL OF THE YEAR'S BEST SF [Merril - 1962]

# F

Face in the Photo, The by Jack Finney.............................................
    (From I Love Galesburg in the Springtime; 1962)
    8th ANNUAL OF THE YEAR'S BEST SF [Merril - 1963]
*Facts in the Case of M. Valdemar, The by Edgar Allen Poe...........AWR  Dec 1845
    GREAT SCIENCE FICTION ABOUT DOCTORS [Conklin & Fabricant - 1963]
Faithful, The by Lester del Rey.....................................ASF  Apr 1938
    FIRST FLIGHT: Maiden Voyages in Space and Time [Knight - 1963]
*Family Resemblance by Alan E. Nourse, M. D. ......................ASF  Apr 1953
    GREAT SCIENCE FICTION ABOUT DOCTORS [Conklin & Fabricant - 1963]
Faq by George P. Elliott............................................HdR  Spr 1952
    THE WORLDS OF SCIENCE FICTION [Mills - 1963]
*Far Centaurus by A. E. Van Vogt....................................ASF  Jan 1944
    GREAT STORIES OF SPACE TRAVEL [Conklin - 1963]
Farmer by Mack Reynolds............................................Glxy  Jun 1961
    WORLDS OF WHEN [Conklin - 1962]
Fastest Gun Dead, The by Julian F. Grow............................If  Mar 1961
    7th ANNUAL OF THE YEAR'S BEST SF [Merril - 1962]
*Feast of Demons, A by William Morrison ps (Joseph Samachson)......Glxy  Mar 1958
    THE EXPERT DREAMERS [Pohl - 1962]
Feeling of Power, The by Isaac Asimov..............................If  Feb 1958
    THE MATHEMATICAL MAGPIE [Fadiman - 1962]
    SPECTRUM II [Amis & Conquest - 1962]
*Figure, The by Edward Grendon......................................ASF  Jul 1947
    FIFTY SHORT SCIENCE FICTION TALES [Asimov & Conklin - 1963]
Filbert is a Nut, A by Rick Raphael.................................ASF  Nov 1959
    PROLOGUE TO ANALOG [J. W. Campbell - 1962]
Final Ingredient, The by Jack Sharkey..............................F&SF  Aug 1960
    ROD SERLING'S TRIPLE W: WITCHES, WARLOCKS AND WEREWOLVES [Serling - 1963]
*Fire Balloons, The by Ray Bradbury.................................Im  Apr 1951
    (Originally appeared under title "In This Sign...")
    CONTACT [Keyes - 1963]
*First Contact by Murray Leinster ps (Will F. Jenkins).............ASF  May 1945
    CONTACT [Keyes - 1963]
First Days of May, The by Claude Veillot...........................Fctn  May 1960
    A CENTURY OF SCIENCE FICTION [Knight - 1962]
First Men, The by Howard Fast......................................F&SF  Feb 1960
    THE WORLDS OF SCIENCE FICTION [Mills - 1963]
    MORE PENGUIN SCIENCE FICTION [Aldiss - 1963]
*Flowers For Algernon by Daniel Keyes..............................F&SF  Apr 1959
    THE HUGO WINNERS [Asimov - 1962]
*Fly, The by Arthur Porges.........................................F&SF  Sep 1952
    FIFTY SHORT SCIENCE FICTION TALES [Asimov & Conklin - 1963]

Mag.   Year

Flying-Flowers by Mikhail Vasilyev............................(No data available)
     DESTINATION: AMALTHEIA [Dixon - 1963]
          (Translated from Russian by Leonid Kolesnikov)
*Fondly Fahrenheit by Alfred Bester...........................F&SF   Aug 1954
     SPECTRUM III [Amis & Conquest - 1963]
*Forgotten Enemy, The by Arthur C. Clarke.....................NW #5  n/d 1949
     MORE PENGUIN SCIENCE FICTION [Aldiss - 1963]
Frances Harkins by Richard Goggin.............................F&SF   Dec 1952
     17 X INFINITY [Conklin - 1963]
Freedom by Mack Reynolds......................................ASF    Feb 1961
     7th ANNUAL OF THE YEAR'S BEST SF [Merril - 1962]
Frog, The by P. Schuyler Miller...............................UW     Oct 1942
     HELL HATH FURY [Hay - 1963]
From The London Times of 1904 by Mark Twain ps (Samuel L. Clemens)..Cny  Nov 1898
     A CENTURY OF SCIENCE FICTION [Knight - 1962]
*Fun They Had, The by Isaac Asimov............................NEA    12/1/51
     FIFTY SHORT SCIENCE FICTION TALES [Asimov & Conklin - 1963]
* F Y I by James Blish.....(From STAR SCIENCE FICTION STORIES #2; F. Pohl - 1953)
     THE MATHEMATICAL MAGPIE [Fadiman - 1962]

*G*

Galactic Chest by Clifford D. Simak...........................OSFS   Sep 1956
     THREE IN ONE [Margulies - 1963]
*Galley Slave by Isaac Asimov.................................Glxy   Dec 1957
     TIME WAITS FOR WINTHROP AND FOUR OTHER SHORT NOVELS FROM GALAXY [Pohl-1962]
Garden in the Void by Poul Anderson...........................Glxy   May 1952
     EXPLORING OTHER WORLDS [Moskowitz - 1963]
Garden of Time, The by J. G. Ballard..........................F&SF   Feb 1962
     THE BEST FROM FANTASY & SCIENCE FICTION: 12th SERIES [Davidson - 1963]
Gentle Vultures, The by Isaac Asimov..........................SSF    Dec 1957
     CONTACT [Keyes - 1963]
Geometrical Disappearance of Dino, The by Raymond Queneau.......................
     (From Exercises in Style; 1958)      (Translated from French by Barbara Wright)
     THE MATHEMATICAL MAGPIE [Fadiman - 1962]
Geometry by Wm. Wordsworth..(From The Prelude; or Growth of a Poet's Mind;  1805)
     THE MATHEMATICAL MAGPIE [Fadiman - 1962]
Ghost Maker, The by Frederik Pohl.............................Bynd   Jan 1954
     BEYOND [Anonymous - 1963]
*Gnarly Man, The by L. Sprague de Camp........................UW     Jun 1939
     THE UNKNOWN [Benson - 1963]
Gold Makers, The by J. B. S. Haldane...........(From The Inequality of Man; 1932)
     GREAT SCIENCE FICTION BY SCIENTISTS [Conklin - 1962]
Golden Horn, The by Edgar Pangborn............................F&SF   Feb 1962
     THE BEST FROM FANTASY & SCIENCE FICTION: 12th SERIES [Davidson - 1963]
Golub-Yavan by Kirill Stanyukovich............................(No data available)
     DESTINATION: AMALTHEIA [Dixon - 1963]
          (Translated from Russian by Leonid Kolesnikov)
*Good Provider, The by Marion Gross...........................F&SF   Sep 1952
     FIFTY SHORT SCIENCE FICTION TALES [Asimov & Conklin - 1963]
*Gostak and the Doshes, The by Miles J. Breuer, M. D. ........Amz    Mar 1930
     GREAT SCIENCE FICTION BY SCIENTISTS [Conklin - 1962]
Great Judge, The by A. E. Van Vogt............................FB #3  n/d 1948
     FIFTY SHORT SCIENCE FICTION TALES [Asimov & Conklin - 1963]
*Great Keinplatz Experiment, The by Arthur Conan Doyle.........................
     (Originally published by Rand McNally; 1895)
     GREAT SCIENCE FICTION ABOUT DOCTORS [Conklin & Fabricant - 1963]

|  | Mag. | Year |
|---|---|---|

Greater Thing, The by Tom Godwin.......................................ASF Feb 1954
    MORE PENGUIN SCIENCE FICTION [Aldiss - 1963]
Green Thumb by Clifford D. Simak............................Glxy Jul 1954
    BEST SF FIVE SCIENCE FICTION STORIES [Crispin - 1963]
Gumdrop King, The by Will Stanton......................................F&SF Aug 1962
    THE BEST FROM FANTASY & SCIENCE FICTION: 12th SERIES [Davidson - 1963]

# H

Hail to the Chief by Sam Sackett.......................................FSF Jun 1954
    THE WEIRD ONES [Howard - 1962]
Hang, Head, Vandal by Mark Clifton.....................................Amz Apr 1962
    8th ANNUAL OF THE YEAR'S BEST SF [Merril - 1963]
Hatchery of Dreams by Fritz Leiber.....................................Fnt Nov 1961
    ROD SERLING'S TRIPLE W: WITCHES, WARLOCKS AND WEREWOLVES [Serling - 1963]
Haunted Space Suit, The by Arthur C. Clarke............................TW 5/11/58
    FIFTY SHORT SCIENCE FICTION TALES [Asimov & Conklin - 1963]
Heart of the Serpent, The by Ivan Yefremov....................(No data available)

    THE HEART OF THE SERPENT [Anonymous - 1961]
      (Translated from Russian by R. Prokofieva)
Heart on the Other Side, The by George Gamow......................ORIGINAL STORY
    THE EXPERT DREAMERS [Pohl - 1962]
*Heavy Planet by Lee Gregor ps (Milton A. Rothman)...................Ast Aug 1939
    THE EXPERT DREAMERS [Pohl - 1962]
*Helen O'Loy by Lester del Rey.........................................ASF Dec 1938
    THE COMING OF THE ROBOTS [Moskowitz - 1963]
Hell-Bound Train, The by Robert Bloch..................................F&SF Sep 1958
    THE HUGO WINNERS [Asimov - 1962]
Hell Hath Fury by Cleve Cartmill.......................................UW Aug 1942
    HELL HATH FURY [Hay - 1963]
*Helping Hand, The by Poul Anderson....................................ASF May 1950
    GREAT STORIES OF SPACE TRAVEL [Conklin - 1963]
Hermeneutical Doughnut, The by H. Nearing, Jr. .......................
    (From The Sinister Researches of C. P. Ransom; 1954)
    THE MATHEMATICAL MAGPIE [Fadiman - 1962]
High Barbary by Lawrence Durrell.......................................Mdm Sep 1961
    7th ANNUAL OF THE YEAR'S BEST SF [Merril - 1962]
*Hilda by H. B. Hickey ps (Herb Livingston).......................F&SF Sep 1952
    FIFTY SHORT SCIENCE FICTION TALES [Asimov & Conklin - 1963]
Hoity-Toity by Alexander Belayev...........................(No data available)
    A VISITOR FROM OUTER SPACE [Anonymous - undated]
      (Translated from Russian by Violet L. Dutt)
Holdout by Robert Sheckley.............................................F&SF Dec 1957
    HUMAN AND OTHER BEINGS [DeGraeff - 1963]
*Holes Around Mars, The by Jerome Bixby................................Glxy Jan 1954
    GREAT STORIES OF SPACE TRAVEL [Conklin - 1963]
Home From the Shore by Gordon R. Dickson..............................Glxy Feb 1963
    8th ANNUAL OF THE YEAR'S BEST SF [Merril - 1963]
Home There's No Returning by C. L. Moore...............(From No Boundaries; 1955)
    (Originally appeared under joint byline Henry Kuttner & C. L. Moore)
    ASLEEP IN ARMAGEDDON [Sissons - 1962]
Honor by Richard Wilson................................................SFQ Feb 1956
    HUMAN AND OTHER BEINGS [DeGraeff - 1963]
Honorable Enemies by Poul Anderson....................................Fw/SFS May 1951
    WAY OUT [Howard - 1963]

Mag.    Year

Hop-Friend by Terry Carr.............................................F&SF  Nov 1962
    THE BEST FROM FANTASY & SCIENCE FICTION: 12th SERIES [Davidson - 1963]
Hottest Piece of Real Estate in the Solar System, The by Arthur C. Clarke........
    (See listing Summertime In Icarus)
Human Man's Burden by Robert Sheckley...............................Glxy  Sep 1956
    12 GREAT CLASSICS OF SCIENCE FICTION [Conklin - 1963]
Hunch, The by Christopher Anvil....................................ASF  Jul 1961
    ANALOG I [J. W. Campbell - 1963]
Hunt the Space Witch by Robert Silverberg.........................SFAd  Jan 1958
    (Originally appeared under pseudonym Ivar Jorgenson)
    GREAT SCIENCE FICTION ADVENTURES [Shaw - 1963]
Hunted Ones, The by Mack Reynolds.................................SFS  Nov 1959
    THE WEIRD ONES [Howard - 1962]
Hunters, The by Walt Sheldon...... .................................Stg  Mar 1952
    FIFTY SHORT SCIENCE FICTION TALES [Asimov & Conklin - 1963]

# I

I Am Tomorrow by Lester del Rey.....................................DSF  Dec 1952
    NOVELETS OF SCIENCE FICTION [Howard - 1963]
I, Robot by Eando Binder ps (Otto Binder)...........................Amz  Jan 1939
    THE COMING OF THE ROBOTS [Moskowitz - 1963]
I'd Give a Dollar by Winston Marks.................................Bynd  May 1954
    BEYOND [Anonymous - 1963]
Ideal, The by Stanley G. Weinbaum............(Excerpts)..............WS  Sep 1935
    A CENTURY OF SCIENCE FICTION [Knight - 1962]
"If The Court Pleases? by Noel Loomis..............................DSF  Jun 1953
    ESCAPE TO EARTH [Howard - 1963]
I'll Build Your Dream Castle by Jack Vance.........................ASF  Sep 1947
    GREAT STORIES OF SPACE TRAVEL [Conklin - 1963]
Immediately Yours by Robert Beverly Hale..........................Mdm  Nov 1961
    7th ANNUAL OF THE YEAR'S BEST SF [Merril - 1962]
Immortality...For Some by J.T. McIntosh ps (James J. MacGregor).....ASF  Mar 1960
    12 GREAT CLASSICS OF SCIENCE FICTION [Conklin - 1963]
Impractical Joke by L. Sprague de Camp........................ FSF #29  n/d 1956
    THE WEIRD ONES [Howard - 1963]
In Human Hands by Algis Budrys.................................SFS #2  n/d 1954
    RARE SCIENCE FICTION [Howard - 1963]
"In This Sign..." by Ray Bradbury.................(See listing The Fire Balloons)
In Tomorrow's Little Black Bag by James Blish....................ORIGINAL STORY
    7th ANNUAL OF THE YEAR'S BEST SF [Merril - 1962]
Infra Draconis by Georgy Gurevish.....................(No data available)
    A VISITOR FROM OUTER SPACE [Anonymous - undated]
    (Translated from Russian by Violet L. Dutt)
Insane Ones, The by J. G. Ballard...................................Amz  Jan 1962
    8th ANNUAL OF THE YEAR'S BEST SF [Merril - 1963]
Intelligence Test by Howard Fast....................................SF+  Jun 1953
    CONTACT [Keyes - 1963]
*Invasion From Mars by Howard Koch........(The radio script of the Orson Welles
    broadcast of H. G. Wells' "The War of the Worlds" over the Columbia broad-
    casting System; October 30, 1938)    (Copyright 1940: Princeton Univ. Press)
    CONTACT [Keyes - 1963]

|  |  | Mag. | Year |
|---|---|---|---|
| Invasion, The by Robert Willey ps (Willy Ley) | | Sup | Sep 1940 |
| THE EXPERT DREAMERS [Pohl - 1962] | | | |
| Iron Man by Eando Binder | | FSF #28 | n/d 1955 |
| THE WEIRD ONES [Howard - 1962] | | | |
| Isolinguals, The by L. Sprague de Camp | | ASF | Sep 1937 |
| FIRST FLIGHT: Maiden Voyages in Space and Time [Knight - 1963] | | | |
| It Becomes Necessary by Ward Moore | | Gent | n/d/a 1961 |
| (Originally appeared under title The Cold Peace) | | | |
| 7th ANNUAL OF THE YEAR'S BEST SF [Merril - 1962] | | | |

## J

| John Sze's Future by John R. Pierce | | ORIGINAL STORY | |
| GREAT SCIENCE FICTION BY SCIENTISTS [Conklin - 1962] | | | |
| Join Our Gang? by Sterling E. Lanier | | ASF | May 1961 |
| ANALOG I [J. W. Campbell - 1963] | | | |
| Jokester by Isaac Asimov | | Inf | Dec 1956 |
| MORE PENGUIN SCIENCE FICTION [Aldiss - 1963] | | | |
| Judas Bomb by Kit Reed | | F&SF | Apr 1961 |
| 7th ANNUAL OF THE YEAR'S BEST SF [Merril - 1962] | | | |

## K

| *Kaleidoscope by Ray Bradbury | | TWS | Oct 1949 |
| GREAT STORIES OF SPACE TRAVEL [Conklin - 1963] | | | |
| Kid Anderson by Robert E. Richardson | | Spc | Spr 1956 |
| (Originally appeared under pseudonym Phillip Latham) | | | |
| GREAT SCIENCE FICTION BY SCIENTISTS [Conklin - 1962] | | | |
| *Killdozer! by Theodore Sturgeon | | ASF | Nov 1944 |
| SPECTRUM III [Amis & Conquest - 1963] | | | |
| Kind of Artistry, A by Brian W. Aldiss | | F&SF | Oct 1962 |
| THE BEST FROM FANTASY & SCIENCE FICTION: 12th SERIES [Davidson - 1963] | | | |
| Kings Who Die by Poul Anderson | | If | Mar 1962 |
| 8th ANNUAL OF THE YEAR'S BEST SF [Merril - 1963] | | | |
| Kiss Precise, The by Frederick Soddy..,........(verse) | | Ntr | 6/20/36 |
| THE MATHEMATICAL MAGPIE [Fadiman - 1962] | | | |
| Kiss Precise, The (Generalized) by Thorold Gosset....(verse) | | Ntr | 1/9/37 |
| THE MATHEMATICAL MAGPIE [Fadiman - 1962] | | | |
| *Knock by Fredric Brown | | TWS | Dec 1948 |
| CONTACT [Keyes - 1963] | | | |
| Knowledge Is Power by H. B. Fyfe | | DSF | Dec 1952 |
| WAY OUT [Howard - 1963] | | | |

## L

| Landscape with Sphinxes by Karen Anderson | | F&SF | Nov 1962 |
| THE BEST FROM FANTASY & SCIENCE FICTION: 12th SERIES [Davidson - 1963] | | | |
| *Large Ant, The by Howard Fast | | FU | Feb 1960 |
| CONTACT [Keyes - 1963] | | | |
| Last of the Spode, The Evelyn Smith | | F&SF | Jun 1953 |
| 17 X INFINITY [Conklin - 1963] | | | |
| Last Year's Grave Undug by Chan Davis | | ORIGINAL STORY | |
| GREAT SCIENCE FICTION BY SCIENTISTS [Conklin - 1962] | | | |

                                                          Mag.     Year
Lastborn by Isaac Asimov.......................(See listing The Ugly Little Boy)
*Later Than You Think by Fritz Leiber.............................Glxy   Oct 1950
    BEST SF FIVE SCIENCE FICTION STORIES [Crispin - 1963]
Law, The by Robert M. Coates......................................Nykr  11/29/47
    THE MATHEMATICAL MAGPIE [Fadiman - 1962]
Learning Theory by James McConnell................................If    Dec 1957
    GREAT SCIENCE FICTION BY SCIENTISTS [Conklin - 1962]
Lenny by Isaac Asimov.............................................Inf   Jan 1958
    THE EXPERT DREAMERS [Pohl - 1962]
Leprechaun by William Sambrot.....................................Escp n/d/a 1962
    8th ANNUAL OF THE YEAR'S BEST SF [Merril - 1963]
Let's Have Fun by L. Sprague de Camp..............................SFQ   May 1957
    RARE SCIENCE FICTION [Howard - 1963]
Liberation of Earth, The by William Tenn ps (Philip Klass)........FSF   May 1953
    MORE PENGUIN SCIENCE FICTION [Aldiss - 1963]
Life-Line by Robert A. Heinlein...................................ASF   Aug 1939
    FIRST FLIGHT: Maiden Voyages in Space and Time [Knight - 1963]
*Limiting Factor by Theodore R. Cogswell..........................Glxy  Apr 1954
    CONTACT [Keyes - 1963]
*Little Black Bag, The by C. M. Kornbluth.........................ASF   Jul 1950
    GREAT SCIENCE FICTION ABOUT DOCTORS [Conklin & Fabricant - 1963]
Living Space by Isaac Asimov......................................SFS   May 1956
    OUT OF THIS WORLD 3 [Williams-Ellis & Owen - 1962]
Long Night, The by Ray Russell....................................Rog   Apr 1961
    7th ANNUAL OF THE YEAR'S BEST SF [Merril - 1962]
Longest Voyage, The by Poul Anderson..............................ASF   Dec 1960
    THE HUGO WINNERS [Asimov - 1962]
Looking Backward by Jules Feiffer..........(cartoon)..............HS    12/10/61
    7th ANNUAL OF THE YEAR'S BEST SF [Merril - 1962]
*Loophole by Arthur C. Clarke.....................................ASF   Apr 1946
    FIRST FLIGHT: Maiden Voyages in Space and Time [Knight - 1963]
Lost Machine, The by John Wyndham ps (John Beynon Harris)..........Amz  Apr 1932
    (Originally appeared under byline John Beynon Harris)
    THE COMING OF THE ROBOTS [Moskowitz - 1963]
*Lost Memory by Peter Phillips....................................Glxy  May 1952
    THE COMING OF THE ROBOTS [Moskowitz - 1963]
    CONTACT [Keyes - 1963]
*Love by Richard Wilson...........................................F&SF  Jun 1952
    HUMAN AND OTHER BEINGS [DeGraeff - 1963]
Loves of the Triangles, The by John Hookham and George Canning....................
    (From The Anti-Jacobin, or Weekly Examiner; 1798)
    THE MATHEMATICAL MAGPIE [Fadiman - 1962]
Luck, Inc. by Jim Harmon..........................................SFS   Nov 1959
    RARE SCIENCE FICTION [Howard - 1963]

# M

MacDonough's Song by Rudyard Kipling............(verse)...........Mpln  Mar 1912
    17 X INFINITY [Conklin - 1963]
*Machine Stops, The by E. M. Forster...........................................
    (From The Eternal Moment and Other Stories; 1928)
    17 X INFINITY [Conklin - 1963]
Mad Moon, The by Stanley G. Weinbaum..............................ASF   Dec 1935
    EXPLORING OTHER WORLDS [Moskowitz - 1963]

                                                              Mag.     Year

*Made in U. S. A. by J. T. McIntosh ps (James J. MacGregor)........Glxy  Apr 1953
    HUMAN AND OTHER BEINGS [DeGraeff - 1963]
Magic Box, The by W. R. Baker.................(verse)
    THE MATHEMATICAL MAGPIE [Fadiman - 1962]
Man From the Big Dark, The by John Brunner......................SFAd  Jun 1958
    GREAT SCIENCE FICTION ADVENTURES [Shaw - 1963]
Man of the Stars by Sam Moskowitz...............................PS  Win 1941
    EXPLORING OTHER WORLDS [Moskowitz - 1963]
Man Who Made Friends with Electricity, The by Fritz Leiber........F&SF  Mar 1962
    8th ANNUAL OF THE YEAR'S BEST SF [Merril - 1963]
Man Without a Planet, The by Kate Wilhelm........................F&SF  Jul 1962
    THE BEST FROM FANTASY & SCIENCE FICTION: 12th SERIES [Davidson - 1963]
Man Without an Appetite, The by Miles J. Breuer, M. D. ...........BV  n/d/a 1916
    GREAT SCIENCE FICTION ABOUT DOCTORS [Conklin & Fabricant - 1963]
Mark Gable Foundation, The by Leo Szilard..(From The Voice of the Dolphins; 1961)
    THE EXPERT DREAMERS [Pohl - 1962]
Map of England and the Absolute, The by George Santayana.......................
    (From Character and Opinion in the United States; 1920)
    THE MATHEMATICAL MAGPIE [Fadiman - 1962]
*Mark of the Beast, The by Rudyard Kipling...........(From Life's Handicap; 1891)
    ROD SERLING'S TRIPLE W: WITCHES, WARLOCKS AND WEREWOLVES [Serling - 1963]
Martian Adventure, A by Willy Ley.............................ASF  Feb 1937
    (Originally aprd under title At the Perhilion under pseudonym Robert Willey)
    GREAT SCIENCE FICTION BY SCIENTISTS [Conklin - 1962]
Martian and the Magician, The by Evelyn E. Smith...............F&SF  Nov 1952
    FIFTY SHORT SCIENCE FICTION TALES [Asimov & Conklin - 1963]
Martian, The by Alexander Kazantsev..........................(No data available)
    A VISITOR FROM OUTER SPACE [Anonymous - undated]
      (Translated from Russian by Violet L. Dutt)
Martian Star-Gazers, The by Frederik Pohl.......................Glxy  Feb 1962
    (Originally appeared under pseudonym Ernst Mason)
    8th ANNUAL OF THE YEAR'S BEST SF [Merril - 1963]
*Martyr, The by Poul Anderson...................................F&SF  Mar 1960
    BEST SF FIVE SCIENCE FICTION STORIES [Crispin - 1963]
Mate in Two Moves by Winston K. Marks...........................Glxy  May 1954
    GREAT SCIENCE FICTION ABOUT DOCTORS [Conklin & Fabricant - 1963]
Mathematician Confided, A — Anonymous........(verse).........(No data available)
    THE MATHEMATICAL MAGPIE [Fadiman - 1962]
Mathematician In Love, The by W.J.M. Rankine..(verse)...(Fr Songs & Fables; 1874)
    THE MATHEMATICAL MAGPIE [Fadiman - 1962]
Mathematician Named Klein, A — Anonymous.......(verse).......(No data available)
    THE MATHEMATICAL MAGPIE [Fadiman - 1962]
Mathematicians, The by Arthur Feldman.............................Amz  Nov 1953
    FIFTY SHORT SCIENCE FICTION TALES [Asimov & Conklin - 1963]
Mathematician's Nightmare, The: The Vision of Professor Squarepoint by
    Bertrand Russell....................(From Nightmares of Eminent Persons; 1955)
    THE MATHEMATICAL MAGPIE [Fadiman - 1962]
Mathematicis Chez Madame Marlette by Elliot Paul.................................
    (From The Last Time I Saw Paris; 1942)
    THE MATHEMATICAL MAGPIE [Fadiman - 1962]
Mathematics For Golfers by Stephen Leacock...........(From Literary Lapses; 1912)
    THE MATHEMATICAL MAGPIE [Fadiman - 1962]
Matter of Ethics, A by J. R. Shango............................. F&SF  Nov 1954
    GREAT SCIENCE FICTION ABOUT DOCTORS [Conklin & Fabricant - 1963]
Maxwell Equations, The by Anatoly Dnieprov....................(No data available)
    DESTINATION: AMALTHEIA [Dixon - 1963]
      (Translated from Russian by Leonid Kolesnikov)

|  | Mag. | Year |
|---|---|---|

*Me by Hilbert Schenck, Jr. ..............(verse)................F&SF  Aug 1959
    THE MATHEMATICAL MAGPIE [Fadiman - 1962]
*Men Are Different by Alan Bloch...(From SCIENCE FICTION THINKING MACHINES; 1954)
    FIFTY SHORT SCIENCE FICTION TALES [Asimov & Conklin - 1963]
Milo and the Mathemagician by Norton Juster....(From The Phantom Tollbroth; 1961)
    THE MATHEMATICAL MAGPIE [Fadiman - 1962]
Minor Ingredient by Eric Frank Russell............................ASF  Mar 1956
    PROLOGUE TO ANALOG [J. W. Campbell - 1962]
Miniver Problem, The by Jan Struther ps (Mrs. Joyce Maxtone Graham)..............
    (From Mrs. Miniver; 1940)
    THE MATHEMATICAL MAGPIE [Fadiman - 1962]
Miniver Problem, The (Solution) by L. A. Graham.................................
    (From Ingenious Problems and Methods; 1959)
    THE MATHEMATICAL MAGPIE [Fadiman - 1962]
Miracle of Rare Device, A by Ray Bradbury.......................Plby  Jan 1962
    THE WORLDS OF SCIENCE FICTION [Mills - 1963]
    8th ANNUAL OF THE YEAR'S BEST SF [Merril - 1963]
Miracle of the Broom Closet, The by W. Norbert ps (Norbert Weiner)..TEN  Apr 1952
    THE EXPERT DREAMERS [Pohl - 1962]
Misfit by Michael Fischer......................................SF+  Dec 1953
    THE COMING OF THE ROBOTS [Moskowitz - 1963]
Misguided Halo, The by Henry Kuttner...............................UW  Aug 1939
    THE UNKNOWN [Benson - 1963]
*Mist, The by Peter Cartur.....................................F&SF  Sep 1952
    FIFTY SHORT SCIENCE FICTION TALES [Asimov & Conklin - 1963]
Modern Hiawatha, The — Anonymous...........(verse)...........(No data available)
    THE MATHEMATICAL MAGPIE [Fadiman - 1962]
*Momento Homo by Walter M. Miller, Jr. ...........................Amz  Mar 1954
    THE WORLDS OF SCIENCE FICTION [Mills - 1963]
Monkey Wrench, The by Gordon R. Dickson........................ASF  Aug 1951
    MORE PENGUIN SCIENCE FICTION [Aldiss - 1963]
Monsters, The by Robert Sheckley..............................F&SF  Mar 1953
    BEST SF FIVE SCIENCE FICTION STORIES [Crispin - 1963]
Monument by Lloyd Biggle, Jr. ...................................ASF  Jun 1951
    ANALOG I [J. W. Campbell - 1963]
Mother of Necessity, The by Chad Oliver...............(From Another Kind; 1955)
    GREAT SCIENCE FICTION BY SCIENTISTS [Conklin - 1962]
*Moxon's Master by Ambrose Bierce...............(From Can Such Things Be?; 1893)
    A CENTURY OF SCIENCE FICTION [Knight - 1962]
Mr. Jinx by Robert Arthur........................................UW  Aug 1941
    THE UNKNOWN [Benson - 1963]
Ms. Found in a Bus by Russell Baker......................N.Y. Times  n/d/a 1962
    8th ANNUAL OF THE YEAR'S BEST SF [Merril - 1963]
Ms Fnd In A Lbry by Hal Draper.................................F&SF  Dec 1961
    17 X INFINITY [Conklin - 1963]
My Dear Emily by Joanna Russ....................................F&SF  Jul 1962
    THE BEST FROM FANTASY & SCIENCE FICTION: 12th SERIES [Davidson - 1963]
My Lady Green Sleeves by Frederik Pohl.........................Glxy  Feb 1957
    HUMAN AND OTHER BEINGS [DeGraeff - 1963]
My Object All Sublime by Poul Anderson.........................Glxy  Jun 1961
    12 GREAT CLASSICS OF SCIENCE FICTION [Conklin - 1963]
My Private World of Science Fiction by Alfred Bester...(article)...ORIGINAL STORY
    THE WORLDS OF SCIENCE FICTION [Mills - 1963]
My Trial as a War Criminal by Leo Szilard......................UCLR  Aut 1949
    7th ANNUAL OF THE YEAR'S BEST SF [Merril - 1962]

# N

|  | Mag. | Year |
|---|---|---|
| Name Your Tiger by Milton Lesser.........................................SFQ | May 1957 |
|     THE WEIRD ONES [Howard - 1962] | | |
| *Narapola by Alan Nelson..............................................Wdg | Apr 1948 |
|     (Originally appeared under title The Origin of Narapola) | | |
|     FIFTY SHORT SCIENCE FICTION TALES [Asimov & Conklin - 1963] | | |
| *Natural State by Damon Knight.......................................Glxy | Jan 1954 |
|     TIME WAITS FOR WINTHROP AND FOUR OTHER SHORT NOVELS FROM GALAXY [Pohl-1962] | | |
| Needed: Feminine Math by Parke Cummings.......(From The Fly in the Martini; 1961) | | |
|     THE MATHEMATICAL MAGPIE [Fadiman - 1962] | | |
| Neutrino Bomb, The by Ralph C. Cooper................................LASLN | 7/13/61 |
|     GREAT SCIENCE FICTION BY SCIENTISTS [Conklin - 1962] | | |
| *Never Underestimate by Theodore Sturgeon...........................If | Jan 1952 |
|     17 X INFINITY [Conklin - 1963] | | |
| Night-Fear by Frank Belknap Long....................................DSF | Oct 1953 |
|     NOVELETS OF SCIENCE FICTION [Howard - 1963] | | |
| Night Piece by Poul Anderson.......................................F&SF | Jul 1961 |
|     THE WORLDS OF SCIENCE FICTION [Mills - 1963] | | |
| Nightmare in Time by Fredric Brown..................................Dude | |
|     7th ANNUAL OF THE YEAR'S BEST SF [Merril - 1962] | | |
| *Nine Billion Names of God by Arthur C. Clarke...................... | |
|     (From Star Science Fiction Stories; Frederik Pohl - 1953] | | |
|     THE MATHEMATICAL MAGPIE [Fadiman - 1962] | | |
| *Noise Level by Raymond F. Jones....................................ASF | Dec 1952 |
|     BEST SF FIVE SCIENCE FICTION STORIES [Crispin - 1963] | | |
| *Not Final! by Isaac Asimov.........................................ASF | Oct 1941 |
|     ASLEEP IN ARMAGEDDON [Sissons - 1962] | | |
| *Not With a Bang by Damon Knight...................................F&SF | Spr 1950 |
|     FIFTY SHORT SCIENCE FICTION TALES [Asimov & Conklin - 1963] | | |
| Note on $\theta$ , $\phi$, and $\psi$ by Michael Roberts.........(verse)...........NS | 3/23/35 |
|     THE MATHEMATICAL MAGPIE [Fadiman - 1962] | | |
| Note on the Einstein Theory, A by Max Beerbohm.....(From Mainly On the Air; 1946) | | |
|     THE MATHEMATICAL MAGPIE [Fadiman - 1962] | | |
| *Now Let Us Sleep by Avram Davidson.................................Ven | Sep 1957 |
|     THE WORLDS OF SCIENCE FICTION [Mills - 1963] | | |
| NRACP, The by George P. Elliott.....................................HdR | Aut 1949 |
|     HUMAN AND OTHER BEINGS [DeGraeff - 1963] | | |

# O

| O'Brien's Table by J. L. Synge...........(From Science: Sense and Nonsense; 1951) | |
|     THE MATHEMATICAL MAGPIE [Fadiman - 1962] | | |
| *Obviously Suicide by S. Fowler Wright..............................Sus | Spr 1951 |
|     FIFTY SHORT SCIENCE FICTION TALES [Asimov & Conklin - 1963] | | |
| *Odd John by Olaf Stapledon.......(Originally published by Methuen and Co.; 1935) | |
|     A CENTURY OF SCIENCE FICTION [Knight - 1962] | | |
| *Of Time and Third Avenue by Alfred Bester........................F&SF | Oct 1951 |
|     A CENTURY OF SCIENCE FICTION [Knight - 1962] | | |
| Omnilingual by H. Beam Piper.......................................ASF | Feb 1957 |
|     PROLOGUE TO ANALOG [J. W. Campbell - 1962] | | |
| On Handling the Data by Henry I. Hirshfield and G. M. Mateyko.......ASF | Sep 1959 |
|     (Originally appeared under byline M. I. Mayfield) | | |
|     BEST SF FIVE SCIENCE FICTION STORIES [Crispin - 1963] | | |

On the Aerodynamic Properties of Addition by Raymond Queneau...................
    (From Exercise In Style; 1958)    (Translated from French by Barbara Wright)
    THE MATHEMATICAL MAGPIE [Fadiman - 1962]
On the Feasibility of Coal-Driven Power Stations by O. R. Frisch.....SA  Mar 1956
    THE EXPERT DREAMERS [Pohl - 1962]
On the Fourth Planet by J. F. Bone...............................Glxy  Apr 1963
    12 GREAT CLASSICS OF SCIENCE FICTION [Conklin - 1963]
One of Those Days by William F. Nolan..............................F&SF  May 1962
    8th ANNUAL OF THE YEAR'S BEST SF [Merril - 1963]
Oneiromachia by Conrad Aiken...............(verse)...................Atl  Oct 1961
    7th ANNUAL OF THE YEAR'S BEST SF [Merril - 1962]
*Or All the Seas with Oysters by Avram Davidson....................Glxy  May 1958
    THE HUGO WINNERS [Asimov - 1962]
Origin of Narapoia, The by Alan Nelson....................(See listing Narapoia)
Oscar by Cleve Cartmill............................................UW  Feb 1941
    FIFTY SHORT SCIENCE FICTION TALES [Asimov & Conklin - 1963]
Other Foot, The by Ray Bradbury....................................NS  Mar 1951
    HUMAN AND OTHER BEINGS [DeGraeff - 1963]
Ottmar Balleau X 2 by George Bamber..................................Rog
    7th ANNUAL OF THE YEAR'S BEST SF [Merril - 1962]
Out of the Cradle, Endlessly Orbiting by Arthur C. Clarke..........Dude  Mar 1959
    (Originally appeared under title Out of the Cradle)
    GREAT SCIENCE FICTION ABOUT DOCTORS [Conklin & Fabricant - 1963]
Over the Abyss by Alexander Belayev........................(No  data available)
    DESTINATION: AMALTHEIA [Dixon - 1963]
        (Translated from Russian by Leonid Kolesnikov)

# P

*Pacifist, The by Arthur C. Clarke.....................................FU  Oct 1956
    THE MATHEMATICAL MAGPIE [Fadiman - 1962]
Pandora's Planet by Christopher Anvil................................ASF  Sep 1956
    PROLOGUE TO ANALOG [J. W. Campbell - 1962]
Paradise Lost at Cambridge by Thomas Jefferson Hogg............(No data available)
    THE MATHEMATICAL MAGPIE [Fadiman - 1962]
Parky by David Rome...........................................SF #48  Aug 1961
    7th ANNUAL OF THE YEAR'S BEST SF [Merril - 1962]
Passage Among the Stars, A by Kaatje Hurlbut........................SEP  5/13/61
    7th ANNUAL OF THE YEAR'S BEST SF [Merril - 1962]
Paul Bunyon Versus the Conveyor Belt by William Hazlett Upson.......FTM  n/d 1949
    THE MATHEMATICAL MAGPIE [Fadiman - 1962]
Peace On Earth by Irving Cox, Jr. ..................................FSF  Jun 1954
    6 AND THE SILENT SCREAM [Howard - 1963]
Perfect Woman, The by Robert Sheckley...............................Amz  Dec 1953
    FIFTY SHORT SCIENCE FICTION TALES [Asimov & Conklin - 1963]
Piebold Hippogriff, The by Karen Anderson...........................Fnt  May 1962
    8th ANNUAL OF THE YEAR'S BEST SF [Merril - 1963]
Pilot Lights of the Apocalypse by Dr. Louis N. Ridenow..............Ftn  Jan 1946
    GREAT SCIENCE FICTION BY SCIENTISTS [Conklin - 1962]
Plague, The by Teddy Keller.........................................ASF  Feb 1961
    ANALOG 1 [J. W. Campbell - 1963]
Planet Named Shayol, A by Cordwainer Smith.........................Glxy  Oct 1961
    7th ANNUAL OF THE YEAR'S BEST SF [Merril - 1962]
Planet of Doubt, The by Stanley G. Weinbaum.........................ASF  Oct 1935
    MORE ADVENTURES ON OTHER PLANETS [Wollheim - 1963]

                                                              Mag.     Year
Planetary Effulgence by Bertrand Russell............(From Fact and Fiction; 1961)
     8th ANNUAL OF THE YEAR'S BEST SF [Merril - 1963]
Please Stand By by Ron Goulart......................................F&SF  Jan 1962
     THE BEST FROM FANTASY & SCIENCE FICTION: 12th SERIES [Davidson - 1963]
Portobello Road, The by Murial Spark...............(From The Go-Away Bird; 1938)
     7th ANNUAL OF THE YEAR'S BEST SF [Merril - 1962]
Portrait of a Mathematician by Christopher Morley..........(verse)..............
     (From The Ballard of New York and Other Poems: 1930-1950; 1950)
     THE MATHEMATICAL MAGPIE [Fadiman - 1962]
Possessed, The by Arthur C. Clarke..................................DSF   Mar 1953
     NOVELETS OF SCIENCE FICTION [Howard - 1963]
Prescience by Nelson S. Bond........................................UW    Oct 1941
     THE UNKNOWN [Benson - 1963]
Prisoner, The by Christopher Anvil..................................ASF   Feb 1956
     BEST SF FIVE SCIENCE FICTION STORIES [Crispin - 1963]
Prize For Edie, A by J. F. Bone.....................................ASF   Apr 1961
     7th ANNUAL OF THE YEAR'S BEST SF [Merril - 1962]
Professor Bern's Awakening by Vladimer Savchenko.............(No data available)
     A VISITOR FROM OUTER SPACE [Anonymous - undated]
          (Translated from Russian by Violet L. Dutt)
Project Hush by William Tenn ps (Philip Klass)....................Glxy  Feb 1954
     FIFTY SHORT SCIENCE FICTION TALES [Asimov & Conklin - 1963]
Prolog by John P. McKnight........................................F&SF  Aug 1951
     FIFTY SHORT SCIENCE FICTION TALES [Asimov & Conklin - 1963]
Prologue to an Analogue by Leigh Richmond.........................ASF   Jun 1961
     ANALOG 1 [J. W. Campbell - 1963]
Propagandist by Murray Leinster ps (Will F. Jenkins)..............ASF   Aug 1947
     GREAT STORIES OF SPACE TRAVEL [Conklin - 1963]
Protective Camouflage by Charles V. De Vet........................SFS   May 1955
     RARE SCIENCE FICTION [Howard - 1963]
Psychophonic Nurse, The by David H. Keller, M. D. ................Amz   Nov 1928
     GREAT SCIENCE FICTION ABOUT DOCTORS [Conklin & Fabricant - 1963]
Pun In Orbit by Hilbert Schenck, Jr. ....................ORIGINAL VERSE
     THE MATHEMATICAL MAGPIE [Fadiman - 1962]
Puppet Show by Fredric Brown......................................Plby  Nov 1962
     8th ANNUAL OF THE YEAR'S BEST SF [Merril - 1963]
Purse of Fortunatus, The by Lewis Carroll ps (Charles Lutwidge Dodgson)..........
     (From Sylvie and Bruno; 1889)
     THE MATHEMATICAL MAGPIE [Fadiman - 1962]
Pushbutton War by Joseph P. Martino...............................ASF   Aug 1960
     PROLOGUE TO ANALOG [J. W. Campbell - 1962]
Pyramid by Robert Abernathy.......................................ASF   Jul 1954
     MORE PENGUIN SCIENCE FICTION [Aldiss - 1963]


                              𝑸


Quake, Quake, Quake by Paul Dehn and Edward Gorey................................
     (From Quake, Quake, Quake; 1961)
     7th ANNUAL OF THE YEAR'S BEST SF [Merril - 1962]
Quaker Cannon, The by Frederik Pohl and C. M. Kornbluth...........ASF   Aug 1961
     7th ANNUAL OF THE YEAR'S BEST SF [Merril - 1962]
*Quest for Saint Aquin, The by Anthony Boucher..................................
     (Original Story From NEW TALES OF SPACE AND TIME; Raymond J. Healy - 1951)
     THE WORLDS OF SCIENCE FICTION [Mills - 1963]
Quick Freeze by Robert Silverberg.................................SFQ   May 1957
     RARE SCIENCE FICTION [Howard - 1963]

| | Mag. | Year |
|---|---|---|

Radiant Enemies, The by R. F. Starzl...............................Arg 2/10/34
    EXPLORING OTHER WORLDS [Moskowitz - 1963]
*Rag Thing, The by David Grinnel.................................F&SF Oct 1951
    FIFTY SHORT SCIENCE FICTION TALES [Asimov & Conklin - 1963]
Random Sample by T. P. Caravan...................................F&SF Apr 1953
    FIFTY SHORT SCIENCE FICTION TALES [Asimov & Conklin - 1963]
Rappaccini's Daughter by Nathaniel Hawthorne......................NEM Apr 1835
    GREAT SCIENCE FICTION ABOUT DOCTORS [Conklin & Fabricant - 1963]
Rations of Tantalus by Margaret St. Clair.........................FU Jul 1954
    WORLDS OF WHEN [Conklin - 1962]
Real People, The by Algis Budrys................................Bynd Nov 1953
    BEYOND [Anonymous - 1963]
Reason by Isaac Asimov...........................................ASF Sep 1941
    A CENTURY OF SCIENCE FICTION [Knight - 1962]
Red Death of Mars by Robert Moore Williams.......................ASF Dec 1961
    MORE ADVENTURES ON OTHER PLANETS [Wollheim - 1963]
*Refugee, The by Jane Rice........................................UW Oct 1943
    HELL HATH FURY [Hay - 1963]
Remember The Alamo! by T. R. Fehrenbach..........................ASF Dec 1961
    (Originally appeared under byline R. R. Fehrenbach)
    ANALOG 1 [J. W. Campbell - 1963]
Report on Grand Central Terminal by Leo Szilard..................UCM n/d/a 1952
    GREAT SCIENCE FICTION BY SCIENTISTS [Conklin - 1962]
*Resurrection by A. E. Van Vogt..................................ASF Aug 1948
    SPECTRUM II [Amis & Conquest - 1962]
Rex by Harl Vincent ps (Harl Vincent Schoepflin).................ASF Jun 1934
    THE COMING OF THE ROBOTS [Moskowitz - 1963]
Ribbon in the Sky by Murray Leinster ps (Will F. Jenkins)........ASF Jun 1957
    GREAT SCIENCE FICTION ABOUT DOCTORS [Conklin & Fabricant - 1963]
Riddle [untitled] — Anonymous..............................(verse)
    (From The Oxford Dictionary of Nursery Rhymes by Iona and Peter Opie; 1951)
    THE MATHEMATICAL MAGPIE [Fadiman - 1962]
Riddle of the Deadly Paradise by Frank Belknap Long..............SFS Nov 1958
    6 AND THE SILENT SCREAM [Howard - 1963]
Ripeness by M. C. Pease..........................................SFS Jan 1955
    RARE SCIENCE FICTION [Howard - 1963]
Root and the Ring, The by Wyman Guin...........................Bynd Sep 1954
    BEYOND [Anonymous - 1963]
Round Trip To Esidarap by Lloyd Biggle, Jr. .......................If Nov 1960
    (Originally appeared under title Esidarap Ot Pirt Dnuor)
    OUT OF THIS WORLD 3 [Williams-Ellis & Owen - 1962]
Runaround by Isaac Asimov........................................ASF Mar 1942
    THE COMING OF THE ROBOTS [Moskowitz - 1963]

## S

Sail On! Sail On! by Philip Jose Farmer..........................Stg Dec 1952
    A CENTURY OF SCIENCE FICTION [Knight - 1962]
Sands Our Abode by Francis G. Rayer...........................NW #84 Jun 1959
    OUT OF THIS WORLD 3 [Williams-Ellis & Owen - 1962]
*Saucer of Lonliness, A by Theodore Sturgeon....................Glxy Feb 1953
    THE WORLDS OF SCIENCE FICTION [Mills - 1963]

```
                                                              Mag.    Year
*Scarlet Plague, The by Jack London..................................ASMM   9/14/13
     ASLEEP IN ARMAGEDDON [Sissons - 1962]
Second Variety by Philip K. Dick.....................................Spc  May 1953
     SPECTRUM II [Amis & Conquest - 1962]
See? by Edward G. Robles, Jr. .......................................Glxy  Jun 1954
     FIFTY SHORT SCIENCE FICTION TALES [Asimov & Conklin - 1963]
*Sense From Thought Divide by Mark Clifton...........................ASF  Mar 1955
     SPECTRUM II [Amis & Conquest - 1962]
Sentiment, Inc. by Poul Anderson.....................................SFS #1 n/d 1953
     THE WEIRD ONES [Howard - 1962]
Sentinel, The by Arthur C. Clarke....................................IOSF  Spr 1951
     (Originally appeared under title Sentinel of Eternity)
     SPECTRUM III [Amis & Conquest - 1963]
Seven-Day Terror by R. A. Lafferty...................................If  Mar 1962
     8th ANNUAL OF THE YEAR'S BEST SF [Merril - 1963]
Ship Who Sang, The by Anne McCaffrey.................................F&SF  Apr 1961
     7th ANNUAL OF THE YEAR'S BEST SF [Merril - 1962]
Shopdropper, The by Alan Nelson......................................F&SF  Jan 1955
     GREAT SCIENCE FICTION ABOUT DOCTORS [Conklin & Fabricant - 1963]
Short Cuts to Success by Ronald A. Knox..............................Slp  Nov 1917
     THE MATHEMATICAL MAGPIE [Fadiman - 1962]
*Short in the Chest by Idris Seabright ps (Margaret St. Clair).......FU  Jul 1954
     17 X INFINITY [Conklin - 1963]
Siema by Anatoly Dnieprov....................................(No data available)
     THE HEART OF THE SERPENT [Anonymous - 1961]
          (Translated from Russian by R. Prokofieva)
Silenzia by Alan Nelson..............................................F&SF  Sep 1953
     17 X INFINITY [Conklin - 1963]
Simian Problem, The by Hollis Alpert.................................F&SF  Jul 1960
     17 X INFINITY [Conklin - 1963]
Singers, The by W. Grey Walter...........(From The Curve of the Snowflakes; 1956)
     THE EXPERT DREAMERS [Pohl - 1962]
Singular Events Which Occured in the Hovel on the Alley off of Eye Street, The
     by Avram Davidson...............................................F&SF  Feb 1962
     THE BEST FROM FANTASY & SCIENCE FICTION: 12th SERIES [Davidson - 1963]
Six Haiku by Karen Anderson.................(verse)................F&SF  Jul 1962
     FIFTY SHORT SCIENCE FICTION TALES [Asimov & Conklin - 1963]
Six Matches by Arkady and Boris Strugatsky.....................(No data available)
     THE HEART OF THE SERPENT [Anonymous - 1961]
          (Translated from Russian by R. Prokofieva)
Sixteen Stones by Samuel Beckett.............................(From Molloy; 1955)
          (Translated from French by Patrick Bowles)
     THE MATHEMATICAL MAGPIE [Fadiman - 1962]
Sky Lift by Robert A. Heinlein.......................................Im  Nov 1953
     A CENTURY OF SCIENCE FICTION [Knight - 1962]
Sleight of Wit by Gordon R. Dickson..................................ASF  Dec 1961
     ANALOG I [J. W. Campbell - 1963]
Small Lords by Frederik Pohl.........................................SFQ  Feb 1957
     THE WEIRD ONES [Howard - 1962]
Snail's Pace by Algis Budrys.........................................DSF  Oct 1953
     WAY OUT [Howard - 1963]
Snip, Snip by Hilbert Schenck, Jr. .............(verse).............F&SF  Sep 1959
     THE MATHEMATICAL MAGPIE [Fadiman - 1962]
*Snulbug by Anthony Boucher..........................................UW  Dec 1941
     THE UNKNOWN [Benson - 1963]
```

|  | Mag. | Year |

Something Green by Fredric Brown..................(From Space On My Hands; 1951)
    EXPLORING OTHER WORLDS [Moskowitz - 1963]
Song Against Circles, A by R. P. Lister.........(verse)............Nykr   5/13/61
    THE MATHEMATICAL MAGPIE [Fadiman - 1962]
Song of the Screw — Anonymous.............(verse)..........(No data available)
    THE MATHEMATICAL MAGPIE [Fadiman - 1962]
Sound Decision by Randall Garrett & Robert Silverberg...............ASF   Oct 1956
    PROLOGUE TO ANALOG [J. W. Campbell - 1962]
Spaceman Cometh, The by Henry Gregor Felson......................F&SF   Apr 1956
    17 X INFINITY [Conklin - 1963]
*Specialist by Robert Sheckley......................................Glxy   May 1953
    CONTACT [Keyes - 1963]
Spectator Sport by John D. MacDonald..............................TWS   Feb 1950
    FIFTY SHORT SCIENCE FICTION TALES [Asimov & Conklin - 1963]
Spontaneous Reflex by Arkady and Boris Strugatsky.............(No data available)
    A VISITOR FROM OUTER SPACE [Anonymous - undated]
       (Translated from Russian by Violet L. Dutt)
Square of the Hypotenuse, The.....(verse)......(From The Film MERRY ANDREW; 1958)
    (Music by Saul Chapling - Lyrics by Johnny Mercer)
    THE MATHEMATICAL MAGPIE [Fadiman - 1962]
*Stair Trick by Mildred Clingerman....................................F&SF   Aug 1952
    FIFTY SHORT SCIENCE FICTION TALES [Asimov & Conklin - 1963]
*Star Bright by Mark Clifton........................................Glxy   Jul 1952
    THE MATHEMATICAL MAGPIE [Fadiman - 1962]
Star-Crossed Lover by William W. Stuart...........................Glxy   Apr 1962
    12 GREAT CLASSICS OF SCIENCE FICTION [Conklin - 1963]
*Star, The by Arthur C. Clarke......................................Inf   Nov 1955
    A CENTURY OF SCIENCE FICTION [Knight - 1962]
    THE HUGO WINNERS [Asimov - 1962]
    BEST SF FIVE SCIENCE FICTION STORIES [Crispin - 1963]
Starcombers, The by Edmond Hamilton...............................SFAd   Dec 1956
    GREAT SCIENCE FICTION ADVENTURES [Shaw - 1963]
Stone From the Stars by Valentina Zhuravleva..................(No data available)
    THE HEART OF THE SERPENT [Anonymous - 1961]
       (Translated from Russian by R. Prokofieva)
Store of the World, The by Robert Sheckley.......................Plby   Sep 1959
    (Originally appeared under title World of Heart's Desire)
    MORE PENGUIN SCIENCE FICTION [Aldiss - 1963]
Story of Sidi Norman, The — Anonymous........................(No data available)
    ROD SERLING'S TRIPLE W: WITCHES, WARLOCKS AND WEREWOLVES [Serling - 1963]
Strange Girl, The by Mark Van Doren
    THE WORLDS OF SCIENCE FICTION [Mills - 1963]
Streets of Ashkalon, The by Harry Harrison...........(See listing An Alien Agony)
Strikebreaker by Isaac Asimov.....................................SFS   Jan 1957
    17 X INFINITY [Conklin - 1963]
Subcommittee by Zeena Henderson...................................F&SF   Jul 1962
    8th ANNUAL OF THE YEAR'S BEST SF [Merril - 1963]
Such Stuff by John Brunner.......................................F&SF   Jun 1962
    8th ANNUAL OF THE YEAR'S BEST SF [Merril - 1963]
Summertime In Icarus by Arthur C. Clarke.........................Vge   Jun 1960
    (Org aprd under title The Hottest Piece of Real Estate In the Solar System)
    GREAT SCIENCE FICTION BY SCIENTISTS [Conklin - 1962]
Sunrise on Mercury by Robert Silverberg..........................SFS   May 1957
    (Originally appeared under pseudonym Calvin M. Knox)
    MORE ADVENTURES ON OTHER PLANETS [Wollheim - 1963]

Superlative Degree, The by Earnest Elmo Calkins......(verse)........SEP   5/16/59
    THE MATHEMATICAL MAGPIE [Fadiman - 1962]
Symbolic Logic of Murder by John Reese...........................EQMM   Oct 1960
    THE MATHEMATICAL MAGPIE [Fadiman - 1962]

# T

T by Brian W. Aldiss.............................................Neb #18   Nov 1956
    FIRST FLIGHT: Maiden Voyages In Space and Time [Knight - 1963]
Ta, Ta, The..................(verse)...................(From Bogey Beasts; 1962)
    (Music by Joseph Charles Holbrooke — Jingles by Sidney H. Sime)
    THE MATHEMATICAL MAGPIE [Fadiman - 1962]
*Talent by Theodore Sturgeon.......................................Bynd   Sep 1953
    BEYOND [Anonymous - 1962]
    FIFTY SHORT SCIENCE FICTION TALES [Asimov & Conklin - 1963]
*Teething Ring by James Causey....................................Glxy   Jan 1953
    FIFTY SHORT SCIENCE FICTION TALES [Asimov & Conklin - 1963]
Temple of Despair by M. C. Pease.................................DSF   Oct 1953
    ESCAPE TO EARTH [Howard - 1963]
Tending To Infinity by J. L. Synge.....(verse)......(From Kandelman's Krim; 1957)
    THE MATHEMATICAL MAGPIE [Fadiman - 1962]
Test by Theodore L. Thomas......................................F&SF   Apr 1962
    THE BEST FROM FANTASY & SCIENCE FICTION: 12th SERIES [Davidson - 1963]
*Test Piece by Eric Frank Russell.................................OW   Mar 1951
    HUMAN AND OTHER BEINGS [DeGraeff - 1963]
Test Stand, The by Lee Correy ps (G. Harry Stine)..................ASF   Mar 1955
    THE EXPERT DREAMERS [Pohl - 1962]
*Testament of Andros by James Blish..............................FSF   Jan 1953
    NOVELETS OF SCIENCE FICTION [Howard - 1963]
Texas Week by Albert Hernhunter.................................FU   Jan 1954
    FIFTY SHORT SCIENCE FICTION TALES [Asimov & Conklin - 1963]
That Mason-Dixon Line by Simon Newcomb........................(No data available)
    THE MATHEMATICAL MAGPIE [Fadiman - 1962]
*That Only a Mother by Judith Merril.............................ASF   Jun 1948
    FIRST FLIGHT: Maiden Voyages In Space and Time [Knight - 1963]
There Is a Tide by Brian W. Aldiss.............................NW #44   Feb 1956
    SPECTRUM II [Amis & Conquest - 1962]
There Is no Defense by Theodore Sturgeon.........................ASF   Feb 1948
    THREE IN ONE [Margulies - 1963]
There Was an Old Man Who Said, "Do..." - Anonymous...(verse)..(No data available)
    THE MATHEMATICAL MAGPIE [Fadiman - 1962]
Things by Zeena Henderson......................................F&SF   Jul 1960
    12 GREAT CLASSICS OF SCIENCE FICTION [Conklin - 1963]
*Third Level, The by Jack Finney..................................Col   10/7/50
    FIFTY SHORT SCIENCE FICTION TALES [Asimov & Conklin - 1963]
Thirty Days Had September by Robert F. Young....................F&SF   Oct 1957
    12 GREAT CLASSICS OF SCIENCE FICTION [Conklin - 1963]
*This Star Shall Be Free by Murray Leinster ps (Will F. Jenkins)....Sup   Nov 1949
    ASLEEP IN ARMAGEDDON [Sissons - 1962]
Three for the Stars by Joseph Dickinson.........................F&SF   Apr 1962
    THE BEST FROM FANTASY & SCIENCE FICTION: 12th SERIES [Davidson - 1963]
Three Mathematical Diversions by Raymond Queneau..............................
    See Listings:  An Exercise In Style: Mathematical
                 On the Aerodynamic Properties of Addition
                 The Geometrical Disappearance of Dino

Mag.     Year

Three Prologues and an Episode by John Dos Passos....................Adt   Spr 1961
    7th ANNUAL OF THE YEAR'S BEST SF [Merril - 1962]
Tiger by the Tail by Poul Anderson.........................................PS   Jan 1951
    MORE ADVENTURES ON OTHER PLANETS [Wollheim - 1963]
*Tiger by the Tail by Alan E. Nourse.....................................Glxy   Nov 1951
    FIFTY SHORT SCIENCE FICTION TALES [Asimov & Conklin - 1963]
*Time Machine, The by H. G. Wells.........................................NwR   Jan 1895
    A CENTURY OF SCIENCE FICTION [Knight - 1962]
Time Waits for Winthrop by William Tenn ps (Philip Klass)..........Glxy   Aug 1957
    TIME WAITS FOR WINTHROP AND FOUR OTHER SHORT NOVELS FROM GALAXY [Pohl-1962]
*Tissue Culture King, The by Julian Huxley.............................Amz   Aug 1927
    GREAT SCIENCE FICTION BY SCIENTISTS [Conklin - 1962]
To a Astronaut Dying Young by Maxine W. Kumin........(verse)........Atl   Dec 1961
    7th ANNUAL OF THE YEAR'S BEST SF [Merril - 1962]
To a Missing Member of a Family Group of Terms in an Algebraical Formula
    by J. J. Sylvester.................(verse)................(No data available)
    THE MATHEMATICAL MAGPIE [Fadiman - 1962]
To Explain Mrs. Thompson by Philip Latham ps (Robert S. Richardson)...... . ......
                                                  ASF  Nov 1951
    THE EXPERT DREAMERS [Pohl - 1962]
To Marry Medusa by Theodore Sturgeon.................................Glxy   Aug 1958
    TIME WAITS FOR WINTHROP AND FOUR OTHER SHORT NOVELS FROM GALAXY [Pohl-1962]
*Tomorrow's Children by Poul Anderson.................................ASF   Mar 1947
    (Originally appeared under joint byline Poul Anderson & F. N. Waldrop)
    FIRST FLIGHT: Maiden Voyages in Space and Time [Knight - 1963]
Top, The by George Sumner Albee...........................................F&SF   Aug 1962
    12 GREAT CLASSICS OF SCIENCE FICTION [Conklin - 1963]
Toy Shop, The by Harry Harrison...........................................ASF   Apr 1962
    8th ANNUAL OF THE YEAR'S BEST SF [Merril - 1963]
Transfusion by Chad Oliver.................................................ASF   Jun 1959
    WORLDS OF WHEN [Conklin - 1962]
Trial of Tantalus, The by Victor Saparin.....................(No data available)
    THE HEART OF THE SERPENT [Anonymous - 1961]
        (Translated from Russian by R. Prokofieva)
*Triggerman by J. F. Bone.................................................ASF   Dec 1958
    PROLOGUE TO ANALOG [J. W. Campbell - 1962]
*Trouble with Water by H. L. Gold.........................................UW   Mar 1939
    THE UNKNOWN [Benson - 1963]
True Confession by F. Orlin Tremaine......................................TWS   Feb 1940
    THE COMING OF THE ROBOTS [Moskowitz - 1963]
Tunnel Ahead, The by Alice Glaser.........................................F&SF   Nov 1961
    7th ANNUAL OF THE YEAR'S BEST SF [Merril - 1962]
Tunnel Under the World, The by Frederik Pohl.......................Glxy   Jan 1955
    MORE PENGUIN SCIENCE FICTION [Aldiss - 1963]
Twenty Thousand Leagues Under the Sea by Jules Verne............(excerpts).......
    (Originally published by G. M. Smith; 1873)
    A CENTURY OF SCIENCE FICTION [Knight - 1962]
[Two] Extracts (untitled) by Mark Twain ps (Samuel L. Clemens)..(No data avble)
    THE MATHEMATICAL MAGPIE [Fadiman - 1962]
Two Weeks in August by Frank M. Robinson.............................Glxy   Feb 1951
    FIFTY SHORT SCIENCE FICTION TALES [Asimov & Conklin - 1963]
Two's a Crowd by Sasha Gilian.............................................F&SF   Jul 1962
    THE BEST FROM FANTASY & SCIENCE FICTION: 12th SERIES [Davidson - 1963]

# U

|  | Mag. | Year |
|---|---|---|

Ugly Little Boy by Isaac Asimov...................................Glxy Sep 1958
    (Originally appeared under title Lastborn)
    THE WORLDS OF SCIENCE FICTION [Mills - 1963]
*Ultimate Catalyst, The by John Taine ps (Eric Temple Bell).........TWS Jun 1929
    GREAT SCIENCE FICTION BY SCIENTISTS [Conklin - 1962]
Ultrasonic God by L. Sprague de Camp.............................Fw/SFS Jul 1951
    NOVELETS OF SCIENCE FICTION [Howard - 1963]
Unfortunate Mr. Morky, The by Vance Aandahl.........................F&SF Oct 1962
    8th ANNUAL OF THE YEAR'S BEST SF [Merril - 1963]
*Unhuman Sacrifice by Katherine MacLean..............................ASF Nov 1958
    A CENTURY OF SCIENCE FICTION [Knight - 1962]
Unsafe Deposit Box, The by Gerald Kersh.............................SEP 4/14/62
    8th ANNUAL OF THE YEAR'S BEST SF [Merril - 1963]
*Ulwelcome Tenant by Roger Dee ps (Roger D. Aycock)..................PS Sum 1950
    .FIFTY SHORT SCIENCE FICTION TALES [Asimov & Conklin - 1963]

# V

Valley of the Four Crosses, The by Igor Zabelin................(No data available)
    DESTINATION: AMALTHEIA [Dixon - 1963]
      (Translated from Russian by Leonid Kolesnikov)
Vanishing Man, The by Richard Hughes.................(From A Moment in Time; 1926)
    THE MATHEMATICAL MAGPIE [Fadiman - 1962]
Verse — Anonymous...............................................................
    (From The Lore and Language of Schoolchildren by Iona & Peter Ople; 1959)
    THE MATHEMATICAL MAGPIE [Fadiman - 1962]
Verse [untitled] by Stephen Barr.........(Original variation of W. Whewell verse)
    THE MATHEMATICAL MAGPIE [Fadiman - 1962]
Verses (Three) [untitled] by L. A. Graham......................................
    (From Ingenious Mathematical Problems and Methods; 1959)
    THE MATHEMATICAL MAGPIE [Fadiman - 1962]
Verse [untitled] by Dr. William Whewell.......................................
    (From Handybook of Literary Curiosities by W. S. Walsh; 1925)
    THE MATHEMATICAL MAGPIE [Fadiman - 1962]
Verses (Four) [untitled] by Frederick Winsor...................................
    (From The Space Child's Mother Goose; 1958)
    THE MATHEMATICAL MAGPIE [Fadiman - 1962]
Via Asteroid by Eando Binder ps (Otto Binder).......................TWS Feb 1938
    (Originally appeared under pseudonym Gordon A. Giles)
    EXPLORING OTHER WORLDS [Moskowitz - 1963]
*Vilbar Party, The by Evelyn E. Smith..............................Glxy Jan 1955
    HUMAN AND OTHER BEINGS [DeGraeff - 1963]
*Vintage Season by Lawrence O'Donnell ps (Henry Kuttner & C.L. Moore)...........
                                                       ASF Sep 1946
    SPECTRUM II [Amis & Conquest - 1962]
Visitor from Outer Space, A by Alexander Kazantsev.............(No data available)
    A VISITOR FROM OUTER SPACE [Anonymous - undated]
      (Translated from Russian by Violet L. Dutt)
Voices of Time, The by J. G. Ballard.............................NW #99 Nov 1960
    SPECTRUM III [Amis & Conquest - 1963]
Vulcan's Hammer by Philip K. Dick............................FSF #29 n/d 1956
    o AND THE SILENT SCREAM [Howard - 1963]

# W

|  | Mag. | Year |
|---|---|---|
| *Walk in the Dark, A by Arthur C. Clarke...........................TWS | Aug 1950 |
|    GREAT STORIES OF SPACE TRAVEL [Conklin - 1963] | | |
| Walk in the Middle of the Air by Ray Bradbury.......................OW | Jul 1950 |
|    FIRST FLIGHT: Maiden Voyages In Space and Time [Knight - 1963] | | |
| War in the Air, The by R. V. Cassill..............................Epch | |
|    THE WORLDS OF SCIENCE FICTION [Mills - 1963] | | |
| Watchful Poker Chip, The by Ray Bradbury..........................Bynd | Mar 1954 |
|    BEYOND [Anonymous - 1963] | | |
| Way in the Middle of the Air by Ray Bradbury........................OW | Jul 1950 |
|    HUMAN AND OTHER BEINGS [DeGraeff - 1963] | | |
| We Are Alone by Robert Sheckley....................................FSF | Nov 1952 |
|    ESCAPE TO EARTH [Howard - 1963] | | |
| We Didn't do Anything Wrong, Hardly by Roger Kuykendall............ASF | May 1959 |
|    PROLOGUE TO ANALOG [J. W. Campbell - 1962] | | |
| *We Don't Want any Trouble by James H. Schmitz....................Glxy | Jun 1953 |
|    FIFTY SHORT SCIENCE FICTION TALES [Asimov & Conklin - 1963] | | |
| *Weapon, The by Fredric Brown......................................ASF | Apr 1951 |
|    ASLEEP IN ARMAGEDDON [Sissons - 1962] | | |
|    FIFTY SHORT SCIENCE FICTION TALES [Asimov & Conklin - 1963] | | |
| West Wind by Murray Leinster ps (Will F. Jenkins)..................ASF | Mar 1948 |
|    THREE IN ONE [Margulies - 1963] | | |
| We Would See a Sign by Mark Rose........................ORIGINAL STORY | |
|    SPECTRUM III [Amis & Conquest - 1963] | | |
| *What If... by Isaac Asimov........................................Fnt | Sum 1952 |
|    GREAT SCIENCE FICTION BY SCIENTISTS [Conklin - 1962] | | |
| What To Do Until the Analyst Comes by Frederik Pohl................Im | Feb 1956 |
|    (Originally appeared under title Everybody's Happy But Me) | | |
|    17 X INFINITY [Conklin - 1963] | | |
| *What Was It? by Fitz-James O'Brien................................Hpr | Mar 1859 |
|    A CENTURY OF SCIENCE FICTION [Knight - 1962] | | |
| *What's He Doing In There? by Fritz Leiber.......................Glxy | Dec 1957 |
|    CONTACT [Keyes - 1963] | | |
| What's It Like Out There? by Edmond Hamilton.......................Stg | Dec 1952 |
|    A CENTURY OF SCIENCE FICTION [Knight - 1962] | | |
| What It Was Moonlight by Manly Wade Wellman........................Unk | Feb 1940 |
|    THE UNKNOWN [Benson - 1963] | | |
| When Lilacs Last in the Dooryard Bloomed by Vance Aandahl.........F&SF | May 1962 |
|    THE BEST FROM FANTASY & SCIENCE FICTION: 12th SERIES [Davidson - 1963] | | |
| *Who Can Replace A Man? by Brian W. Aldiss.........................Inf | Jun 1958 |
|    (Originally appeared under title But Who Can Replace A Man?) | | |
|    A CENTURY OF SCIENCE FICTION [Knight - 1962] (Aprd under original title) | | |
|    BEST SF FIVE SCIENCE FICTION STORIES [Crispin - 1963] | | |
| *Who's Cribbing? by Jack Lewis....................................Stg | Jan 1953 |
|    FIFTY SHORT SCIENCE FICTION TALES [Asimov & Conklin - 1963] | | |
| Who's In Charge Here? by James Blish..............................F&SF | May 1962 |
|    THE BEST FROM FANTASY & SCIENCE FICTION: 12th SERIES [Davidson - 1963] | | |
| Who's There? by Arthur C. Clarke...............................NW #77 | Nov 1958 |
|    OUT OF THIS WORLD 3 [Williams-Ellis & Owen - 1962] | | |
| Wind People, The by Marion Zimmer Bradley..........................If | Feb 1959 |
|    A CENTURY OF SCIENCE FICTION [Knight - 1962] | | |
| *Wings of Night, The by Lester del Rey............................ASF | Mar 1942 |
|    GREAT STORIES OF SPACE TRAVEL [Conklin - 1963] | | |

                                                                    Mag.    Year

Witch Trials and the Law by Charles Mackay........(article).....(excerpts).......
    (From Extraordinary Popular Delusions and the Madness of Crowds; 1841)
      ROD SERLING'S TRIPLE W: WITCHES, WARLOCKS AND WEREWOLVES [Serling - 1963]
With Apologies to Boyal by George Gamow...(From One, Two, Three...Infinity; 1947)
    THE MATHEMATICAL MAGPIE [Fadiman - 1962]
*Wockyjabber by Hilbert Schenck, Jr. ...........(verse)............F&SF  May 1960
      ROD SERLING'S TRIPLE W: WITCHES, WARLOCKS AND WEREWOLVES [Serling - 1963]
Wonderful World of Figures, The by Corey Ford.....................................
    (From Corey Ford's Guide To Thinking; 1961)
    THE MATHEMATICAL MAGPIE [Fadiman - 1962]
*Work of Art, A by James Blish......................................SFS  Jul 1956
    (Originally appeared under title Art Work)
    THE WORLDS OF SCIENCE FICTION [Mills - 1963]
World of Heart's Desire by Robert Sheckley..(See listing The Store of the Worlds)
World of Myrion Flowers, The by Frederik Pohl & C. M. Kornbluth....F&SF  Oct 1961
    HUMAN AND OTHER BEINGS [DeGraeff - 1963]
World Otalmi Made, The by Harry Harrison...........................SFAd  Jun 1958
    GREAT SCIENCE FICTION ADVENTURES [Shaw - 1963]
Worlds of the Imperium by Keith Laumer.........(Excerpts)...........Fnt  Feb 1961
    A CENTURY OF SCIENCE FICTION [Knight - 1962]

# *X - Y*

"X" For "Expendable" by William C. Bailey...........................DSF  Dec 1952
    WAY OUT [Howard - 1963]
*Yesterday Was Monday by Theodore Sturgeon.........................UW  Jun 1941
    THE UNKNOWN [Benson - 1963]
You Are With It! by Will Stanton...................................F&SF  Dec 1961
    A CENTURY OF SCIENCE FICTION [Knight - 1962]
Young Goodman Brown by Nathaniel Hawthorne.........................DR  Dec 1844
    ROD SERLING'S TRIPLE W: WITCHES, WARLOCKS AND WEREWOLVES [Serling - 1963]
Young Lady Named Bright, The by A.H. Reginald Buller....(verse).....Pch  12/19/23
    THE MATHEMATICAL MAGPIE [Fadiman - 1962]
Young Man of Sid. Sussex, The by Arthur C. Hilton............(verse).............
    (From What Cheer — Edited by David McCord; 1945)
    THE MATHEMATICAL MAGPIE [Fadiman - 1962]

## *Miscellaneous*

$\pi$ and The Actuary by W. W. R. Ball...........................(No data available)
    THE MATHEMATICAL MAGPIE [Fadiman - 1962]

# *Alphabetical Author Listing*

## A

Mag.    Year

AANDAHL, VANCE  (2)
    Unfortunate Mr. Morky, The........................................F&SF  Oct 1962
        8th ANNUAL OF THE YEAR'S BEST SF [Merril - 1963]
    When Lilacs Last in the Dooryard Bloomed.......................F&SF  May 1962
        THE BEST FROM FANTASY & SCIENCE FICTION: 12th SERIES [Davidson - 1963]
ABERNATHY, ROBERT  (1)
    Pyramid.........................................................ASF  Jul 1954
        MORE PENGUIN SCIENCE FICTION [Aldiss - 1963]
AIKEN, CONRAD  (1)
    Oneiromachia........................(verse)....................Atl  Oct 1961
        7th ANNUAL OF THE YEAR'S BEST SF [Merril - 1962]
AINE, J. H. ROSNY ps (Honore Boex)  (1)
    Another World...................................................RP  n/d/a 1895
        A CENTURY OF SCIENCE FICTION [Knight - 1962]
          (Translated from French by Damon Knight)
ALBEE, GEORGE SUMNER  (1)
    Top, The.......................................................F&SF  Aug 1962
        12 GREAT CLASSICS OF SCIENCE FICTION [Conklin - 1963]
ALDISS, BRIAN W.  (4)
    Kind of Artistry, A............................................F&SF  Aug 1962
        THE BEST FROM FANTASY & SCIENCE FICTION: 12th SERIES [Davidson - 1962]
    T..............................................................Neb #18  Nov 1956
        FIRST FLIGHT: Maiden Voyages In Space and Time [Knight - 1963]
    There is a Tide................................................NW #44  Feb 1956
        SPECTRUM II [Amis & Conquest - 1962]
    *Who Can Replace A Man?........................................Inf  Jun 1958
        (Originally appeared under title But Who Can Replace A Man?)
        A CENTURY OF SCIENCE FICTION [Knight - 1962]
          (Appeared under original title)
        BEST SF FIVE SCIENCE FICTION STORIES [Crispin - 1963]
ALPERT, HOLLIS  (1)
    Simian Problem, The............................................F&SF  Jul 1960
        17 X INFINITY [Conklin - 1963]
ANDERSON, KAREN  (3)
    Landscape With Sphinxes.......................................F&SF  Nov 1962
        THE BEST FROM FANTASY & SCIENCE FICTION: 12th SERIES [Davidson - 1963]
    Piebold Hippogriff, The........................................Fnt  May 1962
        8th ANNUAL OF THE YEAR'S BEST SF [Merril - 1963]
    Six Haiku...........................(verse)....................F&SF  Jul 1962
        FIFTY SHORT SCIENCE FICTION TALES [Asimov & Conklin - 1963]
ANDERSON, POUL  (14)
    Ballade of an Artificial Satellite............(verse).........F&SF  Oct 1958
        FIFTY SHORT SCIENCE FICTION TALES [Asimov & Conklin - 1963]
    *Call Me Joe...................................................ASF  Apr 1957
        A CENTURY OF SCIENCE FICTION [Knight - 1962]
        SPECTRUM III [Amis & Conquest - 1963]
    *Chapter Ends, The............................................DSF  Jan 1954
        NOVELTS OF SCIENCE FICTION [Howard - 1963]
    Garden in the Void............................................Glxy  May 1952
        EXPLORING OTHER WORLDS [Moskowitz - 1963]

ANDERSON, POUL [Cont'd]             Mag.  Year

 *Helping Hand, The.....................................................ASF May 1950
   GREAT STORIES OF SPACE TRAVEL [Conklin - 1963]
 Honorable Enemies.................................................FW/SFS May 1951
   WAY OUT [Howard - 1963]
 Kings Who Die..............................................................If Mar 1962
   8th ANNUAL OF THE YEAR'S BEST SF [Merril - 1963]
 Longest Voyage, The....................................................ASF Dec 1960
   THE HUGO WINNERS [Asimov - 1962]
 *Martyr, The...........................................................F&SF Mar 1960
   BEST SF FIVE SCIENCE FICTION STORIES [Crispin - 1963]
 My Object All Sublime..................................................Glxy Jun 1961
   12 GREAT CLASSICS OF SCIENCE FICTION [Conklin - 1963]
 Night Piece............................................................F&SF Jul 1961
   THE WORLDS OF SCIENCE FICTION [Mills - 1963]
 Sentiment, Inc. .....................................................SFS #1 n/d 1953
   THE WEIRD ONES [Gold - 1962]
 Tiger by the Tail.......................................................PS Jan 1951
   MORE ADVENTURES ON OTHER PLANETS [Wollheim - 1963]
 *Tomorrow's Children...................................................ASF Mar 1947
   (Originally appeared under byline Poul Anderson & F. N. Waldrop)
   FIRST FLIGHT: Maiden Voyages In Space and Time [Knight - 1963]
ANONYMOUS
 Apothem [untitled]........................................(No data available)
   THE MATHEMATICAL MAGPIE [Fadiman - 1962]
 Culver City Arithmetic Exercise Paper............................Nykr 2/25/61
   THE MATHEMATICAL MAGPIE [Fadiman - 1962]
 Engineer's Yell.....................(verse)............(No data available)
   THE MATHEMATICAL MAGPIE [Fadiman - 1962]
 Mathematician Confided, A..............(verse)..............(No data available)
   THE MATHEMATICAL MAGPIE [Fadiman - 1962]
 Mathematician Named Klein, A................(verse).........(No data available)
   THE MATHEMATICAL MAGPIE [Fadiman - 1962]
 Modern Hiawatha, The.................(verse)..............(No data available)
   THE MATHEMATICAL MAGPIE [Fadiman - 1962]
 Riddle [untitled].....................(verse)...............................
   (From The Oxford Dictionary of Nursery Rhymes by Iona & Peter Opie; 1951)
   THE MATHEMATICAL MAGPIE [Fadiman - 1962]
 Song of the Screw.................(verse).................(No data available)
   THE MATHEMATICAL MAGPIE [Fadiman - 1962]
 Story of Sidi Norman, The
   ROD SERLING'S TRIPLE W: WITCHES, WARLOCKS AND WEREWOLVES [Serling-1963]
 There Was an Old Man Who Said, "Do..."........(verse).....(No data available)
   THE MATHEMATICAL MAGPIE [Fadiman - 1962]
 Verse [untitled].........................................................
   (From The Lore and Language of Schoolchildren by Iona & Peter Opie; 1959)
   THE MATHEMATICAL MAGPIE [Fadiman - 1962]
ANVIL, CHRISTOPHER (3)
 Hunch, The.............................................................ASF Jul 1961
   ANALOG I [J. W. Campbell - 1963]
 Pandora's Planet.......................................................ASF Sep 1956
   PROLOGUE TO ANALOG [J. W. Campbell - 1962]
 Prisoner, The..........................................................ASF Feb 1956
   BEST SF FIVE SCIENCE FICTION STORIES [Crispin - 1963]

| | Mag. | Year |
|---|---|---|

ARTHUR, ROBERT  (1)
  Mr. Jinx.................................................................UW  Aug 1941
      THE UNKNOWN [Benson - 1963]

ASIMOV, ISAAC  (15)
  *Belief..................................................................ASF  Oct 1953
      PROLOGUE TO ANALOG [J. W. Campbell - 1962]
  *Blind Alley.............................................................ASF  Mar 1945
      GREAT STORIES OF SPACE TRAVEL [Conklin - 1963]
  Feeling of Power, The....................................................If  Feb 1958
      THE MATHEMATICAL MAGPIE [Fadiman - 1962]
      SPECTRUM '11 [Amis & Conquest - 1962]
  *Fun They Had, The.......................................................NEA  12/1/51
      FIFTY SHORT SCIENCE FICTION TALES [Asimov & Conklin - 1963]
  *Galley Slave............................................................Glxy  Dec 1957
      TIME WAITS FOR WINTHROP AND FOUR OTHER SHORT NOVELS FROM GALAXY [Pohl-1962]
  Gentle Vultures, The....................................................SSF  Dec 1957
      CONTACT [Keyes - 1963]
  Jokester................................................................Inf  Dec 1956
      MORE PENGUIN SCIENCE FICTION [Aldiss - 1963]
  Lenny...................................................................Inf  Jan 1958
      THE EXPERT DREAMERS [Pohl - 1962]
  Living Space............................................................SFS  May 1956
      OUT OF THIS WORLD 3 [Williams-Ellis & Owen - 1962]
  *Not Final!.............................................................ASF  Oct 1941
      ASLEEP IN ARMAGEDDON [Sissons - 1962]
  Reason.................................................................ASF  Sep 1941
      A CENTURY OF SCIENCE FICTION [Knight - 1962]
  Runaround..............................................................ASF  Mar 1942
      THE COMING OF THE ROBOTS [Moskowitz - 1963]
  Strikebreaker..........................................................SFS  Jan 1957
      17 X INFINITY [Conklin - 1963]
  Ugly Little Boy.......................................................Glxy  Sep 1958
      (Originally appeared under title Lastborn)
      THE WORLDS OF SCIENCE FICTION [Mills - 1963]
  *What If...............................................................Fnt  Sum 1952
      GREAT SCIENCE FICTION BY SCIENTISTS [Conklin - 1962]

AUERBACH, ARNOLD M.  (1)
  Day Rembrandt Went Public, The..........................................Hpr  Jul 1962
      8th ANNUAL OF THE YEAR'S BEST SF [Merril - 1963]

# B

BAILEY, WILLIAM C.  (1)
  "X" For "Expendable"....................................................DSF  Dec 1952
      WAY OUT [Howard - 1963]

BAKER, RUSSELL  (1)
  Ms. Found In a Bus..............................................N.Y. Times  n/d/a 1962
      8th ANNUAL OF THE YEAR'S BEST SF [Merril - 1963]

BAKER, W. R.  (1)
  Magic Box, The..........................................................Hpr  Apr 1928
      THE MATHEMATICAL MAGPIE [Fadiman - 1962]

BALL, W. W. R.  (2)
  Extinction by Subtraction...............................(No data available)
      THE MATHEMATICAL MAGPIE [Fadiman - 1962]

BALL, W. W. R. [Cont'd]                                          Mag.    Year
    π and the Actuary...........................................(No data available)
        THE MATHEMATICAL MAGPIE [Fadiman - 1962]
BALLARD, J. G. (3)
    Garden of Time, The....................................F&SF  Feb 1962
        THE BEST FROM FANTASY & SCIENCE FICTION: 12th SERIES [Davidson - 1963]
    Insane Ones, The.......................................Amz   Jan 1962
        8th ANNUAL OF THE YEAR'S BEST SF [Merril - 1963]
    Voices of Time, The....................................NW #99 Nov 1960
        SPECTRUM III [Amis & Conquest - 1963]
BAMBER, GEORGE (1)
    Ottmar Balleau X2......................................Rog   Mar 1961
        7th ANNUAL OF THE YEAR'S BEST SF [Merril - 1962]
BANISTER, MANLY (1)
    Escape to Earth........................................SFQ   Nov 1957
        ESCAPE TO EARTH [Howard - 1963]
BANKS, RAYMOND E. (2)
    Double Dome............................................Glxy  May 1957
        HUMAN AND OTHER BEINGS [DeGraeff - 1963]
    Ear-Friend.............................................SFS   Mar 1955
        6 AND THE SILENT SCREAM [Howard - 1963]
BARR, STEPHEN (1)
    Verse [untitled] .........(Original variation of Dr. William Whewell verse )
        THE MATHEMATICAL MAGPIE [Fadiman - 1962]
BECKETT, SAMUEL (1)
    Sixteen Stones..............................................(From Molloy; 1955)
        (Translated from French by Patrick Bowles)
        THE MATHEMATICAL MAGPIE [Fadiman - 1962]
BEERBOHM, MAX (1)
    Note on the Einstein Theory, A.................(From Mainly on the Air; 1946)
        THE MATHEMATICAL MAGPIE [Fadiman - 1962]
BELAYEV, ALEXANDER (2)
    Hoity-Toity.................................................(No data available)
        A VISITOR FROM OUTER SPACE [Anonymous - undated]
            (Translated from Russian by Violet L. Dutt)
    Over the Abyss.............................................(No data available)
        DESTINATION: AMALTHEIA [Dixon - 1963]
            (Translated from Russian by Leonid Kolesnikov)
BESTER, ALFRED (3)
    *Fondly Fahrenheit.....................................F&SF  Aug 1954
        SPECTRUM III [Amis & Conquest - 1963]
    My Private World of Science Fiction..........(article).........ORIGINAL STORY
        THE WORLDS OF SCIENCE FICTION [Mills - 1963]
    *Of Time and Third Avenue.............................F&SF  Oct 1951
        A CENTURY OF SCIENCE FICTION [Knight - 1962]
BIERCE, AMBROSE (1)
    *Moxon's Master...............................(From Can Such Things Be; 1893)
        A CENTURY OF SCIENCE FICTION [Knight - 1962]
BIGGLE, LLOYD (JR.) (2)
    Monument...............................................ASF   Jun 1961
        ANALOG I [J. W. Campbell - 1963]
    Round Trip to Esidarap.................................If    Nov 1960
        (Originally appeared under title Esidarap Ot Pirt Dnuor)
        OUT OF THIS WORLD 3 [Williams-Ellis & Owen - 1962]

```
BINDER, EANDO ps (Otto Binder)  (3)                          Mag.    Year
    I, Robot.............................................Amz   Jan 1939
        THE COMING OF THE ROBOTS [Moskowitz - 1963]
    Iron Man............................................FSF #28  n/d 1955
        THE WEIRD ONES [Gold - 1962]
    Via Asteroid........................................TWS   Feb 1938
        (Originally appeared under pseudonym Gordon A. Giles)
        EXPLORING OTHER WORLDS [Moskowitz - 1963]
BISHOP, MORRIS  (1)
    E = MC2..................(verse)................(From A Bowl of Bishop; 1954)
        THE MATHEMATICAL MAGPIE [Fadiman - 1962]
BIXBY, JEROME  (2)
    Can Such Beauty Be?.................................Bynd  Sep 1953
        BEYOND [Anonymous - 1963]
    *Holes Around Mars, The.............................Glxy  Jan 1954
        GREAT STORIES OF SPACE TRAVEL [Conklin - 1963]
BLISH, JAMES  (6)
    Bridge..............................................ASF   Feb 1952
        SPECTRUM II [Amis & Conquest]
    * F Y I .........(From Star Science Fiction Stories #2 - Frederik Pohl; 1953)
        THE MATHEMATICAL MAGPIE [Fadiman - 1962]
    In Tomorrow's Little Black Bag.....................ORIGINAL STORY
        7th ANNUAL OF THE YEAR'S BEST SF [Merril - 1962]
    *Testament of Andros................................FSF   Jan 1953
        NOVELETS OF SCIENCE FICTION [Howard - 1963]
    Who's In Charge Here?...............................F&SF  May 1962
        THE BEST FROM FANTASY & SCIENCE FICTION: 12th SERIES [Davidson - 1963]
    *Work of Art, A.....................................SFS   Jul 1956
        (Originally appeared under title Art Work)
        THE WORLDS OF SCIENCE FICTION [Mills - 1963]
BLOCH, ALAN  (1)
    *Men Are Different.....(From Science Fiction Thinking Machines; Conklin-1954)
        FIFTY SHORT SCIENCE FICTION TALES [Asimov & Conklin - 1963]
BLOCH, ROBERT  (2)
    Cloak, The..........................................UW    May 1939
        HELL HATH FURY [Hay - 1963]
    Hell-Bound Train, The...............................F&SF  Sep 1958
        THE HUGO WINNERS [Asimov - 1962]
BOND, NELSON S.  (1)
    Prescience..........................................UW    Oct 1941
        THE UNKNOWN [Benson - 1963]
BONE, J. F.  (3)
    On the Fourth Planet................................Glxy  Apr 1963
        12 GREAT CLASSICS OF SCIENCE FICTION [Conklin - 1963]
    Prize for Edie, A...................................ASF   Apr 1961
        7th ANNUAL OF THE YEAR'S BEST SF [Merril - 1962]
    *Triggerman.........................................ASF   Dec 1958
        PROLOGUE TO ANALOG [J. W. Campbell - 1962]
BOUCHER, ANTHONY  (3)
    *Ambassadors, The...................................Stg   Jun 1952
        FIFTY SHORT SCIENCE FICTION TALES [Asimov & Conklin - 1963]
    Books..........................................(Special Original Feature)
        7th ANNUAL OF THE YEAR'S BEST SF [Merril - 1962]
        8th ANNUAL OF THE YEAR'S BEST SF [Merril - 1963]
```

BOUCHER, ANTHONY [Continued]                                    Mag.    Year
      *Quest for Saint Aquin, The.....(From New Tales of Space & Time; Healy-!951)
           BEST SF FIVE SCIENCE FICTION STORIES [Crispin - 1963]
           THE WORLDS OF SCIENCE FICTION [Mills - 1963]
      *Snulbug........................................................UW  Dec 1941
           THE UNKNOWN [Benson - 1963]
BRACKETT, LEIGH  (Mrs. Edmond Hamilton)  (2)
      All the Colors of the Rainbow...................................VSF  Nov 1957
           HUMAN AND OTHER BEINGS [DeGraeff - 1963]
      Child of the Sun...............................................PS   Spr 1942
           MORE ADVENTURES ON OTHER PLANETS [Wollheim - 1963]
BRADBURY, RAY  (8)
      *Asleep in Armageddon..........................................PS   Win 1948
           ASLEEP IN ARMAGEDDON [Sissons - 1962]
      Come Into My Cellar............................................Glxy  Oct 1962
           17 X INFINITY [Conklin - 1963]
      *Fire Ballons, The.............................................Im   Apr 1951
           CONTACT [Keyes - 1963]
      *Kaleidoscope..................................................TWS  Oct 1949
           GREAT STORIES OF SPACE TRAVEL [Conklin - 1963]
      Miracle of Rare Device, A......................................Plby  Jan 1962
           THE WORLDS OF SCIENCE FICTION [Mills - 1963]
           8th ANNUAL OF THE YEAR'S BEST SF [Merril - 1963]
      Other Foot, The................................................NS   Mar 1951
           HUMAN AND OTHER BEINGS [DeGraeff - 1963]
      Watchful Poker Chip, The.......................................Bynd  Mar 1954
           BEYOND [Anonymous - 1963]
      Way in the Middle of the Air...................................OW   Jul 1950
           HUMAN AND OTHER BEINGS [DeGraeff - 1963]
BRADLEY, MARION ZIMMER  (I)
      Wind People, The...............................................If   Feb 1959
           A CENTURY OF SCIENCE FICTION [Knight - 1962]
BRETNOR, R.  (I)
      All the Tea in China...........................................F&SF  May 1961
           7th ANNUAL OF THE YEAR'S BEST SF [Merril - 1962]
BREUER, MILES J. M. D.  (3)
      *Appendix and the Spectacles, The..............................Amz  Dec 1928
           THE MATHEMATICAL MAGPIE [Fadiman - 1963]
      *Gostak and the Doshes, The....................................Amz  Mar 1930
           GREAT SCIENCE FICTION BY SCIENTISTS [Conklin - 1962]
      ·Man Without an Appetite, The..................................BV   n/d/a 1916
           GREAT SCIENCE FICTION ABOUT DOCTORS [Conklin & Fabricant - 1963]
BROWN, FREDRIC  (9)
      Armageddon.....................................................UW   Aug 1941
           THE UNKNOWN [Benson - 1963]
      Double Whammy..................................................Bynd  Sep 1954
           BEYOND [Anonymous - 1963]
      Earthman Bearing Gifts.........................................Glxy  Jun 1960
           12 GREAT CLASSICS OF SCIENCE FICTION [Conklin - 1963]
      *Knock.........................................................TWS  Dec 1948
           CONTACT [Keyes - 1963]
      Nightmare in Time..............................................Dude
           7th ANNUAL OF THE YEAR'S BEST SF [Merril - 1962]
      Puppet Show....................................................Plby  Nov 1962
           8th ANNUAL OF THE YEAR'S BEST SF [Merril - 1963]

BROWN, FREDRIC [Continued]                                          Mag.    Year
     Something Green.........................................(From Space On My Hands; 1951)
          EXPLORING OTHER WORLDS [Moskowitz - 1963]
     *Weapon, The............................................................ASF    Apr 1951
          ASLEEP IN ARMAGEDDON [Sissons - 1962]
          FIFTY SHORT SCIENCE FICTION TALES [Asimov & Conklin - 1963]
w/ Mack Reynolds
     *Dark Interlude.........................................................Glxy   Jan 1951
          HUMAN AND OTHER BEINGS [DeGraeff - 1963]
BRUNNER, JOHN  (3)
     By the Name of Man......................................................Neb #17 Jul 1956
          MORE ADVENTURES ON OTHER PLANETS [Wollheim - 1963]
     Man From the Big Dark, The..............................................SFAd   Jun 1958
          GREAT SCIENCE FICTION ADVENTURES [Shaw - 1963]
     Such Stuff..............................................................F&SF   Jun 1962
          8th ANNUAL OF THE YEAR'S BEST SF [Merril - 1963]
BUDRYS, A(lgis) J.  (5)
     Due Process.............................................................ASF    Dec 1960
          12 GREAT CLASSICS OF SCIENCE FICTION [Conklin - 1963]
     In Human Hands..........................................................SFS #2 n/d 1954
          RARE SCIENCE FICTION [Howard - 1963]
     Real People, The........................................................Bynd   Nov 1953
          BEYOND [Anonymous - 1963]
     Snail's Pace............................................................DSF    Oct 1953
          WAY OUT [Howard - 1963]
     Walk to the World.......................................................Spc    Nov 1952
          FIRST FLIGHT: Maiden Voyages In Space and Time [Knight - 1963]
BULLER, A. H. REGINALD F.R.S.  (1)
     Young Lady Named Bright.................................................Pch    12/19/23
          THE MATHEMATICAL MAGPIE [Fadiman - 1962]
BULLOCK, ALICE  (1)
     Asylum..................................................................FSF    Aug 1954
          RARE SCIENCE FICTION [Howard - 1963]

# C

CALKINS, EARNEST ELMO  (1)
     Superlative Degree, The.............(verse).....................SRL    5/16/59
          THE MATHEMATICAL MAGPIE [Fadiman - 1962]
CANNING, GEORGE  (1)
     w/ Hookham Frere
          Loves of the Triangles, The.................................................
               (From The Anti-Jacobin, or Weekly Examiner; 1798)
               THE MATHEMATICAL MAGPIE [Fadiman - 1962]
CARAVAN, T. P.  (1)
     Random Sample...........................................................F&SF   Apr 1952
          FIFTY SHORT SCIENCE FICTION TALES [Asimov & Conklin - 1963]
CARR, TERRY  (1)
     Hop-Friend..............................................................F&SF   Nov 1962
          THE BEST FROM FANTASY & SCIENCE FICTION: 12th SERIES [Davidson - 1963]
CARROLL, LEWIS ps (Charles Lutwidge Dodgson)  (2)
     Apothem [untitled]...........(From Alice's Adventures In Wonderland; 1866)
          THE MATHEMATICAL MAGPIE [Fadiman - 1962]

CARROLL, LEWIS ps (Charles Lutwidge Dodgson) [Continued]          Mag.     Year
    Purse of Fortunatus, The..........................(From Sylvie and Bruno; 1889)
          THE MATHEMATICAL MAGPIE [Fadiman - 1962]
CARTMILL, CLEVE  (2)
    Hell Hath Fury.....................................................UW  Aug 1942
          HELL HATH FURY [Hay - 1963]
    Oscar.............................................................UW  Feb 1941
          FIFTY SHORT SCIENCE FICTION TALES [Asimov & Conklin - 1963]
CARTUR, PETER  (1)
    *Mist, The.......................................................F&SF  Sep 1952
          FIFTY SHORT SCIENCE FICTION TALES [Asimov & Conklin - 1963]
CASSIL, R. V.  (1)
    War in the Air, The.............................................Epch
          THE WORLDS OF SCIENCE FICTION [Mills - 1963]
CAUSEY, JAMES  (1)
    *Teething Ring...................................................Glxy  Jan 1953
          FIFTY SHORT SCIENCE FICTION TALES [Asimov & Conklin - 1963]
CHANDLER, (A.) BERTRAM  (1)     (See listing George Whitley)
    *Cage, The......................................................F&SF  Jun 1957
          12 GREAT CLASSICS OF SCIENCE FICTION [Conklin - 1963]
CHAPLING, SAUL  (1)
    w/ Johnny Mercer
      Square of the Hypotenuse, The...(song)...(From The Film MERRY ANDREW; 1958)
          THE MATHEMATICAL MAGPIE [Fadiman - 1962]
CHURCHILL, WINSTON  (1)
    Apothem [untitled].......................................(No data available)
          THE MATHEMATICAL MAGPIE [Fadiman - 1962]
CLARKE, ARTHUR C.  (14)
    At the End of the Orbit.............................................If  Nov 1961
          THE EXPERT DREAMERS [Pohl - 1962]
    Death and the Senator.............................................ASF  May 1961
          WORLDS OF WHEN [Conklin - 1962]
    *Forgotten Enemy, The...........................................NW #5  n/d 1949
          MORE PENGUIN SCIENCE FICTION [Aldiss - 1963]
    Haunted Space Suit, The............................................TW  5/11/58
          FIFTY SHORT SCIENCE FICTION TALES [Asimov & Conklin - 1963]
    *Loophole........................................................ASF  Apr 1946
          FIRST FLIGHT: Maiden Voyages In Space and Time [Knight - 1963]
    *Nine Billion Names of God...(From Star Science Fiction Stories; Pohl - 1953)
          THE MATHEMATICAL MAGPIE [Fadiman - 1962]
    Out of the Cradle, Endlessly Orbiting........................Dude  Mar 1959
          (Originally appeared under title Out of the Orbit)
          GREAT SCIENCE FICTION ABOUT DOCTORS [Conklin & Fabricant - 1963]
    *Pacifist, The....................................................FU  Oct 1956
          THE MATHEMATICAL MAGPIE [Fadiman - 1962]
    Possessed, The...................................................DSF  Mar 1953
          NOVELETS OF SCIENCE FICTION [Howard - 1963]
    Sentinel, The...................................................10SF  Spr 1951
          SPECTRUM III [Amis & Conquest - 1963]
    *Star, The.......................................................Inf  Nov 1955
          A CENTURY OF SCIENCE FICTION [Knight - 1962]
          THE HUGO WINNERS [Asimov - 1962]
          BEST SF FIVE SCIENCE FICTION STORIES [Crispin - 1963]
    Summertime In Icarus............................................Vog  Jun 1960
      (Org aprd under title The Hottest Piece of Real Estate In the Solar System)
          GREAT SCIENCE FICTION BY SCIENTISTS [Conklin - 1962]

CLARKE, ARTHUR C. [Continued]                                      Mag.    Year
    *Walk in the Dark, A...........................................TWS   Aug 1930
        GREAT STORIES OF SPACE TRAVEL [Conklin - 1963]
    Who's There?................................................NW #77  Nov 1958
        OUT OF THIS WORLD 3 [Williams-Ellis & Owen - 1962]
CLEEVE, BRIAN  (1)
    Angela's Satyr................................................SEP    11/3/62
        8th ANNUAL OF THE YEAR'S BEST SF [Merril - 1963]
CLIFTON, MARK  (3)
    Hang, Head, Vandal..........................................Amz    Apr 1962
        8th ANNUAL OF THE YEAR'S BEST SF [Merril - 1963]
    *Sense From Thought Divide...................................ASF    Mar 1955
        SPECTRUM II [Amis & Conquest - 1962]
    *Star Bright................................................Glxy   Jul 1952
        THE MATHEMATICAL MAGPIE [Fadiman - 1962]
CLINGERMAN, MILDRED  (1)
    *Stair Trick................................................F&SF   Aug 1952
        50 SHORT SCIENCE FICTION TALES [Asimov & Conklin - 1963]
COATES, ROBERT M.  (1)
    Law, The...................................................Nykr   11/29/47
        THE MATHEMATICAL MAGPIE [Fadiman - 1962]
COGSWELL, THEODORE R.  (2)
    Big Stink, The..............................................If     Jul 1954
        HUMAN AND OTHER BEINGS [DeGraeff - 1963]
    *Limiting Factor...........................................Glxy   Apr 1954
        CONTACT [Keyes - 1963]
COLLIER, JOHN  (1)
    *Evening Primrose.........................(From Presenting Moonshine; 1941)
        THE WORLDS OF SCIENCE FICTION [Mills - 1963]
COPPEL, ALFRED  (1)
    Blood Lands................................................DSF    Dec 1952
        WAY OUT [Howard - 1963]
COOPER, RALPH C.  (1)
    Neutrino Bomb, The........................................LASLN   7/13/61
        GREAT SCIENCE FICTION BY SCIENTISTS [Conklin - 1962]
CORREY, LEE ps (G. Harry Stine)  (1)
    Test Stand, The............................................ASF    Mar 1955
        THE EXPERT DREAMERS [Pohl - 1962]
COX, IRVING (E.) JR.  (1)
    Peace On Earth.............................................FSF    Jun 1954
        6 AND THE SILENT SCREAM [Howard - 1963]
CUMMINGS, PARKE  (1)
    Needed: Feminine Math.....................(From The Fly In the Martini; 1961)
        THE MATHEMATICAL MAGPIE [Fadiman - 1962]

**D**

DANCE, CLIFTON L. JR. (M.D.)  (1)
    Brothers, The..............................................F&SF   Jun 1952
        GREAT SCIENCE FICTION ABOUT DOCTORS [Conklin & Fabricant - 1963]
DAVIDSON, AVRAM  (3)
    *Now Let Us Sleep..........................................Ven    Sep 1957
        THE WORLDS OF SCIENCE FICTION [Mills - 1963]

DAVIDSON, AVRAM [Continued]                                    Mag.    Year
    *Or All the Seas with Oysters.......................................Glxy  May 1958
        THE HUGO WINNERS [Asimov - 1962]
    Singular Events Which Occured in the Hovel on the Alley off of Eye Street, The
    ............................................. ....................F&SF  Feb 1962
        THE BEST FROM FANTASY & SCIENCE FICTION: 12th SERIES [Davidson - 1963]
DAVIS, CHAN  (2)
    *Adrift on the Policy Level..........................................................
        (From Star Science Fiction Stories #5; Frederik Pohl - 1959)
        THE EXPERT DREAMERS [Pohl - 1962]
    Last Year's Grave Undug..............................................ORIGINAL STORY
        GREAT SCIENCE FICTION BY SCIENTISTS [Conklin - 1962]
DE CAMP, L. SPRAGUE  (5)
    *Gnarly Man, The.....................................................UW   Jun 1939
        THE UNKNOWN [Benson - 1963]
    Impractical Joke.....................................................FSF #29  n/d 1956
        THE WEIRD ONES [Gold - 1962]
    Isolinguals, The.....................................................ASF  Sep 1937
        FIRST FLIGHT: Maiden Voyages In Space and Time [Knight - 1963]
    Let's Have Fun.......................................................SFQ  May 1957
        RARE SCIENCE FICTION [Howard - 1963]
    Ultrasonic God.......................................................Fw/SFS  Jul 1951
        NOVELETS OF SCIENCE FICTION [Howard - 1963]
DE CONDILLAC, ETIENNE BONNOT  (1)
    Apothem [untitled]...................................................(No data available)
        THE MATHEMATICAL MAGPIE [Fadiman - 1962]
DE MORGAN, AUGUSTUS  (2)
    Apothem [untitled]...........................(From A Budget of Paradoxes; 1872)
        THE MATHEMATICAL MAGPIE [Fadiman - 1962]
    Euler, Diderot, Algebra, and God...........(From A Budget of Paradoxes; 1872)
        THE MATHEMATICAL MAGPIE [Fadiman - 1962]
DE VET, CHARLES V.  (1)
    Protective Camouflage................................................SFS  May 1955
        RARE SCIENCE FICTION [Howard - 1963]
DEAN, ABNER  (1)
    Cartoon [untitled]...........................(From What Am I Doing Here; 1947)
        THE MATHEMATICAL MAGPIE [Fadiman - 1962]
DEE, ROGER ps (Roger D. Aycock)  (1)
    *Unwelcome Tenant....................................................PS  Sum 1950
        FIFTY SHORT SCIENCE FICTION TALES [Asimov & Conklin - 1963]
DEHN, PAUL  (1)
    w/ Edward Gorey
        Quake, Quake, Quake........(verse).......(From Quake, Quake, Quake; 1961)
            7th ANNUAL OF THE YEAR'S BEST SF [Merril - 1962]
DEL REY, LESTER  (4)
    Faithful, The........................................................ASF  Apr 1938
        FIRST FLIGHT: Maiden Voyages In Space and Time [Knight - 1963]
    *Helen O'Loy.........................................................ASF  Dec 1938
        THE COMING OF THE ROBOTS [Moskowitz - 1963]
    I Am Tomorrow........................................................DSF  Dec 1952
        NOVELETS OF SCIENCE FICTION [Howard - 1963]
    *Wings of Night, The.................................................ASF  Mar 1942
        GREAT STORIES OF SPACE TRAVEL [Conklin - 1963]
DEMARE, LEO  (1)
    Cartoon [untitled] ........................... Man's Magazine  n/d/a 1958
        THE MATHEMATICAL MAGPIE [Fadiman - 1962]

(351)

DICK, PHILIP K.  (2)                                             Mag.    Year
    *Second Variety.................................................Spc  May 1953
        SPECTRUM II [Amis & Conquest - 1962]
    Vulcan's Hammer................................................FSF #29  n/d 1956
        6 AND THE SILENT SCREAM [Howard - 1963]
DICKINSON, JOSEPH  (1)
    Three for the Stars...........................................F&SF  Apr 1962
        THE BEST FROM FANTASY & SCIENCE FICTION: 12th SERIES [Davidson - 1963]
DICKSON, GORDON R.  (4)
    Amulet, The...................................................F&SF  Apr 1959
        ROD SERLING'S TRIPLE W: WITCHES, WARLOCKS AND WEREWOLVES [Serling - 1963]
    Home From the Shore...........................................Glxy  Feb 1963
        8th ANNUAL OF THE YEAR'S BEST SF [Merril - 1963]
    Monkey Wrench, The............................................ASF  Aug 1951
        MORE PENGUIN SCIENCE FICTION [Aldiss - 1963]
    Sleight of Wit................................................ASF  Dec 1961
        ANALOG I [J. W. Campbell - 1963]
DNIEPROV, ANATOLY  (2)
    Maxwell Equations, The........................................(No data available)
        DESTINATION: AMALTHEIA [Dixon - 1963]
            (Translated from Russian by Leonid Kolesnikov)
    Siema.........................................................(No data available)
        THE HEART OF THE SERPENT [Anonymous - 1961]
            (Translated from Russian by R. Prokofieva)
DOS PASSOS, JOHN  (1)
    Three Prologues and an Episode................................Adt  Spr 1961
        7th ANNUAL OF THE YEAR'S BEST SF [Merril - 1962]
DOYLE. SIR ARTHUR CONAN  (1)
    *Great Keinplatz Experiment, The.......(Org published by Rand McNally; 1895 )
        GREAT SCIENCE FICTION ABOUT DOCTORS [Conklin & Fabricant - 1963]
DRAPER, HAL  (1)
    Ms Fnd in a Lbry..............................................F&SF  Dec 1961
        17 X INFINITY [Conklin - 1963]
DRYFOOS, DAVE  (1)
    Blunder Enlightening..........................................DSF  Dec 1952
        WAY OUT [Howard - 1963]
DUNN, ALAN  (1)
    Cartoon [untitled]............................................SRL  3/12/55
        THE MATHEMATICAL MAGPIE [Fadiman - 1962]
DURREL, LAWRENCE  (1)
    High Barbary..................................................Mdm  Sep 1961
        7th ANNUAL OF THE YEAR'S BEST SF [Merril - 1962]

# E

EBERHART, SHERI S.  (1)
    Extraterrestrial Triogue on Terran Self-Destruction...(verse)..Glxy  Aug 1961
        7th ANNUAL OF THE YEAR'S BEST SF [Merril - 1962]
ELLANBY, BOYD ps (Lyle G. & William C. Boyd)  (1)
    Chain Reaction................................................Glxy  Sep 1956
        THE EXPERT DREAMERS [Pohl - 1962]
ELLIOTT, BRUCE  (1)
    *Wolves Don't Cry.............................................F&SF  Apr 1954
        ROD SERLING'S TRIPLE W: WITCHES, WARLOCKS & WEREWOLVES [Serling - 1963]

ELLIOTT, GEORGE P.  (3)                                                  Mag.    Year
    Among The Dangs..................................................Esq  Jun 1958
        7th ANNUAL OF THE YEAR'S BEST SF [Merril - 1962]
    Faq.............................................................HdR  Spr 1952
        THE WORLDS OF SCIENCE FICTION [Mills - 1963]
    NRACP, The......................................................HdR  Aut 1949
        HUMAN AND OTHER BEINGS [DeGraeff - 1963]
ELLISON, HARLAN  (1)
    All the Sounds of Fear.......................(From Ellison Wonderland; 1962)
        8th ANNUAL OF THE YEAR'S BEST SF [Merril - 1963]

# F

FARMER, PHILIP JOSE  (1)
    Sail On! Sail On!...............................................Stg  Dec 1952
        A CENTURY OF SCIENCE FICTION [Knight - 1962]
FAST, HOWARD  (4)
    Cato The Martian..............................................F&SF   Jun 1960
        17 X INFINITY [Conklin - 1963]
    First Men, The................................................F&SF   Feb 1960
        THE WORLDS OF SCIENCE FICTION [Mills - 1963]
        MORE PENGUIN SCIENCE FICTION [Aldiss - 1963]
    Intelligence Test.............................................SF+   Jun 1953
        CONTACT [Keyes - 1963]
    *Large Ant, The................................................FU   Feb 1960
        CONTACT [Keyes - 1963]
FEHRENBACH, T. R.  (1)
    Remember The Alamo!...........................................ASF   Dec 1961
        (Originally appeared under byline R. R. Fehrenbach)
        ANALOG I [J. W. Campbell - 1963]
FEIFFER, JULES  (1)
    Looking Backward.................(cartoon).....................HS   12/10/61
        7th ANNUAL OF THE YEAR'S BEST SF [Merril - 1962]
FELDMAN, ARTHUR  (1)
    Mathematicians, The...........................................Amz   Nov 1953
        FIFTY SHORT SCIENCE FICTION TALES [Asimov & Conklin - 1963]
FELSON, HENRY GEORGE (1)
    Spaceman Cometh, The.........................................F&SF   Apr 1956
        17 X INFINITY [Conklin - 1963]
FINK, DAVID HAROLD M.D.  (1)
    *Compound B.......(From New Tales of Space and Time; Raymond J. Healy— 1954)
        GREAT SCIENCE FICTION ABOUT DOCTORS [Conklin & Fabricant - 1963]
FINNEY, CHARLES G.  (1)
    Black Retriever, The.........................................F&SF   Oct 1958
        ROD SERLING'S TRIPLE W: WITCHES, WARLOCKS & WEREWOLVES [Serling - 1963]
FINNEY, JACK  (2)
    Face in the Photo, The........(From I Love Galesburg In the Springtime; 1962)
        8th ANNUAL OF THE YEAR'S BEST SF [Merril - 1963]
    *Third Level, The.............................................Col   10/7/50
        FIFTY SHORT SCIENCE FICTION TALES [Asimov & Conklin - 1963]
FISCHER, MICHAEL  (1)
    Misfit........................................................SF+   Dec 1953
        THE COMING OF THE ROBOTS [Moskowitz - 1963]

(353)

FITZPATRICK, R. C.  (I)                                                          Mag.    Year
     Circuit Riders, The...............................................ASF  Apr 1962
          8th ANNUAL OF THE YEAR'S BEST SF [Merril - 1963]
FORD, COREY  (I)
     Wonderful World of Figures, The...(From Corey Ford's Guide to Thinking; 1961)
          THE MATHEMATICAL MAGPIE [Fadiman - 1962]
FORSTER, E. M.  (I)
     *Machine Stops, The.........(From The Eternal Moment and Other Stories; 1928)
          17 X INFINITY [Conklin - 1963]
FRANKFORT, JAMES  (I)
     Cartoon [untitled]........................................................Vlg  10/12/61
          THE MATHEMATICAL MAGPIE [Fadiman - 1962]
FRERE, HOOKHAM  (I)
     w/ George Canning
     Loves of the Triangles, The...(Fr The Anti-Jacobin, or Weekly Examiner;1798)
          THE MATHEMATICAL MAGPIE [Fadiman - 1962]
FRIEDMAN, STUART  (I)
     *Beautiful, Beautiful, Beautiful!...................................Fut  Mar 1952
          FIFTY SHORT SCIENCE FICTION TALES [Asimov & Conklin - 1963]
FRISCH, O. R.  (I)
     On the Feasibility of Coal-Driven Power Stations..................SA   Mar 1956
          THE EXPERT DREAMERS [Pohl - 1962]
FRUEH, ALFRED  (I)
     Cartoon [untitled] ..................................................Nykr   4/19/58
          THE MATHEMATICAL MAGPIE [Fadiman - 1962]
FYFE, H. B.  (I)
     Knowledge Is Power................................................DSF  Dec 1952
          WAY OUT [Howard - 1963]

# G

GALLUN, RAYMOND Z.  (I)
     Derelict.........................................................ASF  Oct 1935
          THE COMING OF THE ROBOTS [Moskowitz - 1963]
GAMOW, GEORGE  (2)
     Heart on the Other Side, The......................................ORIGINAL STORY
          THE EXPERT DREAMERS [Pohl - 1962]
     With Apologies to Boyal...............(From One, Two, Three...Infinity; 1947)
          THE MATHEMATICAL MAGPIE [Fadiman - 1962]
GARRETT, RANDALL  (I)
     w/ Robert Silverberg
          Sound Decision..............................................ASF  Oct 1956
               PROLOGUE TO ANALOG [J. W. Campbell - 1962]
GILLIAN, SASHA  (I)
     Two's a Crowd.........................................F&SF  Jul 1962
          THE BEST FROM FANTASY & SCIENCE FICTION: 12th SERIES [Davidson - 1963]
GLASER, ALICE  (I)
     Tunnel Ahead, The................................................F&SF  Nov 1961
          7th ANNUAL OF THE YEAR'S BEST SF [Merril - 1962]
GODWIN, TOM  (I)
     Greater Thing, The...............................................ASF  Feb 1954
          MORE PENGUIN SCIENCE FICTION [Aldiss - 1963]

GOETHE (1)               Mag. Year
  Apothem [untitled]........................................(No data available)
    THE MATHEMATICAL MAGPIE [Fadiman - 1962]
GOGGIN, RICHARD (1)
  Frances Harkins...................................................F&SF Dec 1952
    17 X INFINITY [Conklin - 1963]
GOLD, HERBERT (1)
  Day They Got Boston, The..........................................F&SF Sep 1961
    17 X INFINITY [Conklin - 1963]
GOLD, H. L. (1)
  *Trouble With Water...............................................UW Mar 1939
    THE UNKNOWN [Benson - 1963]
GOREY, EDWARD (1)
  w/ Paul Dehn
    Quake, Quake, Quake.......(verse).......(From Quake, Quake, Quake; 1961)
     7th ANNUAL OF THE YEAR'S BEST SF [Merril - 1962]
GOSSET, THOROLD (1)
  Kiss Precise, The (Generalized)............(verse)............Ntr .1/9/37
    THE MATHEMATICAL MAGPIE [Fadiman - 1962]
GOULART, RON (1)
  Please Stand By...................................................F&SF Jan 1962
    THE BEST FROM FANTASY & SCIENCE FICTION: 12th SERIES [Davidson - 1963]
GRAHAM, L. A. (4)
  Miniver Problem, The (Solution)..(From Ingenious Problems and Methods; 1959)
    THE MATHEMATICAL MAGPIE [Fadiman - 1962]
  Verses (Three) [untitled]......(From Ingenious Problems and Methods; 1959)
    THE MATHEMATICAL MAGPIE [Fadiman - 1962]
GRAVES, ROBERT (1)
  Abominable Mr. Gunn, The.....................(From Five Pens In Hand; 1955)
    THE MATHEMATICAL MAGPIE [Fadiman - 1962]
GREGOR, LEE ps (Milton A. Rothman) (1)
  Heavy Planet......................................................Ast Aug 1939
    THE EXPERT DREAMERS [Pohl - 1962]
GRENDON, EDWARD (1)
  *Figure, The......................................................ASF Jul 1947
    FIFTY SHORT SCIENCE FICTION TALES [Asimov & Conklin - 1963]
GRINNEL, DAVID (1)
  *The Rag Thing....................................................F&SF Oct 1951
    FIFTY SHORT SCIENCE FICTION TALES [Asimov & Conklin - 1963]
GROSS, MARION (1)
  *Good Provider, The...............................................F&SF Sep 1952
    FIFTY SHORT SCIENCE FICTION TALES [Asimov & Conklin - 1963]
GROW, JULIAN F. (1)
  Fastest Gun Dead, The.............................................If Mar 1961
    7th ANNUAL OF THE YEAR'S BEST SF [Merril - 1962]
GUIN, WYMAN (2)
  *Beyond Bedlam....................................................Glxy Aug 1951
    SPECTRUM II [Amis & Conquest - 1962]
  Root and the Ring, The............................................Bynd Sep 1954
    BEYOND [Anonymous - 1963]
GUNN, JAMES E. (1)
  Beautiful Brew, The...............................................Bynd Sep 1954
    BEYOND [Anonymous - 1963]

GUREVICH, GEORGY (1)                                              Mag.    Year
    Infra Draconis........................................(No data available)
        A VISITOR FROM OUTER SPACE [Anonymous - undated]
            (Translated from Russian by Violet L. Dutt)

HAASE, JOHN (1)
    Countdown, The.................................................Nykr  10/7/61
        7th ANNUAL OF THE YEAR'S BEST SF [Merril - 1962]
HALDANE, J. B. S. (1)
    Gold Makers, The..........................(From The Inequality of Man; 1932)
        GREAT SCIENCE FICTION BY SCIENTISTS [Conklin - 1962]
HALE, ROBERT BEVERLY (1)
    Immediately Yours..............................................Mdm  Nov 1961
        7th ANNUAL OF THE YEAR'S BEST SF [Merril - 1962]
HAMILTON, EDMOND (3)
    *Dead Planet, The..............................................Stg  Spr 1946
        EXPLORING OTHER WORLDS [Moskowitz - 1963]
    Starcombers, The..............................................SFAd  Dec 1956
        GREAT SCIENCE FICTION ADVENTURES [Shaw - 1963]
    What's It Like Out There?......................................Stg  Dec 1952
        A CENTURY OF SCIENCE FICTION [Knight - 1962]
HARMON, JIM (1)
    Luck, Inc. ....................................................SFS  Nov 1959
        RARE SCIENCE FICTION [Howard - 1963]
HARRISON, HARRY (3)
    Alien Agony, An...........................................NW #122  Sep 1962
        (Originally appeared under title The Streets of Ashkalon)
        MORE PENGUIN SCIENCE FICTION [Aldiss - 1963]
    Toy Shop, The..................................................ASF  Apr 1962
        8th ANNUAL OF THE YEAR'S BEST SF [Merril - 1963]
    World Otalmi Made, The........................................SFAd  Jun 1958
        GREAT SCIENCE FICTION ADVENTURES [Shaw - 1963]
HART, JOHNNY (1)
    B. C. [Cartoon]...............................................NYHT  8/13/61
        THE MATHEMATICAL MAGPIE [Fadiman - 1962]
HAWTHORNE, NATHANIEL (2)
    Rappaccini's Daughter...........................................DR  Dec 1844
        GREAT SCIENCE FICTION ABOUT DOCTORS [Conklin & Fabricant - 1963]
    Young Goodman Brown............................................NEM  Apr 1835
        ROD SERLING'S TRIPLE W: WITCHES, WARLOCKS & WEREWOLVES [Serling - 1963]
HEINLEIN, ROBERT A. (4)
    *"All You Zombies — ".........................................F&SF  Mar 1959
        THE WORLDS OF SCIENCE FICTION [Mills - 1963]
    *Columbus Was a Dope...........................................Stg  May 1947
        FIFTY SHORT SCIENCE FICTION TALES [Asimov & Conklin - 1963]
    Life-Line......................................................ASF  Aug 1939
        FIRST FLIGHT: Maiden Voyages In Space and Time [Knight - 1963]
    Sky-Lift........................................................Im  Nov 1953
        A CENTURY OF SCIENCE FICTION [Knight - 1962]
HENDERSON, ZEENA (3)
    *Ararat.......................................................F&SF  Oct 1952
        OUT OF THIS WORLD 3 [Williams-Ellis & Owen - 1962]

HENDERSON, ZEENA [Continued]                             Mag.    Year

   Subcommittee.....................................................F&SF  Jul 1962
       3th ANNUAL OF THE YEAR'S BEST SF [Merril - 1963]
   Things..........................................................F&SF  Jul 1960
       12 GREAT CLASSICS OF SCIENCE FICTION [Conklin - 1963]

HENSLEY, JOE L. (1)
   And Not Quite Human.............................................Bynd Sep 1953
       ROD SERLING'S TRIPLE W: WITCHES, WARLOCKS & WEREWOLVES [Serling - 1963]

HERBERT, FRANK (2)
   A-W-F Unlimited.................................................Glxy Jun 1961
       17 X INFINITY [Conklin - 1963]
   Cease Fire......................................................ASF  Jan 1958
       A CENTURY OF SCIENCE FICTION [Knight - 1962]

HERNHUNTER, ALBERT (1)
   Texas Week......................................................FU  Jan 1954
       FIFTY SHORT SCIENCE FICTION TALES [Asimov & Conklin - 1963]

HICKEY, H. B. ps (Herb Livingston) (1)
   *Hilda..........................................................F&SF Sep 1952
       FIFTY SHORT SCIENCE FICTION TALES [Asimov & Conklin - 1963]

HILTON, ARTHUR C. (1)
   Young Man of Sid. Sussex, The................(verse)........................
       (From What Cheer — Edited by David McCord; 1945)
       THE MATHEMATICAL MAGPIE [Fadiman - 1962]

HILTON-YOUNG, W. (1)
   *Choice, The....................................................Pch  3/19/52
       FIFTY SHORT SCIENCE FICTION TALES [Asimov & Conklin - 1963]

HIRSHFIELD, HENRY I. (1)
   w/ G. M. Mateyko
      On Handling the Data............................................ASF Sep 1959
         (Originally appeared under byline M. I. Mayfield)
       BEST SF FIVE SCIENCE FICTION STORIES [Crispin - 1963]

HOGG, THOMAS JEFFERSON (1)
   Paradise Lost at Cambridge................................(No data available)
       THE MATHEMATICAL MAGPIE [Fadiman - 1962]

HOLBROOKE, JOSEPH CHARLES (1)
   w/ Sidney H. Sime
      Ta Ta, The................(Song)...............(From Bogey Beasts; 1962)
       THE MATHEMATICAL MAGPIE [Fadiman - 1962]

HOYLE, FRED (1)
   Black Cloud, The.............................(From The Black Cloud; 1957)
       THE EXPERT DREAMERS [Pohl - 1962]

HUBBARD, L. RON (1)
   Devil's Rescue, The.............................................UW  Oct 1940
       HELL HATH FURY [Hay - 1963]

HUGHES, RICHARD (1)
   Vanishing Man, The..........................(From A Moment in Time; 1926 )
       THE MATHEMATICAL MAGPIE [Fadiman - 1962]

HURLBUT, KAATJE (1)
   Passage Among the Stars, A......................................SEP  5/13/61
       7th ANNUAL OF THE YEAR'S BEST SF [Merril - 1962]

HUXLEY, JULIAN (1)
   Tissue Culture King, The........................................Amz Aug 1927
       GREAT SCIENCE FICTION BY SCIENTISTS [Conklin - 1962]

# J

Mag.   Year

JAMESON, MALCOLM  (2)
   *Blind Alley................................................UW  Jun 1943
      ROD SERLING'S TRIPLE W: WITCHES, WARLOCKS & WEREWOLVES [Serling - 1963]
   Double and Redoubled........................................UW  Feb 1941
      THE UNKNOWN [Benson - 1963]
JONES, RAYMOND F.  (2)
   Doomsday's Color-Press.....................................FSF  Nov 1952
      ESCAPE TO EARTH [Howard - 1963]
   *Noise Level...............................................ASF  Dec 1952
      BEST SF FIVE SCIENCE FICTION STORIES [Crispin - 1963]
JOURDAN, D. A.  (1)
   Children of Fortune........................................SFQ  Feb 1957
      6 AND THE SILENT SCREAM [Howard - 1963]
JUSTER, NORTON  (1)
   Milo and the Mathemagician.................(From The Phantom Tollbroth; 1961)
      THE MATHEMATICAL MAGPIE [Fadiman - 1962]

# K

KAZANTSEV, ALEXANDER  (2)
   Martian, The...............................................(No data available)
      A VISITOR FROM OUTER SPACE [Anonymous - undated]
         (Translated from Russian by Violet L. Dutt)
   Visitor from Outer Space, A................................(No data available)
      A VISITOR FROM OUTER SPACE [Anonymous - undated]
         (Translated from Russian by Violet L. Dutt)
KELLER, DAVID H.  M.D.  (1)
   Psychophonic Nurse, The....................................Amz  Nov 1928
      GREAT SCIENCE FICTION ABOUT DOCTORS [Conklin & Fabricant - 1963]
KELLER, TEDDY  (1)
   Plague, The................................................ASF  Feb 1961
      ANALOG I [J. W. Campbell - 1963]
KERSH, GERALD  (1)
   Unsafe Deposit Box, The....................................SEP  4/14/62
      8th ANNUAL OF THE YEAR'S BEST SF [Merril - 1963]
KEYES, DANIEL  (1)
   *Flowers for Algernon......................................F&SF Apr 1959
      THE HUGO WINNERS [Asimov - 1962]
KIPLING, RUDYARD  (3)
   *As Easy as A.B.C..........................................LM   Mar 1912
      17 X INFINITY [Conklin - 1963]
   MacDonough's Song.................(verse)...................Mpln Mar 1912
      17 X INFINITY [Conklin - 1963]
   *Mark of the Beast, The.........................(From Life's Handicap; 1891)
      ROD SERLING'S TRIPLE W: WITCHES, WARLOCKS & WEREWOLVES [Serling - 1963]
KNIGHT, DAMON  (4)
   Babel II...................................................Bynd Jul 1953
      THE WORLDS OF SCIENCE FICTION [Mills - 1963]
   *Cabin Boy.................................................Glxy Sep 1951
      GREAT STORIES OF SPACE TRAVEL [Conklin - 1963]

KNIGHT, DAMON [Continued]                                         Mag.   Year
    *Natural State.................................................Glxy  Jan 1954
        TIME WAITS FOR WINTHROP & 4 OTHER SHORT NOVELS FROM GALAXY [Pohl-1962]
    *Not With a Bang...............................................F&SF  Spr 1950
        FIFTY SHORT SCIENCE FICTION TALES [Asimov & Conklin - 1963]
KNOX, RONALD A.  (1)
    Short Cuts to Success..........................................Slp  Nov 1917
        THE MATHEMATICAL MAGPIE [Fadiman - 1962]
KOCH, HOWARD  (1)
    *Invasion From Mars............The radio script of the Orson Welles broadcast
        of H. G. Wells' The War of the Worlds over the Columbia Broadcasting
        System, October 30, 1938.      (Copyright 1940 Princeton University Press)
        CONTACT [Keyes - 1963]
KORNBLUTH, C. M.  (4)
    *Altar at Midnight, The........................................Glxy  Mar 1952
        FIFTY SHORT SCIENCE FICTION TALES [Asimov & Conklin - 1963]
    Little Black Bag, The..........................................ASF   Jul 1950
        GREAT SCIENCE FICTION ABOUT DOCTORS [Conklin & Fabricant - 1963]
    w/ Frederik Pohl
        Quaker Cannon, The.........................................ASF   Aug 1961
            7th ANNUAL OF THE YEAR'S BEST SF [Merril - 1962]
        World of Myrion Flowers, The...............................F&SF  Oct 1961
            HUMAN AND OTHER BEINGS [DeGraeff - 1963]
KUMIN, MAXINE W.  (1)
    To a Astronaut Dying Young.....................................Atl   Dec 1961
        7th ANNUAL OF THE YEAR'S BEST SF [Merril - 1962]
KUTTNER, HENRY  (2)
    Camouflage.....................................................ASF   Sep 1945
        (Originally appeared under pseudonym Lewis Padgett)
        ASLEEP IN ARMAGEDDON [Sissons - 1962]
    Misguided Halo, The............................................UW    Aug 1939
        THE UNKNOWN [Benson - 1963]
KUYKENDALL, ROGER  (1)
    We Didn't Do Anything Wrong, Hardly............................ASF   May 1959
        PROLOGUE TO ANALOG [J. W. Campbell - 1962]

# L

LAFFERTY, R. A.  (1)
    Seven-Day Terror...............................................If    Mar 1962
        8th ANNUAL OF THE YEAR'S BEST SF [Merril - 1963]
LANIER, STERLING E.  (1)
    Join Our Gang?.................................................ASF   May 1961
        ANALOG I [J. W. Campbell - 1963]
LATHAM, PHILIP ps (Robert S. Richardson)  (1)
    To Explain Mrs. Thompson.......................................ASF   Nov 1951
        THE EXPERT DREAMERS [Pohl - 1962]
LAUMER, KEITH  (1)
    Worlds of the Imperium.....................(Excerpts).............Fnt  Feb 1961
        A CENTURY OF SCIENCE FICTION [Knight - 1962]
LEACOCK, STEPHEN  (2)
    A, B, and C — The Human Element in Mathematics..(From Literary Lapses; 1912)
        THE MATHEMATICAL MAGPIE [Fadiman - 1962]

```
LEACOCK, STEPHEN [Continued]                                       Mag.    Year
    Mathematics for Golfers..........................(From Literary Lapses; 1912)
        THE MATHEMATICAL MAGPIE [Fadiman - 1962]
LEC, STANISLAW JERZY  (4)
    Apothems (Four) [untitled] ....................(From Unkempt Thoughts; 1962)
        (Translated from Polish by Jack Galazka)
        THE MATHEMATICAL MAGPIE [Fadiman - 1962]
LEIBER, FRITZ  (8)
    *Bad Day for Sales, A...........................................Glxy  Jul 1953
        FIFTY SHORT SCIENCE FICTION TALES [Asimov & Conklin - 1963]
    Beat Cluster, The...............................................Glxy  Oct 1961
        7th ANNUAL OF THE YEAR'S BEST SF [Merril - 1962]
    Bleak Shore, The.................................................UW   Nov 1940
        THE UNKNOWN [Benson - 1963]
        HELL HATH FURY [Hay - 1963]
    Bullet With His Name............................................Glxy  Jul 1958
        WORLDS OF WHEN [Conklin - 1962]
    Hatchery of Dreams...............................................Fnt  Nov 1961
        ROD SERLING'S TRIPLE W: WITCHES, WARLOCKS & WEREWOLVES [Serling-1963]
    *Later Than You Think...........................................Glxy  Oct 1950
        BEST SF FIVE SCIENCE FICTION STORIES [Crispin - 1963]
    Man who Made Friends with Electricity, The.....................F&SF  Mar 1962
        8th ANNUAL OF THE YEAR'S BEST SF [Merril - 1963]
    *What's He Doing In There?......................................Glxy  Dec 1957
        CONTACT [Keyes - 1963]
LEINSTER, MURRAY ps (Will F. Jenkins)  (6)
    Exploration Team................................................ASF   Mar 1956
        THE HUGO WINNERS [Asimov - 1962]
        SPECTRUM III [Amis & Conquest - 1963]
    *First Contact..................................................ASF   May 1945
        CONTACT [Keyes - 1963]
    Propagandist....................................................ASF   Aug 1947
        GREAT STORIES OF SPACE TRAVEL [Conklin - 1963]
    Ribbon In the Sky...............................................ASF   Jun 1957
        GREAT SCIENCE FICTION ABOUT DOCTORS [Conklin & Fabricant - 1963]
    *This Star Shall be Free........................................Sup   Nov 1949
        ASLEEP IN ARMAGEDDON [Sissons - 1962]
    West Wind.......................................................ASF   Mar 1948
        THREE IN ONE [Margulies - 1963]
LESSER, MILTON  (4)
    "A" as in Android............................................Fw/SFS  May 1951
        NOVELETS OF SCIENCE FICTION [Howard - 1963]
    Do It Yourself..............................................FSF #33  Sum 1957
        RARE SCIENCE FICTION [Howard - 1963]
    Ennui...........................................................DSF   Dec 1952
        WAY OUT [Howard - 1963]
    Name Your Tiger.................................................SFQ   May 1957
        THE WEIRD ONES [Howard - 1962]
LEWIS, JACK  (1)
    *Who's Cribbing.................................................Stg   Jan 1953
        FIFTY SHORT SCIENCE FICTION TALES [Asimov & Conklin - 1963]
LEY, WILLY  (1)
    Martian Adventure, A...........................................ASF   Feb 1937
        (Originally aprd under title At The Perhilion and pseudonym Robt Willey)
        GREAT SCIENCE FICTION BY SCIENTISTS [Conklin - 1962]
```

LICHTENBERG, GEORGE CHRISTOPHER  (5)                    Mag.    Year
    Apothems (Five) [untitled]............(From The Lichtenberg Reader — Edited
        by Franz H. Mautner and Henry Hatfield; 1959)
        THE MATHEMATICAL MAGPIE [Fadiman — 1962]
LISTER, R. P. (1)
    Song Against Circles, A................(verse)..................Nykr    5/13/61
        THE MATHEMATICAL MAGPIE [Fadiman — 1962]
LOHWATER, A. J.  (1)
    Devil a Mathematician Would be, The......................(No data available)
        THE MATHEMATICAL MAGPIE [Fadiman — 1962]
LONDON, JACK  (1)
    *Scarlet Plague, The.....................................ASMM    9/14/13
        ASLEEP IN ARMAGEDDON [Sissons — 1962]
LONG, FRANK BELKNAP (2)
    Night-Fear.............................................DSF    Oct 1953
        NOVELETS OF SCIENCE FICTION [Howard — 1963]
    Riddle of the Deadly Paradise..........................SFS    Nov 1958
        6 AND THE SILENT SCREAM [Howard — 1963]
LOOMIS, NOEL  (1)
    "If The Court Pleases"................................DSF    Jun 1953
        ESCAPE TO EARTH [Howard — 1963]


# M


MacCREIGH, JAMES ps (Frederik Pohl)  (1)
    w/ Judith Merril
        Big Man with the Girls, A.............................FSF    Mar 1953
            ESCAPE TO EARTH [Howard — 1963]
MacDONALD, JOHN D.  (1)
    Spectator Sport......................................TWS    Feb 1950
        FIFTY SHORT SCIENCE FICTION TALES [Asimov & Conklin — 1963]
MACKAY, CHARLES  (1)
    Witch Trials and the Law.................(article)........(excerpts).........
        (From Extraordinary Popular Delusions and the Madness of Crowds; 1841)
        ROD SERLING'S TRIPLE W: WITCHES, WARLOCKS & WEREWOLVES [Serling — 1963]
MacLEAN, KATHERINE  (1)
    *Unhuman Sacrifice....................................ASF    Nov 1958
        A CENTURY OF SCIENCE FICTION [Knight — 1962]
MANHATTAN, AVRO  (1)
    Crickett Ball, The....................................F&SF   Oct 1955
        FIFTY SHORT SCIENCE FICTION TALES [Asimov & Conklin — 1963]
MARKS, WINSTON K.  (3)
    Double-Take.........................................SFAd   Dec 1953
        (Originally appeared under pseudonym Ken Winney)
        FIFTY SHORT SCIENCE FICTION TALES [Asimov & Conklin — 1963]
    I'd Give a Dollar...................................Bynd   May 1954
        BEYOND [Anonymous — 1963]
    Mate in Two Moves..................................Glxy   May 1954
        GREAT SCIENCE FICTION ABOUT DOCTORS [Conklin & Fabricant — 1963]
MARTINO, JOSEPH P.  (1)
    Pushbutton War.....................................ASF    Aug 1960
        PROLOGUE TO ANALOG [J. W. Campbell — 1962]

MATEYKO, G. M.  (1)                                                        Mag.    Year
    w/ Henry I. Hirshfield
        On Handling the Data............................................ASF  Sep 1959
            (Originally appeared under byline M. I. Mayfield)
        BEST SF FIVE SCIENCE FICTION STORIES [Crispin - 1963]
MATHESON, RICHARD  (1)
    Being..............................................................If   Aug 1954
        ASLEEP IN ARMAGEDDON [Sissons - 1962]
McCAFFREY, ANNE  (1)
    Ship Who Sang, The.............................................F&SF  Apr 1961
        7th ANNUAL OF THE YEAR'S BEST SF [Merril - 1962]
McCONNELL, JAMES  (1)
    Learning Theory....................................................If   Dec 1957
        GREAT SCIENCE FICTION BY SCIENTISTS [Conklin - 1962]
McINTOSH, J. T.  ps (James J. MacGregor)  (2)
    Immortality for Some...........................................ASF  Mar 1960
        12 GREAT CLASSICS OF SCIENCE FICTION [Conklin - 1963]
    *Made In U. S. A. ............................................Glxy  Apr 1953
        HUMAN AND OTHER BEINGS [DeGraeff - 1963]
McKNIGHT, JOHN P.  (1)
    Prolog.........................................................F&SF  Aug 1951
        FIFTY SHORT SCIENCE FICTION TALES [Asimov & Conklin - 1963]
MENCKEN, J. B.  (1)
    Apothem [untitled] .................(From De Charlataneria Eruditorum; 1715)
        THE MATHEMATICAL MAGPIE [Fadiman - 1962]
MERCER, JOHNNY  (1)
    w/ Saul Chapling
        Square of the Hypotenuse, The..(Song)..(From The Film MERRY ANDREW; 1958)
            THE MATHEMATICAL MAGPIE [Fadiman - 1962]
MERRIL, JUDITH  (1)
    *That Only a Mother................................................ASF  Jun 1948
        FIRST FLIGHT: Maiden Voyages In Space and Time [Knight - 1963]
MILLER, LION  (1)
    *Available Data on the Worp Reaction, The......................F&SF  Sep 1953
        FIFTY SHORT SCIENCE FICTION TALES [Asimov & Conklin - 1963]
MILLER, P. SCHUYLER  (1)
    Frog, The..........................................................UW   Oct 1942
        HELL HATH FURY [Hay - 1963]
MILLER, WALTER M.  JR.  (3)
    *Crucifixus Etiam.................................................ASF  Feb 1953
        ASLEEP IN ARMAGEDDON [Sissons - 1962]
    Darfsteller, The.................................................ASF  Jan 1955
        THE HUGO WINNERS [Asimov - 1962]
    *Momento Homo...................................................Amz  Mar 1954
        THE WORLDS OF SCIENCE FICTION [Mills - 1963]
MOORE, C. L.  (1)
    Home There's No Returning........................(From No Boundaries; 1955)
        (Originally aprd under joint byline Henry Kuttner and C. L. Moore)
        ASLEEP IN ARMAGEDDON [Sissons - 1962]
MOORE, WARD  (1)
    It Becomes Necessary.........................................Gent n/d/a 1961
        (Originally appeared under title The Cold Peace)
            7th ANNUAL OF THE YEAR'S BEST SF [Merril - 1962]

MORLEY, CHRISTOPHER (1)                                          Mag.    Year
    Portrait of a Mathematician.............(verse).............................
        (From The Ballard of New York, New York and Other Poems: 1930-1950; 1950)
        THE MATHEMATICAL MAGPIE [Fadiman - 1962]
MORRISON, WILLIAM ps (Joseph Samachson)  (2)
    Bedside Manner.....................................................Glxy  May 1954
        GREAT SCIENCE FICTION ABOUT DOCTORS [Conklin & Fabricant - 1963]
    *Feast of Demons, A................................................Glxy  Mar 1958
        THE EXPERT DREAMERS [Pohl - 1962]
MORTLOCK, BILL (1)
    Apothem [untitled].......................(From Lawyer, Heal Thyself; 1959)
        THE MATHEMATICAL MAGPIE [Fadiman - 1962]
MOSKOWITZ, SAM  (1)
    Man of the Stars...................................................PS  Win 1941
        EXPLORING OTHER WORLDS [Moskowitz - 1963]

# N

NEARING, H.  Jr.  (1)
    Hermeneutical Doughnut, The...................................................
        (From The Sinister Researches of C. P. Ransom; 1954)
        THE MATHEMATICAL MAGPIE [Fadiman - 1962]
NELSON, ALAN  (3)
    *Narapoia.........................................................Wdg  Apr 1948
        (Originally appeared under title The Origin of Narapoia)
        FIFTY SHORT SCIENCE FICTION TALES [Asimov & Conklin - 1963]
    Shopdropper, The..................................................F&SF  Jan 1955
        GREAT SCIENCE FICTION ABOUT DOCTORS [Conklin & Fabricant - 1963]
    Silenzia..........................................................F&SF  Sep 1953
        17 X INFINITY [Conklin - 1963]
NEWCOMB, SIMON  (1)
    That Mason-Dixon Line....................................(No data available)
        THE MATHEMATICAL MAGPIE [Fadiman - 1962]
NOLAN, WILLIAM F.  (1)
    One of Those Days.................................................F&SF  May 1962
        8th ANNUAL OF THE YEAR'S BEST SF [Merril - 1963]
NORBET, W. ps (Dr. Norbert Weiner)  (2)
    *Brain, The........................................................TEN  Apr 1952
        GREAT SCIENCE FICTION BY SCIENTISTS [Conklin - 1962]
    Miracle of the Broom Closet, The...................................TEN  Apr 1952
        THE EXPERT DREAMERS [Pohl - 1962]
NOURSE, ALAN E.  M. D.  (3)
    Counterfeit.......................................................TWS  Aug 1952
        MORE PENGUIN SCIENCE FICTION [Aldiss - 1963]
    *Family Resemblance...............................................ASF  Apr 1953
        GREAT SCIENCE FICTION ABOUT DOCTORS [Conklin & Fabricant - 1963]
    *Tiger by the Tail................................................Glxy  Nov 1951
        FIFTY SHORT SCIENCE FICTION TALES [Asimov & Conklin - 1963]

# O

O'BRIEN, FITZ-JAMES  (I)                                                                          Mag.     Year
    *What Was It?...................................................Hpr  Mar 1859
      A CENTURY OF SCIENCE FICTION [Knight - 1962]
O'DONNELL, LAWRENCE ps (Henry Kuttner & C. L. Moore)  (I)
    *Vintage Season.................................................ASF  Sep 1946
      SPECTRUM II [Amis & Conquest - 1962]
OLIVER, CHAD  (2)
    Mother of Necessity.............................(From Another Kind; 1955)
      GREAT SCIENCE FICTION BY SCIENTISTS [Conklin - 1962]
    Transfusion.....................................................ASF  Jun 1959
      WORLDS OF WHEN [Conklin - 1962]
ORWELL, GEORGE ps (Eric Blair)  (I)
    Apothem [untitled] .............................(From Animal Farm; 1945 )
      THE MATHEMATICAL MAGPIE [Fadiman - 1962]

# P

PANGBORN, EDGAR  (2)
    *Angel's Egg....................................................Glxy  Jun 1951
      A CENTURY OF SCIENCE FICTION [Knight - 1962]
    Golden Horn, The................................................F&SF  Feb 1962
      THE BEST FROM FANTASY & SCIENCE FICTION: 12th SERIES [Davidson - 1963]
PAUL, ELLIOT  (I)
    Mathematics Chez Madame Mariette.......(From The Last Time I Saw Paris; 1942)
      THE MATHEMATICAL MAGPIE [Fadiman - 1962]
PEASE, M. C.  (2)
    Ripeness........................................................SFS  Jan 1955
      RARE SCIENCE FICTION [Howard - 1963]
    Temple of Despair...............................................DSF  Oct 1953
      ESCAPE TO EARTH [Howard - 1963]
PHILLIPS, A. M.  (I)
    Extra Bricklayer, The...........................................UW  Sep 1940
      HELL HATH FURY [Hay - 1963]
PHILLIPS, PETER  (3)
    *Counter Charm..................................................SInt  Spr 1951
      FIFTY SHORT SCIENCE FICTION TALES [Asimov & Conklin - 1963]
    *Dreams Are Sacred..............................................ASF  Sep 1948
      SPECTRUM III [Amis & Conquest - 1963]
    *Lost Memory....................................................Glxy  May 1952
      THE COMING OF THE ROBOTS [Moskowitz - 1963]
      CONTACT [Keyes - 1963]
PIERCE, JOHN R.  (I)
    John Sze's Future...............................................ORIGINAL STORY
      GREAT SCIENCE FICTION BY SCIENTISTS [Conklin - 1962]
PIPER, H. BEAM  (I)
    Omnilingual.....................................................ASF  Feb 1957
      PROLOGUE TO ANALOG [J. W. Campbell - 1962]
POE, EDGAR ALLEN  (I)
    *Facts in the Case of M. Valdemar, The.........................AWR  Dec 1845
      GREAT SCIENCE FICTION ABOUT DOCTORS [Conklin & Fabricant - 1963]

POHL, FREDERIK  (7)     (See also listing James MacCreigh)          Mag.    Year
    Ghost Maker, The....................................................Bynd   Jan 1954
        BEYOND [Anonymous - 1963]
    Martian Star-Gazers, The............................................Glxy   Feb 1962
        (Originally appeared under pseudonyn Ernst Mason)
        8th ANNUAL OF THE YEAR'S BEST SF [Merril - 1963]
    My Lady Green Sleeves...............................................Glxy   Feb 1957
        HUMAN AND OTHER BEINGS [DeGraeff - 1963]
    Small Lords.........................................................SFQ    Feb 1957
        THE WEIRD ONES [Howard - 1962]
    Tunnel Under the World, The.........................................Glxy   Jan 1955
        MORE PENGUIN SCIENCE FICTION [Aldiss - 1963]
    What to do Until the Analyst Comes..................................Im     Feb 1956
        (Originally appeared under title Everybody's Happy But Me)
        17 X INFINITY [Conklin - 1963]

    w/ C. M. Kornbluth
        Quaker Cannon, The..............................................ASF    Aug 1961
            7th ANNUAL OF THE YEAR'S BEST SF [Merril - 1962]

POLYA, G.  (3)
    Apothems (Three) [untitled] .....................(From How to Solve It; 1945)
        THE MATHEMATICAL MAGPIE [Fadiman - 1963]

POPE, ALEXANDER  (1)
    Dunciad, The: An Heroic Poem in 3 books.....(Excerpts-verse)....DP  5/18/1728
        THE MATHEMATICAL MAGPIE [Fadiman - 1962]

PORGES, ARTHUR  (2)
    Emergency Operation.................................................F&SF   May 1956
        GREAT SCIENCE FICTION ABOUT DOCTORS [Conklin & Fabricant - 1963]
    *Fly, The...........................................................F&SF   Sep 1952
        FIFTY SHORT SCIENCE FICTION TALES [Asimov & Conklin - 1963]

PORGES, PAUL PETER  (1)
    Cartoon [untitled] .................................................ALM    Jul 1955
        THE MATHEMATICAL MAGPIE [Fadiman - 1962]

# Q

QUENEAU, RAYMOND  (3)
    Exercise in Style: Mathematical, An............(From Exercises in Style; 1958)
        THE MATHEMATICAL MAGPIE [Fadiman - 1962]
    Geometrical Disappearance of Dino, The.........(From Exercises in Style; 1958)
        THE MATHEMATICAL MAGPIE [Fadiman - 1962]
    On the Aerodynamic Properties of Addition......(From Exercises in Style; 1958)
        THE MATHEMATICAL MAGPIE [Fadiman - 1962]
            (Original appearance of all stories translated from French by
                Barbara Wright)

# R

RANKINE, W. J. M.  (1)
    Mathematician in Love, The.........(verse).......(From Songs and Fables; 1874)
        THE MATHEMATICAL MAGPIE [Fadiman - 1962]
RAPHAEL, RICK  (1)
    Filbert is a Nut, A.................................................ASF    Nov 1959
        PROLOGUE TO ANALOG [J. W. Campbell - 1962]

```
RAYER, FRANCIS G.  (1)                                              Mag.    Year
    Sands Our Abode.........................................NW #84  Jun 1959
        OUT OF THIS WORLD 3 [Williams-Ellis & Owen - 1962]
REED, KIT  (1)
    Judas Bomb..............................................F&SF   Apr 1961
        7th ANNUAL OF THE YEAR'S BEST SF [Merril - 1962]
REESE, JOHN  (1)
    Symbolic Logic of Murder................................EQMM   Oct 1960
        THE MATHEMATICAL MAGPIE [Fadiman - 1962]
RENARD, JULES  (1)
    Apothem [untitled].....................(From Histories Naturelles; n/d/a)
        THE MATHEMATICAL MAGPIE [Fadiman - 1962]
REYNOLDS, MACK  (6)
    *Business, As Usual, The................................F&SF   Jun 1952
        A CENTURY OF SCIENCE FICTION [Knight - 1962]
        FIFTY SHORT SCIENCE FICTION TALES [Conklin - 1963]
    Earthlings Go Home!.....................................Rog    Aug 1962
        8th ANNUAL OF THE YEAR'S BEST SF [Merril - 1963]
    Farmer..................................................Glxy   Jun 1961
        WORLDS OF WHEN [Conklin - 1962]
    Freedom.................................................ASF    Feb 1961
        7th ANNUAL OF THE YEAR'S BEST SF [Merril - 1962]
    Haunted Ones, The.......................................SFS    Nov 1959
        THE WEIRD ONES [Howard - 1963]
    w/ Frederic Brown
        *Dark Interlude.....................................Glxy   Jan 1951
            HUMAN AND OTHER BEINGS [DeGraeff - 1963]
RICE, CHARLES D.  (1)
    Cupid with an Adding Machine............................TW     9/18/60
        THE MATHEMATICAL MAGPIE [Fadiman - 1962]
RICE, JANE  (1)
    *Refugee, The...........................................UW     Oct 1943
        HELL HATH FURY [Hay - 1963]
RICHARDSON, ROBERT S.  (1)        (See also listing Philip Latham)
    Kid Anderson...........................................Spc    Spr 1956
        (Originally appeared under psuedonym Philip Latham)
        GREAT SCIENCE FICTION BY SCIENTISTS [Conklin - 1962]
RICHMOND, LEIGH  (1)
    Prologue to anaAnalogue.................................ASF    Jun 1961
        ANALOG 1 [J. W. Campbell - 1963]
RIDENOW, LOUIS N.  (1)
    Pilot Lights of the Apocalypse..........................Ftn    Jan 1946
        GREAT SCIENCE FICTION BY SCIENTISTS [Conklin - 1962]
ROBERTS, JANE  (1)
    Chestnut Beads, The.....................................F&SF   Oct 1957
        ROD SERLING'S TRIPLE W: WITCHES, WARLOCKS & WEREWOLVES [Serling - 1963]
ROBERTS, MICHAEL  (1)
    Note on θ , φ , and ψ ...............(verse)..........NS     3/23/35
        THE MATHEMATICAL MAGPIE [Fadiman - 1962]
ROBINSON, FRANK M.  (1)
    Two Weeks in August....................................Glxy   Feb 1951
        FIFTY SHORT SCIENCE FICTION TALES [Asimov & Conklin - 1963]
```

ROBLES, EDWARD G. JR.  (I)                                                    Mag.    Year
    See?...........................................................Glxy  Jun 1954
        FIFTY SHORT SCIENCE FICTION TALES [Asimov & Conklin - 1963]
ROCKLYNNE, ROSS  (I)
    At the Center of Gravity.......................................ASF  Jun 1936
        EXPLORING OTHER WORLDS [Moskowitz - 1963]
ROME, DAVID  (I)
    Parky......................................................SF #48  Aug 1961
        7th ANNUAL OF THE YEAR'S BEST SF [Merril - 1962]
ROSE, MARK  (I)
    We Would See a Sign.....................................ORIGINAL STORY
        SPECTRUM III [Amis & Conquest - 1963]
RUSS, JOANNA  (I)
    My Dear Emily..................................................F&SF  Jul 1962
        THE BEST FROM FANTASY & SCIENCE FICTION: 12th SERIES [Davidson - 1963]
RUSSELL, BERTRAND  (2)
    Mathematician's Nightmare, The: The Vision of Professor Squarepoint..........
        (From Nightmares of Eminent Persons; 1955)
        THE MATHEMATICAL MAGPIE [Fadiman - 1963]
    Planetary Effulgence..........................(From Fact and Fiction; 1961)
        8th ANNUAL OF THE YEAR'S BEST SF [Merril - 1963]
RUSSELL, ERIC FRANK  (4)
    Allamagoosa...................................................ASF  May 1955
        THE HUGO WINNERS [Asimov - 1962]
        GREAT STORIES OF SPACE TRAVEL [Conklin - 1963]
    Appointment at Noon...........................................Amz  Mar 1954
        FIFTY SHORT SCIENCE FICTION TALES [Asimov & Conklin - 1963]
    Minor Ingredient..............................................ASF  Mar 1956
        PROLOGUE TO ANALOG [J. W. Campbell - 1962]
    *Test Piece....................................................OW  Mar 1951
        HUMAN AND OTHER BEINGS [DeGraeff - 1963]
RUSSELL, RAY  (I)
    Long Night....................................................Rog  Apr 1961
        (Originally appeared under title The Exploits of Orgo)
        7th ANNUAL OF THE YEAR'S BEST SF [Merril - 1962]

# S

SACKETT, SAM  (I)
    Hail to the Chief.............................................FSF  Jun 1954
        THE WEIRD ONES [Howard - 1962]
SAMBROT, WILLIAM  (I)
    Leprechaun...............................................Escp n/d/a 1962
        8th ANNUAL OF THE YEAR'S BEST SF [Merril - 1963]
SANDERS, WINSTON P.  (I)
    Barnacle Bull.................................................ASF  Sep 1960
        ANALOG I [J. W. Campbell - 1963]
SANTAYANA, GEORGE  (I)
    Map of England and the Absolute, The..................................
        (From Character and Opinion in the United States; 1920)
        THE MATHEMATICAL MAGPIE [Fadiman - 1962]
SAPARIN, VICTOR  (I)
    Trial of Tantalus, The.....................................(No data available)
        A VISITOR FROM OUTER SPACE [Anonymous - undated]
            (Translated from Russian by Violet L. Dutt)

```
SCHENCK, HILBERT  JR.  (4)                                        Mag.    Year
   *Me..............................(verse).....................F&SF  Aug 1959
       THE MATHEMATICAL MAGPIE [Fadiman - 1962]
   Pun In Orbit....................(verse).....................ORIGINAL VERSE
       THE MATHEMATICAL MAGPIE [Fadiman - 1962]
   Snip, Snip......................(verse).....................F&SF  Sep 1959
       THE MATHEMATICAL MAGPIE [Fadiman - 1962]
   Wockyjabber.....................(verse).....................F&SF  May 1960
       THE MATHEMATICAL MAGPIE [Fadiman - 1962]
SCHMITZ, JAMES H.  (1)
   *We Don't Want Any Trouble...............................Glxy  Jun 1953
       FIFTY SHORT SCIENCE FICTION TALES [Asimov & Conklin - 1963]
SCHOENFELD, HOWARD  (1)
   *Built Up Logically......................................Retort  Win 1949
       FIFTY SHORT SCIENCE FICTION TALES [Asimov & Conklin - 1963]
       (Appeared under title Built Down Logically)
       MORE PENGUIN SCIENCE FICTION [Aldiss - 1963]
SEABRIGHT, IDRIS ps (Margaret St. Clair)  (2)
   *Egg a Month from All Over, An...........................F&SF  Oct 1952
       FIFTY SHORT SCIENCE FICTION TALES [Asimov & Conklin - 1963]
   *Short in the Chest......................................FU  Jul 1954
       17 X INFINITY [Conklin - 1963]
SHANGO, J. R.  (1)
   Matter of Ethics, A......................................F&SF  Nov 1954
       GREAT SCIENCE FICTION ABOUT DOCTORS [Conklin & Fabricant - 1963]
SHARKEY, JACK  (1)
   Final Ingredient, The....................................F&SF  Aug 1960
       ROD SERLING'S TRIPLE W: WITCHES, WARLOCKS & WEREWOLVES [Serling - 1963]
SHECKLEY, ROBERT  (8)
   Ask a Foolish Question...................................SFS #1  n/d 1953
       6 AND THE SILENT SCREAM [Howard - 1963]
   Holdout..................................................F&SF  Dec 1957
       HUMAN AND OTHER BEINGS [DeGraeff - 1963]
   Human Man's Burden.......................................Glxy  Sep 1956
       12 GREAT CLASSICS OF SCIENCE FICTION [Conklin - 1963]
   Monsters, The............................................F&SF  Mar 1953
       BEST SF FIVE SCIENCE FICTION STORIES [Crispin - 1963]
   Perfect Woman, The.......................................Amz  Dec 1953
       FIFTY SHORT SCIENCE FICTION TALES [Asimov & Conklin - 1963]
   *Specialist..............................................Glxy  May 1953
       CONTACT [Keyes - 1963]
   Store of the World, The..................................Plby  Sep 1959
       (Originally appeared under title World of Heart's Desire)
       MORE PENGUIN SCIENCE FICTION [Aldiss - 1963]
   We are Alone.............................................FSF  Nov 1952
       ESCAPE TO EARTH [Howard - 1963]
SHELDON, WALT  (1)
   Hunters, The.............................................Stg  Mar 1952
       FIFTY SHORT SCIENCE FICTION TALES [Asimov & Conklin - 1963]
SILVERBERG, ROBERT  (4)
   Hunt the Space Witch.....................................SFAd  Jan 1958
       (Originally appeared under pseudonym Ivar Jorgenson)
       GREAT SCIENCE FICTION ADVENTURES [Shaw - 1963]
   Quick Freeze.............................................SFQ  May 1957
       RARE SCIENCE FICTION [Howard - 1963]
```

SILVERBERG, ROBERT [Continued]           Mag. Year
  Sunrise on Mercury..................................................SFS May 1957
    (Originally appeared under pseudonym Calvin M. Knox)
    MORE ADVENTURES ON OTHER PLANETS [Wollheim - 1963]

  w/ Randall Garrett
    Sound Decision.................................................ASF Oct 1956
      PROLOGUE TO ANALOG [J. W. Campbell - 1962]
SIMAK, CLIFFORD D. (5)
  *...And the Truth Shall Make You Free..........................FSF Mar 1952
    NOVELETS OF SCIENCE FICTION [Howard - 1963]
  Big Front Yard, The...........................................ASF Oct 1958
    THE HUGO WINNERS [Asimov - 1962]
  Earth for Inspiration.........................................TWS Apr 1941
    THE COMING OF THE ROBOTS [Moskowitz - 1963]
  Galactic Chest................................................OSFS Sep 1956
    THREE IN ONE [Margulies - 1963]
  Green Thumb...................................................Glxy Jul 1954
    BEST SF FIVE SCIENCE FICTION STORIES [Crispin - 1963]
SIME, SIDNEY H. (1)
  w/ Joseph Charles Holbrooke
    Ta, Ta, The..............(Song)..............(From Bogey Beasts; 1962)
      THE MATHEMATICAL MAGPIE [Fadiman - 1962]
SMITH, CORDWAINER (2)
  Ballard of Lost C'Mell, The...................................Glxy Oct 1962
    12 GREAT CLASSICS OF SCIENCE FICTION [Conklin - 1963]
  Planet Named Shayol, A........................................Glxy Oct 1961
    7th NNUAL OF THE YEAR'S BEST SF [Merril - 1962]
SMITH, EVELYN E. (4)
    D
    A
 *[BAXBR]...........................(From Time To Come; August Derleth - 1954)
    B
    R
    OUT OF THIS WORLD 3 [Williams-Ellis & Owen - 1962]
  Last of the Spode, The........................................F&SF Jun 1953
    17 X INFINITY [Conklin - 1963]
  Martian and the Magician, The.................................F&SF Nov 1952
    FIFTY SHORT SCIENCE FICTION TALES [Asimov & Conklin - 1963]
  *Vilbar Party, The............................................Glxy Jan 1955
    HUMAN AND OTHER BEINGS [DeGraeff - 1963]
SMITH, GEORGE O. (1)
  Amateur in Chancery...........................................Glxy Oct 1961
    THE EXPERT DREAMERS [Pohl - 1962]
SMITH, H. ALLEN (1)
  Achievment of H. T. Wensel, The...............................SRL 5/21/60
    THE MATHEMATICAL MAGPIE [Fadiman - 1962]
SODDY, FREDERICK (1)
  Kiss Precise, The...................(verse)...................Ntr 6/20/36
    THE MATHEMATICAL MAGPIE [Fadiman - 1962]
SPARK, MURIAL (1)
  Portobello Road, The..........................(From The Go-Away Bird; 1958)
    7th ANNUAL OF THE YEAR'S BEST SF [Merril - 1962]
ST. CLAIR, MARGARET (1)  (See also listing Idris Seabright)
  Rations of Tantalus...........................................FU Jul 1954
    WORLDS OF WHEN [Conklin - 1962]

```
STANTON, WILL   (3)                                                    Mag.    Year
   *Barney............................................................F&SF   Jul 1954
      FIFTY SHORT SCIENCE FICTION TALES [Asimov & Conklin - 1963]
   Gumdrop King, The.................................................F&SF   Aug 1962
      THE BEST FROM FANTASY & SCIENCE FICTION: 12th SERIES [Davidson - 1963]
   You are with It!..................................................F&SF   Dec 1961
      A CENTURY OF SCIENCE FICTION [Knight - 1962]
STANYUKOVICH, KIRILL   (I)
   Golub-Yavan, The..........................................(No data available)
      DESTINATION: AMALTHEIA [Dixon - 1963]
         (Translated from Russian by Leonid Kolesnikov)
STAPLEDON, OLAF   (I)
   *Odd John.....................(Originally published by Methuen & Co.; 1935)
      A CENTURY OF SCIENCE FICTION [Knight - 1962]
STARZL, R. F.   (I)
   Radiant Enemies, The..............................................Arg    2/10/34
      EXPLORING OTHER WORLDS [Moskowitz - 1963]
STEINBERG, SAUL   (3)
   Cartoon..........(Titled Alligator Walking Line)...(From THE LABYRINTH; 1960)
      THE MATHEMATICAL MAGPIE [Fadiman - 1962]
   Cartoon.............(Titled Man in Cube).........................Nykr   9/10/60
      THE MATHEMATICAL MAGPIE [Fadiman - 1962]
   Cartoon.............(Titled Question Mark on a Seesaw).......Nykr   7/23/60
      THE MATHEMATICAL MAGPIE [Fadiman - 1962]
STRUGATSKY, ARKADY   (3)
   w/ Boris Strugatsky
      Destination: Amaltheia......................................(No data available)
         DESTINATION: AMALTHEIA [Dixon - 1963]
            (Translated from Russian by Leonid Kolesnikov)
      Six Matches................................................(No data available)
         THE HEART OF THE SERPENT [Anonymous - 1961]
            (Translated from Russian by R. Prokofieva)
      Spontaneous Reflex.........................................(No data available)
         A VISITOR FROM OUTER SPACE [Anonymous - undated]
            (Translated from Russian by Violet L. Dutt)
STRUTHER, JAN ps (Mrs. Joyce Maxtone Graham)   (I)
   Miniver Problem, The..................................(From Mrs. Miniver; 1940)
      THE MATHEMATICAL MAGPIE [Fadiman - 1962]
STUART, WILLIAM W.   (I)
   Star-Crossed Lover................................................Glxy   Apr 1962
      12 GREAT CLASSICS OF SCIENCE FICTION [Conklin - 1963]
STURGEON, THEODORE   (8)
   Ether Breather...................................................ASF    Sep 1939
      FIRST FLIGHT: Maiden Voyages In Space and Time [Knight - 1963]
   *Killdozer!......................................................ASF    Nov 1944
      SPECTRUM III [Amis & Conquest - 1963]
   *Never Underestimate............................................If     Jan 1952
      17 X INFINITY [Conklin - 1963]
   *Saucer of Loniiness, A.........................................Glxy   Feb 1953
      THE WORLDS OF SCIENCE FICTION [Mills - 1963]
   *Talent.........................................................Bynd   Sep 1953
      BEYOND [Anonymous - 1963]
      FIFTY SHORT SCIENCE FICTION TALES [Asimov & Conklin - 1963]
   There is no Defense.............................................ASF    Feb 1948
      THREE IN ONE [Margulies - 1963]
```

STURGEON, THEODORE [Continued]             Mag.  Year

STURGEON, THEODORE [Continued]

 To Marry Medusa...............................................................Glxy Aug 1948
   TIME WAITS FOR WINTHROP & 4 OTHER SHORT NOVELS FROM GALAXY [Pohl-1962]
 *Yesterday Was Monday.....................................................UW Jun 1941
   THE UNKNOWN [Benson - 1963]

SYLVESTER, J. J. (1)
 To a Missing Member of a Family Group of Terms in an Algebraical Formula.....
     (verse)          (No data available)
   THE MATHEMATICAL MAGPIE [Fadiman - 1962]

SYNGE, J. L. (3)
 Euclid and the Bright Boy.............(From Science: Sense and Nonsense; 1951)
   THE MATHEMATICAL MAGPIE [Fadiman - 1962]
 O'Brien's Table......................(From Science: Sense and Nonsense; 1951)
   THE MATHEMATICAL MAGPIE [Fadiman - 1962]
 Tending to Infinity.......(verse)............. (From Kandelman's Krim; 1957)
   THE MATHEMATICAL MAGPIE [Fadiman - 1962]

SZILARD, LEO (3)
 Mark Gable Foundation, The..............(From The Voice of the Dolphins; 1961)
   THE EXPERT DREAMERS [Pohl - 1962]
 My Trial as a War Criminal.............................................UCLR Aut 1949
   7th ANNUAL OF THE YEAR'S BEST SF [Merril - 1962]
 Report on Grand Central Terminal....................................UCM n/d/a 1952
   GREAT SCIENCE FICTION BY SCIENTISTS [Conklin - 1962]

# T

TAINE, JOHN ps (Eric Temple Bell) (1)
 *Ultimate Catalyst, The..............................................TWS Jun 1929
   GREAT SCIENCE FICTION BY SCIENTISTS [Conklin - 1962]

TENN, WILLIAM ps (Philip Klass) (5)
 *Brooklyn Project....................................................PS Fal 1948
   17 X INFINITY [Conklin - 1963]
 Down Among the Dead Men..............................................Glxy Jun 1954
   HUMAN AND OTHER BEINGS [DeGraeff - 1963]
 Liberation of Earth, The.............................................FSF May 1953
   MORE PENGUIN SCIENCE FICTION [Aldiss - 1963]
 Project Hush.........................................................Glxy Feb 1954
   FIFTY SHORT SCIENCE FICTION TALES [Asimov & Conklin - 1963]
 Time Waits for Winthrop..............................................Glxy Aug 1957
   TIME WAITS FOR WINTHROP & 4 OTHER SHORT NOVELS FROM GALAXY [Pohl-1962]

THOMAS, THEODORE L. (2)
 Day of Succession....................................................ASF Aug 1959
   A CENTURY OF SCIENCE FICTION [Knight - 1962]
 Test................................................................F&SF Apr 1962
   THE BEST FROM FANTASY & SCIENCE FICTION: 12th SERIES [Davidson - 1963]

TREMAINE, F. ORLIN (1)
 True Confession......................................................TWS Feb 1940
   THE COMING OF THE ROBOTS [Moskowitz - 1963]

TWAIN, MARK ps (Samuel L. Clemens) (3)
 Extracts (Two) [untitled] ..............................(No data available)
   THE MATHEMATICAL MAGPIE [Fadiman - 1962]
 From The London Times of 1904.......................................Cny Nov 1898
   A CENTURY OF SCIENCE FICTION [Knight - 1962]

# U

UNTERMAYER, LOUIS  (1)                                                    Mag.    Year
    Einstein: A Parody in the Manner of Edw-n Markh-m..........(verse)..........
        (From Collected Parodies; 1926)
        THE MATHEMATICAL MAGPIE [Fadiman - 1962]
UPSON, WILLIAM HAZLETT  (1)
    Paul Bunyon Versus the Conveyor Belt.............................FTM  n/d 1949
        THE MATHEMATICAL MAGPIE [Fadiman - 1962]

# V

VAN DOREN, MARK  (1)
    Strange Girl, The
        THE WORLDS OF SCIENCE FICTION [Mills - 1963]
VAN VOGT, A. E.  (5)
    *Black Destroyer.................................................ASF   Jul 1939
        FIRST FLIGHT: Maiden Voyages In Space and Time [Knight - 1963]
    *Enchanted Village..............................................OW    Jul 1950
        ASLEEP IN ARMAGEDDON [Sissons - 1962]
    *Far Centaurus.................................................ASF   Jan 1944
        GREAT STORIES OF SPACE TRAVEL [Conklin - 1963]
    Great Judge, The...............................................FB #3  n/d 1948
        FIFTY SHORT SCIENCE FICTION TALES [Asimov & Conklin - 1963]
    *Resurrection..................................................ASF   Aug 1948
        SPECTRUM II [Amis & Conquest - 1962]
VANCE, JACK  (1)
    I'll Build Your Dream Castle...................................ASF   Sep 1947
        GREAT STORIES OF SPACE TRAVEL [Conklin - 1963]
VASILYEV, MIKHAIL  (1)
    Flying Flowers............................................(No data available)
        DESTINATION: AMALTHEIA [Dixon - 1963]
           (Translated from Russian by Leonid Kolesnikov)
VEILLOT, CLAUDE  (1)
    First Days of May, The.........................................Fctn  May 1960
        A CENTURY OF SCIENCE FICTION [Knight - 1962]
           (Translated from French by Damon Knight)
VERNE, JULES  (1)
    Twenty Thousand Leagues Under the Sea...............(excerpts)..............
        (Originally published by G. M. Smith; 1873)
        A CENTURY OF SCIENCE FICTION [Knight - 1962]
VINCENT, HARL ps (Harl Vincent Schoepflin)  (1)
    Rex............................................................ASF   Jun 1934
        THE COMING OF THE ROBOTS [Moskowitz - 1963]

# W

WALLACE, F. L.  (2)
    Accidental Flight..............................................Glxy  Apr 1952
        TIME WAITS FOR WINTHROP & 4 OTHER SHORT NOVELS FROM GALAXY [Pohl-1962]
    Bolden's Pets..................................................Glxy  Oct 1955
        GREAT SCIENCE FICTION ABOUT DOCTORS [Conklin & Fabricant - 1963]

```
                                                              Mag.   Year
WALTER, W. GREY  (1)
    Singers, The.....................(From The Curve of the Snowflakes; 1956)
         THE EXPERT DREAMERS [Pohl - 1962]
WEINBAUM, STANLEY G.  (3)
    Ideal, The...............(excerpts)..........................WS  Sep 1935
         A CENTURY OF SCIENCE FICTION [Knight - 1962]
    Mad Moon, The...............................................ASF  Dec 1935
         EXPLORING OTHER WORLDS [Moskowitz - 1963]
    Planet of Doubt, The........................................ASF  Oct 1935
         MORE ADVENTURES ON OTHER PLANETS [Wollheim - 1963]
WELLEN, EDWARD  (1)
    Deadly Game..................................................If  May 1962
         8th ANNUAL OF THE YEAR'S BEST SF [Merril - 1963]
WELLMAN, MANLY WADE  (1)
    When It was Moonlight.......................................UW  Feb 1940
         THE UNKNOWN [Benson - 1963]
WELLS, H. G.  (2)
    *Crystal Egg, The..........................................NwR  May 1897
         A CENTURY OF SCIENCE FICTION [Knight - 1962]
    *Time Machine, The.........................................NwR  Jan 1895
         A CENTURY OF SCIENCE FICTION [Knight - 1962]
WHEWELL, DR. WILLIAM  (1)
    Verse [untitled].................................................
         (From Handy-book of Literary Curiosities by W. S. Walsh; 1925)
         THE MATHEMATICAL MAGPIES [Fadiman - 1962]
WHITE, JAMES  (2)
    Apprentice, The..........................................NW #99  Nov 1960
         OUT OF THIS WORLD 3 [Williams-Ellis & Owen - 1962]
    Christmas Trombone........................................F&SF  Jan 1962
         8th ANNUAL OF THE YEAR'S BEST SF [Merril - 1963]
WHITLEY, GEORGE ps (A. Bertram Chandler) (1)  (See listing A. Bertram Chandler)
    Change of Heart............................................Fnt  May 1962
         8th ANNUAL OF THE YEAR'S BEST SF [Merril - 1963]
WILHELM, KATE  (1)
    Man Without a Planet, The................................F&SF  Jul 1962
         THE BEST FROM FANTASY & SCIENCE FICTION: 12th SERIES [Davidson - 1963]
WILLEY, ROBERT ps (Willy Ley) (1)   (See also listing Willy Ley)
    Invasion, The.............................................Sup  Sep 1940
         THE EXPERT DREAMERS [Pohl - 1962]
WILLIAMS, BEN AMES  (1)
    Coconuts..................................................SEP  10/9/26
         THE MATHEMATICAL MAGPIE [Fadiman - 1962]
WILLIAMS, RALPH  (2)
    Business as Usual, During Alterations.....................ASF  Jul 1958
         PROLOGUE TO ANALOG [ J. W. Campbell - 1962]
    *Emergency Landing........................................ASF  Jul 1940
         FIFTY SHORT SCIENCE FICTION TALES [Asimov & Conklin - 1963]
WILLIAMS, ROBERT MOORE  (1)
    Red Death of Mars.........................................ASF  Jul 1940
         MORE ADVENTURES ON OTHER PLANETS [Wollheim - 1963]
WILLIAMSON, IAN  (1)
    *Chemical Plant........................................NW #8  Dec 1950
         CONTACT [Keyes - 1963]
WILSON, RICHARD  (2)
    Honor.....................................................SFQ  Feb 1956
         HUMAN AND OTHER BEINGS [DeGraeff - 1963]
```

WILSON, RICHARD [Continued]                                            Mag.    Year
  *Love...........................................................F&SF  Jun 1952
        HUMAN AND OTHER BEINGS [DeGraeff - 1963]
WINSOR, FREDERICK (4)
  Verses (Four) [untitled] ........(From The Space Child's Mother Goose; 1958)
        THE MATHEMATICAL MAGPIE [Fadiman - 1962]
WINTER, J. A. M.D. (1)
  Expedition Mercy.............................................ASF  Nov 1948
        GREAT SCIENCE FICTION ABOUT DOCTORS [Conklin & Fabricant - 1963]
WORDSWORTH, WILLIAM (1)
  Geometry.................(From The Prelude; or Growth of a Poet's Mind; 1805)
        THE MATHEMATICAL MAGPIE [Fadiman - 1962]
WRIGHT, S. FOWLER (1)
  *Obviously Suicide...........................................Sus  Spr 1951
        FIFTY SHORT SCIENCE FICTION TALES [Asimov & Conklin - 1963]
WYNDHAM, JOHN ps(John Beynon Harris) (4)
  Asteroids, 2194, The........................................Rpnt - Amz  Jan 1961
        (Originally appeared under title The Emptiness of Space NW #100 Nov 1960)
        7th ANNUAL OF THE YEAR'S BEST SF [Merril - 1962]
  Consider Her Ways..............................(From Sometime Never; 1956)
        BEST SF FIVE SCIENCE FICTION STORIES [Crispin - 1963]
  *Dumb Martian...............................................Glxy  Jul 1952
        OUT OF THIS WORLD 3 [Williams-Ellis & Owen - 1962]
  Lost Machine, The...........................................Amz  Apr 1932
        (Originally appeared under byline John Beynon Harris)
        THE COMING OF THE ROBOTS [Moskowitz - 1963]

# Y

YEFREMOV, IVAN (1)
  Heart of the Serpent, The...................................(No data available)
        THE HEART OF THE SERPENT [Anonymous - 1961]
        (Translated from Russian by R. Prokofieva)
YOUNG, ROBERT F. (2)
  Dandelion Girl, The.........................................SEP    4/1/61
        7th ANNUAL OF THE YEAR'S BEST SF [Merril - 1962]
  Thirty Days Had September...................................F&SF  Oct 1957
        12 GREAT CLASSICS OF SCIENCE FICTION [Conklin - 1963]

# Z

ZABELIN, IGOR (1)
  Valley of the Four Crosses, The.............................(No data available)
        DESTINATION: AMALTHEIA [Dixon - 1963]
            (Translated from Russian by Leonid Kolesnikov)
ZHURAVLYOVA, VALENTINA (2)
  Astronaut, The..............................................(No data available)
        DESTINATION: AMALTHEIA [Dixon - 1963]
            (Translated from Russian by Leonid Kolesnkov)
  Stone from the Stars........................................(No data available)
        THE HEART OF THE SERPENT [Anonymous - 1961]
            (Translated from Russian by R. Prokofieva)

# SCIENCE FICTION

*An Arno Press Collection*

## FICTION

About, Edmond. **The Man with the Broken Ear.** 1872

Allen, Grant. **The British Barbarians:** A Hill-Top Novel. 1895

Arnold, Edwin L. **Lieut. Gullivar Jones:** His Vacation. 1905

Ash, Fenton. **A Trip to Mars.** 1909

Aubrey, Frank. **A Queen of Atlantis.** 1899

Bargone, Charles (Claude Farrere, pseud.). **Useless Hands.** [1926]

Beale, Charles Willing. **The Secret of the Earth.** 1899

Bell, Eric Temple (John Taine, pseud.). **Before the Dawn.** 1934

Benson, Robert Hugh. **Lord of the World.** 1908

Beresford, J. D. **The Hampdenshire Wonder.** 1911

Bradshaw, William R. **The Goddess of Atvatabar.** 1892

Capek, Karel. **Krakatit.** 1925

Chambers, Robert W. **The Gay Rebellion.** 1913

Colomb, P. et al. **The Great War of 189—.** 1893

Cook, William Wallace. **Adrift in the Unknown.** n.d.

Cummings, Ray. **The Man Who Mastered Time.** 1929

[DeMille, James]. **A Strange Manuscript Found in a Copper Cylinder.** 1888

Dixon, Thomas. **The Fall of a Nation:** A Sequel to the Birth of a Nation. 1916

England, George Allan. **The Golden Blight.** 1916

Fawcett, E. Douglas. **Hartmann the Anarchist.** 1893

Flammarion, Camille. **Omega:** The Last Days of the World. 1894

Grant, Robert et al. **The King's Men:** A Tale of To-Morrow. 1884

Grautoff, Ferdinand Heinrich (Parabellum, pseud.). **Banzai!** 1909

Graves, C. L. and E. V. Lucas. **The War of the Wenuses.** 1898

Greer, Tom. **A Modern Daedalus.** [1887]

Griffith, George. **A Honeymoon in Space.** 1901

Grousset, Paschal (A. Laurie, pseud.). **The Conquest of the Moon.** 1894

Haggard, H. Rider. **When the World Shook.** 1919

Hernaman-Johnson, F. **The Polyphemes.** 1906

Hyne, C. J. Cutcliffe. **Empire of the World.** [1910]

**In The Future.** [1875]

Jane, Fred T. **The Violet Flame.** 1899

Jefferies, Richard. **After London; Or, Wild England.** 1885

Le Queux, William. **The Great White Queen.** [1896]

London, Jack. **The Scarlet Plague.** 1915

Mitchell, John Ames. **Drowsy.** 1917

Morris, Ralph. **The Life and Astonishing Adventures of John Daniel.** 1751

Newcomb, Simon. **His Wisdom The Defender:** A Story. 1900

Paine, Albert Bigelow. **The Great White Way.** 1901

Pendray, Edward (Gawain Edwards, pseud.). **The Earth-Tube.** 1929

Reginald, R. and Douglas Menville. **Ancestral Voices:** An Anthology of Early Science Fiction. 1974

Russell, W. Clark. **The Frozen Pirate.** 2 vols. in 1. 1887

Shiel, M. P. **The Lord of the Sea.** 1901

Symmes, John Cleaves (Captain Adam Seaborn, pseud.). **Symzonia.** 1820

Train, Arthur and Robert W. Wood. **The Man Who Rocked the Earth.** 1915

Waterloo, Stanley. **The Story of Ab:** A Tale of the Time of the Cave Man. 1903

White, Stewart E. and Samuel H. Adams. **The Mystery.** 1907

Wicks, Mark. **To Mars Via the Moon.** 1911

Wright, Sydney Fowler. **Deluge: A Romance** and **Dawn.** 2 vols. in 1. 1928/1929

# SCIENCE FICTION

## NON-FICTION:
### Including Bibliographies, Checklists and Literary Criticism

Aldiss, Brian and Harry Harrison. **SF Horizons.** 2 vols. in 1. 1964/1965

Amis, Kingsley. **New Maps of Hell.** 1960

Barnes, Myra. **Linguistics and Languages in Science Fiction-Fantasy.** 1974

Cockcroft, T. G. L. **Index to the Weird Fiction Magazines.** 2 vols. in 1 1962/1964

Cole, W. R. **A Checklist of Science-Fiction Anthologies.** 1964

Crawford, Joseph H. et al. **"333": A Bibliography of the Science-Fantasy Novel.** 1953

Day, Bradford M. **The Checklist of Fantastic Literature in Paperbound Books.** 1965

Day, Bradford M. **The Supplemental Checklist of Fantastic Literature.** 1963

Gove, Philip Babcock. **The Imaginary Voyage in Prose Fiction.** 1941

Green, Roger Lancelyn. **Into Other Worlds:** Space-Flight in Fiction, From Lucian to Lewis. 1958

Menville, Douglas. **A Historical and Critical Survey of the Science Fiction Film.** 1974

Reginald, R. **Contemporary Science Fiction Authors,** First Edition. 1970

Samuelson, David. **Visions of Tomorow:** Six Journeys from Outer to Inner Space. 1974